All, too, will bear in mind this sacred
principle that, though the will of the
majority is in all cases to prevail, that
will, to be rightful, must be reasonable;
that the minority possess their equal
rights, which equal law must protect,
and to violate which would be oppression.

THE CONSENT OF THE GOVERNED

THE *Second Edition* CONSENT OF THE GOVERNED

John C. Livingston Sacramento State College

Robert G. Thompson Sacramento State College

THE MACMILLAN COMPANY, NEW YORK

COLLIER-MACMILLAN LIMITED, LONDON

PREFACE

*R*EVISING A BOOK, we have discovered, is not simply a matter of bringing it up to date and correcting errors. What started out to be a tune-up soon revealed the desirability of a complete overhaul. Our original idea—that the perspectives of democratic theory and the problems of mass democracy provide the most adequate framework for an introductory treatment of American government and politics—remains the basis of the book..We hope to have succeeded in sharpening and clarifying the development of these themes by major surgery on the first eight chapters, which included complete reorganization of the sequence as well as thorough redrafting of the presentation of the materials. A new chapter has been added (Chapter Eight) on the ideological dimensions of policy-making. The chapter on the Presidency is completely new. The remaining chapters have been extensively revised and rewritten.

Special note should be made of the fact that the treatment of civil liberties, civil rights, and due process is dispersed through the book, rather than concentrated in specific chapters. We have considered, and decided against, the latter approach because we have not wanted to sacrifice the advantages of relating these issues to the processes and institutions through which they are debated and defined. In the revision, however, we have concentrated the treatment of civil liberties in Chapter Seven and the treatment of civil rights and due process in Chapter Sixteen.

In the process of reviewing the first edition and preparing the second we have had the benefit of high-quality criticism and comment from many sources. The advice of Professors Earl Segrest, Gerald McDaniel, and Richard Hughes of the Department of Government at Sacramento State College has been both generous and helpful, as has been that of Professor Martin Birnbach of San Jose State College. Specific and exceptionally useful criticism of the first edition came from Professors Rocco J. Tresolini of Lehigh University, John H. Schultz of Fullerton Junior College, E. Thomas Chapman, Jr., of the University of Michigan, Christopher Dyer-Bennet of Chico State College, Allan Dionisopoulos of Northern Illinois University, J. Ben Stalvey of the University of Miami, John W. Ellsworth of California State College, Hayward, and Stanley V. Anderson of the University of California, Santa Barbara.

Mr. Robert Patterson has been the very model of what an editor should be, completely adamant about our meeting deadlines and mercifully forgiving about their not being met. Ethel Livingston has translated our intolerably messy handwriting into typewritten manuscript with tolerance and skill. Pamela Thompson and Michael Livingston have read proof with rare discernment and patience. Our families have put up with more than families should be asked to bear. Finally, as in the first edition—it seemed to work out well—each of us assigns responsibility for errors to the other.

J. C. L.
R. G.T.

TO THE STUDENT

*T*HIS BOOK, we think you will find, differs from the typical textbook in at least three important and fundamental respects.

First, it is not a comprehensively descriptive seed-catalog-style book. It assumes that facts become meaningful only when they are put into a conceptual framework. Descriptive materials, therefore, are selected for their relevance to what we hope are important questions. The problems we have set for you require critical analysis rather than memorizing.

Second, we start with the premise that we do not already know what democracy means—except that it requires citizens to confront the question for themselves. We have sought to provide a basis for understanding the theoretical questions that must be faced in this effort, an introduction to some of the alternative answers that have been offered, and an analysis of the implications of these answers for the organization of American politics. We hope that these raw materials will permit you to define your own role as a citizen.

Third, the tradition of textbook writing dictates that authors make a concerted effort to avoid or conceal their biases. We have scandalously ignored this tradition, and it will be a very dull scholar indeed who fails to discern our unreconstructed majoritarian leanings, our skepticism about the politics of group compromise, or our unconcealed distress over professional manipulation of political preferences. We do not mean to apologize for our biases; we have regarded our obligations in this respect to be to set them down with a full exposition of the grounds on which we hold them and to provide a fair and accurate presentation of alternative positions. The burden is therefore on you to examine them critically.

We have tried, above all, to convey a sense of the intellectual excitement that can be the exclusive privilege of free men in a free society. This experience requires that one become engaged in the exercise of freedom, that new problems and new perspectives broadening one's horizons be welcomed. We have tried to open some windows; we can only hope the vistas are inviting enough to help you on your own ways to understanding.

CONTENTS

THE CRISIS OF DEMOCRATIC POLITICS

. . . in which it is argued that there is a deep disorder in our political system.

An understanding of this disorder requires analysis of **The Anatomy of Political Crises.** Politics involves power because it provides processes for resolving conflicts among incompatible desires, interests, opinions, and values. When these processes occur through institutions of government, the resulting policies inevitably favor some persons over others and yet are binding on all. Every political system, therefore, faces

> **The Problem of Legitimacy.** A political system acquires legitimacy when its citizens recognize its commands as an exercise of legitimate authority, rather than the imposition of sheer power, and when they feel a psychological and a moral obligation to obey. Modern governments appeal for the loyalty of their citizens to **Normative Theories** or philosophies that support and justify their political institutions. These normative theories claim to answer the basic political questions of *how* political decisions ought to be made, *who* ought to make them, and *what* limits there ought to be on political authority. The answers to these questions will determine what conflict-resolving methods are accepted as legitimate and what roles various actors in the political drama are expected to play.
>
> **Democracy as Normative Theory** must provide answers to these questions if democratic institutions are to be accepted as legitimate by citizens. It is in this context that we confront

The Crisis of Legitimacy in American Politics, which is reflected in a deep and widening

> **Gulf Between Theory and Practice,** between the traditional norms of democratic theory and the actual processes of democratic politics. This gulf is clearly revealed in the character of policy-making, in the role of citizens, and in the roles of politicians and political parties.
>
> **The Crisis in Policy-making** may be measured by the distance between the traditional norm of rational public debate of a public interest and the

1

actual processes of basing public policies on compromises of organized private interests. Policy-making tends to be dominated not by debate of alternatives but by a climate of moderation that protects the "mainstream" of general agreement on the *status quo* against proposals for change; voters are offered echoes, not choices; and those critics who challenge the moderate middle are dismissed as extremists. Second, there is a

Crisis in the Obligations of Citizenship because the actual behavior of citizens tends not to reflect those qualities that traditional theory regarded as necessary to make citizens into rulers. Citizens were obligated to play a public role: to sit in rational, moral, and independent judgment on the common good; in practice they seem to have become the manipulated masses who abandon their roles as democratic rulers in favor of other attitudes toward politics. Recently the behavior of citizens, in increasing numbers, has been characterized by apathy, egoism, and extremism. These qualities are reflected in **The Retreat from Politics** in which politics is seen as corrupt or as unrelated to the more important concerns of private life; in **The Politics of "What's-in-it-for-me?"** in which votes are "purchased" in exchange for private and personal benefit; and in **The Politics of the Spleen** in which suspicion, hatred, and fear replace the democratic climate of mutual trust and respect that makes rational disagreement and controversy possible. Finally, there is a

Crisis in the Obligations of Leadership. Traditional democratic theory expected leaders to speak for "those who are voiceless," to stand for something, and to have the courage to risk defeat to promote their principles; modern political campaigns tend to be based not on issues but on appeals to private interests and on personality images created by public-relations firms; politicians tend to make winning of elections their primary goal and to make full use of the new techniques of **The Engineering of Consent** through psychological manipulation.

These gaps between theory and practice add up to a **Crisis in Democratic Politics,** which presents a fundamental challenge to traditional democratic theory, to be examined further in the next chapter.

It did not come easily to one who, like myself, had known the soft air of the world before the wars to recognize and acknowledge the sickness of the Western liberal democracies. Yet, as we were being drawn into the second of the great wars, there was no denying, it seemed to me, that there is a deep disorder in our society which comes not from the machinations of our enemies and from the adversities of the human condition but from within ourselves.

WALTER LIPPMANN

Chapter One

THE CRISIS OF
DEMOCRATIC POLITICS

*I*N THE YEARS since 1955, when he wrote these words,[1] Mr. Lippmann's concern has been widely shared by scholars and intellectuals. It has been reflected, too, in the less sophisticated but equally significant sense of political malaise felt by increasing numbers of common men. That average citizens often feel frustrated, angry, or alienated in the face of political processes is not surprising, for scholars themselves are not agreed on a diagnosis of the deep disorder in democratic governments, on how deep the disorder is, or on how it is to be remedied.

[1] Walter Lippmann, *The Public Philosophy* (New York: Mentor, 1955), p. 12.

This situation provides us with the conditions from which an effort to understand American government and politics must begin. Our starting point must be a recognition that the practices and realities of democratic politics have been undergoing profound and even revolutionary changes. As a result, we have reached a point where "to speak today of the defense of democracy as if we were defending something which we knew and had possessed for many decades or many centuries is self-deception and sham."[2] The political system under which we now live is not what democracy was presumed to mean in the past. It is, in many respects, essentially new, and many of the values and slogans inherited from the past are no longer reflected in our current political institutions. We are entitled, in the circumstances, to take neither the good health of American political institutions nor the adequacy of our inherited democratic ideals for granted.

The Anatomy of Political Crisis

We begin our approach to an understanding of American politics, then, on the assumption that the task is to confront and deal with a political system in a state of fundamental crisis. To say that the crisis in democratic politics is fundamental is to say that it involves a deep and widening gulf between the values and ideals that have been traditionally employed to explain and justify the political system and the actual operation of the system. Why the existence of such a gulf is an important matter becomes clear when we examine the nature of politics itself.

THE NATURE OF POLITICS

In the broadest sense, a situation may be said to be political when it contains individuals and groups with incompatible and conflicting interests, desires, or values. Political processes are those procedures used to resolve such conflicts. When political conflict occurs, it is impossible that all those with claims will be treated equally in the resolution of their differences. Any conceivable solution of differences will favor some individuals or groups over others. For this reason, politics is always concerned with power, with the exercise of discretion over the behavior of others, and with the ability to shape common policies and decisions binding on others in accordance with one's own desires. Politics, thus defined, is not confined to the arena of government. It is present in the

[2] E. H. Carr, *The New Society* (Boston: Beacon, 1957), p. 76.

conflicts, and the means of resolving them, in families, churches, corporations, labor unions, fraternities, universities—indeed, in every sort of social organization. Wherever there is conflict, there is politics.

POLITICS AND GOVERNMENT

We are concerned especially with that particular sphere of politics in which conflicts are viewed as affecting the interests of the entire community and in which public policies regulating the conflicts are accordingly brought into being or modified. The processes by which such public policies are formulated operate through the institutions of government. The formal structure of government includes legislatures, courts, executive officers, and administrative agencies. Informally, there is a wide range of other agencies and groups the central purposes of which are related more or less closely to the desire to influence the formal institutions of government in ways seen as desirable by their members: pressure groups, political parties, the mass media of communications.

The line between the private (or internal) politics of a fraternity, labor union, or corporation and the public politics of governmental policy-making is never fixed. What starts out as a private dispute—the conflict between labor and management within the corporation, for example—may be transferred to the public arena at whatever time it comes to be viewed as involving the political interest of the entire community. When this happens, the sphere of the conflict is extended and the political techniques employed come to be those that are relevant to influencing the governmental process. Sometimes this occurs because it is seen by one or several of the parties in a private conflict as an effective strategy for getting their way. Sometimes it is the result of third parties insisting successfully that the conflict involves a public interest that cannot be protected in the accommodations worked out by private interests. However it occurs, when a dispute is put into the governmental arena, its resolution becomes a matter of public policy to be embodied in law and administrative rulings applicable to all and enforced by the coercive power of the community.

Every political system, then, has two central characteristics: it formulates public policies that allocate power, influence, prestige, and wealth among conflicting forces in society; and the resulting policies have behind them the coercive force of society. There are many different ways of resolving disputes and conflict in society. When the interests or goals of two parties are incompatible, the solution may be provided, for example, by the rule of the stronger, by the verdict of an elite, by majority decision, by bargaining and compromise, or by invocation of established and traditional rules that prescribe the rights and obligations of the competing parties.

Power exercised through government means the ability to forbid and compel actions on the part of citizens and subjects. Democratic governments, too, are coercive in this sense, and their coercive power may always be brought to bear on individuals in order to maintain civil peace and protect the general welfare; to punish individuals for the violation of laws by depriving them of life, liberty, or property in accordance with defined legal procedures; to impose compulsory taxation requiring monetary contributions to the public treasury; and to acquire private property for public use after just compensation is made.

POWER AND AUTHORITY: THE PROBLEM OF LEGITIMACY

Government always "plays favorites" in the making of policy. Victory in the political struggle carries with it control over, or a disproportionate share in, decisions favoring some individuals or groups over others and yet binding on all. But why should those who do not fare well in the struggle, or lose out altogether, abide by the decisions that are made? The answer cannot be that "might makes right"; the proposition that power is its own justification has been advanced by a few philosophers, but it has never served as the basis for a political system in any society. Nor could it ever serve to deter those who lose out from seeking to become powerful enough to overthrow the system.

The fundamental political problem is always that of seeking to support the structure of political power with the voluntary support of those who are governed. Talleyrand is reported to have said to Napoleon: "You can do everything with bayonets, Sire, except sit on them." Pacifists and martyrs have always understood the same point: the desire to rule by brute force can always be frustrated by a people determined not to obey. For then, force must eliminate resistance and in the end there is no one left to be ruled. The same point—that the regular exercise of political power cannot rest basically on force—is expressed in the statement of a more recent observer that the art of ruling "is not so much a question of the heavy hand as of the firm seat."[3]

Before any political regime can be considered stable, the exercise of

[3] Jose Ortega y Gasset, *The Revolt of the Masses* (New York: Norton, 1957, 25th anniversary ed.), p. 127.

power in that regime must be judged to be legitimate by the majority of those over whom it is exercised so that their participation in its processes and their acquiescence in the execution of its laws is a matter of willing obligation, not of brute force or the threat of force. A substantial portion, at least, of those who are ruled obey not out of fear but because they feel they ought to. This is what we mean when we call a government legitimate; those subject to its commands regard them as bearing the stamp of rightful authority rather than sheer power. Often, the claim to legitimacy is neither rational nor consistent, but it is always an effort to create a psychological and moral sense of obligation as the basis for the citizen's obedience to law and his loyalty to the regime.

LEGITIMACY AND NORMATIVE THEORY

A political system may be accepted by its citizens as legitimate simply on the basis of habit, custom, and tradition. Thus in many so-called primitive societies political practices are sanctioned because they have existed from time immemorial and are sanctified by time-honored myths and legends. A fairly common myth endows the rulers with legitimate authority by tracing it back to a divine or semidivine god-king who was the founder of the tribe. But in the modern world origin-myths and custom have been replaced by explicit models or philosophies —sometimes called ideologies—that seek to translate political power into legitimate authority. When the cake of custom is crumbled, some explicit theoretical model must be invoked to justify a particular system of allocating political power.

The political quest of modern man comes to focus in the relationship of power to justice, reason, and morality. It is a quest for a solid ground on which man might stand to assert that some particular means of determining public policy translates power into authority; makes the exercise of power nonarbitrary; controls, mediates, or limits power by making it subservient to justice, reason, and morality. Fascism, Communism, democracy, liberalism, conservatism—all are efforts to construct theoretical models that would support the assertion that a particular political system provides a means of substituting reason, justice, or morality for human will or whim in public policy.

For men to put the question of political legitimacy to themselves assumes that man has a choice. It assumes the possibility of a distinction between what is and what ought to be. It assumes some possibility of human control over human destiny. The question itself reflects a recognition of the fact that man, unlike other animals, has cut himself off or been cut off from nature and from custom and is thus faced with the necessity of choice. Deprived of instinct or habit as sure and unconscious guides to action, man faces the problem of seeking a rational or moral ground for behavior. He asks how he ought to behave and why. To answer this question, he cannot avoid putting other questions to himself: What kind of creature is he? Where is the substitute for instinct to be found: in subjectively given inner drives, emotions, and passions: in an objective, transcendental reality where exist immutable and eternal principles of truth and morality accessible to human faith or reason: in the fallible and tentative conclusions resulting from human reflection on human experience?

Out of such questions as these is the conscious study of government born. And in man's efforts to find answers and apply them to the problem of power does it live. Each such effort rests on assumptions about the nature of man, of truth, of history, and of society. On these assumptions are built answers to the basic questions of politics: *How* (on what basis, by what methods) ought political decisions be made? *Who* ought to make them? What are the limits, if any, on the exercise of political authority? These are the normative questions of politics; theories that supply answers to them are normative theories. That is to say, they do more than describe how people do in fact behave politically; they seek to *prescribe* how people *ought* to behave. Normative theories contain norms or standards for making judgments about what ought to be; they seek to justify some desirable or ideal state of affairs.

DEMOCRACY AS NORMATIVE THEORY

Democracy, for example, is a normative theory because it makes certain assertions about how government ought to be organized. It asserts that the masses of the people themselves ought to play an important role in the making of policy. It asserts that the powers of government are inherently limited and that there are certain areas of private judgment and action that ought to be exempted from governmental regulation. But these normative statements about how government ought to be organized and limited are not self-evidently true. Autocratic and elitist theories of government argue that the *real* interests of the people (as distinct from what they may think is good for them) can only be interpreted and promoted by a single individual or a small group of individuals who are alleged to have access to Truths not available to others. If there is some body of Absolute Truths, if most men are precluded from seeing them or acting on them by their innate sinfulness, and if there is a group of men who may be counted on to discern the Truth more fully and to act more selflessly than others, then an elitist theory of government will make sense.

Authoritarian models of government, by vesting power in an elite, challenge the democratic ideal of popular participation in the making of policy. Similarly, totalitarian models of government challenge the democratic idea that the powers of government must be limited to protect the rights of individuals and groups in society. Totalitarian theory justifies governmental control over all aspects of social and individual life on grounds that such control is necessary for the achievement of a blueprint for social and individual perfection.

The Crisis of Legitimacy in American Politics

In the preceding two paragraphs we have written as if there were clear and widespread agreement on the meaning of the theory of democracy. But this is not really the case. At the root of our current predicament are two fundamental facts of modern political life: (1) there is a wide gulf between our traditional theories and our current political practices, and (2) the democratic ideals that historically gave both justification and direction to democratic practices are themselves now in dispute so that any discussion of democracy requires that we deal with conflicting theories of democracy.

THE GULF BETWEEN THEORY AND PRACTICE

There are striking gaps between model and reality, between the norms and values to which our allegiance to democratic theory commits us and the actual processes of American politics. By way of clarification, consider the following examples of such dichotomies:

1. **The American Dilemma.** Among the premises of eighteenth-century thought, reflected clearly in the language of the Declaration of Independence, were the doctrines of natural rights and of human equality. Yet these ideals were never applied, until very recently, to the condition of the Negro in the United States. Under the institution of slavery, the Negro was simply treated as an exception. The end of slavery meant the extension of the promise of equality to the Negro, a promise that the political system had to fulfill if it were to retain its

claim to legitimacy. For a hundred years the promise went unfulfilled but never ceased to torment the American political conscience. The meaningful steps that have been taken in the last decade have been possible, indeed inevitable, because the promise was deeply embedded in our political faith. That faith justifies and makes legitimate the claim of civil rights groups to "Freedom Now"; outside of some areas in the South where the faith has never been accepted, it reduces those who would resist the movement to the plea, "Not so fast." It is significant that the urgency of the movement has been intensified as the gulf between theory and reality has been clearly and generally perceived. The resulting strains on the body politic—the use of techniques of civil disobedience and of direct political action and the occasional breakdown of law and order—should not be surprising. They are the normal consequences of a crisis involving the legitimacy of the political system.

2. **Public Interest or Group Compromise.** If the American dilemma of race were the only instance of a basic gap between ideal and reality, our problems would be much simpler than, in fact, they are. But there are others equally as fundamental. For example, we still profess ourselves to be committed to the idea of a public interest, a conception of the general or common welfare, which it is the function of our political system to seek out and implement. Yet, the most striking characteristic of our actual politics is that the struggle for power is dominated by special-interest groups, each bent on advancing its own special claims; actual policies tend to be compromises of these partial and self-interested claims. Thus, while our generally accepted normative ideas about democracy require that public policies reflect the considered and public-spirited judgments of individual citizens, the actual policy-making process is more often simply a response to the organized pressures of interest groups. To approach the same issue from a different direction, we may also say that whereas our inherited ideals call for rule by a majority whose opinions are the result of a rational debate of issues, our actual processes of public policy-making are more often the result of bargains negotiated among organized groups.

3. **Independent Voters or Manipulated Masses.** Similarly, our normative ideals define the ballot box as the supreme institution of democracy and require that the citizen cast his vote knowledgeably and independently. But, in recent years, the rapid growth of techniques of psychological manipulation and the application of the methods and morality of advertising to political campaigns have seemed to turn the

electorate into a mass market for the merchandising of public images created by professional public-relations men. Moreover, if the voter is easily manipulated, it is because citizens no longer act out the roles that traditional democratic theory required of them; that is, they were to give serious attention and study to public problems, seeking to formulate a judgment in the best interest of the entire community. In practice, however, voters tend to behave not as citizens but as private persons, seeing politics as a device for promoting their private and special interests against those of other individuals and groups. The result is an electorate that can be manipulated by appeals to private desires and passions, rather than a public to which reasoned arguments about public policy can be addressed.

4. The Engineered Consent of the Governed. The dominance of interest groups, the prevalence of compromise among them as a way of making policy, and the refinements of the techniques of psychological manipulation rob the citizen of his traditional role as governor and make a mockery of the traditional ideal of government by the consent of the governed. That ideal, as it was propounded in our political folklore, has meaning only where consent is freely and independently given by rational, public-spirited citizens. Under modern conditions of political advertising and manipulation, it has become possible to talk of the engineering of consent by an elite of experts and professional politicians. Consent that is thus engineered is difficult to distinguish in any fundamental way from the consent that supports modern totalitarian governments. Were the manipulated voter to become the normal voter, the government he supports could hardly be said to rest on his consent in any traditional sense of that word.

As these four very broad examples indicate, the most fundamental beliefs in our traditional democratic faith are now challenged by our political practices. The inconsistencies add up to a crisis because they go to the very heart of democratic doctrine, involving as they do the nature of the policy-making process, the role of citizens, and the behavior of politicians and political parties. We will get a clearer view of the dilemma of American politics at midcentury by examining in closer detail the conflict between ideal and reality in each of these areas.

THE CRISIS IN POLICY-MAKING

It is an obvious and inescapable fact that American society confronts difficult and complex problems: discrimination directed against ethnic and religious minorities; poverty, which characterizes from a fourth to a third of American families; rat-infested urban slums and general urban blight; inadequate medical care; unemployment aggravated by the pressures of automation; foreign tensions and the threat of nuclear war; organized crime; and increasing delinquency rates. One need not be a Cassandra to recognize that America has not yet become the "Good Society" or the "Sane Society." There is a long and difficult agenda on the way to becoming what President Lyndon B. Johnson calls the "Great Society." These facts do not, in themselves, constitute a crisis in the political order. Democracy never promised a Utopia. The crisis lies in a widespread perversion of what democracy did promise: a procedure through which men could work rationally, peacefully, and creatively toward the solution of their problems.

The essence of democratic procedure was held to be reasoned debate of alternative solutions to public problems. It offered a unique solution to the problem of power conflict, a solution that would control conflict without seeking to eliminate it. It was a method of creating unity out of diversity without seeking to create uniformity. Perhaps the central characteristic that distinguished it from all other forms of government lay in the fact that it recognized the legitimate place and function of an opposition. A leading modern political scientist has expressed clearly this underlying premise of popular government:

> Above everything, *the people are powerless if political enterprise is not competitive.* It is the competition of political organizations that provides the people with the opportunity to make a choice. Without this opportunity popular sovereignty amounts to nothing.[4]

This process claimed to enable men to correct their mistakes, to free themselves from the necessity of drifting with the tide of events, to make men the masters of their own destinies, to substitute reason for violence, discussion for warfare, and conscious control for undirected drift.

Public Debate and the Politics of Moderation. How, then, do the current processes of American democracy measure up to this standard? A dramatic illustration of the gulf between ideal and reality in policy-making was afforded when, on March 25, 1964, Senator Fulbright, Democrat from Arkansas, rose on the floor of the United States Senate to make a major speech on the need for re-examination of the "myths" on which American foreign policy had rested in the period after World War II. The circumstances surrounding his speech and its consequences

---

[4] E. E. Schattschneider, *The Semisovereign People* (New York: Holt, Rinehart and Winston, 1960), p. 140. Italics in original.

are intriguing. In the first place, it was made in the solemn setting of what in the American political folklore has often been called "the greatest deliberative body in the world." The same scene had been the setting for the great Webster-Hayne debates and for the parliamentary and forensic abilities of such leaders as Clay, Benton, Calhoun, George W. Norris, and Robert A. Taft.

But when, in 1964, Senator Fulbright addressed himself to what is generally recognized as one of the great and fateful and perplexing problems of our time, it was almost literally true that he "addressed himself": few Senators remained in the chamber. His speech, which might have been the signal for a great debate of a fateful issue, had almost no political consequences. In response to the proddings of the press, his fellow Democrats, including the incumbent President, disavowed his views without challenging them or pleaded ignorance on grounds that they had not heard the speech. His Republican colleagues either took the latter course or labeled the speech "irresponsible." Almost no politician took up the challenge, and the course of Senate proceedings was almost totally unaffected.

Senator Fulbright's experience is not unique. When, on rare occasions, a sustained debate on an issue occurs in the Senate, it is not always clear that the effect of the debate is the formulation of alternatives or the clarification of the issue under consideration. Senator Joseph S. Clark, Democrat from Pennsylvania, recently described the atmosphere surrounding the Senate debate over the ratification of the test-ban treaty with the Soviet Union in 1963:

> . . . with few exceptions during the twelve days of debate on the treaty, the discussion consisted of set speeches made to an almost empty chamber. There were thirty-odd Senators present when Senator William Fulbright opened the "debate." That was the high-water mark. When I spoke in support of the treaty, there were three Senators on the floor. Senator Barry Goldwater made one of the principal speeches against the treaty to a Senatorial audience of four. Senator John Stennis drew six. When Senator Strom Thurmond called for a "live" quorum before he made his speech, it took almost an hour to round up the fifty-one Senators. As soon as they answered to their names they left the chamber. By the time Senator Thurmond got into the body of his speech, there was no one on the floor except the presiding officer and a junior Republican Senator who was present to protect Republican interests against sudden and unexpected attack.[5]

[5] Senator Joseph S. Clark, "A New Kind of Election," *Harper's Magazine*, May, 1964, pp. 76, 78. Earlier in the same article Senator Clark had pointed out that much of the "debate" had bypassed the real issues: "There was an enormous amount

The quality of Congressional debate clearly falls short of what our inherited ideals would require. But it is even rare for issues to be debated at all on the floor of the Senate and much rarer still in the House of Representatives. Walter Lippmann has repeatedly criticized the Congress for creating an impasse that brings the government to a standstill by frustrating and blocking the efforts of Presidents to deal creatively with such pressing national problems as unemployment and economic growth, tax reform, and civil rights. Lippmann's criticism is that Congress has developed procedures that "smother and strangle" presidential proposals without debate and before they can come to a vote:

> But to my mind the process of smothering measures in committees is a subversion of the principles of representative government. It is a subversion in that it prevents public debate. Yet debate is the great educator of democratic peoples. It is a subversion in that it prevents a decision by a vote, which is the sovereign principle of democracy.[6]

These and similar criticisms of Congress have become commonplace in recent years, and they are mirrored in more general criticism of the character of American politics. If democracy requires reasoned debate of significant alternatives, then clearly political parties must provide for the organization of political competition. The party system has come in for the same kind of criticism that has been directed against Congress. The two major parties, in this view, have jostled with each other to occupy the center of the political road in the three decades since the end of the New Deal reforms. Their common rallying cry has come to be "Moderation." Even though the rhetoric of party politicians has included exhortations to join a "Great Crusade," to embark on a "New Frontier," or to rise to the challenges of a "Great Society," such phrases have floated down the slow current of the mainstream of a general consensus that no drastic innovations were necessary or desirable. During these years the term *extremism* came into common currency as a device for putting those who argued for fundamental changes beyond the pale of legitimate controversy. Both parties concentrated on locating and occupying the middle ground that would express the general consensus

---

of poking around in corners alleged to be dark and mysterious for the purpose of unmasking sinister Russians bent on setting off nuclear explosions on the other side of the moon, where the Communists could see what was going on but we couldn't."

[6] Walter Lippmann, "A Critique of Congress," *Newsweek*, January 20, 1964, p. 18.

of Americans, and it was no accident that this consensus resembled more and more a defense of the *status quo.*

Choices and Echoes. In 1964 the Republican party broke sharply from this precedent and nominated a presidential candidate who offered the voters a "choice, not an echo."[7] Yet even then no real issues were very clearly joined. There were two major reasons. Candidate Goldwater, who had promised a campaign based on the domestic policies advanced in his book, *The Conscience of a Conservative,* and the foreign policies propounded in his *Why Not Victory?* responded to adverse early reactions in both areas and ended up basing his campaign on such tried and proven noncontroversial issues as public and official morality and law and order.[8] The second reason that real issues tended not to emerge was that the Democrats made extremism the issue—a charge to which the Goldwater candidacy was vulnerable, though the campaign blurred the distinction between the tactics and outlook of extremist groups and mere opposition to existing policies. Republicans, including National Chairman Dean Burch, complained about the refusal of the opposition to engage in debate. The Democrats won a resounding victory by moving further to occupy the center that the Republicans had vacated. The result was a new triumph for moderation and the public avoidance of conflict and controversy.

But democratic theory has not been predicated on the avoidance of conflict; it has always been proclaimed to provide a procedure through which conflicts can be resolved after their bases have been thoroughly explored through rational debate and formulated into alternatives for political choice. In this process political parties play a key and decisive role. Theirs is the responsibility to formulate and defend alternatives. Without the political competition they are capable of providing, policy tends to become rigidly inflexible and responsible government, in the traditional sense, to become impossible.

THE CRISES IN THE OBLIGATIONS OF CITIZENSHIP

The model for the resolution of political conflicts whose broad outlines are sketched in the preceding section was built on certain assumptions

---

[7] The phrase is the title of Phyllis Schlafly's widely circulated campaign paperback, *A Choice Not an Echo* (Alton, Ill.: Pere Marquette Press, 1964).

[8] Barry Goldwater, *The Conscience of a Conservative* (New York: Victor, 1960); *Why Not Victory?* (New York: McGraw-Hill, 1962).

concerning the nature of man and society and of human knowledge. Like all models that justify political systems, it made legitimate certain techniques in the struggle for power and proscribed others. In order for its political processes to operate, it laid down certain norms for the behavior of participants in those processes. Specifically, democratic theory contained a set of specifications regulating the behavior of citizens and politicians.

Democratic theory asserted that legitimate political power stems from and must be continuously responsible to the people who comprise the citizenry. Democratic citizens play a dual role: they are rulers when they make the laws or elect those who will make them; they are subjects when they obey the laws they have participated in making. In his role as subject the democratic man was to be protected by a whole range of guarantees against administrative arbitrariness and unfairness. These guarantees had been built up over several generations of Anglo-American legal tradition; they are enumerated in the Bill of Rights of the Constitution. As we will see in later chapters, these guarantees have always been fragile and precarious because of a continuing tendency to deal with unpopular individuals—for example, Communists, Fascists, habitual criminals—by denying them due process of law. But our main concern here is with the other role of the citizen—his role as ruler—and with the question of how closely the actual behavior of citizens fits the requirements of traditional theory.

Citizens as Rulers. The central requirement of democratic citizens as rulers was clearly expressed by President Kennedy in his inaugural address. Recently elected to the highest office in the United States, by a hairline margin of votes, the handsome young President called upon his countrymen to "ask not what your country can do for you, but what you can do for your country." President Kennedy's exhortation to his people was a poetic expression of what democracy had always demanded of its citizens: that they be, in part of their lives at least, public men; that they enter the public arena not exclusively in pursuit of their private desires and interests, but in order to ensure that justice prevails in the affairs of men and in order to promote the common interest. The early theorists of democracy had argued that if self-serving monarchs and despots are not to be trusted, neither is a self-seeking majority. If reason and morality are to prevail in public policy, then democratic citizens must seek to be reasonable and moral in their public roles.

The impact of Kennedy's words—they became perhaps his best remembered phrase—reflected a deep-seated recognition of how far democratic citizens have departed from the role demanded of them by their traditional faith. Status striving and the pressures of private affluence in the years after World War II had tended to make the successful pursuit of personal material gain the recognized cultural standard of individual success. It was not surprising that the affluent way of life had spilled over into politics to exhibit a pattern of political motivation in which opportunism and personal interest were dominant. A culture whose values prompt it to rely on the slogan "Drive Safely: The Life You Save May Be Your Own" to minimize what others have called "murder on the highways" was quite likely to produce a pathological supply of egoistic self-seeking in politics. "What's in it for me?" would seem to be the logical political corollary of the "Affluent Society."[9]

At the same time it would be inaccurate to imply that the norms of democracy required citizens always to behave like Plato's philosopher-kings. Democracy always recognized a tension in individual citizens between the private pursuit of personal wealth, prestige, influence, and favor and the public-spirited pursuit of justice and welfare for all. This tension is ubiquitous and, as Joseph Tussman puts it, is an enduring characteristic of democratic politics:

> At the heart of political life there is an inescapable tension between interest and duty, between the inclinations of private life and the obligations of the public role. Attempts to resolve the tension from either direction are failures. On the one hand, attempts to absorb the individual into his public role so that there is no recalcitrant remainder founder on the fact that man is, after all, an animal, a striving biological organism with a particular identity. No matter how "social" or "mature" or "integrated" he may be he cannot abolish the difference between the immediate and the remote, the particular and the general, "my own" and "theirs" or even "ours." No theory about the identity of individual and social can quite conceal the difference. Similarly, attempts to dissolve the public role and its demands into the private individual and his interest do not survive much exposure to the plain facts of social life. The conflict between interest and obligation cannot be conjured away: political life will always involve us in moral dilemmas.[10]

[9] The phrase is from the title of an influential book: John K. Galbraith. *The Affluent Society* (Boston: Houghton-Mifflin, 1958). One of the clearest expressions of this tendency was the promise of several business concerns to pay bonuses to their employees if the 1964 Republican candidate, Senator Goldwater, was elected President. (*Sacramento Bee*, November 1, 1964, p. A2.)

[10] Joseph Tussman, *Obligation and the Body Politic* (New York: Oxford, 1960), p. 18.

Democratic theory recognized the dilemma Tussman describes. It was, in fact, a theory of politics aimed at resolving the conflict between individualism and community, not by depriving man of the rights and liberties necessary for his private pursuits, but by containing them within community standards. The standards themselves, to be considered legitimate, were to follow from public debate of public problems in which citizens transcended their private lives sufficiently to participate in a public-spirited and rational manner. The realities of current American politics contradict this ideal in three significant ways.

The Retreat from Politics. In the first place, a large and apparently growing number of citizens have retreated altogether from the political arena and have come to see politics as "dirty" and corrupt, a game played by the wealthy and the powerful for their own purposes in which the common man is powerless and stands only to disrupt his domestic tranquility. The resulting withdrawal from politics not only keeps one out of the smoke-filled rooms, it reflects usually a callous indifference and dispassionate aloofness from the troubles of one's fellow citizens. It is a social as well as a political attitude. Men come to see themselves as islands unto themselves and seek their rewards and enjoyments in the small circles of their private lives.

Shocking illustrations of this withdrawal from social responsibility have occurred with increasing frequency in recent years. On March 13, 1964, a twenty-eight-year-old woman was knifed to death in a suburban area of Long Island in a struggle that lasted nearly an hour while thirty-eight persons heard her screams for help but ignored them in favor of their television sets or their beds. On May 4, an eighteen-year-old secretary was raped and beaten in broad daylight in the Bronx while forty witnesses watched silently without feeling enough obligation to interfere or even to call for help. The outbreak of such incidents prompted police officials around the country to remind us that a major difficulty in their efforts to enforce the law is the tendency for citizens to avoid becoming involved. Private citizens, in their cocktail party and living room conversations, recounted examples from their own experience of the same lack of concern, the same dispassionate withdrawal of individuals into their private worlds.

This desire to avoid becoming involved in the problems of others is more than a social characteristic; it has profound political implications. It reveals a lack of the same sense of public obligation that would prompt and enable a democratic citizen to forego private desires and run the risks involved in responsible political participation. The ancient Greek lawgiver Solon described the basic precondition of both social and political responsibility in his maxim that justice depends on the capacity of citizens to feel wrongs suffered by anyone as wrongs suffered by themselves. Politically, because he is a participant in a regime that rests on popular sovereignty, democratic man is morally involved in the misdeeds and injustices of government. There is no way in a democratic society for this responsibility to be transferred.[11]

The Politics of "What's-in-It-for-Me?" Not all those who lack a sense of democratic obligation retreat from the political arena. Others see politics as a means to the advancement of their private interests and desires. This is true of individuals, groups, and political constituencies. So far has this approach to politics come to prevail that some political scientists see the American political process frankly as a system of organized bribery in which votes are exchanged for personal favors; for support of higher parity payments for farmers, a higher minimum wage for labor, or lower taxes for stockholders; or for a new highway or dam in a candidate's district. Thus both noninvolvement and the pursuit of private gain in politics operate to undermine the sense of obligation that traditional democratic ideals required of the citizen.

The Politics of the Spleen. The third way in which the realities of current American politics contradict the norms of democratic citizenship is almost the reverse of the noninvolvement and the self-seeking participation we have been describing. In recent years a growing minority of citizens have become involved with a vengeance that destroys rational politics. For not only did democratic political obligation require the engagement in public affairs of its citizens, it required that participation be rational and respectful of the integrity and the views of other citizens. Perhaps the ultimate restraint on the carrying on of political conflict was the assumption that individual citizens would act with integrity and within the framework of mutual honesty and trust. Hatred, fear, suspicion, and a conspiratorial view of politics are as destructive of democratic ideas of obligation as is a total retreat from public affairs.

Another recent event provides a graphic illustration of the extent to which these forces are operative. Mrs. Madalyn Murray had instituted a suit claiming that the recitation of prayers in the schools of Maryland (Baltimore) constituted an establishment of religion contrary to the

[11] A fascinating analysis of this problem is to be found in Edmond Cahn, *The Predicament of Democratic Man* (New York: Macmillan, 1961).

First Amendment to the Constitution. When the Supreme Court upheld her claim, a national furor was touched off. For her part, Mrs. Murray lost her job and was unable to find another, despite the fact that she had a law degree and seventeen years' experience as a psychiatric social worker. Her two sons were beaten and stoned. Thousands of "involved" citizens wrote her abusive and threatening letters. One said, "You filthy atheist. Only a rat like you would go to court to stop prayer. All curses on you and your family. Bad luck and leprosy disease upon you and your damn family."[12]

Increasingly, in recent years, citizens who have had the courage to stick their necks out on controversial issues have had to bear the brunt of threatening and abusive anonymous telephone calls and poison-pen letters. Public officials, too, have been subjected to the same pressures. On May 2, 1963, Republican Senator Thomas Kuchel from California felt compelled to draw the attention of his Senate colleagues and the public to the mail he had been receiving. In a memorable Senate speech he quoted from what used to be described as "crank mail" but which was then pouring into his office at the rate of about six thousand letters each month. The burden of most of this mail was the demand that the Senator: "Get the United States out of the U.N. Stop all foreign aid. Repeal the income tax. Abandon NATO and bring our troops home from Europe." Senator Kuchel described it as "fright mail." Its tone was hysterical, fearful, conspiratorial, hateful, suspicious, and intemperate. As he made clear, Senator Kuchel was appalled by the mood and approach of the letters, not the position taken on substantive issues:

> Let us, by all means, debate, as reasonable and rational and realistic people, the successes and failures of the United Nations and foreign aid.
> But let us not do it on the basis of childish slogans or the inane premise that they are Communist programs adopted by a Communist or pro-Communist Government in Washington.[13]

The climate of American public life was further revealed when Senator Kuchel's speech was widely heralded as an act of extraordinary courage. And so it turned out to be. For the reaction was an enlarged torrent of abuse, filth, threat, and calumny that far exceeded in vitriol and unrestraint the original attacks. The Senator responded with a

---

12 *Saturday Evening Post*, July 11, 1964, p. 86.
13 *Congressional Record*, May 2, 1963, pp. 7215-21.

subsequent speech in which he revealed the new excesses of the "fright peddlers."

The same political temper was apparent in the battle for the Republican presidential nomination in 1964, particularly in the California primary where New York Governor Rockefeller was campaigning as the leader of a stop-Goldwater coalition and in the Republican convention. At the convention the behavior of the zealots, particularly in the gallery, when Rockefeller rose to speak in support of the insertion of an antiextremist plank in the platform provided an object lesson for television viewers in the perversion of political enthusiasm.

The Case of the Disappearing Citizen. What are the implications of these phenomena for democratic politics? On the one side are the apparently growing numbers of citizens who are morally apathetic, dispassionate spectators who retreat from involvement and public responsibility or whose interest in politics is confined to considerations of "What's in it for me?" On the other side, also in apparently growing numbers, are the new political activists who enter the political arena with their fangs bared and with a lust for the blood and reputations of those who oppose them. In this crush between the retreat from political responsibility and the politics of the spleen, between dispassionate withdrawal and unrestrained passion in politics, where is the ideal of the citizen who is both passionate and responsible, committed and reasonable? The traditional democratic idea envisioned men who can and do disagree, but whose disagreements are contained in the framework of a reasoned dialogue that assumed a mutual respect for the dignity and integrity of all. "Integrity of views," said Jefferson, "more than their soundness, is the basis of mutual esteem." To some significant extent this model of civic decency in the relations of citizens with one another has been rendered irrelevant by those who renounce civic obligation, and it has been destroyed by those who regard decency as weakness or appeasement. As a result it becomes possible for us to speak of a crisis in the obligations of democratic citizenship.

THE CRISIS IN THE OBLIGATIONS OF LEADERSHIP

When we come to consider how it was that our inherited democratic ideals expected politicians to behave, we are on somewhat more uncertain ground. Why, in one version of the democratic theory, do we need leaders at all? If the people are to be sovereign, then all that is necessary is that they have agents who will do their bidding. In this grass-roots, Jacksonian interpretation, public officials should be recruited from the ranks of Mr. Average Voter; no special competence, training, or commitment is either necessary or desirable. This version of democratic doctrine holds that the proper responsibility of the politician is simply to ascertain what his constituents desire, at least what a majority of them desire, and then to act on it. He has no real responsibilities of leadership, no obligation to have ideas and principles of his own, no responsibility to participate in a political dialogue that is an important part of the education of citizens.

It is such ideas as these that led Charles Frankel to make the following observations:

> If I were to identify the most serious defect of received democratic theory, I would say it is the tendency to suppress the significance of leadership in a democracy. The crucial question is the recruitment and distribution of leaders. Are the best people in a given society willing to go into politics? Do they find the public life a satisfying and rich one? Is it too punishing? Is the morality or the code of politics one from which they would retreat? . . . Where are the leaders of those who are voiceless? Where are the moralists? Where, if you will, are the poets?[14]

Politicians as Leaders. Professor Frankel is challenging the ideal of the democratic politician as errand boy for his constituents' desires. But this ideal was not the only, or the major, interpretation of the role of leadership in democracy. Indeed, the ideal of an issue-oriented, reason-dominated process for resolving disputes and the ideal of informed, public-spirited citizens both required something more of those who aspire to political leadership. These ideals required that politicians stand for something, that they have the courage of their convictions even at the risk of political defeat, that they feel obligated to argue publicly their differences with their opponents and to seek to persuade voters to their positions. Only thus could citizens become knowledgeable about the issues and be presented with significant alternatives. Controversy and alternatives were viewed as key elements in democratic policy-making, and it was regarded as the politician's job to provide them.

This latter interpretation of the meaning of leadership in democratic

---

[14] Senator J. William Fulbright, and others, *The Elite and the Electorate* (Santa Barbara, Calif.: The Fund for the Republic, 1963), pp. 10-11.

theory is perhaps the dominant one in the expectations of Americans. It is often expressed in various and sometimes apparently incongruous forms. In the columns of American newspapers during the 1964 presidential campaign, for example, a persistent theme ran through many of the "Letters to the Editor," which amounted to this: "I don't necessarily agree with everything Goldwater stands for, but at least I know where he stands." The clear implication was that Senator Goldwater ought to have been supported because he alone lived up to the fundamental criterion by which democratic politicians should be judged; he alone had both the required convictions and the courage necessary to stand and argue publicly for them. The frequency of such appeals attests to the fact that the ideal they express is still widely held. The late President Kennedy, then a senator, expressed the same ideal in his book *Profiles in Courage*, in which he traced the contributions to American politics of a series of men who, as the cover copy on the paperback edition expresses it, "at crucial times in our history, risked their personal and public lives to do the one thing that seemed in itself right."[15]

Profile or Courage? If this ideal is regarded as part of our authentic political heritage, there is, again, reason for profound concern about the actual state of affairs in our practical politics. We may doubt that Senator Goldwater stands out as a lone beacon of civic virtue in a darkness of political obsequiousness and cynical vote-mongering. We may question whether the typical American politician is an expedient trimmer completely lacking in conviction or totally willing to conceal his convictions from the voters in order to further his own political career. But we must take into account the fact that the absence of meaningful public debate and significant alternatives has led some citizens to such cynical campaign humor as the slogan "Vote No for President," and that there is some substance to the complaint that underlies the slogan. One disenchanted observer of American politics was even led to suggest that there was "more profile than courage" exhibited in Kennedy's own later conduct in his successful quest for the presidential nomination.

The typical political campaign is *not* distinguished by controversy

---

[15] John F. Kennedy, *Profiles in Courage* (New York: Pocket Books, 1957). The ideals described in the book still reflect the political faith of large numbers of Americans as shown by the fact that it has remained on the best-seller list almost continuously since its publication and by the popular television series based on it.

over real issues or by the public defense of political principles by contending candidates. Campaigns may be aimed at "belly issues"; they may be based on promises to do good for everybody; they may appeal subtly to bigotry, prejudice, and fear. Slogans abound: "Tippecanoe and Tyler Too"; "Back to Normalcy"; "A Fair Deal"; "A Square Deal"; "I Will Go to Korea"; "Get the Country Moving Again"—all aimed at filling the partisan silos with votes. They attempt to strike or capture a mood among the electorate that will result in the broadest kind of favorable response without running the risk of alienating any significant group of voters. The content of the appeal seems irrelevant, as long as the jump spark is made between the candidate's pitch and the citizen's vote. A candidate who seeks to stick to the issues and to aim at the reason of the voters is often accused of talking over their heads.

"Losing Isn't Anything." Perhaps the heart of the matter is that it has become an unwritten rule of American political practice that the purpose of entering politics is to win an election. A highly successful and influential politician, the Speaker of the California State Assembly, Mr. Jesse M. Unruh, spoke frankly for this view of the politician's role:

> . . . some of my more skittish friends once in a while chide me for wanting to win a little too badly. They tell me "Jess, winning isn't everything." To this I readily accede. Winning isn't everything but losing isn't anything. . . .[16]

Mr. Unruh's clever formulation expresses an attitude toward politics with which most politicians would probably agree. But it clashes head-on with an important traditional ideal of what a democratic politician should be and do. Winning, zealously pursued, can destroy the integrity of both candidate and voter. Under the conditions of mass society, described in a later chapter, it is likely to lead especially to the non-controversial, moderate posture of the man who seeks to please everyone. This, in turn, leads to the demise of significant political dialogue.

The general complaint that politicians are long on "profile" and short on principles and courage is not a new phenomenon in American politics. The muckraking author Frank Norris, in *The Octopus*, a widely read novel written in 1901, made the same charge. In his description of what he then regarded as the "new-style" politician, he implied that things used to be better. Note the graphic contrast in Norris' view of the new and the traditional styles of politics in the following description:

[16] Address by Jesse M. Unruh to the San Francisco Democratic Associates, January 17, 1963. Mimeographed, p. 1.

> Lyman, Magnus's eldest son, . . . told himself he was a born poli-
> tician, was diplomatic, approachable, had a talent for intrigue, a gift
> for making friends easily and, most indispensable of all, a veritable
> genius for putting influential men under obligations to himself. . . .
> The largeness of his father's character, modified in Lyman by a counter
> influence of selfishness, had produced in him an inordinate ambition.
> Where his father during his political career had considered himself
> only as an exponent of principles he strove to apply, Lyman saw but the
> office, his own personal aggrandizement. He belonged to the new school,
> wherein objects were not obtained before senates and assemblies, but
> by sessions of committees, caucuses, compromises and expedients. His
> goal was to be in fact what Magnus had been only in name—gover-
> nor.[17]

If the gulf between traditional democratic theory and political reality
is not new, what makes it an urgent problem now? Why may it now
be regarded as a crisis in which the stakes are the fundamental character
of our political system? The major justification for making such an
assertion is that in recent years a whole new array of techniques has
been added to the arsenal of political power, as a result of which the
problem of manipulation is more dramatically obvious and the process
more efficient and successful.

The Engineering of Consent. In 1952, an American political party
for the first time turned over the conduct of its national campaign to
professional experts in persuasion when the Republicans engaged the
services of a leading Madison Avenue public-relations firm. In 1956
the Democrats followed suit, and the American public was treated to
the first of what was to become a quadrennial national contest between
rival experts in the fine arts of winning votes and influencing voting
decisions. The techniques, and most of the experts themselves, were
borrowed directly from the world of commercial advertising and mass
communication. The same firms were often involved in selling breakfast
cereal and "fastback" cars along with political candidates, and with
the same methods.

Our modern vocabulary of campaigning reflects the character of
these techniques: we speak of the image of a candidate that is projected
to a mass audience rather than of who the candidate *is* and what he
thinks; candidates may be said to be packaged for audience appeal in
the same way that products are; voters are treated as consumers of
campaigns, their votes as purchases that measure the effectiveness of the

---

[17] Frank Norris, *The Octopus* (New York: New American Library, 1964), p. 49.

sales campaign; voters will buy this, not that; the electorate is divided by the professionals into "target groups"; and so on.

Over three hundred years ago the great, controversial Genevan political philosopher Jean Jacques Rousseau lamented that the prospects for a free and democratic society were darkened by the fact that "the arts of pleasing have been developed into a system. The question is no longer whether a man is honest, but only whether he is clever." Rousseau's diagnosis was premature, as recent developments in "the arts of pleasing" and persuasion show. And the new system is supported by a whole new array of "scientific" and technological gimmicks. Consider, in addition to the techniques of modern public relations, the following recent developments.

The Uses of Public-Opinion Polls. Public-opinion polls, developed in their modern scientific form in the 1930's, were originally used in politics almost exclusively to predict the outcome of elections. Recently they have found two more significant uses. In the first place, a legislator may have polls conducted of his constituents on particular issues in order to decide how to cast his vote in the legislature. The politician who uses polling techniques in this way may have no political conscience of his own; he may conscientiously define his role as errand boy for his constituents. Or he may resolve conflicts between his conscience and his constituents' wishes with the convenient rationalization offered by one state legislator: "If you don't vote your district, you won't be back to vote your conscience." In either case, the poll has become a technological substitute, of great efficiency and effectiveness, for both conscience and courage on the part of the politician.

The "People Machine." The second, related, modern use of public-opinion-polling techniques is both more sophisticated and more devastating in its effect on the ideals that traditionally defined the role of the democratic politician. In the 1960 presidential campaign the Democrats engaged the services of a corporation founded by a group of academic specialists in the various aspects of the scientific study of voting behavior. They were engaged to advise the Kennedy organization on which campaign tactics and appeals would be most effective. The answers were obtained from a modern, high-speed computer into which experts had fed a "model" of the voting public, broken down into the factors that earlier studies had shown to be related to voting behavior, and data on attitudes gathered from polling. The objective was to estimate "the relative gain or loss to be obtained from adopting one strategic alternative over another."[18] The approach of the Kennedy campaign to the religious issue in 1960 was based on the predictions generated by the machine.[19]

The basic technique involved here was not new. Public-opinion polling has been used for many years by public-relations firms in shaping a merchandising campaign for a product, and it has been used for the same purpose in political campaign management.[20] The significance of the refinements of this technique is that it may soon be possible, if it is not now, to turn over the planning of a campaign to electronic computers. A nationwide contest for high public office between IBM, RCA, and Westinghouse electronic computers would make a new and fascinating spectator sport. But it would make a candidate's convictions a nuisance and his courage irrelevant. It would, indeed, come near making the candidate superfluous.[21]

The Crisis of Democratic Politics

In the preceding sections we have developed the thesis that there is a widespread and deepening incompatibility between political realities in the United States and our inherited democratic ideals. We have described these conflicts as parallel crises in policy-making, in citizenship, and in civic leadership. If that were all there is to our present political condition, it would be reason enough for concern. But, in fact, these conflicts have raised a more fundamental question: Are those

[18] Ithiel de Sola Pool, Robert P. Abelson, and Samuel L. Popkin, *Candidates, Issues, and Strategies: A Computer Simulation of the 1960 Presidential Election* (Cambridge, Mass.: M.I.T. Press, 1964), p. 44. This book, whose authors were involved in the project, is an explanation and defense of the technique.

[19] See Thomas Morgan, "The People Machine," *Harper's Magazine*, January, 1961, pp. 53-57. The Simulmatics Corporation, described above, was the real-life basis of Simulation Enterprises, the firm described in the late political scientist Eugene Burdick's novel that satirizes this whole process: *The 480* (New York: McGraw-Hill, 1964). In an appendix Burdick lists the actual 480 groups or "targets" used in the 1960 campaign.

[20] The purpose, in the jargon of Madison Avenue, is "to discover what makes them salute." In the more antiseptic language of academic research, the goal is "to discover what issues have saliency for the voters." An accurate translation of both seems to be "to find out how the attitudes, desires, and wants of voters can be manipulated."

[21] These developments have for some time offered material for the satirical political novel. In addition to Eugene Burdick's *The 480*, John G. Schneider had a master political ad man dream up a fictitious pregnancy for a presidential candidate's wife in *The Golden Kazoo* (New York: Dell Publishing Company, 1956), and Shepherd Mead outdid them all with a total society organized and kept happy by computer in *The Big Ball of Wax* (New York: Simon and Schuster, 1954).

traditional ideals still valid and viable? Ought we to reaffirm or ought we to re-examine and reformulate them?

Those historic ideals, like all ideals, rested on certain assumptions about knowledge, man, and society; it was on those assumptions that our normative prescriptions for the character of policy-making and the behavior of citizens and politicians were fashioned. These assumptions have been widely challenged, and often repudiated, in recent years. At the root of our current predicament lies uncertainty and controversy over what model of political life democratic men ought to aspire to; we are no longer in agreement on what democracy means, on what political institutions and processes best serve it, on what kinds of behavior it requires of its citizens and its politicians. To these problems we turn in the next chapter.

Chapter Two

THE CHALLENGE TO DEMOCRATIC THEORY

... which examines recent proposals that our traditional normative ideas, rather than our actual political practices, require modification.

These challenges to traditional assumptions of democratic theory argue, specifically, that

the idea of a public interest assumed an objective moral order that human reason and discussion could discover; moral relativism (the view that values and preferences are subjective, emotional phenomena not subject to rational tests) is a more adequate assumption. Similarly,

the concept of *Citizenship* in the traditional model rested on assumptions that are naive, overoptimistic, and unrealistic; any workable system of democracy must be built on assumptions that recognize the dominant role played by egoism and irrationality in human behavior. Finally,

the traditional concept of *Leadership* threatened political stability and order by assuming principled and courageous leaders who would divide the electorate into warring factions; the moderate, manipulative politician is necessary to keep political conflict within the bounds of peaceful, orderly, democratic consent.

In addition to these philosophical attacks on traditional assumptions of democratic theory, the crisis has produced efforts to find an easy way out through *Attractive Myths* that have been offered as solutions, including

The Myth of Simple Solutions, which holds that our problems have only been made to appear complex; at heart they are simple and will yield to moral determination and good will.

The Conspiracy Myth, which attributes problems to a conspiracy of evil, determined men and divides the world into those who oppose the conspiracy and those who are its tools or "dupes." The belief in simple solutions and the belief in conspiracies are related and are involved in the recent growth of extremism.

The Myth of a Religious Solution, which holds that our difficulties are due to a general moral decline that can be remedied only by a return to common religious belief and which proposes to bring this about through vague symbols of a "common-denominator faith," which puts God on the side of the *status quo*.

The Myth of Capitalistic Democracy, which insists on the necessity of a capitalist economic system in a democracy and which makes capitalism a vague referent for efficiency and prosperity, and thus puts the *status quo* beyond the reach of public criticism.

The inadequacy of these myths is seen to inhere in the fact that they are efforts to define **Democracy as Anticommunism.** Meaningful efforts to distinguish democracy from communism must rest on a view of the **Meaning of Democracy** that provides

as an alternative to authoritarianism (a form of government that concentrates authority in one man or in an elite), the concept of **The Open Society** in which political participation rests on belief in the procedural values of free conscience, communication, and association. A meaningful theory of democracy must also provide

an alternative to totalitarianism (an all-embracing ideology that sets standards of belief and behavior in all areas of social life) in **Pluralism** (a society in which the interests and opinions of citizens are left to individual and group initiative).

An open, pluralistic society rests on procedural values that make criticism of all substantive beliefs and institutions legitimate. These values are currently threatened by both

Moderates and Extremists. The climate of moderation creates pressures toward conformity and defenses of the *status quo* that stifle debate and treat dissenters as extremists; **Extremism** subverts the network of mutual trust and honest communication on which the Open Society depends.

Democratic politics requires a distinction between extremism, which is incompatible with the procedural universals of democracy, and radicalism (substantive proposals for fundamental changes in social institutions), which is not. A pervasive spirit of moderation is likely both to produce extremists and to confuse them with radicals.

Here, as elsewhere, our predicament requires a searching re-examination and reappraisal of the meaning of democracy.

*I do not believe in democracy, but I am perfectly willing to admit
that it provides the only really amusing form of government ever
endured by mankind.*

H. L. MENCKEN

Chapter Two

THE CHALLENGE TO DEMOCRATIC THEORY

WHAT IS DEMOCRACY? We use the word nearly every day; we invoke it to settle arguments; we often reaffirm our faith in democratic principles and processes; we proclaim that democracy is superior to any other form of government. But it becomes more apparent every day that the term is used with widely divergent meanings, that the same person often means contradictory things by it, that we really are not at all sure we know what we are talking about.

The Crisis in Democratic Theory

Our perplexity is due in part, no doubt, to the philosophical difficulties inherent in the effort. Talented minds have pondered over the centuries the questions that now must concern us. But in part, also, our perplexity is due to our not having faced up to the problem. The first step is to recognize the inconsistencies in our ideas about democracy. We commit ourselves to democracy—meaning a process by which the fruits of reasoned debate of public problems are translated into policy by majority rule; we reaffirm our faith in our democratic system—meaning the process by which the private desires of most citizens are reflected in policy through compromises engineered among interest groups. The roots of this and similar contradictions are to be found in the conflict between the assumptions underlying traditional democratic theory and the assumptions implicit in current political realities. We will get closer to our problem by examining briefly this conflict of assumptions with respect to the making of policy and the roles of citizens and politicians.

POLICY-MAKING: PUBLIC INTEREST OR PRIVATE BENEFITS?

Underlying the first of these conceptions was the assumption that there is an objective moral order that human reason and discussion can discover. The public interest, in its most fundamental meaning, was that part of this moral order that applies to the ordering of men's political relations. It was to be discovered and clarified through the processes of reasoned debate, and it was to serve as the criterion by which the special interests and claims of individuals and groups were to be judged. On these assumptions men can decide rationally, though never finally or perfectly, on how justice and morality are to be embodied in public policies. The same processes of rational discussion will permit us to rectify mistakes and continuously to adjust social institutions to meet changing situations.

What, then, are we to make of the fact that present political realities tend to reflect a situation in which public policies express only bargains hammered out on the anvil of compromise by private groups each with its special interest to promote? What are we to make of the facts that these bargains do not reflect a concern with a public interest and that they enable us to respond with half measures, at best, to pressing public problems? Many modern critics tell us that we ought not be overly concerned. They argue that it is foolish and naïve to lament the absence of these traditional virtues from politics. Indeed, the virtues never really existed, for the concept of a public interest was always a myth. There is, in this view, no objective moral order that reason is capable of exploring or a public interest of expressing. Propositions about public morality—about what is best for everyone—cannot be rationally tested or discussed. They are prejudices, feelings, emotions; not arguable assertions.

This moral relativism is a widely held conclusion, in one or another form, in modern society. Applied to democratic theory, it leads to the conclusion that the traditional ideal of processes through which the common good is debated and embodied in policies is logically meaningless and practically dangerous. It concludes that political society is nothing but a variety of partial interests and conflicting desires. The organization of these interests and the accommodation of their rival claims in ways satisfactory to none but acceptable to all is the function of democratic politics. In this view it is dangerous to demand more from a political system than ours now produces. America is a pluralistic society, that is, a society composed of a wide range and variety of relatively autonomous economic, religious, sectional, ethnic, and cultural interests. Such a society must move slowly, and not too deliberately, into the future, since centrifugal forces constantly threaten to pull it apart by substituting intransigent rivalry and warfare for politics.

If highly rationalized and moralized "solutions" to national problems cannot get a hearing, if instead public policies emerge out of the interplay and compromise of all the diverse interests that would be affected, moralizers and idealists may be offended. But this is the only way to safeguard civic peace from the constant threat of political warfare in a pluralistic society. *Compromises, deals, bargains* are not as noble-sounding terms as *rational debate* and *the public interest*. But, in this view, they are more consistent with the nature of human values and knowledge. They are the only real and tested alternative to government by outright coercion.[1] This position finds nothing seriously or fundamentally wrong with existing political processes. It argues, instead, for basic changes in our expectations and demands on the system. It argues that our normative ideas of democracy, not our actual political processes, are in need of revision.

CITIZENSHIP: PUBLIC OR PRIVATE MAN?

The traditional obligations of citizenship, described in chapter 1, rested on the eighteenth-century view of human nature, which saw man

---

[1] The intellectual and academic development of this theory of democracy is treated in Chapter 3. For a literary panegyric to it, see Allen Drury's novel, *Advice and Consent* (Garden City, N.Y.: Doubleday, 1959).

as essentially a rational, infinitely improvable political animal who could be trusted to govern himself. The growth of psychology as a scientific discipline has led many to conclude that this view of man was hopelessly unrealistic and overoptimistic. An adequate definition of the possibilities and limitations of political man, many have concluded, must start from more realistic and pessimistic assumptions that take into account the dominant role of irrationality and selfishness in human behavior. In both secular and religious terms, recent political theorizing has been characterized by a rediscovery of sin. Many have been led to the conclusion that the role accorded to the people in traditional democratic thought was based on a tragically overoptimistic view of human motivations and capabilities.

Similarly, the dominant eighteenth-century view saw society as merely a mechanical collection of atomistic individuals and saw government, accordingly, as a device for registering their free, spontaneous, and uncoerced decisions. But the growth of scientific sociology and cultural anthropology has led to an increased recognition of the role of language, culture, group life, status, and social class in shaping the expectations, desires, and personalities of individuals. We have relearned the ancient wisdom that man is a social animal; in the language of modern behaviorism, all human behavior is "conditioned" behavior. From this view, we ought not be shocked to discover that the democratic voter does not behave in the rational, free, independent way prescribed by traditional theory; he is, after all, only human. Moreover, we may even be thankful that he falls short of such demands, for if he tried to behave in the manner required by traditional standards, the political temperature would be likely to rise too high for a healthy, functioning political system. Here again, in this perspective the problem comes to be that of revising and refashioning our ideas of what standards democracy requires.[2]

LEADERSHIP: IDEALISM OR MODERATION?

On the role of politicians, too, similar objections to traditional theory have been raised. Did it demand too much of human nature? Was it not a dangerous ideal even if it were possible to realize it? Did not the demand for principled and courageous politicians offer a standing invitation to the extremist, the zealot, and the bigot to enter the political

[2] This question is dealt with in detail in Chapter 10.

lists to capitalize on men's passions and fears? Would it really take very many of such ideal politicians to divide the electorate into warring factions and to destroy the processes of peaceful transfer of power among competing politicians and political parties?

The case for the new-style, moderate, manipulative politician is an attractive one in a highly interdependent, complex, and affluent society. It confronts the simple, idealistic ethic of our inherited theory with the sophisticated lore by which the art of the possible is pursued. The faith of the Founders quails and hesitates before the realities of power in the vast, complex, pluralism of current American politics. Can we afford to romanticize the posture of the idealist who loses his cause by refusing to stoop to the arts of political maneuver?

The measure of our dilemma lies in this: we no longer have any sure guides to politics that seem to us unchallengeable. A case can be made —and has been—against our traditional ideals and in defense of the behavior of the manipulative politician. What is wrong with the politics of maneuver and manipulation? *Why* is the use of public-relations techniques, polls, and computers undesirable? The politician who uses them to win office is, after all, only trying to please and to appeal to the electorate; the scientists and public-relations experts and computers only help him to know what people want. The new-style politician gives people what they want, at least what a large majority of them want, and if that isn't democracy, what is?

Well, what is? It is a subtle, complex, and difficult question. It is a question that goes to the heart of our political ideals and of our political system. The fact that we have now to ask it reveals that our ideals themselves have come unglued. A nation that knows, with clarity and certainty, how its citizens and its politicians ought to behave may justifiably be said to be living in a period of normalcy, even if many of its citizens fall short of the ideal. A nation that is uncertain, troubled, divided, and confused about the values that are to be used to guide the behavior of its citizens and politicians in its public life may justifiably be said to be living in a period of political crisis.

Four Attractive Myths

The crises described above have led in recent years to a great deal of intellectual and emotional ferment. We have tended to become self-conscious and self-critical about our social and political institutions. The press, Hollywood, and sometimes television have taken up themes related to our general predicament. And an imposing number of penetrating and scholarly critical appraisals have appeared in recent years, many of which we will encounter in subsequent chapters.

At the same time tension and frustration have resulted in efforts to find a quick and easy way out of our difficulties. We discuss below some of these recent efforts to find a simple touchstone that will resolve our perplexities and restore order, confidence, and tranquillity to our political system. All these panaceas are attractive because of their simplicity; for this reason they are widely held. At the same time, each of them rests on a myth that distorts either the American past or the complexity of our current condition. Because they are both false and inadequate, they tend only to deepen and aggravate the real problems besetting us. By subjecting them to analysis here we hope to preclude later their getting in the way of the more searching and difficult analysis that is necessary.

THE MYTH OF SIMPLE SOLUTIONS

A curious law that often seems to operate in politics might be expressed this way: the number of oversimplified solutions offered to social problems is positively correlated with the complexity of the problems. Examples abound in the middle of the twentieth century: "states' rights" or a civil rights act will solve the race problem; job training and vocational education will solve the problem of unemployment; education will solve the problem of automation; more rigorous penalties will solve the problem of increasing crime rates; selling the slogan "The Family Who Prays Together Stays Together" will significantly reduce divorce rates.

But perhaps the clearest and most dangerous example is to be found in the area of foreign policy, where simple solutions have more than kept pace with the increasing complexity of reality. It is not our purpose here to resolve the question of what American policy toward communism and the rest of the world ought to be. Our point is that the position of the United States in the world after World War II raised difficult and complex questions that put tremendous strains on our political system. A cautious foreign policy seeking to feel its way through the complexities of a new international drama for which history offered us few direct guides to action was destined to create frustration and opposition. The United States became the most powerful nation in the world at just that time when the rules and conditions for the effective exercise of international power were undergoing radical changes. In an arena that had always been complex, the conditions for the exercise of power were rapidly and radically altered. More than ever the chances were immeasurably increased for slips between the cup and the lip in matters of power and influence.

In this new setting the communist world was our mortal enemy, sworn to bury us in the process of the universal victory of communism. Then, in the language of the title of Senator Goldwater's book, why not victory over communism? In order to propose that our problems were amenable to the simple solution of a policy of victory, it was necessary first to assume that the problems themselves were simple. The world had to be viewed as a simple battleground between communism on the one hand and democracy or the free world on the other and the assumption had to be made that if only communism had never been invented, we should not have had any significant or perplexing problems to confront. Among the obvious factors that this simple view of the situation leaves out of account are these: the impact of nuclear weapons and intercontinental delivery systems and the threat of total annihilatory war; the anticolonial revolution; the rise of nationalism in the emerging nations; the struggle for equality of the colored peoples against the racism that had been inherent in European supremacy in the colonial areas; the "revolution of rising expectations" that accompanied the demand for industrialization and political and social reform in these areas; the growing heterogeneity of the communist world and the changes in Soviet policy after Stalin's death; and the fact that *democracy* or the *free world* hardly describes accurately the situation of many of our allies.

Take, for example, this last point. Consider what you would make of an announcement that a certain foreign government that had come into power by violent revolution had taken

> steps to tighten government control over the population which included the following: censorship of the press and all public information media, controls on travel and goods distribution, enlarged authority of detention and house arrest, unlimited search rights in private houses, a ban on strikes and demonstrations or meetings contrary to public order, and the death penalty after an urgent trial before a military court for persons caught in terrorist activity.[3]

This would be an accurate description of the steps taken to consolidate power after a communist take-over—in Castro's Cuba, for

[3] *San Francisco Chronicle*, August 8, 1964, p. 8.

example. But as a matter of fact, it is taken verbatim from the news-paper account of the decrees issued on August 7, 1964, by Premier Nguyen Khanh of South Vietnam whose regime we were supporting financially, militarily, and morally. In a speech announcing the decrees the Premier called on the people of North Vietnam to "stand up and overthrow the dictatorial party rule" of their communist government.[4]

This is not a unique situation. It is, rather, illustrative of one aspect of the world we confront that is not shaped by our dreams and desires. The most persuasive answer to the demand for total victory is that the world is not that simple. It is not in our power to exercise that degree of control over people and events in a world shaken by the fundamental changes described earlier.

It may or may not be the case that a policy of greater firmness in our relations with communism in Southeast Asia or Berlin or Cuba would be desirable; that is not the question. The point is that any rational case for a firmer, more aggressive policy would have to argue from the complex realities of international politics, the attitudes of our allies, the fatal consequences of nuclear war, the role of democratic values in foreign policy, and the consequences of the application of a given policy of greater firmness in a particular situation. On the last point, for example, it is a minimal condition of rationality to recognize that the Soviet response to President Kennedy's nuclear threat over Cuba in October 1962 does not provide a model for our diplomacy everywhere. Soviet response to a similar American posture in Berlin or the eastern European satellites would obviously be based on a different set of calculations. And it is by no means clear that Chinese and Soviet reactions would be identical.

Simple solutions ordinarily rest on dividing the world into polar opposites in moral terms. Problems become simple when they can be attributed to evil forces and motivations and when it is assumed that completely virtuous alternatives are available. The international struggle, for example, appears simple when it is assumed that our total goodness justifies any means to eradicate the total evil of communism. Similarly, from the other extreme of the political spectrum, the reverse argument is often applied. Thus, in the recent literature of the extremist left, the Viet Cong is described as a noble movement for national independence and self-determination, and the brutality

---

[4] *Ibid.* While "U. S. officials declined comment on details of the measures . . . one high official said, 'if this results in an increased mobilization and a better prosecution of the war effort it seems like a good step.' "

of its tactics is ignored; the atrocities of the South Vietnamese government and American bombing are pictured as the exclusive sources of evil in the situation. From this polarized morality it is an easy step to the simple solution of American withdrawal from every area of the world in which communists threaten a "war of national liberation."

A general argument for simple solutions is not very often explicitly made. When it is, it almost inevitably contains a basic anti-intellectual bias, for if our problems are really simple and if simple solutions are readily available, it must be the intellectuals—*eggheads* is the pejorative term—who have needlessly confused us. Thus, in the 1964 presidential campaign a widely read paperback proclaimed that, according to the

> . . . peculiar line of egghead reasoning, present-day problems are so complex that we must have sophisticated—not simple solutions.
>
> Contrary to this argument, civilization progresses, freedom is won, and problems are solved because we have wonderful people who think up simple solutions![5]

The author's simple solution to all the perplexities of foreign policy is a "firm stand," and there are similar simple solutions for most other problems too. The right men, she concludes, "can cut through the egghead complexities in Foggy Bottom and solve these problems for us."[6]

It is not surprising that those who hold that simple solutions are available but not invoked are ordinarily led to the conclusion that stupid or evil men must be at the heart of our difficulties. Thus we are led to a second and closely related myth—the myth that an evil conspiracy has occupied the centers of political power.

THE CONSPIRACY MYTH

Amid the frustrations and tensions induced by prolonged depression, runaway inflation, and defeat in war, Adolph Hitler came to power in Germany by persuading large numbers of Germans that their problems were entirely the result of a dual conspiracy: an international conspiracy of the Jews to control and exploit all other "races" and an

---

[5] Phyllis Schlafly, *A Choice Not an Echo* (Alton, Ill.: Pere Marquette Press, 1964), p. 81. Mrs. Schlafly's book became almost a bible for Senator Goldwater's right-wing supporters. A total of 1,600,000 copies of the first two editions in 1964 were distributed, and Mrs. Schlafly herself delivered the message in person over national television during the campaign. According to a Republican national committeeman, the distribution of a half-million copies in California prior to the primary "was a major factor" in the Goldwater victory.

[6] *Ibid.*, p. 83.

international communist conspiracy to control the world. These conspiracies provided the internal enemies—Jews and communists—against whom German aggression could be directed with impunity.

Hitler did not invent the conspiratorial view of history and politics, and it did not die with the defeat of nazism. Indeed, a distinguished American historian has reminded us recently that conspiracy myths are not a new phenomenon in the United States.[7] Hofstadter points out that there have been imagined "conspiracies" against the government by Masons, Catholics, and government officials, as well as communists. He cites Senator Joseph McCarthy's 1951 statement that the federal government was riddled with subversives engaged in "a conspiracy of infamy so black, that when it is finally exposed, its principals shall be forever deserving of the maledictions of all honest men."[8] Included in McCarthy's indictment were such men as Secretary of State George C. Marshall, a distinguished American who had served as the highest ranking general of the American army during World War II.

In the basic text of the John Birch Society, *The Politician*, Robert Welch provides a more recent example:

> On January 20, 1953, Dwight Eisenhower was inaugurated as the 34th President of the United States. He thus became, automatically and immediately, captain and quarterback of the free-world team, in the fight against communism. In our firm opinion he had been planted in that position, by communists, for the purpose of *throwing the game*.
>
> It is extremely shortsighted to assume that the most cunning, deceptive, and ambitious gangsters the human race has ever known would not, with world rulership as their goal, contrive to have their opposition double-crossed at some stage by the leader of the opposition.

There is more. John Foster Dulles, the late secretary of state, becomes "a communist agent"; his brother Allen, formerly director of the Central Intelligence Agency, is the "most protected and untouchable supporter of communism, next to Eisenhower himself, in Washington"; Milton Eisenhower is, "the chances are strong," President Eisenhower's "superior and boss within the Communist party. For one thing, he [Milton] is obviously a great deal smarter."[9]

This, of course, is the conspiracy from which the extremist right

---

[7] Richard Hofstadter, "The Paranoid Style in American Politics," *Harper's Magazine*, November, 1964, p. 77.

[8] *Ibid.*

[9] Robert Welch, *The Politician* (privately published, 1958), Chap. 12.

has volunteered to save the nation. But they have no monopoly on conspiracy theories. At the other end of the political spectrum, where they meet, is the communist myth that all problems and the processes of democratic government really conceal a gigantic conspiracy of the capitalist class to maintain and consolidate their control of social and economic institutions. Conspiracy myths are the common denominator of the divergent views of the one-gallus racial bigot hiding in his bed-sheet, the black nationalist preaching that "whitey" is the devil, the little old lady in tennis shoes whose life is dedicated to frustrating the communist effort to poison us by putting fluorides in our drinking water, and the communist who sees religion and political democracy as fronts behind which capitalists keep the masses enslaved and exploited.

In still other shapes the conspiracy myth is more subtle and therefore, perhaps, more attractive. For example, the view that the civil-rights movement is the work of the communist conspiracy is the official view of some state legislatures and public officials in the South and is widely held in other parts of the country as well. Like all conspiracy myths, this one starts from some undeniable facts: there is a communist party in the United States; its members do seek to exploit racial unrest. But here, as in all such cases, the question is whether the alleged conspiracy is either necessary or helpful in explaining the events at issue. It would be truly a "mad, mad world" and our dilemma as democrats would be curious indeed if we required the belief in a communist conspiracy to explain why an oppressed group of people have organized to fight for equality of opportunity and "freedom now." Their demands are, after all, the historic promises of American life. It would be strange, indeed, if the communist party had to be blamed for efforts to invoke and realize those promises. To explain the civil-rights crisis as communist-inspired and -motivated requires the belief that all ideas and actions directed to social reform can be and must be explained by fitting them into the catchall basket of communism. But any rational analysis of the civil-rights struggle will disclose that it involves a wide range of persons and groups who are distinguished by a variety of beliefs about both goals and methods. To insist that they are to be treated solely in terms of whether they are for or against a communist conspiracy is to distort reality in a way that makes any rational evaluation of the issue impossible.

A more general and still more subtle form of conspiracy myth has had important effects on American politics in recent years. This is the myth that holds the internal communist conspiracy responsible for the growth in the functions of government and for increases in governmental intervention in the economy. The facts out of which this myth has been fabricated are that members of the American communist party have actively worked for, have set up communist front organizations to work for, and have involved themselves in noncommunist organizations working for, these programs. Economic liberals shared with communists many specific goals: for example, public housing, Medicare, slum clearance and redevelopment, government protection of union organization and collective bargaining, social security, unemployment compensation, and publicly owned utilities. On these facts there was built the myth that economic liberalism, the New Deal, and the welfare state constitute progressive steps toward socialism and that democratic socialism is simply a way station on the road to communism. Pink became a political color that linked democratic liberals and socialists with communists. Thus, a communist conspiracy was alleged to be responsible for the liberal reforms of the twentieth century—or, if the communists were not responsible for these reforms, they were at least tainted with red.

The absence of a viable noncommunist socialist movement in the United States and the unwillingness of liberal politicians to risk their careers by rising to a public defense of the small democratic socialist minority in the country contributed to the result. Lacking the courage or the insight to protest the assimilation of democratic socialists into the communist conspiracy, liberals were powerless to protest against the next step in the logic of conspiracy, which made *them* its tools and dupes. Their failure to protest or to use the conspiracy theme as the occasion for a re-examination of the meaning of democratic values contributed to that shameful era of the early fifties known as *McCarthyism*, in which thousands of loyal Americans were pilloried and abused for their alleged relation to an alleged conspiracy. The issue has not died, because the conspiracy myth has never been squarely faced in the public dialogue.[10] The evidence that would support the great leap from the fact that Communists do conspire to the conclusion that political events are caused by their conspiracy has never been

[10] It led in the 1964 campaign to bumper strips with the message: "Socialist or Republican: Which Are You?"

demanded. Hence, this is a source of tension that continues to strain the political system and constantly to threaten to substitute a holy war against conspirators and their tools and dupes for a politics of discussion of the underlying problems.[11]

A parallel attack has been made in recent years on conservatives and reactionaries by identifying them with an alleged conspiracy of extremists of the radical right. The American Nazi party, Texas oil millionaires, some large industrialists, the military, the Minutemen, and others have been alleged to be engaged in a conspiracy to undermine American freedom. Sometimes leading public officials have been charged with being their agents or dupes—J. Edgar Hoover has been a target in some left-wing circles. From there, the pattern of the argument is the same: The alleged conspiracy is using for its nefarious purposes such arguments as states' rights, the elimination of the income tax, attacks on the Supreme Court and demands for the impeachment of its justices, demands for the reduction of the national debt, and the elimination of government intervention in the economy. Those who support these positions are alleged to be tools of the conspiracy. Although the term has not been used, the clear implication is that *creeping fascism* would be the result if any of their proposals were to be adopted. The words are different; the tune is the same. The technique is as subversive of democratic values in one case as in the other. As Hofstadter puts it:

> The paranoid spokesman sees the fate of conspiracy in apocalyptic terms—he traffics in the birth and death of whole worlds, whole political orders, whole systems of human values. He is always manning the barricades of civilization. He constantly lives at the turning point. Like religious millennialists he expresses the anxiety of those who are living through the last days and he is sometimes disposed to set a date for the apocalypse. ("Time is running out," said Robert Welch in 1951. "Evidence is piling up on many sides and from many sources that October 1952 is the fatal month when Stalin will attack.")[12]

Those who believe in conspiracy tend to engage not in politics but in holy warfare, and they treat the opposition, even within their own party, as "the enemy within." The result of losing an election for this group is not disappointment but confirmation of the view that the

---

[11] A prime example of conspiracy literature, a copiously documented "proof" of treason in high places, is John A. Stormer's *None Dare Call It Treason* (Florissant, Missouri: Liberty Bell Press, 1964). It was widely distributed in the 1964 campaign.

[12] Hofstadter, *op. cit.*, p. 82.

conspiracy was even more vicious and deeply entrenched than they had assumed. As one citizen put it in a "Letter to the Editor" after the 1964 election: "The die is cast. Dreams of foreign ideology have finally overcome the republic, its principles and ideals."[13]

The dual myths that there are simple solutions to our problems and that only a conspiracy prevents us from applying them are the roots of the recent growth of extremism in the United States. Extremism represents the politics of frustration and fantasy. Yet somehow it has a disturbing grip on an alarming number of Americans. Its significance, moreover, exceeds its own impact, for it is an index of milder forms of intolerance, unreason, and rejection of democratic values. It calls our attention to the perilous condition of the fundamental principles of the democratic creed. It is a measure of the extent to which men no longer agree on or support the principles that make government by consent possible.

THE MYTH OF A RELIGIOUS SOLUTION

It is sometimes argued that our political problems merely reflect a general moral decline in society and that this moral decay is itself due to our having strayed from the religious faith of earlier generations. The cure for our political ailments, then, is a public return to religious (or Judeo-Christian or Christian) faith. Like so much of modern analysis of political problems, this formula is often conceived as the only effective way of distinguishing our system from, and achieving victory over, communism. Thus, this argument is often accompanied by the redundant charge that the most significant characteristic of communism is its "Godless atheism."

It is of course clear that religion—specifically the Judeo-Christian religious tradition and, more specifically still, Christianity—has played a major formative role in the development of Western civilization and Western-type democracy. Surely no understanding of our cultural and political history is possible without an accounting of the vital role played by religious belief. But this is not at all equivalent to saying that democracy requires and rests on religious belief. However tempting it may be, it is not legitimate to argue that since the communist creed is atheistic and defines religion as "the opiate of the masses," the

---

[13] *Sacramento Bee*, November 6, 1964.

democratic concept of human dignity must rest on religion and require a belief in God.[14]

The dangers and consequences of this identification of democracy with religious belief were illustrated in the very beginnings of the democratic movement. One of the most influential of its philosophers was the Englishman John Locke. He wrote to justify the "Glorious Revolution" of 1688, which established the fact that the King was not above the law and was to be responsible to the Parliament. His ideas on natural rights and representative government became, in Jefferson's phrase, "the commonsense of mankind" and exerted a profound influence on American democrats. But in his defense of freedom, in his essay *On Toleration*, Locke applied the premise that religious belief is necessary to morality, and therefore to responsible citizenship. His conclusion was that atheists are to be excluded from the regime of religious toleration in democratic societies.

Locke's argument graphically illustrates the consequences of insisting that religious belief is necessary to democratic citizenship. He formulated his conclusions broadly enough to encompass all or most religious beliefs (he would also exclude Catholics from the regime of toleration on grounds that they owe loyalty to a foreign power). Within this framework, governments should not interfere with the individual's freedom of choice. Yet, a significant group of other alternatives—atheism, agnosticism, or humanism, for example—could legitimately be foreclosed. Specifically, a modern Socrates, Thomas Paine, Justice Holmes, or Clarence Darrow would be read out of democratic society.

The tendency of modern Americans to adopt Locke's argument is revealed in the current way of speaking of freedom of religious belief as a basic tenet of American democracy. What this clearly implies is the existence of a variety of established and respectable religious faiths, and the right of the individual to freedom of choice in deciding among them. This is a quite different meaning of freedom of conscience in this area from, for example, Jefferson's statement in that landmark of

[14] We refer to the facile and superficial pleas for a watered-down, empty religious consensus. There are, on the other hand, some penetrating and thoughtful men who argue, from one or another religious point of view, that some particular religious insight is necessary to the democratic spirit and outlook. Among these are Jacques Maritain, *Man and the State* (Chicago: University of Chicago Press, 1951); John H. Hallowell, *The Moral Foundation of Democracy* (Chicago: University of Chicago Press, 1954); and Reinhold Niebuhr, in any of his stimulating books. The important point is that none of these men conclude that believers have a right to force their views on, or to deny full citizenship and civil liberties to, nonbelievers.

religious liberty the Act for Establishing Religious Freedom in Virginia (1786). That act did not provide for the freedom of men to make a choice between alternative institutionalized modes of worship or even for their freedom to worship God in their own ways. It provided, rather, in carefully chosen words, "that all men shall be free to profess, and by argument to maintain, *their opinions in matters of religion.*" An atheist, an agnostic, or a humanist has "opinions in matters of religion" that this way of stating the matter protects. The distinction between these two positions was made dramatically clear in the 1964 Congress when an effort was made to amend the Civil Rights Act to exclude atheists from its protection!

Perhaps we can get a clearer view of this question by examining the attitudes of communist Russia to religion. In February 1918, about three months after the Communists had taken power in the Soviet Union, a decree was issued with this provision: "Every citizen may profess any religion or none at all. Any legal disabilities connected with the profession of any religion or none are abolished." In its separation of church and state and its assertion of freedom of belief and expression, this decree parallels the Virginia Statute of Religious Freedom. But as the Communists cemented their control of the Soviet state, as rival political parties were made illegal, and as the leaders of the party established themselves as the official interpreters of the meaning of socialist doctrine, there were changes in Soviet policy.

The Marxist interpretation of religion as a device to offer the workers "pie-in-the-sky-by-and-by," and thus take their minds off their troubles here and now, led to official efforts to eliminate religious belief and religious congregations. The new political reality was reflected in the Soviet Constitution of 1936. That document still provided for freedom of religious *belief*, but freedom "of propaganda" (that is, freedom of expression) was reserved exclusively for antireligious views. Unlike some other provisions of the Soviet Constitution, this one generally has been reflected in political practice. Americans would not be fooled by a pretense of guaranteeing freedom of belief while providing that only certain views are entitled to be expressed. Obviously there is no genuine freedom for the religious point of view under these conditions. What we need to ask ourselves is whether identifying democracy with religion does not put nonreligious views under the same disabilities and restraints.

The heart of the problem seems to be that Communists who insist on official atheism and believers who demand an official commitment to religion share a common assumption: a society, as a society, must choose between atheism and religion. From the point of view of this assumption, anyone who argues for the open society must appear as a camouflaged proponent of, or at least a dupe of, the dreaded position of the enemy. Thus, a Communist reading this chapter will dismiss it as a concealed plea for religion, and some American readers doubtless will interpret it as a skillfully concealed defense of communism or of atheism.

"Religion (atheism) is the creed of capitalism (communism); who except a capitalist (communist) sympathizer, would defend equality for the religious (atheist)?" The words may be interchanged; the argument is the same. What it fails to recognize is that there is another possibility, a position holding that the basis for political loyalty need not and ought not to contain any commitment whatever on the question of religion, except the commitment to the fullest possible freedom of belief and expression. It may be, as some have argued, that men are so constituted that such a society will not satisfy the emotional need for common substantive symbols or the moral restraints for behavior that only final truths can provide. But the position must be recognized as a possibility that is logically at odds with the positions of both Communists and advocates of religion-based democracy.

Finally, we need to recognize that the major force behind the effort to enforce a religious test of citizenship comes not from religious zealots but from the moderate middle. It does not demand acceptance of any clear or specific religious faith, but only some vague, undefined common-denominator symbols that put God on the side of the *status quo*. D. W. Brogan, an English observer, made the point effectively:

> For it is a belief of mine, reinforced by my last few months in the States, that the real religion of the mass of the Americans (including many Catholics) is America. By "under God," they don't mean under God but along with God (who is, of course, always judging the other nations, not the Americans).[15]

The effect of this type of religious conformity is to reinforce an unthinking kind of loyalty to prevailing political institutions, as well as to discourage all inquiry into religious questions, and even any serious and meaningful religious commitment.

[15] D. W. Brogan, "The Church Views the Nation," *Saturday Review*, October 29, 1960, p. 19.

THE MYTH OF CAPITALISTIC DEMOCRACY

A fourth recent tendency is to hold that a capitalist economic system is the fundamental requirement for democratic government. This proposition, like the one that links democracy with religion, suffers the defects of its origin. Usually, it is a result of the effort to define democracy as the negative of the attributes of communism. Thus, if communism means public ownership and socialist planning, democracy requires, therefore, a free-enterprise economy.

Like the religious argument, this one is parochial and rooted in one aspect of the American experience. Capitalism, like religion, *is* an important part of our tradition, but that tradition includes other opposing elements as well. And there are other countries in whose democratic traditions anticapitalism has played the dominant role. Certainly, there are many examples of noncommunist, socialist movements whose loyalty to political democracy cannot be questioned. We can hardly afford to sweep under the rug the British, Scandinavian, western European, Indian, and many other socialist parties, nor ought we to presume to read them out of democratic politics. (For those who join the religious and economic arguments, the difficulties are compounded by the fact that in many democratic nations there are Christian Socialist parties!)

Moreover, for most of the uncommitted peoples of the world, capitalism is, for valid historical reasons, identified with colonialism and white supremacy. So far as the appeal of democracy to these peoples is concerned, to link it necessarily with capitalism is to give it the kiss of death. What is more, the democratic socialism of other democratic nations has often been their main bulwark against communism. The Communists themselves recognize this and often tend to regard the noncommunist Socialists as their major enemies.

The phrases *capitalistic democracy* and *democratic capitalism* are themselves fairly new to American history, having become current only in the period since World War II. During most of the American tradition, the spokesmen for the idea of democracy have been opposed to industrial capitalism. Jefferson, for example, was convinced that democracy required the economic climate of an agrarian society of small, independent landholders. The rise of industrial capitalism met with constant attack from the camp of those democratic reformers who saw in it a threat to the independence and the fraternity that, in their view, democracy required. Again, it is one thing to argue that capitalism

—at least the modified kind of "mixed economy" that currently prevails in the United States—is compatible with democracy; it is quite another to argue that capitalism is the *only* economic system compatible with democracy.

The relation of political democracy to forms of economic organization is a complicated problem. Most often those who talk of capitalist democracy are exceedingly vague about what is meant by capitalism. The growth of the giant corporation, the accompanying growth of labor bureaucracy, the shift in emphasis from production to sales and service, the central role of human relations in modern industry, governmental economic controls required by the Cold War—these and other developments make the old capitalist shibboleths of *laissez faire*, competition, the law of supply and demand, and the sovereign consumer largely irrelevant. The result is that the plea for a necessary connection between democracy and capitalism is bound to be an ambiguous one. As in the case of the religious argument, such ambiguity serves broadly to put the *status quo* beyond the reach of public criticism. It is a doctrine even more inimical to the democratic requirement of open debate than it would be if its proponents were clear about what they meant by capitalism. For in that event, because their doctrine would refer to a specific set of ideals and institutions, it could more effectively be challenged by rival *ideas*. But where, as seems to be the case, what is being defended is simply the moderate's preference for whatever we now have, ideas and ideals will appear as irrelevant or—worse yet— dangerous to morale and social harmony. In the climate generated by a public commitment to capitalism as a vague referent for efficiency and prosperity, any ideological attack on the *status quo*, even a very conservative appeal to the historical meaning of capitalism itself, may appear as vaguely subversive and out of order. The result may be not simply to declare specific ideas and principles dangerous but also— and this is a far more corrosive tendency—to regard all ideas as irrelevant.

DEMOCRACY AS ANTICOMMUNISM

It would be comfortingly simply if any one, or any combination, of these myths was an adequate basis for understanding the political world we live in and for guiding us through its perplexities. In an important way, however, each myth falsifies reality and takes us down blind alleys. Taken singly or together, they obstruct our understanding of where we are and cripple our efforts to decide where we want to go. Their effect and often, one suspects, their intent are to deal with opposing opinions not by rational analysis and discussion, but by labeling them subversive of Americanism or destructive of truths that are assumed to be sacred and unquestionable.

As the analysis in Chapter 1 should have made clear, there are fundamental problems in our political system that have no direct connection with the communist challenge. The fact is that quite apart from the issue of communism, we do not share a common view of what democracy means. There are wide gaps between our traditional ideas and our current practices, and the traditional ideas themselves are now subject to uncertainty, confusion, and controversy. The myths we have examined represent efforts either to attribute all our difficulties to communism or to resolve them by identifying democracy with institutions assumed to be opposite to those of communism. There are two central fallacies in this procedure that make these myths dangerous as well as misleading. In the first place, the idea of democracy is older than communism; men explored and defended its assumptions and values and wrote them into the Declaration of Independence and the Constitution more than a half-century before Marx published *The Communist Manifesto*. As we will see in subsequent chapters, to a considerable extent the problems debated by early democrats are the same ones we are now called upon to face. It is hardly reasonable to suppose that we can find easy answers by allowing communism to pose the questions. The real question is not "How can we be anti-communists?" It is, rather, "What approaches to society and politics are appropriate for democratic men?"

The second fallacy is more dangerous. It lies in allowing communism to provide not only the questions but the answers as well. The effort is to construct a blueprint for democracy that is the opposite of communism, but the result is to create a picture of democracy that turns out to be not the genuine opposite of communism, but its mirror image. We will see in the next section why this is the case.

The Meaning of Democracy: An Alternative View

The myths we have been examining are not adequate bases for a definition of democracy. Their very inadequacies, however, may lead us to some fundamental principles that distinguish democratic from authoritarian and totalitarian systems. In this view, the most significant characteristics of communist governments are their authoritarian (or dictatorial) nature and their totalitarian tendencies. Democratic governments, on the contrary, are seen to rest on the concepts of the open society and pluralism. A closer look at these distinctions may serve as a starting point to clarify both the essential features of democracy and the nature of the communist challenge.

DEMOCRACY AS THE OPEN SOCIETY

Every system of government allows some room for criticism and argument. Every pattern of political organization leaves some alternatives open to individuals. There are areas of public debate and there are options left open to individuals in even the most authoritarian governments. But the authoritarian character of the regime is revealed in the fact that the areas left open to public debate and the options available to individuals are themselves determined by the authoritative decisions of an elite. Among other things, this means that the boundaries of permissible public initiative and controversy will vary over time, a fact likely to dampen the enthusiasm of citizens for seizing such opportunities as may, at a given time, be available. What it is permissible to think and say today may next week become subversive obstructionism.

(Something of a parallel nature occurred in the United States after World War II when political activities considered legitimate in the 1930's came to be retroactively labeled subversive. Although never on anything like the level of conformity in totalitarian countries, one effect was to discourage people from any political involvement that might, at some time in the future, be publicly labeled subversive. The safe course in the circumstances was not to join anything or take any position on controversial matters.)

In modern authoritarian societies, the official ideology is itself always beyond criticism; the fundamentals of the political order that it establishes and justifies are never open to public debate. In communist regimes, the validity of the materialist view of reality, the role of class struggle as the dynamic of history, and the truth of atheism may not be publicly challenged. Nor may the basic allocation of political power and the arrangements for making political decisions be challenged. The meaning and proper interpretation of the ideology remain matters for authoritative pronouncement by an elite presumed to have access to truth not available to ordinary citizens.

In a democracy, by contrast, the meaning of democracy itself—the assumptions appropriate to it and the political processes and institutions needed to implement it—remain open questions. There can be no permanent agreement because there is no authoritative source of dogma with an official corps of interpreters to whom matters can be referred when people disagree. This is the basic meaning of the concept of an open society. Its implications can be clarified by considering some of the concepts developed by anthropologists in their analyses of comparative cultures.[16]

Many anthropologists use the term *cultural universals* to describe those basic beliefs that hold a society together by giving the lives of its members a common meaning and significance. These beliefs are the central source of cultural conformity; they are shared by all, or nearly all, adult members of the society; and their acceptance is a condition for full membership and participation in the social life of the community. Cultural universals are to be contrasted with alternatives—that is, the existence of optional patterns of belief and behavior available to individuals and groups within the culture. Universals and alternatives are related inversely to each other; when a particular aspect of behavior is governed by a universal belief, alternatives cease to exist in that area. For example, if monogamy is a cultural universal, the option of plural marriages is not available. It is not available in the sense that ordinarily its practice would be met with social disapproval and punishment. In a deeper sense, the universals are so thoroughly internalized in the process of growing up that plural marriage would ordinarily seem so unnatural as not to be regarded as a possibility.

Now if the argument we have made about the open character of even the most fundamental questions in a democracy is valid, does this imply that there are no universals in a democratic society? If there are democratic universals, what are they? How are they distinguished from the universals of authoritarian societies? In answering these questions we must not lose sight of the conclusion reached by all students of human culture that society rests fundamentally on the existence of shared attitudes, beliefs, and values. Unless people perceive the world in substantially the same way, unless they evaluate human actions similarly, society is impossible. Unless the activities of the individual have some larger meaning in the shared purposes of others, the cement

[16] The concepts we employ were developed by Ralph Linton in *The Study of Man* (New York: Appleton-Century-Crofts, 1936), p. 272 ff.

that holds societies together is missing. What is the cement in the democratic social fabric?

As our earlier analysis has suggested, we would argue that there are no *substantive* universals in democracies, no specific beliefs such as religion or capitalism, which make particular kinds of behavior or institutions necessary to democracy. There are, however, commitments to certain *procedural* universals. These are the *absolutes*, if the term is to be used at all, of democratic society.

The procedural universals of democracy are summed up in the traditional freedoms: freedom of conscience and of belief, freedom of speech and of press, freedom of association, freedom from arbitrary acts of government officials. These freedoms define the conditions of the open society. Freedom of belief and freedom of expression are the means by which any attempt authoritatively to enforce the acceptance of substantive conclusions or to insist on the finality of any institution may be challenged. Their purpose is to make possible endless controversy about such matters. They are the bulwark against all forms of authoritarianism.

Procedural freedoms clearly imply some common values. Freedom of inquiry and criticism implies the obligation for individuals to carry on the quest for truth and justice. Freedom of speech implies the obligation to speak honestly, while incorporating the faith that speech is a means to rational truth. Freedom of conscience implies the responsibility for integrity in one's beliefs and the obligation to submit one's conclusions to public criticism. In turn, the right of criticism imposes the obligation to deal fairly and honestly with opposing views. It will be recognized that these procedural values are incompatible with the simple solutions and the conspiracy myths described earlier.

These universals embody the procedures and attitudes that are necessary to the human quest for truth and justice in social life. The dilemma of democracy is rooted in the fact that the quest is never consummated, at least for the society as a whole. Democracy implies that not the truth, but the unending quest for it, will make a society free. Of course, life compels the individual in his quest to arrive at some conclusions. It is obviously demanding much of human nature for men to refrain from imposing their beliefs on their fellows and to value the processes of inquiry more highly than their own conclusions.

Although this is a formidable condition, it is clearly not an unattainable one. Something like this bound Athenian citizens together and was the basis for Athenian patriotism. And the same ties were important in binding together American statesmen of the formative period. To be sure, no democratic heaven was ever achieved in which significant numbers of men stuck consistently to Socrates' cardinal principle that it is only the "examined life" that is worth living. Socrates, after all, drank hemlock for his reward. The first session of the Congress under the Constitution reached an impasse in which all business was suspended because of the bitterness generated by the conflict over the funding of the national debt. Just eight years after the Constitution was adopted, the Alien and Sedition Acts were passed making it a crime publicly to criticize elected officials. When the Jeffersonians sought to repeal them in 1800, business in the United States Senate came to a halt as the Federalists drowned out their opponents' arguments by scraping their feet on the chamber floor. We must be wary, then, of overidealizing the Founding Fathers. And yet, the entire tradition of American democracy reflects the vitality of the notion that all substantive questions in a democracy are open questions.

At the same time, this doctrine has been under constant attack from one direction or another. Jeffersonians identified democracy with a rural, agrarian way of life and insisted that commercial and industrial activities were fundamentally incompatible with necessary democratic virtues. After the Civil War there were other efforts to identify the democratic creed with unlimited industrial competition and the survival of the fittest.

Thus, whereas the ideal of democracy requires that all universals be procedural rather than substantive and that all questions (including the meaning of democracy itself) be at least potentially open ones, there are always forces in every society working in the opposite direction. There is a tendency to identify prevailing and orthodox beliefs with democracy. In addition, there are tendencies in every society to rewrite the past to make it accord with currently fashionable prejudices.

These practices of freezing presently respectable conclusions into absolutes and of translating tradition into substantively unifying myths pose constant challenges to the openness of a democratic society. The myths examined earlier will be recognized as important examples of current tendencies in this direction. Simple solutions and conspiracy charges make genuine discussion impossible and destroy the climate of trust that is necessary for dissent. The effort to identify religion or capitalism with democracy would, if successful, make these into universals of American society and restrict the range of alternatives in these areas. As these examples show, free thought and free speech are in constant competition with all other claimants to a place in the universals of a democratic society. Ironically, the effort to distinguish democracy from communism through substantive universals opposite to those of the communists moves us, in a fundamental sense, closer to the communist system.

One qualification to the ideal of the open society needs to be made: it is neither necessary nor likely (nor, from the point of view of social stability, desirable) that *all* matters *will* be in dispute at all times. It is only necessary that they be potentially open. Thus, for a time in the period after the Civil War unregulated private enterprise served as a largely unchallenged framework for the growth of the American economy. There were, however, protest movements among farmers and industrial workers. Toward the end of the century, the growth of monopoly and unscrupulous treatment of labor and consumers led to the beginnings of regulatory legislation. Efforts were made —in the press, the pulpit, and the Supreme Court—to identify the absolute rights of private property with Americanism and democracy in order to put reform movements, including the organization of labor unions, beyond the pale of legitimate protest. The efforts failed; the right to dissent and to propose reforms in this area prevailed.

In the realm of political ideas, the present century saw an unlimited faith develop in the political capabilities of the people. This idea became, except for a few unpopular conservative critics, an unchallenged and unexamined premise of political debate. On this basis, the cure for the ills of democracy was held to be more democracy. The application of the premise to politics took the form of the extension of the franchise, movements directed against "bossism," establishment of direct primaries, and initiative, referendum, and recall provisions. Terms like *elite* and *aristocracy* became epithets. Yet, even this assumption that democracy means direct responsiveness to popular wishes was not made immune to dissent and argument. This assumption is now, as it has not been for many years, under vigorous attack. That it can now be challenged without the issue of loyalty or patriotism being raised is the real test of the openness of American society.

DEMOCRACY AS PLURALISM

Totalitarianism, like other political terms, has been variously defined. The common element in these definitions is the emphasis on a situation in which the state defines the standards of thought and regulates activity in every sphere of social life. The totalitarian state operates from an authoritative, all-embracing ideology that furnishes answers to all human problems and standards of taste and judgment in all human relations. For example, communism is not simply a political and economic theory. Such basic concepts as dialectical materialism and class struggle are used to justify and prescribe specific attitudes on religion, legitimate patterns of marriage and family life, good and bad art, and correct principles of genetics. Potentially, the ideology is all-inclusive.

To know that a person is a Communist is to know his attitudes toward such areas of experience as the arts, religion, the press, marriage, leisure, and labor unions. No similar information can be deduced from the knowledge that a person is a democrat. He may be a Catholic, a Baptist, a Jehovah's Witness, or an atheist; a partisan of progressive jazz, folk music, Bach, or "pop" tunes; a subcriber to the belief that the progressive income tax is legalized robbery or that there are too many tax loopholes for the wealthy. Moreover, he may belong to organizations to advance his varying interests and opinions. And these organizations are not required to answer to the demands of an official, all-inclusive ideology.

In this contrast with totalitarianism, the meaning of political pluralism becomes clear: a society in which government does not prescribe the interests or opinions of its citizens and in which, therefore, forms of group life may flourish at the initiative and discretion of citizens.

It is obvious that the procedural freedoms are the condition for a pluralist society. Freedoms of thought and speech are the roots from which the spontaneity and initiative of citizens spring. In addition, without freedom to associate with others to promote common interests and without freedom from arbitrary actions of government, intellectual freedom could never be reflected in social and political reality.

MODERATES AND EXTREMISTS: STRANGE BEDFELLOWS

The values necessary to an open, pluralistic society are currently under attack from both the moderation of the middle and the extremism of left and right in American politics. Moderation as a political style and compromise as a political process accept and operate within the general framework of existing social and economic institutions. The political environment they create is not hospitable to dissent or to innovation. Indeed, it is an environment that, as we have suggested, is likely to treat dissenters as extremists. It is also conducive to translating traditions and widely shared attitudes into defenses of the *status quo* that stifle public debate and close off the processes of individual inquiry, judgment, and choice. These pressures toward conformity in thought and action are exemplified by recent tendencies to define democracy so that it requires a common but meaningless religious faith and a common belief in the existing capitalist economic system. Within this climate efforts to promote a rational dialogue are smothered under the blanket of moderation and drowned out in the process of interest-group compromise.

At the same time, when issues are discussed, extremist offerings of oversimplified solutions and allegations of conspiracy pollute the very spring of democratic dialogue. The open, pluralistic society in its traditional meaning assumed mutual trust and a network of free discussion and honest communication. These conditions are subverted by the politics of manipulation in a climate of moderation; they are destroyed by the politics of extremism.

EXTREMISM, RADICALISM, AND DEMOCRATIC POLITICS

Extremism, as we use the term, is distinguished by attitudes and approaches to politics that are incompatible with the mutual trust, respect, and processes of reasoned discussion required by democracy. But, as we have suggested, the meaning of the term has been distorted because it has been defined from the perspective of the moderate middle. In that context *extremism* becomes almost synonymous with *radicalism*. This dangerously misleading process is reflected in the use of the term *radical right* to describe right-wing extremist movements. But radicals—those who propose fundamental and far-reaching changes in the institutions of society—are not necessarily extremists. They may meet all the tests of democratic citizenship. Their radicalism, indeed, is as likely to meet those tests as are more moderate approaches. Radical views may include a defense of *laissez faire* or of socialism, a proposal to limit the authority of the Supreme Court or to impeach its chief justice, an argument to eliminate or to make more progressive the income tax, to dismantle completely the welfare state or to adopt a full-fledged system of socialized medicine, a plan for unilateral disarmament or preemptive war. The only democratic test is whether the proposals are offered in a form and manner in which they are susceptible of rational examination and discussion in an atmosphere of integrity and mutual trust. If they are, they are radical simply in the sense that they contemplate a basic change in public policy. If they are not, they are extremist in the sense that their effect is to undermine the very processes by which policy is formulated in democratic society. Radicalism, then, of either the left or right, is not incompatible with democracy. In fact, a healthy democracy requires, and is likely to produce, radicals—particularly in a period of rapid social change.

The distinction between radicalism and extremism is important because it tends to be muddied or eliminated by the politics of moderation and compromise. The operational system of American politics, we have argued, proceeds within a broad framework of consensus on policy. This consensus accommodates the interests of the major organized groups in society and trades upon the apathy and self-interest of large numbers of citizens. Its pervasive spirit of moderation sets the tone for the response to all views that pose a fundamental challenge to the *status quo*. The recent tendency has been to lump them all together and to dispose of them with the label "extremist": Socialist and Communist, economic conservative and the swastika-adorned neo-Nazi, pacifist and "comsymp," interventionist and nuclear war hawk. A healthy democracy would be polite, if not hospitable, to radicals who accept its fundamental procedural values. A political system that makes room only for moderates is likely, we may suspect, to produce a pathological oversupply of genuine extremists.

THE NEED FOR REAPPRAISAL

Our analysis in the first two chapters has pointed to a dual crisis in democratic politics: the existence of a large and apparently widening gap between our traditional democratic ideals and political realities; and the emergence of disagreement and debate over the meaning, the validity, and the adequacy of those ideals.

In Chapter Three we will consider the gulf between theory and practice by examining the consequences for politics of the growth of an affluent *mass society*. The complex of social and historical tendencies summed up in the phrase *mass society* has resulted in the development of political attitudes and relations that are fundamentally incompatible with our inherited democratic ideals. Political reality, of course, never perfectly mirrored the demands of normative theory. Our purpose will be to examine some recent social, cultural, and economic developments that have tended to widen the gap.

Chapter Four returns to the fundamental problems in democratic theory that have been precipitated by widespread concern over the state of disrepair of the political system. There we examine several of the conflicting models that have been proposed to close the gap between theory and practice. We seek to clarify the assumptions they embody, the solutions they offer, and the issues over which they contest. Only so is it possible to get to the heart of the crisis in democratic politics and, at the same time, to acquire the intellectual tools necessary for systematic and critical understanding of the present state of American politics.

Chapter Three

THE POLITICS OF MASS SOCIETY

. . . in which the growth of mass society and the development of mass man are described, and their implications for democratic theory and democratic practice are explored.

A *Profile of Mass Man* is drawn in which he is pictured as
> *The Other-Directed Man,* who seeks to conform his behavior to the constantly changing expectations of others rather than to internalized standards of right and wrong;
> *The Consumption-Oriented Man,* who consumes standardized, mass-produced goods and standardized attitudes and preferences conveyed by the mass media of communications and who does not mind being manipulated to satisfy the demands of advertising; and
> *The "Organization Man,"* whose destiny is shaped by the large-scale organizations in which he lives and works and who substitutes the social ethic of togetherness for the older Puritan ethic of individualism.

These attitudes are shaped by **The Characteristics of Mass Society** which are described as
> *Anomy,* which is a condition of rootlessness and normlessness caused by the absence of emotionally satisfying social ties and in which individuals are forced into "the weightless irrelevance of their personal affairs";
> *Conformity,* which differs from the conformity of earlier societies because it is not rooted in stable or sanctified patterns of behavior. "It does not occur" to the mass man "to have any inclination, except for what is customary" in styles and fashions;
> *Alienation,* which causes man to feel estranged from the world and to develop a sense of futility and powerlessness; and
> *Anxiety,* which is a state of undefined, unfocused fear that may in some circumstances lead to extremist, irrational, and unrestrained political behavior.

The Philosophical Premises of Mass Man are next examined and their political implications are developed:

Ethical Relativism, the belief that normative propositions cannot be tested or verified, is seen to be the natural posture of the mass man, and the ways in which it is incompatible with traditional democratic theory are developed. And

The Mechanistic View of Man as a machine whose behavior is the inevitable result of psychological conditioning is described as the basis for the manipulative techniques that characterize the politics of mass democracy.

The effect of mass society—its characteristics and its beliefs—on political behavior is reflected in

The Politics of Mass Democracy in which the mass man as citizen sees politics as a "spectator sport" in which he is powerless; yet he acquiesces in its processes because his private stake in an affluent society is sufficiently provided for; the mass man as politician emerges as a broker who serves as go-between for pressure groups and as a middle-of-the-road moderate who is the ideologically missing man and who manipulates the electorate through techniques of public relations; and political decisions are the result of group bargaining and compromise (brokerage), and campaigns are conducted with the techniques of advertising. While these may be called the typical processes of mass democracy,

Mass Society also produces **Extremism,** a phenomenon that is clarified by a description of

The Authoritarian Personality, an interrelated set of attitudes that results when alienation increases beyond a certain point to produce neurotic anxieties that release destructive impulses incompatible with democratic methods and values.

Finally, the conflict between the tendencies of **Mass Society** and the norms of democratic theory is seen to pose the question whether modifications in our traditional normative model of democracy are necessary. This question requires an analysis of alternative theories of democracy, to which the next chapter is devoted.

Instead of the comradeship of persons all of whom are their genu-
ine selves, we have the spurious friendship of a gang whose motto
is, "You scratch my back and I'll scratch yours."

KARL JASPERS

Chapter Three

THE POLITICS OF
MASS SOCIETY

*M*ORE THAN A CENTURY AGO, Alexis de Tocqueville, an astute
European observer of the American experiment in self-government, was
pessimistic about its success. A democracy founded on liberty and
equality, he concluded, faces new and difficult perils:

> . . . the species of oppression by which democratic nations are
> menaced is unlike anything which ever before existed in the world:
> Our contemporaries will find no prototype of it in their memories
> . . . the old words despotism and tyranny are inappropriate; the
> thing itself is new; and since I cannot name it, I must attempt to
> define it.

I seek to trace the novel features under which despotism may appear in the world. The first thing that strikes the observation is an innumerable multitude of men all equal and alike, incessantly endeavoring to procure the petty and paltry pleasures with which they glut their lives. Each of them, living apart, is as a stranger to the fate of all the rest—his children and his private friends constitute to him the whole of mankind; as for the rest of his fellow citizens, he is close to them, but he feels them not; he exists but in himself and for himself alone; and if his kindred still remain to him, he may be said at any rate to have lost his country.[1]

Written in 1835, after a visit to the United States, Tocqueville's *Democracy in America* has been recognized as a classic in recent years, primarily because he put the problem of tyranny in a democracy in a new light. In his analysis of the dangers to freedom, he forecast the tendencies and problems of mass society. Tocqueville argued that, contrary to the views of the Founding Fathers, the real problem of freedom lies not in the danger that a majority will tyrannize a minority by forcing its will or opinion on them, but in the social pressures on all men to conform to prevailing mass attitudes. This tyranny of mass opinion, he predicted, will result in a new variety of despotism—a "servitude of the regular, quiet, and gentle kind" that may even appear to its victims as a form of freedom. "Sovereignty of the people" may still seem to exist even after the people have been spared "all the care of thinking" necessary to make their participation as citizens meaningful.

Tocqueville predicted the development of the social basis of mass society: the transition from a society of individuals or of identifiable social classes into an undifferentiated mass whose consent to be governed is engineered by politicians whose power rests on their ability to curry favor with the masses. Most careful recent observers agree that Western society generally, and America in particular, stand at a watershed and that the underlying changes in the fabric of society first described by Tocqueville are fundamental, even revolutionary. Herbert Muller has summarized much of this concern:

Let us spell out the worst about this notorious mass-man and his mass-culture. He has a meager idea of the abundant life, confusing quantity with quality, size with greatness, comfort with culture, gadgetry with genius. He has as little appreciation of pure science as of the fine arts, and as little capacity for the discipline that both require;

[1] Alexis de Tocqueville, *Democracy in America*, Phillips Bradley, ed. (New York: Knopf, 1948), p. 318.

although he may stand in awe of them his real veneration goes to the engineers and inventors, the manufacturers of True Romances and Tin Pan Alley airs. He is frequently illiberal, suspicious of "radical" ideas, scornful of "visionary" ideals, hostile to "aliens"; in America he has developed a remarkable vocabulary of contempt that manages to embrace most of mankind—the nigger, the mick, the chink, the wop, the kike, *et cetera*. He is the chief foe of the individualism he boasts of, a patron of standard brands in tastes and opinions as in material possessions, with a morbid fear of being thought queer or different from the Joneses; individuality to him is "personality," which may be acquired in six easy lessons or his money back, is then turned on to win friends and influence people, and is confirmed by the possession of "personalized" objects, which are distinguished only by having his initials on them. In short, he appears to be a spoiled child, fundamentally ungrateful to the scientists, political philosophers, social reformers, and religious idealists who have given him his unprecedented opportunities. He is therefore the natural prey of advertisers, politicians, millionaire publishers, and would-be dictators.[2]

Much of the discussion of mass society has centered on the question of whether the rise of the mass man to political power has paralyzed the efforts of the elect—the *saving remnant*, in the prophet Isaiah's term—to protect the values of civilization. In our view this is a false issue. The mass man described by Muller is not a member of the masses as distinguished from the upper classes; he is, rather, the characteristic victim of mass society. Neither money, nor social position, nor education is proof against these pressures. As subsequent analysis will show, the pressures of mass society are characteristic of urban, industrial, secular society, and they operate on all social strata in that environment. We are talking, then, about a cultural condition, not about a revolt of the masses against the excellence, civility, and honor that it has always been the fancied task of an elite to protect from vulgar meddling.

To what extent is Muller's profile of mass man an accurate description of actual Americans in the middle of the twentieth century? As Muller himself insists, it is at most a half-truth.[3] What follows in this chapter is intended not as an accurate description of all Americans or of dominant traits of most Americans, but as a description of significant *tendencies* in modern society that aggravate the rift between democratic ideal and reality. The threat these tendencies pose to democracy is our central concern. How far they have advanced, whether

2 Herbert Muller, *The Uses of the Past* (New York: Oxford, 1952), p. 232.
3 See below, page 91.

they are inevitable and irreversible—these are important questions but beyond the scope of our concern in this chapter.

A Profile of Mass Man in Mass Society

The word *mass* pervades the modern vocabulary. We speak of mass society, the mass media, mass markets, mass production, mass consumption, mass education. A complex network of historical changes—social, cultural, economic, political, intellectual—has made this usage of the word possible and inevitable. We cannot pretend here to provide an extensive account of these historical forces. Our purpose is the more limited one of seeking to clarify the major tendencies in the social character of the mass man and to examine their effect on politics.

THE OTHER-DIRECTED MAN

The mass man has been described by David Riesman as "other-directed" in contrast to the "inner-directed" man of an earlier period.[4] The behavior of the inner-directed man was governed by internal norms or values. His course through life was directed by the values—largely imposed by parents and Church—that had come to form the content of his conscience. These values, interiorized in the process of growing up, functioned in a manner analogous to the gyroscope, giving his behavior a self-contained equilibrium and direction.

The other-directed man, by contrast, has no fixed or definite standards of taste or judgment. He wants above all to belong, to be liked, not to stand out from the crowd. He seeks to conform his behavior to the constantly changing expectations of others, rather than to any internalized standards of right and wrong. The analogy here is not the gyroscope, but radar. In search of cues from the groups to which he belongs, he sends out signals and guides his behavior by what he interprets to be the expectations of his fellows. Professor Ray Ginger makes the same point in his study of Chicago when its leading public figures were such controversial men as the radical Governor Peter Altgeld and Clarence Darrow. However unlovely in certain respects these men's personalities may have been, the question they put to themselves was, "Am I right?" This is to be contrasted with the question that appears to dominate the lives of current residents of suburbia: "Am I covered?"[5]

---

[4] David Riesman and others, *The Lonely Crowd* (Garden City, N.Y.: Doubleday, 1950).

[5] Ray Ginger, *Altgeld's America* (New York: Funk and Wagnalls, 1958).

Other-directedness is a total approach to life—it shapes man's attitudes to the world of consumption, to the world of production, to the world of ideas, to the world of human relations. In every area of life the problem for the other-directed person is to adjust to his surroundings, never to change his surroundings to fit his own desires and values. As he confronts the endless series of choices that living in a complex society involves, he displays an exaggerated tendency to conform to the standards of the group with which he happens, at the time, to be associated. He is constantly vulnerable to the changing, shifting tides of preference and opinion. In ideas, as in clothes, he is an avid follower of current fashion. Above all, he wants to be popular, to be well liked.

The typical other-directed mass man is adaptable and adjustable; he is likely to adopt a tolerant attitude toward changes in the details of his daily life, his friendships, and his preferences. It does not follow, however, that he is also likely to be tolerant of deviant, nonconforming behavior. He may be tolerant of ethnic and religious minorities who follow the patterns of middle-class standards, but his tolerance is not likely to extend to beatniks, civil-rights activists, Communists, Birchers, atheists, Jehovah's Witnesses, peace marchers, pacifists, or any kind of "winger" of the right or left.

In the politics of mass society, these qualities affect the relationship of politicians to the electorate. It is not simply that those relations are manipulative; the manipulative appeals themselves tend to focus around personalities and noncontroversial standards—*honesty, sincerity,* and similar catchwords—rather than around issues and principles of public policy. This is, perhaps, due to the fact that politicians, as well as other elite groups in modern society, tend also to be other-directed men who themselves lack a set of guiding political principles. They may even be seeking to give the public what it wants—or, perhaps more accurately, to divine the lowest common denominator of its wants—in a psychological sense. "Democratic republics," Tocqueville predicted, "extend the practice of currying favor with the many and introduce it into all classes at once." The result is, as Tocqueville foresaw, a government that still seems to rest on the consent of the governed, but in which that consent is no longer the product of conscious, reasoned choice of social goals and policies.

THE CONSUMPTION-ORIENTED MAN

Modern America is characterized by widespread material ease and comfort beyond the wildest dreams of past generations. This material affluence means not simply an increase in the absolute economic level of life, but the creation of an economic and cultural climate in which a constantly increasing and accelerating standard of consumption has come to be a reasonable expectation for a majority of the population. But whereas the dream of man for centuries had been the elimination of economic poverty and drudgery in order to free man for other and higher pursuits, economic abundance has not seemed to have that effect. Modern men seem, if anything, more preoccupied than ever with the realm of making and consuming. They seem, if anything, less often to have the opportunity for the "disclosure of 'who' in contradistinction to 'what' somebody is."[6]

The crucial fact is that, as far as the majority of persons in the modern economy is concerned, economic activity has come to be oriented toward consumption rather than production. The tendency has been to induce men to see themselves as consumers and to view consumption of the products and services of an ever-increasing standard of living as the goal of life. The products themselves are mass-produced and mass-consumed, which is to say that they are highly standardized, highly stylized, and rendered rapidly obsolescent. Men tend to regard themselves and others as cogs in the social apparatus that organizes the accelerating cycle of consumption, as players of the roles required in an affluent society.

The consumption orientation to life is promoted and reinforced by the dominant role of the mass media of communications in shaping attitudes and life styles. Here, the contrast with the situation of earlier "inner-directed" men is dramatic. In eighteenth-century America communication was by word of mouth, by the handbill and the pulpit, or by local newspapers with relatively small circulation. These were vehicles through which individual ideas, attitudes, and opinions were transmitted. Man's knowledge of the world came to him packaged in other men's attitudes toward it. The availability of a variety of attitudes seemed to impress on every man the obligation to arrive at his own understanding and commitments; at the same time, there were readily available means for communicating these to others.

---

[6] The phrases from Hannah Arendt, *The Human Condition* (Garden City, N.Y.: Doubleday Anchor Books, 1958). This book, despite its heaviness of style, is perhaps the most provocative analysis available of the developments we are considering here. Her general conclusion is that modern society "is a society of laborers which is about to be liberated from the fetters of labor, and this society does no longer know of those higher and more meaningful activities for the sake of which this freedom would deserve to be won" (p. 5).

The growth of the mass media (radio, television, metropolitan newspapers relying on nationwide press services, the mass-circulation magazines) has had a profound effect on this historic condition. So far as his knowledge of the world is concerned, information and attitudes come to modern man in the unctuous voices of news reporters or in the studied, balanced views of commentators. There is little expression of opinion, and men in this highly organized society come to distrust their own opinions. They tend, instead, to receive impressions as spectators or consumers of news in a situation in which there is little opportunity and less inducement to answer back.

The mass media are addressed to mass audiences. This conditions their content: "they are concerned not with finding an audience to hear their message but rather with finding a message to hold their audience." The result is an effort not to antagonize anyone (anything either controversial or unpleasant is to be avoided) or to leave anyone out (also to be avoided are subjects of special interest and treatment of any subject at higher levels of maturity or subtlety than can be handled easily by the mass audience).

The crucial fact about the modern mass media—magazines, newspapers, radio, television—is that they are dominated by advertising, this for the simple reason that advertising pays the bills. With respect to radio and television, the only contribution of the consumer is the price of his receiver. In the case of magazines and newspapers, in many cases, "the real situation is that the advertiser buys the magazine for the 'purchaser,' and what the purchaser pays as the 'price' of the magazine is really only a kind of qualifying fee to prove that he is a bona fide potential consumer and not a mere deadhead on whom this handsome advertising spread would be wasted."[7]

It is the hold of advertising on the mass media that gives the latter their distinctive character, and advertising is perhaps the most distinctive institution of the mass society. We are talking here of advertising in its modern form as a device for stimulating consumption and the desire to consume, not as mere information giving. It is in this sense that advertising is not only an institution, but one of those few crucial institutions that serve as "instruments of social control."[8]

Society controls individual behavior primarily through those central

[7] David M. Potter, *People of Plenty* (Chicago: University of Chicago Press, 1954), p. 180.
[8] *Ibid.*, p. 176 ff.

institutions that define the individual in a distinctive way and induce him to conceive of himself in the same way. Historically, the Church, the democratic political system, and *laissez faire* capitalism, for example, offered models of man as a creature of God, as a rational participant in political life, and as an independent producer. Advertising conceives man as consumer and encourages him to so conceive himself. The model of man as consumer demands that he have no set standards of taste and judgment. Participation in the consumption of standardized, mass-produced goods and services requires that individual tastes and values be fluid and manipulable. It is, therefore, the enemy of those older institutions that encouraged men to cling to traditional values or consciously to formulate their own standards. Advertising "has joined the charmed circle of institutions which fix the values and standards of society," but "it has done this without being linked to any of the socially defined objectives which usually guide such institutions in the use of their power."[9]

To put it bluntly, much of modern advertising and public relations involves lying or dissembling or both. The stimulation of consumer demand often involves making things seem what they are not: a deodorant is made to seem a cure for loneliness or a candidate is made to seem a father figure, for example. To put a good face on things is very often a matter of concealing or distorting their real natures. The use of words to cajole and to manipulate desires destroys the integrity of the language itself. And because language is the most effective means men have for communicating, the corruption of the language is at the same time the corruption of human relations. Integrity and trust are destroyed. How, asks Joseph Tussman, can we teach our children integrity, when our language no longer has that quality? How can we teach them the necessary integrity of language when we support, even honor, professional liars and dissemblers?

A rough measure of the extent to which these tendencies are reflected in American life is revealed in the fact that by 1951, the total outlay for advertising in the United States had come to exceed the total spent on primary and secondary education. In short, society spends more of its resources on the manipulation of its members as consumers than it does on their education as citizens.[10] Meanwhile, social adjustment and the consumer orientation to life have influenced the curriculum of the

[9] *Ibid.*, p. 177.
[10] *Ibid.*, p. 178.

schools themselves. For example, curricula in home economics and business education are often designed to educate the student in his role as consumer. It should not be surprising if increasing numbers of people come to regard the purchase of a new automobile as a more important decision than the election of a President.

THE "ORGANIZATION MAN"

The social and economic framework within which individuals struggle for status and popularity has undergone profound changes in recent years. The Horatio Alger myth of rags-to-riches, which was exemplified in the lives of such industrial giants as Andrew Carnegie and Henry Ford, no longer adequately describes the life chances of Americans. Instead, ". . . opportunity, as measured by the chances of success in building up a major enterprise of one's own, has given way to opportunity measured by advancement in the bureaucratic elites."[11]

A new white-collar class of bureaucrats whose destinies lie within the organization has tended to replace the older middle class of independent businessmen and members of the professions. Whyte describes this new class as "organization men," chiefly characterized by the fact that they have abandoned the older Puritan ethic of individualism for the social ethic of togetherness, harmony, and moderation. Organization men, says Whyte, "tend to equate the lone individual with psychic disorder."[12] Like Riesman's other-directed man, the organization man is a team player who has surrendered his own individuality to the organization as the necessary price for eligibility to climb in its ranks. He is a good committee member, an unassertive moderate, and an all-round good fellow.

Climbing in the organizational ranks provides the major arena in which men compete for status and prestige. But this organizational politics also operates within the framework of the social ethic; the result is characterized by Riesman as a pattern of "antagonistic cooperation." Manipulation replaces the traditional bureaucratic principles of hier-

---

[11] S. M. Lipset, *The First New Nation* (New York: Basic Books, 1963), p. 129.

[12] William H. Whyte, *The Organization Man* (Garden City, N.Y.: Doubleday, 1956). The expatriate American philosopher George Santayana drew a similar picture in his conclusion that ". . . a man finds his life supervised, his opportunities preempted, his conscience intimidated, and his pocket drained. Every one he meets informs him of a new duty and presents him with a new subscription list. At every turn he must choose between being incorporated or being ostracized." George Santayana, "Liberalism and Culture," in *Soliloquies in England and Later Soliloquies* (New York: Scribner's, 1922).

archy and a chain of command. An experienced management training consultant has recently described the basic principle of organizational success: study the boss rather than the job. In his words, "Your boss is king-maker. You need him with you to help you move up, for it is almost impossible to do so without his recommendation. Therefore it is vitally important for you to study him, learn everything you can about him and his motivations. . . ."[13] Meanwhile, presumably, the boss is learning everything he can about you and your motivations in order to use you effectively in his own further rise up the ladder. The necessary price of being able to use the boss is not minding that he is, at the same time, using you. This is the point of Erich Fromm's comment that, instead of loving people and using things, modern man has come to use people and love things.

Collectively, large-scale organizations are characterized by an over-riding concern with the morale of their members. In the human relationships of modern organizational life it may not be seriously misleading to see morale as a substitute for morality. The growth of the corporation has been accompanied, as Riesman argues, by a concern with human relations as the central organizational problem. Internally, this has meant the rapid expansion of personnel departments and harmony programs designed to secure the happiness and emotional well-being of employees.

Externally, the problem becomes one of public relations—to create and merchandise a favorable image of the organization. Virtually every large organization—including manufacturing corporations, government agencies, labor unions, and even universities—has a public-relations department carefully nurturing an image. Specialized firms offering public-relations skills and services have even acquired the collective name of *Madison Avenue*. In both its internal and external expressions, this concern with people as the problem assumes that the process of persuasion is essentially psychological, thus promoting a conception of man that is clearly incompatible with the traditional democratic faith in individual rationality and autonomy.

Moreover, the organization man carries the qualities that stand him in good stead at the office to his home in suburbia where his easy congeniality leads him into the P-TA, civic improvement clubs, and service organizations. But not into partisan politics. Partisan political

[13] Edward J. Hagarty, *How to Succeed in Company Politics: The Strategy of Executive Success* (New York: McGraw-Hill, 1964).

activity means controversy and divisiveness. The man who is committed to the proposition that all truth lies somewhere between competing claims to it, and that moderation is always the best policy, is not likely to be attracted to a partisan politics of issues. The political style of the mass man is characterized by withdrawal from conflict and controversy. Moderation between opposing points of view and the harmonious accommodation of rival interests seem to be the appropriate attitudes.

Individuals who increasingly confront these forces in their organizational lives are likely to carry over the same attitudes and expectations into the realm of politics. Enmeshed in organized bureaucracies demanding their uncritical loyalties, cogs in the wheels of intricate and highly interdependent organizations whose purposes and goals seem beyond their, or any men's, control or direction—such men are not likely to see politics as a vehicle through which society and the future may be consciously subordinated to human purpose.

The Characteristics of Mass Society

The character traits of the mass man we have been describing are related to the underlying conditions of the society in which he lives. The mass man is other-directed because he is socially isolated and rootless; his is the face in the "lonely crowd" because he has been cut off from meaningful and emotionally satisfying relations with those whose elbows he rubs. He is the product of those historical forces that undermined the formative influence and emotional ties of family, town, and class and of religious, occupational, professional, and social allegiances. The term used by sociologists to describe this phenomenon of rootlessness—of the loss of deeply emotional social and ideological ties—is *anomy*.[14]

ANOMY ·

Anomy in modern society means that man is more mobile, both geographically and socially, than perhaps men have ever been before. But his very mobility, while it increases the frequency of his contacts with others, decreases their intensity and their meaning. The mass man

[14] The term *anomie* was first used by the French sociologist Emile Durkheim to describe the conditions of a society in which traditional values and norms had broken down without any new ones taking their place. The term has come into wide enough use that it is often written in anglicized form as *anomy*, the usage adopted here.

is rootless in the sense of lacking membership in groups that give meaning to life by providing common purposes and values, shared emotional meanings, and relatively fixed patterns of status and role for the individual. In earlier societies these were a source of individual self-identity and self-esteem. At the same time, the mass man lacks roots in the sense of having lost the capacity to believe in the existence of an objective moral order that transcends both individual desires and cultural traditions. For the moral absolutes of the past, the mass man substitutes morale; for the quest for truth and justice, he substitutes the quest for harmony. Having abandoned fixed standards of taste and preference, he is willing prey to constantly changing mass styles and fashions.

One critic provides a telling illustration of how these pressures affect traditional occasions and even the very young:

> The coming of Valentine's Day no longer means that the boy brings, shyly or boldly, to some girl he has mooned over all year a lacy heart and a declaration of love; but that every kid under pressure brings every other kid in his entire class some machine-produced greeting remembered the day before at the Five-and-Ten.[15]

Socially, intellectually, and spiritually, the mass man is radically isolated. Yet his isolation—his freedom from the emotional and moral ties of genuine community—does not make him an autonomous individual. He does not fill the void created by the weakening of deep social ties with a sense of self-identity and purpose developed out of his own reflection. He does not substitute his own standards and values for those of tradition, habit, and social prejudice. Lacking a sense of purpose, he retreats into his private world or seeks to overcome boredom in a continuing search for fun. Hannah Arendt has graphically made the point in her description of what happened to the survivors of the valiant French underground Resistance at the end of World War II:

> After a few short years they were liberated from what they originally had thought to be a "burden" and thrown back into what they now knew to be the weightless irrelevance of their personal affairs, once more separated from "the world of reality" by . . . the sad opaqueness of a private life centered about nothing but itself.[16]

[15] Leslie A. Fiedler, "Voting and Voting Studies," in Eugene Burdick and Arthur Brodbeck, eds., *American Voting Behavior* (New York: Free Press, 1959), p. 196.
[16] Hannah Arendt, *Between Past and Future* (New York: Viking, 1961), p. 4.

The anomy that characterizes life in a mass society is related to changes in the basic institutions of character formation. There is wide agreement among anthropologists, sociologists, and social psychologists that the early years of childhood and the child-rearing practices of every society are crucial to the process of forming adult character traits. A review of the changes in childhood experience that are related to the growth of anomy is beyond our purpose here. Very generally, however, as our discussion of advertising indicated, the primary instruments of socialization in the past—the family, the Church, and the school— are generally believed to have declined in their influence over the development of the child. At the same time, the mass media (particularly television) and association with other children of the same age (peer groups) have come to play an enlarged role in the shaping of character. The effect is that those forms of direct adult control, and particularly parental control, by which traditional values were imparted to a new generation have been attenuated. At the same time, the newer influences of the mass media and the transitory and relatively superficial relations within peer groups operate to reinforce the anomy created by the urbanizing, secularizing tendencies of modern society.

CONFORMITY

The typical other-directed mass man described above is obviously a compulsive conformist. Keeping up with the Joneses is the common-sense expression of his attitude toward life. And its key characteristic is that those who live by it have lost the capacity to make independent choices. Faced with the possibility of making his own choices, he avoids those situations in which choices must be made; he seeks to "escape from freedom" into the anonymity of the crowd.[17] Lacking any basis for formulating his own style of life or his own political principles, he "chooses" to do what is popular or accepted. John Stuart Mill described this condition a hundred years ago in the following terms:

> In our times, from the highest class of society down to the lowest, everyone lives as under the eye of a hostile and dreaded censorship. Not only in what concerns others, but in what concerns only themselves, the individual or the family do not ask themselves—what do I prefer? or, what would suit my character and disposition? or, what would allow the best and highest in me to have fair play, and enable

[17] The phrase is the title of the influential and pathbreaking study by psychiatrist and social philosopher Erich Fromm, *Escape from Freedom* (New York: Holt, Rinehart and Winston, 1941).

it to grow and thrive? They ask themselves, what is suitable to my position? What is usually done by persons of my station and pecuniary circumstances? or, (worse still) what is usually done by persons of a station and circumstances superior to mine? *I do not mean that they choose what is customary, in preference to what suits their own inclination. It does not occur to them to have any inclination, except for what is customary.*[18]

We need to recognize, of course, that mass society is not unique in its demands for conformity. Every society produces social agreement on attitudes, desires, and values. This is a necessary precondition for society; it is the very essence of the process of socialization through which individuals are inducted into a culture.[19]

We have noted that in earlier, simpler societies the community norms of belief and behavior provided the individual with roots. "But those roots not only anchored, they imprisoned. Communal values and norms were clear, unambiguous—and stifling."[20] The values and attitudes of inner-directed men were generally created in this kind of environment; they were conformists too, but with a difference. Because their conformity was rooted in the values transmitted by family, Church, and the small community, they seldom felt the sense of aimlessness and rootlessness associated with anomy. Moreover, they often encountered other values and styles of life derived from other subcultures in an atmosphere in which their own values were tested. In these encounters an individual might choose to modify his own values and attitudes. Whether he did or not, he was likely to feel that the opportunity for individual choice and decision had been present and used. The prevailing democratic ideology encouraged, even required, him to make the choice. As Justice Holmes put it, "To have examined one's own most cherished assumptions is the mark of a civilized man." In any event, he was likely to believe that his ideas were his own. As a result, in order to influence his behavior it was necessary to appeal to his values or to modify them.

The conformity of mass society is different in kind. Here, conformity is a matter of social adjustment: individuals adjust to the expectations

---

[18] John Stuart Mill, *On Liberty*, Alburey Castell, ed., (New York: Appleton-Century-Crofts, 1947), p. 61. Italics added.

[19] As cultural anthropologists have told us, the very process of learning a language is an indoctrination into seeing the world in certain ways: "Every language is at the same time a philosophy." See, especially, Weston La Barre, *The Human Animal* (Chicago: The University of Chicago Press, 1954), pp. 163-207.

[20] Leonard J. Fein, ed., *American Democracy: Essays on Image and Realities* (New York: Holt, Rinehart and Winston, 1964), p. 74.

of their peers because of the vague desire to be popular and the fear of being different. "If you want to get along, go along," a current slogan puts it. Perhaps the heart of the matter is that where social approval becomes the major or exclusive goal of the individual, conformity does not require the sacrifice of other goals or values. Consequently mass man can be easily manipulated by appeals to his fear of being different, to his anxiety about social approval, and to his desires for material affluence and escape from the meaninglessness of his life.

Conformity in mass society is dictated by rapidly changing fads and fashions of one's peers. Because it is a matter of doing what everyone else is doing, and because the individual conforms for psychological rather than ideological reasons, there seems to be no visible source of authority. It is, therefore, more difficult for the individual to detect the psychological coercion involved in the process or to resist it. Individuals for whom social adjustment and approval are the ultimate goals are incapacitated even to recognize as tyranny those "regular, quiet, and gentle" forms of manipulated but voluntary acquiescence in a standardized life.

It may be the case, for this reason, that the conformity of mass man is self-generating and cumulative in a sense not true of earlier modes of conformity. Where preferences and attitudes are developed on the basis of what will sell or what will be popular, no one appears to be establishing them. Like Topsy, and in a manner analogous to the growth of custom in primitive society, they just grow and change.[21] This process of continuous but impersonal change adds powerfully to the feelings of normlessness, rootlessness, and personal impotence described earlier. The resulting anxieties and frustrations may well have the effect of making more compulsive the drive to keep up with what others are likely to be doing.

Some critics have argued that the standardization of preferences and attitudes in a mass democracy is also likely to mean that the norms of conduct, precisely because they are not formulated or imposed by an elite, are likely to mean the reign of mediocrity.[22] Norms that result

[21] In the terminology of sociologists, they are *crescive*, rather than consciously *enacted*.

[22] ". . . the commonplace mind, knowing itself to be commonplace, has the assurance to proclaim the rights of the commonplace and to impose them wherever it will. . . . the mass crushes beneath it everything that is different, everything that is excellent, individual, qualified and select." Jose Ortega y Gasset, *The Revolt of the Masses* (New York: Norton, 1957, 25th anniversary ed.), p. 18.

from a desire to please everyone are likely to mean the repudiation of ideas of excellence in all areas of life. In such circumstances the pursuit of excellence, since it cannot by definition be achieved by a mass audience, will court resentment and lead to maladjustment for the individual.

ALIENATION

Another term often used to describe the condition of man in modern society—one closely related to anomy—is *alienation*. Whereas anomy refers to the condition of normlessness or rootlessness, alienation describes feelings of estrangement from the world and a sense of futility and powerlessness. The alienated person no longer feels that he plays any significant role in society or that his life matters. The historical roots of the increase in alienation in modern society are complex, and various social philosophers have traced it to different causes. Karl Marx, in his earliest writings, saw alienation as the inevitable outgrowth of changes in the character of work. The growth of a money economy and of industrial processes made it impossible for the worker to derive any personal satisfaction from or to control the conditions of his work. When labor became a commodity to be bought and sold on the market, man himself became an object to be used by others. He lost the sense of his own identity because he could no longer translate his energy and resourcefulness into products that were objective representations of his personality. Georg Simmel, a German sociologist, found that industrial society destroyed man's sense of self-identity through the increasing degree of specialization and the fracturing or breaking up of the person into a series of separate roles.

Others have found the major source in the growth of the city, which destroyed the close contacts, the sense of interdependence, and the shared communal values of the small community and estranged men from one another. This development freed the individual from the tyranny of local norms—anyone who has grown up in a small town will know how stifling and repressive these can be—but it did not prepare him to exercise his new-found freedom. Instead, the new urban man found himself unfettered but without any clear idea of who he was and with a deep-seated feeling of impotence, helplessness, and bewilderment.[23]

---

[23] Here, as elsewhere in this chapter, we are developing the critic's view of mass society. There are, of course, dissenters. On this point, for example, there are those

Whatever its causes, the political significance of alienation in mass society is to be found in the accompanying feelings of frustration, impotence, and anxiety. The meaning of alienation for political life has been defined as follows:

> Political alienation is the feeling of an individual that he is not part of the political process. The politically alienated believe that their vote makes no difference. This belief arises from the feeling that political decisions are made by a group of political insiders who are not responsive to the average citizens, the political outsiders. Political alienation may be expressed in feelings of powerlessness, meaningless-ness, estrangement from political activity, and normlessness.[24]

What is at stake is the basic democratic idea that individuals have the power to control their own lives and that men collectively can be history-makers. This sense of mastery over events has been undermined by the sheer size of social institutions of all sorts, by the impersonality of bureaucratic organization, by the complexity of modern problems, and by the development of nuclear weapons that impersonally threaten to terminate history. The resulting feeling of helplessness in the face of things and events contributes powerfully to mass man's sense of futility. The alienation that results may produce the retreat from poli-tics discussed in the first chapter, or it may under other circumstances lead to anxiety and political extremism.

ANXIETY

Mass society is often said to be anxiety-producing and mass man to be anxiety-ridden. The word *anxiety* describes a state of diffuse, vague, and unfocused fears. Anxiety gives rise to the felt need for action to reduce or control the fears. But because the individual has no clear notion of the causes, extent, or limits of the threat, the actions he takes do not succeed in reducing his anxiety. Indeed, they are as likely to heighten it. Thus, the other-directed mass man, afflicted by anxious fears about the emptiness and meaninglessness of his life, seeks security in efforts to be liked by everyone. But no amount of acting on the cues he picks up about the expectations of others succeeds in reducing

---

who argue that the city created the possibilities of pluralism, individual diversity, and choice. What the critic of mass society sees as anonymity and alienation has been seen by others as freedom and individuality. See, for example, Daniel Bell, *The End of Ideology* (New York: Collier Books, 1961), pp. 13-38.

[24] Murray B. Levin, *The Alienated Voter* (New York: Holt, Rinehart & Winston, 1960), pp. 61-62.

his anxiety. The resulting behavior does not alleviate or satisfy the needs that gave rise to it.

Not all fears and insecurities reflect what we are describing as anxiety. Fear that is a response to a known, identified, focused, limited threat is likely to lead to nonneurotic responses that promise to reduce the threat. The political implications of this distinction have been clarified by a comparative study of totalitarian and democratic propaganda during World War II. The fear to which nazism supplied a response was the undefined, unfocused fear of alleged communist and Jewish conspiracies. Hitler's speeches were an emotional call for action, total unrestrained action requiring total obedience, against a total enemy. By contrast, Churchill's speeches to the British people were more factual; they defined the danger, outlined alternatives, and proposed ways of dealing with it. His speeches, the authors of the study conclude, "contributed to the prevention of an inexpediently large and rapid increase in anxiety; unknown danger was transformed into a danger known in kind and extent."[25]

If the conditions of mass society produce anxiety in neurotic forms, we have reason to be concerned. Many of the tendencies we have examined would seem to work in this direction. The common man feels impotent in the face of events that threaten radically to transform his life but over which he has no control and of which he has very little understanding. He has no clear ideas of the causes of these events but he feels impelled to control them. He has no basis for making moral judgments about what to do about them, but he feels an obligation to judge.

In such a situation the alienated and impotent are likely to experience anxiety, which disposes them "to engage in extreme behavior to escape from these tensions."[26] Thus, alienation in mass society may create anxieties that lead to direct methods of "irrational and unrestrained" political action.[27] Such actions often take bizarre and inconsistent forms. For example, in the presidential campaign of 1964 the individuals and groups most frequently expressing fear of a powerful central government also expressed concern over the decline in morality and respect for law and order. Thus, the same persons who

[25] Ernst Kris and Nathan Leites, as quoted by Daniel Bell in Fein, *op. cit.*, p. 71.
[26] William Kornhauser, *The Politics of Mass Society* (New York: Free Press, 1959), p. 32.
[27] *Ibid.*

demanded a return to states' rights also called upon the national government to accept responsibility for restoring law and order to city streets and parks. More serious examples of the political consequences of neurotic anxiety are reflected in some of the conspiracy myths described in the preceding chapter.

The Philosophical Premises of Mass Man

The developments sketched above have been accompanied by changes in some of the basic philosophical assumptions on which men build their views of the world. Explicitly or implicitly, the mass man embodies in his behavior the assumptions of ethical relativism and a mechanistic conception of the nature of man. In the following sections the meaning and the social and political implications of these assumptions are briefly explored.

ETHICAL RELATIVISM

Ethical relativism, simply defined, is the position that where men's desires or values differ, there is no external, objective way of deciding who is right. *"De gustibus non est disputandum,"* the Romans put it. ("There's no disputing tastes.") All moral principles or values are really assertions of personal, subjective, emotional desires. There is no distinction between what a person desires and what is objectively desirable. In the words of the British philosopher Bertrand Russell: "Questions as to 'values' lie wholly outside the domain of knowledge. That is to say, when we assert that this or that has 'value,' we are giving expression to our own emotions. . . ."

Both as an intellectual position and as a practical approach to life and politics, the growth of the relativistic attitude can be related to many historical sources. Here we distinguish three such forces, which, while they do not add up to an adequate historical explanation, may shed some light on the meaning and implications of the relativist position: the growth of secularism, the rise of scientific method, and the increase in knowledge about human behavior and culture.

It is now a commonplace that one of the central distinguishing characteristics of our age is that we live in a *secular* culture. Most earlier cultures, by contrast, were *sacred* cultures. The basis of this distinction lies in the character of the norms and sanctions for behavior in society. In sacred cultures religious or spiritual beliefs pervade all of life, and almost every human activity is judged by its compatibility with the system of sacred beliefs and its contribution to the religious values of the culture. In a secular culture, on the other hand, behavior is judged by reference to norms having no divine or sacred source but resting instead on such worldly or temporal bases as reason, experience, efficiency, or expediency. It is obvious that our world has become increasingly secular since the seventeenth century. The attack on medieval political theory and on the doctrine of the divine right of kings and the rise of democratic theories were themselves efforts to secularize politics —that is, to separate it from sacred or religious beliefs.

It is undeniable that in the secular age in which we live, men in large numbers have abandoned belief in the absolute truths of religious faith, at least as reliable guides to social conduct. A recent study of the attitudes of American college students concludes that, while they "normally express a need for religion," their religious beliefs do "not carry over to guide and govern important decisions in the secular world. Students expect these to be socially determined. . . ."[28] The result appears to have been, notwithstanding the recent religious revival in America, that increasing numbers of men are no longer able to embrace the intangible truths of the spirit as authoritative standards for social and political behavior. Men's social, economic, and political values seem increasingly to have come to rest on other than religious foundations. This did not mean immediately, and it does not require logically, that men were forced to the conclusion that, in Herbert Muller's phrase, "unless we are standing on the Rock of Ages, we are standing on nothing." Indeed, the men of the eighteenth century were convinced that they still had solid, if not quite sacred, ground to stand on—the ground of natural rights and truths derived from reason. Thus, the secularization of politics did not immediately lead to value relativism.[29] Relativism became a common and popular conclusion only with the impact of scientific method and the fruits of its application to human behavior.

The relativistic attitude toward values stems in part from what is perhaps the most prevalent interpretation of the meaning and character of scientific method. In this view, science is held to be purely descriptive, to permit only statements about the world as it is, never conclusions that express a preference about how it ought to be. It is

---

[28] Philip E. Jacob, *Changing Values in College* (New York: Harper, 1957), p. 2.

[29] It is remarkable, perhaps, in retrospect, that the conclusion of skepticism and relativism was so seldom drawn in the eighteenth century. David Hume, a Scotch philosopher (1711–1776), was pre-eminent and almost alone in arguing the relativist cause in politics.

impossible, according to this position, to get to an "ought" statement from any number of "is" statements. "Ought" statements express and refer to our internal feelings and desires, not to the external world; hence, they can never be verified or tested empirically. On these grounds, many philosophers have turned over the study of values to the psychologists. The conclusion is that values are purely subjective and simply relative to one another.

As a practical approach to life and politics, relativism probably owes most to a general understanding of cultural relativity. The inquiries of modern social science have systematically shown what increasing contact among cultures has revealed to common sense: human beings are in fact much more plastic than they formerly were assumed to be. The central tenet of the modern study of culture, the only hypothesis that makes human behavior intelligible, is the proposition that human behavior is learned; that, by and large, human beings behave the way they do and value the things they do because they have learned to act and think in these ways in the cultures in which they were reared. The tremendous diversity of cultural beliefs and practices seems to reinforce the view that there is nothing either right or wrong, but culture makes it so. There is, after all, almost no kind of activity regarded by any society as good that is not also regarded by some other society as bad.

It is obviously tempting to go from the facts of cultural relativism to the conclusion of complete moral relativism, and from the inescapable conclusion that human behavior occurs within a cultural context to the position that therefore the individual can never transcend the values of his culture. Similarly, it is easy to see how the evidence that cultures in the past have sought to justify the exercise of power through a wide variety of appeals to God, nature, history, and race leads to the conclusion that all such efforts are, and must be, equally fraudulent. The political philosophy of the past, including democracy in its historic form, seems only to reinforce the view. To paraphrase the late anthropologist E. A. Hooton, man has insisted on playing the game of politics, not only with an ace up his sleeve, but with the smug conviction that God put it there. So, in the words of another anthropologist:

> We have come to suspect that even our own deepest beliefs and our most cherished convictions may be as much the expression of an unconscious provincialism as are the fantastic superstitions of the savage.[30]

[30] Clyde Kluckhohn, *Mirror for Man* (New York: McGraw-Hill, 1949), p. 20.

Ethical relativism is the natural posture of the mass man. He is vulnerable to pressures to conform to prevailing styles and attitudes because he has ceased to appeal to any other authority to justify his behavior and attitudes, or even to believe that any such appeal is possible. Having rejected the authority of standards outside himself derived from religion or tradition or reason, the mass man

> . . . is satisfied with himself exactly as he is. Ingenuously, without any need of being vain, as the most natural thing in the world, he will tend to consider and affirm as good everything he finds within himself: opinions, appetites, preferences, tastes.[31]

If mass man is satisfied with thinking the first thing that comes into his head, his relativistic assumption that preferences need not be defended with reasons makes it likely that the source of the things that come into his head will be the things that others whose esteem he values seem to believe and prefer.

For the individual, relativism would seem to lead in the direction of political apathy or feelings of alienation rooted in the belief that politics cannot be a means to meaningful control of the environment. Apathy—*political quietism* it has been called—will be recognized as one of the alleged characteristics of mass man. Perhaps his thoroughly relativistic outlook helps to explain his "cool" attitude toward politics and his vulnerability to the shifting tides of mass opinion.

It should be obvious that ethical relativism is incompatible with traditional ideas about the meaning and defense of democracy. The Declaration of Independence rested on truths asserted to be self-evident and on rights held to be inalienable. The processes of government established under these principles were held to provide a means for men to resolve the moral issues of public life through reasoned debate. The rhetoric of the American democratic tradition asserted that politics was to be concerned with moral issues: with the solution of social problems (what is a social problem except a discrepancy between what is and what ought to be?); with the *reform* of existing evils; with making *progress* toward a more desirable state of affairs; with protecting men's natural *rights*; with rectifying *injustices*. Our traditional ideas about democracy were heavy with value-laden words, and the underlying assumption was that men, through sincere and reasoned inquiry and discussion, could discover values worth pursuing.

[31] Ortega, *op. cit.*, p. 62.

The very term *republic* expressed these convictions, for it was derived from the Latin *res publica* which had meant the public or common concerns. A democratic government, our earlier traditions informed us, was a government whose purpose was the promotion of the common good, the public interest. *The public interest* is not an easy term to define, but it is a tremendously important one because, more than any other, it sums up the traditional way in which democratic theory has sought to translate power into legitimate authority. It is meaningful, first of all, in what it intends to exclude: the public power of government is not to be used to promote private, exclusive, or personal interests. It may be legitimately employed only where the goals it serves are common goals that are publicly approved. Neither the rich nor the poor, for example, can have any right to use government in order to weigh the scales of taxation in their favor. Arguments for or against more or less steeply graduated schedules of taxation must be made on the basis of the requirements of justice and the welfare of the entire community. This basic faith in the powers of reason and reflection to solve fundamental conflicts of interest in society is the root meaning of the public interest.

Relativism is incompatible, of course, with any concept of a public interest that might be used to discriminate among the claims of clashing private interests. Relativism, if taken seriously, would make it impossible to find any ground for preferring the interests of any group over any other—even, it would seem, for favoring the rights of Negroes over those of bigots or the claims of his victims over those of the dope peddler. All interests must be accepted as equally legitimate. Appeals to the public interest appear to be simply the gloss all private interests use to conceal their special claims. It becomes impossible, therefore, to speak meaningfully about social problems, reform, progress, or a public interest, since all these traditional terms imply the existence of some dependable notion of what is desirable.

THE MECHANISTIC VIEW OF MAN

Much the same sort of analysis might be made for the increasingly prevalent view that human nature is infinitely plastic and that men are essentially like machines and will react in determined ways to external stimuli. The distinguishing characteristic of a machine is that it does not make choices of goals or purposes that modify its own behavior. Consequently, if one understands the principles and mechanism of its operation, it becomes possible to cause it to operate in ways that the operator regards as desirable.

The typical modern form of a deterministic, mechanistic view of man, like all things modern, tends to be secular rather than religious and to have its sources in psychology rather than theology. It sees man, not as an actor in some preordained divine scheme of things, but rather as an organism operating in accordance with certain internal psychological mechanisms that automatically translate external stimuli into determinate forms of response. Just as access to the plot of the divine drama would have enabled one to predict the behavior of the actors, so also it is assumed that knowledge of the internal psychological mechanisms will permit complete prediction of human behavior. To be sure, this is a different kind of machine, the only machine that has sensations of freedom and choice, but these are held to be illusions that stand really for the incompleteness of our knowledge of the determining mechanisms. Unlike the deficiencies in our knowledge of the divine plan, these are potentially remediable. Moreover, also unlike the earlier theological interpretation, the expansion of our knowledge permits not only prediction but also control of behavior. Human nature is infinitely plastic; men can be conditioned and manipulated into almost any form of behavior, provided only that our knowledge of the determining mechanisms is accurate enough and our control of external conditions thorough enough.

The mechanistic view of man is rooted in popular interpretations of the ideas of "all three of the great teachers of the nineteenth century—Darwin, Marx, Freud." The result is a "sort of secular Calvinism" that holds human behavior to be completely determined.[32] It seems likely that popular interpretations of the findings of psychoanalysis have provided the major reinforcement of the mechanist position. Freudian psychology introduced the concept of the unconscious, a concept that permitted explanation of many aspects of individual behavior not theretofore explicable. Essentially, this concept suggests that beneath the level of consciousness there are personality forces at work— drives, frustrations, conflicts, and so on—that are so threatening to the sense of self-importance and identity that they are repressed in consciousness. Yet they often operate to determine behavior in quite

[32] Joseph Wood Krutch, *The Measure of Man* (New York: Grosset and Dunlap, 1953), p. 37. Krutch's book is in part a reply to behavioral psychologist B. F. Skinner's mechanistic utopia, *Walden Two* (New York: Macmillan, 1948).

irrational or nonrational ways and completely without the awareness of the individual. Although Freud himself, and most other students of psychoanalysis, did not draw the conclusion that no individual ever knows the real motivations for his behavior and that therefore the intellect is simply an excuse hunter for concealed drives and mechanisms, many versions of the popularization of psychoanalysis have arrived at this conclusion.

After Freud, "it was soon discovered not only that the gross symptoms of insanity are the manifestations of irrational psychological processes but that in all human behavior intellect plays a role subordinate to that of the blind and irrational emotions."[33] From this point of view, reason appears to have been given to man not, as in traditional democratic theory, to direct his thought and action, but rather to conceal and camouflage the hidden forces of the unconscious that really do direct it. At best then, when men disagree, rationality is a cloak that may be useful "merely as a camouflage to conceal the real nature of the process of persuasion," which is inherently psychological rather than logical.[34]

This approach to human behavior led to the discovery that the democratic voter, like other men, can be most effectively reached not by rational argument but by appeals addressed to his subconscious desires, drives, and tensions. It led also to the development and refinement of the techniques of psychological manipulation. But even more important, the allegedly scientific character of the theory of mechanism served to offer a firm ground for the justification of the use of the techniques. For if all appeals turn out to be emotional rather than rational, psychological manipulation and conditioning appear as the only—and, therefore, the democratic—alternative to rule by a traditional elite or by physical coercion. As one political scientist has put it:

> Nor does the practice of manipulation render this country any less a democracy. Democracy describes a system based on the free consent of the governed. If this consent is engineered, it certainly does not make it any the less consent. And it is doubtful if it is any the less free for its being the product of manipulation.[35]

[33] Franz Alexander, *Our Age of Unreason* (Philadelphia: Lippincott, 1942), p. 24.
[34] The phrase is from E. H. Carr, *The New Society* (Boston: Beacon, 1957), p. 72. Carr provides a very readable analysis of the effects of this assumption on traditional democratic theory.
[35] Andrew Hacker, "Liberal Democracy and Social Control," *The American Political Science Review*, December, 1957, p. 1022.

But, of course, for those who do not accept the relativistic assumptions on which this analysis rests, manipulation is "less democratic" and manipulated consent is "less free." Their ideas of consent continue to be rooted in the traditional ideal of a *public*, rather than a mass, sitting in rational judgment on alternative policies.[36]

The Politics of Mass Democracy

Unless his anxieties have assumed neurotic proportions and have taken a political direction, mass man as citizen is likely to be politically apathetic and alienated. When he participates in politics he is likely to adopt a moderate, middle-of-the-road posture, shying away from party-oriented or issue-oriented controversy. This general political attitude has been described as one of "acquiescent *powerlessness*":

> For the members of the lonely crowd, politics is a spectator sport; for the organization men, patterns of life and work are determined by an amoral institution; for the exurbanite, participation is social or civic, rather than partisan; and for all, the fruits of a surfeit of honey are sufficient exchange for removal from the decision-making process.[37]

The mass man as politician is likely to assume the role of representing the narrow interests of his constituency rather than positions on the issues in the broader community. In the legislative arena he will be an astute horse trader in behalf of his constituents' interests. Where his constituents' interests are in conflict, he will play the role of neutral middleman, seeking to work out compromise arrangements satisfactory to all. His public face will be cast in the image constructed for him by the professional public-relations firm he has retained to guide his campaigns. If he has any strong convictions on public issues,

[36] See, for example, Carr, *op. cit.*, and especially C. Wright Mills, *The Power Elite* (New York: Oxford, 1956). It is an interesting footnote to this debate that many of the experts in manipulation seek to dodge the issue and have it both ways. Thus, one of the leading authorities says, "The responsible leader . . . must apply his energies to mastering the operational know-how of consent engineering and to outmaneuvering his opponents in the public interest." William L. Bernays, *Public Relations* (Norman: University of Oklahoma Press, 1952), p. 161. The appeal to a public interest, in the premises, is completely spurious. For where reason has been ruled out as the basis of political debate, the public interest can only serve as camouflage for the power aspirations or the rationally indefensible biases of the consent engineer.

[37] Hacker, *op. cit.*, fn. 16, p. 1023. Books to which phrases in the statement refer include, in addition to Riesman, *op. cit.*, and Whyte, *op. cit.*, A. C. Spectorsky, *The Exurbanites* (Philadelphia: Lippincott, 1955) and Russell Lynes, *A Surfeit of Honey* (New York: Harper, 1957).

he will publicly play them down. The cardinal rule will be inoffensive-ness: never say anything that might alienate any significant group of voters. His stance will be in the middle of the road; his byword, *moderation*; all in all, he is the ideological missing man.

After the election, the same process that shaped the party platforms and the positions of the candidates operates to shape policy in the legislature. The basic process is, of course, the bargaining and compromise of rival interests. The basic rule of the game is that no important interest may be adversely affected without its consent.

Under these conditions, the majority that puts candidates and parties into office determines only *who* the official policy-makers will be; it does not determine *what* policies will be implemented. These will be the result of group bargaining and compromise. A. Lawrence Lowell, a political scientist and president of Harvard University, foresaw in 1913 the development of an "age of brokers" and an "age of advertisement."[38] *Brokerage* describes the process of resolving the conflict of interests in mass democracy; *advertisement* describes the techniques of organizing and engineering consent in the electoral process. Thus the basis on which candidates are elected (advertisement) no longer has anything to do with the way in which public policy is formed (compromise). The vote ceases to be a means of influencing or controlling policy.

Mass Society and Extremism

The placid comforts of suburban life, protected by a benevolent consensus on moderation, seem compensation enough for the typical mass man's political powerlessness. If he is rootless and alienated, his frustration is likely to take the form of political cynicism or apathy accompanied by willingness to accept the results of the brokerage process. There are, however, in apparently growing numbers, atypical citizens whose frustrations are pyramided into anxieties and for whom the call to politics is a call to do battle against the forces of evil. *Extremism* is the appelation recently given this brand of politics. It is a significant political phenomenon not only because of its recent growth, but because it threatens the rights and liberties necessary to democratic decision-making.

[38] A. Lawrence Lowell, *Public Opinion and Popular Government* (New York: Longmans, Green, 1913), pp. 58-61.

Who is the extremist? How is he related to mass society? In what ways does he threaten the fundamental principles of the democratic system? We may shed some light on these questions by examining the personality characteristics that seem to be reflected in extremist behavior.

THE AUTHORITARIAN PERSONALITY: A PROFILE

Political observers in recent years have been keenly interested in outlining the profile of the authoritarian personality[39]—that is, the cluster of interrelated attitudes and behaviors that are incompatible with the democratic process. These authoritarian characteristics rarely define a particular individual; perhaps most people possess some of them in some degree. They do tend, however, to constitute a syndrome (characteristic symptoms found together) that, undiluted by more gracious, conflicting qualities, leads to undemocratic behavior.

The set of attitudes that make up the authoritarian personality and their political implications may be briefly described as follows:

"People Can't Be Trusted." The motives of other people are suspect and their ability to make their own decisions is questioned. There is a tendency to see social problems as due to the human weakness or wickedness of others and to believe that coercive solutions are necessary. This generally low estimate of human nature leads to a distrust of democratic officials, to a contempt for the ability of the masses to participate in self-government, and to a general cynicism about the integrity of democratic processes and serious doubts about the ability of democracy to solve problems and to deal with social crises.

"The World Is a Jungle." All social situations must involve super-ordination or subordination: "Does he submit to me, or do I submit to him?" This heirarchical view of society carries along with it a contempt for weakness and a respect for strength. Politically, it leads to a

[39] Among the leading works in this area are the pathbreaking books by Theodore Adorno and others, *The Authoritarian Personality* (New York: Harper & Row, 1950); Gabriel Almond, *The Appeals of Communism* (Princeton, N.J.: Princeton University Press, 1954); Erich Fromm, *Escape from Freedom, op. cit.*; Eric Hoffer, *The True Believer* (New York: Mentor Books, 1958); Christie R. Jahoda and Marie Jahoda, eds., *Studies in the Scope and Method of "The Authoritarian Personality"* (New York: Free Press, 1954); Robert E. Lane, "Political Personality and Electoral Choice," *American Political Science Review*, March, 1955, pp. 173-90; Robert E. Lane, *Political Ideology: Why the American Common Man Believes What He Does* (New York: Free Press, 1962); Herbert McClosky, "Consensus and Ideology in American Politics," *American Political Science Review*, June, 1964, pp. 361-82; Milton Rokeach, *The Open and Closed Mind* (New York: Basic Books, 1960).

desire to dominate others seen as weaker than oneself and a desire to submit to strong leaders.

Intolerance of Ambiguity. There is a tendency to be uncomfortable in the presence of uncertainty and complexity, a tendency to be compulsive, inflexible, and unyielding and to hold rigid opinions and ideas. These attitudes often express themselves in a rejection of political pluralism, in a denial that there is any place in politics for compromise, and in a desire for simple, final, and forceful solutions to complex problems.

"Are You for Me or Against Me?" This is a tendency to divide the world into the "good guys" and the "bad guys," the "we" and the "they." Attitudes of suspiciousness and hostility are directed against outsiders. This attitude decreases the capacity for empathy (that is, the sympathetic understanding of others) and thus reduces the sense of obligation to respect the rights of others. The ability to put oneself in another's place, we have already noted, is a basic underpinning of the democratic sense of justice. In the authoritarian personality that ability is restricted to the narrow group that shares fully one's own views. The result is an intolerance of intellectual or cultural differences and an inability to believe that either compromise or rational discussion is a legitimate means of dealing with conflict. At the same time this attitude promotes the tendency to attribute everything that goes wrong to a conspiracy of the others.

"Intellectuals Think Too Much." Another authoritarian attitude is a basic anti-intellectualism. Intellectual activity tends to be regarded as useless at best, dangerous at worst. It is impractical and leads to noncomformity, atheism, moral relativism, and disloyalty. Eggheads are not to be trusted. These attitudes are often accompanied by a tendency to seek supernatural rather than scientific explanations. Politically, they reinforce the tendency to demand final, simple solutions and to derogate the role of reason in political affairs.

The Tendency to Stereotype. This is the attitude that sees others as members of groups, attributes characteristics to the groups, then judges others to be worthy or unworthy depending on the valuation of the qualities attributed to the group. It is, of course, this attitude that underlies racist movements in politics, but it will be recognized also as an attitude capable of extension to the poor, the capitalists, and other social groupings as well. In any of its forms it is likely to result in the belief that not all persons are entitled to the same fundamental rights and liberties.

The Authoritarian Personality and Mass Society

The authoritarian personality suffers from a loss of identity and self-esteem that would seem to be associated with the anomy and alienation of mass society. Feeling inadequate and disliking himself, he is very often the quickest to aggress against others or to project his own suppressed inadequacies on them. Eric Hoffer, using the phrase from Genesis II, "and slime they had for mortar," as a point of analogy, describes the role these anxieties play in mass movements:

> We have seen the acrid secretion of the frustrated mind, though composed chiefly of fear and ill will, acts yet as a marvelous slime to cement the embittered and disaffected into one compact whole. Suspicion too is an ingredient of this acrid slime, and it too can act as a unifying agent.
>
> The awareness of their individual blemishes and shortcomings inclines the frustrated to detect ill will and meanness in their fellow men. Self-contempt, however vague, sharpens our eyes to the imperfections of others. We usually strive to reveal in others the blemishes we hide in ourselves. Thus when the frustrated congregate in a mass movement, the air is heavy-laden with suspicion. There is prying and spying, tense watching and a tense awareness of being watched.[40]

Alienation in its milder forms produces apathy and withdrawal and makes its victim an easy target of manipulation. Increased beyond a certain point it produces neurotic anxiety, which releases destructive impulses and hostilities that are incompatible with democratic methods. Such anxiety furnishes the raw material for recent extremist movements.

Mass Society and Democratic Theory

We need to reemphasize that the picture we have sketched of the mass man cannot be offered as an accurate or adequate portrait of American society. As Muller says, following his description quoted earlier:

> Yet he is much more than this, else he would never have got where he has. The "mass-man" is also a bogey—a monstrous abstraction that conceals the infinite varieties of common men, in interest, ability, character, and aspiration. It conceals all the degrees in culture, the frequent lustiness of the low-brow, the earnestness of the middle-brow. In particular it conceals the idealism that underlies the

[40] Eric Hoffer, op. cit., p. 114.

obvious materialism. This expresses itself in such commonplace sentiments as that every man ought to have a fair chance—a very novel
commonplace, in the light of history. In times of crisis it has enabled
such loyalty, fortitude, and unpretentious heroism as won the Battle
for Britain. At all times it inspires an enthusiasm for vast cooperative
enterprises, kindles the energy and imagination that have made the
kingdom of common men the most adventurous in history. "An idealist working on matter" Santayana has called the American; and his
fine enthusiasm might be touched to finer issues. Meanwhile it is
again an inhuman spirituality that cannot see idealism in the effort
to eliminate the poverty and wretchedness once accepted as the will of
God, and to enable all men to enjoy the material well-being once
enjoyed only by a privileged few—by aristocrats who could afford
to exalt noneconomic interests and values because they took for
granted their wealth and luxury, and seldom had to earn it.[41]

Certainly, as a factual description, the picture we have painted is
greatly overdrawn—how greatly may be judged better in the light of
subsequent chapters. But as a model that clarifies the direction in
which recent tendencies are leading us, it may provide us with a
perspective necessary both to understand and to evaluate the present
condition of our political system. As E. H. Carr has put it, "We shall
not begin to understand the problems of mass democracy unless we
recognize the serious elements of truth in it, unless we recognize how
far we have moved away from the conditions out of which the democratic tradition was born."[42]

The democratic theory that became dominant in America held that
government should reflect the will of the masses of the people expressed
through majority rule. The will of the majority was expected to produce
objective principles of reason and justice to be applied to the settling
of disputes. According to this theory, the sovereign voter was required
to play certain roles. He was supposed to be interested in public issues,
able to discuss them, willing to expose himself to information and argument contrary to his own beliefs, and committed to judging issues on the
basis of principles that reflect not simply his own personal interests
but also the common good.

This theory leads democratic man to assume "that he has the right
to feel politically powerful, meaningful and moral."[43] Mass society
produces conditions in which these political expectations are not met.

[41] Muller, *op. cit.*, pp. 232-33.
[42] Carr, *op. cit.*, pp. 73-74.
[43] Levin, *op. cit.*, p. 73.

The citizen feels himself an alien in a political structure in which he has no legitimate role. Thus, either democratic theory or mass society may be regarded as the cause of alienation. That is, the roles of citizens derived from democratic ideals may be utopian and unrealistic, in which case the cure for the frustrated expectations of citizens is the development of a more realistic model; or the traditional model may be valid, in which case the cure is a reform of the political structure that prevents these expectations from being realized.

How far should modern man accept the political conditions of mass society as inevitable or desirable? Is compromise a necessary evil to be minimized as far as possible, or a positive good to be maximized as the democratic way of resolving conflict? Is psychological manipulation the only real alternative to physical coercion in the organization of consent? In general, do the ideals of traditional democratic theory, when understood in an adequate theoretical context, still provide valid norms for judging the political system? These questions can only be answered in the light of the models of democratic theory that compete for our allegiance and the philosophical assumptions that underlie them. This is the objective to which the next chapter is addressed.

Chapter Four

THE CONFLICT OF
DEMOCRATIC THEORIES

. . . in which the meaning of democracy is examined by comparing the liberal, conservative, and brokerage models.

The central question in democratic theory is treated as

> **The Problem** of preventing the tyranny of **Faction** (a group of citizens united to promote their economic interests or their passions). In a democracy this problem becomes one of preventing a factious **Majority** from tyrannizing minorities. So fundamentally different are the approaches to this problem taken by current theories of democracy that we may speak of *"The Warfare of Democratic Ideals."* There are three major models, all with roots in the American tradition, which offer competing solutions to the problem of faction and majority tyranny:

The Liberal Theory of Democracy argues that government should be organized so as to enable the majority to rule. It adds that

> **Majority Rule** is legitimate only when majority opinion has resulted from free and open debate of **The Public Interest;** and when
>
> **The Rights of Minorities** to the procedural freedoms that permit dissent and opposition are protected. The liberal belief that a majority can be expected to respect these rights requires
>
> **An Optimistic View of Man's Potentialities,** at least in the sense that they can be cultivated through political participation and education. Respect for rights of minorities would also be promoted by the belief that they are **Natural Rights.**
>
> **Who,** the liberal asks finally, **Would Stand Guard Over the Guardians?** All alternatives to majority rule, the question implies, have the effect of removing error from rational criticism.

The Conservative Theory of Democracy, in contrast, is pessimistic about human nature and argues for

> **The Need for Restraints on Human Frailty,** including constitutional restraints that will prevent a majority from ruling; exorbitant faith in the rational capacities of man will destroy reason itself;

The Need for Tradition, which will restrain the struggle for power, and the need for a sense of *Community,* which can unite men in a common cause;

The Need for Hierarchy and a limited, responsible *Aristocracy* motivated by a sense of *noblesse oblige* as a basis for social and political order. On these assumptions conservatives find the solution to government by consent in

A *System of Checks and Balances* that pits factions against one another and that provides for a limited elected aristocracy not directly subject to the changing interests and passions of the majority.

The Theory of Democracy as Broker Rule rejects both majority rule and the principles of balance and limited aristocracy. It argues that

Politics Is a Struggle for Power, the basis of which is the rivalry of

Organized Groups that seek to gain access to centers of decision-making. This group competition for power is kept in equilibrium where interests are not highly moralized and where there is overlapping of group membership. The group struggle for power must be resolved through processes of

Bargaining, Negotiation, and Compromise in which politicians play the role of *Brokers,* if political stability is to be reconciled with change and if liberty is to be preserved.

Finally, the liberal, conservative, and broker models of democracy are compared and contrasted, and the prospects for a realistic theory of democracy that would still provide norms for the measurement of real-world achievement are evaluated.

Compromise, n. Such an adjustment of conflicting interests as gives each adversary the satisfaction of thinking he has got what he ought not to have, and is deprived of nothing except what was justly his due.

AMBROSE BIERCE
(*The Devil's Dictionary*)

Chapter Four

THE CONFLICT OF DEMOCRATIC THEORIES

*T*HE GROWTH of mass society, described in Chapter 3, has created a crisis in democratic politics. At issue is the legitimacy of our political system. There is disagreement, we have noted, over how far along the road to the politics of mass society we have traveled. But it is clearly far enough to prompt questions as to where we are headed and why, and even to prompt such reactions as, "Oh! I thought you were driving." There is, indeed, a growing recognition that no one is driving, that we are drifting, and that we have already drifted far from the moorings of our traditional democratic ideals.

One important consequence of these developments is that we are forced to return to the fundamental question of the meaning of democracy. The central problem is the same one that has always faced democratic theory: In an open, pluralistic society, how is the exercise of power to be limited and controlled so that it will be accepted as legitimate authority by those who are asked to obey? This was the issue over which men contended in the debate over the form to be taken by the new government after the Revolution. Perhaps no one has ever stated the problem more clearly than did James Madison in the tenth number of *The Federalist Papers*.[1]

The Problem of Faction and Majority Tyranny

Madison, sometimes called the Father of the Constitution, addressed himself to the problem of tyranny in systems of government that derive their power from the people. There are, he argued, certain "mortal diseases" that are peculiar to popular governments and under which such governments "have everywhere perished." He describes these "diseases" as "instability, injustice, and confusion," and he argues that they all have a common source in the danger that the "public councils" will be dominated by the "spirit of faction."

Madison defines a faction as "a number of citizens, whether amounting to a majority or minority of the whole, who are united or actuated by some common impulse of passion, or of interest, adverse to the rights of other citizens, or to the permanent and aggregate interests of the community." Madison was describing the two threats to popular government with which philosophers had been concerned since democratic Athens: the danger that the power of government would come to be used to advance the selfish interests of an economic class or the emotional excesses of a mob.

The problem of faction is rooted in the conditions of an open and pluralistic society. "Liberty," says Madison, "is to faction what air is to fire." When men are left free to organize to pursue their own economic interests, it is inevitable that what we now call pressure groups will seek to influence and control public policies; when men are en-

[1] *The Federalist Papers* were a series of eighty-five essays written under the pseudonym of *Publius* by Alexander Hamilton, James Madison, and John Jay, and published in New York newspapers in 1787. Their purpose was to promote the ratification of the proposed Constitution in the New York convention. They are available in many different editions.

couraged to form their own opinions, it is inevitable that men's opinions will sometimes be dominated by their emotional passions. The danger of faction, therefore, cannot be eliminated; what must be done is to prevent the factious spirit (economic interests or emotional fears and hatreds) from controlling the government. For rule by faction, whether the faction be a minority or a majority, would be tyranny.

The problem in a democracy, as Madison clearly saw, was how to avoid tyranny by a *majority*: "If a faction consists of less than a majority, relief is supplied by the republican principle, which enables the majority to defeat its sinister views by regular vote." A well-organized and determined minority faction may "clog the administration" and even "convulse the society," but it will not be able to "mask its violence under the forms of the Constitution." The problem of democratic republics, then, is how "to secure the public good and private rights"—that is, minority rights—against a factious majority. And to do it without sacrificing "the spirit and form of popular government."

Here, in 1787 in the debate over the form of the new government, was perhaps as clear a statement as has ever been offered of the central problem of how a system of popular government is to be made legitimate. Unanimity on issues of public policy rarely exists; the spirit of democracy requires that a majority prevail over a minority; then how is it possible to guard against the danger that the majority's voice will reflect its economic interests, its whims, its passions?

Periodically, since 1787, the issue has been rephrased and reformulated, but its essence remains the same. Thomas Nixon Carver put it forcefully, if bitterly, in his comment that "there are few things more democratic than a lynching bee, where everybody is satisfied except a small and insignificant minority of one."[2] The problem was formulated even more clearly by A. Lawrence Lowell in the following analogy:

> If two highwaymen meet a belated traveller on a dark road and propose to relieve him of his watch and wallet, it would clearly be an abuse of terms to say that in the assemblage on that lonely spot there was a public opinion in favor of a redistribution of property. Nor would it make any difference, for this purpose, whether there were two highwaymen and one traveller, or one robber and two victims. The absurdity in such a case of speaking about the duty of the minority to submit to the verdict of public opinion is self-evident; and it is not due to the fact that the three men on the road form part of a larger community, or that they are subject to the jurisdiction of a common

[2] Quoted in Arthur A. Ekirch, *The Decline of American Liberalism* (New York: Longmans, Green, 1955), p. 220.

government. The expression would be quite as inappropriate if no organized state existed; on a savage island, for example, where two cannibals were eager to devour one shipwrecked mariner. In short the three men in each of the cases supposed do not form a community that is capable of a public opinion on the question involved.[3]

Although our descriptive language has been modified—we speak of factions as economic interests, pressure groups, or extremist movements —the problem posed by Madison, Carver, and Lowell is still the crucial one for democratic theory, and it is at the heart of the controversy that has developed in recent years.

"The Warfare of Democratic Ideals"[4]

The course of recent debate over the meaning of democracy has revealed genuine, fundamental, and widespread disagreement on how the problem raised by Madison is to be solved. Although it involves some oversimplification, the major solutions that have been offered may be described as: (1) the liberal theory of majority rule; (2) the conservative theory of balanced government; (3) the theory of minorities or broker rule.

All three of these theories have roots reaching far back in our political history. The Founding Fathers were not, as this common designation might suggest, agreed on fundamental questions of political theory. The conflict over the adoption of the Constitution was, as we shall see, in large measure a struggle between conservative and liberal solutions to the problem of faction. The conflict was not permanently resolved; it was glossed over, and with the rise of mass society a strikingly different model of democracy was developed that has taken the form of the now widely held theory of minorities or broker rule.

These three theories do not exhaust the possibilities, but they do contain the major alternative ways in which men seek to solve the problems of how a government "of the people, by the people, and for the people" is to be organized. In this section we attempt to present a broad overview of how each of these three models responds to the problem of faction. In the sections that follow we will look more closely at the philosophical assumptions that underlie these models and at their implications for the organization of the political system.

[3] A. Lawrence Lowell, *Public Opinion and Popular Government* (New York: Longmans, Green, 1913), pp. 2-3.
[4] The phrase is the title of a penetrating and excellent analysis of the philosophical issues in democratic theory: Francis M. Myers, *The Warfare of Democratic Ideals* (Yellow Springs, Ohio: Antioch Press, 1956).

THE CONSENT OF THE GOVERNED

The democratic idea of government began in a revolt against the power of kings and dictators and against hereditary and self-appointed aristocracies. It challenged as arbitrary all power that did not spring from the will of those who are governed. In the language of the Declaration of Independence, governments exist to secure man's "unalienable rights," and they derive their "just powers from the consent of the governed." This is the bedrock democratic test of legitimacy.

But how is popular consent to be organized and registered? This is the question to which our three models of democratic politics offer opposing answers: (1) The answer proposed by the liberal model is majoritarian, libertarian, and optimistic. Liberalism is majoritarian in its insistence that government be organized so as to enable the majority to rule; public policies should be formulated by public officials who reflect the opinions of the majority. Liberalism is libertarian in its argument that majority opinion should flow from the free, open, unencumbered debate of ideas, and that minorities retain the right to oppose the majority view. It is optimistic in its belief that the opinions of majorities formed in this free market of ideas will be the result of reasoned choice rather than of a factious spirit. (2) The conservative model of democracy, in contrast, is pessimistic and argues for balance and the need for a responsible aristocracy. Conservative democracy is pessimistic in its belief that the factious spirit will almost always govern the behavior of both majorities and minorities. It finds the solution to government by consent in a system that checks factions against one another and balances them, and in a limited, controlled, responsible aristocracy elected by the people but not directly subject to their changing interests and passions. (3) The broker model of democracy rejects both majority rule and the principles of balance and limited aristocracy. It argues that what Madison called factions are the basic elements in democratic politics. The proliferation of organized groups, representing all manner of interests, is inevitable in a pluralistic society. These groups all seek to influence public policy. The resulting struggle for power must be resolved through the process of bargaining, negotiation, and compromise.

Rule by majority; a balance of social forces in which a limited, responsible aristocracy can play a guiding role; rule by compromise—these are the three major alternative answers to the meaning of consent in the American tradition. Because they still provide the major alternative bases for judging actual political processes, a closer analysis and contrast of their assumptions and arguments seems justified.

THE LIBERAL THEORY OF DEMOCRACY

The central tenets of the liberal model of democracy are that government should be so organized as to facilitate the expression of majority opinion and its implementation in public policy. Thomas Jefferson summed up the liberal position in the assertion that "the will of the majority is in all cases to prevail" and in the qualification that the will of the majority "to be rightful must be reasonable." The qualification —that rule by a majority is only *legitimate* when the majority's will has resulted from an appeal to reason—clearly recognizes the possibility of majority tyranny. If the majority will reflects its passions or its interests, it is not "reason-able"—that is, open to rational argument. In such a case, the minority would have no moral obligation to obey. Thus, liberal democracy does not assume that the voice of the majority is the voice of God or that there is some magic in the figure 50 per cent plus 1, which automatically confers on a majority the right to impose its decisions on a minority. Majority rule requires something more than a mere counting of noses; there is no reason except superior force why minorities should accept the right of a factious majority to have its way.

Majority Rule and the Public Interest. Jefferson's qualification that the will of the majority must be "reasonable" if it is to be legitimate implies not only that the majority must have been created by rational discussion, but also that the will of the majority must express an opinion on the public interest. The citizen must be more than merely "rational" since reason might be used to rationalize self-interest or to conceal passions; the citizen's rational faculties must be used to judge between conflicting views of how justice can be done for everyone, how the common good and the public welfare can best be defined and promoted.

There are obvious perils in this concept of a public interest, for every authoritarian regime is supported by an idea of the general will or the real interests of the whole society. If it is assumed that the real interests of all men are ultimately in accord, and that this common interest is knowable, the practical conclusion would seem to be a single political party to embody and translate into reality the interest of all. For this reason it has sometimes been argued that the concept leads logically to political authoritarianism.

In their development of the concept of a public interest, the spokesmen for majority rule sought to avoid both the anarchistic consequences of individualism and natural rights and the totalitarian consequences of the doctrine that there is a final, ultimate, universal good that transcends individual opinions of what is good. The public interest is not something that can be known finally or ultimately. The conditions of society and human knowledge are constantly changing. Men's ideas about justice and the good life change too. The assertion of a public interest is another way of stating the faith that men can control and direct these processes of social and historical change by subjecting them to social goals and values evolved out of the processes of inquiry and public debate.

But if the public interest can only be arrived at by the opinions of men, it is necessary that men in their political activity concern themselves with questions that transcend their own immediate and personal interest. It is necessary that men have opinions about the public interest rather than simply desires about their private interests. The purpose of democratic politics is a continuing debate of, and temporary definitions of, the goals of public policy. The debate is a continuing one because the progress of the human mind assumes that human reason is fallible, but corrigible. The debate is meaningful because conflicting views of the public interest can be put to the test of reasoned discussion.

Another way of stating this qualification on the right of the majority to rule is to say that it is the *opinion* of the majority on the question of what is best for all that has a right to prevail. What the liberal assumes is the existence of what C. Wright Mills has called the "liberal public" and which he defines as "a body of reasoning men to whom reasoned appeals can be made." The liberal's citizen is a public man, as distinguished from the private man seeking his own interests or following his own emotional tendencies. In his private life his interests and passions find inevitable expression, but when he functions as ruler, they are transcended by his effort to act on his opinions about what will serve the public good. As Thomas Paine put it:

> As to the prejudices which men have from education and habit, in favour of any particular form or system of Government, those prejudices have yet to stand the test of reason and reflection. . . . We have but a defective idea of what prejudice is. It might be said that until men think for themselves the whole is prejudice, and not opinion: For that only is opinion which is the result of reason and reflection.[5]

[5] Thomas Paine, *The Rights of Man* (New York: Dutton, 1951), p. 148.

A majority that is factious—that is, organized on the basis of an appeal to emotion or on the basis of a private interest or a coalition of private interests—can make no claim that its authority over recalcitrant minorities is legitimate. A majority of debtors organized to reduce the interest rate, a rural majority organized to push a farm program, or a coalition of private interests organized to promote some accommodation of their interests are impossible to distinguish from Lowell's highwaymen. Where voters are organized as classes or as masses, from this point of view, there can be no legitimate authority, and the minority may be expected to continue its allegiance to the system only so long as effective possibilities of revolt are not open to it.

Majorty Rule and Minority Rights. If it is the "reason-able" character of majority opinion that gives it legitimacy, the basis of the minority's obligation is clear. The minority is obligated to obey the laws passed by a majority, but not to believe that the majority or its laws are correct. The final political loyalty of both majority and minority is to the *process* through which majority opinion is formed and continuously tested. In that process conflicting opinions confront one another in free and open debate. The process of majority rule puts limits on the power of temporary majorities and guarantees rights for temporary minorities. Thus, majority rule requires vigorous protection of those freedoms that make effective opposition possible: the right to full and equal political participation, free speech, a free press, religious freedom in the sense that religion is regarded as a matter of private conscience rather than public concern, freedom of association and peaceable assembly, and freedom from arbitrary enforcement of the laws. These rights and liberties are regarded by the liberal democrat not as gifts of a tolerant majority, but as the necessary conditions that give a temporary majority the moral right to rule at all. Any violation of them undermines the process of majority rule itself. If the majority uses its power to curtail dissent or to coerce belief in its views, it ceases in the liberal sense to be a majority. It may remain a majority in numbers, but there ceases to be any way of knowing whether it would continue to be a majority if its views had to meet the test of open challenge and free controversy. The majority that deprives minorities of their civil rights and liberties has lost its claim on the obligation of minorites and its right to rule.

The built-in restrictions on majorities limit both their formal and informal power. A majority can have no right to pass laws limiting the dissenter's freedom to criticize. Neither can it have any right to enact laws that seek to influence or control the minds and opinions of the public. It cannot, for example, set up a ministry of propaganda or seek to control the media of communications in behalf of its own views. Nor can it legitimately pass laws making its own conclusions into official or public tests of loyalty. This is the basis, for example, for the liberal democrat's opposition to the insertion of the phrase "under God" into the Pledge of Allegiance. This was an attempt by a religious majority to ensure that it would continue to be a majority by removing the issue from the realm of private judgment and free discussion.

The limits on majorities extend to more informal abuses of power as well. They include efforts by majorities to deprive minorities of their rights by the use of public office in a way that subjects minorities to informal social punishment, loss of reputation, or economic sanction. Liberal democrats object on this ground, for example, to many of the activities of legislative investigating committees in recent years that have had the effect of impugning the loyalty of dissenters and subjecting them to social punishment, even though they were innocent in the eyes of the law. This kind of informal, extralegal abuse of majority power has a long history. In 1794, the Whisky Rebellion in western Pennsylvania was widely attributed by the Federalist party to a conspiracy led by American agents of French radicalism. A resolution was introduced in the House of Representatives putting the blame on the newly organized "Democratical Societies" that formed the basis of the opposition Jeffersonian party. The resolution of censure read:

> We cannot withhold our reprobation of the self-created societies, which have risen in some parts of the Union, misrepresenting the conduct of the Government, and disturbing the operation of the laws, and which, by deceiving and inflaming the ignorant and the weak, may naturally be supposed to have stimulated and urged the insurrection.[6]

James Madison offered the liberal democrat's reply to this resolution in the following argument:

> He conceived it to be a sound principle, that an action innocent in the eye of the law could not be the object of censure to a legislative body. . . . Opinions are not the objects of legislation. You animadvert on the abuse of reserved rights: how far will this go? It may extend to the liberty of speech, and of the press. It is vain to say that this indiscriminate censure is no punishment. If it falls on classes, or individuals, it will be a severe punishment. . . .[7]

---

[6] Quoted by Irving Brant in "The Bill of Rights and the Radical Right," *Northwest Review*, Winter, 1963, p. 17.

[7] Quoted from the *Annals of Congress* in *ibid*.

We may summarize the liberal view of majority power and minority rights in the proposition that both the legitimate authority of a majority and the inviolable rights of minorities are defined by the process of free, rational debate through which majorities are formed. Minorities have a right to be considered, and majorities an obligation to consider them, as the loyal opposition.

We have examined the implications of Jefferson's provision that the will of the majority is only legitimate when it has resulted from an appeal to reason. This qualification admits the possibility of majority tyranny and defines the conditions that must be met if minorities are not to be tyrannized. But liberal democrats have agreed with Jefferson that "the will of the majority is in all cases to prevail." Thus, while liberals have insisted on minority rights, they have left them in the hands of the majority. "The people," Jefferson argued, may not always be the wisest, but they are "always the safest repository of their own liberties." This position seems almost patently self-contradictory. Will not majorities, unless they are somehow restrained by institutional or legal checks, almost inevitably exceed their legitimate powers and deprive minorities of their "equal rights"? Will they not, too often for safety and political stability, use their power to promote their own economic interests or be led by a demagogue into irrational excesses? Historically the theory of liberal democracy has avoided these conclusions by the position it has taken on the nature of man and society.

The Liberal View of Man. Majority rule obviously requires an optimistic view of human nature: it conceives man as an independent, rational, moral agent, capable of participating in public affairs. Only an optimistic view of man's potentialities would venture to make every man a ruler and to trust the rights of minorities to the keeping of the majority.

At the same time, liberals have never been so unsophisticated as to think that all men *are* such independent, rational, and benevolent individuals. As one of their revolutionary spokesmen, Samuel Adams, put it, "power is intoxicating; and men legally vested with it too often discover a disposition to make ill use of it and an unwillingness to part with it."[8] Early liberals described the source of the tendency to use political power for personal ends as "avarice and ambition," a phrase that recurs constantly in the writings of the liberals of Jefferson's generation. "Where avarice and ambition beat up for recruits," said John Taylor,

[8] Harry Alonzo Cushing, ed., *The Writings of Samuel Adams* (New York: Putnam's, 1904–1908), Vol. IV, p. 214.

"too many are prone to enlist,"[9] and "it is the thirst of avarice and ambition for wealth and power that we have to withstand."[10]

If liberals did not assume that men are always rational and responsible moral agents, how did they defend majority rule? In the first place, they did assume that moral choice is real and meaningful, that man's fate will depend on the choices he makes, and that man is *capable* of making responsible, reasoned choices. Second, their doctrine of the moral, rational individual is not so much a description of man as a statement of a value judgment. They were developing a normative, rather than a descriptive, model of politics. They did not assume rationality; they *preferred* it. They regarded the searching, questing individual human mind as the source of the dignity of mankind. Man's capacities for reason and choice among conflicting values they viewed as his highest qualities, the cultivation of which is the noblest object of society and government. Liberals regarded a representative majoritarian democracy as a superior form of government because of its commitment to the freedom and cultivation of the human mind.

They were espousing an ideal *for* individuals, an ideal clearly expressed in a later historian's description of Philip Freneau, a crusading Jeffersonian editor: "He had no vanity, no ambition for place or power, and no fear of either. He wore no man's collar and he was no man's man. He was a law unto himself."[11] But if independence was one aspect of the ideal individual, moral responsibility was equally important. Man has a right to make his own choices, to determine for himself what kind of life is worth living, and to arrive at his own conclusions about the ways existing social conditions need to be modified. He has a corresponding responsibility to develop for himself his intellectual and moral capacities.

They were insisting that individualism must not and need not be allowed to degenerate into self-centered egotism, that the free society requires men able, in the language of Joel Barlow, to participate in politics as "moral associates." This is the same proposition that underlies the description of Athenian democracy in Pericles' celebrated funeral oration: "We do not allow absorption in our own affairs to interfere with participation in the City's: we yield to none in independence of

[9] John Taylor, *Inquiry into the Principles and Policy of the Government of the United States* (New Haven, Conn.: Yale University Press, 1950), p. 71.
[10] *Ibid.*, p. 124.
[11] Claude G. Bowers, *Jefferson and Hamilton* (Boston: Houghton Mifflin, 1925), p. 160.

spirit and complete self-reliance, but we regard him who holds aloof
from public affairs as useless."

The liberal defense of majority rule, then, requires only a limited
and cautious optimism about human nature. With an early Puritan
democrat, the Reverend John Wise, it asserts that "man is not so wedded
to his own interest but that he can make the common good the mark
of his aim."[12] This assumes that every person must judge for himself
what is offered to him as a citizen, and that he is potentially at least
capable of judging with reference to broader considerations than his
own immediate, or even long-range, selfish interests. These potentialities
must be cultivated and developed through education; hence education
ranks at the top of the liberal's scheme of social institutions, and universal, free education came to be regarded as a condition of the liberal
society.

The Liberal Doctrine of Natural Rights. The liberal idea of natural
rights played a peculiarly important role in the justification of majority
rule by providing a basis for the protection of the rights of minorities.
Majorities might be expected to exercise restraint if they regard the
rights due minorities as natural rights to which all men are categorically
entitled. The doctrine of natural rights holds that all individuals, by
the very fact that they are all endowed with the faculty of reason and
the capacity for moral choice, are endowed with rights that transcend
existing political institutions.

The history of political theory is swollen with speculation about what,
specifically, these rights include. From time to time self-preservation, free
expression, acquisition of property, free association, tyrannicide, and
disobedience to unjust laws have been held to be on the list of rights
that are natural, and therefore unalienable. In a world affected by the
tendencies of mass society described in the preceding chapter, the whole
idea is often dismissed as a historical curiosity, not worthy of serious
consideration. Still, Americans often express the idea in such phrases
as "They can't do that to me"; "It's a free country"; or, "I've got my
rights." Although such statements are substantively imprecise, they
embody the idea that the individual has rights that go beyond mere
legal guarantees or concessions but belong to him because he is a man.

Despite the variations on what these rights are and the confusion as

---

[12] John Wise, A *Vindication of the Government of New England Churches*
(1717), reprinted in *The People Shall Judge* (Chicago: University of Chicago Press,
1949), Vol. I, p. 32.

to their source, liberal democrats have tended to have a fairly clear idea of their content and significance. They have generally regarded as bedrock the freedoms of conscience, speech, writing, and assembly. Sometimes these "truths" were asserted to be "self-evident," a claim the meaning of which has never been very clear. More often they have been held to be natural in a dual sense. First, they are derived from nature in the sense that they are the rights necessary to the cultivation and expression of the highest qualities in man's nature. The second sense in which they may be held to be natural is that they follow from the nature of society. The central characteristic and the permanent condition of society is change. One might as well expect a man to wear the clothes that fitted him as a boy, Jefferson argued, as to expect one generation to live under the conditions and institutions that fitted another. Intellectual and political freedom is the necessary means by which men can give rational direction to this natural process of social change. Jefferson's close political ally John Taylor summed up this dual justification of the natural right to intellectual liberty:

> Man's thoughts, suffered to flow, furnish the purest streams of human happiness, Dam'd up by law, they stagnate, putrify, and poison. To his characteristic qualities of speaking and writing, all man's social discoveries and improvements are owing. *Qualities which distinguish him from the brute creation, must be natural rights;* and those which are the parents of social order, must be useful and beneficial. Why should governments declare war against them?[13]

At bottom, the liberal doctrine of natural rights comes down to a defense of those minority rights necessary to make the process of majority rule legitimate. They add up to the warning to every majority that Jefferson expressed so clearly in his *Notes on Virginia*: Only the "acts of the body" and never "the operations of the mind" should be "subject to the coercion of the laws."

To argue that the rights of conscience, speech, and press are absolute is to argue that all other specific rights and obligations—all social and political institutions—are tentative and open to critical inquiry. This is the significance of natural rights. The appeal to nature is simply the

---

[13] Taylor, *op. cit.*, p. 413. Jefferson developed the same view when he proposed that "questions of natural right are triable by their conformity with the moral sense and reason of man." Quoted in John Dewey, *Thomas Jefferson* (New York: Longmans, Green, 1940), p. 16.

effort of liberal thought to examine all traditional institutions, "to bring them before the bar of reason to justify themselves."[14]

The chief functional significance of natural rights, particularly freedom to inquire, was to deny that any particular form of government or form of social inequality could be justified as being natural. As the Reverend John Wise, who had developed the theory of natural rights in Puritan New England, expressed it: "There is no particular form of civil government described in God's word; neither does nature prompt it."[15] All social institutions, he held, are the product of "human and rational combinations"; hence, all alike are open to human criticism and change. The final faith of this position is Jefferson's statement in the *Notes on Virginia*: "it is error alone which needs the support of government. Truth can stand by itself."

Who Would Stand Guard over the Guardians? We may summarize our description of the liberal defense of majority rule thus far as follows: Rule by a majority is more likely to result in rational and morally defensible decisions than is rule by any minority. This is true, not because the majority includes more people, but because the majority has been created out of the process of reasoned debate of alternatives and because the errors of a majority can be more readily corrected. If the majority is mistaken, the consequences of acting on its opinion will reveal its weaknesses and strengthen the arguments of its opponents. All of this, of course, assumes that the majority's opinions are reasoned and principled, and that they are formed under conditions that make criticism and the free expression of ideas possible. But the majority may be motivated by economic interest or swayed by emotion, and it is likely to be tempted to entrench itself in power by limiting the freedoms of its potential opponents. While granting the reality of these dangers, the liberal model would entrust both reason and minority rights to the care of majorities. This requires an optimistic view of the possibilities of human nature when men are properly educated to the responsibilities of citizenship. And it counts heavily on the self-restraint that will be shown by majorities who believe that the rights of minorities are natural and unalienable rights that inhere in all men.

There is one final aspect of the liberal case. Nothing that has been said above requires the belief that majority rule is a perfect solution

---

[14] Morris R. Cohen, *American Thought: A Critical Sketch* (New York: Free Press, 1954), p. 124.
[15] Wise, *op. cit.*, p. 31.

to the problem of how men are to be governed; it is only the best of the alternatives available. This is an important point because it explains why, finally, the liberal declines to put limits on the power of majorities. What are the alternatives? Only, it would seem, empowering some other body than the majority to decide when the majority is legitimate and when it is not. But who is to be trusted with the power to entertain appeals from majority decisions and to restrain a factious or tyrannical majority? "Have we then," asked Jefferson, "found angels in the form of men?" If we are to trust a set of guardians, then who will stand guard over the guardians?

To this unanswerable question the liberal model adds another point. Where the majority rules, minorities can always appeal their decisions to the court of public opinion. This appeal is an appeal to reason and to moral conscience. (Even the tactics of nonviolent disobedience of the law are moral appeals, and they may reflect a commitment to reason, but, in Karl Jaspers' phrase, "reason exasperated" by the majority's intransigence.) But if there is another court of appeal than public opinion—whatever the body who make it up—the appeal must be not to reason or conscience but to the authority, the judgment, or the wisdom of the appeal body.

Liberalism finds two difficulties in this. If the appeal is to be effective, the decision of the reviewing agency must be accepted as final and authoritative; the majority must have no recourse to argument to overturn its decision. And therefore, if it is wrong—and why should it always be right?—there is no appeal to reason to correct its error. Second, any body to whom appeals from majority decisions could be carried would have to be charged with the responsibility for defining the meaning of reason and for protecting the rights and liberties that the system requires. But to make any elite responsible for these matters is to relieve citizens themselves and their political representatives from responsibility —indeed, it is even likely to encourage irresponsibility. If there is an agency that can be trusted to curb men's excesses and judge the reasonableness of their decisions, then why should men not say: "Let us pursue our interests and our impulses unrestrained; an elite will tell us when we have overstepped the bounds of reason and will curb our abuses." In the long run, not even the wisest, most responsible Supreme Court can safeguard the liberties or ensure the rationality of a people who, having shifted responsibility to the court, no longer feel themselves bound to listen to reason, to act on principle, or to respect and protect the rights and liberties on which the system depends. This is the meaning of Jefferson's argument, quoted earlier, that the people themselves are the safest keepers of their own liberties.

The argument we have been examining might even be put in the form attributed to Winston Churchill: "Democracy is the worst form of government ever devised by the minds of men—except for all other forms of government devised by the minds of men." Most liberals would prefer, no doubt, a less cynical, more hopeful way of making the point. Still, the pessimistic case emphasizes the fact that the liberal model is not as utopianly optimistic as it appears at first glance. In the final analysis, the liberal case comes down to the argument that majority rule is the decision-making process more likely than any other to bring to bear on public policy the best rational and moral judgment—fallible but improvable—men are capable of making.

THE CONSERVATIVE THEORY OF DEMOCRACY

Fortunately for the intellectual future of America, the colonial period produced a truly remarkable number of able men who brought their talents to bear on the problem of organizing the new government after independence. The liberal theory of democracy had eloquent spokesmen, and they were countered by equally formidable partisans of a conservative persuasion. The issues were sharply drawn and clearly expressed.

Conservatives challenged the validity of liberal theory at three major points: (1) It underestimates the role of irrationality and egoism in human behavior and fails to provide adequate safeguards against them; (2) it undermines the necessary place of tradition and a sense of community in maintaining social order and civic decency; and (3) it fails to recognize the need for hierarchy and aristocracy in society.

The Need for Restraints on Human Frailty. Conservatives see the liberal faith in rational majorities as unrealistic and irresponsible. Liberalism overestimates the power of reason and the rational capacities of individual men and underestimates the human tendency to self-interest and passion. The conservative view of man does not regard him as completely depraved; it sees him, rather, as a paradox. His natural tendencies are predatory and antisocial, and they constantly threaten to break down the civilized barriers that keep them in precarious restraint. In conflicts between reason and passion or between self-interest and public-spiritedness, man's natural vices are always likely to prevail.

All men "may have some affection for the public," John Adams reasoned, but it is equally true that "there are few who love the public better than themselves."

The view of man expressed by Adams was not new to political theory, but it was unusual for such assumptions to be part of the intellectual equipment of democratic theorists. On it Adams and other conservatives built the theory of conservative democracy. Their theory is *democratic* because it does not entrust power to an elite who are assumed to be exempt from the frailties that afflict other men and because it does not rule out man's ability to participate in government if adequate safeguards are built into the system. It is a *conservative* theory of democracy in that it rejects the view that men are likely to behave rationally and morally in a liberal political system. Where liberals argue that government should be organized so that it can be effectively controlled by citizens, conservatives contend that human nature needs also to be controlled and restrained by government and by society.

This fundamental difference in the liberal and conservative appraisals of human nature should not blind us to some values they share in common. Most important, perhaps, they share the belief that the struggle for power must be subordinated, as far as possible, to reason and the public interest and the belief that, as far as possible, freedom should prevail. They differ on how these goals are to be attained and on how much is possible.

In the conservative view the liberal faith in human rationality is fatal to reason itself. The capacity of men to submit their beliefs and actions to the test of reason is too rare and capricious a gift to rely on for the control of the lust for power and self-aggrandizement. If reason is to play a role in political affairs, it must have a limited place in a political system that uses other means—tradition, religion, habit, deference to established institutions, balance—to control the potential evil and unreason in the human psyche.

So also with the goal of freedom. If rights and liberties are regarded as natural and protected only by the promise that they will appeal to men's reason and sense of justice, they will have no protection whatever. Self-restraint provides no restraint at all on men who are likely to invade the rights of others whenever the opportunity presents itself. What is necessary is to restrict the opportunity. Unless society and a carefully contrived constitution provide such restraints, the liberal effort to create unlimited liberty will produce a tyranny that will eliminate all liberty.

Thus, by its extravagant hopes, liberalism will destroy both reason and liberty. We can have a maximum of both only if we recognize that man's first or original nature is their natural enemy. On this analysis recent conservatives have laid the blame for the rise of modern totalitarian regimes on the liberal doorstep.[16]

Through all of the conservative attitudes runs the emphasis on the necessity of government as a device for controlling the factious tendencies in all men. Liberals have wanted the people to control the government; conservatives have insisted that government must be arranged to control the evil in people. Liberals have had faith that popular participation in democratic government serves to make men less self-centered and more rational; conservatives have rejected the idea that man's nature can be reformed through politics. Majoritarian democracy, conservatives were convinced, could lead only to political convulsion. This ought not be interpreted to mean that they were opposed to popular government as such, or to civil liberties. They were, in fact, often eloquent spokesmen for as much of popular control of government and as much of civil liberties as might be, in their view, compatible with the restraint of man's innate will to power and self-seeking and his natural susceptibility to demagogic appeals. But their assumptions about human nature made them skeptical about how much was possible. They were convinced that a government neither could, nor should, be made to rest on the freely formed opinions of men, particularly common men. This conviction rested on the view that men do not often have opinions; they are more likely to have desires, appetites, and interests. The doctrine of the original depravity of man produced, in the minds of conservatives, an open distrust of the procedures of free public discussion as the *basic principle* of government, even though it remained for them a cherished principle and a positive good.

The Need for Tradition and Community. The conservative authors of *The Federalist* noted that "man is very much a creature of habit" (No. 27) and held that the solid basis of any government must be, at least for the masses of men, habitual obedience and reverence for the existing mechanisms of government rather than the appeal to reason implied in the liberal position. The Constitution would become a genuine instrument of government, *Federalist* No. 49 argued, when

---

[16] See, for example, William Y. Elliot, *The Pragmatic Revolt in Politics* (New York: Macmillan, 1928) and Daniel J. Boorstin, *The Genius of American Politics* (Chicago: The University of Chicago Press, 1953).

it had acquired "that veneration which time bestows on everything, and without which perhaps the wisest and freest governments would not possess the requisite stability." It concluded that even "the most rational government will not find it a superfluous advantage to have the prejudices of the community on its side."

On this analysis, a society that is committed to the liberal theory of democracy must fail to enlist the necessary support of its citizens. Men require something more than a commitment to reasoned choice to hold them together. In order to give purpose to their lives and institutions, they require the emotional satisfactions derived from membership in a community whose bonds are full of spiritual and moral meaning. The symbols of political society—the flag, the Pledge of Allegiance, the patriotic holidays, the national myths and rituals, and national shrines and memorials—must serve as substitutes for reason. They must be so pregnant with emotional meaning that they pull all strata of the community together through deeply charged emotion, shared values, and common purposes. A nation, the conservative argues, is not a debating society, and the liberal's effort to make it one fails because it does not fulfill the emotional and spiritual needs of individuals to share a common faith in a larger community. The failure of a liberal society to fill this need produces the mediocrity and conformity of mass society, rather than the free and enlightened individuals the liberal expected to produce. In the final analysis, the conservative would contend, the tensions, frustrations, and anxieties of life in mass society are produced by the inadequacy of liberal theory. The result is likely to be citizens ripe for the emotional appeals of mass movements led by a man on horseback.

The Need for Hierarchy and Aristocracy. The conservative sees in the liberal's faith in popular majorities and belief in natural rights a fatal attack on the hierarchy and the principle of aristocracy that are necessary to social justice and the protection of the public interest. The ideal of equality of participation in politics would undermine the foundations of service and responsibility that a natural aristocracy must supply. Conservatives have always tended to believe that, in every society of men, there are the "better sort," the "middling sort," and the "poorer sort."[17]

Inequality is natural; therefore, a stratified society is natural. Those

[17] Clinton Rossiter, *Conservatism in America* (New York: Knopf, 1955), p. 81.

who possess the greatest talents must be in a position to use them for the benefit of all. At the same time, the conservative's aristocracy is not an elite that can be trusted with uncontrolled power. The aristocrat is a man of naturally superior talent, educated to exercise prudence in judgment and motivated by a sense of *noblesse oblige* to put his talents in the service of the community. Still, the aristocrat is cut from the same human cloth as everyone else; he is no less susceptible to abusing power in the service of his own avarice and ambition. As John Adams said, men "are all of the same clay." While an aristocracy may have "more knowledge and sagacity, derived from education, and more advantages for acquiring wisdom and virtue," still, when it comes to "usurping other's rights," they are "equally guilty." Adams' conclusion is the essence of the conservative position, "No wise man will trust either with an opportunity. . . ."

Every class of men, Adams argued, has "waged everlasting war against the common rights of man": "So has human nature, in every shape and combination, and so it ever will." The aristocracy, of course, is always in a minority. Since it is rooted in the natural inequalities among men, it is entitled to a higher position in society. But because aristocrats, like all men, are selfish and corrupt by nature, they cannot be trusted to rule without restraints. Because an aristocracy is motivated by pride, it is tempted to use the power of government to increase artificially its wealth and prestige. The result would be minority tyranny. But the pride of the nobility is matched by the "vulgar malignity and popular envy" of the masses. If the majority of the common people were allowed to rule, they would use their power to take from the few what rightfully belongs to them. The result would be majority tyranny.[18]

The Conservative Solution: Balance and a Limited Aristocracy. Early America presented unique problems to the conservative argument for community and hierarchy. The American revolution was essentially liberal in its goals and aspirations. There was no inherited and tradition-bound system of class or status—indeed, such an idea was repugnant to the stated aims of the revolution. And the vast unexploited frontier with its resources of free land not only provided an outlet for economic pressure but encouraged the development of a liberal society in its mammoth regions.

[18] Charles Francis Adams, ed., *The Works of John Adams* (Boston: Little and Brown, 1850–1856), Vol. VI, pp. 417-20.

In the absence of tradition and a stable class structure, American conservatives were forced to find other solutions. They found them in the principles of balanced government and limited aristocracy. The principle of balance seeks to solve the problem of faction by pitting power against power, ambition against ambition, self-interest against self-interest. Every effort to establish just and orderly government, John Adams argued, "has been found to be no better than committing the lamb to the custody of the wolf, except that one which is called a balance of power."[19]

The device that seemed capable of restraining the potential evil in all men was a carefully contrived constitution, which, through the system of checks and balances, would frustrate and neutralize the efforts of every class of men to invade the rights of others. Such a system would make it impossible for either majority or minority factions to rule. It would thus permit, in one of Adams' favorite expressions, the rule of "a government of laws, and not of men."

Conservatism, unlike the theory of broker rule to be examined in the next section, is not content to allow public policies to reflect simply a balance of private interests. Conservatives are interested in neutralizing the influence of factions by a system of checks and balances, so that some elbow room may be provided for the influence of reason and the public interest. Public decisions, in the language of Madison in *Federalist* No. 10, must reflect "rules of justice" and protect the liberty of all rather than simply mirror the power positions of "rival parties." The "public councils" must be directed by considerations of justice and the public welfare. And this function must be performed by limited, controlled aristocrats.

The spirit of popular government requires that public officials be elected. But the principle of aristocracy requires that the method of election be indirect—through what Madison called "the successive filtration of popular power." The objective must be to "refine and enlarge the public views, by passing them through the medium of a chosen body of citizens, whose wisdom may best discern the true interests of their country, and whose patriotism and love of justice will be least likely to sacrifice it to temporary or partial considerations."[20]

Conservatives have disagreed about who is to perform this aristocratic function, but they have agreed that the power must be ultimately,

[19] *Ibid.*, p. 431.
[20] The quotation is from James Madison in *The Federalist* (No. 10).

but not directly, controlled by the citizens. Thus, in the principle of a balanced constitution and in the role of limited aristocracy the dangers of democracy can be controlled while the greatest possible degrees of rationality and liberty are promoted.

The Rise of the Politics of Minorities Rule

The conflict between liberal and conservative ideas provided the framework within which the debate over the Constitution and much of our subsequent constitutional and political history has occurred. As we will see in the next chapter, the Constitution adopted in 1789 was a conservative document. In its cardinal principles of checks and balances, federalism, and judicial review, it established conservative bulwarks against the political power of majorities. Liberals carried on a running battle to surmount these barriers to the popular will. Their victories were reflected in the rise of political parties with a mass base, in the majoritarian reforms of the Jeffersonians, the Jacksonians, and the Civil War, and in the constitutional amendments that provided for civil liberties, universal suffrage, and the direct election of senators. Thus, it is tempting to view American political history as the progressive modification of the conservative constitutional system in the direction of majority rule.

Yet, the striking fact is that nearly all competent observers of the system agree that the actual tendencies of American politics have led in a quite different direction. As we have seen, by 1913 the character of our political life had changed so much that A. Lawrence Lowell could describe the political future as an "Age of Advertisement" and an "Age of Brokers." Lowell saw in "the same conditions that have caused the great development of advertising, where the mass of the public must be reached," the factors that produced the political broker "in the class of transactions which affect a smaller class of persons."[21]

Very early in their development Lowell recognized the two central characteristics of the politics of mass society: the manipulation of a mass electorate and the tendency of politicians to play the role of brokers who serve as go-betweens among conflicting interest groups.

Modern political scientists almost unanimously accept the picture drawn by Lowell as the most adequate *descriptive* model of more recent

[21] Lowell, *op. cit.*, p. 60.

American politics. Indeed, Lowell's use of the term *broker* was prophetic, for the model is now commonly referred to as *broker rule*. The political system described by this phrase differs sharply from both the liberal and conservative models. The majority does not rule, nor does a balancing of factions neutralize their drives for power and allow room for guidance by a responsible aristocracy. As one political scientist has put it, "The making of government decisions is *not* a majestic march of great majorities united upon certain matters of basic policy." Neither does it reflect the conservative intent of our constitutional arrangements. Instead, "it is the steady appeasement of relatively small groups."[22] We cannot describe American politics as either majority or minority rule, or as a mixture of the two. It is, rather, a system in which minor*ities* rule, in which policies reflect the compromises agreed to by organized minority groups through a process of bargaining. "In the American system decisions are made by endless bargaining; perhaps in no other national political system in the world is bargaining so basic a component of the political process."[23]

In this process governmental policies are determined by shifting coalitions of minorities, rather than by either a majority or a minority. These minorities spring up naturally in an open society to promote the interests of citizens. The major groups are economic and reflect the farm, business, and labor interests, and their subgroups and subinterests. But there are also geographical, sectional interests (the South, the West, and the Northeast, for example) and ethnic and religious interests (Catholics, Protestants, Jews, Irish, Negroes, for example). Votes and support are traded among the interests. In the Congress, their supporters often constitute voting blocs on issues that affect their interests. The rules of the Congress, the committee structure, the seniority system, and the filibuster in the Senate facilitate their maneuvering.

The process also extends to the Presidency: a candidate cannot hope to win election with the solid opposition of any major group. Political parties put together a package that contains something for everybody and straddle the fence on issues in order to avoid alienating or offending any important group.

The over-all result is that organized groups come to exercise a veto

[22] Robert A. Dahl, *A Preface to Democratic Theory* (Chicago: University of Chicago Press, 1956), p. 146.

[23] *Ibid.* There are those who argue that there is in practice, a ruling elite; perhaps the best case for this view is made by C. Wright Mills in *The Power Elite* (New York: Oxford, 1956).

on political decisions. Their veto is limited and conditional on their willingness to be "reasonable" and to accept the rules of the game. How effective this veto power is will depend on how influential and powerful the group is. But the crucial fact is that government can act only with the express consent of the organized groups.

Broker rule has been proposed as both a descriptive model of actual American politics and a normative model of democracy. Nearly all political scientists accept it as the most adequate model for describing the political system, but there is sharp disagreement on whether the system is a good one. Philosophical liberals and conservatives attack the politics of broker rule and propose reforms that would bring political processes more nearly into line with their own normative models. Inevitably so, for broker rule leaves little place for enlightened and rational citizens, for tradition, or for guardianship of an aristocracy; it leaves none at all for a public interest. It finds in group interests the basic data of politics. And it makes the compromising and balancing of group claims the uniquely democratic solution to the problem of politics. Both the fact that it is already widely held and the fact that it claims to justify some of the major tendencies of modern political life entitle it to serious and systematic consideration. It is to this normative model of democracy as minorities rule that we now turn.

THE THEORY OF DEMOCRACY AS BROKER RULE

The theory of broker rule is a defense and justification of modern political processes. Some of the elements of the practice that broker rule describes are as old as politics; but the term itself is new, and the philosophical theory it stands for has only been widely held in very recent decades. As a theory of politics, broker rule was first developed by John C. Calhoun.[24] Long-time Senator from South Carolina and Vice-President of the United States from 1825 to 1832, Calhoun was another in the long line of politician-philosophers so prominent and distinctive in the American tradition (and, ironically, perhaps destined to be casualties in the development of the very system of broker rule that Calhoun advocated).

In Calhoun's view, there are no abstract standards of public interest or justice that men, whether a majority or a minority, can be relied on

---

[24] Calhoun's ideas were developed in "A Disquisition on Government," in Richard K. Kralle, ed., *The Works of John C. Calhoun* (New York: Appleton-Century-Crofts, 1954), Vol. I.

to discover or apply. For when men's desires and interests are at stake, one man's opinions are as good as another's, one man's interests as legitimate as any other's. Human values, in short, are rationalizations of interests and desires. They are, from any rational point of view, simply incommensurable. For if any man or group of men is allowed to judge, he must simply prefer his own interest against others. He will, to be sure, dress up his decision in the language of moral justification, but this must be recognized for the rationalization it is bound to be. All interests, and accordingly all competing social groups, must be taken to have been born equal.

On these assumptions, it necessarily follows that majority rule—and, of course, minority rule as well—is sheer coercion. The noncoercive use of the powers of government requires the equal treatment of all organized groups. Equality of treatment cannot be guaranteed through a static equilibrium established in a constitution, or through reliance on Madison's "representatives whose enlightened views and virtuous sentiments render them superior to local prejudices and to schemes of injustice." No static balance is possible because there is no way of determining objectively when the conflicting forces are in equilibrium; this is a judgment that would have to be made by men, and like all human judgments, it would inevitably express self-interest. The only alternative to force in government, Calhoun concluded, is the process of securing the universal assent of all rival interests to every proposed public policy—that is, the process of compromise. A genuinely constitutional government, one that would control the human propensity to use others for one's own purposes, must ensure that all public policies reflect compromises voluntarily agreed to by the factions themselves.

Applying this theory to the sectional conflict of his own day, Calhoun worked out the principle of the "concurrent majority," which involved giving each of the major sectional interests an absolute, constitutionally protected right of veto over any proposed legislation. The irony of Calhoun's role in American history is that, even in its larger meaning, his theory of democracy as compromise had few takers and remained largely outside the framework of American political theory for at least another seventy or eighty years.

The reason for this is not simply that he was on the losing side of the slavery issue. What he presented was a radically different model of democratic politics, one in which the pursuit of truth and public morality no longer was regarded even as a possible goal of political life. It made factional strife the exclusive reality of politics and argued that the only problem was to keep any interest from winning.

In its broader context Calhoun's theory went unsupported because it represented a radical attack on the objectives of politics as these were conceived in both liberal and conservative thought. His theory proposed that: "The aim of a political organization was not to educate men, but to deploy them; not to alter their moral character, but to arrange institutions in such a manner that human drives would cancel each other or, without conscious intent, be deflected towards the common good."[25] Men whose ideas were dominated by liberal and conservative definitions of the purpose of government could not accept the conclusion that "morality was absent from politics or that it might come about automatically" through the compromises of conflicting interests.[26]

It seems reasonable to conclude that developments involved in the growth of mass democracy, described in the last chapter, were responsible both for the increasing prevalence of the politics of broker rule and for the fact that increasing numbers of Americans have come to accept it as a normative theory. As T. V. Smith says, it was Calhoun's peculiar lot "while losing his cause to win his case," for although slavery was doomed, the political theory he devised to protect it has become the orthodox defense of current American political institutions.

The Modern Theory of Broker Rule. The model of broker rule in its modern form represents a refinement and elaboration of Calhoun's ideas.[27] Its major assumptions and arguments include the following: (1) Politics is a struggle for power. (2) The elements in this struggle in a democracy are organized interest groups. (3) The stability of democratic politics requires overlapping membership in groups and the selection of legislators, administrators, and judges who will define their roles as mediators of group compromise. (4) Democracy cannot operate

---

[25] Sheldon S. Wolin, *Politics and Vision* (Boston: Little, Brown, 1960), p. 389.

[26] Alfred De Grazia, *Public and Republic* (New York: Knopf, 1951), p. 248. De Grazia concludes his comment with, "even though everyday politics affirmed the idea as a working principle." But it is not clear whether "everyday politics" affirmed that "morality was absent from politics" or that morality "came about automatically" from the clash of private interests. It makes a difference, and the second possibility sounds more like a kind of magic than something that "everyday politics" could "affirm."

[27] The first modern statement of the theory was developed by Arthur F. Bentley in 1908 in *The Process of Government* (republished at Bloomington, Ind.: Principia Press, 1949). Like Calhoun, Bentley had little impact when first published. In recent years both Calhoun and Bentley have been rediscovered and republished.

under other than brokerage techniques. These elements of the broker-age model are examined briefly below.

Politics as Power. To the theorist of compromise, the scientific study of politics must confine itself to the study of power relationships. Underlying this assertion is the assumption that values are psychological data, the primary purpose of which is to camouflage and rationalize interests, needs, and desires. From this point of view, it is a mistake to believe that principles can play any real causal role in politics. As Bentley put it, "It is the power of the underlying interests which pump all the logic into theory that theory ever obtains." The devastating effect of this proposition on the traditional liberal model is obvious. The trouble with the liberal view of democracy was that, in it, "the political community had some of the characteristics of an Oxford debating society, policy emerging from endless argument, with reason presiding in the speaker's chair."[28]

According to the theory we are considering, this is a hopelessly utopian dream, even as an ideal, because it rests on a mistaken view of the nature of politics. It makes any understanding of the actual political processes of democracy impossible. A legislature, for example, can never be understood as long as it "is taken for what it purports to be—a body of men who deliberate upon and adopt laws." To dis-cover where "the real law-creating work is done" it is always necessary to trace any policy from "its efficient demand [by an interest group or groups] to its actual application." When this is done, it will always turn out that the legislature was not "Moses the law-giver" but "merely Moses the registration clerk."[29] If the legislature fails accurately to reflect the balance of power among groups in the political arena, the function will be taken over by the President or the courts; hence, the fluctuation over time in their respective influence.

For the same reasons, the traditional concern for the pursuit of the public interest becomes meaningless. Where the struggle for power is held to be the only political reality, the public interest cannot "describe any actual or possible political situation within a complex nation." Accordingly, it can never be more than "a tremendously useful pro-motional device."[30]

[28] Earl Latham, *The Group Basis of Politics* (Ithaca, N.Y.: Cornell University Press, 1952), p. 6.
[29] Bentley, *op. cit.*, p. 163.
[30] Latham, *op. cit.*, pp. 50-51.

The Group Basis of Politics. Brokerage theory assumes that interest groups are the basic elements in the political system. An interest group has been defined by one exponent of the theory as "any group that, on the basis of one or more shared attitudes, makes certain claims upon other groups in the society for the establishment, maintenance, or enhancement of forms of behavior that are implied by the shared attitudes."[31] It is true, of course, that organized interests—groups characterized by interaction and organized to exert pressure on centers of decision-making—tend to proliferate in a pluralistic, free society. No one denies this. It is what Paul Appleby meant when he said that "noses count in politics but noises do too. Big noises count extra." But what group theory asserts is that politics is nothing but the struggle of interest groups: "The only opinion, the only will, which exists is the opinion, the will, of special groups."[32] From this perspective, political society is seen only as a process of group competition for power.

As we have noted, American politics in the twentieth century seems to fit the model of group rivalry and compromise rather well. To understand the significance of this fact we need to get a clearer view of what group theory implies and what other approaches to politics it excludes. It denies, in the first place, that the ballot box can be the primary means by which sovereign, choice-making individuals hold the exercise of governmental power responsible. The people elect their leaders by majority vote, but the vote is a ratification of a coalition of interests. Political competition in elections serves not to give voters a clear-cut choice of policies but to ensure that all organized groups will have access to potential officeholders, and thus to increase the size, number, and variety of minorities whose interests will have to be considered by those who make policy. The proponents of group theory assert that it "does not lose sight of the individual," since groups may be seen as existing to fulfill the desires, wants, and values of the individual.[33] But they do see the group as both the source of individual attitudes and the channel through which they are given political effect. They see government as *responding* to the desires of individuals by reflecting the competing demands of interest groups, rather than as *responsible* to the individual's convictions about public issues. They hold that "we cannot

[31] David Truman, *The Governmental Process* (New York: Knopf, 1951), p. 33.
[32] John Dickinson, "Democratic Realities and Democratic Dogmas," *American Political Science Review*, May, 1930, p. 291.
[33] Latham, *op. cit.*, p. 54.

correctly describe the actual operations of democratic societies in terms of the contrasts between majorities and minorities. We can only distinguish groups of various types and sizes, all seeking in various ways to advance their goals, usually at the expense, at least in part, of others."[34] As a leading spokesman for the theory puts it:

> The legislative vote on any issue tends to represent the composition of strength, *i.e.*, the balance of power, among the contending groups at the moment of voting. What may be called public policy is the equilibrium reached in this struggle at any given moment, and it represents a balance which the contending factions or groups constantly try to weight in their favor.[35]

The legislature serves as referee in the group struggle, "ratifies the victories of the successful coalitions, and records the terms of the surrenders, compromises, and conquests in the form of statutes." Insofar as the legislature does more than umpire the game and serve as a cash register, it is not because a majority political party translates its principles into policy. It is rather that legislatures are groups themselves and "show a sense of identity and consciousness of kind that unofficial groups must regard if they are to represent their members effectively."[36]

Group Conflict and Stable Equilibrium. Where interest groups have free access to centers of decision-making, where interests tend to be economic rather than ideological and doctrinaire, and where all interests respect the rules of the game, the result is presumed to be a condition of equilibrium. This condition among competing interests is held, in the group theory of politics, to constitute justice in democratic societies. The whole system of group equilibrium will be a stable one only if all the important groups in society accept the basic rule of compromise and refrain from doing serious violence to the interests of other groups.

Most groups, however, would like to have their own complete way. The problem is how to ensure that the process of compromise is not blocked by stalemate and does not degenerate into warfare. Broker theorists solve the problem through reliance on: (1) the preservation of the rules of the game through the number and variety of groups in a pluralistic society; (2) the role of the politician as broker; and (3) the phenomena of overlapping membership and potential groups.

---

[34] Dahl, *op. cit.*, p. 131.
[35] Latham, *op. cit.*, p. 36.
[36] *Ibid.*, p. 37.

The Rules of the Game. In a pluralist society the sheer number and variety of competing interests will operate to restrain the demands made by any one of them. Because no group or combination of groups can hope to constitute a majority, none can afford to be

> . . . intransigent or doctrinaire. It must make every conceivable effort to compromise, relying on its veto only as a last resort. For if any player wields this weapon recklessly, the game will break up—or all the other players will turn on him in anger, suspend the rules for the time being, and maul those very interests he is trying so desperately to protect.[37]

The Politician as Midwife. Broker theory also sees an important role for the politician in ensuring that, amid the struggle of each group to have its way, a new way is created that "is the way of neither, in which each gets enough of what it wants to observe a truce in the spirit of sportsmanship. . . ."[38] It is the democratic politician's task to enforce compromise by devising these new ways. Politicians are society's "generalized specialists in conciliation"; it is their role to invest "the legislative process with the accolade of moral midwifery."[39] If he is to perform his function effectively, the legislator must make the following assumptions: (1) "all major interests in a given society are equally legitimate"; (2) "representatives of the great legitimate interests are equally honest"; and (3) "ideals (justice, for example) cannot be invoked to settle issues that involve quarrels as to what the ideals are."[40] These are the assumptions that make it possible for the legislator—or the administrator or the judge—to maintain the neutrality that an effective conciliator must possess.

Overlapping Membership and Potential Groups. The third condition that ensures stability lies in the fact that "no single group affiliation accounts for all of the attitudes or interests of any individual except a fanatic or a compulsive neurotic."[41] Individuals belong to many groups with the result that group membership is overlapping. The fact of overlapping membership guarantees that no group can command

---

[37] John Fischer, "Unwritten Rules of American Politics," *Harper's Magazine*, November, 1948, p. 30.

[38] T. V. Smith, *Discipline for Democracy* (Chapel Hill: University of North Carolina Press, 1942), p. 105.

[39] T. V. Smith, "Compromise: Its Context and Limits," *Ethics*, October, 1942, p. 2.

[40] T. V. Smith, *The Legislative Way of Life* (Chicago: The University of Chicago Press, 1940), p. 26.

[41] Truman, *op. cit.*, p. 508.

the total loyalty of its members and that, therefore, its demands on other groups will be less drastic and its leaders more amenable to compromise. If the leadership of any group seeks to go too far, its members, who may also belong to other groups that would be hurt thereby, will balk and curb its ambitions. An individual may even belong to directly opposed groups, "as when a man who belongs to a local improvement association that is demanding the repaving of a neighborhood street is also a member of a taxpayer's group that is opposing an appropriation for this purpose."[42] This condition of overlapping and contradictory memberships ensures that the rules of the game will be respected.

In some cases, group theorists agree, overlapping membership may not always be extensive enough to "obviate the possibility of irreconcilable conflict"—in the case of labor unions and the National Association of Manufacturers, for example.[43] Overlapping membership may be inadequate, in which case the "relative stability" of the political system is to be explained by "the second crucial element, . . . the concept of the unorganized interest or potential interest group."[44] An "unorganized interest" refers to people with shared attitudes and expectations who are not yet organized to make demands on other groups. The claim is that organized interests, recognizing the possible serious disturbances to the system that might result "if these submerged, potential interests should organize," provide "some recognition of the existence of these interests" and give "them at least a minimum of influence." For similar reasons, such groups as churches, which are not organized to exert political pressure, will still wield political influence because the politically powerful groups recognize and respond to their potential political mobilization.

The Case for Broker Rule: A Summary. The theory of broker, or minorities, rule has wide support among political scientists and among Americans generally. Its central arguments may be summarized under the following points:

1. Broker rule is the only alternative to coercion. We will either have politicians who can "rise above principle" in order to serve the higher "principle of toleration and compromise," or we will have an authoritarian system that inflicts "upon the people bodies of fixed principles without counting the desires of the people."[45] In a system of minorities

---

[42] *Ibid.*, p. 157.
[43] *Ibid.*, p. 510.
[44] *Ibid.*, p. 511.
[45] Latham, *op. cit.*, p. 224.

rule, no one gets everything he wants, but everyone gets something. Since it is impossible for any group of men, even a majority, to be sure that they know what is good for others, this is as close as men can come to securing justice for all. Every tyranny in history has rested on the power of those who claimed to know how others should live and what they should want. But certainly democracy requires us to accept what men want as the only test of what is good for them. Then all desires should be entitled to expression and all interests should have access to and exert influence on those who make decisions. It may be painfully difficult for men to give up high-sounding symbols like the "public interest" and the "common good." But, even if they cannot, we may be thankful for a political system that requires them to participate in compromises that prevent any group from running roughshod over the interests of others.

2. In a diverse, pluralistic society, the politics of broker rule is "the price of union."[46] Any effort to organize democratic politics on the basis of reason and principle would threaten to divide society into warring factions organized around radically opposed ideological principles. Civil liberties are not likely, in these circumstances, to survive the temptations offered the winner, and defeat must appear intolerable to the vanquished. Submission is possible for the loser only when the stakes are low, and this requires that the major interests in society be recognized in the winning coalition. If, in the political struggle, "the desire to accomplish one's purpose turns into a desire to annihilate one's opponent, the outcome is civil war." Therefore, it is necessary that the game not be played for principles: "Material interests can be compromised, principles cannot. A man who sensibly will not fight his neighbor over depredations in his garden will fight him over being called a liar."[47] The American Civil War, the political parties of France, and the communist and fascist movements provide examples of the instability of political situations in which the competing forces command the ideological loyalty of their members.

Broker rule controls power by diffusing it, thus making tyranny impossible and stability likely. At the same time it provides conditions

---

[46] The phrase is the title of a classic exposition of the theory. See Herbert Agar, *The Price of Union* (Boston: Houghton Mifflin, 1950).

[47] Jacques Barzun, *The House of Intellect* (New York: Harper, 1959), p. 146. Barzun's is an interesting position. He seems to want to protect the purity of the "house of intellect" against the corrupting influence of politics. One may doubt, however, whether the life of reason will long be honored in a society that has given up hope of making its politics rational.

that facilitate the further healthy growth of pluralistic diversity. Broker politicians, seeking to win election, will give access to power to newly organized groups. Thus broker rule encourages, as well as reflects, diversity and pluralism. And, at the same time, it provides the flexibility that is necessary in a dynamic society.

3. Broker rule reflects the basic satisfaction with the *status quo* of a vast majority in our affluent, middle-class, suburbanized, secularized society. While the conformity, the aimlessness, the mediocrity of this style of life have been satirized and caricatured by its critics, the other side of the same coin of mass society provides "the right to privacy, to free choice of friends and occupation, . . . a plurality of norms and standards, rather than the exclusive and monopolistic social controls of a single dominant group." The "arrival at a political dead center" does not mean the end of diversity and pluralism, but the widening of the opportunities for it made possible by the widespread affluence of American life.[48]

If large numbers of citizens are apathetic about the outcome of political contests, this merely reflects a widespread satisfaction with the system. The old ideological warfare is dead because the issues on which it was fought—economic oppression and privation, political disfranchisement—have been largely won. These conditions make broker rule possible. Who should be unhappy about it?

4. Broker rule rests on a realistic appraisal of man. The case for this view of the limitations of human nature in politics has been forcibly put by Robert Dahl:

> In a rough sense, the essence of all competitive politics is bribery of the electorate by politicians. How then shall we distinguish the vote of the Soviet peasant or the bribed stumble-bum from the farmer who supports a candidate committed to high support prices, the business man who supports an advocate of low corporation taxes, or the consumer who votes for candidates opposed to a sales tax? I assume that we wish to exclude expressions of preference of the first kind but to include the second. For if we do not exclude the first, then any distinction between totalitarian and democratic systems is fatuous; but if we exclude the second, then surely no examples of even the most proximate democracies can be found to exist anywhere. We can hardly afford to read the human race out of democratic politics.[49]

Moreover, if we demand more than this of man, we are likely to get less. A stable and orderly society in which the rights of all are

---

48 Daniel Bell, *The End of Ideology* (New York: Free Press, 1960), p. 30.
49 Dahl, *op. cit.*, pp. 68-69.

protected is more likely to be built upon the recognized self-interests of organized groups and honest brokers than upon the dreams of self-righteous ideologues and zealots.

The Liberal and Conservative Responses. The model of minorities rule differs from traditional democratic theory in fundamental ways. Its basic assumptions are different, and, consequently, it envisions radically different roles and functions for citizens, politicians, interest groups, political parties, and governmental agencies. It is not surprising, then, that those who are still committed to the traditional views should have reacted warmly to the development of broker theory. Some of their most common responses have been these:

1. By ruling out a concept of a public interest transcending the bargains of organized groups, the broker model provides no way to solve the social problems that continue to exist or to develop public support for policies that the national interest requires. Social problems do exist—poverty, urban blight, crime, delinquency, inadequate education, segregation, and discrimination are examples—and there is no reason to believe that bargaining among organized groups will even recognize their existence. In the politics of broker rule, as Michael Harrington has observed, the poor do not get wealthier; they become "invisible."[50] Even gradual approaches to solving the problem of poverty —or to any other social problem—depend first on its recognition as a problem in which the entire community has a moral concern. Moral involvement in public problems cannot be generated out of group bargaining. "To approach decision in the bargaining spirit," Joseph Tussman reminds us, "is to confuse 'solving' with 'getting.' "[51]

2. The recognition of a public responsibility for the solution of problems requires political leadership. Effective leadership is difficult to secure in even the best of circumstances in a pluralistic, multigroup society. As Sir Henry Maine put it, "the mincing of political power into very small morsels naturally makes the wire puller the leader."[52] The theory of broker rule makes the task impossible by defining the ideal politician as the one who listens most closely, and responds most readily, to the demands and desires of all of his constituents. This concept of the role of the representative incapacitates him for leadership. The alternative is the role that Edmund Burke defined for himself.

[50] Michael Harrington, *The Other America: Poverty in the United States* (Baltimore: Penguin Books, 1963).

[51] Joseph Tussman, *Obligation and the Body Politic* (New York: Oxford, 1960), p. 117.

[52] Quoted in Lowell, *op. cit.*, p. 62.

Burke, an eighteenth-century British philosopher and politician, told his Bristol constituents in 1774 that their representative's "unbiased opinion, his mature judgment, his enlightened conscience, he ought not to sacrifice to you, to any man, or to any set of men living." In Burke's view a representative should act on his own conscientious principles, whether or not this happened at a given time and on a given question to correspond with the desires or will of his constituents.

Although Burke built a conservative philosophy of democracy on this principle, the principle itself is not necessarily a conservative one. In fact, the liberal system of majority rule cannot operate otherwise. Unless the representative has a set of principles he is unwilling to sacrifice to public opinion, even at the high and unpleasant cost of defeat, he cannot stand for anything for which he can be held responsible. The question is whether he is held accountable at periodic intervals to majority vote at the conclusion of an electoral process in which he has defended his principles, and his record in applying them, against alternative principles and proposals. A contest among candidates all of whom promise to do what everybody wants would provide no means for society to debate what a majority ought to want.

The conception of the democratic politician as a public-opinion poller, with his ear to the ground and his nose to the wind, has grown out of a corruption of traditional doctrine that substituted the desires of the public for their reasoned judgment and a compromise of private interests for controversy over the public interest. Its fatal consequence is that problems go undefined and therefore unresolved. No doubt a democratic society needs the specialists in compromise whom T. V. Smith called its "moral midwives." Without them the clash of honest and principled men might be too sharp to permit peaceful resolution. But such men are not currently in short supply. Our political peril is that, however necessary midwives may be to the birth of public policy in a creative democratic system, not many live births are likely to occur at a midwives' convention.

3. The system of broker rule fails to provide the stability and order it promises. The reasons for this are partly contained in the first two arguments already described. Problems are not attended to; leadership is not available to define the public interest in their solution or to develop programs for their amelioration; they continue to fester and to generate discontent.

The stability of a broker regime is threatened in another way. The evidence seems to show that the zealot and the bigot—the true be-lievers—who pose the threat to democratic processes represent person-ality patterns that are reactions to certain ego-threatening or frustrating life experiences. Every society seems to provoke these symptoms in some of its citizens. The anomy and normlessness and the accompanying alienation and anxiety of mass democracy may produce a more-than-average number of such personality types. The recent rash of extremist groups in American politics seems to reinforce this interpretation.

4. Compromise, contrary to the claims of broker theory, is not likely to protect the rights of the unorganized. The case for compromise as the basic democratic principle is an attractive one. Everyone gets part of what he wants except for the unorganized. Here is the first apparent gap in the theory. The solution it offers the unorganized, who never get dealt in to the fair deal, is a simple one: organize. This is no solution at all for the individual whose expectations in politics can only be satisfied by an organized partisan debate of policy alter-natives. Beyond this, it is not even clear that it is very helpful advice for those who are at an economic disadvantage because of their lack of organization.

There is some evidence to suggest that organization is often not so much the means to influence as a result of it. In American politics, the important interest groups have most often been able to organize effectively only *after* their claims were given public recognition as being in harmony with a public interest. For example, business interests were able to organize for effective political action after they had grown strong in a climate that held private enterprise to be necessary to promote maximum economic welfare for all. Effective farm organiza-tion occurred after the independent farmer had become a symbol of American ideals and, indeed, largely after the government had under-taken to facilitate recruitment of membership for what became the largest farm organization. The period of effective labor organization followed the passage of the Wagner Act in 1936, which gave labor, as a matter of justice, the necessary legal and political help. None of this would have been possible under a brokerage system, and, where such a system is in operation, advising the unorganized to organize is some-thing like prescribing that a drowning man should learn to swim. What he clearly requires is some fairly active concern for his welfare on the part of the bystanders who are swimmers.

The unorganized general public constitutes a special and difficult problem for the theory. The celebrated political cartoonist Herbert Block has pointed to one aspect of the problem:

> We don't need to be concerned about pressure groups, according to one pleasant theory, because they tend to balance each other off. That would be comforting if it were true. But too often the only balance that's achieved is the lightening of John Public's pockets on both sides at the same time.[53]

5. Broker rule in general, and group theory in particular, fail to enlist the human loyalties, energies, and potentialities that modern governments require. The groups required by group theory are not really even aggregations of individuals; the condition of overlapping membership requires that they be collections of the partial interests of individuals. Furthermore, the system will be more stable the more schizophrenic are its citizens—the more, that is, they hold to conflicting interests that they make no effort to rank or reconcile. It is tempting to note that while there is an old axiom that holds that two heads are better than one, this is not such an obvious advantage when they are on the same person, as they seem to be here.

From either the liberal or the conservative points of view the theory of broker rule does, indeed, "read the human race out of democratic politics." For the liberal, it does so explicitly because it rests on a theory of human nature that sees the individual as a collection of interests, desires, and preferences as these are reflected in his group memberships rather than as a conscious, reasoning animal making judgments on public issues. Similarly, it loses sight of the individual in the traditional conservative sense. The concept of group membership required by the theory fragments and makes trivial the social relationships of the individual, robbing him of that sense of established status in a well-ordered society that earlier conservative theories of balance had sought to protect.

The model of broker rule is willing to take human nature as it finds it in mass society—egoistic, consumption-oriented, group-adaptive. It is willing to accept the tendency of the mass man to conceive of himself as a consumer and a conformist to group fashions. It denies the conservative demand that government ought to control man's passions and his egoism by denying that self-gratification is evil. It promises, as did the classical economic theory of *laissez faire*, that public virtue will emerge

[53] Quoted in Robert A. Horn, *Groups and the Constitution* (Stanford, Calif.: Stanford University Press, 1956), p. 165.

from the compromise of private vices. It repudiates the liberal conviction that politics ought both to permit and to encourage man to see himself as a rational participant in shaping his collective destiny.

For the liberal, what is missing from American politics, and what is needed, is "a responsible political system which will reflect the will of the majority and which will enable the citizens to hold identifiable rulers accountable for policy decisions."[54] Responsibility, in Bailey's sense, is at the heart of the liberal doctrine of progress, of faith in man's ability to control his own social destiny and to shape the future to fit human values. The principle of compromise is incompatible with this faith in progress as consciously controlled and directed change; policy that is the result of compromise does not constitute a consciously defined direction into the future. From the liberal point of view, compromise is aimless, or power-directed, drift.[55]

From the conservative point of view, a regime of compromise undermines the capacity of leaders for statesmanship and the capacity of followers to believe in the ultimate truths of what Walter Lippmann has called the "public philosophy." Compromise itself, from the conservative assumptions, can only operate where it is underwritten by a basic social consensus on ultimate values enshrined in tradition and a stable social system.[56] The rule of compromise as a basic principle, by its encouraging men to follow their interests and their impulses and by its dissolving all the traditional restraints on power-motivated man, must ultimately destroy the constitutional order itself.

We cannot, as even broker theorists agree, simply define democracy as the way most people behave. What we must look for, in the words of Professor Dahl, are the "conditions that may be used as limits against which real world achievement can actually be measured." Dmocracy, that is to say, is a set of ideals to be approximated as nearly as possible. If the ideals of democracy must be, in some sense, unreal, it has been the historic office of political theory to insist that they be genuinely heroic as well. We ought not settle now, when the need for values is greater than ever, for a theory that offers no resistance to

---

[54] Stephen K. Bailey, *Congress Makes a Law* (New York: Columbia University Press, 1950), p. 239.

[55] For a comprehensive critique of the theory of compromise from a liberal perspective, see Myers, *op. cit.*

[56] For a similarly comprehensive critique of compromise from a conservative position, see John H. Hallowell, *The Moral Foundation of Democracy* (Chicago: The University of Chicago Press, 1954).

those pressures which increasingly encourage mass men to repudiate their own humanity in their roles as citizens.

THEORIES OF DEMOCRACY: A SUMMING UP

In this chapter we have centered our attention on the philosophical problems involved in democratic theory and on the major efforts to develop theoretical solutions. The picture we have drawn is grossly oversimplified, and it is important to understand in what ways. Three possible sources of distortion seem worth noting:

1. American democratic ideas have generally developed in response to practical issues of policy. To extract the ideas from the context of political controversy in which they developed, as we have done, involves limitations that need to be kept in mind.

2. Political theories do not, in historical fact, fall anywhere so neatly into categories as we have implied. Oversimplification need not mean serious distortion, however. The best insurance against this is a constant alertness to the fact that the real world of ideas is more complex than can be fitted into any neat categories. If we are to discharge our responsibilities as citizens we must commit ourselves, however tentatively, to some model of how democratic politics ought to operate, and then seek to bring political reality closer to our ideals.

3. No normative model of democracy is ever perfectly mirrored in political reality. Many of the characteristics of mass democracy and of broker rule have always existed in the United States. Politics in American democracy has always involved a considerable amount of brokerage: parties have always tended, among other things, to accommodate the interests and claims of rival social and economic interests; the party platforms have reflected the political horsepower of organized groups; some politicians have tended to define their role as political brokers. The practices we have been describing are not new. But they will only be the *essence* of the political process in a mass democracy that accepts them as legitimate and inevitable. Men have lived in the past in a political system whose normative demands required that they see themselves as responsible participants in formulating the rules of their common life. To some extent (and that was all anyone could ever hope for), they have lived up to that ideal. If it ceases to live as an ideal, if it is replaced by a new ideal that encourages and legitimatizes private claims and manipulative appeals, we may expect that compromise will indeed become the *essence* of democratic politics. The pressures of mass society seem to lead in that direction.

Chapter Five

THE CONSTITUTION:
DEMOCRATIC BATTLEGROUND

. . . which analyzes the Constitution as a battleground for the conflict between liberal and conservative theories of democracy.

The conflict between liberal and conservative theories of democracy has recently focused on whether the *Constitution* established a *Democracy* or a *Republic.* Historically, the Constitution is seen as

A *Conservative Counterrevolution* against the majoritarian ideas of liberals. Both liberals and conservatives believed in

Constitutionalism, but whereas *Conservatives* desired a written document to assure a system of balanced liberty in which power would be pitted against power, *Liberals* wanted it to guarantee government responsible to the majority and to protect natural rights for minorities.

The result was a tolerable document, the very ambiguity of which meant that the *Constitutional Settlement* would permit continuing struggle over the interpretation of its basic principles.

The principle of *Separation of Powers and Checks and Balances* had different purposes when viewed from conservative and liberal perspectives:

As a *Conservative Doctrine* it was incorporated into the Constitution to make majority control of the government difficult or impossible; whereas in the

Liberal Prescription for *Divided Power* and *Popular Sovereignty* its purposes were to ensure that the powers of government would not be removed from popular control and that reason rather than passion would dominate public discussion.

The Principle of Federalism sets out the broad outlines for dispersing political power by distributing it between national government and the states.

Whether, at the Convention, federalism was merely a necessary *Compromise* between representatives of large and small states or whether it was a desired principle of government is still a debatable question; but conservatives came to regard it as a bulwark of checks and balances, while liberals saw it as a means of maximizing the individual citizen's ability to participate in government at the state and local levels.

The principle of *Limited Government,* which exempts areas of *Individual Liberty* from *Governmental Power,* is inherent in constitutionalism. The American Constitution, especially in its Bill of Rights, provides protection for
Political Rights (the right to vote in honest elections, to run for office, to petition the government), and
Civil Liberties (the rights to speak, read, worship, and assemble freely), which *Citizens* must have if they are to be *Rulers.* Another category of
Civil Rights protects *The Rights of Citizens as Subjects.* These provisions guarantee the citizen fair and equal treatment before the law and restrain the government from arbitrary or irresponsible use of power.
While there was agreement that some protection of these rights was necessary, there was no clear American consensus on how *Authority and Liberty* were to be reconciled. Whereas conservatives tended to believe that toleration would only be produced by a multiplicity of sects and interests, liberals relied on the capacity of majorities to believe in the principle of liberty for the protection of freedom for minorities.

The principle of *Judicial Supremacy,* which makes the courts the final and authoritative interpreters of the Constitution for the other branches of government, is not explicitly provided in the Constitution but was effectively assumed by the Supreme Court. As a check on majority rule it raised a fundamental issue between liberals and conservatives.

These four constitutional principles have provided a *Continuous Battleground* for debate over the organization of government and its relationship to citizens, and this is examined in the next two chapters.

Reduced to the form of a definition, this is the meaning of the term, spirit of our constitution—the will of the people, expressed through an organization by balanced power. Every man, therefore, who would compare any given provision, with the spirit of our constitution, ought not to recur to principles of abstract liberty, but to principles of balanced liberty.

JOSIAH QUINCY

Chapter Five

THE CONSTITUTION: DEMOCRATIC BATTLEGROUND

By NOW it should be evident that there was a substantial difference between the liberal and conservative views of democracy. From their divergent opinions on the nature of man, liberals and conservatives drew different conclusions on how government should be structured. The liberal's faith in majorities of rational men called for a strong legislature where rational debates would clarify issues so that a majority could decide with final authority. Conservatives, on the other hand, argued that majority decisions are likely to be self-interested, passionate, and irrational and must be checked within a system of balanced power.

137

The Constitution of 1789 was the result of reconciling a variety of theoretical and practical considerations into a document that would establish an enduring framework of government. In the main, however, the structural features set out in the Constitution were reflective of the conservative view of human nature described in earlier chapters. In this chapter we discuss four constitutional principles of government that have given form and content to American government. They are (1) separation of power and checks and balances, (2) federalism, (3) limited government, and (4) judicial supremacy. Most Americans are familiar with these principles, but there is still a lack of clarity about their intent and consequences.

This chapter will be concerned primarily with definitions of these principles and some of the controversies surrounding their meaning. In the next chapter their historical development will be considered.

The Constitution: Democracy or Republic?

The Constitution is an arrangement of political power so that it is (1) separated into three branches (legislative, executive, and judicial); (2) dispersed through federalism, which establishes "states' rights" by making state governments supreme in their own constitutionally established spheres of authority; (3) limited so that individuals have certain rights and liberties beyond governmental control; and (4) watched over by a judiciary culminating in the United States Supreme Court, which has final authority to interpret the meaning of the Constitution of the United States.

There is no general agreement, however, on the over-all character of the government that has developed under these constitutional principles. Is the United States a "democracy" based upon liberal doctrine, or is it a "republic" in which majoritarianism is held in restraint and balanced by conservative principles?

As the Constitution approaches its two-hundreth anniversary, the question of whether it should be interpreted in a "democratic" or "republican" way continues to form a center of political controversy. It appears in debates on graduated income taxes, civil rights, law enforcement, public welfare, civil liberties, and, more recently and perhaps most sharply, state legislative reapportionment. Beneath the myths and slogans lies a deep concern on the part of conservatives over the movement of the nation toward liberal democracy. They see, in the development of the welfare state, in the rise of the President as a popular leader, and in the liberal tendencies of recent Supreme Court decisions, a serious breakdown in the checks on majority rule and the demise of responsible aristocratic leadership. Even more, many responsible conservatives see "mobocracy" to be inherent in the principle of "one man, one vote" and other movements toward egalitarian and libertarian interpretations of the Constitution. To the extremist element outside the pale of responsible politics, *democracy* has become a contemptuous term, and any movement in that direction is regarded as a conspiracy, closely linked with the threat of communism. Robert Welch, leader of the John Birch Society, reflected this view in his charge that Chief Justice Earl Warren "has taken the lead in converting this country to democracy."[1]

Mr. Welch's pained outcry contains a modicum of truth. Chief Justice Warren and enough of his Supreme Court colleagues to form a majority have done much to move the country toward a more majoritarian definition of democracy. This fact has become most apparent in a series of recent decisions in which the Court has required the reapportionment of state legislatures to satisfy the basic principle of "one man, one vote."[2]

Among the many issues raised by these decisions was the democratic idea that all citizens should be equally represented in their state legislatures. Chief Justice Warren, for the Court, has stated this clearly:

> Legislators represent people, not trees, or acres. Legislators are elected by voters, not farms or cities or economic interests. As long as ours is a representative form of government, and our legislatures are those instruments of government elected directly by and directly representative of the people, the right to elect legislators in a free and unimpaired fashion is a bedrock of our political system.[3]

Chief Justice Warren was not speaking for a unanimous court. His colleague Justice Harlan did not agree that the principle of "one man, one vote" should take precedence over the principle of federal relationships, which permits the states to determine who should be represented in their legislatures. In his dissent, he said:

> These decisions cut deeply into the fabric of our federalism. What must follow from them may eventually appear to be the product of

[1] Robert Welch, quoted in a mimeographed report by Attorney General Stanley Mosk to Governor Brown of California, July 7, 1961, p. 2.

[2] *Baker* v. *Carr*, 369 U.S. 186 (1962) was the first of a series of cases in which the Court held that legislative reapportionment must satisfy the "equal protection of the laws" provision of the Fourteenth Amendment to the Constitution. This interpretation requires states to use population as the basis of representation.

[3] *Reynolds* v. *Sims*, 377 U.S. 533 (1964).

State Legislatures. Nevertheless, no thinking person can fail to recognize that the aftermath of these cases, however desirable it may be thought in itself, will have been achieved at the cost of a radical alteration in the relationship between the States and the Federal Government, more particularly the Federal Judiciary. Only one who has an overbearing impatience with the federal system and its political processes will believe that that cost was not too high or was inevitable.

Since its entry into the reapportionment controversy, the Court has aroused considerable debate over the nature of American democracy. Should it be egalitarian and majoritarian or does it rest on the principle of balanced power? Political columnist Raymond Moley, for example, argued that the Court's original decision calling for reapportionment rested on "an assertion which involves a principle basic in the American system. That is that this is a democracy rather than a republic. Indeed, every sort of prudent device was incorporated in the Constitution to prevent such a degeneration. Of all people, Supreme Court Judges should know that."[4]

The argument ebbs and flows and involves all three branches of government as well as state and local government. We need to keep clearly in mind, then, as we approach an analysis of the constitutional framework within which American government operates, that the meaning of the Constitution was not settled once and for all in 1787. The issues that divided men then divide them still.

THE CONSTITUTIONAL CONVENTION: CONSERVATIVE COUNTERREVOLUTION

To a considerable extent, conservatives have history on their side. The men who convened at Philadelphia in 1787 to draft the Constitution were involved in what has sometimes been called a "counterrevolution" against the liberal democratic tendencies of the revolution. They were solid men of property and, while Charles A. Beard's famous economic analysis of their motivations may go too far, it is clear that they intended to protect the property rights of the minority from popular majorities, as well as to guard against what they saw as the excesses and injustices resulting from the excessively democratic tendencies of many of the states.

Those who framed the Constitution did, indeed, intend to establish a republic, one purpose of which was to render majoritarian democracy impossible. It was not simply that they wanted the will of a

4 *Newsweek*, April 16, 1962, p. 116.

majority to be expressed through representatives rather than directly; on this point, there was general agreement. The Jeffersonians were in accord with the view, expressed by Madison in *The Federalist* (No. 10), that "the public voice, pronounced by the representatives of the people" may well be "more consonant to the public good" than if pronounced directly. The framers of the Constitution wanted a government in which the majority would not rule either directly or indirectly. They regarded majority rule as no safeguard at all against the danger of faction.

The device that promised to curb majorities, and at the same time to prevent minority rule, was a carefully contrived Constitution. To that end the men at Philadelphia turned their attentions and their considerable talents.

As we noted earlier, there were other leading Americans whose political philosophy was majoritarian. If the Constitutional Convention was dominantly a conservative gathering (and it was), it was still true that the document had to be ratified by duly elected conventions in the states. Here the liberal democrats could bring the full force of their influence to bear.

How, then, could a Constitution and a system of government be built out of disagreement? There are two general answers to this question: (1) While they disagreed about solutions, liberals and conservatives were in agreement that some form of government was necessary to preserve the independence of the new nation in a hostile world. (2) The principles of the new Constitution were sometimes ambiguous, so that the question of their legitimate meaning remained in doubt.

CONSTITUTIONALISM: LIBERAL AND CONSERVATIVE

Liberals and conservatives agreed that a written Constitution was necessary, although for different reasons. From the conservative point of view, only a set of restraints on the will to power of all groups could succeed in pitting power against power, thus ensuring a system of "balanced liberty." And these restraints could only be permanently effective if a written document put them on a level above the strategies of the contestants in the day-to-day political struggle. For the liberals, the necessity for a written Constitution followed from their commitment to the principles of representation and majority rule. If the people were not to govern directly, there must be constitutional restraints to curb the powers of their representatives and to limit the natural temptation of officials to exceed their commissions from the people. At the same time, the majority principle required that the civil liberties necessary to its operation be spelled out in a basic document that would underscore their fundamental priority.

THE AMBIGUITY OF THE CONSTITUTIONAL SETTLEMENT

The solutions worked out in the constitutional debate were ambiguous. In some cases (the federal compromise between large and small states and the three-fifths compromise between free and slave states),[5] they were clearly compromises that sacrificed the purity of the principles of all the contestants. In other more important cases, wherein they were not compromises but the elaboration of conservative principles, the meaning of the principles was not at all clear, so that the intentions of the Founders has been a matter of dispute ever since. As a consequence, men of radically different principles could all claim that the Constitution was sufficiently in accord with their philosophies to be tolerable. Even those who opposed its adoption—and it was adopted by only a narrow majority of a small percentage of the citizenry —found it tolerable enough to forestall rebellion.

The ambiguity in the meaning of the Constitution has contributed to a continuous dialogue and has resulted in different interpretations at different times. In the next chapter we will see how different interpretations have resulted from different circumstances. Now, however, we turn to a definition of the four constitutional principles and a consideration of the issues at stake at the time of their adoption.

Separation of Powers and Checks and Balances

The principle that the powers of government should be separated and put in the care of different persons was not, of course, an American invention. The development of the rule of law as a limit on the power of the king in England had implied, as it inherently does, the development of an independent judiciary that makes it possible for citizens to

---

[5] The compromise beween large and small states provided equal representation of the states in the United States Senate, while the House of Representatives would reflect representation by population although each state was guaranteed one representative. The three-fifths compromise provided that only three fifths of the slaves, referred to as "other persons," were to be counted as population for representation in the House of Representatives. See Constitution, Art. 1, sec. 2, para. 3.

bring suit in the courts against governmental officials for exceeding their authority. Before Montesquieu, with whose name the principle is ordinarily associated, John Locke had noted that "it may be too great a temptation to human frailty, apt to grasp at power, for the same persons who have the power of making laws to have also in their hands the power to execute them." The Founding Fathers were familiar with both Montesquieu and Locke, and they were practiced in the arts of government under a system of separation of powers since both the colonial governments and most of the states after independence had practiced it. As a principle it was widely accepted, though the question of its meaning and purpose was in dispute.

The principle itself is not explicitly stated in the Constitution; it is, rather, implied in the structure of government. The first three articles define the exercise of legislative, executive, and judicial powers, respectively:

> All legislative powers herein granted shall be vested in a Congress of the United States, which shall consist of a Senate and House of Representatives.
> The executive power shall be vested in a President of the United States of America.
> The judicial power of the United States shall be vested in one Supreme Court, and in such inferior courts as the Congress may from time to time ordain and establish.

The basic principle underlying this system is clear. In Madison's words, "the accumulation of all powers, legislative, executive, and judiciary in the same hands" must be prevented if tyranny is to be avoided. But this does not mean, as it is often interpreted and as the wording of the Constitution quoted above seems to imply, that *only* legislators are to exercise legislative power, the President executive power, and the courts judicial power. In any such arrangement, if it could be instituted, no effective government at all would be possible, for the executive might refuse to enforce laws passed by the Congress or the decisions of the courts. Effective government under these conditions would tend to make the legislative power supreme, for the power to formulate and modify basic policy must take precedence over the powers to administer it and to interpret it. This is clearly not what the Founding Fathers were after; indeed, many of them saw the Constitution as a means of remedying the defects of some of the state governments in which the legislature had become pre-eminent.

The key to the constitutional system is not the principle of separation of powers but the principle of checks and balances. The principle of checks and balances implies an intermixture of powers that will permit the several branches of government to check one another and, particularly, to establish checks on the legislative power. The only way in which the President and the courts can put checks on the legislature is to provide for them to share in the legislative power. Again, in Madison's words, "the great security against a gradual concentration of the several powers in the same department consists in giving to those who administer each department the necessary constitutional means and personal motives to resist encroachment on the others."

The President shares in the legislative power by virtue of his right to veto legislation, but Congress may, by two-thirds vote, still have its way. The Senate has the power to refuse to confirm the President's nominations of persons to fill executive and judicial offices or to approve treaties negotiated by the executive. Congress may decline to appropriate funds for any executive agency. The courts, in their power to decide the constitutionality of acts of Congress, are exercising legislative power. Congress may initiate amendments to the Constitution to overcome a judicial veto. More commonly, the President with the consent of the Senate may make appointments to the Supreme Court as vacancies occur that will have the effect of modifying future Court decisions. Or, as President Roosevelt unsuccessfully proposed in 1937, Congress and the President may enlarge the size of the Court in order to reverse the Court's decisions. Although this last technique is clearly within the range of constitutional possibilities, it failed because it still seemed to most Americans to violate the principle that each branch of government should be in a position to defend its own prerogatives.

In addition to these mutual checks that the three branches may bring to bear on one another, Congress itself is divided into two houses—the principle of bicameralism—and each house has an absolute veto on the other. But this still does not exhaust the ramifications of the principle. Additional mutual checks are provided for by the fact that the different branches of government have different modes of election and hold office for terms of different length. The House of Representatives was popularly elected for a two-year term; the Senate elected by the state legislatures for staggered six-year terms; the President elected by the electoral college for a four-year term; and the judges appointed by the President, with the concurrence of the Senate, for life during good behavior.

Finally, the principle of federalism (that is, the constitutional division of powers between the national and state government, which will be discussed later) may also be considered as an internal check on the powers of government. Federalism probably reflected a necessary compromise between those who favored strong national government and those who were sympathetic to, and jealous of, the rights of the states. Yet, in *The Federalist* (No. 51), federalism is defended as a "double security . . . to the rights of the people. The different governments will control each other at the same time that each will be controlled by itself." In this view, federalism would bulwark checks and balances.

Why this elaborate scheme of intermingling governmental power among the several branches, yet leaving each in a position to maintain and defend its own prerogatives? What was its purpose? Here we have a perfect illustration of the way in which the ambiguity of a principle made agreement on it possible. The principle itself was almost universally accepted. As the authors of *The Federalist* said, "The separate and distinct exercise of the different powers of government . . . to a certain extent is admitted on all hands to be essential to the preservation of liberty." The purpose and meaning of the principle were widely disputed. Although it is something of an oversimplification, we may say that generally the two positions and two interpretations in conflict reflected the conservative and liberal philosophies.

CHECKS AND BALANCES AS A CONSERVATIVE DOCTRINE

Madison, in *The Federalist* (No. 10), seemed to rely primarily upon "the great variety of interests, parties, and sects" in an "extended republic" to prevent "a coalition of the majority of the whole society . . . on any other principles than those of justice and the common good." The Constitution is full of what are called, in *The Federalist* (No. 51), "auxiliary precautions" the intent of which was not simply to curb tyrannical abuses of majority power but to make majority rule impossible. The key to this system is checks and balances. The voice of a majority might find expression in the popularly elected House of Representatives (although property qualifications on the suffrage were counted on even here to keep the completely indigent and those without property from having a direct voice). The House was to be checked by an indirectly elected Senate, sitting for longer terms, who were expected to reflect a more aristocratic and conservative point of view.

To conservatives like John Adams, the President was to play the lofty role of impartial umpire between the interests of the masses as represented in the House and the interests of a natural aristocracy represented in the Senate. Other conservatives looked to the Court to serve as a final barrier against an impassioned majority. In order to prevent a minority from becoming tyrannical, "a dependence on the people" is necessary, but a majority can never be depended upon to treat minorities equitably. The solution to the problem of power is to divide it and balance it. As John Taylor, foremost liberal polemicist, almost sneeringly put it, the conservative panacea was ". . . doctor Balance, venerable with the rest of antiquity . . ."[6]

Jefferson, in his *Notes on Virginia*, raised the question of what was to be done when the several departments, "being perfectly coordinate by the terms of their common commission," should come into disagreement about the limits of their powers or when one poached on the powers of the others. His answer, consistent with the liberal majoritarian position, was "an appeal to the people themselves, who, as the grantors of the commission, can alone declare its true meaning, and enforce its observance." For conservatives this was no appeal at all, since, as Madison argued in *The Federalist* (No. 49), the legislature as the department closest to the people is likely to emerge victorious. Even if, through unusual circumstances,

> . . . the public decision might be less swayed by prepossessions in favor of the legislative party . . . still it could never be expected to turn on the true merits of the question. It would inevitably be connected with the spirit of pre-existing parties, or of parties springing out of the question itself. . . . The *passions*, therefore, not the *reason*, of the public would sit in judgment. But it is the reason of the public, alone, that ought to control and regulate the government.

The reason of the people, this argument suggests, is never to be found in the voice of a majority. Instead, it is embodied in the great object of "maintaining the constitutional equilibrium of the government," which is the only safeguard against the peculiar liability of popular governments to majority tyranny.

THE LIBERAL PRESCRIPTION: DIVIDED POWER AND POPULAR SOVEREIGNTY

Majoritarians were also in favor of a system of checks and balances. Indeed, they saw it as a necessary means to ensure majority rule as

---

[6] John Taylor, *Inquiry into the Principles and Policy of the Government of the United States* (New Haven, Conn.: Yale University Press, 1950), p. 61.

well as a precaution to be certain that the voice of a majority would be the voice of reason rather than passion. Where they controlled state governments, they had often set up a plural executive to be such a safeguard. Always this was done within the framework of legislative supremacy, in order to preserve the majority principle. They were unwilling to concede that the dangers of majority tyranny could be averted by making it impossible for the majority to rule. The reason of the people was still to be expressed only in the vote of the people, not in virtual representation by a guiding aristocracy or by a constitutional equilibrium. They were careful to distinguish their theory of the division of power from those conservative theories that sought the guarantees of freedom in a balancing of class interests or social forces. Thus John Taylor argued:

> Mr. Adams considers our division of power, as the same principle with his balance of orders. We consider these principles as opposite and inimical. Power is divided by our policy, that the people may maintain their sovereignty; by the system of orders, to destroy the sovereignty of the people. Our principle of division is used to reduce power to that degree of temperature, which may make it a blessing and not a curse. . . .[7]

For the liberal, the checks and balances system was an insurance against men of power exceeding their commissions from the people. Taylor was explicit: "We do not balance power against power. It is our policy to reduce it by division, in order to preserve the political power of the people, by forbearing to excite the ambition and avarice of individuals."[8]

In addition to ensuring that political power was responsible to the people, the separation of powers served as a check on factious majorities by encouraging adequate deliberation of public issues. The liberal case for it on these grounds was put most convincingly by John L. O'Sullivan, a liberal journalist, in an issue of the *Democratic Review* of 1837:

> We are opposed to all self-styled "wholesome restraints" on the free action of the popular opinion and will, other than those which have for their sole object the prevention of precipitate legislation. This latter object is to be attained by the expedient of the division of power, and by causing all legislation to pass through the ordeal of successive forms; to be sifted through the discussions of coordinate legislative branches

[7] *Ibid.*, p. 356.
[8] *Ibid.*, p. 171.

with mutual suspensive veto powers. *Yet all should be dependent with equal directness and promptness on the influence of public opinion; the popular will should be equally the animating and moving spirit of them all.*[9]

Much of the subsequent discussion of the system of checks and balances has centered around its function in providing a cooling-off device that would permit the taking of an appeal "from the people drunk to the people sober." Here again, what looks at first glance like a basic agreement between liberals and conservatives turns out, on closer analysis, to conceal fundamental differences. Hamilton put the conservative case for the delaying function of checks and balances in *The Federalist* (No. 71):

> It is a just observation, that the people commonly intend the public good. This often applies to their very errors . . . when occasions present themselves, in which the interests of the people are at variance with their inclinations it is the duty of the persons whom they have appointed to be the guardians of those interests, to withstand the temporary delusion in order to give them time and opportunity for more cool and sedate reflection.

In interpreting Hamilton's position, we must not lose sight of the warning that George Mason had given to the members of the Convention: "Notwithstanding the oppression and injustice experienced among us from democracy, the genius of the people is in favor of it, and the genius of the people must be consulted." On other occasions, Hamilton had described the people as a "great beast." He clearly did not believe that popular delusions would always be temporary. More fundamentally, as the quotation from *The Federalist* (No. 71) makes clear, the real interests of the people are to be defined by their guardians, not directly by public opinion itself.

For the liberal, the distinction between the interests of the people and their inclinations was to be defined by reasoned appeals to the people. For the conservative, the public good must be protected by balance and by a successive filtration of power through indirect election that creates guardians of the people's real interests. Time for full reflection and consideration does not constitute a sobriety test for public opinion in this view. Either sobriety is impossible and the best society can do is pit a drunken majority against drunken minorities (which

[9] Quoted in Mason, *Free Government In the Making* (New York: Oxford, 1949), p. 447. Italics added.

tended to be Madison's position), or a guiding aristocracy must be trusted to tell the majority when it is sober (which tended to be Hamilton's position). Both these positions are conservative, and they are to be distinguished from the liberal policy of preventing precipitate legislation within a framework in which public opinion remains the only permissible court of appeal. Here, as elsewhere in the constitutional framework, agreement was possible because to a considerable extent liberals and conservatives used the same words but interpreted them differently.

Liberals, for their part, failed to some extent to appraise seriously enough the threat posed to their position by the conservative principle of balance. They did so because, while they insisted that majorities must rule, they did not want them to do much ruling. Generally, liberals were the spokesmen for a philosophy of agrarianism—that is, the view that the conditions of the small agricultural community with relative equality of wealth were necessary for democracy to flourish. Agrarianism implied an economic policy of *laissez faire*. Liberals tended to oppose the development of industrialism and urbanization; they found the virtues of individual independence and autonomy to be uniquely related to an agrarian, frontier environment; and, under these conditions, they saw little need for government to do very much. For many of them, even government construction of internal improvements, like roads and canals, was an unjustified interference with individual initiative and independence.

Given these limitations on public policy, even a conservative theory of checks and balances seemed not to pose a major threat. If the functions of government were to be limited to the maintenance of order and the conduct of foreign affairs, and if all else was to be left to the initiative of self-sufficient individuals, it was reasonable to assume that the major threat to the responsible exercise of power was the danger of public officials exceeding their commissions. In a world in which there were no corporations, no large cities, and no networks of mass communication and transportation, it was reasonable to assume that the major problem in making government responsible was to provide safeguards to its potential abuse. Especially was it reasonable to a generation in revolt against too much government and arbitrary governmental intervention in the affairs of individuals. Under the changed conditions of economic and social life, brought about by industrialization and urbanization, liberals and conservatives changed positions on this issue. But in the context of American society in the latter part of the eighteenth century, the liberal belief in *laissez faire* made the system of checks and balances appear to be relatively innocuous.

The idea of equilibrium by checks and balances was, as we have noted, augmented by federalism, which would require the federal government to share power with the states. The liberals and conservatives also differed over federalism, and it is to this we turn next.

The Principle of Federalism

Our very national designation—the United States of America—makes it clear that fifty states are united to form a nation and that the result is a federal union. Federalism, a second constitutional principle, is a way of organizing the distribution of political power between a central or national government, on the one hand, and the governments of the areas into which the nation is divided (states, provinces, cantons, and so on), on the other. At the one extreme is the unitary state in which all political power is centralized in the national organs of government, and all subsidiary governments are the creatures of the national government. Great Britain is an example. At the other extreme is the confederation in which all political power is ultimately in the hands of the constituent states, and the national government is their creature with no independent powers of its own. American government under the Articles of Confederation (1781–1789) was an example.

THE BROAD OUTLINES OF AMERICAN FEDERALISM

Federalism stands between these two extremes, distributing power between a national government and the states in such a fashion that both have substantial powers and both are bound by the terms of the arrangement. In the American system this is accomplished in the written Constitution, and the allocation of powers to nation and states therein provided may be formally altered only through a process of amendment in which both the national and state governments participate. The broad outline of this political relationship is stated in the Tenth Amendment: "The powers not delegated to the United States by the Constitution, nor prohibited by it to the States, are reserved to the States respectively, or to the people."

"The powers . . . delegated to the United States by the Constitution" are those that define the powers of the Congress (Art. I, sec. 8), the President (Art. II, sec. 2), and the national courts (Art. III, sec. 2).

The relationship between national and state governments seems as explicit and clear as a written document could make it. The national Congress may legislate and the President may act only where there is an express or implied grant of power in these articles of the Constitution. All other powers of government are reserved to the states. Yet the whole problem of states' rights has led to endless controversy, and is an exceedingly complicated one. The relationship, seemingly so explicitly defined in the Constitution, has been modified continuously by interpretation, statutes, custom, and usage. It is constantly being contested in Congress and in state legislative halls throughout the land; in the courts, both state and national; in bureaucracies of various sorts; in election campaigns; and by ballots. The principle of federalism like that of checks and balances has been a principle only in the sense of marking out an arena of controversy, of defining an issue around which the struggle to define democracy has continued to revolve.

AMERICAN FEDERALISM: COMPROMISE OR PRINCIPLE?

In the Constitutional Convention federalism was a compromise, and a necessary one; without it, it is unlikely any stable government at all could have been formed. The Connecticut Compromise (so called because it was formulated by Dr. William Samuel Johnson of that state) sought a middle ground between those who would retain the full sovereignty of the individual states and those who wanted a strong national government. In Dr. Johnson's words: "The two ideas embraced on different sides, instead of being opposed to each other ought to be combined; that in one branch the people ought to be represented; in the other the states." This compromise laid the groundwork for the reconciliation of the interests of larger and smaller states, stifled most objections to a national government with real power, and paved the way for the elaboration of the federal system. As Madison noted in *The Federalist* (No. 37), the result was that "the convention must have been compelled to sacrifice theoretical propriety to the force of extraneous considerations" because of "the interfering pretensions of the larger and smaller States."

A recent critic has warned us: "It is rather muddleheaded to romanticize a necessary bargain into a grand principle of democratic politics."[10] The warning, however trenchant, is a little tardy. The

[10] Robert A. Dahl, *A Preface to Democratic Theory* (Chicago: The University of Chicago Press, 1956), p. 118.

bargain described above by Madison as an unavoidable compromise that could not be supported by theoretical propriety had already in *The Federalist* (No. 51) become an example of the application of a principle. In that issue (written less than a month after No. 37) the federal principle had already become part of the conservative system of checks and balances and an auxiliary precaution against factious majorities:

> In the compound republic of America, the power surrendered by the people is first divided between two distinct governments, and then the portion allotted to each subdivided between distinct and separate departments. Hence, a double security arises to the rights of the people. The different governments will control each other, at the same time that each will be controlled by itself.

Federalism had thus become an important part of the system whereby ambition could be made to counteract ambition. From the conservative point of view, the most important aspect of federalism was that it removed political power from the states where democratic tendencies were most marked and where, sometimes, agrarian majorities ran wild (at least as conservatives were inclined to define *wildness*). Madison, in *The Federalist* (No. 51), summed up the conservative view of the danger of democracy in state governments and the advantages of a federal union:

> It can be little doubted that if the State of Rhode Island was separated from the Confederacy and left to itself, the insecurity of rights under the popular form of government within such narrow limits would be displayed by such reiterated oppressions of factious majorities that some power altogether independent of the people would soon be called for by the voice of the very factions whose misrule had proved the necessity of it.

The federal principle itself thus was counted upon to operate as an additional bulwark against majority tyranny and an additional safeguard of the rights of a propertied minority. At the same time, the preference of liberal democrats for decentralized government and retention of political power in the states reflected their own political and economic assumptions. They feared a strong national government supporting high duties on imports and, in general, dedicating itself to the interests of the wealthy class and the large landholders.

Despite their general opposition to giving power to a national government, liberals gradually accepted the federal structure. Again, as in the case of checks and balances, their acceptance of federalism followed from their interpretation of its meaning and effect in the light of liberal principles. They saw the states as laboratories of political science in which their new experiments in government could be conducted, tested in practice, and copied in other states when they proved successful. They saw the union as necessary for the protection of newly won independence, but they did not intend that the new national government should do very much. The liberal hope that the states would become laboratories of political science has come to fruition. But the liberal of the eighteenth century might be somewhat disturbed at some of the political innovations states have brewed in their laboratories. Federalism, as the next chapter will make clear, has been a complication in securing the protections of limited government for all citizens everywhere.

Limited Government

The third major principle of American constitutionalism is that the powers of government are limited by the rights and liberties of the governed. This principle is inherent in the very idea of *constitutional* government. As we have already seen, it is the purpose of a constitution to limit and restrain the exercise of political power; a constitution is a system of "effective, regularized restraints."[11]

The eighteenth century, with its faith in the process of establishing governments on a rational basis and its philosophy of natural rights, was an age of constitution-making. Americans, in particular, were experienced in the art of writing constitutions and impressed by the fruits of living under a fundamental body of law defining the scope and limits of governmental power. One of the first groups of settlers had begun their adventure by agreeing to the Mayflower Compact. The political history of the Colonies had been, in some measure, a story of conflict over the terms of written colonial charters and the rights of Colonists as subjects of the unwritten British constitution. In the process, the basic doctrine that citizens retain rights *against* the government as well as rights of *access to* the government came to be a widely shared article of the American political faith.

[11] Carl J. Friedrich, *Constitutional Government and Democracy* (Boston: Ginn, 1946). As Friedrich maintains, a government is rendered constitutional by "establishing and maintaining effective restraints upon political and more especially upon governmental action" (p. 121).

GOVERNMENTAL POWER AND INDIVIDUAL LIBERTY

The essence of constitutionalism, as we have suggested, is that the powers of government shall be restrained to protect the liberty of citizens. In a democracy, the citizen plays a dual role: he is at the same time subject and ruler; he is bound by the laws that he participates in making.[12] The limitations that a democratic constitution places on a government relate to the dual roles of citizenship. They ensure that the citizen as ruler is guaranteed those rights that are necessary if he is to be able to influence and control the government. And they protect the citizen as subject from arbitrary treatment by those temporarily in control of the instruments of government.

CIVIL LIBERTIES: THE RIGHTS OF CITIZENS AS RULERS

The role of the citizen as ruler in a democratic society quite obviously starts with certain political rights. The fundamental one is the right to vote in regularly scheduled elections in which the ballot is secret and the results are honestly counted and announced. The right to vote also implies the right to run as a candidate and to participate in the selection of candidates for public office.

These political rights are a necessary, but not a sufficient, basis for the democratic role of the citizen as ruler. They might even exist in a framework in which the citizen participates in politics but does not in any real sense control the government. Political rights themselves may even be the means by which citizens can be induced to troop to the polls to participate in a public ritual that permits them to be blamed for subsequent developments over which they exercised no real choice. There is a distinction between voting and political participation as social acts, on the one hand, and participation that involves choice and responsibility, on the other. The mere existence of political rights does not permit us to distinguish between free and unfree elections or between free and engineered consent of the governed. It is scarcely possible to doubt, for example, that the Communist party in the Soviet Union could afford the secret ballot, regular elections, and honestly counted returns. Whether or not they always do so is not the point:

[12] Joseph Tussman develops this distinction in an interesting and provocative way in his *Obligation and the Body Politic* (New York: Oxford, 1960).

we stress here only that to do so would not seriously prejudice the controlling power of the Communist party apparatus.

If political rights are not enough, what more is required? Again, we return to the crucial and fundamental matter of dissent. Democratic participation requires alternatives and the opportunity to choose. The existence of choice, in its turn, depends upon the fundamental right to dissent and to seek to persuade and join with others in an effort to make one's dissenting opinions prevail.

The class of rights that undergird and guarantee the possibility of dissent, and, therefore, of alternatives and genuine choice, are generally described by the term *civil liberties*. They are the fundamental rights in the sense that they guarantee the openness and the competitive politics that are the basic conditions of democratic citizenship. In the United States, they are stated succinctly in the First Amendment to the Constitution and are often summed up as the First Amendment Freedoms. They guarantee that the national government shall have no power to interfere with the intellectual freedom of citizens or with their freedom to associate with one another in common pursuit of their intellectual commitments and purposes. In the language of the Amendment itself:

> Congress shall make no law respecting an establishment of religion, or prohibiting the free exercise thereof; or abridging the freedom of speech, or of the press; or the right of the people peaceably to assemble, and to petition the government for a redress of grievances.

In addition to the fundamental guarantee therein provided, there are other sections of the Constitution whose purpose is to guarantee civil liberties. The Second Amendment, protecting the "right of the people to keep and bear arms," while no longer relevant, should probably be put in that category. Certainly the definition of treason in Article III, section 3, was and continues to be an important limitation on one of the means by which political controversy and criticism might be curtailed. It provides the following:

> Treason against the United States, shall consist only in levying war against them, or in adhering to their enemies, giving them aid and comfort. No person shall be convicted of treason unless on the testimony of two witnesses to the same overt act, or on confession in open court.

This section closes off what had been, in the history of government, an important means by which the state could rationalize its silencing of critics and its restraints on free thought and discussion. Treason has ever been the political counterpart of the charge of heresy in religious organizations. It is the means by which otherwise permissible criticism can be put beyond the pale of legitimate discussion and critics made to appear the enemies of society.

The gravity of the evil that the framers were seeking to guard against, and its fundamental incompatibility with democratic politics, were revealed in the period following World War II when aspirants for public office accused the members of the opposition party of "twenty years of treason"—a charge that, if made successfully, would have effectively ended competitive politics. This threat did not end with the demise of *McCarthyism*, a term coined from the name of Senator Joseph McCarthy who shook America to its roots by extravagant and reckless charges of "Communists in government."[13] The challenge of communism continues to lead groups on the radical right to the conclusion that socialists, leftists, New Dealers, and liberals all aid and abet the cause of communism and are, therefore, parties to treason. In defining treason as giving aid and comfort to the enemy and carefully defining the proof necessary for conviction, the Founding Fathers sought to remove this weapon from the struggle for power. These limitations on government assume that there are rights that inhere in individuals and have logical and moral priority over government, rights that no government is morally entitled to interfere with or curtail.

CIVIL RIGHTS: THE RIGHTS OF CITIZENS AS SUBJECTS

When we view the democratic citizen in his role as subject, we encounter a different class of rights derived from the ideal of a government of laws or equality before the law. Ordinarily designated *civil rights*, as distinct from civil liberties, these restraints on government protect the individual from arbitrary, personal, or irresponsible use of governmental power. The basic principle that men who make and administer the laws are themselves subject to the laws was established early in the struggle for constitutional democratic government in England (England, of course, has no written constitution; this is a good example of an unwritten constitutional principle). The principle was established when it was decided that the King was not above the

---

[13] For an account of McCarthyism, see Richard H. Rovere, *Senator Joe McCarthy* (New York: Meridian, 1960).

law—that is, that he could not rule by arbitrary decree or exact punishment except through the regularized procedures of established laws.

The limitations in the American Constitution that fall into this category may be thought of as seeking to achieve the protection of the individual as subject against arbitrary acts of government through the establishment of three principles:

1. The Ultimate Power of Government to Coerce Individuals—to Deprive Them of Property, or Liberty, or, in the Final Extremity, Life—May Only Be Employed for Violations of Established, Definite Laws. The following provisions of the Constitution contribute to the accomplishment of this purpose.

Article I, section 9, prohibits Congress from inflicting punishment on individuals by legislative act and without judicial proceedings (bills of attainder); from passing retroactive legislation to punish an act that was not a crime at the time it was committed or from retroactively increasing the penalties for a crime or making conviction easier (ex post facto laws). These guarantees of civil rights are closely connected with civil liberties. The arbitrariness involved in bills of attainder and ex post facto laws not only deprives individuals of equal justice; such laws are also one potential means by which political dissenters might be punished for their dissent and political controversy suppressed. Similarly, in modern totalitarian regimes, the substitution of decrees and the secret police for regularly established courts of law is a major instrument for enforcing conformity.

The Fifth Amendment prohibits the taking of private property for public use "without just compensation," and the question of whether compensation is just may be appealed from political officials into the courts. It makes an even more general provision: "No person shall be . . . deprived of life, liberty or property, without due process of law. . . ."

The Eighth Amendment prohibits excessive fines and "cruel and unusual punishments."

The purpose of these limitations is to provide for individuals a range of predictability within which individual responsibility can operate. For even though ignorance of the law is no excuse, unless it is possible for the individual to know clearly what the law is, and what the penalties for its violation are, there can be no range within which the individual can plan his own life and make his own choices. Making choices requires the possibility of anticipating consequences of alternative paths of action. If the government can change the rules retroactively or modify them so that they apply differently to different individuals, this condition no longer is present.

The basic principle was clearly formulated by Justice Jackson in his concurring opinion in the 1952 case in which the Supreme Court invalidated President Truman's seizure of the steel industry.[14] The authority of the government under the Constitution, Justice Jackson asserted, "reaches so far as there is law"; the due process provision of the Fifth Amendment guarantees "a private right that authority shall go no farther." These principles, Jackson continued, "signify about all there is of the principle that ours is a government of laws, not of men, and that we submit ourselves to rulers only if under rules." They are the minimum condition that must be met in order that "the public may know the extent and limitations of the powers that can be asserted, and persons affected may be informed from the statute of their rights and duties."

2. In the Use of Its Coercive Power, Government May Not Unnecessarily Invade the Privacy of Individuals. This principle is embodied in the following constitutional provisions.

Article I, section 9, provides that the writ of habeas corpus may not be suspended except under conditions of "rebellion or invasion."

The Fourth Amendment guarantees "the right of the people to be secure in their persons, houses, papers, and effects, against unreasonable searches and seizures" and provides that warrants may be issued only "upon probable cause."

The Fifth Amendment protects individuals against "double jeopardy."

The Sixth guarantees defendants a "speedy" trial.

The Eighth prohibits "excessive bail."

These provisions protect the individual from harassment by the police; from search or arrest "on suspicion"; from the necessity of living in constant fear of the law-enforcing agencies of government.

3. When Accused of a Crime, the Individual Is Entitled to Be Judged Fairly and Impartially and to Have Available the Means to His Defense. The guarantees of this principle, as they apply to federal criminal cases, are contained in the Fifth and Sixth Amendments. The Fifth Amendment requires indictment by a grand jury and protects the individual from being compelled "to be a witness against himself."

---

14 *Youngstown Sheet and Tube Co. v. Sawyer,* 343 U.S. 579 (1952).

The Sixth Amendment guarantees the accused the right to a public trial by an "impartial jury" in the state and district where the crime was committed, the right to be informed of the charges against him, the right to confront hostile witnesses and to subpoena friendly witnesses, and the right to a defense counsel.

It should be noted that not all these restrictions apply equally against the states, although many state constitutions contain like provisions. Most of the limitations on government in the United States Constitution are directed only to the national government. This is true of the entire Bill of Rights. In the next chapter, we discuss how the Supreme Court, in its interpretation of the due-process clause of the Fourteenth Amendment, which limits state governments, has applied most of the Bill of Rights to the states.

The importance of the civil rights that are guaranteed by the foregoing three principles would be difficult to exaggerate. If we need any reminding, the rise of modern totalitarian regimes emphasizes both their importance and the intimate relation between the guarantees of freedom of thought and speech and association, on the one hand, and the limitations on arbitrary acts of government, on the other. For the single most significant characteristic of modern totalitarianism is its use of terror as an instrument of governing. Terror is the means by which effective criticism of the regime is precluded. Terror rests, in Hannah Arendt's phrase, on the elimination of the "legal personality"[15] of citizens. It rests, that is to say, on systematic destruction of any legal order in which the rights and duties of individuals are clearly defined, and on the nonexistence of orderly procedures for establishing individual guilt or innocence. Terror, to be effective, must be anonymous, and it must destroy any important areas of predictability for the individual. Punishment by the state must be unrelated to any specific acts that an individual has committed or failed to commit. Punishment must be arbitrary from the point of view of individual moral responsibility.

It is not, of course, arbitrary from the point of view of the movement: To be a Jew in Nazi Germany was, by definition, to be implicated in a conspiracy against the laws of race. But the point is that the legal order of a democratic society consists of regularized laws that make specific acts punishable, and it embodies procedures that require

---

[15] Hannah Arendt, *The Origins of Totalitarianism* (New York: Harcourt, Brace, 1951). See especially Chap. 12, "Totalitarianism in Power."

proof of individual responsibility. Such a legal order is the first line of defense against government by terror and a necessary foundation for the freedoms of thought and expression that make responsible government possible.

AUTHORITY AND LIBERTY: AN AMERICAN CONSENSUS?

The tone of our discussion thus far might suggest that in the provision for limited government and individual rights and liberties we have at last located a bedrock principle on which our forefathers were agreed and from which our common political faith springs. It turns out, however, that this is true only in the same limited sense in which there has been agreement on the other principles of checks and balances and federalism. It is no less true of limited government that we are closer to the truth if we see it as defining a problem rather than as posing a solution. Again there was agreement on the principle in spite of—or, perhaps more accurately, because of—disagreements over its meaning.

The conflict among the Founding Fathers should be immediately apparent from the circumstance that most of the rights we have been discussing are included in the first ten amendments to the Constitution, rather than in the body of the document itself. For conservatives, the system of balanced power set out in the document was as far as it was realistically possible to go in the direction of guaranteeing liberty; the Bill of Rights would do no harm, but neither would it do much good. In this view, liberty is to be discovered in the interstices of a balance of power, not in pronouncements that presume to declare fundamental truths. For liberals the Bill of Rights was the essence of constitutionalism, and freedom was to be achieved only by men who were consciously committed to it as a basic and enduring principle.

Toleration versus Liberty. The conflict dividing the Founding Fathers on this issue was a fundamental one that reverts to the underlying philosophical issues that defined the conservative and the liberal positions. With respect to the problem of freedom, the two major positions are to be found in the conservative theory of toleration and the liberal theory of natural rights.

The approach of liberal democratic theory to this question we have already quite fully explored. The liberal faith in reason and the liberal commitment to natural rights led to the conclusion that liberty is something that men directly pursue and explicitly value. The free society is one in which the supreme value of freedom is the cardinal principle to which citizens are committed. Ultimately, from the liberal point of view, it is only the dedication of free men to civil liberties that can effectively safeguard them. The rights of the individual will only be safe when other individuals accept Henry David Thoreau's principle that "under a government which imprisons any unjustly, the true place for a just man is also a prison."

From the conservative view of human nature and the conservative concern for social order and stability, the liberal faith in a commitment to abstract principle was a frail reed upon which to rest men's liberties. A modern conservative has put their case aptly in the argument that freedom is essentially a by-product of toleration and comes to exist only in a "happily tolerant era," such as under those conditions in the Rome of the Antonine emperors as described by Gibbon: "The various modes of worship, which prevailed in the Roman world, were all considered by the people, as equally true; by the philosopher, as equally false; and by the magistrate, as equally useful." Gibbon concluded, "Thus toleration produced not only mutual indulgence, but even religious concord."[16] What Gibbon found to be the secret of religious toleration—a multiplicity of competing sects all of which accept the legitimacy of the others and none of which can hope to prevail—some of the Founding Fathers saw as the key to toleration generally. Madison expressed the argument clearly in *The Federalist* (No. 51):

> In a free government the security for civil rights must be the same as that for religious rights. It consists in the one case in the multiplicity of interests, and in the other in the multiplicity of sects. The degree of security in both cases will depend on the number of interests and sects . . .

Civil rights and liberties, in this view, are not to be maintained by an appeal to abstract principle. If they are to prevail, it will be in spite of, not because of, what men seek in politics. If there is a wide enough variety of interests and desires in political competition, ambition may be made to counteract ambition. Civil rights and liberties are only to be protected because no group has the power to curtail liberties of others, not because any group is committed to a principle

---

[16] Quoted in Daniel Boorstin, *The Genius of American Politics* (Chicago: The University of Chicago Press, 1953), p. 135.

that would protect others' liberties. The most that might be hoped for is that men who have lived for a long time in a carefully balanced pluralistic society may come even to see the policy of live and let live as a desirable one.

The distinction between the idea of toleration and the idea of freedom was developed by early liberals. "Toleration," Tom Paine argued, "is not the *opposite* of Intolerance, but is the *counterfeit* of it. Both are despotisms." Whereas intolerance "assumes to itself the right of withholding Liberty of Conscience,"[17] toleration no less despotically assumes the right of granting it. "Liberty of conscience," Paine argues, is not to be granted or denied by government to individuals; it is a natural right antecedent to government. And only if it is regarded as such will it be possible for individuals to control, and not to be controlled by, their government.

A political system that rests on the toleration of a broad plurality of groups, it might be pointed out, is one that is likely to be inhospitable to new ideas that propose far-reaching changes in society. Groups that have come to tolerate one another are likely to share an interest in maintaining the *status quo*, in which each is likely to have a vested interest. Thus, it is just those groups and individuals whose liberties are most in need of protection who are most likely not to find it.

In a regime of religious toleration, for example, it is the prevailing, conventionalized modes of religious worship that are mutually indulged. Precisely what is not indulged is the belief of those individuals who question the assumptions shared in what Gibbon called the "religious concord" of mutually tolerant religious beliefs. Similarly, where there is mutual indulgence between labor and management groups, there is likely to be little tolerance for those who would criticize the *status quo* in any fundamental way.

Toleration, in short, is a conservative prescription for a condition of equilibrium among the several interests in a society. Where it is successfully achieved, the privacy and the liberty of individuals are protected from assaults by others. Liberty is to be ensured and protected by diversity. A carefully devised constitution that will ensure a balance among rival groups will protect men against themselves and their own innate tendencies to deprive others of their liberties. The liberal view, on the other hand, put its faith in the capacities of man's reason to

[17] Thomas Paine, *The Rights of Man* (New York: Dutton, 1951), p. 64.

discover and his good will to enforce the natural rights by which opinion, thought, speech, and writing are taken to be immune from governmental restriction. Men will have liberty when men take liberty to be the first principle of society and government. Otherwise, what will be tolerated is just those moderate and orthodox views that do not in any significant way challenge the *status quo* and that do not, therefore, stand in any real need of defense.

Judicial Supremacy

Clashes over the meaning of limited government, as well as other constitutional principles, require decision. Final decisions are often necessary, but if the principles of checks and balances, federalism, and limited government cause conflicts that must be resolved, who has final authority to decide them? The answer in the United States is that the Supreme Court does. The distinctive character of the Court's role is that it includes the power to decide authoritatively and finally on the constitutionality of the acts of the Congress and the executive. Because the decision of the Court is authoritative and binding on the other agencies, we have used the phrase *judicial supremacy* rather than the more common but less descriptive caption of *judicial review*.

Moreover, among the founders of the Constitution it was only the question of the final and binding character of the decisions of the federal courts that was at issue. There was general agreement that, in its absolutely necessary function of interpreting the statutes passed by Congress, the courts should have also the right to declare their findings with respect to whether statutes were compatible with the meaning of the Constitution. The issue was whether the courts' interpretation of the Constitution was to prevail over the views of other agencies that, under the doctrine of checks and balances, were equal and coordinate branches of government. The issue was not whether the courts should have a right to *review* the constitutionality of acts of Congress, but whether, in this function, *supremacy* should mark their findings.

The Constitution itself, of course, is silent on this question. In Article III, sections 1 and 2, it provides only the following:

> The judicial power of the United States shall be vested in one Supreme Court, and in such inferior Courts as the Congress may from time to time ordain and establish. . . .
> The judicial Power shall extend to all Cases, in Law and Equity,

arising under this Constitution, the Laws of the United States and Treaties made, or which shall be made, under their Authority;—to all Cases affecting Ambassadors, other public Ministers and Consuls; —to all Cases of admiralty and maritime Jurisdiction;—to Controversies to which the United States shall be a Party;—to Controversies between two or more States. . . .

The power of the Court to nullify an act of Congress as contrary to the Constitution was successfully asserted by the Court itself in the case of *Marbury* v. *Madison*,[18] but from the beginning some had argued that this power of the Court was inherently implied in the new system of government. On the surface, the arguments were those developed by Chief Justice Marshall in *Marbury* v. *Madison*. The Constitution, his decision held, expresses law that has a higher standing than ordinary legislation; hence, acts contrary to the Constitution must be void; hence, the Court must hold them to be invalid. In this view, a written constitution becomes meaningless unless the courts exercise the power authoritatively to maintain its provisions. Behind these legalistic arguments, however, stood the conservative political assumptions of the Federalists. The doctrine of judicial review was seen as a necessary barrier to the legislative supremacy of popular majorities, which, despite the check and balance system, might come to control the other agencies of government. Against the onslaught of majority attack, the courts might be expected to protect the rights of minorities, as well as to enshrine national supremacy over states' rights.

The political, rather than legal, character of the argument for judicial supremacy was clear in the very circumstances in which it was asserted. The first legislation to reorganize the judiciary was passed in 1801, at the close of John Adams' administration, in order to carry out clearly partisan designs. It reduced the number of justices on the Supreme Court in order to maintain Federalist control, and it created new inferior federal courts to which Federalist justices could be appointed by the outgoing administration. It was the validity of one of these midnight appointments that was at issue in *Marbury* v. *Madison*. Moreover, John Marshall, who delivered the opinion of the Court in the case, was a Federalist, appointed Chief Justice at a late hour to keep Jefferson from making the appointment.

For the liberal, constitution-making and constitutional interpretation were viewed as political, not legal, acts. Since a constitution is of funda-

[18] 1 Cranch 137 (1803).

mental importance, it is all the more necessary that those who make and interpret it be responsible to public opinion. Liberals granted, of course, that a written constitution must be respected if it is to be meaningful. But they denied that judges are peculiarly able to make such judgments. Liberals and conservatives alike were agreed on the necessity for the independence of the judiciary if equal justice was to be ensured, but the very independence of the judiciary made it, for liberals, the worst possible place to locate final political authority. Judges must be counted on for even-handed administration of the laws. "But," John Taylor added, "the instant an individual is removed from the legislative or executive departments into the judicial, his nature is supposed to have been regenerated, his errors are sanctified, his intrigues are overlooked, and his responsibility commuted for the universal refuge of imposture, 'God and his own conscience.' "[19]

From the liberal assumptions, judicial supremacy would put popular majorities in the position of a Caspar Milquetoast and the Court in the position of his wife: "I make all the major decisions and my wife makes all the minor ones; of course, she decides which questions are major ones." That is to say, the Court would be in the position of choosing what questions the popular agencies of government were competent to decide upon. But, if this was inadmissible, liberals were divided on the alternatives. Some looked to the separation of powers; with Andrew Jackson they would say to the Chief Justice (in connection with a later case), "John Marshall has made his decision, now let him enforce it." Others were more inclined to look to the federal principle and to the power of the legislatures in the several states as a counter to the political power of the courts.

Today there is little question about, but much dissatisfaction with, the supremacy of judicial decisions. The Court almost continually has been the center of controversy, for it is the nature of the judicial process to hear and resolve controversies brought to the bar of justice. In later chapters, we shall deal with the Court's place in American government and the various roles it plays in the political process. In no other country, particularly one with democratic government, does the judiciary play such a central and significant role in the political, economic, and social life of the society.

[19] Taylor, *op. cit.*, pp. 198-99.

Constitutional Principles: Continuous Battleground

The four principles of the Constitution discussed in this chapter—checks and balances, federalism, limited government, and judicial supremacy—have been the focal points of the development of American government. Debate about their meaning has continued unabated through the almost two hundred years of the government's existence. The character, size, and complexity of the United States have changed significantly during this time. There have been some changes in the Constitution itself, but it has proved remarkably durable. Its durability is no doubt partly due to the ambiguity of the meaning of principles it established.

In the next chapter we trace some of the significant historical interpretations of the meaning of these principles. We also deal with the role of the Supreme Court as interpreter of the Constitution throughout the many phases of American history. Wars, both civil and foreign, economic upheavals, technological changes, and the nagging social problems of racial relationships, poverty, and ignorance have all put the four constitutional principles to a test. Problems still exist. So do the four constitutional principles, and, as we shall see, a beleaguered Supreme Court copes mightily with their meaning.

CONSTITUTIONAL DEVELOPMENT: THE CONTINUING STRUGGLE
Checks and Balances and Federalism

... which discusses the historical development of the constitutional principles of checks and balances and federalism.

The principle of *Checks and Balances* has been modified substantially by historical developments that have changed its meaning and undermined its conservative intent.

The Rise of Political Parties cut across the separated (legislative, executive, and judicial) powers that were designed to check one another. Political parties provide the potential means for controlling all of the branches of government and bringing a consistent majority point of view to bear on public affairs.

Constitutional Changes to Make the Several Agencies Responsible to the electorate further weakened checks and balances. The Twelfth Amendment to the Constitution, which makes the President and Vice-President popularly elected officials, and the Seventeenth Amendment, providing for the direct election of senators, have both enhanced the possibility of popular control by a majority.

Changes in Usage and Practice That Facilitate Majority Rule include such factors as the judicial self-restraint that the Supreme Court imposed upon itself in order to give the widest possible latitude to congressional and executive action; the increasing power of the executive branch of government; and the establishment by Congress of independent regulatory commissions that are empowered to exercise legislative, executive, and judicial powers within the limits of a broad congressional statement of public policy.

All three of these developments have modified and made more liberal—that is, more directly responsible to the majority—the original conservative idea of checks and balances.

Federalism originally involved a difference between liberals and conservatives on the strength of the national government in relation to the government of the states. Conservatives advocated a strong central government; liberals

167

emphasized states' rights. Early Supreme Court decisions tended to bulwark the conservative idea of a strong national government, and the Civil War finally resolved the issue in favor of the predominance of the federal union. Since then there has been continuous development of the

Instruments of National Power. The national government has been strengthened by the interpretation and use of the *War Power* (the power to provide for the national defense), which becomes almost limitless in an age of total war and cold war; the power to regulate *Interstate Commerce,* which has provided the national government with the constitutional basis for enacting economic and social legislation and making it applicable to almost the entire economic activity of the nation; and the power to tax and spend for the *General Welfare,* which has provided the basis for the provision of federal funds to and the imposition of federal control over the quality of such state programs as highway construction, welfare, public health, and unemployment insurance.

The Growth of National Power through congressional and executive action under these provisions has resulted in a steady and continuous increase in regulation of economic life. Recent years have also seen the growth of

National Power by Judicial Command. The Supreme Court has extended the national power over the states with increasing rapidity in the areas of civil rights and liberties. The Court has required state governments to provide "equal protection" of their laws (under the Fourteenth Amendment) to all of their citizens and has required, under the same provision, that states provide equal representation for all citizens in both houses of their legislatures.

Similarly, the Court has increasingly used the due-process and equal-protection clauses of the Fourteenth Amendment to require that states extend guarantees of the *Bill of Rights* to all their citizens; increasingly, state laws and practices that abridge those rights have been declared unconstitutional.

Thus, *The Fourteenth Amendment* has been made the basis of a new federalism in which the Court has emerged as the primary force in the extension of national power to preserve the rights and liberties of citizens.

The Constitution was not framed merely to guard the States against danger from abroad, but chiefly to secure union and harmony at home; and to accomplish this end it was deemed necessary, when the Constitution was framed, that many of the rights of sovereignty which the States then possessed should be ceded to the General Government; and that in the sphere of action assigned to it, it should be supreme and strong enough to execute its own laws by its own tribunals, without interruption by a State, or from State officials.

CHIEF JUSTICE ROGER B. TANEY

Chapter Six

CONSTITUTIONAL DEVELOPMENT: THE CONTINUING STRUGGLE
Checks and Balances and Federalism

THE CONSTITUTIONAL PRINCIPLES of separation of powers and checks and balances, federalism, limited government, and judicial supremacy have done much to shape the course of American history. The meaning of these principles has changed at different historical junctures under the impact of slavery, industrialization, economic depression, urbanization, war, mass communication, and many other phenomena. Controversy over their meaning has been one of the most enduring and characteristic qualities of American government—as indeed it should be in a democracy. Such controversy will no doubt continue as long as the government lasts—at least as long as it remains true to its democratic spirit. This chapter and the one following examine in broad outline the historical development and the current status of the controversy over these four constitutional principles.

Checks and Balances: Historical Development

The principle of checks and balances has always been ambiguous. The actual constitutional arrangements intended to implement it have been modified, sometimes by constitutional amendment, but more often by interpretation, usage, and the growth of extraconstitutional political mechanisms. These changes have reflected the liberal view of the purpose of separation of powers. As liberalism adopted a more positive attitude toward the role of government, particularly in economic affairs, the constitutional restraints on majority action seemed to liberals more oppressive and indefensible. The resulting changes in the American political system that have played the most direct and important role in undermining the conservative principle of checks and balances are described below.

THE RISE OF POLITICAL PARTIES

From the beginning, effective liberal government required that there be some means of cutting across the separation of powers—that is, some means of raising the same issues of public policy in all the branches of government so that all were equally responsive to popular will. The political instrument that almost immediately arose to provide continuity and cohesiveness to public policy and a framework for public debate was the political party. Parties were formed to put the same political philosophy and political organization in control of all public offices. Not provided for in the Constitution, they arose as the means by which coherent principles and programs could compete for temporary control of the government. As such, competitive political parties were a powerful weapon of majoritarian democracy; their effect was to undermine the foundations of the conservative constitutional edifice.

CONSTITUTIONAL CHANGES TO MAKE THE SEVERAL AGENCIES DIRECTLY RESPONSIBLE

The conservative doctrine of balance, as we have noted, relied in part on indirect election in order to carry out Madison's idea of a "successive filtration" of the popular will. Liberal reforms written into constitutional amendments have all but eliminated this conservative safeguard. The Twelfth Amendment, and the custom that binds electors to vote for the presidential and vice-presidential candidates who have secured the largest number of popular votes in their states, have made the President a popularly elected official. (It is, of course, still possible for a President to be elected by a minority.) The Seventeenth Amendment made senators directely elected.

Whereas, for the most part, O'Sullivan's liberal plea that all the branches of government should be "equally dependent on the popular will" has been realized, the same is not true of his argument that this should be so "with equal promptness." Their different terms of office still operate to heighten the possibility of a President representing one party and a Congress the other, or of the two houses of Congress being in the control of different parties. Proposals for constitutional reform to remedy this defect (from the liberal viewpoint) have often been made, but not successfully.

CHANGES IN USAGE AND PRACTICE THAT FACILITATE MAJORITY RULE

There are, in this category, three developments that have contributed to undermining the constitutional equilibrium: judicial self-restraint after 1937, the growth in the power of the Presidency, and the development of regulatory commissions.

We will examine the role of the Supreme Court in the system of checks and balances in a later chapter. Now we need only note that the Court came to be the major check on majority government and, after the Civil War, the conservative bulwark against majority attacks on the property rights of minorities. The Court's continued reluctance, since 1937, to set aside statutes as unconstitutional in areas other than civil liberties and civil rights has meant the decline of another conservative safeguard.

Second, the steady growth in the power of the Presidency, to be examined in detail later, saw the emergence of that office as a potential spokesman for a national majority and made it possible for campaigns involving nationwide issues to be fought at a national level. At the same time the growth of the President's role as national legislative leader, with strong Presidents able to exert considerable leadership in the legislative process, cuts across the separation of powers between those two branches in the interest of a popularly supported legislative program.

(At the same time, of course, the wide acceptance of the principle of separation of powers itself set important limits on the powers of the President, as Franklin D. Roosevelt discovered when he sought unsuccesfully to purge congressmen who had opposed his program.

The third development to be considered here is the rise of the regulatory administrative agency. This 'device, unknown to the Constitution, was the major means used by Congress to implement programs designed to regulate various aspects of the economy in response to the demands of national majorities. Beginning with the Interstate Commerce Commission in 1887, the independent regulatory commission became the institutional device most often used to enforce the public interest in such areas of the economy as the control of monopoly and trade practices (Federal Trade Commission, 1914), the quality of foods and drugs (Pure Food and Drug Administration, 1906), the sale of corporate securities (Securities and Exchange Commission, 1934), and the interstate distribution of electric power and natural gas (Federal Communications Commission, 1934).

At the same time, the states instituted similar commissions to regulate in the public interest a range of intrastate activities, including recent fair-employment-practices commissions designed to ensure the public interest in equality of economic opportunity regardless of race. In every case these agencies resulted from public discussion of what were taken to be public issues, and in most cases the decision to institute them can be construed as a majority decision enforced on a recalcitrant minority—indeed, on a minority that usually claimed that its liberties were being abrogated by a tyrannical majority.

In establishing federal regulatory commissions, Congress made them independent of the rest of the executive establishment: the commissioners who head these agencies may not be removed by the President except for causes prescribed by Congress; the decisions of the commission are not reviewed and may not be vetoed by the President. At the same time, the commissions themselves exercise legislative, executive, and judicial powers. Under a broad congressional statement of public policy, the commissions develop administrative rules and regulations that have the force of law; they are themselves charged with the responsibility of applying and administering the law and the regulations; and in the course of discharging these obligations, they prosecute offenders, hear cases, and hand down decisions. It is on these grounds that their functions have been referred to as quasi-legislative and quasi-judicial.

Congress, of course, may redirect or terminate any of these agencies at any time and commission decisions are reviewable on issues of law in the regular courts. But the important thing for our purposes here is that the functions of regulatory agencies cut across the traditional separation of powers and that they developed as applications of a view of the public interest supported by a popular majority.

The constitutional restraints on majority rule embodied in the doctrine of checks and balances have been, in large measure, circumvented and nullified by the developments we have discussed: the popular election of senators and reform in the electoral college, the rise of political parties, the self-imposed restraint of the Supreme Court after 1937, the supremacy of national government over the states, the growth of the governmental commission, and the increase in the power of the Presidency.

The remarkable fact is that these reforms have not succeeded in producing the political system that Jefferson and subsequent liberal reformers envisioned, and it seems very doubtful that modification of such remaining constitutional barriers as differential terms of office and the Electoral College would transform the system into one closer to the traditional liberal model. At the same time, the conservative hopes of the Constitution-makers have been no less frustrated: our political system does not maintain a constitutional equilibrium of economic classes, nor does it provide for the indirect election of an aristocracy who will be "proper guardians of the public weal." (The phrase is from the tenth *Federalist*.) The result has been neither liberal nor conservative in the traditional sense, but rather the politics of minorities rule.

The principle of checks and balances expressed the conservative assumptions and hopes of those who formulated it; it was modified by amendment and usage in the light of the quite different assumptions and hopes of majoritarians. But, at any given time, the practical meaning and working of political and constitutional mechanisms will reflect the assumptions and hopes of the participants.

If checks and balances has not worked out as anticipated by either liberals or conservatives, neither has federalism. In the next section, we shall see how historical circumstances, unanticipated for the most part, have worked to complicate federal relationships to the point where liberal and conservative positions on a strong central government have reversed almost completely.

Federalism: Historical Development

The early conflict between conservative and liberal interpretations of federalism centered on two issues: how powerful the national government was to be, and how conflicts between national and state governments were to be resolved. The first great conservative political party, led by Alexander Hamilton and John Adams, called itself the Federalists; the Jeffersonian liberals began their party career as the Anti-Federalists. The names concealed more than they revealed about the differences between them. The central question was not whether a federal system should prevail, but whether the federal division of power in the Constitution should be loosely or strictly interpreted. The Federalists, because they wanted to expand the national government, argued for a loose construction of the language enumerating its powers; the Anti-Federalists wanted to confine the powers of the national government to a strict and literal reading of the constitutional text.

The debate was first set off when, in 1790, Alexander Hamilton, as Washington's secretary of the treasury, proposed the establishment of a national bank. There was no such grant of power in the Constitution; Hamilton argued it was a power that, under the language of the final clause of Article I, section 8, could be inferred to be "necessary and proper for carrying into execution" the powers that were expressly granted. The issue was decided by the Supreme Court in 1819 in favor of the Federalist position. In *McCulloch* v. *Maryland*,[1] the Court upheld the constitutionality of the second national bank (the charter of the first expired in 1811 without its ever having been tested in the courts) by accepting Hamilton's argument. In his decision, Chief Justice Marshall argued that the grants of power to Congress to lay and collect taxes, regulate commerce, coin and borrow money, and provide for the national defense are to be viewed as broad ends or goals of government activity, and that, therefore, they imply the existence of the power to do whatever may be "necessary and proper" for their accomplishment.

Thus, he held that whereas Congress was given no express power to charter a bank, its decision to do so was clearly a means to the accomplishment of the broad ends it is constitutionally empowered to promote. "Let the end be legitimate," Marshall summarized, "Let it be within the scope of the Constitution, and all means which are appropriate, which are plainly adapted to that end, which are not

[1] 4 Wheaton 316 (1819).

174

prohibited, but consist with the letter and spirit of the Constitution, are constitutional."

The Court threw its authoritative weight behind the Hamiltonian argument for loose construction, and the doctrine that the national government has "implied" and "resultant" powers to be inferred from those expressly enumerated became the basis for its growth in later years. The Hamiltonian argument came back, ironically, to haunt a new generation of conservatives when the instruments of the national government were controlled by liberals who undertook to use them to limit and regulate, rather than to promote, the interests of business. In changed circumstances, liberals and conservatives reversed sides on the question of states' rights and national power, which suggests again that the question has never been a matter of fundamental political principle for any of the contestants.

The real issue has always been fundamentally that of marking out the legitimate boundaries of the power of popular majorities. Jeffersonians opposed national power when they saw it as a vehicle for protecting the property interests of a minority; they supported and used it when they saw it as an instrument of majority rule. Conversely, conservatives supported national power when they saw it as a check on the factious tendencies of local majorities; they opposed it and invoked the symbols of states' rights when majorities clamored for federal regulation of railroads and other reforms that invaded the property interests of minorities. When the high-sounding symbol of states' rights is invoked in political conflict, American history would seem to tell us, we would do well to take it only as window dressing, as a clue that some important conflicts of interests and principles are involved, but never as a statement of what the conflict is really about.

The second major issue over which the Federalists and Anti-Federalists (or Jeffersonian Republicans) contested the meaning of federalism involved the question of the nature of the Union itself. The Constitution is silent on whether the Union it established is indissoluble and on whether a state is obligated to comply with national legislation that it regards as unconstitutional. Did a state have the right voluntarily to secede? Did it have the right to nullify a national action as it applied to the citizens of the state? Did it have the right to interpose legislation of its own contrary to federal legislation in order to prevent the latter from being enforced within the state?

These are all now, in a sense, dead issues; never resolved through political debate, they were for all practical purposes laid to rest on the bloody fields of the Civil War. Cries of "nullification" and "interposition" echoed across the land from some southern states in the aftermath of the Supreme Court's desegregation decision, but they were cries from a buried past. They were, however, very live issues until they were settled by trial of arms. For the conservative, national power could operate within the confines of the constitutional equilibrium; there were no such safeguards on the power of the states. It was the very purpose of the federal union to limit and contain the factious majorities that might develop in the states. It was, therefore, unthinkable that a state could secede or that a temporary majority in a state could nullify national legislation. On the other hand, for the liberal the federal principle could only operate to safeguard liberty and popular government when the national government was not supreme. He saw the federal principle as another device for ensuring that all government reflected maximum participation of popular majorities.

John Taylor stated the liberal view most clearly in his argument:

> The best restraint upon legislative acts tending to the destruction of a true republican government, consists of the mutual right of the general and state governments to examine and controvert before the public each other's proceedings.[2]

To modern ears this sounds more like a recipe for anarchy than for a "true republican government." Again, however, the argument becomes a more sensible one if we bear in mind that, historically, liberals expected that all government, national and state, would need do very little.

The initial battle in this struggle over the nature of the Union centered around the Alien and Sedition Acts. Federalists, alarmed about the influence of the Jacobin ideas of the French Revolution on the Jeffersonian societies, and seeking to cement their hold on the reins of government, passed these acts in 1798. Their effect was to make it a crime to criticize the government or its (then Federalist) officials. Jefferson and Madison, who had by this time become a staunch Jeffersonian and Jefferson's closest political compatriot, countered by drawing up the Virginia and Kentucky Resolutions and inducing the legislatures of those two states to adopt them. The resolutions rested squarely on Taylor's interpretation of federalism. They declared the acts to be unconstitutional, a clear usurpation of power by the national

[2] John Taylor, *Inquiry into the Principles and Policy of the Government of the United States* (New Haven, Conn.: Yale University Press, 1950), p. 556.

Congress, and thus, insofar as Virginia and Kentucky were concerned, null and void. The Virginia Resolution went further by proposing that states had the right to "interpose" contrary statutes as an exercise of their sovereignty to make enforcement of national law impossible within the state. Virginia and Kentucky called on the other states to adopt similar resolutions. The issue and conflicting political philosophies underlying it were clarified in this contest, and the Sedition Act was allowed to lapse after Jefferson was elected President. The Alien Act was never enforced.

At the Hartford Convention of 1814, the New England states' threat to secede because of the harm suffered by shipping interests in the War of 1812 illustrates how the federal principle became embroiled in the struggle of economic interests as well. So also does the extended debate between Senators Webster and Hayne in 1830. Here the threat of nullification arose over dissatisfaction in the South with the Tariff of Abominations of 1828. Senator Hayne, spokesman for the agricultural interests of the South, argued that tariff legislation passed in the interests of northern manufacturers was intolerably oppressive to the southern states and that, under the Constitution, nullification constituted a legitimate weapon with which a state could defend its vital interests. By this time, the issue of federalism had become so entangled in the struggle of economic interests and their moralistic rationalizations that it is difficult to discern what fundamental political principles, if any, were at issue. The debate was conducted over such matters as whether the Constitution had been created by the people as citizens of the United States or by the people as citizens of their respective states and whether, therefore, the national government was the agent of the whole people or of the people acting through their states. But the arguments had become legalistic, and states' rights seemed to be a mantle that could be, and was, donned by every interest that felt itself threatened by action in the national arena.

The issue of the nature of the federal union was settled when it became the battleground of forces that were moral as well as economic in the sectional rivalry that found its climax in the Civil War. Thereafter, the nature of the union was settled as an "indestructible Union, composed of indestructible states";[3] the question of what the national government should do and what is better left to the initiative and discretion of the states continued, of course, to be a source of controversy

---

[3] *Texas* v. *White*, 7 Wall 700 (1869).

in American politics. Much of that controversy has been characterized by legalistic pleadings about the intent of the Founding Fathers that serve only to conceal or obscure the conflict of economic interests that lie at the heart of the matter. The invocation of states' rights in the controversy over the right to exploit tidelands oil in the years between 1947 and 1953 is a case in point. Partly, also, controversies have reflected efforts to deal with the very difficult problem for majoritarian theory of *which* majority should rule when there is a conflict between the majority views in local and larger political arenas. The control of alcoholic beverages and racial segregation illustrate this problem.

Finally, the controversy between national power and states' rights at times involves the traditional question of how the powers of government should be distributed so as to maximize freedom in society. To a considerable extent, the issue of federal aid to education would seem to turn on a fundamental controversy over this basic question. Perhaps the chief weaknesses of a federal system are that conflicts over the respective limits of national and state power promote a legalistic approach to issues ("Who has the constitutional prerogative?" rather than "What ought to be done?") and that, at the same time, the invocation of states' rights serves to conceal the interests and principles that are in conflict.

THE INSTRUMENTS OF NATIONAL POWER

The history of American federalism is the record of the aggrandizement of power at the national level. The national government, restricted by the Constitution to those powers expressly delegated to it or implied therein, has come to exercise authority that would have astounded even the most ardent advocates of national supremacy at Philadelphia. Brought back to the America of the 1960's, eighteenth-century Americans would find it hard to believe that the intervening changes could have been accomplished without extensive constitutional revision. Yet, only the Sixteenth Amendment, which made the income tax constitutional, directly expanded the powers of Congress and the President over economic life. Otherwise, the power emanating from Washington has grown slowly and informally, through constitutional interpretation and usage. This growth has come largely in response to the facts that industrialization and the changed position of America in the world have raised new issues to the level of national debate and that the pressures of majority opinion and of organized interests have undermined that portion of the doctrine of checks and balances embodied in the federal structure of government.

Most of the growth of national power has been justified on the constitutional grants of power to Congress "to lay and collect taxes, duties, imposts, and excises, to pay the debts and provide for the common defense and general welfare of the United States," "to regulate commerce with foreign nations and among the several states, and with the Indian tribes," and to declare war and provide for national defense. It is certainly worth asking, however, just how far the war power, the commerce power, and the taxing power can be stretched without making the federal limitations on the national government meaningless. Have they been stretched beyond all reasonable and meaningful limits?

The War Power. There seems to be little question concerning the power of the national government to provide for the national defense and to declare and wage war. The national government has acquired vast power over the economy in discharging its war powers, not because of willful conspirators in Washington, but because of the changing requirements of national defense and the changed character of warfare. War has become total war; defense now means total economic and social mobilization, not because of the aspirations of power-hungry bureaucrats or advocates of socialist planning, but because of the technology of war itself. Who can doubt that national survival in the current contest with international communism involves the rate of growth of the economy, the capacity of the educational system to produce the skills and abilities necessary to a viable democratic order as well as an expanding economy, or the elimination of racial discrimination and segregation in all aspects of American life? Total war means total mobilization.

Some of these activities may be undesirable on other grounds. Indeed, the warfare state may even be incompatible with the maintenance of democracy in the long run. But, with respect to the question of the constitutional power of the national government, the nature of modern war means that the war power has become almost total power. The question is no longer whether the national government has the constitutional right to interfere in all aspects of economic and social life; modern war has virtually eliminated federalism as a system of constitutional restraints on the power of the national government. In one of its aspects this development is a healthy one. If there is no longer, in most matters, a *constitutional* question of what Congress has a legal right to do, there is still a political question of what and how much the national government should be asked to do. If we are forced to decide these questions as matters of public policy rather than as explications of a constitutional text, we shall have put the issues where, in a democratic society, they belong—squarely in the center of political controversy and debate.

The Commerce Power and the Power to Tax and Spend for the General Welfare. Historically, the age of total war was clearly ushered in by World War II. Already, however, the power of the national government had been greatly expanded in the direction of the welfare state. The government had enacted legislation designed to regulate economic life; it had gone into business itself in some areas, most especially in the production and distribution of electrical energy and in the provision of recreational facilities in the national park system; it had undertaken to plan the use and development of natural resources; it had erected a system of social-security measures including old age and survivors' insurance, unemployment compensation, and minimum wage and child labor statutes.

Mainly, these measures were made under the grant of power to Congress to regulate interstate commerce and to tax and spend money for the general welfare. It should be noted here that there is no general grant to the national government of police power (that is, power to protect and advance the public "health, safety, welfare, and morals"). Thus, the national government may not enact legislation dealing with housing, wages, pornographic literature, or prostitution simply because the Congress and the President believe that such measures would contribute to the general welfare. It may, however, establish regulations on interstate commerce that have the effect of accomplishing these objectives. It may, for example, prohibit the movement in interstate commerce of goods produced in enterprises that pay less than an established minimum hourly wage. Or it may prohibit the use of the mails to defraud, even though there is no power to prevent fraud as contrary to the best interests of society.

The power to regulate interstate commerce turned out to be formidable. It has been used to justify national legislation designed not only to promote, control, and prohibit specific kinds of economic activity, but also to implement national policy on conditions of labor, the "white-slave" traffic, racial discrimination, and so on. Moreover, interstate commerce has been defined so broadly by Congress and the courts that it includes virtually all economic activity. The power to regulate interstate commerce extends to the power to regulate the affairs of small businesses engaged, for example, in selling rock and gravel products in a local market. Similarly, a farmer who grows only enough grain to feed his own livestock is nevertheless defined as being engaged in interstate commerce. Generally, the only persons who are excluded from national legislation regulating interstate commerce are those who, in the wording of the legislation, are deliberately excluded by Congress.

Is this an arbitrary and conscienceless abuse of the clear language of the Constitution? Not, it would seem, if we define commerce with relation not merely to a word in the Constitution, but with relation to the interdependent network of activity in a modern industrialized economic system. The rock and gravel delivered by our local business-man may be used by steel companies and other firms engaged in producing for an interstate market; it may be part of a roadbed that supports the vehicles engaged in the intricate system of transportation underlying the national economy. The farmer producing his own grain for his own livestock is affecting, nevertheless, the interstate market for grain and for livestock. All business is interstate business because of the nature of the industrial and commercial system. The extent to which it ought to be subjected to promotion, regulation, or even abolition is a political rather than a narrowly constitutional or legal question in a modern, interdependent economy.

Similarly, the national government may tax or borrow and spend money, both directly and indirectly, for welfare purposes, even though it has no power in the Constitution directly to promote those purposes. Thus, during the Depression of the 1930's, the national government created and financed work programs designed to provide immediate relief for the unemployed, although there is no direct grant of such authority in the Constitution. Many of the "alphabet" agencies—the CWA (Civil Works Administration), PWA (Public Works Administration), WPA (Works Progress Administration), CCC (Civilian Conservation Corps), NYA (National Youth Authority)—represented national efforts to use the powers to tax, borrow, and spend to stimulate a flagging economy.

The national power to tax and spend may also be employed indirectly through the technique of grants-in-aid. Through this device, the national government makes funds available to the states for specific purposes, usually with a provision that requires the states to match the federal contributions at some stated percentage thereof from their own revenues.

The Social Security Act of 1935 was based on this principle, which has since been extended beyond welfare to such programs as highway development, urban redevelopment, and vocational education and rehabilitation. Sometimes, as notably in the employment security program, federal funds are made available to the states on a tax rebate system, wherein state agencies collect unemployment security taxes for the federal government, which in turn gives most of it back to the states to make unemployment insurance payments in amounts set by state legislatures.

The use of federal money in welfare and other programs may involve more or less of national government control, but in every instance grants-in-aid involve some measure of national initiative and control. In rare instances, national power has been used to stimulate state activity from which the national government hopes later to withdraw. Thus, Congress invested heavily in grants-in-aid to the states in venereal disease control and treatment programs, later cutting back its financial contributions in the hope that states would undertake to continue the programs on their own.

Whenever the national government undertakes to contribute financially to state programs—whether in highway construction, welfare, health, employment security, or resource development—state legislatures and local officials are left with less discretion than they would otherwise have. State agencies accepting federal welfare money must comply with all sorts of rules and regulations that they might otherwise prefer to do without. Specifically, in this program, all employees working for a welfare agency using federal funds must be under a merit system with an established, graduated wage scale that serves to frustrate traditional spoils operations in many states; all grants must be the same regardless of race, creed, or place of origin, which is incompatible with traditional double living standards in some states; specific limitations are set on the various ways in which states may define residence in order to determine eligibility for aid; matching formulae must be met; and a plethora of reports must be submitted to Washington.

These restrictions, designed to ensure compliance with minimum national standards, are bound to seem vexatious to state and local officials. Sometimes protests from the states are loud and insistent enough to induce Congress to yield to the views of the states. A good example was the Jenner Amendment to the welfare appropriation in

1954, which enabled states to print publicly the names of welfare recipients—a practice previously forbidden by the terms of federal legislation authorizing welfare grants to the states.

THE GROWTH OF NATIONAL POWER

How are we to account for the relentless increase in the powers of the national government? Aside from the imperatives of national defense and economic interdependence, how are we to explain the development of a range of national programs that affect almost all aspects of social life? It is important to distinguish between two general sources of demands for the expansion of national governmental power: the effort to use politics to resolve pressing public problems and the effort on the part of organized groups to secure governmental protection and promotion of their interests. The distinction is between policies undertaken to serve some conception of the public interest and governmental programs created out of the push and haul of rival economic interest groups. The distinction is important, even though it is often difficult to apply it in practice.

A system of old-age pensions, for example, may reflect the philosophical conclusion that a free-enterprise economic system in modern society destroys family responsibility for the care of the aged at the same time that it makes it impossible for most persons to provide for their own security. On the other hand, an increase in the amount of the pension may reflect the demands of politically potent senior citizens either organized as a pressure group or seen by politicians as constituting a voting bloc important in the next election. The approach to social security may take the form of issue- and principle-oriented debate, or it may be interest-motivated. The extensive growth in the power of government in this century has reflected both motivations; underlying them both are some deep and far-reaching changes in American society and economic life.

Industrialism and *Laissez Faire*. The traditional order drew heavily on occurrences in the fateful year of 1776. A British economist, Adam Smith, published his *Inquiry into the Wealth of Nations*, a book that shook the foundations of traditional economic institutions as much as the American Revolution disturbed political ones. In it, Smith set forth a radical economic doctrine advocating a *laissez faire* economy and proposing that free competition in the market place would provide an automatic regulator of economic activity. The functions of government were to be confined to keeping the domestic peace, enforcing private contracts, and securing the nation against attack. *Laissez faire* expresses one of the dominant themes in the American political folklore. Its literal meaning—"to let alone"—expresses a commitment to individualism and to the belief that a powerful government is the major source of threats to individual freedom of choice and action. It seemed to promise a society in which all economic activity would be determined by the impersonal forces of supply and demand; economic processes would be regulated "as if by an unseen hand," rather than by the visible hands of men who had economic power.

The idea of an economy in which no man could have power over another man's sustenance or behavior fitted into the Jeffersonian agrarian ideal. The new American nation nurtured itself on Smith's doctrine, modifying it a bit with tariffs and other deviations from time to time. After the Civil War the theory was carried over, with modifications, to justify a rapidly developing corporate, industrial society.

The results, however, were not quite what Smith had predicted. The rapidly growing industrial machine was accompanied by the cycle of "boom and bust," a widening gulf between poor and rich, the economic whip that created a twelve-hour day in the new steel mills, the specter of child labor, the growth of new urban slums, and the wholesale corruption of politics by the new men of wealth.

Not until the Depression of the 1930's did these forces have their full impact. That decade saw an astounding increase in the powers of the national government. Prolonged mass unemployment was the triggering mechanism. But the responsibilities assumed by the government went beyond the obligation to provide work temporarily and ensure full employment over the long run. It also undertook or expanded programs designed to protect investors and consumers against abuses of economic power; devised a social-security program; conducted a program of integrated river valley development in the Tennessee Valley and embarked on other programs of electric power and resource development; established government agencies to make loans to farmers and undertook to ensure that farm income maintained parity with non-farm income; guaranteed the right of labor to organize and bargain collectively with employers; established minimum wage levels in industry; eliminated child labor; and provided limitations on working conditions of employed women. These activities were financed mainly from the proceeds of a federal income tax, the rates of which were made increasingly progressive.

These increases in the powers of the national government seem clearly to have been directed to the solution of problems occasioned by the concentration of economic wealth and power under unregulated capitalism. The response was at the national level because the problems were national in scope. The problems of an interdependent, industrial economy do not yield to local solutions.

Federal and State Action. In some instances, the national government stepped in because state governments, for reasons rooted in their historical development, were unwilling to act. By and large, state governments in recent years appear to be more susceptible to the pressures of the most powerful interests and less responsive to popular demands for economic reform. Most often, the most powerful interests are property interests. The result is reflected, for example, in the structure of state and local, as contrasted with national, tax systems. The national income and corporation taxes are progressive; states and local communities rely mainly on sales, excise, and property taxes that are proportional or even regressive in their effects. (A progressive tax taxes higher incomes at higher rates; a regressive tax takes a lower percentage of higher incomes).

Partly, the susceptibility of state governments to the pressure of business and property interests is due to the overrepresentation in state legislatures of rural areas that tend to be economically conservative. This condition may change substantially when legislatures are reapportioned so that urban areas gain strength. But partly, also, the condition is a function of the limitations inherent in local efforts to deal with an economic system that is national in organization and scope. Thus, states are in competition with one another to attract business and industry on which the level of income in the state will depend. To do this, local governments often appropriate public funds to chambers of commerce to be spent on advertising the community's attractions for industry. Most state governments have agencies of their own for this purpose. The success of these efforts generally depends on whether the state offers a favorable climate for business. In addition to such matters as the availability of power, cheap transportation, land, and a skilled labor force, a favorable tax structure with correspondingly low levels of welfare expenditures and the absence of a regulatory climate inimical to business freedom are also important.

Historically, after the Civil War, states competed with one another to see who could offer the most favorable conditions for business in their incorporation laws. More recently, the competition has extended to the whole range of tax, labor relations, regulation, and welfare activities. The states continue to find themselves in a situation in which there are very real pressures toward subordination of the public interest to private interests of corporate business or labor. Perhaps it would be more accurate to say that there is relentless pressure on the states to identify private business interests with the public interest, to accept what was for a long time the leading slogan of the business lobbies: "What Helps Business Helps You."

Pressure and Principle. The national government is under no such limitation. Because it is coextensive with the economy, it is uniquely able to avoid being divided and ruled by economic interests. It is uniquely capable of ensuring that the economy is in the service of public goals. Although ordinarily these facts are not readily recognized, it seems likely that they underlie most of the debates about national power and states' rights. Those who identify the business interest with the public interest are likely to invoke the slogan of states' rights and eulogize the virtue of government that is close to the people. For those who take a different view, the national government seems in reality to be closer to the people than are the governments of the states.

We do not mean to imply that all the activities of the national government are undertaken in pursuit of a public interest that stands above the private claims of powerful groups or that, specifically, all federal programs that intervene in the economy are undertaken in order to ensure that private economic power is made to serve public purposes. At the national level too, government often simply responds in a brokerage fashion to private pressures, and national politicians often identify the balancing of private claims with the public interest. At the least, other interests than business—labor, for example—are likely to get a more even break in Congress than in state legislatures. At the most, national government in the present circumstances is capable of transcending all the private claims in order to deal with national problems created by industrialization and urbanization.

In practice, pressure politics and principled politics are both operative in national consideration of most issues, although one or the other may at different times be dominant. This matter is considered in greater detail in subsequent chapters. Our main concern now is to point to the greater difficulty at the state level of conducting government on any basis other than a response to private interests and to the pressures on state governments to favor the business interest over others. In any decision about whether a particular responsibility should be undertaken at the national or state level, these considerations should be an important element. They are not the only considerations involved, of course. Big government means big bureaucracy, red tape, inflexibility of rules, the danger of officiousness in the attitudes of public officials, and the narrowing of diversity and variety in the national life. What this re-emphasizes, above all, is that the constitutional principle of federalism is not an oracle to which one can appeal for a solution to the problem of which levels of government should be relied on in particular cases. We are now called upon to debate the kinds of questions that the founders themselves debated. Here again, our heritage is not a constitutional catalogue of answers to political questions; it is, rather, one of controversy and of conditions that make continuing political debate possible.

NATIONAL POWER BY JUDICIAL COMMAND

In the previous section, we were concerned with the growth of national power by actions of Congress and the President. This growth has been gradual and steady as a result of circumstances that require the national government to act. There have been other expansions of federal power as well. Most significantly this has been done through judicial interpretation of the due-process and equal-protection-of-the-laws clauses of the Fourteenth Amendment to the Constitution.

This extension of national power by decisions of the federal courts is reflected most vividly in problems of civil rights for minority groups. Many of the crucial stages of the civil rights movement have been the result of Supreme Court interpretations of the Fourteenth Amendment, which have required state governments to provide equal protection of their laws for all citizens regardless of race, creed, or place of national origin. This same doctrine of equal protection has also been asserted to guarantee all citizens equal representation in both houses of their state legislatures—"one man, one vote"—which has precipitated another domestic controversy.

Recent Supreme Courts have extended national authority in other areas as well. Most importantly, the Court has abandoned its earlier position of judicial restraint in the interpretation of the meaning of the due-process-of-law clause of the Fourteenth Amendment. In recent years the Court has ruled that due process includes an increasing number of the provisions of the first eight amendments and, therefore, that state governments are limited in their powers by the authority of the Bill of Rights.

THE BILL OF RIGHTS AND THE STATES

The broad outline of the federal relationship is stated in two constitutional amendments, the tenth and the fourteenth. The ideas about federal relationships provided by these amendments have been the source of much conflict.

The Tenth Amendment says:

The powers not delegated to the United States by the Constitution, nor prohibited by it to the States are reserved to the States respectively, or to the people.

The much interpreted and adjudicated section 1 of the Fourteenth Amendment declares:

All persons born or naturalized in the United States and subject to the jurisdiction thereof, are citizens of the United States and of the State wherein they reside. No State shall make or enforce any law which shall abridge the privileges or immunities of citizens of the United States; nor shall any State deprive any person of life, liberty, or property, without due process of law; nor deny to any person within its jurisdiction the equal protection of the laws.

The Tenth Amendment was part of the Bill of Rights proposed by the first Congress and ratified in 1791. The Fourteenth Amendment was added to the Constitution in 1868 as one of the post-Civil War amendments designed to end slavery.

The conflict inherent in these two amendments is a conflict of states' rights versus national authority. The Tenth Amendment restricts federal activities to those areas where specific authorization is granted, and it permits states to act in all areas where they are not specifically restricted. This is, in short, a clear expression of states' rights.

The Fourteenth Amendment is a potential instrument for the nationalization of the rights and privileges of all citizens. Indeed, this was its intent but, through early Supreme Court interpretation of its meaning, the nationalization of these rights by use of the Fourteenth Amendment has been slow.

Before discussing the development of the Fourteenth Amendment as a vehicle for extending the Bill of Rights to the states, it should be pointed out that the states' rights principle was a well-grounded tradition in American government. The Supreme Court bulwarked this tradition in 1833 when a controversy over whether the Fifth Amendment applied to the states came before it.[4]

The language of the Fifth Amendment does not, like that of the First Amendment, specifically restrict only the power of Congress. The opening words of the Fifth Amendment are "no person shall . . . ," followed by restrictions on government actions which would deprive an individual of his right to indictment by a grand jury, protection against double jeopardy, privilege against self-incrimination, guarantee of "due process of law," and promise of just compensation for property taken for public use.

It was the last clause of the Fifth Amendment providing for just compensation which was before the Court. The City of Baltimore, in paving its streets, diverted water from an area under a wharf owned by one Barron. This diversion of water diminished the wharf's value since it could no longer be used to service ships. Barron sued the city and was awarded a judgment of $4,500. The city appealed and the highest appellate court in the state reversed the decision. Barron then appealed to the United States Supreme Court claiming a violation of his rights under the Fifth Amendment, which forbids the taking of private property without just compensation. In his last constitutional decision, Chief Justice John Marshall stated that the question was "of great importance, but not much difficulty" and ruled that "the Fifth Amendment must be construed as restraining the power of the general government, not as applicable to the states." Barron's plea then was dismissed for lack of jurisdiction.

For many decades, the Barron rule prevailed and state legislatures had only to answer to their own constitutions and their own courts in the enactment of laws in the field of civil liberties and in the enforcement of their legal codes. Some states jealously guarded these liberties, or some of them, while others were less prone to preserve them when dangerous ideas were expressed or when people assembled for unpleasant or annoying reasons. Even religion was curtailed by some states or local governments when unpopular cults appeared to challenge the established order.

It was not until seven years after its passage that the Fourteenth Amendment was given its initial interpretation and any fears that states had of an onslaught of national control were judicially calmed.[5]

[4] *Barron* v. *Baltimore*, 7 Peters 243 (1833).
[5] *The Slaughter House Cases*, 16 Wall 36 (1873).

The decision in this case not only held back an extension of the federal Constitution to the states through the Fourteenth Amendment, but it virtually killed the privileges-and-immunities clause of the Amendment. This was done in spite of the established historical fact that this clause was intended to extend all ordinary rights and liberties of citizens to the states.[6] So thoroughly was this clause put to rest that it has never been revived. But while "privileges and immunities" has yet to be used as a test for complete incorporation of the first eight amendments into the Fourteenth Amendment, some ten justices have argued, at various times, that it should be revived and used.[7]

From the Slaughter House Cases until the 1930's, the Fourteenth Amendment lay dormant as a means of extending the federal Constitution to the states. It was awakened in 1925 when the Court, although refusing to negate a state law claimed to interfere with a free press, stated:

> For present purposes, we may and do assume that freedom of speech and of the press—which are protected by the First Amendment from abridgment by Congress—are among the fundamental rights and "liberties" protected by the due process clause of the Fourteenth Amendment from impairment by the states.[8]

The dictum in the Gitlow opinion foreshadowed a new era in the evolution of federal-state relations under the Fourteenth Amendment. Where an earlier Court had declined to incorporate the first eight amendments into the Fourteenth through the privileges-and-immunities clause, the Gitlow opinion opened a new door. The due-process clause was to become a vehicle for absorbing the first eight amendments into the Fourteenth and enforcing them against state actions.

Six years after the Gitlow decision, the Court held a state law completely invalid as an offense to freedom of the press by including the First Amendment in the "liberty" protected against state infringement by the due-process clause of the Fourteenth Amendment.[9]

By 1940, the Court had fully absorbed all the provisions of the First Amendment into the Fourteenth. The Court still declined, however,

---

[6] Robert E. Cushman, *Leading Constitutional Decisions* (New York: Appleton-Century-Crofts, 12th ed., 1963), p. 52.

[7] See Justice Douglas' concurring opinion in *Gideon* v. *Wainwright,* 372 **U.S.** 355 (1963), and footnote 2 in *Malloy* v. *Hogan,* 12 L.ed. 2d 653 (1964).

[8] *Gitlow* v. *New York,* 268 U.S. 652 (1925). The Court's opinion on the due-process clause was an *obiter dictum*—that is, an opinion on an issue not necessary to the decision in the case.

[9] *Near* v. *Minnesota,* 283 U.S. 1 (1931). The law negated was a Minnesota statute allowing prior restraint of publication if officials deemed it necessary.

to incorporate all the protections of Amendments Two through Eight. In 1937, the Court had distinguished between what it would incorporate and what it would not. In response to a plea to incorporate the Fifth Amendment protection against self-incrimination, the Court, in an opinion written by Justice Cardoza, refused on the grounds that "the right to trial by jury and immunity from prosecution except as the result of an indictment may have value and importance. Even so, they are not *the very essence of a scheme of ordered liberty* . . . what is true of jury trials and indictments is true also, as the cases show, of the immunity from compulsory self-incrimination."[10]

The test used by the Court in this case—whether a particular right is necessary to a "scheme of ordered liberty"—became an important precedent. In subsequent decisions, however, the Court's interpretation of it changed drastically. Freedom from compulsory self-incrimination, for example, which Cardoza had held not to be necessary to ordered liberty, has since been incorporated into the Fourteenth Amendment.[11]

In recent years, on a case-by-case basis, the Court has gradually applied most of the provisions of the Bill of Rights to the states. The important milestones in this process include the following:

1925—The Fourteenth Amendment can be used to extend First Amendment liberties to the states.

1931—A state statute abridging freedom of the press was held unconstitutional for violating the First Amendment's protection of a free press.

1940—The religious clause of the First Amendment was extended to the states.

1962—A state statute making it a crime to be addicted to the use of narcotics was held to be cruel and unusual punishment in violation of the Eighth and Fourteenth Amendments.

1963—Fourth Amendment procedural guarantees regarding arrests, searches, and seizures were extended to the states.

1963—The Sixth Amendment requirement of right to counsel in criminal proceedings was required of all states.

1964—The Fifth Amendment privilege against self-incrimination was applied to the states.

1965—The Sixth Amendment's provision for the right of an accused person to confront witnesses against him was incorporated into the Fourteenth Amendment.

[10] *Palko* v. *Connecticut*, 302 U.S. 319 (1937). Italics added. See also Chap. 16.
[11] *Malloy* v. *Hogan*, 12 L.ed. 2d (1964). See also Chap. 16.

Some students of the judicial process feel it will not be long before the Supreme Court incorporates all of the first eight amendments into the Fourteenth. It is possible that the privileges-and-immunities clause could be revived as a vehicle for their blanket incorporation. The trend, since 1925, has been, with occasional steps backward or aside, in this direction. It could, of course, stop or even reverse itself if future justices on future Courts so decide.

THE FOURTEENTH AMENDMENT AND A NEW FEDERALISM

Increasingly, the Fourteenth Amendment has become a strong instrument for securing civil rights and liberties for all citizens in all states. The recent use of this provision has embroiled the Court in some of the most heated controversies in its history. Even the casual observer of American life realizes that judicial interpretation of the Fourteenth Amendment has caused a revolutionary break with the past and has instituted changes in the whole fabric of national life that can never be turned back. This Amendment, as interpreted by the courts, probably will be an important key to federal-state relationships for a long time to come.

Utilization of the due-process clause had opened the door to the nationalizing of civil rights and liberties. The door was pushed even wider when, in later cases, the Court used the equal-protection-of-the-laws provision to end racial segregation[12] and to reapportion state legislatures.[13]

In some ways it is ironic that the Supreme Court is forcing us to be free and equal in the liberal meaning of those terms. This is hardly what the Founders, favoring a strong judiciary, had in mind. The effect of the judicial interpretation of the Fourteenth Amendment in the area of incorporating the Bill of Rights also has had an impact on the historical development of limited government to which we turn in the next chapter.

[12] *Brown* v. *Board of Education*, 347 U.S. 483 (1954).
[13] *Baker* v. *Carr*, 369 U.S. 186 (1962), *Reynolds* v. *Sims*, 32 LW 4535 (1964), and numerous subsequent cases.

CONSTITUTIONAL DEVELOPMENT:
THE CONTINUING STRUGGLE . . .
Limited Government and Judicial Supremacy

. . . which extends the historical development of the Constitution to the principles of limited government and judicial supremacy.

The development of **Limited Government** is in large measure a history of judicial interpretation of the scope and limits of individual rights, particulary of those liberties found in the First Amendment (speech, press, assembly, and religion). In interpreting these provisions the courts have had to deal with the following questions:

Is *Freedom of Speech Absolute or Relative,* and if it is relative, what criteria are to be used to judge when it can be curtailed? In its history the Court has devised several standards for judging exceptions to the rule of absolute freedom, none of which has proved satisfactory to all of the justices or to observers of the judicial process.

How are the demands of **Civil Liberties** to be weighed against the requirements of **Public Order?** In this area the Court is called upon to adjudicate the right to assemble in order to listen to speeches, to demonstrate, to picket, or to carry on other lawful purposes and to weigh this right against the rights of others to order and privacy.

What limitations may be put on **Civil Liberties** in order to protect **Public Morality?** Here the Court is called upon to determine whether censorship of the press (which includes radio, movies, and television) is warranted in order to protect the public morality and decency and, where it is permitted, to assure that the criteria and procedures involved are not arbitrary.

Do the First Amendment's religious provisions require A *"Wall of Separation"* between **Church and State?** This question involves the Court in such issues as school prayers and Bible reading, the inclusion of "under God" in the Pledge of Allegiance, public aid to parochial schools, and the rights of conscientious objectors. Because religion permeates so many phases of American life and because it is a highly sensitive issue, the Court always finds itself the center of controversy regardless of how it interprets the religious clause of the First Amendmend or where it locates the wall.

In all of these areas *Civil Rights and Liberties* are the subjects of *Continuing Debate* before the people and its governmental tribunals, particularly the judiciary. The defense of liberty is a difficult and unending problem in a democracy because limitations on freedom are usually directed against unpopular ideas and individuals. This suggests that in the long run liberty can only be defended by an enlightened public opinion.

The *Development of Judicial Supremacy* is the history of the role of the Supreme Court as final arbiter in determining the meaning of the Constitution. In this process, one central question has been whether

Judicial Power is to be used as *Brake or Accelerator.* At times the Court has lagged behind the temper of the nation and at other times it has been in the forefront of social change. Prior to 1937, it served as a brake on social and economic reform; since that time it has accelerated, or forced, change in a liberal, egalitarian direction. The changing posture of the Court has dramatized the fact that

Judicial Supremacy in a democratic system poses a *Political Dilemma:* the power of the judiciary sets limits on majority rule; yet it sometimes operates to protect those liberties that make majority rule legitimate. Whether the Court is the safest or wisest repository of this power involves the basic questions that have divided liberals and conservatives.

Judicial interpretation in recent years has made the Constitution more liberal, more egalitarian, more sensitive to the rights and liberties of all. The Court has established *National Standards of Justice* and extended them to the states, mainly through the *Fourteenth Amendment* and, in so doing, has made political decisions in the guise of deciding legal questions. This is the role forced on the Court by the principle of *Judicial Supremacy;* political repercussions from the Court's decisions have raised the question of the validity of the principle itself.

The history of its principles reveals above all that ours is a *Living Constitution.* There is no consensus on its meaning. Its historical course has seemed to move mainly in the direction of majoritarian theory but, ironically, with a conservative institution, the Court, taking the lead. But, in any event, constitutional principles do not exclusively define political reality. To these other forces and processes the next chapters turn.

194

The Court is forbidden by the Constitution to consider anything but concrete cases, involving the real interests of particular litigants. In a civilization growing less human all the time, with budgets beyond the grasp of men and weapons that can wipe out continents, surely there is a special value in an institution that focuses on the individual.

ANTHONY LEWIS

Chapter Seven

CONSTITUTIONAL DEVELOPMENT: THE CONTINUING STRUGGLE

Limited Government and Judicial Supremacy

THE STRUGGLE for civil liberties always raises the question of the nature of freedom. Should freedoms of conscience, speech, assembly, and press extend to everyone, including those who would destroy a government that guarantees these liberties? Is freedom absolute or is it to be "balanced" against some "reasonable" standard of "common morality," "order," "tranquillity," "safety," or "security"? Must it meet a test of "utility" or can freedom really be subjected to such a test and still be freedom? The Bill of Rights has involved all of these questions and probably always will, for it is the nature of a free society to continually submit its freedom to disputations and tests.

Limited Government: Historical Development

The limitations on Congressional interference with speech and writing were not long in being tested. Reacting to vigorous criticisms of the government and some of its officials, the first Federalist Congress passed the Alien and Sedition Acts designed to gag loose talk and inflammatory speech. The effect and the purpose of the Sedition Law were to reduce the limits of speech and press in the United States to those set by the then-prevailing English common law of seditious libel. Its provisions asserted the right of the state to punish those who wrote any statements that tended to expose public magistrates to hatred, contempt, or ridicule. As Blackstone, the great British authority on the common law, put it, the laws must be protected against any tendency to disturb the public peace "by stirring up the objects of them to revenge, and perhaps to bloodshed." Truth was no defense in these proceedings; only intent was important, and the administration of the Sedition Act assumed that bad intent could be inferred from a tendency to undermine the popularity of an official.

The Federalist support of the Sedition Act reflected their view that government must control as well as reflect the opinions of the people. To control the potential turbulence of the masses they felt it necessary to reduce the meaning of the First Amendment to the English common law. This meant putting limits on political discussion in order to maintain a veil of majesty and reverence around civil authority.

The Sedition Act loomed large in the election John Adams referred to as the "revolution of 1801." In a significant sense that election was a victory for Jefferson's view "that the opinions of men are not the object of civil government, nor under its jurisdiction."[1] Jefferson, in his first inaugural address, no doubt had these laws in mind when he said:

> If there be any among us who would wish to dissolve this Union or to change its republican form, let them stand undisturbed as monuments of the safety with which error of opinion may be tolerated where reason is left free to combat it.

Jefferson gave further meaning to his position when, as President, he pardoned all those who had been convicted under the Act.

[1] For an exhaustive study of the Alien and Sedition Laws, see James Morton Smith, *Freedom's Fetters* (Ithaca, N.Y.: Cornell University Press, 1956).

After the Alien and Sedition Act, the First Amendment's command that Congress "shall make no law . . ." was well enough observed that the Supreme Court did not rule on any important civil liberties cases involving congressional action until World War I. During this time, Congress, as did much of the general public, took the Bill of Rights quite casually. When the drums of war began to roll, a Sedition Act was passed by Congress and approximately nineteen hundred people were prosecuted under it for alleged subversive activity or criticism of the federal government. Many radical publications were denied mailing privileges, and groups advocating a variety of political innovations were cast under a cloud of suspicion. Private citizens broke their German dishes, and the common American hamburger became Salisbury steak. After the war and in reaction to the Bolshevik Revolution in Russia, repressive limitations on civil liberties were continued in the country's first "red scare." As one authority put it:

> The First Amendment had no hold on people's minds because no live facts or concrete images were then attached to it. Like an empty box with beautiful words on it, the Amendment collapsed under the impact of terror of Prussian battalions and terror of Bolshevik mobs. So the emotions generated by the two simultaneous cataclysms of war and revolution swept unchecked through American prosecutors, judges, jurymen and legislators.[2]

FREE SPEECH: ABSOLUTE OR RELATIVE?

Since the end of World War I, a steady flow of cases arising under the First Amendment have been before the Supreme Court. A vast literature on the meaning of civil liberties has also been developed. The range of judicial and scholarly opinion on the subject is now immense. The core of the problem—for judges, legislators, or citizens—is whether democracy is best served by balancing First Amendment freedoms against other values such as national security or by taking an absolutist position for uninhibited freedoms in the areas covered by the First Amendment. One of the most influential advocates of the absolute sanctity of the First Amendment has argued that free speech must extend to everyone:

> There are no exceptions—Communists, Socialists, Fascists, Democrats, Republicans, the foolish, the wise, the dangerous, the safe, those

[2] Zechariah Chafee, Jr., *Thirty-Five Years with Freedom of Speech* (New York: Roger N. Baldwin Civil Liberties Foundation, 1952), p. 4.

who wish to overthrow the state, those who wish to keep it as it is. There is no reason to curb freedom of speech in time of danger or in war. . . . The time of danger is exactly the time to show people that you mean what you say.[3]

Such a pure view of freedom to speak has not, however, been very widely accepted in periods of crisis or danger, real and imaginary. During World War I, the general secretary of the Socialist Party was arrested and convicted under the Espionage Act of 1917 for mailing pamphlets to draftees urging them to oppose the draft. His appeal eventually went to the Supreme Court, which unanimously upheld his conviction.[4] "In many places and ordinary times," said Justice Holmes for a unanimous Court, "the defendants in saying all that was said in the circular would have been within their constitutional rights." But, he added:

> The question in every case is whether the words used are used in such circumstances and are of such a nature as to create a *clear and present danger* that they will bring about the substantive evils that Congress has a right to prevent. It is a question of proximity and degree.[5]

Holmes's relativism was a rigid relativism and his qualification of freedom would only apply in situations as serious as war or imminent violence. Words, then, had to be a proximate cause of serious consequence—"triggers of action," as Judge Learned Hand once called them. But even a rigid relativism in the law leaves open the door for further exceptions to the absolutist's position. Men were convicted and some went to jail for their words under the "clear and present danger" test.[6]

Later, however, Holmes and his colleague Louis D. Brandeis, dissenting from the views of a majority of the Court, attempted to demonstrate that the clear-and-present-danger test did offer protection of the individual and imposed limits on how far the provisions of the First Amendment could be stretched. In *Abrams et al.* v. *United States*,[7] the

---

[3] Alexander Meiklejohn, *Free Speech and Its Relation to Self-Government* (New York: Harper, 1948), p. 50. On p. 27, he says, "To be afraid of ideas, any ideas, is to be unfit for self-government."
[4] *Schenck* v. *United States*, 249 U.S. 47 (1919).
[5] *Ibid.* Italics added.
[6] *Frohwerk* v. *United States*, 249 U.S. 204 (1919), and *Debs* v. *United States*, 249 U.S. 211 (1919). The opinions of the Court in these cases were written by Holmes. Although the words *clear and present danger* were not used, the test of the Schenck case seems to have been applied.
[7] 250 U.S. 616 (1919).

two dissented sharply from the conviction of another group of pamphleteers. Holmes's dissent, in which Brandeis concurred, attempted to clarify the limits of the clear-and-present-danger test:

> I never had any reason to doubt that the questions of law that alone were before this court in the cases of Schenck . . . Frohwerk . . . and Debs . . . were rightly decided. I do not doubt for a moment that by the same reasoning that would justify punishing persuasion to murder, *the United States constitutionally may punish speech that produces or is intended to produce a clear and imminent danger that will bring about forthwith certain substantive evils* that the United States constitutionally may seek to prevent. The power . . . is greater in time of war. . . .[8]

Holmes added some persuasive arguments to his dissent and warned against making exceptions to the First Amendment unless the "emergency . . . makes it immediately dangerous to leave the correction of evil counsels to time." But the majority was not deterred from upholding this and other similar convictions.[9] In subsequent cases, as a majority of the Court further expanded the limits of permissible punishment of speech under the "bad tendency" test, Holmes dissented eloquently. "Every idea," he reminded his colleagues, "is an incitement."[10]

Out of the judicial use of the clear-and-present-danger test and the extension of the due-process clause of the Fourteenth Amendment to the states grew the doctrine of the "preferred position." This doctrine, championed by Justices Murphy and Rutledge, held that the usual presumption of validity given to state legislation does not apply to laws restricting freedom of speech, press, or assembly. This approach, as developed by Justice Rutledge, still held that civil liberties must be balanced against domestic tranquillity and national security, but it argued that the presumption must be in favor of liberty rather than its suppression. Rutledge put it this way:

> This case confronts us again with the duty our system places on this court to say where the individual's freedom ends and the State's power begins. Choice on that border, now as always delicate, is perhaps more so where the usual presumption supporting legislation is balanced by the preferred place given in our scheme to the great, the indispensable democratic freedoms secured by the First Amendment. That

---

[8] *Ibid.* Italics added.
[9] *Schaefer* v. *United States,* 251 U.S. 466 (1920), and *Pierce* v. *United States,* 252 U.S. 239 (1920).
[10] *Gitlow* v. *New York,* 268 U.S. 652 (1925).

priority gives these liberties a sanctity and a sanction not permitting dubious intrusions.[11]

Rutledge then brought in the clear-and-present-danger test when he stated, "Any attempt to restrict those liberties must be justified by clear public interest, threatened not doubtfully or remotely, but by clear and present danger."

This formula is not acceptable, of course, to those who argue the absolute inviolability of First Amendment liberties. It has also come under attack by those who regard it as too restrictive. Its most severe critic was Justice Frankfurter, who called it a "deceptive formula" unreasonably limiting the power of legislatures.

The preferred position, like all other judicial tests, was another attempt to find an exception to the absolute exercise of free speech. It left the door open for the Court to decide when a clear and present danger existed and then to determine when "the individual's freedom ends and the State's power begins."

None of these tests has ever proved satisfactory, and there are some interesting cases illustrating the difficulty the Court confronts when the issue is clearly drawn. One of them was *Terminiello* v. *Chicago*.[12] Terminiello was a defrocked Catholic priest who specialized in anti-Semitic tirades and splenetic blasts at both the Roosevelt Administration and the Roosevelt family. He was a disciple of hatemonger Gerald L. K. Smith. At the time of his arrest, he was speaking to a large audience of believers while a mob of nonbelievers picketed the building outside, charged the doors, and threw rocks at the windows of the auditorium.

Terminiello was subsequently arrested under a city ordinance for causing a riot. He was later convicted and his conviction was upheld by the Illinois appellate courts. The Supreme Court reversed the Illinois courts on the ground that the ordinance was faulty. Justice Jackson, recently returned from his duties as allied prosecutor at the Nuremberg war crime trials of high-ranking nazis, dissented sharply. He held the incident "was a local manifestation of a world-wide and standing conflict between two organized groups of revolutionary fanatics, each of which has imported to this country the strong-arm technique developed in the struggle by which their kind has devastated Europe." In answer to the majority of the Court, Jackson had this to say:

[11] *Thomas* v. *Collins*, 323 U.S. 516 (1944).
[12] 377 U.S. 1 (1949).

This court has gone far toward accepting the doctrine that civil liberty means the removal of all restraints from these crowds and that all local attempts to maintain order are impairments of the liberty of the citizen. The choice is not between order and liberty. It is between liberty with order and anarchy without either. There is danger that, if the court does not temper its doctrinaire logic with a little practical wisdom, it will convert the constitutional Bill of Rights into a suicide pact.

The concern Justice Jackson expressed was reflected in a series of decisions, made by the Supreme Court during the 1950's, dealing with the relationship of free speech to subversion. One of these cases involved a test of a provision in the Taft-Hartley Act requiring all union officials to sign a noncommunist affidavit.[13]

The Court, speaking through Chief Justice Vinson, upheld the loyalty oath provision on the ground that it was a reasonable protection of the security of the nation. Vinson said that if constitutional government ". . . is to survive it must have the power to protect itself against unlawful conduct and, under some circumstances, incitements to commit unlawful acts. Freedom of speech thus does not comprehend the right to speak on any subject at any time."

Justice Jackson in a concurring opinion made a distinction between the Communist party and other political parties and concluded that the requirement of an affidavit was reasonable for the Communist party because it advocates the overthrow of the government. Justice Black, who holds a different view of the First Amendment, dissented on the ground that "not the least of the virtues of the First Amendment is its protection of each member of the smallest and most unorthodox minority."

Another case in which the Court was faced with the problem of curtailing free speech was *Dennis* v. *United States*.[14] Dennis and ten other Communists had been convicted under the Smith Act of 1940, which made advocacy of the overthrow of the government by force or violence a crime. Chief Justice Vinson spoke for the Court and again argued that national security is essential to any kind of freedom. He said:

Overthrow of the government by force and violence is certainly a substantial enough interest for the government to limit speech. Indeed this is the ultimate value for any society, for if a society cannot

[13] *American Communications Association* v. *Douds,* 339 U.S. 382 (1950).
[14] 341 U.S. 494 (1951).

protect its very structure from armed internal attack, it must follow that no subordinate value can be protected.

Vinson's decision again brought a sharp dissent from Justice Black, who challenged the whole concept of "reasonableness," which was emerging as a judicial test to limit free speech:

> So long as this court exercises the power of judicial review of legislation, I cannot agree that the First Amendment permits us to sustain laws suppressing freedom of speech on the basis of Congress' or our own notions of mere "reasonableness." Such a doctrine waters down the First Amendment so that it amounts to little more than an admonition to Congress. The Amendment as so construed is not likely to protect any but those "safe" or orthodox views which rarely need its protection. . . .

The issue of curtailing free speech came up again in *Feiner* v. *New York*,[15] when a zealous graduate student from Syracuse University was arrested for haranguing a comparatively small crowd on the streets of Syracuse. Chief Justice Vinson, speaking for the majority and using the test of reasonableness, said he agreed with the trial court's findings that a "clear danger of disorder" existed and that Feiner had defied the police officers who told him to stop speaking after a member of the audience threatened to do it himself. But what price do we pay for order? The consequences of casting freedom to speak, however violently, against the desire for order and tranquillity, and having the former give way to the latter, are disturbing to many believers in democratic theories of government. If this were to be the test, all one would have to do to stop a speech would be to mill around the speaker in a disorderly fashion.

The Vinson Court was sharply divided on the issue of civil liberties. The fear of cynical use of liberty to cover up plans to curtail democracy and the assertion that it is the unpopular and noxious opinions that must be protected if freedom of speech is to mean anything are fundamental differences in political philosophy. Under Chief Justice Warren, the Court has been more favorably disposed to First Amendment freedoms. The trend established in the Douds, Dennis, and Feiner cases was temporarily halted in *Yates* v. *United States*.[16] In this case, the Court held that the Smith Act, under which Dennis had been convicted, did not outlaw the abstract theory of overthrow of the government. Justice Harlan said that to be punishable under the Smith Act advocacy must

[15] 340 U.S. 315 (1951).
[16] 354 U.S. 298 (1957).

go beyond a mere belief in "violent revolution" and must urge others "to do something, now or in the future, rather than merely to believe something." Justice Black, with the concurrence of Justice Douglas, went further to state: "The First Amendment provides the only kind of security system that can preserve a free government—one that leaves the way open for people to favor, discuss, advocate or incite to causes and doctrines however obnoxious and antagonistic such views may be to the rest of us."

The relativism inherent in the test of reasonableness was subsequently further developed into the judicial doctrine of balance. In the Barenblatt case, Justice Harlan, speaking for the court, made both national security and free speech relative and put the Court in the role of umpire. Upholding Barenblatt's conviction, he commented: "We conclude that the balance between the individual and the governmental interests here at stake must be struck in favor of the latter, and that therefore the provisions of the First Amendment have not been offended."

Justice Black responded with this:

> To apply the court's balancing test under such circumstances is to read the First Amendment to say "Congress shall pass no law abridging freedom of speech, press, assembly, and petition, unless Congress and the Supreme Court reach the joint conclusion that on balance the interest of the Government in stifling these freedoms is greater than the interests of the people in having them exercised." This is closely akin to the notion that neither the First Amendment nor any other provision of the Bill of Rights should be enforced unless the court believes it is *reasonable* to do so.

Others have criticized the procedure of balancing the claims of individuals under the First Amendment against a public interest in national security on grounds that, where the conflict is defined in this way, the public interest will always overbalance the private claim. In their view, if a balance test is to be applied, it is not the *individual claim* to free speech but the *public interest* in maintaining freedom that should be weighed against other public goals. Quite clearly under this proposal the First Amendment side of the scales would be more heavily weighted.

The conflict over the meaning of free speech and of civil liberties generally often becomes intense and bitter. Individuals and groups who would restrict civil liberties to defend other values have sometimes been accused of bigotry or fascism by opponents. Those who argue for the primacy and inviolability of civil liberties have often been charged with abetting or sympathizing with the aims of the unpopular groups whose rights they defend. The American Civil Liberties Union has been for many years the leading organization dedicated to a defense of civil liberties against any intrusion or curtailment. Despite the fact that the ACLU numbers among its membership prominent Americans of different political persuasion, and often defends radicals of the right as well as of the left, it was attacked by Senator McCarthy as an instrument of subversion and listed by a committee of the California State Legislature as a subversive organization. More recently several groups, including the California Department Convention of the American Legion, have urged that the ACLU be investigated by a congressional committee. In periods of national insecurity, apparently, the question is even raised of whether civil liberties should be extended to those who argue for the inviolability of civil liberties!

At this point, perhaps we do reach a bedrock democratic principle. While the meaning and limits of civil liberties remain open questions, the principle of complete freedom to debate those questions is absolutely required. Within that framework there will be those who will say, with Judge Learned Hand, that the prohibitions of the First Amendment are "no more than admonitions of moderation." Others will reply, with Justice William O. Douglas, that "the idea that they are no more than that has done more to undermine liberty in this country than any other single force."[17]

CIVIL LIBERTIES VERSUS PUBLIC ORDER

Freedom of assembly is a corollary of freedom of speech. Free speech would be an empty liberty if one could not peaceably assemble an audience to hear the words spoken. But assemblies are not always peaceable, and when people assemble they may, in some circumstances, infringe on the liberties of others—the right not to listen, for example.

Every government must maintain the right and ability to use its police power to maintain public order. Legislatures and courts have real difficulty in finding a test for making exceptions to the right of assembly. Incitement to riot and disturbing the peace are vague criteria for limiting this right.

Does a city government have a right to prohibit any assemblies in streets and parks without a permit from a city director of public safety? The Supreme Court invalidated one such ordinance in Jersey City,

---

[17] William O. Douglas, *The Right of the People* (New York: Doubleday, 1958), p. 45.

New Jersey, on the ground that it gave one man, the director of public safety, the right to determine what assemblies could be held, which actually gave him the arbitrary power to restrict free speech.[18] The question of how far freedom of speech and assembly may be limited by ordinances designed to prevent breaches of the peace, however, has never been clearly resolved in public discussion or in the decisions of the courts.

A particularly difficult problem of free speech and assembly involves ordinances designed to curtail the use of sound trucks and other amplifying devices and the distribution of handbills that are subsequently tossed on the streets and become litter. One of the more interesting cases was *Saia* v. *New York*,[19] which involved the Jehovah's Witnesses —a group often appearing before the Supreme Court. Saia, a minister of this sect, lost his permit to use sound amplifiers because of complaints. Nevertheless, he continued his broadcasts and was soon arrested, tried, and convicted. His appeal eventually went to the Supreme Court.

Justice Douglas again took the purist position and held the law in violation of free speech, but Frankfurter dissented, pleading that uncontrolled noise was an "intrusion into cherished privacy" of people who might like to sit quietly in the park without benefit of Jehovah's Witness doctrine. The case is interesting because it put into clear focus the conflict between the rights of the speaker and the rights of people who do not wish to hear the message. Sound equipment extends free speech to areas in which it may not be welcome and makes the listener a captive, as many citizens who complain about the loud and raucous noises coming from a nearby commercial area have discovered. A logical extension of Douglas' reasoning could, as Justice Jackson put it in his dissent, "render life unbearable."

In a case decided the following year the Court reversed its position and upheld a Trenton, New Jersey, ordinance preventing "loud and raucous" sound trucks from using the public streets.[20] Justice Reed supported the "loud and raucous" criterion as a valid exercise of the police power, although he would not go so far as his colleague Justice Jackson, who would have upheld the right of a city to keep all sound trucks off the public streets. The Court has recognized here a conflict between the right of speech and a counterclaim of privacy. No clear solution has been devised by the courts or by public discussion.

[18] *Hague* v. *Committee for Industrial Organization*, 307 U.S. 496 (1939).
[19] 334 U.S. 558 (1948).
[20] *Kovacs* v. *Cooper*, 336 U.S. 77 (1949).

CIVIL LIBERTIES AND PUBLIC MORALITY

Freedom of speech and freedom of the press may come into conflict also with the exercise of the police power to safeguard the public morality. Here again, the issue is whether the power of government should be applied to behavior or to ideas expressed in speech or writing. If censorship is admitted to be legitimate, the problem is how to construct criteria for determining when words are pornographic or salacious or when they "appeal to a prurient interest." Unfortunately for the courts, they are often called upon to rule on the constitutionality of moral postulates written into the law by self-righteous legislators.

Historically, there seems to have been a distinctive American tendency to write into the law anything and everything that a majority thought to be moral. Many foreign observers of American society, ranging from Alexis de Tocqueville to Gunnar Myrdal, have been interested in our concern with law and our "worship of the Constitution." Myrdal had this to say:

> Americans are accustomed to inscribe their ideals in laws, ranging from their national Constitution to their local traffic rules. American laws thus often contain, in addition to the actually enforced rules (that is "laws " in the ordinary technical meaning of the term), other rules which are not valid or operative but merely express the legislators' hopes, desires, advice or dreams.[21]

An examination of the laws, both statutory and judge-made, of the United States and of many individual states would bear out Myrdal's thesis. In a society that describes itself with the oft-repeated phrase that it is "a government of laws," there has been an almost literal translation of this to mean that there ought to be a law on every possible subject. We find, for example, that for a while Americans sought to prevent the consumption of alcoholic beverages by an amendment to the United States Constitution, that the Constitution of California limits boxing matches to ten rounds, that in Kansas it is against the law to swallow snakes and other reptiles in public, and that a successful suicide is a crime in many places.

Such enactments ordinarily express the moral indignation or the code of ethics of enough lawmakers or a highly vocal pressure group to get the law on the books. They seek to regulate behavior in areas regarded by others as essentially matters of private judgment and con-

---

[21] Gunnar Myrdal, *An American Dilemma* (New York: Harper, 1944), p. 14.

cern. When such moral postulates are enacted into law, they are often inadequately enforced and violations are common and sometimes flagrant. The hip-flask, speakeasy, and organized bootleg crime during the Prohibition Era attested to the fact that many Americans did not regard even the Constitution as a legitimate source of authority over this aspect of their private lives.

The enacting of a code of personal morality into law can also produce some interesting moral hairsplitting, both by legislatures and by the courts. Gambling, in all states but Nevada, is prohibited in many of its forms. But often we find that betting on horses is legal although the slot machine, crap table, and roulette wheel are outlawed and smashed with zeal if discovered. It cannot be gambling that is bad, then, but specific forms of it. There has been much interesting legislative debate attempting to distinguish between the moral implications of the dog race and the horse race; the former is against the law and the latter is legal in many states.

The major burden of moral exegesis, however, falls on the courts. When a legislature passes a law against pornography, the court must decide whether *Lady Chatterley's Lover* is a pornographic book. Courts will be called on to decide what portions of the bare anatomy will appeal to a prurient interest, and the same courts may decide that the latest "sex kitten's" sweater, while covering the flesh but enticingly accentuating what is underneath, is permissible. The courts' dilemma, however, is an expression of the confusions and inconsistencies in the moral attitude of society and of the difficulties of seeking to apply the law to areas of private taste and judgment.

One approach developed by the courts, and adhered to until 1961, was the rule that "prior restraint" of what might appear in print was contrary to the meaning of a free press under the First Amendment.[22] Laws of libel and slander, the Court held, protect people who may have private cause for action after publication. To suppress publication of any material was held to be a basic interference with a free press. For a long time this principle was not seriously challenged. In 1961, however, the Court departed substantially from this principle when it upheld a city ordinance permitting censorship of movies before they could be displayed.[23] The case involved the moving picture *Don Juan*, which the distributors had refused to submit to the censors. Justice Clark wrote the opinion for the five-man majority and, in upholding

[22] *Near* v. *Minnesota*, 283 U.S. 697 (1931).
[23] *Times Film Corporation* v. *City of Chicago*, 81 S. Ct. 391 (1961).

the censorship ordinance, stated: "It has never been held that liberty of speech is absolute."

Chief Justice Warren dissented sharply in a long opinion that went deeply into the history of censorship. He argued: "The decision presents a real danger of eventual censorship for every form of communication be it newspapers, journals, books, magazines, television, radio or public speeches." Concluding his opinion, he made a strong plea for a more rigorous interpretation of the First Amendment: "No more potent force in defeat of [First Amendment] freedom could be designed than censorship. It is a weapon that no minority group, acting through government, should be allowed to wield over any of us."

It is not clear whether the majority of the Court intended the new doctrine to extend to preventing a publication from being issued. Nor is it certain that the case will have the effect of reopening the whole question of prior censorship in the future. The Court has recently held that any censorship by states must guarantee adequate procedural safeguards and must be done quickly.[24] Where censorship is admitted, the problem of ensuring that the criteria employed are not arbitrary is a most difficult one. There are those who argue that it is not insuperable; others insist that no amount of logic and thought can eliminate the essential arbitrariness of the censor's role.

CHURCH AND STATE: A "WALL OF SEPARATION"?

The First Amendment to the Constitution directs Congress to make "no law respecting an establishment of religion, or prohibiting the free exercise thereof." The idea of separation of church and state, moreover, has been expanded into the states by the Supreme Court's use of the Fourteenth Amendment to order states to guarantee their citizens religious freedom. The "exercise" of religion quite consistently has been kept free by the courts but the "establishment" clause has caused difficulty. For example, prior to 1962, students in School District No. 9 in New Hyde Park, New York, were directed to start each school day with a prescribed appeal to God. The official prayer was composed by the State Board of Regents and was recommended to school districts for moral and spiritual training of students. It was a generalized, nonsectarian prayer worded as follows:

24 *Freedman* v. *Maryland*, 33 LW 4211 (1965). No specific procedure was prescribed by the Court, although it pointed out that it had upheld a New York statute that provided an injunctive procedure in *Kingsley Books* v. *Brown*, 354 U.S. 436 (1957).

Almighty God, we acknowledge our dependence upon Thee, and we beg Thy blessings upon us, our parents, our teachers, and our Country.

After School District No. 9 adopted this prayer officially, the parents of ten of the pupils challenged it as an official establishment of religion. After losing their case in the New York courts, the parents appealed to the United States Supreme Court, which ruled in their favor by holding the regents' prayer unconstitutional under the establishment clause of the First Amendment.[25]

The reaction this case was soon to cause was not unanticipated, for in his opinion for the Court, Justice Black said:

It has been argued that to apply the Constitution in such a way as to prohibit state laws respecting an establishment of religious services in public schools is to indicate a hostility toward religion or toward prayer. Nothing, of course, could be more wrong.

Black's fears that the public would incorrectly interpret the decision as an expression of "hostility toward religion" were not unfounded. The reaction was loud, sometimes violent, and often questionable in terms of Christian ethics. "They have taken God out of the schools and put the Nigras in," cried a southern senator, coupling his indignation over the prayer decision with his segregationist views.[26] The kind of vitriolic reaction described in Chapter 1 exploded all over the country. The already beleaguered Court heaped coals on the fire a year later with a further decision in which an eight-man majority held readings from the Bible in public schools to be a "religious exercise" and therefore, unconstitutional.[27] Reaction to these cases had an almost immediate political impact. Several constitutional amendments were proposed to "put God back into the schools" and to curtail the powers of the Supreme Court. The 1964 Republican Party platform contained a plank supporting a constitutional amendment to reverse the Court's decision, and creeping atheism was ranked along with creeping socialism as a political call to arms.

The Supreme Court's action in these cases was another chapter in a long controversy over the role of religion in a democratic society. Much of this controversy has revolved around schools, since, at the time of

[25] *Engle* v. *Vitale,* 370 U.S. 421 (1962).
[26] H. Frank Way, Jr., *Liberty in the Balance* (New York: McGraw-Hill, 1964), p. 78.
[27] *School District* v. *Schempp,* 203 U.S. 374 (1963).

these decisions, some forty states and the District of Columbia had Bible readings and prayers in schools, and ten of these states required such exercises by law.[28]

The controversy over the relationship of church and state is an old one in American history. The provision of the First Amendment preventing the federal government from enacting any law respecting the establishment of religion was a "unique American experiment in the development of religious freedom and the separation of church and state."[29] Before its adoption, the Colonies had engaged in many discriminatory policies against members of certain religious orders, and some Colonies had established churches. Virginia officially recognized the Church of England, while Massachusetts, New Hampshire, and Connecticut were Congregationalist. In the matter of religious tests for holding office, only the constitutions of the states of New York and Virginia excluded religious affiliations from consideration, although New York as a colony had at one time excluded Catholics and Jews from suffrage. In Massachusetts and Maryland, only Christians could be governors; in four other states the governor had to be a Protestant.

Some fundamental questions were resolved by the religious clause of the First Amendment. It clearly ruled out a state-supported church of any kind, and it precluded religious tests for public office or for the exercise of political rights. But if the religious clause restricted Congress, it did not restrict state and local government until 1940, when the Fourteenth Amendment was used to extend the religious clause to the states.[30]

Congress itself does not always heed meticulously the command that it shall make no law affecting the establishment or free exercise of religion. For example, many people feel that the insertion of "under God" in the Pledge of Allegiance has an effect on the free exercise of religion because it inhibits the freedom of those who choose not to worship God. Atheism, it can be argued, is an exercise of religion, albeit a negative one, and should be respected in secular oaths. In a 1957 decision a New York court had ruled that, since the flag salute is not compulsory and no one is compelled to recite it, "under God" is not offensive to the First Amendment.[31] The Supreme Court was petitioned

[28] Way, *op. cit.*, p. 79.

[29] Rocco J. Tresolini, *American Constitutional Law* (New York: Macmillan, 1959), p. 369.

[30] *Cantwell* v. *Connecticut*, 310 U.S. 296 (1940). Art. VI, sec. 3 of the Constitution prohibits religious tests as a qualification for holding public office.

[31] *Lewis* v. *Allen*, 159 N.Y.S. 2d, 807 (1957).

to rule on the issue in 1964, but it declined to do so. Any ruling by the Court, already beleaguered by the religious issue, surely would have caused a considerable controversy. In fact, religion and the pledge of allegiance had twice rocked the Court severely. In 1940, during a period of preparation for war, some children of Jehovah's Witnesses were expelled from school for failing to salute the flag and recite the Pledge of Allegiance. When the case eventually came before the Supreme Court, it upheld the expulsions.[32] There was a sharp reaction to this decision, and in a subsequent case three years later Justices Black, Douglas, and Murphy who had voted with the majority stated that *Gobitis* had been "wrongly decided." They joined Justice Stone, who had dissented, and Justices Rutledge and Jackson, who joined the Court after the decision, to reverse the case.[33] In his opinion for the Court, Justice Jackson stated:

> If there is any fixed star in our Constitutional constellation, it is that no official, high or petty, can prescribe what shall be orthodox in politics, nationalism, religion, or other matters of opinion, or force citizens to confess by word or act their faith therein. If there are any circumstances which permit an exception, they do not now occur to us.

The public outcry which followed this opinion leads to the suspicion that separation of church and state simply cannot be established by the courts. It must be important to the people and must have substantial support of organized religious institutions if it is to become meaningful. Many religious sects do support the doctrine of separation, vigorously defend the Supreme Court's decisions, and oppose efforts to amend the Constitution that come as an aftermath of those decisions.

The "wall of separation," in Jefferson's phrase, is still under construction and there are many areas where it would be hard to build. "In God We Trust" is imprinted on our coins; the Bible is used to administer official oaths; adoption laws are geared to religious beliefs in several states; chaplains are part of our armed forces; and the United States Supreme Court opens its sessions with the court crier intoning "God save these United States and this honorable Court." In short, the Christian religion and its ethical code permeate American life. Other religions are, of course, free to organize without interference, as the Jewish, Buddhist, Mohammedan, and other churches will attest. The

---

[32] *Minersville School District* v. *Gobitis*, 310 U.S. 586 (1940).
[33] *West Virginia State Board of Education* v. *Barnette*, 319 U.S. 624 (1943).

"wall" has not been erected as yet so that it is always clearly visible, although the Supreme Court has generally tried to keep it from being torn down where it does exist.

The question of separation has arisen in several other ways. Again, public schools have often been the focal point of the controversy. In 1947, the Supreme Court held five to four that states may use public funds to transport students to nonprofit and parochial schools.[34] Justice Black's opinion ended with this statement about the "wall": "The First Amendment has erected a wall between church and state. That wall must be kept high and impregnable. We could not approve the slightest breach. New Jersey has not breached it here."

Four justices did think it had been breached, and there has been more adjudication on this matter by the Court. The next year, in *McCollum v. Board of Education*,[35] the Court held unconstitutional a released-time law permitting school buildings to be used for the teaching of various religious ideas while students not wishing to participate in the Catholic, Protestant, or Jewish instruction were not released from their secular instruction. There was some argument over the wall analogy and Justice Jackson, although concurring, felt that clearer legal principles must be provided than those given by Black or the wall might become as "winding as the serpentine wall designed by Mr. Jefferson for the University he founded." There was a good deal of bitterness in some church circles over this decision.

The released-time idea was not completely knocked down by the Court, however. It was upheld in *Zorach v. Clauson*,[36] wherein a New York plan called for released-time religious instruction *away* from the school buildings on written request of the parents. The Zorach decision may have reflected a judicial reaction to the storm of protest generated by the McCollum decision, since 1952 was a time of growing religious influence. On this question, as on others, there is now considerable precedent on both sides of the question of how high the wall should be.

Another major issue involving a continuous debate is the question of whether, and under what conditions, government is entitled to regulate behavior that flows from religious conscience. Religious groups, the Supreme Court long ago asserted, may not engage in activities offensive to public morals.[37] But this doctrine is not as clear as it sounds.

[34] *Everson v. Board of Education*, 330 U.S. 1 (1947).
[35] 333 U.S. 203 (1948).
[36] 343 U.S. 306 (1952).
[37] *Reynolds v. United States*, 98 U.S. 145 (1879).

In 1944, the Court returned a case to lower courts because of its reluctance to interfere with religious freedom.[38] In this case, the issue was whether the defendant acted as leader of a religious sect or as a religious racketeer. The Court could not order him to çease his practices without undertaking to define religion. To do so would make the government, via the judiciary, the arbiter of religious activity.

Conscientious objectors also raise the issue of freedom of religious belief. Every conscription law since World War I has granted exemption from military service to conscientious objectors as defined by statute. From time to time, the courts have had to decide just what a conscientious objector is, and some six thousand men, two thirds of them Jehovah's Witnesses, were held prisoner during World War II because they did not meet the legal definition of objectors.

These and many other questions are raised by the religious clause of the First Amendment. They suggest, above all, that even the most fundamental principles of democratic government cannot be authoritatively defined by a constitution or a corps of official interpreters.

CIVIL RIGHTS AND LIBERTIES: CONTINUING DEBATE

We have examined very sketchily a few of the issues connected with the meaning and limits of the freedoms of speech, press, assembly, and religion. Changing conditions have given rise to new issues and new interpretations. The problem of defending civil liberties is also the problem of defining them. Since they are the liberties that make citizens also rulers, their defense must always be at the top of the agenda of a democratic society. What makes their defense difficult is that limitations on civil liberties are nearly always directed against unpopular and unorthodox ideas. In these circumstances it is easy to lose sight of the basic principle that liberty is always and exclusively for unpopular minorities. Freedom of thought is exclusively for those who think otherwise. There is never any problem of civil liberties for those who think and speak and write the thoughts that are orthodox at the time. *Every* society provides liberties for those who accept its prevailing ideas.

What this suggests is that civil liberties can be protected only when the majority is committed to the principles of liberty and their application to minorities. A similar range of issues arises in connection with the civil rights guaranteed by the other provisions of the Bill of Rights.

[38] *United States* v. *Ballard*, 322 U.S. 78 (1944).

These are dealt with subsequently.[39] In this area the problems generally arise as conflicts between the guarantees of due process of law and demands for more rigorous and efficient law enforcement. It is the person apprehended by the police, the person suspected of having committed a crime, who stands in need of the protections of due process. He is likely to get them only where the law-abiding majority is committed to due process for *all*.

In the American political system, the courts are the final arbiters of the meaning and limits of the Bill of Rights. But cases come to the courts because of the ordinances passed by city councils, laws passed by state legislatures and Congress, and the acts of public officials. Moreover, the courts respond, in the long run, to the political and intellectual climate of the country. No institutions can long protect the civil liberties of a people who become indifferent to them or who come to value other goods more highly.

In 1947, the President's Committee on Civil Rights reported that it was essential to see that "all Americans are familiar with the fundamental rights to which they are entitled and which they owe one another." The report went on to say:

> This is not the case at present. In October, 1946, the National Opinion Research Center at the University of Denver, asked a cross-section of our adult population a series of questions about the Bill of Rights. Only one out of five Americans had a reasonably accurate knowledge of what is in the first 10 Amendments to the Constitution. Completely confused and inaccurate descriptions were offered by 12 per cent. More than a third had heard of the Bill of Rights but could not identify it in any way. Another third had not even heard of it. The NORC also reported that "Even among the best informed people, however—the more privileged, educationally, economically, and occupationally—less than a majority can satisfactorily identify the Bill of Rights." There is no excuse for this kind of ignorance.[40]

In the period since the Committee wrote we have seen the rise and fall of Senator McCarthy and the hunt for subversives, the social and political agonies of the school desegregation decision, congressional combat on civil-rights legislation, and a reassertion of a stronger attitude toward maintaining civil rights and liberties by further extension of the Fourteenth Amendment to bring state laws into line with the Bill of Rights as interpreted by the Supreme Court.

Nothing in this history suggests that the issues have been resolved or

[39] See Chap. 16.
[40] President's Committee on Civil Rights, *To Secure These Rights* (Washington, D.C.: Government Printing Office, 1947), pp. 134-35.

the threats to civil rights and liberties eliminated. Nor is it likely that they ever will be. Even the continuation of the controversy and the struggle, however, will depend on the existence of a public proud of its rights and liberties and alert to their abuse. To live in a democratic society is to share in responsibility for the continuing interpretation and enactment of its basic principles. In this sense, the Constitution was not written and adopted in 1789; it is being "written" and enacted by every generation of democratic citizens.

Judicial Supremacy: Historical Development

The preceding sections of this chapter have dealt with many aspects of the Supreme Court's role in interpreting the Constitution. In this section, we will look more closely at the political problems caused by the principle of judicial supremacy. As we have seen, the Supreme Court, by the very definition of its duties, cannot avoid controversy. Sometimes the Court has dodged important controversial issues, but not often. Whether the Court is slowing the momentum of the other branches or units of government or whether it is plunging them into unsought problems, the Court is always a focal point of controversy.

JUDICIAL POWER: BRAKE OR ACCELERATOR?

On January 6, 1937, President Franklin Roosevelt declared to Congress, "The judicial branch also is asked by the people to do its part in making democracy work." When President Roosevelt made this statement, he was at the crest of his popularity, having been elected by the greatest electoral vote in history some two months previously. The "nine old men" on the Supreme Court had been hostile to New Deal legislation designed to pull the United States out of a grinding economic depression. More than this, however, the President was of the opinion that the Court was not merely interpreting the Constitution but imposing outmoded economic theories on the whole society because of a collective personal hostility toward his program. Justification of his charge was to be found in the written opinions of Supreme Court justices themselves. Justice Holmes became known as the "great dissenter" over just such issues, and he undoubtedly would have agreed with the caustic dissent of Justice Stone when he said, "it is difficult to imagine any grounds other than our own economic predilections" for holding a New York minimum wage law invalid.[41]

41 *Morehead* v. *New York*, 298 U.S. 587 (1936).

President Roosevelt's challenge to the Court's power to wreck the New Deal took the form of presenting Congress with an imaginative plan to change the structure of the Supreme Court.[42] His proposal did not directly challenge the Court's power to review legislation, but it would have given him the opportunity to appoint enough justices sympathetic to his program to ensure its judicial approval.

Roosevelt lost this issue but ultimately won his case. The Court, no doubt aware of widespread hostility to its political and economic doctrines, imposed upon itself a new self-restraint and began to look more favorably at social legislation. Also, time inevitably worked to the President's advantage, and he was able to appoint justices more sympathetic to his programs.

The battle over the judiciary in the thirties involved different issues and different parties than the conflict in the sixties. Some thirty years ago, political commentators often used the then-apt phrase *judicial lag* to describe the conservatism of the Supreme Court. Now the problem is reversed; the Court, according to its critics, no longer lags but races ahead toward a more egalitarian and liberal society. Ironically, the power and prestige of the Supreme Court came to fruition during the terms of the long-tenured and conservative Chief Justices John Marshall (1801–1835) and Roger B. Taney (1836–1864). When the Court eventually made its transition from a bulwark of conservatism to an active champion of liberal democracy, the power and prestige of the Court were so deeply rooted in our system of government that it was able successfully to resist serious threat, even though it became the center of stormy controversy. It also should be noted that the Supreme Court has generally contained sharply divided viewpoints even though the majority may be solidly conservative or liberal.

The present Supreme Court has its opposing forces of liberals and conservatives, which have been quite closely balanced. The current liberal majority is by no means an overwhelming one, and the conservatives are quite articulate in expressing their views. Many of the cases involving states' rights, civil rights, and civil liberties have raised sharp disagreement among the justices. The old issue of subjective jurisprudence, which bothered Justice Stone, has risen again, but this time, it is the conservative side of the Court that objects. In a recent

[42] Roosevelt's proposal would have allowed him to appoint an additional justice to the Court when any member of the Court reached the retirement age of seventy whether or not the justice retired. This would have given Roosevelt six appointments and the New Deal a clear track ahead.

decision requiring reapportionment of state legislative districts, Justice Stewart, in dissent, had this to say:

> The Court's draconian pronouncement, which makes unconstitutional the legislatures of most of the states, finds no support in the words of the Constitution, in any prior decision of this Court, or in the 175 year political history of our Federal Union. With all respect, I am convinced these decisions mark a long step backward into that unhappy era when a majority of this Court were thought by many to have convinced themselves and each other that the demands of the Constitution were to be measured not by what it says, but by their own notions of wise political theory.[43]

The problem Justice Stewart has raised takes us back again to the role of the Supreme Court in a democratic society. If we use this case as an example to put the power of the Court in juxtaposition with the issue before it—in this instance whether urban votes should count as much as rural votes in state legislatures—what should the Court do? Is there an injustice in current practice incompatible with democratic concepts of equality? Should the Court let other tribunals decide the issue? Whatever it does, there will be a reaction, for the very nature of the decision—in both its moral and its power context—raises serious questions.

JUDICIAL SUPREMACY: A POLITICAL DILEMMA

The course of Court decisions has placed both liberals and conservatives in an awkward position. When liberals react favorably to the Court's recent decisions, they implicitly abandon their dedication to majority rule and acknowledge the essentially conservative authority of the judiciary to declare the law. When conservatives react negatively, they abandon their view that a powerful judiciary is essential for the preservation of traditional values. President Roosevelt's attempt to modify the Supreme Court to ensure acceptance of his liberal economic programs is not much different from the conservatives' attempt to restore states' rights by limiting jurisdiction of the Court, either by statute or by constitutional amendment.

Criticism of the judiciary is always most intense when the courts decide a sensitive public issue. Declaring tradition illegal and demanding change, as the courts have done in recent civil rights, civil liberties, and reapportionment decisions, not only makes new laws but requires an

[43] *Lucas* v. *Forty-Fourth Assembly of Colorado*, 377 U.S. 713 (1964).

adjustment in public morality. Judicial supremacy, as we shall see more thoroughly in Chapter 16, makes the Court an oracle of public morality. It is when moral declarations become frozen into legal authority that judicial supremacy becomes bothersome to many observers. Morris R. Cohen stated that it is "characteristic of the American system to make judges' view of public morality the law of the land." He went on to say that while liberals assumed that individual conscience should be the seat of judgment on the morality of the law, the development of judicial supremacy

> has changed this moral right of the people into a legal right of the judiciary. From the anarchy that would follow if every individual felt free to disobey what seemed to him an unjust law, we have been saved by a doctrine of judicial absolutism or infallibility. Presumably whatever a majority of the Supreme Court decides not only is the law but is also the original intention of the people, and conforms to the eternal principles of justice, or at any rate to the principles recognized by Anglo-Saxons since they roamed in the German forests.[44]

Mr. Cohen's position is well taken, but there remains the difficult problem of what to do when the public does not address itself to crucial moral questions. Former Supreme Court Justice Goldberg rose to this question in arguing that the attacks on the Court are based on a series of myths. He dispelled the first "myth" of usurpation by the Court of the power of judicial review by arguing that such power is inherent in a written constitution. He then took up the "myth" that the Court is incompatible with democratic government:

> The next great myth is that, even though judicial review was intended and is sanctioned, it is, nevertheless, undemocratic and, therefore, to be regarded with alert suspicion and its exercise to be dimly viewed. The argument has an obvious, albeit superficial, appeal. The justices are appointed for life and not elected by the people for limited terms, as the President and Congress are. The latter, so the argument goes, being representative of the popular will, should have their way —otherwise democracy will be forsaken; a guardianship, however benevolent, negates popular government.
>
> This reasoning, however, overlooks the first facts about our Constitution—that its source is the people and that, as Dean Roscoe Pound once said, it is meant to restrain "not individuals alone, but whole people." It is they who mandated that the individual be protected and safeguarded in his constitutional rights even against the

[44] Morris R. Cohen, *American Thought: A Critical Sketch* (New York: Free Press, 1954), pp. 143-44.

popular will of the moment as voiced by the legislature or the executive. Our courts were entrusted with the responsibility of judicial
review, in large part, to protect individuals and minorities in their
fundamental rights against abridgement by both government and majorities.[45]

Implicit in former Justice Goldberg's defense of the Supreme Court
is a recognition that moral issues cannot be ignored and that judicial
power must be used to resolve them if the other branches of government,
or the states, ignore them. The Court itself has often been torn over
the choice between self-restraint and self-assertion. The very nature of
a written Constitution and a federal system puts the judiciary in a
position of great potential power. And, as Fred Rodell, an authority
on the courts, puts it, an overabundance of self-restraint has as many,
if not more, adverse effects in a government structured on checks and
balances. He says:

> More significantly, the argument for judicial self-restraint on the
> grounds of vulnerability is, in essence, circular and self-defeating.
> What it adds up to is: Let us not use our power lest we lose our
> power. But power let go by default might as well be lost. What the
> argument neglects to take into account—and what Franklin Roosevelt
> overlooked when he proposed his Court-packing plan—is the immense
> prestige of the Court as an institution. Regardless of popular, and
> passing, indignation at this or that decision, its prestige is bound to
> protect it from any but minor incursions on its authority.
> At any rate, it is clear that the new majority of the Warren Court
> will have none of this timidity. They see nothing to be gained and
> much to be lost in declining to use the power which no one—save
> a few crackpots—denies is theirs. Even in the unlikely event that a
> constitutional amendment or Congressional action should reverse or
> temper the more extreme parts of the recent reapportionment rulings,
> there would still remain a substantial achievement in bringing about
> a more truly representative government—something that would never
> have happened if the advice of the self-restrainers had been heeded.[46]

There is little question that the judiciary is well established in the
American political system. But its final authority of interpretation of
the Constitution is potentially hazardous. Perhaps a system that permits
nine men to write thoughtful opinions for perusal by all who care to read
them has some advantages. But a court that has final authority, and uses

[45] Arthur J. Goldberg, "The Court Sits in the Center of the Storm," *New York
Times Magazine*, November 8, 1964, p. 30.
[46] Fred Rodell, "The Warren Court Stands Its Ground," *New York Times
Magazine*, September 27, 1964, p. 121.

it aggressively, to defend the rights and liberties of minorities may even in the long run weaken the sources of popular support and responsibility for the preservation of freedom. The liberal is likely to be haunted by the fear that liberty is, finally, only safe in the keeping of citizens who believe in it.

Conservatives, when they are consistent, are likely to agree with Peter Viereck that the ultimate question is whether we are to be ruled by men in black robes (the justices) or men in white sheets (the members of such bigoted organizations as the Ku Klux Klan). The old issues that divided liberal and conservative reassert themselves. Judicial supremacy, like the other articles of American constitutionalism, turns out to be unfinished business on the agenda of democratic discussion.

The Living Constitution

At this point, we come to some seemingly reasonable conclusions from the historical development of constitutional principles. First, there is no fixed consensus, nor is there likely to be, on what these principles mean.

Second, while conservatives protest the course of events, the interpretation of these constitutional principles shows a definite trend toward majoritarian democracy—a trend that probably will not be sidetracked.

Third, there is irony in the fact that there is no consistent pattern of liberal and conservative views of these principles. Liberals, inconsistently but happily, watch a conservative instrument, the Supreme Court, demand civil rights, liberties, and equality for all citizens. Conservatives, on the other hand, become vocal champions of the Jeffersonian doctrines of states' rights, minimum government, and the rights of popular majorities.

Fourth, the Constitution and its principles cannot be viewed as a description of political reality. There are many other forces and institutions to be looked into before the political system emerges with any degree of clarity.

THE IDEOLOGICAL CLIMATE OF
AMERICAN POLITICS

. . . which examines the way in which the absence of ideological differences in American politics has the effect of clothing the constitutional skeleton in the flesh of broker rule.

Ideologies (related clusters of attitudes toward issues of public policy) are the means by which **Issue Conflicts** can be presented to voters for meaningful choice. They need not be dogmatic or rigid; in American politics the basic conflict is often described as right wing–left wing, Republican-Democratic, *conservative-liberal* (italics are used to distinguish these as ideological positions from their meaning as philosophical theories). They are the means of organizing the competitive politics on which democracy depends. **The Ingredients of Liberal and Conservative Ideology** are policy positions on both domestic and foreign-policy issues.

In the area of **Domestic Policy, Economic Liberalism** accepts the reforms of the New Deal and subsequent welfare state, regulatory, and tax programs that use the power of the federal government to extend opportunities to the underprivileged; **Economic Conservativism** sees past increases in governmental power as necessary evils, at best, and opposes further increases in the name of individual initiative and self-reliance. There tends to be little of explicit ideology in the attitudes of either *liberals* or *conservatives*: pragmatic, piecemeal responses to specific problems are the common *liberal* posture; *conservatives* reply, "Not so fast."

In the area of **Foreign Policy** the distinction is less clear-cut, largely for historical reasons. But in general terms the *liberal* position inclines to accept the possibilities of coexistence and to rely on and favor strengthening the United Nations; the *conservative* position looks to a firmer military stand against communism and greater reliance on American strength and independence. These differences are muted, however, by the bipartisan consensus in which American foreign policy operates.

The ideological conflict between *liberalism* and *conservatism* has its roots in the **Historical Background** of industrial society. In the United States the issue is complicated and confused by the role played by the concept of **Laissez Faire** ("to let alone"; no government interference in economic affairs), to which both *liberals* and *conservatives* have professed loyalty. Confusion has resulted from the fact that the phrase was used in nineteenth-century *liberal* defense of individualism in an agrarian setting, which pitted **Man Against Nature**; it is also used by *conservatives* to defend a system of industrial competition that pits **Man Against Man** and in which the winners acquire power over others. Confronted with an interdependent corporate economy, *liberal* loyalites shifted **From Laissez Faire to the Welfare State.** But, unlike the welfare state in the European democracies, American *liberals* developed pragmatic programs that were specific responses to acute problems and to the pressures of organized groups and blocs of voters. The charge of "creeping socialism" fails to recognize that there was more pragmatism and brokerage than ideology in these programs; the result has been an irrelevant dialogue in which the *conservatives* win the battle of rhetoric while *liberals* win nonideological victories through political maneuver. The confusing result of this historical background is that

Political Competition tends not to be based on **Ideological Configurations.** While the Republican Party is generally supported by *conservatives* and the Democratic Party by *liberals*, the parties, with rare exceptions, "mastered Same-Speak years ago" as they moved to the center and seemed to embrace an American "consensus ideology" in which brokerage politics has free play. Within this framework it is assumed that, in the area of domestic concerns, **Reasonable Men** will participate in reaching **Sensible Bargains.** Thus, negotiation, consensus, and artful compromise come to be accepted as the "legislative way of life." Both economic *liberals* and economic *conservatives* find that ideological arguments are irrelevant at the bargaining table; they tend, instead, to identify themselves with different coalitions of interest groups. The political strength of the *liberal's* group support is countered by the free-enterprise rhetoric supporting the *conservative's* groups. Thus, in the environment of **Brokerage Politics** there is little room for meaningful **Political Dissent.** The **Moral American,** finding himself a **Political Outcast,** has increasingly taken to the streets in frustration and protest. The basic question is whether the regular processes of the political system can be made to find room for him.

Democracy is a competitive political system in which competing leaders and organizations define the alternatives in such a way that the public can participate in the decision-making process.

E. E. SCHATTSCHNEIDER

Chapter Eight

THE IDEOLOGICAL CLIMATE OF AMERICAN POLITICS

THE CONSTITUTION has proved a dynamic, flexible framework for American politics. Within its broad outlines conflicting models of democracy have competed for dominance. But the actual operation of a political system always reflects more than constitutional and philosophical factors. Every political system will reflect the cultural, ideological, and psychological climate in which it operates. For this reason the political behavior we describe as democratic is only likely to occur in a society whose culture disposes citizens to play the required roles. Conversely, the actual politics of any people will reflect its cultural attitudes, personality characteristics, and life styles. Which of the democratic models American politics will most nearly approximate will depend on these underlying cultural characteristics. In an earlier chapter the growth of mass society and the political attitudes and roles associated with it were described. In the current chapter we examine the typical behavior of Americans as they engage in the process of making decisions on public issues within the constitutional framework.

Issue Conflict and Ideology in American Politics

Political competition, the hallmark of democratic policy-making, has somehow to be organized. The alternatives must be narrowed down—to two in a two-party system—when they are presented to the electorate for choice. Since there are many specific issues of public policy, the people are necessarily limited to choosing between broad, general directions of policy. These considerations put the importance of political ideology into focus. *Ideology*, as we are using the term here, refers to a related cluster of attitudes on questions of public policy. An ideology "equips the individual to perceive the connectedness of many superficially diverse events and relate them to one another coherently."[1] Similarly, ideology permits political parties to present to voters competing packages of specific proposals coherent enough to make meaningful electoral choice possible. We often describe these competing ideologies as Republican and Democratic, right wing and left wing, "liberal" and "conservative."

THE INGREDIENTS OF LIBERAL AND CONSERVATIVE IDEOLOGY

Until now we have been using the words liberal and conservative to describe basic philosophies of democracy and the attitudes toward political processes and institutions that follow from them. The primary concern of such theories is the question of *how* policies are to be formulated. But this is not the only—perhaps not even the most common—usage of the terms. In common parlance *liberal* and *conservative* most often refer to positions people take on the question of *what* policies should be adopted.[2]

[1] Angus Campbell and others, *The American Voter* (New York: Wiley, 1960), Chap. 8.

[2] To distinguish these two uses of the terms, we put *liberal* and *conservative* in italics when they refer to ideological or policy positions. At the same time, the philosophical and ideological expressions of liberalism and of conservatism have some common roots, as subsequent discussion will make clear.

Policy *liberals* and *conservatives* have divided over both domestic and foreign policy issues. Attitudes tend to fall into patterns on these questions although they are not always connected. A particular person may be a *liberal* on foreign-policy questions and a *conservative* on domestic issues. The factors that make this possible will become apparent as we look more closely at the common meaning and content of the terms *liberal* and *conservative* in these policy areas.

Economic Liberalism and Conservatism. The central issue here is the question of the extent and limits of the role of government in the economic and social life of the nation. On the one side are the self-professed *liberals* who accept the economic reforms of the New Deal, the Fair Deal, the New Frontier, and the Great Society, and who would push ahead cautiously in enlarging the power of the federal government to solve current problems. The policy *liberal* regards the reforms of the past—including social security, unemployment compensation, the federal reserve system, business and public utility regulation, federal power and regional development programs, and national government responsibility for maintaining high levels of employment—not as necessary evils but as positive goods. He justifies them as means of enlarging the opportunities and extending the freedom of groups who had been historically deprived and disadvantaged. And he looks to government, especially to the federal government, for the initiative in meeting such current problems as civil rights, educational opportunity, rates of economic growth, the amelioration of poverty, protection against the high medical costs of the aged, mass transportation problems in urban areas, and urban blight.

Democratic Senator Eugene McCarthy, a leading contemporary *liberal* argues that modern liberalism is responsive to issues as they arise and is not a doctrinaire ideology. He says:

> The liberal movement in this century is identified and associated with the New Deal of the first two Roosevelt Administrations. The New Deal involved political and economic changes which were a response to urgent practical demands, rather than the fulfillment or advancement of an ideology or a doctrinaire theory of political, economic and social organization.
>
> Roosevelt's program provided for the pooling of social risks, as in the case of Social Security, and the pooling of economic risks, as in the case of the Federal Deposit Insurance program. It included such projects as the Tennessee Valley Authority and the hydro-electric developments in the Far West. In each case, the decision was based

on practical considerations—the development and distribution of power, for example, or the related problems of navigation and flood control—rather than on an ideological demand for social ownership or collectivization.[3]

This practical and optimistic *liberalism* contrasts with the *conservative* response to similar economic issues. The policy *conservative* regards the increase in the power and functions of the federal government over the past several decades as a necessary evil, at best. In the main, he accepts them, but reluctantly and sadly. He sees the increasing size and power of a federal bureaucracy as limiting the initiative, self-reliance, and freedom of individuals. He is inclined to regard the increasing national debt as dangerous and to believe that governmental expenditures are unproductive as such and can be justified only where they are used to expand the opportunities for private investment. While the *liberal* sees little danger in the growth of governmental bureaucracy, his *conservative* counterpart is similarly unconcerned about a burgeoning corporate bureaucracy. Andrew Hacker has described the attitudes of *conservatives* on these and related questions in the following way:

> Unions, for example, symbolize for him the mass man, led either by "crooks" (Hoffa) or "Socialists" (Reuther). The trade unionist demands across-the-board raises for everyone in a particular job classification regardless of a person's competence or contribution to productivity. Conservatives identify with management, and visualize their own promotions and raises as due to their unique qualifications. It is galling to see hoards of blue-collar workers coming up in the world *en masse.*
>
> By the same token, the political power of the unions appears threatening, for it is clear that labor wishes to tax hard-working citizens so as to establish a welfare state for those unwilling to provide for themselves. The resentment against taxes is based on the feeling that this money ends up supporting the indolent (through unemployment compensation), the improvident (with public housing and medical care) and the immoral (by aid to unmarried mothers and illegitimate children). The conservative in America today sees himself beleaguered by powerful and insolent groups hoping to use government as an instrument to tax and destroy.[4]

As Hacker points out, the *conservative's* stand on the issue of labor reflects an ideological identification with corporate management, the

Magazine, September 1, 1963, p. 8.

[3] Eugene J. McCarthy, "The Liberal: What He Is and Isn't," *New York Times* [4] Andrew Hacker, "Inquiry into the New Conservatism," *New York Times Magazine,* February 16, 1964, p. 7.

new "better sort," which in turn has roots in the philosophical conservative's acceptance of social hierarchy. In the same way the *liberal's* support for labor expresses an ideological identification with those nearer the bottom of the socioeconomic ladder, which has its roots in the philosophical liberal's egalitarian beliefs.

Basically, however, Senator Eugene McCarthy's argument that there is little of either ideology or philosophy, at least explicitly, in the attitudes of *liberals* applies to *conservatives* as well. Pragmatic, piecemeal efforts to ameliorate specific problems are the common *liberal* posture; *conservatives* tend to reply, "Not so fast."

Foreign Policy: Liberal and Conservative. In the area of foreign policy, the effort to distinguish a *liberal* and a *conservative* position is more difficult, largely for reasons rooted in the historical development of the American role in world affairs.

From the first administration of George Washington until the end of World War II, when the United States became a member of the United Nations, American foreign policy was basically founded on the avoidance of foreign entanglements. *Splendid isolation* was a term invoked to describe American policy, and it was reasonably descriptive of the *conservative* position on foreign affairs. There were, of course, such modifications as the Monroe Doctrine, which put the United States on the side of hemispheric protection from foreign intervention. The history of the Monroe Doctrine illustrates the difficulty of describing foreign policy in ideological terms. Theodore Roosevelt, a progressive in domestic affairs, developed big-stick diplomacy in his interpretation of the Doctrine; Franklin Roosevelt reversed this position with his good-neighbor policy; under the Eisenhower administration new forms of meddling in the internal affairs of Latin American countries were developed through the activities of the CIA.; President Kennedy's Alliance for Progress re-emphasized the good-neighbor approach but was accompanied by a continuation of undercover involvement in hemispheric regimes; President Johnson's intervention in the Dominican Republic in 1965 seemed to herald a return, under modern conditions, to the first Roosevelt's policies of intervention. It is difficult to discern here any consistent relationship between the foreign and domestic policies of Presidents whom we would label *liberal* and *conservative*.

Aside from hemispheric protection, however, isolation has been generally described as the historic *conservative* position, particularly between World Wars I and II when the United States refused to join the

League of Nations. The term applied primarily to political involvement, since *conservatives* tended to support the expansion of American commercial interests all over the world. Competition for markets and commodities occasionally led the business community to call for governmental assistance, and the *conservatives* modified their isolationist views to include the idea that "the flag follows business." In some instances striking inconsistencies developed from the nation's refusal to involve itself in international politics while, at the same time, it protected economic adventures.

Following World War I, *liberal* and *conservative* ideologies on foreign affairs were more clearly developed. President Wilson expounded involvement in foreign affairs in league with all other nations. His hopes of putting the United States into the League of Nations became part of the *liberal* credo but were dashed by the *conservative* refusal to ratify America's entry. A series of little wars leading up to World War II widened the breach. Ethiopia and Spain were to be a testing ground for fascist might, Manchuria for the Japanese military machine. In this setting *liberals* tended to argue for policies of intervention to halt the growth of fascism; *conservatives* favored a policy of isolation and neutrality to avoid American involvement in the war. In the hands of President Roosevelt the nation's posture shifted gradually to the support of our eventual allies as Hitler's armies swept across France and posed an imminent threat to Great Britain.

The development of the Cold War after World War II posed new problems for American policy and settled finally the issue of isolationism. The United States emerged as one of the world's two great powers, locked in bipolar conflict with the Soviet Union and its allies. The United States reacted with a vigorous assertion of its leadership of the "free world." Foreign military and economic aid and political and military alliances were forged as means of countering communist expansion. These policies were developed with bipartisan support under the maxim that "politics stops at the water's edge." Initiated under President Truman, they have been continued in the administrations of Eisenhower, Kennedy, and Johnson.

In these circumstances it is difficult to distinguish foreign-policy positions along *liberal* and *conservative* lines. In opposition, *liberals* criticized the "brinkmanship" of President Eisenhower and Secretary of State Dulles; in power, Kennedy went to the very edge of the nuclear brink in Cuba. President Johnson, domestic *liberal*, escalated American military involvement in South Vietnam and intervened unilaterally in the Dominican Republic. His foreign policies in 1965 won their strongest support from *conservatives*, their sharpest criticism from *liberals*.

Isolation, we have said, is a dead issue. The question that has emerged revolves around the character of American involvement. Within this context it is still possible to distinguish a basic difference between *liberal* and *conservative* positions. The *liberal* is inclined to see the struggle with communism as primarily ideological, political, and economic; the *conservative* as primarily military. The *liberal* would adopt a limited view of American capabilities in the world, directing major attention to the strengthening of democratic regimes wherever possible and relying more heavily on the United Nations and other forms of multilateral alliances. The *conservative* is more likely to put his trust in American military power and the provision of military support for anticommunist governments. The *liberal* contemplates coexistence with communist regimes and sees Titoism as the most effective available alternative in some areas of the world. The *conservative* is more inclined to see communism as a monolithic evil to be opposed everywhere. In oversimplified terms, peace becomes the *liberal* policy; defeat of communism the *conservative* policy.

This division, however, is blurred both in Congress and in national politics generally by the bipartisan consensus within which foreign policy operates. Debate on American foreign policy is discouraged, and when it occurs, it is outside the framework of party controversy in which domestic policies are formulated. Unlike economic policies, the issues themselves do not easily fit into the brokerage process. The result is an uneasy truce between policy *liberals* and *conservatives* to keep foreign affairs out of the arena of public debate. Policy differences, rooted in the perspectives of *liberals* and *conservatives*, find no clear political expression.

The Historical Background of American Ideology

Ideological *liberalism* and *conservatism* have their roots in the social and economic history of industrial society. At the same time this historical background is the source of contemporary ideological confusion. The problems involved in an effort to understand the historical context of modern policy conflicts are complex and difficult.

Perhaps the dominant theme in the American political tradition is expressed in the idea of *laissez faire*. In no other nation in the world has this idea had the force and the persistence it has had in American political folklore. It has played a critical role in American history, yet it has always been an ambiguous symbol. What areas of individual life are to be let alone? In what circumstances is governmental intervention and control justified? The answers to these questions have been quite different in different historical periods. The term itself has been claimed by those who call themselves *conservatives* and by self-professed *liberals*. A brief review of the evolution of the idea of *laissez faire* might help us to understand current conflicts over policy and to see more clearly the relation between philosophical and policy liberalism and conservatism.

LAISSEZ FAIRE: MAN AGAINST NATURE OR MAN AGAINST MAN?

The ideal that came to dominate American life in the period from the enactment of the Constitution to the Civil War reflected the aspirations and the attitudes of the yeoman farmer and the independent merchant of the frontier. The ideal was expressed in the view of the Jeffersonians that the least government is the best government. The belief that individuals should be as free as possible from governmental restraints extended from civil liberties into economic pursuits. The Jeffersonian concept of *laissez faire* was built on the view that the agrarian life on the frontier was uniquely favorable to the development of individual independence and self-reliance. The economic conditions of the day seemed to support this view. At the time of the adoption of the Constitution more than 95 per cent of the population lived on farms or in small towns. The typical farmer owned his own land or expected to acquire it and he worked it with the aid of his family. Wealth was fairly equally divided with no extremes of riches or poverty. Commerce was conducted by small merchants. It was, in short, an entrepreneurial system of individual ownership, small farms, and shopkeepers.

Given these conditions Jeffersonians could well argue that the individual would have the best opportunity to develop his potential where he was left to his own devices. Even more importantly, the promise of these conditions was a society organized to prevent any man from acquiring economic power over the lives of others. On the frontier man would pit his individual talents, energies, and creativity against nature. The degree of his success would have no bearing on the opportunities available to other men. It is important to understand that the early American ideology of *laissez faire* was a doctrine of men against nature rather than a system of competition between men for wealth and power. Competition with the forces of nature, then, challenged man to the development of his individual talents and provided favorable circumstances for the fullest development of his individual personality.[5]

The Jeffersonian argument for *laissez faire* was not doctrinaire. Government was looked upon as a useful device for promoting the common interests of common men; it was to be feared and resisted when it promoted the interests of a monied or social aristocrary. Thus, canal and road building were generally looked upon as legitimate functions of the national government, and education was seen as a desirable obligation for state and local governments.

The philosophical conservatives were not enamored of weak government for obvious reasons. Government must be responsible for looking after all of the interests in society as well as all of its social classes. In Hamilton's economic programs conservatives found the means for protecting the economic interests of the wealthy from the rabble at the same time that wealth was put in the service of building national power and prestige. Thus, paradoxically in the light of later developments, philosophical conservatives were advocates in the early years of a strong, centralized, paternalistic government; liberals, of weak, decentralized government with minimal powers.

How are we to explain this apparent paradox? Are modern *liberals* and *conservatives* inconsistent? To answer these questions we must look to a quite different interpretation of *laissez faire*, which developed after the Civil War. This is the ideology of business enterprise, developed to justify a rapidly developing system of industrialism built on free enterprise and competition. Like the earlier agrarian doctrine of *laissez faire*, it calls for government to leave economic activity to private ownership and discretion. But in two fundamental ways it differs from the older Jeffersonian ideas. It was designed, in the first place, to justify a system in which business enterprises struggled with one another for dominance rather than a struggle of man against nature. The stakes were wealth and power and one man's gains were another man's losses. Competition was ruthless with few holds barred. It was no game for weaklings.

A second and more fundamental difference is to be found in the

[5] See Henry Bamford Parkes, *The American Experience* (New York: Knopf, 1947).

different assumptions about human nature underlying *liberal* and *conservative* theories of *laissez faire*. As a defense of industrial capitalism, *laissez faire* is rooted in the view that man is egocentric and materialistic: man, it is held, will strive for superiority or success if there is something in it for him. Without the motivation of economic gain he will fail to produce as much private wealth and, consequently, public benefit. Thus, government should stay out of economic activity in order to give free reign to all of man's egocentric desires. An "unseen hand," in Adam Smith's words, will guide economic activity in such a way that private vices will be automatically translated into public virtues. Egoism, with its natural allies of ambition, avarice, and acquisitiveness, is the key, then, to this view of human nature. And it is this view that has come to underlie the modern defense of *laissez faire*. Harry K. Girvetz has reminded us that, although intellectuals reject egoism as an acceptable basis for evaluating human behavior,

> . . . it is equally apparent that egoism continues to survive as the accepted theory of motivation among people in general and practical men of affairs in particular. We are likely to be told that everyone asks the question, "What's in it for me?" except a few "starry-eyed idealists," and even they, the "realist" sagely assures us, have their ax to grind if we only knew.[6]

Egoism is a substantially different view of man than that held by Jeffersonian liberals. Consequently, the modern doctrine or *laissez faire* cannot be interpreted as a logical extension of the Jeffersonian position. Whereas eighteenth-century liberals wanted to let man alone so he could be free to conduct his life in an unencumbered and rational way, the modern *conservative* wants him to be let alone so he will be motivated to compete, to prove his worth in the struggle for status and wealth, and, in the process, to create a maximum supply of goods in the economy.

The economic evolution of the United States has been one of a continuous shift from an agrarian, small business, and entrepreneurial society to a large mass society geared to consumption of standardized goods produced by gigantic corporations. Individuals now find themselves increasingly in the employ of one of these large organizations, and the "organization man" has replaced the private owner of a small farm or business. Under these conditions private enterprise is dominated

---

[6] Harry K. Girvetz, *The Evolution of Liberalism* (New York: Collier Books, 1963), p. 34.

by corporations that are, in effect, private governments. Jeffersonian liberals hoped that private economic power could be eliminated in an agrarian utopia. Confronted with its seemingly ineradicable presence, the philosophical liberal must insist that it be curbed or controlled. The test for the liberal is to find a means to eliminate economic power or to subordinate it to a public interest defined by the political decisions of free and equal citizens.

Historically, philosophical liberals were led to seek to destroy monopolistic power through the antitrust acts and to regulate and control it when it could not be eliminated. Faced with the problems of economic power, unemployment, and poverty, they turned to such modern *liberal* programs as welfare measures, public power development, currency control, utility regulation, and regional development programs. *Laissez faire* ceases to be legitimate, the liberal argues, when its practical result is human misery or when it becomes irresponsible to majority control in the public interest.

The modern *conservative* ideology of *laissez faire* is also incompatible with philosophical conservatism. While the philosophical conservative would agree that the egoistic drives of avarice and ambition are an ineradicable part of man's nature, he would insist that they be harnessed and controlled by social institutions. An economic system that is anti-traditional and that encourages the expression of human vices is profoundly unconservative in a philosophical sense.

While philosophical conservatives are unable, consistenly, to defend *laissez faire*, they have good reason for criticizing the development of the *liberal* welfare state. They distrust the concentration of power, especially its concentration in the hands of self-interested majorities. They are likely to prefer a system that diffuses economic power and establishes a system of economic checks and balances, with labor, consumers, and owners exercising countervailing power over one another and with government being entrusted to maintain the rules of the game. Sometimes they have tended to see in the new managerial elite of the large corporations a socially responsible and restrained aristocracy.[7]

Similarly, philosophical conservatives will resent the redistribution of wealth and the leveling tendencies inherent in *liberal* policies of taxation and public expenditure. Such policies penalize ability and industry, reward indolence, and thus destroy incentive. Above all, conservatives

[7] See, for example, the editors of *Fortune* in collaboration with Russell W. Davenport, *U.S.A.: The Permanent Revolution* (New York: Prentice-Hall, 1951).

will be concerned about the collectivistic tendencies that produce a powerful and power-hungry public bureaucracy whose control over individuals threatens to become total.

FROM LAISSEZ FAIRE TO THE WELFARE STATE

As we have already noted, issue-oriented *liberalism* in the United States has been a pragmatic, nonideological response to glaring and unavoidable problems demanding action. The New Deal and its subsequent extensions have been a series of specific responses to acute problems. The New Deal's legislative monument to the welfare state, the Social Security Act, was not enacted, as were many such programs in Europe, as a result of consciously articulated radical theory. This measure became law in response to a breakdown in the economic system. The Act, like most American laws, was forged out of the pushing and hauling of interest groups and amended to minimize or neutralize potential opposition. The law alleviated the economic problems but by no means solved them. Subsequent amendments have been designed to cope with new circumstances or to satisfy the demands of interest groups or blocs of voters. The process can perhaps best be characterized as *action on* rather than broad efforts at *solution of* economic problems.

European observers of the American political process have been quick to understand its pragmatic quality. From the European point of view our social security and welfare programs cannot accurately be called a welfare state.[8] The European welfare state is based on the provision of a statutory floor under income below which no person is allowed to fall. Government guarantees a certain minimum standard of living to *all* citizens to which they are felt to be entitled simply by virtue of their being human and in need therefore of minimal conditions compatible with individual dignity. In the United States, by contrast, there is no such statutory floor. "Instead there is a net which catches most of those who fall, but through whose holes a person in need may slip, to be succored, presumably, by private charity."[9] The American system, these men argue, is more appropriately labeled "the social-security state," which reflects the group basis of American politics and

[8] See the analysis of two British political scientists: D. W. Brogan and Douglas V. Verney, *Political Patterns in Today's World* (New York: Harcourt, Brace and World, 1963), pp. 106-12.

[9] *Ibid.*, p. 107. As the authors point out, there is a curious anomaly in the United States: the Veterans Administration is a "small-scale welfare state," which meets with almost no opposition.

the brokerage process of formulating public policy. Unlike its European counterparts it has not resulted from ideologically oriented political movements in American politics.

This distinction has not been generally recognized in American political controversy. *Welfare state* has been an epithet applied to American *liberalism* in the rhetoric of *conservatives*, embellished by appeals to *laissez faire* and expressed fears of creeping socialism and the destruction of the "American way."

The ideological radicalism some *conservatives* profess to find in *liberal* reforms has never been respectable in the United States. Americans have failed generally to understand such radical movements as democratic socialism, and their very ignorance has cast a spell over American politics. The socialism of most other modern democracies is commonly not distinguished from the Marxist socialism of totalitarian states, and the fear of creeping socialism inhibits rational discussion of public problems. The result of this irrelevant dialogue is that labels replace arguments. At the same time the widespread abandonment of *laissez faire* and economic individualism in practice is accepted only apologetically and usually by being ignored. One consequence is that *liberals* tend to secure their reforms through expertness in the arts of legislative maneuver, while *conservatives* win by default on the battleground of political rhetoric. Nearly all politicians pay public homage, for example, to the balanced budget while *liberal* spending programs continue to increase the public debt. The result is a "creeping schizophrenia" in the American political personality.

Another consequence of this ideological confusion is that the center of gravity of American politics and the freedom of maneuver of even the *liberal* politicians tend to be toward the right of the ideological spectrum. The *conservative* bias in our politics is revealed in the fact that even the most moderate *liberal* is open to the scornful charge of "creeping socialist."

Social legislation in the United States will undoubtedly continue to be spliced together at the brokerage table even though our dialogue will cause many of the negotiators to move toward the right of the table. The brokerage solution is already clearly evident in our social enactments. Federal social-service programs are limited to clearly defined groups. And while the old age, survivors, and disability insurance programs (the social-security program) now covers 95 per cent of the population, the excluded 5 per cent includes those groups least well organized and most in need.[10] The same group process is reflected in medical care. While the *conservative* parties of Europe now support general public programs to provide access to medical care to all, not until 1965 did the American Congress pass a Medicare bill, and then it was one that covered only the aged. Presumably *liberals* hope to extend the coverage eventually to everyone, but the process is likely to be one of gradual inclusion of other groups through the back door to preclude the ideological issues from being squarely faced. American *liberals* are more akin to European conservatives in their piecemeal approach to social legislation. European liberals have few American counterparts; fewer still play influential roles in practical politics.

From any genuinely radical perspective the American political process appears as effective as the application of a series of Band-Aids where major surgery is called for. To borrow an old British phrase, we "muddle through," but our muddling is accompanied by irrelevant rhetorical flourishes that serve as a rear-guard action against change and preclude the more comprehensive debate of social problems that their seriousness requires. There is competition in our politics to be sure, but in the process of organizing this competition, further blurring of ideological differences occurs.

Political Competition and Ideological Configurations

The terms so far used to describe ideological differences lose much of their coherence in the arena of political conflict. Competition for votes between the two political parties, whose very designations, Republican and Democrat, supposedly represent ideological differences, often results in blurring the distinction between ideological clusters of attitudes. As we shall see in the next chapter, American parties make little pretense of representing clearly defined ideological positions. While Republicans tend to gain support of *conservatives* and Democrats call themselves the party of *liberalism*, there is much truth in Joseph Roddy's comment that both parties "mastered Same-Speak years ago."[11] "Same-Speak" leads the parties to seek an all-encompassing consensus, with the result that not only are philosophical liberals and conservatives frustrated in their search for a spiritual home, but ideological *liberals*

[10] While the states provide a floor in their general assistance programs, these have languished with the development of federal categorized assistance programs and, in many states, are "quite inadequate for the purpose." *Ibid.*

[11] "What Is a Liberal? What Is a Conservative?" *Look,* July 28, 1964, p. 21.

and *conservatives* suffer the same difficulty in finding a clear representation of their attitudes. Parties, in short, seek a consensus that transcends right wing–left wing, Republican-Democrat, or *conservative-liberal* ideologies in order to capture votes. The result is ideological bewilderment for the average voter. It is difficult, for example, to discover a clue to the Democrats' ideology from President Johnson's description of himself:

> I am a liberal, a conservative, a Texan, a taxpayer, a rancher, a businessman, a consumer, a parent, a voter, and not so young as I used to be, nor as old as I expect to be—and I am all these things in no fixed order . . . at the heart of my own beliefs is a rebellion against the very process of classifying, labeling and filing Americans under headings.[12]

President Johnson's campaign in 1964 sought a reconciliation of traditional ideological positions into a larger, albeit vague, ideology encompassing all of the qualities he attributed to himself in the description quoted. The votes he garnered in the election demonstrated a high degree of success in building not only a new ideology broad enough to embrace previous differences, but also a new confederation of previously hostile power groups. His administration further broadened this consensus among conflicting ideologies and interest groups: *liberals, conservatives*, business, labor, peace advocates, war hawks, civil-rights leaders, welfare state supporters, and civil libertarians all lined up behind the Great Society. Most remarkable of all, however, was the lack of effective criticism by any of these groups of the domestic policies of the Johnson administration, at least in its early stages. This was no doubt related to the voluminous legislative output, which included something for everyone—civil-rights legislation, antipoverty bills, tax reductions, environmental beautification, federal aid to education, and Medicare. Who could complain? How could opposition to such varied legislative abundance be effective?

While the Republican party, which had allied itself with the ideological right in 1964, was preoccupied with rebuilding during the postelection period, its members seemed to have learned from their defeat that there is only one effective American ideology—that is, only one that can be appealed to for political power. An American ideology seemed to be emerging as a "consensus" of all ideologies. Sometimes called "mainstream," it is an eclectic cluster of ideas so broad that

[12] *Ibid.*, p. 21.

meaningful competitive politics becomes difficult, if not impossible. It is within this broad consensus that brokerage politics takes root. Since the broad outline of politics is agreed upon, the only thing left is to wheel and deal within the system. The ideological dissenters find themselves increasingly confined to small clusters of fringe groups whose sole purpose is to utter wistful protests to the philosophical and logical inconsistencies of the consensus ideology underlying brokerage politics.

Ideological configurations are not completely obliterated. The political parties are still nominally representative of enough differences to develop some campaign issues. As a result, *liberals* and *conservatives* generally fall in and march to the polls behind the leadership of the Democrats and Republicans, respectively. Within the parties a continuing struggle goes on over the question of how much ideological identity the party should have. Republican *conservatives* took over the party in 1964 to save it from the "me-tooers" and the apostles of the mainstream. In 1965 Democratic *liberals* in the Senate bolted the Johnson consensus and missed upsetting it by only two votes on an anti-poll-tax amendment to Johnson's voting rights bill.

BROKERAGE POLITICS: "REASONABLE" MEN AND SENSIBLE BARGAINS

If the American ideology has become one of a broad consensus on a basic ideology, one may well ask what all the political shouting is about. To illustrate the nature of our current political controversy, and at the risk of some repetition of what appears elsewhere in the text, it might be well to diagnose some of the factors dividing policy *liberals* and *conservatives* operating in a brokerage context, particularly on economic issues.

There is little question that our politics heats up considerably on economic issues. Politicians, to be sure, disagree on foreign issues, but the crisis nature of foreign policy, the tradition of bipartisanship, and executive dominance of international affairs tend to prevent boiling. Domestic economic policy is the arena of the nation's most flashy political pyrotechnics. Kenneth Galbraith suggests the following explanation of this phenomenon:

> Economic questions, which must be taken to include those involving economic power, have been the major subject of dispute over most of our national history. It is true that on occasion moral questions (the inherent rights and wrongs of slavery, or whether a man's re-

sponsibility as his brother's keeper should encompass his sobriety) have agitated us rather deeply. . . . Yet, year in and year out, it is the question of economics—the manifold issues surrounding collective bargaining, the problems of farm price policy, tariffs, public spending, taxation, and the regulation of business—which provide us with the bread and butter of political controversy. It is these that give us our daily diet of insinuation, indignation and insult. As a people, we react violently to the suggestion that we are materialistic. We aver strongly that we are not. But in searching for the long-standing pre-eminence of economic issues as objects of political controversy, it is perhaps fair to say that we are intelligently sensitive to political activity in the vicinity of our pocketbooks.[13]

In spite of the clanging din of controversy, modern *liberals* and *conservatives* no longer view economic controversies as class struggles. After the indignation and insults subside, the politicians generally sit down, red-faced with anger perhaps, and strike their bargains. The operational politics of brokerage takes place at the bargaining table. This is particularly true, as we shall see in detail in a later chapter, of the legislative branch of government where negotiation, consensus, and artful compromise are increasingly accepted as the "legislative way of life."[14]

If we look at a hypothetical bargaining table where a hypothetical tax bill is being considered, perhaps we can get a clearer idea of the broker-age process. Few of the negotiators will be brokers in the pure sense—that is, most of them will probably have some recognizable policy objective. All, or most, of them will realize that when they sit down to settle the issue they will not get all they would like. After all, this is a bargain and one must be willing to concede part of the loaf, although one hopes and expects to get more than a thin slice. Different negotiators will settle for greater or lesser portions. At the far right of the table will sit those few who may indignantly leave the negotiations to wage an ideological battle against the result if business interests and the well-to-do are burdened to support the poor. At the left of the table will sit those few who will bolt unless the resulting tax rates are more progressive. The center of the table will be occupied by the brokers and the moderates—moderate in the sense that they will keep trying

[13] John Kenneth Galbraith, *Economics and the Art of Controversy* (New York: Vintage Books, 1960), pp. 5-6.
[14] The phrase is the title of a book by a leading exponent of the philosophy of compromise: T. V. Smith, *The Legislative Way of Life* (Chicago: The University of Chicago Press, 1940).

for a bargain, as well as in the sense that their policy commitments are less intense. Even the moderates will try for the best deal possible, although most of them will feel that any bargain is better than none at all—"at least we have a bill" is not an uncommon reaction of legislators emerging from bargaining sessions.

In addition to general ideological commitments, loyalties to interest groups will be represented in the bargaining (often, but not always, such group loyalties will coincide with the politician's ideological commitments). The resulting bargain is likely to be struck near the center of the conflicting interests and positions. In the case of a tax bill the bargain is likely to be described by the old adage of "plucking the feathers from the goose with the fewest squawks."

Economic Liberals and Brokerage Politics.   The *liberal* who appears at the brokerage table is generally distinguished by the set of organized groups he represents or favors in contrast to his conservative counterpart. The *liberal's* allegiance may be dictated by general ideological attitudes, the characteristics of his constituency, his profession or business, or his drive for power and prestige. To earn the name of *liberal* he will probably have a policy identity with certain issues. He would, for example, probably vote prolabor, antitrust, or, if he is daring, anti-tax exemption for various businesses. If he wants to cut a big *liberal* swath, he may adopt a cause that has little organized pressure behind it one way or the other—for example, he might oppose capital punishment or censorship legislation. On large economic issues he undoubtedly would have something to say, but he could seldom be expected to advocate a solution very far removed from the one likely to be supported by a consensus. In confronting the poverty of more than 20 per cent of the population he would no doubt be willing to extend various forms of relief, but he would be unlikely to suggest that the solution to the problem requires fundamental changes in our attitudes, values, or institutions. He would vote for slum clearance but would hardly demand that slum dwellers be relocated in adequate housing rebuilt with public funds. In short, the nagging, recurring, perennial difficulties of the society are never confronted head-on. There is seldom a meaningful dialogue in which the *liberal* broker boldly lays bare the tragic problems of society for all to see. If he is tempted, he will probably consider carefully the high cost of quixotic acts of courage that could retire him from politics forever. As the late President Kennedy pointed out, he knows very well that courageous congressmen have won public renown for courage but have lost all chance for the Presidency in the process of gaining their reputation.[15]

It was the traditional liberal's obligation to look deep into social problems and search for rational solutions to them. It would be difficult to imagine Thomas Jefferson calmly suggesting a program of relief packages to alleviate the grinding poverty in West Virginia and other depressed areas or piously voting a trickle of dollars for the retraining of unemployed victims of automation. Traditional liberals would consider that these crucial and pressing public problems call for an examination of the basic principles of the social structure. Unlike the broker, they would be uninterested in whether the poor and unemployed were organized into interest groups. The traditional liberals, in short, assumed a different purpose for politics, a different kind of citizen, and a different sense of political obligation than does the liberal broker dealing in economic issues.

Modern economic *liberals*, we have suggested, tend to see their function generally as representing a different set of organized groups than their conservative counterparts. For eighteenth-century majoritarian philosophy they substitute the nineteenth-century utilitarian slogan of the "greatest good for the greatest number." But the greatest good for the greatest number comes to be interpreted as an alliance with organizations that have large numbers because of a broad-based membership, such as organized labor. To be prolabor is to be *liberal*; to be antilabor is to be *conservative*.

The economic *liberal's* attachment to the little guy is usually to organized little guys. The real little guys, those who fall through the social-security net mentioned earlier, get his sympathy, maybe even his vote, but not his soul or his career. His identity with particular groups causes him to overlook much chicanery and self-seeking in their political activity. Thus, many self-styled *liberals* refuse to confront some of the more crass demands of the organizations they support and which, in turn, support them. For *liberals*, labor tends to be an untouchable group to whose demands they respond with knee-jerk alacrity.

Economic Conservatives and Brokerage Politics. The policy *conservative*, like the *liberal*, operates from certain vaguely defined ideological premises. His social outlook is generally suspicious of and hostile to the programs of the welfare state. On any given issue property rights are likely to be his first line of defense, states' rights his second. He

---

[15] John F. Kennedy, *Profiles in Courage* (New York: Pocket Books, 1957).

starts with a presumption against governmental efforts to regulate social relationships or to intervene in economic decisions. This basic defense of individual initiative and independence is not likely, however, to extend to official patriotic, religious, and moral regulation embodied in loyalty oaths, deference to God in the flag salute, mandatory patriotic and religious exercises in the schools, and the suppression of pornographic or indecent literature.

Translated into brokerage terms, however, the position of the economic *conservative* tends to be distinguished from that of his *liberal* counterpart by his attachment to a different segment of the power structure. While the *liberal* waxes eloquent over the plight of the little man, the *conservative* is equally eloquent over the dependence of society on the virtues of the affluent and the successful. The *liberal's* concern is expressed in his support of the organizations that speak for the interests of lower socioeconomic groups; the *conservative* is usually found on the side of such groups as manufacturers, organized medicine, real estate, private power companies, and the military. As a negotiator in the brokerage system, the policy *conservative* is willing to deal in power trades. His position is strengthened by the affluence of the groups he represents, although the present wealth of labor and other *liberal* groups makes this distinction less meaningful than it used to be. He benefits also from the fact that the mass media tend to support his position, though on this score, too, the scale is more nearly balanced than it has been historically. His major bargaining weakness stems from the fact that his groups lack the numerical strength of the *liberal* forces. His bargaining position, therefore, does not have behind it the potential threat of retaliation at the polls. But money and the influence of the communication media work well to offset numbers if they are skillfully used in techniques of public persuasion. All things considered, including the conservative tone of our political rhetoric and the ideological consensus within which bargaining operates, the *conservative* broker goes into a bargaining situation well enough braced by power to wield the veto power Calhoun correctly defined as the essence of the bargaining situation.

The *conservative* broker, lacking the support of groups with numerical strength, backs his negotiation with rhetorical appeals to the ideology of *laissez faire*. His attack on his *liberal* opponents focuses on the paternalism of their welfare programs, the centralizing and bureaucratic tendencies of their reliance on Washington, and the leveling effects of their use of tax programs for egalitarian purposes. Senator Goldwater's analysis of the income tax, for example, embodied these appeals:

> The graduated tax is a *confiscatory* tax. Its effect, and to a large extent its aim, is to bring down all men to common level. Many of the leading proponents of the graduated tax frankly admit that their purpose is to redistribute the nation's wealth. Their aim is an egalitarian society—an objective that does violence both to the charter of the Republic and the laws of Nature. We are all equal in the eyes of God but we are equal *in no other respect*. Artificial devices for enforcing equality among unequal men must be rejected if we would restore that charter and honor those laws.[16]

A rhetoric that includes appeals to God, Republic (capitalized), and Nature (also capitalized) is a formidable weapon against a *liberalism* that has become thoroughly pragmatic and nonideological. It permits *conservatives* to cover the power groups they represent with the mantle of free enterprise and the American way, while the *liberal* seems to stand exposed as a defender of selfish interests. When, for example, a question arose whether the federal government or private enterprise, in this case American Telephone and Telegraph, should build the Telstar orbiting relay system, the merits of the case were buried under an avalanche of rhetoric about free enterprise. *Liberals* argued that the profit as well as the product was likely to be astronomical, but private business carried the day. The best the *liberals* could muster against the *conservative* appeal to free enterprise was the poetry of the Democratic Senator from Louisiana, Russell B. Long:

> This star is here to make a buck,
> It's here for monopoly;
> Tell all the poor people they're out of luck,
> A man's got to pay to see.[17]

At the state and local levels, especially, self-seeking group interests are often effectively guised under the cloak of free enterprise. *Liberal* brokers, seeking justification for serving the desires of their groups, have difficulty in finding a response that can effectively counter the *conservative* appeal to a widely held political folklore.

In summary, the economic *conservative's* approach to politics differs little from that of his *liberal* counterpart in its method of operation. *Conservatives* may appear to be somewhat less willing to compromise

[16] Barry Goldwater, *The Conscience of a Conservative* (Shepardsville, Ky.: Victor, 1960), p. 64.
[17] *Congressional Record*, August 15, 1962, p. 15531.

or to rely more on stale dogmas in making their case. But even here, old-style labor baiters, as well as free-swinging *liberal* opponents of Wall Street, have generally departed the political scene. The apparent ideological fervor of *conservative* politicians turns out most often to be a weapon of negotiation. The chief difference is to be found in the choice of groups each tends to support in the bargaining process.

BROKERAGE POLITICS AND POLITICAL DISSENT

One economic analysis of the current tendency of politicians to operate as brokers within a pressure system holds that the American economy is organized into power blocs that act as countervailing checks upon one another in such a way that none of them can dominate the scene.[18] Many *liberals* rally to this idea and justify their allegiance to a select set of pressure groups as being representatives of power blocs that must act as countervailing powers to those championed by their adversaries. This serves as a rationale for stopping short of rational political dialogue. Power becomes the key to politics. The morality of power politics is the morality of advocacy: to give one's best for the segment of power represented in the hope that it will get fair treatment in the final bargain. Compromise of power thus becomes a moral principle, and rationality comes to be equated with equilibrium of the political power structure.

If the resulting struggle for power is to be kept within bounds of peaceful negotiation, it must be a struggle over how the pie is to be sliced; there is no room at the table for those who want to change the menu itself. As an able exponent of the theory has put it, "Democratic government will work to full advantage only if all the interests that matter are practically unanimous not only in their allegiance to the country but also in their allegiance to the structural principles of the existing society."[19]

The unanimous "allegiance to the structural principles of the existing society" of "all the interests that matter" has been powerfully reinforced by the development of what Fred J. Cook has called the warfare state.[20] The role of defense appropriations and expenditures in the economy after World War II gave rise to what President Eisenhower in his Farewell Address described as the "military-industrial complex." But

[18] See John K. Galbraith, *American Capitalism: The Concept of Countervailing Power* (Boston: Houghton Mifflin, 1952).
[19] Joseph A. Schumpeter, *Capitalism, Socialism, and Democracy*, 3rd ed. (New York: Harper, 1950), p. 296.
[20] Fred J. Cook, *The Warfare State* (New York: Macmillan, 1962).

the alliance that has a stake in defense expenditures is broader than the leaders in the Pentagon and the large industrial corporations. Any curtailment of defense production affects not only the munitions entrepreneurs but the people who work in defense plants and the unions representing them. An almost irresistable alliance develops when pressure is exerted by labor groups, munitions manufacturers, and military personnel to continue arms production. Economic *liberals* respond to labor's interests and its fear of unemployment, while economic *conservatives* are prone to favor the manufacturers and the military. In every political constituency there are tremendous pressures to keep the payrolls of military installations and defense-related industry in town. This multiplicity of motives to continue production leads to a defense program consisting of various proportional ingredients of employment, profit, "pork," and defense requirements. Any rational appraisal of arms production thus becomes blurred, even irrelevant, and *liberals* as well as *conservatives* appropriate generously for a public interest quite unlike that championed by philosophical liberals or conservatives. In the politics of the warfare state, allegiance to the country and support of its existing structural principles become almost indistinguishable. An attack on the latter (which democratic theory had always held to be legitimate) tends to be seen as subversive of the former.

Ideologically, brokerage politics is mainstream politics. The *conservative* politician's professed ideological commitment to individual freedom tends to be limited in practice to those individuals who conform to prevailing standards of economic and cultural life. Beatniks, bearded students, and demonstrators against war or segregation are likely to get only his contempt and perhaps the advice that a bath, a shave, and sartorial correctness would change their perspectives. Nor is the *liberal* politician likely to contest this analysis. Mainstream politics is not kind to dissenters.

At the same time the benevolent consensus on moderation, in the face of the complex problems of the modern world, is likely to breed dissent. One observer, who is famous for other than social insight, nevertheless put it well:

> Unless we manage to clarify ourselves, unless we learn to think and reason and communicate and behave as *social creatures* rather than mobs of greedy, grabbing, frightened animals, we're all going to wind up face to face with a little thing called catastrophe much sooner than we even realize.[21]

[21] Artie Shaw, *The Trouble with Cinderella* (New York: Collier Books, 1963), p. 348.

THE MORAL AMERICAN: A POLITICAL OUTCAST

If all of the ideological and philosophical tributaries to American democracy flow into the mainstream and on into a vast sea of consensus, where do those who wish to be moral men in a moral world find a source of political expression? The regular procedures of American politics now offer little place for the person committed to intellectual integrity or to a consistent ideological approach to issues. Such a person is likely derisively to be labeled an egghead, a purist, or an idealist who is simply too unsophisticated for the hurly-burly of the real political world where "the art of the possible" is pursued at the bargaining table.

There are signs, however, that many Americans are not content to accept the political order as it is now conceived and as it now operates. Their voices have been heard in protest against the war in Viet Nam; they march on a southern capitol and conduct sit-ins around defense plants; they push baby carriages in peace marches; they assemble and speak in protest over the bureaucratic ineptness of college administrators, the impersonality of the "multiversity," and the irrelevance of the curriculum; they refuse to answer questions before legislative investigating committees. Many of these acts constitute overt disobedience to legal authority, but they have been justified by their practitioners as the only means of making a meaningful political point. To take moral arguments to the existing political and governmental establishments, it has been argued, would be an absurd exercise in futility. The existing order contains no mechanisms for registering rational or moral challenges to the *status quo* it is dedicated to preserve. If there is an avenue of moral protest available, it is to be found in the judiciary, to which one may appeal only if he has a case; and the most direct way to ensure a case is to have oneself arrested. For this reason alone, it will not do to dismiss all demonstrations as extremism. They may represent radicalism, as that term was defined in an earlier chapter, but more likely, perhaps, they reflect sheer frustration with the bland, absorbent, and condescending politics of moderation in which a strong moral argument evokes little more than a lifted eyebrow or a tolerant smile from professional politicians.

We are not arguing that everyone who has a grievance should take to the streets; our purpose is to emphasize that an understanding of recent increases in the incidence of direct political action must recognize that the all-embracing ideology we seem to be developing in our politics tends to rule out regular opportunities for meaningful philosophical or ideological debate. To modify the existing structure of politics by engaging oneself in it is, of course, possible. The capture of the Republican Party in 1964 by an alliance of dedicated people embracing an arch-conservative ideology and right-wing extremists proves that it is possible to capture and rebuild an old, staid, political party. Yet the failure of this attempt was partly due to the fact that the majority of Americans seem to resist any movement away from a broad ideological consensus and political brokerage.

There is a unique sensitivity in a democratic system of government, however, which may work to overcome the increasing discontent of people seeking a more moral politics. If the demand for political integrity continues, it is very possible that candidates may begin to take a more courageous stand on issues. It is, in short, quite possible for a democratic society to demand and receive more from its politics and politicians than it has been getting in recent history. The fundamental requirement is that citizens redefine their roles and modify their expectations.

PARTIES, PRESSURE GROUPS, AND PUBLIC RELATIONS

... which is concerned with informal political institutions that are nonetheless vital to the American political process.

American politics especially, because of its brokerage character, operates within the framework of *The Pressure System,* the network of organized groups seeking to influence policies and decisions in ways favorable to their interests. The increasing influence of pressure groups and their methods of operation have diminished the importance of

The Old Order of Politics in which the political *Machine,* the party *Boss,* and the rivalries of *Sectionalism* played dominant roles. The development and conflict of pressure groups with national interests have largely replaced the parochial basis on which the old order was organized.

Within the pressure system there are different *Types of Pressure Groups,* representing a wide range of economic, social, religious, and cultural interests. Some are organized around narrow private interests; others seek public policy goals that will bring no direct, special benefit to the group's membership; some reflect a combination of both private and public interests. However,

Recent Changes in the Pressure System indicate an increase in the relative strength and influence of private-interest economic groups; a tendency for groups to be less inclined to justify their objectives as being in the public interest; and a tendency for group leadership to be less responsive to the membership.

The Activities of Pressure Groups extend beyond direct efforts to influence government officials; they include propaganda campaigns directed at the general public, or segments of it, and designed to create a favorable image that can be converted into political strength. In these efforts there is usually a close connection between *Money and Influence.*

Although they have many characteristics in common, it is important to understand the distinction between *Political Parties* and *Pressure Groups:*

The goal of American political parties is to select candidates for public office and to get them elected; therefore, they must be more broadly representative in their membership and objectives than pressure groups. At the same time

The Relationship of Pressure Groups to Political Parties is ambiguous: parties welcome support from the pressure system; yet, if they hope to win elections, they cannot afford to become the obvious captives of particular groups.

Fundamentally, the relationship between parties and pressure groups will be determined by the importance of

Political Ideology in the behavior of *Political Parties.* Historical *Party Differences* have sometimes been sharp; in other periods they have almost completely disappeared. The absence of distinct philosophical or ideological differences in the recent past has led to labeling the American parties *Tweedledee* and *Tweedledum.* Despite some continuing, and significant, differences (and with the exception of the 1964 campaign), parties have been brought closer together as they have become

Brokerage Parties for Brokerage Politics. Parties have increasingly developed a brokerage approach to their chief activities of selecting candidates, building platforms and programs, conducting campaigns, and organizing legislatures. The result is a tendency for both parties to accommodate the interests of all major groups into similar bargains. These tendencies, while bringing the parties closer together, have also served to diminish and make more difficult

The Role of Third Parties, which, in the past, have often served as catalysts of basic changes in the programs of the major parties.

As part of the same process through which modern parties have taken on a brokerage character, *The Rise of Public Relations* has revolutionized the relationship of parties and politicians to the public.

Public-Relations techniques, borrowed from the advertising industry, have played an increasingly prominent role in selecting and selling candidates and issues; the *Politician* increasingly surrenders to the *Professional Expert* control over the choice of tactics, techniques, and goals. As a result,

The Impact of Public Relations on American Politics raises serious questions: while it can be argued that the public is better informed through the use of these techniques, its capacity to make meaningful choices seems not to be enhanced.

The questions raised by these developments have led to proposals *For Reform* of political parties to make them more effective instruments of responsible, majority government; a *Case Against Reform* has been made by those who accept the postulates of broker rule.

America is, therefore, in a very real sense the land of many parties. France cannot match the 100 or so parties of the United States. These various state organizations are, however, in loose coalition and once every four years are frozen into unity by a brief spell cast by what is called the National Convention. In a few days of frenzy, men of varied views meet and agree not upon a doctrine . . . but upon a man, or rather two men, the candidates for president and vice-president. Having performed this midwifery and hammered out a party platform, the party leaders disperse, hoping that the politician they have selected will not alienate too many of the party's supporters or depart too much from the platform hopefully presented to him.

D. W. Brogan and Douglas V. Verney

Chapter Nine

PARTIES, PRESSURE GROUPS, AND PUBLIC RELATIONS

THE LEXICON of modern politics is heavy with words denoting moderation. *Consensus, mainstream, responsible liberalism, dynamic conservatism, middle-of-the-road,* and *conservatism-with-a-heart* are a few of the phrases floating on the autumn air during election years. The target of these verbal reinforcements of stability is mass man. Until the Republicans' classic failure of 1964, recent political campaigns were most noted for their inoffensive appeals, bland issues, and split-level platforms designed to appeal to a large middle-class market.

When the Republicans daringly ventured into the angry fringes of extremism, there was shock among the party's old "pros" and nervousness among the professional managers of that strange crusade. Candidate Goldwater himself knew he was treading dangerous paths, and his tactics moved from his preconvention senatorial posture of defender of the right, in both a political and moral sense, to a more moderate, if not muddled, position. A gloss of "aw-shucks," regular-guy appeal was hastily applied to the candidate by his public-relations advisers. Lines were cast into the mainstream for votes, and Goldwater's public statements became a peculiar mishmash of contradictions. And, while moderates were unsuccessfully courted, his right-wing admirers became upset. Was the candidate selling out to soft-headed liberalism? One of Goldwater's more articulate admirers angrily charged that concessions to moderation at the expense of conscience were odious. He said:

> A society that seduces the conscience by sweet reason is one thing; but ours is developing into a society that harpoons the conscience, and tows it right into the maws of the mother vessel, there to be macerated and stuffed into a faceless can.
>
> The enemies of the human spirit are outpacing even the population explosion, and it becomes harder and harder to fight them down. It is so much easier to succumb, and there are so many formulae for doing so gracefully, and the great conscience-shriver is the wink on Univac's face on election night.[1]

The election night wink of Univac was for Goldwater's opponent. President Johnson had campaigned for a consensus to build a Great Society in a peaceful world and had won hands down. Specifics were lacking, but the Democrats had successfully mined the American middle. All the Republicans had won was the old solid South, a political reject of the Democrats, which the Republicans had courted on a states' rights appeal that, applied to the civil-rights issue, was little more than a thinly veiled racism.

Many things accounted for the Republican defeat in 1964, but among them was a reaction to a politics of departure from the middle. The postelection agony among Republicans has come to focus on techniques of getting the party back into the moderate position it occupied during the Eisenhower years. Moderate Republicans urged a return to the realities of modern politics—to a recognition that, while they could not be all things to all men, they had to be many more things to many

[1] William F. Buckley, Jr., "We Want Our Politicians to Be Hypocrites," *Saturday Evening Post*, October 17, 1964, p. 12.

more men if they were to have any hope of winning. They could not, in short, afford to become a small band of romantics who would take political positions antagonistic to large segments of the organized pressure system.

The election statistics furnished glaring proof. Johnson won by 13 per cent more than Kennedy had in 1960. His majority included a nearly three-to-one landslide in the cities with their heavy concentrations of ethnic groups and labor strength; he carried 72 per cent of the Catholic vote as against the 63 per cent won by Kennedy, the nation's first Catholic President; he won by a fantastic nineteen to one among low-income voters, by two to one in the middle-income brackets, and even received 49 per cent (13 per cent more than Kennedy) of the upper-income vote; the Negro vote, which had been fairly evenly split in 1960, went to Johnson by 96 per cent; even the normally Republican suburbs went to Johnson by 59 per cent.

New York's Republican Senator Jacob K. Javits foresaw this disaster over a year before election when he argued that the choice facing the Republicans was between a narrow, unrealistic ideological position or one of "accommodating the whole spectrum of Republican thought." He preferred the latter course so that

> . . . the Republican party will retain its historic institutional character, and thus its force as an agent of creative partisanship. It will continue to be a party that is national in scope, broadly representative in membership, sensitive to the pulse of American life, temperate in instinct and practical in its work habits.[2]

Senator Javits' plea for a practical moderation invites analysis of the role of political parties in a society composed of voters and organized interest groups who oppose radical shifts in public policy. There is much logic to his position in light of the voting behavior of Americans to be described in the next chapter. His argument is also valid in relation to the role of organized presure groups as formulators or vetoers of public policy.

The Pressure System

Organizational life, as described in earlier chapters, has many social consequences that affect man's political life. Mass society is character-

[2] Jacob K. Javits, "To Preserve the Two-Party System," *New York Times Magazine*, October 27, 1963, p. 5.

ized by large mechanisms of cogs and wheels meshed together to achieve a mass-produced end product. If the individual's economic life is increasingly destined to be a cog or wheel in one of these organizations, his political life tends to fit a similar mold. These very organizations composing corporate life are not only economic units but they become political units in the maze of pressure groups seeking a favorable climate for their activities.

In the pressure system one sees these organizations busily working at politics. Often large organizations are organized into even larger ones for political purposes. We find, for example, numerous oil companies uniting as the petroleum institute, while numerous private power companies join forces as the power lobby. Even greater combinations of strength result, however, when the petroleum institute and power lobby agree, after due negotiation by their brokers, to unite for the passage of a bill. Certain combinations of interests are irresistible; in most state legislatures a coalition of labor, industry, and education could have things pretty much their own way. While it is not characteristic of group life to find such organizations together, there is always a possibility that skillful give and take by their representatives can arrange a joint effort for some political goal of mutual interest to all participants in the deal.

The operation of the pressure system, with its units of power endlessly rearranging themselves into coalitions for the support or defeat of particular issues, reflects the character of organized group life and the increasing homogeneity of American life. As a result, the pushing and hauling of economic groups has increasingly replaced the older bases of political conflict. The pressure system has emerged from the old sectional, class, and ethnic political organizations, which are rapidly fading as significant political forces.

THE OLD ORDER OF POLITICS: MACHINE, BOSS, AND SECTIONALISM

Before the curtailment of immigration to the United States, politics was characterized by the organization into machines of newly arrived ethnic groups who settled mainly in the cities. Running the machine was usually a boss, who pulled various levers of the mechanism so it would grind out victories at the polls. The machine was organized so that district leaders and ward heelers, friends and agents of the boss, would fan out through the political jurisdiction to keep everyone happy or at least in line. Machines based their strength on organizing un-assimilated ethnic and immigrant groups as well as economically under-privileged people. The machine distributed jobs, groceries, buckets of coal, clothing, or a few dollars to its clients. It also arranged for wakes, funerals, and marriages for the faithful, the poor, the Irish, the Catholics, the Poles, and the Jews. When it was time to vote, the favor was usually returned.

In the past, the machine and its boss have often been powerful enough to control and deliver the politics of a city or a state. Curley of Boston, "Big Bill" Thompson of Chicago, Hague of Jersey City, and Crump of Memphis were some of the colorful figures who were powerful enough to demand and receive consideration in the selection of candidates and the development of the platforms of the national party.

The boss and his machine, however, are rapidly going out of date. An analysis of New York City politics—the historic home of Tammany Hall, the strongest and most enduring of the machines—reveals the forces at work to undermine their traditional sources of strength and change their character. One study[3] found that the district leader, the key to the machine's traditional organization and power, has become a mere functionary of a system in which real power has gravitated into the hands of the top party leaders, municipal bureaucrats, public-relations firms, and leading businesses that contract with the city. The result, according to these observers, is a shift from a system that with all its faults was responsive to the people (particularly to the poorest and most disadvantaged part of the population) to a system that is almost completely removed from their desires and grievances.

The authors of this study point out that, in 1959, New York had more than 600,000 people on its municipal payroll and argue that, unlike the traditional boss, this powerful bureaucracy was increasingly dedicated to serving its superiors rather than the people of the city. The poorest citizens seeking relief for their poverty or their grievances now deal with a vast and impersonal bureaucracy rather than with a sympathetic (for whatever reasons) and personal boss. With respect to the new system that has replaced the old machine, the authors hold that "power speaks only to power." They go on to argue that:

> The power is of many kinds and degrees, but its varying forms have one thing in common. It is derived from the top, not from the bottom.

[3] Fred J. Cook and Gene Gleason, "The Shame of New York," *The Nation,* October 31, 1959, pp. 261-321.

The men who control the $2 billion-a-year city government deal only with their counterparts—with the men who wield millions in private finance, with the men whose fortunes control all the large media of public opinion, with the new emperors of Madison Avenue who, through the cultivation of the technique of making a rancid herring smell sweet, have become the go-between in every big deal.

This, say the authors, has left the district leader

> . . . shorn of his functions as the Lord Bountiful and guardian of his people; and as he has lost this elemental reason for existence, he has been deprived of the influence his following used to give him with the men upstairs. No longer is he the source of food to the starving, jobs for the needy. Welfare is administered by one of those great, impersonal city agencies directed from the top of City Hall. The finding of jobs is the function of the employment bureau. The services that cater to the most fundamental needs of the people now filter down from the top. One cannot understand what is happening in today's New York unless one understands the significance of this change.[4]

This is not the place to argue the relative merits of ward heelers and bureaucrats, but these authors have indicated that New York City politics, like politics in many other places, has been turned upside down —that is, the local party leaders tend to become functionaries in a system in which power and influence flow downward. The result has been to make a bureaucracy of the political system, which increasingly ignores the sentiment, however self-seeking or illogical, of the people. Rather than being responsive to public sentiment, the new powers in politics ignore it, or, if they cannot ignore it, they manipulate or engineer it with professional skill to serve their ends.

The old political boss, more often corrupt than not and usually completely indifferent to a public interest defined in any way but expediency, at least heard the voice of the oppressed and responded some- how. Not many people weep as the corpses of machines are laid to rest, but the homogenized brokerage politics that is taking its place also seems to concentrate power, albeit in different places, and operates with as much cynicism as the machine. Whereas the machine, for reasons of its own power, responded to the needs of unorganized individuals with problems, brokerage politics offers to see that the demands of organized groups—the National Association of Manufacturers, the

[4] *Ibid.*, p. 262.

AFL-CIO, the Farm Bureau Federation, and the others—are all responded to in rough proportion to their political power.

TYPES OF PRESSURE GROUPS

In addition to the increase in their number, size and organizational structure, interest groups have undergone other significant changes that contribute to the dominance of the brokerage process. In order to see what these changes are, we need to distinguish between two general types of pressure groups. There is a difference between the organization devoted to securing differential economic or status advantages for its members and the one devoted to promoting some particular public principle in which its members have no stake other than their intellectual commitment. We may label these two types as "private-interest groups" and "public-interest groups" to distinguish their central concerns. Examples of the first type are the private power lobby (the Association of American Light and Power Companies), the real estate lobby (National Association of Real Estate Boards), the AFL-CIO, and the Farm Bureau Federation. Examples of public-interest groups are the American Civil Liberties Union, the American League to Abolish Capital Punishment, the Planned Parenthood Association, the American Association for the United Nations, and the John Birch Society. The test, as a leading political scientist has recently put it, is a dual one: whether the benefits sought by the organization are exclusive or nonexclusive; whether membership is open or confined to those with a common, exclusive interest. His illustration of the difference deserves further consideration:

> Is it possible to distinguish between the "interests" of the members of the National Association of Manufacturers and the members of the American League to Abolish Capital Punishment? The facts in the two cases are not identical. First, *the members of the A.L.A.C.P. obviously do not expect to be hanged.* The membership of the A.L.A.C.P. is not restricted to persons under indictment for murder or in jeopardy of the extreme penalty. *Anybody* can join A.L.A.C.P. Its members oppose capital punishment although they are not personally likely to benefit by the policy they advocate. The inference is therefore that the interest of the A.L.A.C.P. is not adverse, exclusive or special. It is not like the interest of the Petroleum Institute in depletion allowances.[5]

[5] E. E. Schattschneider, *The Semisovereign People* (New York: Holt, Rinehart & Winston, 1960) p. 26.

This distinction is admittedly difficult to draw in practice. Some pressure groups are a combination of both material interest and general interest. For example, veterans' groups like the American Legion work strenuously for such clientele benefits as pensions, home loans, and educational benefits while, at the same time, they lobby for anticommunist legislation, loyalty programs, and other measures of a general application.

In addition, most private-interest groups clothe their claims in an appeal to principle. Sometimes the claim is too disingenuous or naïve to be credible: "What's good for General Motors is good for the country." Often, however, such claims deserve a hearing: "The depletion allowance is necessary to create the incentive for oil exploration on which America's defense capability and economic future rest." Sometimes, too, what appears to be a public-interest group is a front for a private interest. A "facts forum" may be subsidized by Texas oil millions, or a committee to promote constitutional government may derive its sustenance from large corporations.

RECENT CHANGES IN THE PRESSURE SYSTEM

Despite these difficulties in application, the distinction is crucial to an understanding of recent changes in the composition and pattern of pressure groups. These changes, in turn, have had important consequences for the role of pressure groups in the political system.

There appears to have been, in the first place, an increase in the number and importance of private- as against public-interest organizations. Historically, public-interest groups have played an important role in influencing political parties and legislatures to adopt their principles. The abolition societies, the Women's Christian Temperance Union, the Daughters of the American Revolution, the Suffragettes, and the Anti-Saloon League are obvious examples. The Izaak Walton League played an instrumental role in securing conservation policies at the turn of this century. There are still such groups in existence, and they continue to be politically active. But their relative number and influence have declined, and they now operate on the fringes of the political arena with little chance of being considered by politicians or parties as spokesmen for a principle. Instead, they are seen as featherweight organizations to be weighed into the balance of interest with the heavyweight economic interest groups. The effect of this development is exaggerated by the tendency of legislators to define their role as neutral brokers. When they do so, the influence of pressure groups is almost entirely dependent on the amount of heat they can generate. For the broker-legislator, heat is heat no matter who applies it. The American Civil Liberties Union and the American Friends Service Committee enter the arena armed with matches, the private-interest groups with blowtorches.

Second, private-interest groups are less likely to define and justify their private interests in terms of public principles. Business groups—chambers of commerce, trade associations, and the National Association of Manufacturers, for example—formerly defended their interests as entitled to legitimate expression because the entire community had a stake in the creation of an economic system based on private enterprise, competition, and *laissez faire*. In recent years, chambers of commerce seem more concerned with local prosperity even where this means coming to the defense of local examples of creeping socialism—government dams, arsenals, power facilities, and other projects that bring payrolls and prosperity to the local scene. The steel industry seeks legal authorization of basing-point pricing, not on the grounds of a competitive system with which it is obviously incompatible, but on the obligation of representatives of steel-producing states to safeguard the economic prosperity of their constituencies. The effectiveness of this appeal can be judged by the following: when this issue came to a vote in the House, all but two members of Pennsylvania's fifteen-man Democratic delegation voted to legalize the system, even though it very obviously conflicts with traditional party positions on monopoly and economic concentration.[6]

It would appear that private-interest groups generally see themselves as rivals in a contest for advantage, entitled to be given a fair weighting rather than to have their claims to a public interest considered.

Third, interest groups less and less represent identifiable, conscious interests of *individuals* and more and more are becoming compromises engineered by the professional bureaucracy of the organization. Labor unions, for example, tend to be *responsive* to the conflicting desires of their membership as these are interpreted by the leadership, rather than *responsible* for consciously determined goals. Thus, skilled craftsmen have a stake in promoting wage differentials based on skill; women workers want maternity benefits and equal pay for equal work; night workers want greater shift differentials; elderly members want better

[6] Earl Latham, *The Group Basis of Politics* (Ithaca, N.Y.: Cornell University Press, 1952). See especially Chaps. 4 and 5.

pension provisions. Union leaders, like politicians, attempt to reconcile the pressures so as to contribute to the stability and growth of the organization.

The same process characterizes the shaping of the demands of trade associations, associations of government employees, and other organizations. In short, private interests too are brokerage houses, rather than instruments for defining and pursuing conscious goals of public policy or for reflecting the opinions of their members. Collectively, they constitute a mart in which parties and politicians tend to play the neutral role of referee.

ACTIVITIES OF PRESSURE GROUPS

The objective of pressure groups is to influence public policy in some desired direction. The techniques that will promote that objective are varied: gaining access to and influence in the centers where governmental decisions are made, developing favorable attitudes among the public at large and in other groups, or influencing the nomination and election of favorably disposed candidates. In their efforts to influence directly the making of governmental policies, pressure groups operate within and before legislative bodies at the federal, state, and local levels. In their efforts to affect policy administration and interpretation, they appear before regulatory commissions and other administrative agencies.

The agent of the pressure group is the lobbyist. We will describe and analyze his activities in a later chapter on the legislative process. Here we only note that the lobyist may be a member of the organization he represents or he may be a skilled public-relations expert, ex-legislator, or career lobbyist retained by the organization to achieve certain objectives for a fee—sometimes a flat fee and sometimes a contingency fee based upon his success.

The lobbyist, however, is only a small part of pressure-group operation. The House of Representatives Select Committee on Lobbying Activities reported:

> Our investigation has convinced us that the business of influencing legislation is dominated by group effort, and that individual activities by persons known as "lobbyists" are subordinate. Much of the money expended to influence legislation is spent in pamphleteering or advertising to obtain legislative aims. We . . . believe that the printed word is much more extensively used by organizations as a means of pursuing legislative aims than personal contacts with legislators

by individual lobbyists. . . . Lobbying activities of this kind increasingly overshadow the traditional techniques of contact and persuasion.[7]

Interest groups distribute printed materials not only to those people who make the final decisions but also to influential individuals and groups. Businessmen, teachers, medical practitioners, and members of labor unions and other organizations are constantly receiving pamphlets from various pressure groups. Often they bear the open invitation to write one's congressman, legislator, or executive official to express one's agreement with the cause. Recipients of this barrage of material might wonder about its effectiveness as they toss large quantities of it into the wastebasket, but the amount of mail received by legislators attests to its influence in activating many of those who receive it.

Pressure groups work to win elections for sympathetic candidates as well as to influence legislation after election. An example of their effectiveness is described in R. Craigin Lewis' account of the intensive efforts of the medical profession to support candidates of its choice.[8] In the Florida Democratic primary contest between Claude Pepper and George Smathers in 1950, Senator Pepper was an advocate of national health insurance. He told the Florida physicians flatly that he was "sticking by the administration's health plan. I just don't care about your 2,000 votes."

The reaction of the physicians was quick and effective. The health insurance plan had already been tainted with the label "socialized medicine" in a national advertising campaign sponsored by the American Medical Association. In Florida, doctors from all parts of the state contributed a hundred dollars apiece, and their wives staged a series of fund-raising parties to sweeten the treasury. Mr. Lewis describes the results:

> Professional reserve melted away. Doctors got out their patient lists, dashed off hundreds of personal letters. From Tallahassee to Ponce de Leon, people began to tell each other, "My doctor thinks it's a good idea to vote for Smathers." Some patients wrote answering notes that gave M.D.'s a rare glimpse of their own influence: "Didn't know you were interested. I assure you I'll vote for him . . ." "Received your card and am going to please you. Hadn't even planned to register."

[7] *House Report No. 3239* (Washington, D.C.: Government Printing Office, 1951), p. 3.

[8] "New Power at the Polls: The Doctors," *Medical Economics*, January, 1951, pp. 73-79.

On election day, medical workers phoned every professional man in the state before noon. More than 70 per cent, they found, had already voted. In some small towns every phone number in the book was called. By the time the primary balloting was over, George Smathers was a shoo-in.[9]

Money and Influence. Activities of pressure and interest groups cannot be conducted without considerable amounts of money. How much they spend depends upon several factors: (1) the availability of revenue—that is, some have steady and abundant sources of funds while others rely upon hand-to-mouth collection of contributions; (2) how anxious they are to achieve results—for example, a particular bill before a legislative body might present a fundamental threat or opportunity and generate an all-out effort; (3) how much good-will advantage might be expected to accrue from supporting causes peripheral to the group's major interest—for example, support given to education or higher teachers' salaries; and (4) how much chance of success is predictable.

It is difficult to get a reliable estimate of total expenditures of pressure groups because their activities take so many different forms. Attempts have been made by Congress and many states to require financial reporting by lobbying groups, but these laws are so written that reporting requirements are easily evaded and figures reported never tell the full story. For example, many organizations assign employees to supply information that can be interpreted not to be influence. In any event, lobbying is just a part of the over-all activity; it by no means tells the story of the total expenditures.

Lobbying expenditures are interesting, however, as a very rough and grossly understated index of who spends what. In 1960 ten organizations reported spending more than $75,000 on lobbying before Congress. Fifteen other groups reported spending in excess of $50,000. These included veterans, labor, farmer, business, professional, and educational organizations. Other lobbies registered before Congress range from the Associated Third Class Mail Users ($13,200.03 reported) to the West Coast Inland Navigation District ($2,507.10 reported) and include all types of organizations and activities.[10]

The scope and strength of the pressure system, and the dominance within it of private interest groups, serve to underscore some of the forces that promote the processes of minorities rule. The underlying

[9] *Ibid.*, pp. 76-77.
[10] *Congressional Quarterly*, May 5, 1961, p. 771 ff.

problem, first clearly set out by Madison, remains: how to devise the means for subordinating the conflicting claims of private groups to a public interest without destroying the pluralism out of which the pressure system inevitably grows. The supremacy of the party system, it would seem, offers the major alternative to the supremacy of the pressure system.

Political Parties

Although political parties and pressure groups are both interested in acquiring political power and although they are closely related to one another, they are distinguished by a key difference: parties organize the electorate in elections. They are instruments for organizing majorities. No matter how much or how little parties are organized along ideological lines, it is in the nature of party organization to select nominees and to seek to elect them to public offices. In a two-party system, as we have mentioned, the parties are likely to be broad-based groups able to appeal to a fairly wide range of interests and philosophies. Within this framework the party operates to select its candidates and help them successfully through the campaigns and elections.

Pressure groups are neither so broad nor so open. They do not run candidates—officially, at any rate—although they give strong support to those they believe will be favorably disposed to their aims. They cannot pretend to the breadth of appeal or the comprehensiveness of program that would qualify them to enter the lists to carry a slate of candidates into office. They concentrate, rather, on influencing the position of the parties and the decisions of official agencies of government.

The other major distinction of concern to us here is that although pressure groups seek to *influence* the government, the political parties seek to *organize* and *control* it. We noted earlier that political parties have undermined the system of separation of powers in their efforts to control all of the governmental agencies. Because they organize political power, the parties are the central institution of a democratic society. Responsible government is possible only where parties compete for the right to organize and control the government by offering alternative candidates and programs to the electorate.

This distinction is illustrated by the occasional efforts of pressure groups to behave like political parties. Sometimes, a group that lacks either a broad set of principles for dealing with issues or a broad-gauged appeal to a wide range of other groups has tried to achieve its aims by organizing as a party. Prohibitionists, successful with the Eighteenth Amendment as a pressure group in the Anti-Saloon League, organized themselves as a party after its repeal. Vegetarians are another example. In the nature of the case, neither group has those characteristics necessary for appealing to the electorate as a party or organizing the government if successful.

THE RELATIONSHIP OF PRESSURE GROUPS TO POLITICAL PARTIES

It is axiomatic in modern American politics that the parties have to live with the pressure system. It is also true that certain pressure groups are firmly attached to each of the major parties and serve a vital function of supplying money for the ever-increasing costs of campaigns. Labor is solidly and financially with the Democratic party and business is, or was until 1964, a rich uncle of the Republicans. Many other pressure groups align themselves with varying degrees of enthusiasm with the parties, although many of them prefer to remain aloof from partisan affairs so that they can apply their heat and financial lubricants to members of either party who will vote for the group's interests. Generally, however, pressure groups tend to favor the outlook of one of the two major parties and feel that by investing in partisan politics they can bulwark their power.

While parties welcome alliances with pressure groups, they must guard against the danger of falling captive to one or a few interests. Leonard Hall, Republican national chairman during the Eisenhower period, lamented that the Republican party's dilemma after the disaster of 1964 was to make the party something more than a collection of white, Anglo-Saxon, protestant businessmen, and that it "must make itself attractive to minority groups—not just the Negro minority but all others as well." His view was echoed by Senator Thruston Morton, who said at the time there was no use speculating about the 1968 Republican campaign because "the party must be completely rebuilt."[11] Both men are keenly aware of the fact that the Republican party needs votes and that it must gain voter appeal by broadening its base of support. Part of the Republican problem is that much of the pressure system moved

[11] Ralph McGill, "News Behind the News," *Sacramento Bee*, April 5, 1965, p. B-22.

over to the Democratic party in 1964, and the Republicans must lure them back. But how? In order to attract their support, the Republicans will have to advocate policies that threaten to alienate the groups now controlling the party, a process made easier by the fact such organizations have no place else to go. Rebuilding the party means putting some new planks in its platform, clearing out some of the dry rot, and redesigning its obsolete architecture. This, of course, is not a simple task, for the Democrats are not likely to lend a hand—indeed, they will do everything they can to delay construction, even to stealing the planks.

An example of the Republican dilemma is the abandonment of their party by ethnic minority groups, which Mr. Hall mentioned. These groups tend to vote in blocs for relatively clear-cut political objectives. For a long time the Republican party had done as much, if not more, than the Democrats to promote the objectives of the Negro. Republican administrators at all levels of government had often supported fair-employment-practice bills, antidiscrimination laws, and housing legislation. The Eisenhower administration worked for the passage of civil-rights legislation and supported the Supreme Court's order to desegregate schools. In 1960 the Republicans had roughly half of the Negro vote and might have had considerably more if the campaign had been more sharply directed toward the civil-rights issue. The Republicans, in short, had a record of Negro support and an opportunity to improve it. But they lost it in 1964 to the extent that the Democrats received 96 per cent of the Negro vote, a high price for Republican victories in the five states of the deep South. Measured in power, the Democrats made a good swap; measured in morality, their gains were considerable.

But if the Republicans woefully assess their problems arising from the organized support they have lost, the Democrats must concentrate on difficulties ahead arising from the support they have gained. Democrats have never been known for the orderliness of their affairs. Brawling among themselves in "utter incoherence," as Theodore Roosevelt put it over fifty years ago, is still characteristic of the strange bedfellows who call themselves Democrats—southerners, labor groups, civil libertarians, Americans for Democratic Action, a few industrialists, peace advocates, and eggheads are found in various combinations at Democratic conclaves. To many observers of the mid-sixties it is out of character for the Republicans to be engaged in internal warfare and rebuilding while the Democrats enjoy a comforting consensus bulwarked by fat majorities at the polls. Some of the pressure groups lured into the Democratic party in reaction to extremism may find their new environment uncomfortable even under the masterful orchestration of President Johnson, who can get his party to play in tune if anyone can. Too many divergent interests within a party create difficulties which stem from the nature of American political parties, to which we turn next.

POLITICAL IDEOLOGY AND POLITICAL PARTIES

So far our discussion has centered on the relation between political parties and pressure groups in the busy and occasionally seamy process of snaring votes. There is no discounting the importance of winning elections, and professional politicans are prone to put victory ahead of principles if the two collide. This attitude is more likely to prevail where parties are not effectively organized and where partisan differences are not clearly defined. The individual politician under these conditions is more likely to feel that his success will depend on his own personal talents for maneuver.

American parties tend to be mixed bags of principles and interests containing something for everybody. There is a significant difference between the policy positions of the leaders of the parties, as we shall see in the next chapter. But these differences are likely to be muted in the public faces the parties present and in the behavior of party members in office. The exigencies of getting elected and the dominant influence of the pressure system ordinarily operate to reduce the policy differences between the parties.

Within the parties these same influences produce some interesting results which tend to confuse further the differences between them. One acute student of American parties has described the result as a "four-party system." He argues that there is a presidential and congressional wing within each of the two major parties. Presidential parties represent the policy *liberals* within each party, while congressional parties represent the *conservatives*.[12] These differences are due in large measure to the differences in the relationship of congressmen and Presidents to the electoral process and to the pressure system.

Congressmen represent localized interests while presidential candidates must appeal to the entire nation. As a result congressmen tend

[12] James MacGregor Burns, *The Deadlock of Democracy* (Englewood Cliffs, N.J.: Prentice-Hall, 1963), pp. 257-64. See also his "Goldwater Challenges the '4-Party System,'" *New York Times Magazine*, June 28, 1964, p. 7.

to articulate constituent and group interests more than national interests. This situation has the effect of making the congressional wing of each party the more conservative since broad-based national programs often work against local interests. Texas Democrats in Congress, for example, tend to find it necessary to support legislation favorable to the oil industry, while a Democratic President's tax program might involve the reduction or elimination of the depletion allowance. California congressmen's enthusiasm for the state's defense industry collides with a national administration's program for economy in defense appropriations. Southern Democrats in the Congress, whatever their personal views, react to constituency pressure to resist the extension of civil-rights legislation. Midwestern representatives, whatever their party, are not enthusiastic about proposed agricultural reforms. Vested interests, in short, tend to be defended by congressmen more than by Presidents. Presidential candidates, appealing to a national constituency, are more able to speak for the interests of the unorganized and to address themselves to national problems. The conditions of a nationwide election seem to elicit some measure of such appeals, and until very recently presidential candidates were rarely selected from the ranks of congressmen.

The recent presidential candidacies of men with congressional experience—Kennedy, Nixon, Johnson, Goldwater—have blurred this distinction. Liberal Republican congressmen are raising their voices, and congressional Democrats have recently muted the influence of their southern far right and have moved increasingly in the Congress to a *liberal* position on domestic affairs. Ironically, on foreign policy *liberal* Democratic congressmen have taken the lead in criticizing a Democratic President and, to his discomfort, forced him to depend on *conservative* Republican support.

Despite all of these tendencies to weaken the meaning of party identification and the influence of parties on policy, the differences in ideological orientation between the parties, perhaps somewhat sharper now than they have been for years, cannot be ignored. Public policy that results from the progovernment orientation of the Democrats will differ from that resulting from the antigovernment approach of the Republicans. The numerous liberal legislative proposals and enactments of the Johnson administration, which has enjoyed a comfortable majority in Congress, would hardly be expected from a Republican president with a similar partisan majority in Congress.

Party Differences: The Historical Situation. In the past, the conflict between the two American parties appears to have had both social class and ideological dimensions. In a significant sense we have had a *conservative* and a *liberal* party. There have been periods, such as the "Era of Good Feelings" during the administrations of Presidents John Quincy Adams and Monroe, when the distinction between the parties became so blurred as to eliminate party lines almost entirely. But after 1828, the old party lines were re-established. They had had their origins in the first conservative party, the Federalists, which drew its strength from "well-to-do farmers, urban merchants, persons of English extraction, and members of such high-status churches as the Congregationalists and the Episcopalians." The Federalists were opposed by the Jeffersonian Republicans, whose support was based on the "urban workers, poorer farmers, persons of non-English background such as the Scotch-Irish, and members of the (then) poorer churches like the Presbyterians and the Catholics."[13]

These basic, class-oriented distinctions continue to furnish the centers of gravity of the two parties. The Whigs, who took over the mantle of the conservative party from 1836 to the eve of the Civil War, drew their strength from the old Federalist sources. The Democrats continued to be the party of the poorer classes and the waves of immigrants. After 1865, the Republicans inherited both the support and leadership of the northern Whigs. A writer in the 1860's said of the politics of New York, from 1828 onward: "The mass of large and little merchants have, like a flock of sheep, gathered either in the Federalist, Whig, Clay, or Republican folds. The Democratic merchants could have easily been stored in a large Eighth Avenue railroad car."[14]

In the latter part of the nineteenth century, the social cleavage of the parties was blurred somewhat by the tension between small farmers and urban workers and by the Negro issue, but the basic distinction remained. Recent studies of the class basis of historical party loyalties confirm Charles Beard's comment in 1917 that "the center of gravity of wealth is on the Republican side while the center of gravity of poverty is on the Democratic side."[15]

These differences in social-class composition of the parties have been

[13] Seymour Martin Lipset, *Political Man* (Garden City, N.Y.: Doubleday, 1960), p. 292.
[14] Quoted in *ibid.*, p. 293.
[15] Quoted in V. O. Key, *Politics, Parties and Pressure Groups*, 4th ed. (New York: Crowell, 1958), p. 235.

accompanied by ideological differences. In a meaningful sense, there have tended to be, particularly in periods of crisis, real differences in the positions of the parties. The Democrats have been the *liberal* party in the sense that they have generally pursued policies that would provide the disfranchised with access to political power and the disadvantaged with access to economic opportunity. The early stages of the conflict reflected the fundamental differences between philosophical liberals and conservatives. De Tocqueville described the conflict between the parties, in the 1830's, in this way: "The deeper we penetrate into the inmost thoughts of the parties, the more we perceive that the object of one is to limit and that of the other to extend the authority of the people."[16] The authority of the people was extended by the progressive elimination of restrictions on popular control, such as the indirect election of senators, and by the creation of devices for bringing government closer to the people, such as the initiative, referendum, and recall.

As these battles were won and the character of the political system transformed in the direction of the liberal model of majority rule, the emphasis in party rivalry shifted to the conflicts between economic *liberalism* and *conservatism* described in an earlier chapter. It focused on programs directed toward labor reform, control of monopolies, progressive income taxes, aid to the farmer, minimum-wage legislation, unemployment compensation, social security—the whole network of social legislation covered by the term *welfare state*.

The ideological base of the parties is also affected by the outlook of organized groups supporting them. Ideologically oriented groups that want government to embrace their position search for a party they can support and that will support them. The activities of their members will have some affect on the party's position. In 1964, for example, the decision of civil-rights groups to affiliate with the Democrats surely had something to do with party ideology, just as did the support of the John Birch Society (or at least of its members) for the Republican Party.

While it is possible, then, to discern ideological differences between the two parties, the demands of winning elections and of accommodating group pressures tend to discourage an emphasis on these differences. Much of the time and effort of the parties is devoted to strategy—one-upping the opposition—to the point that party differences are deliberately obscured, if not forgotten.

[16] Alexis de Tocqueville, *Democracy in America*, Phillips Bradley, ed. (New York: Knopf, 1948), Vol. I, p. 168.

American Parties: Tweedledee and Tweedledum?   Alice in *Alice in Wonderland*, encounters two characters who are mirror likenesses of each other: Tweedledee and Tweedledum. This, said Lord Bryce, the Victorian observer of American politics, is the character of American political parties. So apt was his analogy that it is still commonly used to emphasize the similarity of the parties in the United States.

We have already encountered several features of American two-party politics that operate to conceal or gloss over the differences between the parties. It may be useful at this point to summarize the factors contributing to this result.

1. A fundamental reason for a narrowing of party differences is rooted in the nature of the two-party system in a mass democracy. Both parties must be mass parties, and their approach to issues must be eclectic if they are to have a chance to win. As one expert has put it, "The first consideration of the party is to get elected, and the second to get re-elected."[17] The path to election and power in a multigroup society is a winning coalition of groups, and it is this coalition that defines the position of the parties. Since both parties share the same exclusive objective of getting elected, the character of the coalitions they engineer is likely to differ only very marginally.

Two-party competition in a brokerage political system means that the Republicans simply cannot allow themselves to become an exclusive club for white, Anglo-Saxon, Protestant businessmen who would like to repeal the income tax. Nor can the Democrats allow themselves to fall captive to the lunchpail demands of labor unions. In brokerage politics the base of operation must be broad. Tweedledee, Tweedledum—an echo not a choice—is inherent in building voting strength, and parties will continue to go a-courting among the organized for endorsements, contributions, and the basic political staple, votes. Not theoreticians or philosophers but brokers and public-relations technicians will furnish the requisite attitudes and skills. But under the economic conditions of the past, the liberal party has had a built-in advantage: its programs carried an economic appeal to the lower classes, which have always been a majority. The conservative party must win working-class support to bolster its chances of winning elections. To do so, it has had to accept the reforms of the liberal party. Republicans in the 1950's, for example, did not urge the repeal of New Deal and Fair Deal reforms. Candidate Eisenhower, in 1952, promised the farmers 100 per cent of parity, and

[17] Henry B. Mayo, *An Introduction to Democratic Theory* (New York: Oxford, 1960), pp. 90-91.

President Eisenhower pushed through Congress with Democratic support significant extensions of the social-security program. In 1960 Nixon shied away from direct attacks on the liberal establishment and sought to appeal to ethnic minorities for support. Inevitably, if the parties seek to keep alive their chances of winning, they are likely to behave like giant businesses competing for the same mass market. The differences among their products will be marginal and marked mainly by the packaging rather than the content.

2. Awareness of the differences that do exist between the parties is much sharper among party leaders than among rank-and-file voters. The results of one study disclosed that while only 10 per cent of the political leaders could not name an issue that divides the parties, 45 per cent of the electorate could not do so.[18] Given this situation, the chore of campaign managers is to blur the differences between the parties in order to appeal to the uncommitted and to avoid offending the committed. The party then becomes primarily a vehicle for winning power.

Moreover, as we will see in the next chapter, most Americans do not vote on the basis of the issues. Approximately half of the electorate have no clear idea of what their opinions are, as revealed by the fact that 48 per cent "do not know in which direction they would turn if the parties were reorganized to reflect ideological differences more clearly."[19] Insofar as they are influenced by issues, the rank-and-file of the voters tend not to disagree very widely. They tend to oppose changes in either direction, and such disagreement as exists does not correspond closely with party allegiance. As a result Republican followers are closer to Democratic leaders in their opinions on issues than they are to Republican leaders.[20] Under these conditions, for the Republican party to offer the voters "a choice, not an echo" is to court electoral disaster. If proof were needed, the Goldwater hard-conservatism campaign in 1964 provided it: the Johnson majority was a huge 62 per cent, the largest in recent history and larger even than Roosevelt's 1936 victory over Landon.

3. The inherent characteristics of a two-party system are exaggerated in the United States by the loosely confederative nature of the national parties. On the surface, the formal party structure seems to provide for a considerable degree of centralized authority. In fact, however, the

[18] McClosky and others, "Issue Conflict and Consensus Among Party Leaders and Followers," *American Political Science Review,* June, 1960, p. 372.

[19] *Ibid.,* p. 372.

[20] *Ibid., passim.*

central organs of the party are relatively powerless, and the parties tend to be loose coalitions of sectional, economic, ethnic, religious, and local political groupings. The primary responsibility of the national committees is to plan and conduct the party presidential nominating conventions every four years. They are not, in any important sense, policy bodies. The conventions themselves are the scene of a complex interplay of the parties' officeholders, leaders of city and state machines, leaders of important interest groups, and, increasingly, the leading candidates who have successfully built up an imposing public image and public support in the preconvention campaigns. In all this elaborate and complex jockeying for power, there are no mechanisms out of which a clear picture of party policy might emerge. It may almost be said there is no national party organization, at least in the sense of an authoritative and powerful national organ of the party that defines party policy, exerts a significant influence on the selection of candidates for national office, or influences the behavior of its members who hold national office.

American political parties reflect the pluralism of American society and the federalism of the constitutional structure. They must bridge local, state, and national interests. Except for the personal influence of an incumbent President, there is no effective national party center that could establish policy and program and enforce discipline or communicate party positions to party members.

4. The parties, as we have seen, are internally divided on policy issues by such factors as the historical link between the Democrats and the South, and the conflict in Republican ranks between small and medium-sized businessmen and the newer corporate managerial class. Perhaps more important is the tendency described above of the presidential and congressional wings within each party to take divergent policy positions.

At the national level, insofar as there is a national party leader, it is the President, who is leader when his party is in power. The party out of power tends to be identified with its representatives in the House and Senate. The control of the national party by out-party congressmen is largely a matter of their filling what would otherwise be a vacuum. Understandably, they resent and oppose the development of any formal party organization that would provide the machinery for developing national party policy and for disciplining those party officeholders who do not support it.

One effect of the control of national parties by their incumbent congressmen is to move the party system in the direction of the brokerage model. Incumbent politicians, of all people, are most likely to regard the winning of elections as both the proximate and the ultimate end of politics. Where they control a party, the purpose of the party is likely to be defined exclusively as the winning of elections. In a society of strong and well-organized private-interest groups this is likely to mean, in Professor Bailey's phrase, "a politics of 'boodle' and accommodation." In the second place, as we will see more fully in a later chapter, legislators become members of a "club" in which they share certain outlooks and attitudes as well as procedures for moderating differences and reconciling disagreements. The rules of the club are no doubt necessary to maintain the mutual respect and indulgence required by the legislative task. But, at the same time, if carried over into control of party affairs, they can hardly fail to have the effect of making the parties more noncommittal on matters of policy, and less inclined to the kind of proposing and opposing that makes responsible government possible.

The parties, in short, are weak and decentralized. The formal structure does not provide for effective national organization; real power gravitates into the hands of state and local organizations and of the parties' officeholders. The result is to make it less possible for the parties to give direction to government policy or to maintain an independence from interest groups. Organized minorities have an open arena in Congress largely because of the lack of party leadership and discipline. The over-all consequence is a party system approaching the brokerage model.

5. A fifth factor is an increasing deference of American parties to the nonpartisan bias, which has characterized a large segment of the electorate. No doubt this bias is caused by a typically American deep-rooted aversion to power. It has sometimes—as in the case of the "Citizens for . . ." and the "Independents for . . ." organizations—led the parties to present a more noncommittal face to the voters than their real differences would justify. Occasionally, this bias leads a party to offer itself to a popular hero, rather than to select one of the tried-and-true party leaders as a candidate. The most recent example was the wooing of General Eisenhower by both parties on the assumption that his prestige, popularity, and nonpartisanship would provide a strong coattail whereby the party and its other candidates could be pulled into office. For the Republicans, who finally did convince him to run, this proved to be a sound prediction. Two years later, however, when Eisenhower was not a candidate, the Democrats regained control of Congress.

The Role of Third Parties. No adequate analysis of the American party system is possible without a consideration of the role of minor parties, particularly of those that have arisen from time to time to challenge the two major parties from a broad ideological position. Historically, third parties have often furnished the lever by which one of the major parties has been moved to change its position, with a consequent intensification of major-party competition. Thus, in the 1890's, much of the program of the People's Party (the Populists) was taken over by the Democrats under the leadership of William Jennings Bryan, only to have Teddy Roosevelt "steal all of Bryan's thunder" for the Republicans in 1904. Subsequently, Roosevelt himself led a third-party movement to further his reforms. The Progressives made a creditable showing at the polls in 1912, syphoning off enough Republican votes to ensure the election, by a plurality, of Woodrow Wilson.

The most recent national third-party effort occurred in 1948. The Progressive party, led by Henry Wallace, attempted to attract liberals on the plea that the two major parties offered no real choice, particularly in the area of foreign policy. In this case, the effort was a signal failure. It had no visible impact on the positions of the major parties, partly because Wallace, for reasons that have never been clear, permitted Communists to take control of, and wreck much of, the organization.

Third parties have served in the past as a lever on the two-party system in another way. By furnishing opportunity for voters to cast a protest vote, reflecting their dissatisfaction with the "me-tooism" of the major parties, they have caused the latter to respond by increasing somewhat the difference between their respective centers of gravity. This was particularly true of the Socialist party, which polled nearly a million votes in 1920. Many a registered Democrat and Republican found in Eugene V. Debs, and later in Norman Thomas, an opportunity to protest. Not all the Socialist vote was mere protest, by any means. The planks in the Socialist platform, almost without exception, found their way into the platforms of one of the two major parties.

Many factors in recent years have made it more difficult for third parties to organize and less likely that the effort will be made. For example, the complexity and variety of state laws governing the appearance of parties on the ballot, the sheer growth in size of the electorate and the costs of reaching it, and the irrelevance to modern problems of many of the aspects of such traditional ideologies as socialism and capitalism. If the prospects for third-party organization are diminishing, as they seem to be, the political system will be deprived of what has been historically a major stimulus to controversy between the major parties.

The Rise of Public Relations

In describing preparations for the 1950 congressional campaigns, the New York *World Telegram* ran a story under the headline: "The Hucksters Take Over GOP Campaign."[21] The story had symbolic significance: the decade of the 1950's seems to mark the large-scale introduction into politics of the uses of the mass media and of the techniques employed to merchandise mass-produced articles in a culture of mass consumption. The story itself described the advertising paraphernalia that the National Committee and Congressional Campaign Committees were making available to Republican candidates: dramatized radio spot announcements, newsletters, street interview techniques, and visual aids of various sorts.

In 1952, both television and Madison Avenue made their first large-scale entrance into presidential politics when both party conventions became carefully staged television spectaculars. Television coverage was concentrated in metropolitan areas and available to more than 50 per cent of the voters of the nation.[22]

During the campaign, the Republican party was represented by the prominent New York advertising agency of Batten, Barton, Durstine and Osborn, whose professional influence was evident in the use of media, the treatment of issues, budgeting, strategy, and timing in the campaign. The Democratic standard-bearer, the late Adlai Stevenson, dissented vigorously from the public-relations trend with the observation that "the idea that you can merchandise candidates for high office like breakfast cereal is the ultimate indignity to the democratic process."[23] In 1952, the Democrats made little use of professional persuaders, and those they used had less voice in policy decisions. By 1956, however, the Democrats had been converted. They retained an advertising agency of their own and organized the campaign in close consultation with the professional public-relations men. The age of the advertising men in politics had apparently arrived. By the beginning of the 1960's, candi-

---

[21] Vance Packard, *The Hidden Persuaders* (New York: McKay, 1957), p. 155.

[22] Charles Thomson, *Television and Presidential Politics* (Washington, D.C.: The Brookings Institution, 1956), p. 1.

[23] Quoted in Packard, *op. cit.*, p. 172.

dates for even the humblest of offices were no more likely to enter the fray without hired professional help than an old-style politician would have been to forget the birthdays of his leading constituents.

THE ROLE OF PUBLIC RELATIONS IN POLITICS

Very early in this process, one of the first and most successful of the experts in campaign management, Clem Whitaker of California's Whitaker and Baxter, noted that "managing campaigns founded on sound public relations principles and using every technique of modern day advertising is no longer a hit or miss business directed by broken down politicians."[24] Whitaker's statement points to the pervasive influence of the professional expert in a campaign, but it does not very precisely define his role. Is he an essentially neutral expert who gives technical advice on the relative effectiveness of alternative techniques and approaches, prepares publicity releases that dramatize and maximize the audience for the candidate's position, and provides access to—besides serving as a contact with—the mass media? Or is he also cast in a policy-making role, creating the image of the candidate to be projected to a mass audience and helping to select the issues to be emphasized?

Perhaps this distinction between technical advice and policy-making is too pat. There are some fairly obvious ways in which technical advice operates to shape policy in a campaign. The expert, for example, may advise a politician that he cannot hold a television audience for a fifteen-minute speech, and that ten- to thirty-second spot announcements provide the most efficient use of limited campaign funds. Obviously nothing very meaningful can be said about complex social issues in twenty seconds, even if the time is devoted to a brief statement by the candidate himself. Still less can be said if it is used for professionally produced animated cartoons.

The intent of this technical advice is to saturate the audience by repeating the candidate's name or by identifying him with some simple and homely virtue. Insofar as issues are dealt with at all, they are given in capsule form, set forth in slogans, and relieved of intellectual content. The 1952 presidential campaign offers some instructive examples. The campaign plan called for candidate Eisenhower to deal with issues through a series of very brief, taped, and uncomplicated interviews. A voice would present the candidate with an issue; he responded in "short, simple and hopeful" terms. For example:

[24] Quoted in William Lee Miller, "Can Government Be Merchandized?" *Reporter*, October 27, 1953, p. 12.

VOICE: Mr. Eisenhower, can you bring taxes down?

EISENHOWER: Yes. We will work to cut billions in Washington spending and bring your taxes down.

Or:

VOICE: Mr. Eisenhower, what about the high cost of living?

EISENHOWER: My wife Mamie worries about the same thing. I tell her it's our job to change that on November 4th.[25]

The Republicans reportedly spent about $1,500,000 on forty-nine of these station-break spots in selective parts of the nation in the final three weeks of the campaign.[26] The Democrats, although they spent only a small fraction of that amount, countered with spots of their own. One of these went as follows: "Sh-h-h-h-h. Don't mention it to a soul, don't spread it around . . . but the Republican Party was in power back in 1932 . . . 13,000,000 people were unemployed . . . bank doors shut in your face. . . ."[27] Not even the most enthusiastic huckster could claim this to be a meaningful debate of issues.

It seems that the over-all purpose of public relations in politics is to set the issues of the campaign in such a way that they are no longer issues in the traditional sense. Here again, the 1952 campaign is instructive. The Republicans were "successful in establishing with the voter their definition of the issues at stake, . . ." which were "the government's handling of the Korean War, subversives in government agencies, and corruption." Polls demonstrated their success in making these important to voters.[28]

But are these really *issues?* The war and corruption themes were essentially charismatic appeals ("I will go to Korea"; the moral crusade) on universally desired goals. In neither case was there any hint of policy or program for dealing with the issue, or even efforts at defining the character and causes of the evils under attack. In the case of the subversion issue in government, the party traded on the climate created by Senator Joseph McCarthy and sought to read the opposition out of the democratic political arena ("Twenty Years of Treason" was one campaign theme).

This is a presentation of issues that are no longer issues. The appeal

[25] Stanley Kelley, Jr., *Professional Public Relations and Political Power* (Baltimore: Johns Hopkins Press, 1956), p. 189.

[26] *Ibid.*, p. 190.

[27] *Ibid.*, pp. 190-91.

[28] *Ibid.*, p. 200.

is addressed to stimulating emotional reactions, so that no one will be alienated and so that opposition is difficult or impossible. Much the same might be said of some of the issues created by the Democrats in the 1960 campaign. "Getting this country on the move again" is hardly a controversial position on a real issue. The issues, so framed, bear more than a superficial similarity to the issue of eating a "breakfast of champions" or preventing cavities. We do not mean to imply that this was all there was to either the Democratic or the Republican campaigns. We are here examining only the impact of advertising techniques on politics. Politicians have by no means surrendered all control to professional persuaders. What we are arguing is that when public-relations techniques have determined the character of campaigns, there has been a tendency to define real issues out of existence.

Occasionally, the professionals have even identified one of their problems as a tendency of the candidate to upset his image, which has been carefully built up, or to take positions on issues that have a negative effect on the campaign. Thus Whitaker observed that "an automobile is an inanimate object; it can't object to your sales talk—and if you step on the starter, it usually runs. A candidate on the other hand can and does talk back."[29] Another public-relations consultant commented about "the generality of candidates": They "only know they're ambitious and not much else. We take them from there."[30]

In 1964 the presidential candidates of both parties talked back to their enthusiastic advertising men and repudiated some of their more flamboyant gimmicks. The Democrats had selected the advertising firm of Doyle, Dane, Bernback, Inc., to handle their campaign because President Kennedy, shortly before he was assassinated, had been taken with the firm's clever Volkswagon ads.[31] The agency confronted the problem of how to dramatize and emotionalize the nuclear war issue. The result was a television shot showing a pretty little girl picking petals from a daisy with a male voice in the background counting backwards. Sandwiched between regular programs, the little girl came on the screen with her daisy and the man counted—ten, nine, eight—until he reached zero when the screen erupted in a loud explosion replete with flash and mushroom cloud. In the background President Johnson's voice said, "These are the stakes." "Unfortunate," Democratic Vice-Presidential

[29] *Ibid.*, p. 222.
[30] *Ibid.*, p. 234.
[31] Pete Hamill, "When the Client Is Candidate," *New York Times Magazine*, October 25, 1964, p. 31.

Candidate Hubert Humphrey admitted, after a shocked public registered strong protest at such poor taste. Candidate Goldwater was more caustic:

> The homes of America are horrified and the intelligence of Americans is insulted by weird television advertising by which this Administration threatens the end of the world unless all-wise Lyndon is given the nation for his very own.[32]

The commercial was called off.

Later in the campaign Republican strategists had similar difficulties with one of their advertising productions. An allegedly disastrous decline in national moral standards had become a prime "issue" in the Republican campaign. Russell Walton, publicity director for Citizens for Goldwater-Miller, candidly described to a strategy conference how this problem was to be exploited by the production of a film entitled *Choice*. A stenographic record reports Walton to have said:

> People who were brought up in the small towns and on the farms, especially in the Midwest, have a built-in prejudice against the city. . . . This film will obviously and frankly just play on their prejudices. . . . We want to just make them mad, make their stomachs turn . . . take this latent anger and concern . . . build it up, and subtly turn and focus it on the man who drives 90 miles an hour with a beer can in his hands.[33]

Choice fulfilled its promise. Violence on the streets, girls in topless bathing suits, race riots, stripteasers, delinquents, and covers of pornographic books appeared along with a careening car driven by a man resembling President Johnson who tossed beer cans out of the window of the speeding vehicle. John Wayne and Raymond Massey, two of Hollywood's virile conservatives, spoke about the decadence of our lives and urged everyone to vote against this decadence by electing Senator Goldwater.

Goldwater was shocked. "It is nothing but a racist film," he said, and ordered further showings stopped under threat of repudiation. The film was withdrawn in spite of efforts to revive it by the "Mothers for a Moral America," who supported the Republican candidate.

There were other tasteless efforts by advertising firms during the 1964 campaign which raised serious question about the use of advertising as a legitimate political technique. Many politicians found that they shared the public's revulsion toward such brazen attempts at mass

32 *Ibid.*
33 *Newsweek*, November 2, 1964, p. 25.

manipulation. The question that seemed to emerge was whether the proud claims by advertising men that they could successfully feel the nation's pulse needed re-examination.

Not all political public-relations men, however, are as cynical as the producers of these two ill-fated television spectaculars. Many of them sincerely believe that they are producing a wider familiarity with the candidates and with political questions than would otherwise be possible. In any event, our concern is not with their motivations but with the impact of the new techniques on political processes. One result seems to be a contribution to producing candidates who fit the description the late Governor Long of Louisiana gave to one of his opponents: "He won't say nothing, he won't promise nothing, and if he gets in he won't do nothing."[34] At the same time, it is an open question, of course, whether this is an improvement over the type of old-style boss that Long himself epitomized.

The Politician and the Professional Expert. Public-relations techniques are those of reaching and moving mass audiences. As such, they are in considerable measure the by-products of a consumption-oriented mass society generally, and of the domination of mass media by advertising in particular. Politicians are forced to compete for the attention of the voter with the entertainment provided in the mass media by other advertisers. In the circumstances, it would be surprising if they did not turn for help to those who have been successful in these media. The politician is uncertain about what approaches will be most effective, and he operates always within a very limited budget. The costs of campaigning are increased by the new media through which he must communicate, and the decisions on how to use very limited funds become more difficult.

The politician may not be certain that the experts know very clearly about the relative effectiveness of various techniques (it is very possible that no one as yet knows very much about it), but his own uncertainty is likely to lead him to trust those who have at least mastered the maze of technical detail involved in a candidate's getting access to mass audiences. Another factor that sometimes operates to increase the candidate's willingness to put his campaign in the hands of a professional is pressure exerted on him by large contributors to his campaign who have also relied on public relations in their own enterprises.[35] Sometimes

[34] Quoted in A. J. Liebling, "A Reporter at Large: The Great State," *New Yorker*, June 4, 1960, p. 74.
[35] Kelley, *op. cit.*, p. 205.

large campaign contributions are made in the form of direct payments for professional consultation or management.

THE IMPACT OF PUBLIC RELATIONS ON AMERICAN POLITICS

It seems obvious that the intrusion of professional public-relations techniques into all stages of campaigns has far-reaching consequences. But the precise nature of these consequences is not so obvious. There are differences of opinion, for example, on how these changes are affecting the voter, how they are influencing the type of candidate likely to enter politics and likely to be elected, and more broadly what they do to traditional models of democratic politics.

As a result of the use of public-relations techniques in the mass media, it has been contended, the average American citizen is becoming less apathetic, better informed, and more rational. One authority, for example, has recently claimed that television

> . . . brought about an infinite broadening of public participation in our democratic processes. It has given all Americans a clearer understanding of trends and issues. It has given them a personal acquaintance with their leaders and with those who aspire to leadership. It has increased the degree of independent thinking. . . . It has resulted in balloting based more on reason than on emotion.[36]

Whereas some people credit professional public relations with reducing apathy, its low level of intellectual content and its emotive appeal have been justified by others as techniques necessary to capture the attention of an apathetic, gullible, and ill-informed citizenry. As one professional remarked of the use of faulty and misleading statistics, "Jello isn't very solid either, but they sell a hell of a lot of it."[37] The difficulty with this rationalization is that these qualities of the citizen are not simply the stimuli to public-relations techniques; they are also a consequence of their use. The mass media, as we have seen, constitute instruments of social control and character formation. When they are the vehicles for modern consent engineering, they induce people to see themselves as consumers of candidates and issues rather than as political participants shaping public policies.

Under the necessity of mass audience appeal, it is inevitable that the choice of candidates should come to be made on different grounds.

[36] Sig Mickelson, "TV and the Candidate," *Saturday Review*, April 16, 1960, p. 14.
[37] Quoted in Kelley, *op. cit.*, p. 234.

Availability is the term used to describe the qualities that give a presidential candidate a good chance of being elected. The available candidate in the past was white, Protestant, from a large and pivotal state, and not identified too closely with particular interests or with either wing of the party. President Kennedy laid the religious criterion to rest in 1960. Still, it was these traditional criteria that were being applied when, during the campaign, the story went around that the ideal Democratic vice-presidential candidate would be "a dirt-farmer from Kansas named Martin Luther" (Kennedy, of course, was a wealthy Catholic from industrial New England).

These traditional criteria seem to be yielding to new ones: a well-known name, a good television personality, personal ability to finance and organize the pre-sales campaign and the build-up. Stanley Kelley, on whose study we have relied heavily in this section, even suggests that the political public-relations man may become a "talent scout."

If the development of public relations techniques has debased the coin of democratic debate, it is also true that the mass media present opportunities for political education never before even approximated. The mass media have created a national public, which makes it possible to confront national issues. As the Kennedy-Nixon debates in 1960 made clear, television could be a flexible and useful vehicle for the organization of competitive politics. Properly used,[38] it could put candidates on their mettle in ways not heretofore possible.

The all-important question is what the politicians, the audience, and the parties imagine their roles in the new media to be. Whether they contribute to genuine political debate and to a more responsible political system will depend on what models of democracy inform the behavior of the participants. We see no reason to abandon the conclusion that, where the media are dominated by public-relations techniques, the tendency will be to cheapen and make trivial political debate and to contribute to what has been termed a politics of *organized irresponsibility.* The political uses of public relations techniques, however, will depend largely on the character of political parties. Because parties are central to the process of responsible government, the concluding section of this chapter considers recent proposals for their reform.

[38] As follow-up polls after the 1960 debates revealed, "the debates were more effective in presenting the candidates than the issues." Earl Mazo and others, *The Great Debates* (Santa Barbara, Calif.: Fund for the Republic, 1962), pp. 2-3.

Political Parties: The Case for Reform

So far we have discussed political parties as collections of divergent interests overlaid with a general and highly diluted ideological approach to the proper role and limits of governmental activity. Clear ideological differences between the parties can hardly be expected to emerge from their internal diversity or from the Tweedledee-Tweedledum tactics employed in campaigns. To those who are still committed to traditional ideas of what democracy should be, these conditions destroy the possibility of meaningful choice, make responsible government impossible, and produce alienation and the retreat from politics that threaten the democratic process.[39]

One reform offered to correct this situation is to realign parties on a liberal and conservative basis. This would allow southern Democrats and conservative northern Republicans to unite against liberals of both the Democratic and Republican parties. This view is popular with many students of politics, who see sharper ideological differences as a means of enabling the two parties more effectively to organize responsible political competition. One observer has commented that "mean-nothing parties may reduce political heat, but they also dampen interest," and that "when parties decline in meaning there is a tendency toward leader-worship. The voter gropes for a label better than 'In' or 'Out.' Where he can't find a principle he grabs a personality."[40]

The objective of sharpening party differences on principle is usually pursued through proposals to strengthen the national parties and make them more disciplined on the European model. In parliamentary systems with highly disciplined parties such as those of Great Britain, individual legislators, and cabinet officials who first have to be elected to the legislature, adhere closely to party programs which have been clearly formulated and carefully spelled out in campaigns. If they desert their party on a crucial issue, they risk defeat for the government and the calling of a new election. American politicians have no such restrictions since they are elected for fixed terms. After they win office,

---

[39] Historically, the debate over party reform was stimulated by a committee of the American Political Science Association: "Toward a More Responsible Two Party System," *American Political Science Review* (Supplement), September, 1950. This report precipitated a lively and continuing debate over the questions of how much difference there is between the parties and how much there should be. See, for example, Julius Turner, "Responsible Parties: A Dissent from the Floor," *American Political Science Review*, March, 1951, pp. 143-52.

[40] Richard L. Strout, "Should Parties Mean Something?" *The New Republic*, April 12, 1954, pp. 8-10.

they can roam back and forth on issues more or less at will, because American parties have few disciplinary measures they can take against their mavericks. As we shall see in later chapters, legislators in the American system are noted for their freedom from party control, but much of the reason for this is that the party has no clear-cut program to which it is committed. What program there is comes from the executive, who may or may not be a member of the majority party in the legislature. Executive programs are not party programs. They tend to be made up after election and may or may not include planks from the platform of the campaign.

It is one thing, however, to say parties should be more disciplined and responsible, but it is another to devise means of making them so. Much of this difficulty results from the way political parties are organized, and some reformers think that a basic overhaul of party structure would accomplish this purpose. Stephen K. Bailey lists nine changes, most of them structural, that he believes are in order.[41] They are (1) broadly based sources of party finance, (2) two-party competition in all states, (3) national advisory councils and staffs for each party, (4) office space for the national parties in Washington, (5) eight-year terms for senators, (6) party policy committees in Congress, (7) modification of the congressional seniority system, (8) repeal of the Twenty-Second Amendment limiting the president to two terms, and (9) a roster of executive talent within each party. Bailey's recommendations are a combination of basic reforms, such as eight-year terms for senators and repeal of the Twenty-Second Amendment, and the trivial, such as office space in Washington. Their common purpose, however, is to put some muscle into the presently flabby parties and to move the political system in the direction of the majoritarian model.

Much of the weakness of parties can be attributed to their confederative nature. The states and their subdivisions (precincts, wards, cities, and counties) are the basic organizational units. National party headquarters sputter along between elections and provide little policy leadership, which falls to the President and/or Congress. Structural reforms might strengthen party organization and discipline, but it is not certain that stronger parties would automatically be less likely to play the roles of Tweedledee and Tweedledum on policy issues. This, we would argue, remains the chief problem. Its roots lie deeper than the structural flaws

[41] Stephen K. Bailey, *The Condition of Our National Political Parties* (Santa Barbara, Calif.: The Fund for the Republic, 1962), pp. 12-16.

in national political parties; they are to be found in the dominant role of public relations in political campaigns and, perhaps, in the fact that moderation is the political way of life of man in mass democracy. If so, political parties, the potential instruments for organizing a system of political debate and rule by popular majorities, will continue to be ineffective for the purpose. In the past, they have been weak and decentralized except where a popular and strong President or presidential candidate could align them behind his political program. Given the basic climate of moderation, which seems to have roots deep in the social and intellectual changes we have examined, the recent similarity of the parties may be unlike the temporary lulls in party controversy that have occurred in the past.

The likelihood of a restoration of more vital partisan debate is further reduced by the tendency of voters and candidates alike to regard legislators as representatives of their constituency's interests rather than as representatives of identifiable positions on national issues. This tends to make the campaign for the Presidency, addressed to a national electorate, the only forum for the debate of national issues. Certainly, this accounts for much of the increase in the power and prestige of the Presidency in this century.

However, mass democracy exerts pressure on presidential candidates to act as brokers of private interests on a larger scene. Even if the pressures are resisted, presidential candidates alone, in a system of separation of powers with decentralized parties, cannot provide responsible government. The coalitions in Congress, and the supremacy of interests over parties there, will continue to obscure party differences and frustrate party competition. The role of the presidential contest is an important factor in keeping alive issue-oriented controversy in party politics. But, in the final analysis the prospects for more responsible party competition probably depend on American citizens redefining their own roles and their expectations of and demands on the political system.

THE CASE AGAINST REFORM

The argument for party reform, of course, assumes the desirability of the liberal model of democracy. From the perspective of the broker model the present system serves us well. Those who accept it argue that there is no demand from the electorate for more clear-cut party differences on policy, and that it is fortunate this is the case. Greater differences between the parties would only confuse the meaning of election returns since there is inadequate ideological consistency among voters.[42] It would also prejudice the stability of the political system. "We have a political system that is kind to losers," and this is "not necessarily a bad thing." If people voted for the parties only because they agreed with their stands on a wide range of issues, then changes in public opinion or in party positions might result in "great swings in party strength." The result might be the destruction of the two-party system, and consequently any choice at all would be eliminated.

The present system operates effectively to give voters what they want. What party reformers end up arguing is that "voters *ought* to want big and clear choices from the Presidential parties."[43] Perhaps so, but until they do idealists ought to content themselves with a system that gives voters what they, in fact, do want and that provides a stable and progressive way of responding to their expressed needs and desires.

Finally, the present system also provides for flexibility and change. Party controversy is sporadic and cyclical, the significant differences occurring in periods of crisis. Typically, one party responds to certain demands in society that are not being met. If the party wins with its innovation, the other party emulates it, and the parties become more alike again. Thus, in cyclical fashion the political system moves from consensus to consensus and a very satisfactory combination of stability and flexibility is achieved.

THE FUTURE OF PARTY GOVERNMENT

Democracy demands that political power and public policy be made responsible ultimately to the people: "The people shall judge." But judge what? Who are the people? And through what political instruments is their voice to be registered and made effective?

By now, it should be clear that democrats are by no means agreed on what the legitimate and proper role of the people is. "The people," meaning "the many," may participate as one of the counters in a system of constitutional checks and balances, as found in the conservative model; "the people," meaning "the electorate," may dictate the broad outlines of public policy through party debate and majority rule, as found in the liberal model; "the people," organized into pressure groups,

[42] The argument that follows is based largely on Nelson W. Polsby and Aaron B. Wildavsky, *Presidential Elections* (New York: Scribner, 1964), Chap. 4.
[43] *Ibid.*, p. 175.

may rule through the principles of compromise and the mutual accommodation of their conflicting interests, as found in the brokerage model; "the people," as a mass audience, may choose among competing merchandising appeals in much the same way they choose a toothpaste or a breakfast cereal.

It is clear that political power has shifted from the people in the first or conservative sense to the people in one of, or a combination of, the latter three senses. Whether or not he ever did, the American common man has long since ceased to regard the House of Representatives as his branch of government, speaking for his interests and opinions in a delicately balanced constitutional order. From Jacksonianism to the present, Americans have regarded all the agencies of political power, including and perhaps especially the Presidency, as vehicles of their will. Probably this process is, for all practical purposes, irreversible. If so, the real question is the extent to which "the people" organized as a public, "the people" organized as interest groups, or "the people" organized as a media market have inherited power.

The sense in which the people rule will be determined by the character of pressure groups, political parties, and the mass media, and by the pattern of their relationships. Political parties are the potential instruments through which a public may be organized to assert the primacy of public goals over private claims. In a pluralist society, group man can always be counted on to be articulate; mass man, a product of recent social change, reacts to the calculated slogans and issueless techniques of political merchandising. Public man, the ideal of traditional theory, is almost completely inarticulate unless his voice is organized politically through political parties with principles that stand above the interests and dominate the political uses of the mass media.

When the realities of political life are viewed in this way, much of the frustration and cynicism that so often leads to an "escape from freedom" can be avoided. In a pluralist society, pressure groups are a desirable and inevitable means through which persons petition their government. From the extremist right and the extremist left alike come proposals to solve the problems of democracy by eliminating the pluralism and openness that produce pressure groups or professional persuaders. Typically, their appeal is to transcend competitive politics, to find something better than politicians, to go above the strife of party controversy. It may be possible—in our view, it is both possible and desirable—to transcend the clash of private groups and to find alternatives to the competition of political hucksters. But the only approach consistent with democracy must look to the reorganization of political competition through politicians and parties. Appeals to rise above partisan politics turn out, on analysis, to reflect a loss of faith in democracy itself.

Still less can the politician be made the villain in the piece (assuming that one finds present practices less than satisfactory). If he too often succumbs to the temptation to dodge his way through the conflicting interests, if he listens too earnestly to the siren songs of the political advertising men, it may be for the sake of his political survival. In other words, he may be trying to give constituents what he believes they want. And his successes may reaffirm this judgment.

Few politicians have adopted completely these conceptions of their role. American political history is full of examples of courage of a political sort. But political courage will be more common when it is politically rewarded. The roles of politician and citizen are interdependently related. Again, the character of the party system plays a crucial role in defining both.

Chapter Ten

CITIZENS AND VOTERS

. . . wherein the political behavior of Americans is examined to see how well they measure up to the requirements of traditional democratic theories, which demanded that they (1) share in a consensus on the basic procedural universals, and (2) disagree in an informed, rational, and tolerant manner on ideological issues of policy.

Citizens were expected to serve *as the Custodians of the Procedural Rights and liberties* (civil liberties, equality of political and civil rights, and due process of law) on which democracy depends. Studies of public opinion, however, show that there is:

> *Widespread Cynicism about Democratic Processes* and about the ability and equal rights of people to participate in government; *Widespread Agreement* on democratic values when they are stated in the most general and abstract terms, but this support disappears when they are applied to concrete situations involving unpopular causes or groups; *Greater Understanding* of and more intense belief in democratic values among *Leaders* (those who are politically active and influential) than among *Followers*. The data suggest that popular understanding and support of the democratic creed is not sufficient to permit citizens to be very adequate guardians of its fundamental values.

Within the framework of agreement on procedural values, *The Citizen as Voter* was expected to participate in a competitive politics of issues. Effective participation required him to be

> *Interested.* Recent studies, however, disclose an increase in political *Apathy.* They suggest further, that apathy is attributable to the threats posed by politics to the individual ego, to a sense of alienation from politics, and to feelings of political futility—all of which are associated with the conditions of mass society. The interested voter was also expected to make
>
> *Informed, Principled, and Independent Choices.* Studies of voting behavior reveal striking contrasts between the demands of democratic theory and the behavior of American voters with respect to each of these norms. A large majority of voters cast ballots with almost no

information about the issues or the positions of the candidates and parties; the information of a sizable minority is based on misperceptions. Of those voters who are accurately informed and vote on the isssues, a sizable proportion evaluate the issues in relation to immediate material benefits to them rather than on any

Principle. Campaigns are dominated by appeals to private interests rather than to a public interest, with the result that a significant number of votes are cast on the basis of **Visceral Responses** to the candidates and the campaigns. Voting decisions are not often **Independent,** but are based on habit, socioeconomic status, group loyalties, and geographical and regional characteristics.

A **Profile of Voting Preferences** discloses the extent to which the American electorate fails to measure up to the demands of democratic theory: even by very loose definitions only about one tenth of the eligible citizenry votes in an interested, informed, principled manner. What emerges is a picture of the typical voter as threatened into apathy, incapacitated by ignorance, manipulated by group pressures, and motivated by private interests. The hope for traditional ideals of democracy seems to lie in the differences disclosed by recent studies between

The Elite and the Electorate. Just as political leaders showed greater agreement on and more intense belief in the democratic procedural universals, so do they come much closer to meeting the democratic demand for principled, informed disagreement on issues. Moreover, Republican and Democratic party leaders disagree significantly on a range of issues involved in the *conservative-liberal* cleavage. Thus, measured by both tests of democratic theory, only a small political elite seems even reasonably well to meet its demands.

These findings suggest we have reached an **Impasse in Democratic Theory.** Are we to conclude that, because citizens have not measured up to the demands of the theory, the system has not worked? Or that, because the system works, the theory is in need of revision? Those who argue the latter make

The Case for the Irrational Voter, arguing that, because voters and leaders behave the way they do, the system is able to reconcile consensus with cleavage and stability with flexibility, and to provide for the peaceful conciliation of group interests. Other theorists respond with

The Case for Traditional Democratic Theory, which challenges these claims and argues· the need for a meaningful consensus to protect democratic values.

We may say that if the political education of the average American voter is compared with the average voter in Europe, it stands high; but if it be compared with the functions which the theory of American government lays on him, which its spirit implies, . . . its inadequacy is manifest.

JAMES BRYCE

Chapter Ten

CITIZENS AND VOTERS

TRADITIONAL THEORIES of democracy put a heavy burden on citizens. Democracy has generally been assumed to depend upon citizens who (1) share in a consensus on basic procedural values, and (2) disagree in an informed, rational, and tolerant manner on policy questions.

In the last two decades, sociologists, social psychologists, and political scientists have turned their attentions to the problem of describing and explaining the behavior of voters. As a result of the growing body of research in this area, it is now possible for us to make some generalizations about how effectively citizens measure up to these two requirements.

The most general observation we can make is that the evidence suggests a wide gulf between the traditional model of the democratic voter and his actual behavior.

The Citizen as Custodian of Democratic Values

How much faith does the typical American have in the processes of democratic decision-making? How deeply committed is he to the principle of equal political and civil rights on which popular government depends? How widely does he share and how deeply does he feel an obligation to accept and respect nonconformity? How committed is he to due process of law?

Recent studies permit us to make some significant generalizations about the state of American public opinion on these questions:[1] (1) There is widespread cynicism about democratic processes and the ability and the right of people to participate equally in self-government. (2) Although there is general agreement on democratic values when they are stated in the most abstract and general terms, this support tends to disappear when these democratic norms are applied to specific, concrete situations. (3) There is much greater understanding of and more intense belief in democratic values among those who are politically active and influential (leaders) and among those with higher incomes and more education than among the masses (followers).

These generalizations, and their implications, may be clarified by looking more closely at the attitudes of Americans toward the basic democratic norms of equality of political and civil rights, civil liberties, and due process.

EQUALITY OF POLITICAL AND CIVIL RIGHTS

When Americans are asked about the desirability of maintaining a democratic system, they are almost unanimous in their assent. But when the questions ask about equality of political rights or the ability of

[1] The studies on which we have relied most heavily are Samuel A. Stouffer, *Communism, Conformity and Civil Liberties* (Garden City, N.Y.: Doubleday, 1955); Herbert McClosky, "Conservatism and Personality," *American Political Science Review*, March, 1958, pp. 27-45; V. O. Key, *Public Opinion and American Democracy* (New York: Knopf, 1961); James W. Prothro and C. W. Grigg, "Fundamental Principles of Democracy: Bases of Agreement and Disagreement," *Journal of Politics*, Spring, 1960, pp. 276-94; Seymour Martin Lipset, *Political Man* (Garden City, N.Y.: Doubleday, 1960); Robert E. Lane, *Political Ideology: Why the American Common Man Believes What He Does* (New York: Free Press, 1962); Herbert McClosky, "Consensus and Ideology in American Politics," *American Political Science Review*, June, 1964, pp. 361-82.

people to vote intelligently, this consensus evaporates. One study found a majority of voters opposed to allowing a Communist to run for local public office or to take office if he were legally elected.[2] Another found that a majority of the general electorate agreed with these statements:

> "The main trouble with democracy is that most people don't really know what's best for them."
> " 'Issues' and 'arguments' are beyond the understanding of most voters."
> "It will always be necessary to have a few strong, able people actually running everything."
> "Regardless of what some people say, there are certain races in the world that just won't mix with Americans."

Agreement with these statements reflects a distrust of the ability of people to govern themselves and a disbelief in equality of political rights. The size of the majority that expressed agreement varied from 50.4 to 62.3 per cent. The same questions were put to political influentials (in this case the delegates and alternates to the Democratic and Republican Conventions of 1956). Their responses were more democratic on every statement. The proportion of this group expressing agreement with the statements quoted above, for example, ranged from 37.2 to 42.5 per cent.[3] Thus, while the responses of political influentials were more democratic than those of the general electorate, even here there was nothing approaching a consensus on these issues.

CIVIL LIBERTIES

Much the same situation characterizes attitudes toward the basic freedoms to dissent and criticize that are protected in the First Amendment. In one study, conducted during the height of the McCarthy period in 1954, 30 per cent would not permit speakers to advocate public ownership of railroads or major industries, 60 per cent would deny freedom of speech to atheists, 45 per cent would prohibit the publication of socialist newspapers.[4] Public-opinion polls have shown that a majority (over 60 per cent) believe atheists should not be allowed to teach, radical books should be removed from libraries, and Communists should be prevented from speaking or even from holding jobs. At the same time, all the studies agree that the leaders of organizations, including even the

[2] Prothro and Grigg, *op. cit.*
[3] McClosky, "Consensus and Ideology in American Politics," *op. cit.*, p. 369.
[4] Stouffer, *op. cit.*

Daughters of the American Revolution and the American Legion, hold more democratic beliefs than the membership of their organizations.

In one recent study, when democratic values were expressed in general terms, over 75 per cent of the electorate supported them (the percentage ranged from a low of 77 per cent who agreed that freedom of conscience should include freedom to be an atheist, to a high of 94.3 per cent who agreed that no matter what a person's political beliefs are, he is entitled to the same legal rights and protections as anyone else). But, again, when these general statements were translated into specific terms, the consensus disappeared. More than one third of the electorate agreed that "a man oughtn't to be allowed to speak if he doesn't know what he's talking about," and one half felt that "a book that contains wrong political views cannot be a good book and does not deserve to be published." By contrast, fewer than 18 per cent of the politically active and influential agreed with either of these statements.[5]

DUE PROCESS OF LAW

A third area of fundamental democratic values involves the ideal of equality before the law and the rights of the criminally accused. Here again, there is greater support for the guarantees in the Bill of Rights when they are stated abstractly; when the internal security of the nation or law and order seem threatened or when persons championing unpopular causes need protection, the average citizen is less likely to see the importance of the principles. For example, one fourth of the electorate agreed with the statement: "In dealing with dangerous enemies like the Communists, we can't afford to depend on the courts, the laws and their slow and unreliable methods." Only 7.4 per cent of the influentials expressed agreement with this statement, showing again the greater tendency of the politically active minority to support a democratic order.[6]

We may summarize these findings by concluding that a large proportion of the electorate has failed to understand and accept the underlying ideas and principles on which a democratic system rests. In every case the political elite, while not unanimous, endorses these principles in greater measure than the masses.

The undemocratic responses to many of these questions will be recognized as reflecting the alienation, anxiety and frustration promoted

[5] McClosky, "Consensus and Ideology in American Politics," *op. cit.*, p. 367.
[6] *Ibid.*

within a mass society. These tendencies are further revealed in the fact that a majority of citizens believe that "many politicians are bought off by some private interest," that "the people who really run the country do not even get known to the voters," that "a few people will always run things" no matter what the people think, that "most politicians don't . . . really mean what they say," and that "there is practically no connection between what a politician says and what he will do once he gets elected." These views reflect a deep sense of alienation from the political process. They also suggest a widespread cynicism about democatic politics. But for most voters this alienation has not yet produced the anxieties and self-doubts that lead to political activism and extremist behavior. Over 89 per cent of these same voters say they "usually have confidence that the government will do what is right."[7] Confused, apathetic, superficial, powerless, but acquiescent seem to be the adjectives that describe these attitudes toward politics. Yet, if the preservation of democratic values depends on a consensus among the electorate, the outlook is dim. We shall come back to this question after we have examined how well the average voter fulfills the second demand that traditional democratic theory made upon him.

The Citizen as Voter

Traditional democratic theory not only demanded a consensus on values, but it made certain assumptions about and placed specific demands upon the citizen as voter. Within the framework of agreement on *how* public policies are to be formulated, it was expected that citizens would disagree on *what* policies are to be adopted. In his political role of helping shape public policy, the citizen was required to be interested in and informed about public issues and capable of making independent, reasoned, principled choices among competing programs for dealing with the issues.

We are already familiar with the model from which these requirements stemmed. In it, the appeal of politicians was presumed to be to citizens who were vitally concerned about public affairs; who voted on the basis of their opinions about issues rather than on their special interests or on vague and irrelevant emotional appeals; and who had a knowledge of the issues and arguments necessary to an individual judgment. In short, the voter was presumed to perform an act of independent and informed choice among alternative principles of the public good. His

[7] *Ibid.*, p. 370.

vote was not to be determined by habit, or the determinism of social status, religion, sex, age, income, or family or group pressures; nor was it to be seriously affected by emotional response to personalities or glittering but meaningless generalities.

Only in comparatively recent years has this ideal picture been tested against reality. From the point of view of traditional theory, the results of these recent studies are disastrous.

THE VOTER: INTERESTED OR APATHETIC?

More voters turn out on election day in totalitarian than in democratic countries, and in no other major democratic nation is participation at the polls so limited as in the United States. This is the more surprising because the United States was the first nation to achieve universal adult suffrage. Yet 60 per cent of the eligible electorate is considered a good turnout in presidential elections (only in 1952, 1956, and 1964 did the figures go this high), and in local elections it often goes as low as 10 per cent. Moreover, many of those who do vote are herded to the polls by interested parties or pressure groups. They are not highly motivated and often vote more out of a sense of civic obligation (a feeling that is stimulated by popular pressures ranging from a nation-wide campaign organized by the Advertising Council of America to active efforts by the Boy Scouts to shame their elders into voting) than out of real and sustained interest in public affairs. In 1952, when Eisenhower was elected on the slogan of "Communism, Corruption, and Korea," a relatively large percentage of the electorate turned out to vote, but only 37 per cent of the public said they were "very much interested" in the campaign, and 28 per cent said they were "not much interested."[8]

Voting is only one avenue of political participation. But if the other possible means by which the average citizen can influence politics are considered—reading and listening to campaign materials, talking politics with friends and associates, contributing financially to parties and candidates, and working actively in political campaigns—it is still apparent that "a decline in political participation has been occurring in the United States concomitant with the emergence of a 'nonpartisan' set of attitudes toward the political process."[9]

Both apathy and nonpartisanship operate to reduce the popular basis

[8] Angus, Campbell, Gerald Gurin, and Warren E. Miller, *The Voter Decides* (Evanston, Ill.: Row, Peterson, 1954), p. 34.
[9] Samuel J. Eldersveld and others, "Research in Political Behavior," in Eulau, Eldersveld and Janowitz, *Political Behavior* (New York: Free Press, 1956), p. 72.

of democratic consent for governmental policy: apathy for obvious reasons, and nonpartisanship because party leadership and the competition of the parties provide the means to responsible government. Nonpartisanship very likely is promoted by some of the same causes that underlie the growth of political apathy, and in many cases it may even be simply a more respectable way of expressing one's apathy. Thus, for example, that apparently growing body of voters who regard themselves with pride as independents contains a large proportion who turn out not really to care very much one way or another. The independent is usually the least interested and motivated voter, and he is in fact very likely not to vote at all. Recent research discloses that "the more strongly the voter favors or opposes parties and candidates, the more interested he is in the election."[10] When partisan commitment is weakened, interest is decreased.

There is much about the causes and character of political apathy that we do not know. However, recent research gives us clues as to some of the factors involved. It also suggests that political apathy in some of its dimensions is not simply a response to politics but reflects those more deep-seated social and cultural developments, which we have earlier described as mass society. Research in this area has identified three sources of apathy, all associated with mass society: (1) withdrawal from politics because of the threats that it may pose to the individual, (2) disengagement, which is the result of feelings of alienation from politics, and (3) apathy that reflects a sense of futility.[11]

Politics as a Threat to the Individual. For whatever truth there is in Reisman's analysis of the mass man as other-directed, it is obvious that it should operate in the direction of increasing political apathy and disinterest. For political choice is inherently a divisive process, basically at odds with the longing for harmony. Participation in partisan and controversial political activity may be seen as a potential source of disapproval in the groups with which one associates. Typical of this attitude is the following response of an interviewee in a recent study: "We don't discuss politics much. I think it's sort of like religion. It's personal, and I don't like to get into arguments. When politics comes up in conversation I always say—'Let's talk about something else.' "[12]

It is true, on the other hand, that occupational and other groupings

---

[10] Bernard R. Berelson, Paul F. Lazarsfeld, and William N. McPhee, *Voting* (Chicago: University of Chicago Press, 1954), p. 25.
[11] Our analysis is based extensively on Morris Rosenberg, "Some Determinants of Political Apathy," *Public Opinion Quarterly*, Winter, 1954, pp. 349-66.
[12] *Ibid.*, p. 352.

may be a strong source of support for political participation. A labor union, as well as a trade association or a professional organization, may exert pressures on the individual to participate actively in politics for certain causes or candidates. More loosely, where there is political agreement among occupational associates this tends to support political interest and involvement by the members. In this connection, one of the most significant results to come out of research into voting behavior relates to the important effects of cross pressures on the individual. A voter is subjected to social cross pressures when his environment is not politically homogeneous. He may find himself in political conflict with his wife or his family, with his close associates or his neighbors, or with the members of religious and social groups to which he belongs. There is a strong tendency for most people to associate in face-to-face groups mainly with persons who share the same political dispositions, but when conflict does occur, one possible response is to avoid making a choice by withdrawing from political participation. This is likely to be especially true of those persons who can find a sense of their own worth only in the approval of others, an attitude that in the opinion of many observers is characteristic of mass society.

In addition to the threatening social and occupational consequences which may promote apathy, interest in politics ordinarily involves the individual in situations in which he risks being shown up as wrong or as uninformed in one way or another. It involves exposing oneself to the risk of ego deflation.[13] Just as some persons enter politics to enjoy the ego inflation that goes with being in the know and the chance to rub an occasional elbow with celebrities and to engage in the game of name dropping, so others stay out because of the hazards to personality. This type of person, when asked whether he discussed political questions, commented: "No, since I don't understand too much about politics, I just keep my mouth closed. . . . I don't think I am capable enough to take an active part. I just feel I lack the ability. . . . I don't know what would be required of me."[14]

Probably, the number of people who see the controversy of politics as undesirable and threatening has been increasing in recent years. As one political scientist has put it:

> By withdrawal the citizen may avoid a painful choice. He does not have to choose between two reference groups with different policies; he does not have to bring together in his own mind mutually

[13] *Ibid.*, p. 353.
[14] *Ibid.*, pp. 353-54.

incompatible ideals which are all dear to him; he does not have to risk alienating friends, customers, superiors, or in-laws; he does not have to expose himself to incompetence. All around him are people who are also apathetic who give him reassurance that he is not too derelict in his duties in this behavior.[15]

Perhaps it is significant that the word *apathy* is derived from a Greek word meaning to *not suffer*.

The Alienated Voter. Political interest and activity imply the existence of effective incentives for the individual citizen. Political questions and issues, that is to say, must be felt to have some significance for the individual. He must be able to see that these questions, or for that matter politics itself, relates to his life and to his important concerns in one way or another. There is evidence that this condition is lacking for many people in contemporary politics.

In the traditional democratic model, we should recall, politics was viewed as the arena in which men could control their collective destinies. Politics was a means by which society could be continuously adapted to men's moral purposes and public goals. A paradox of recent society is that while politics increasingly affects men's lives as the boundaries of governmental activity are expanded, the individual's feeling of control and competence and his sense of mastery over the future seem to have diminished: ". . . people no longer feel confident that they can affect their destiny, in anything that matters, by political action, individual or collective."[16] When people are asked about issues in campaigns there is always a sizable "don't know" response; this often means really "don't care."[17] And not caring stems from an inability to see direct and important consequences affecting oneself or society from the victory of one side or the other.

These attitudes may even characterize persons who are politically active in campaigns. One study found that even active party workers are "not typically motivated by ideological concerns or plain civic duty"[18] but by the sources of ego inflation noted above. This suggests that even among those who are politically active, for a great many the psychological incentives are social rather than political. Political issues themselves often seem to many persons abstract, distant, and impersonal.

[15] Robert E. Lane, *Political Life* (New York: Free Press, 1959), p. 47.
[16] David Riesman and Nathan Glazer, *Faces in the Crowd* (New Haven, Conn.: Yale University Press, 1952), p. 33.
[17] Berelson, Lazarsfeld, and McPhee, *op. cit.*, p. 309.
[18] *Ibid.*, p. 307.

As contrasted with family, job, and friends, the subject matter of politics seems not to relate to their personal lives.

Political campaigns must be pitched to those whose votes are likely to be influenced. Especially is this true of the minority party (that is, the party that has a minority of registered adherents). Both parties must, of course, seek to activate their partisans and ensure that they get to the polls. But the majority party must also seek to hold its potential waverers, and the minority party must make these marginal supporters of the opposition its major target. There is an especially high proportion of apathetic persons among this very group of un-decideds. The result is that campaigns tend to be keyed to those sorts of appeals likely to activate voters who have a heightened sense of alienation. This leads campaigns to be increasingly personalized and emotionally flavored in competition with other media of mass enter-tainment. The marginal voter tends to exert even more than his due share of influence on campaign techniques and strategy. And this in-fluence is exerted in directions other than rigorous analysis of public issues or sustained debate of a public interest.

Apathy and Futility. In addition to the threatening personal conse-quences of politics and alienation, a third major source of political apathy is the sense of individual powerlessness to affect the course of po-litical decisions, the belief that the individual vote really makes no dif-ference anyway, and the conviction that political power is wielded by an elite that is not genuinely susceptible to the influence of the average citizen and voter.

These feelings of futility may arise from several sources. They may be rooted in the feeling of being dwarfed by the size of the electorate as when the individual feels that his is only an insignificant single vote destined to be overwhelmed by the huge number of the votes and voices of other participants. Or they may reflect the individual's feeling that he is weak in relation to powerful and usually anonymous forces—a vague "they" who make up the City Hall crowd or the political machine or simply the government—who will continue to run things as they wish and for their own benefit, despite anything that citizens might do at the polls. Or they may stem from a conviction that the parties do not offer the voters real alternatives, that pressure groups are the real, effec-tive agencies of politics, and that the role left for the individual as voter is accordingly negligible. Finally, they may flow from a resentment at being made the objects of manipulation by high-powered opinion engineers.

The attitude that a single vote cannot be important when there are large numbers of voters going to the polls is a common one. The size of modern electorates does tend to make the influence of the individual voter appear *deceptively* small. We say *deceptively* because it is not the total vote that the individual must compete against in order to be effective, but rather the number constituting the margin between the candidates. Where over seventy million people vote in a presidential election, the influence of a single vote looks small indeed. But where elections are won by as little as one vote per precinct in the country, the picture appears quite different. Yet sizable numbers of people continue to believe, with this respondent, that "voting doesn't make that much difference. What can an individual do about it? He can't really do much. My vote will always count, yet one vote one way or the other doesn't make much difference."[19]

Those who, for whatever reasons, develop a sense of futility about the role of the average citizen in politics are likely to have their views reinforced by the financial aspects of political campaigns. Especially as the costs of campaigning continue to rise, those who see themselves as powerless are likely to regard all campaign contributions as purchases of special favors. Witness the comment of one person on a Boston campaign for mayor: "He spent too much money campaigning. I thought of where all those funds came from."[20]

Feelings of futility about politics are related to demographic characteristics in the population. Thus, the person who believes that he can exert a significant influence on politics is likely to be college-educated, from upper-income and higher-status occupational groups, male, white, and residing outside the South in a metropolitan area. A heightened sense of futility is associated with the following characteristics: grade-school education, female, Negro, low income, unskilled workers and farmers, southern residents, and residents of rural areas.[21]

In part, these results reflect the objective access of different groups to political power and influence. People of higher socioeconomic status are more likely to know, or to know persons who know, successful politicians; they are more likely to have experienced situations in which efforts at political influence have been successful. Persons of lower socio-

[19] *Ibid.*, p. 355.
[20] Murray B. Levin, *The Alienated Voter* (New York: Holt, Rinehart & Winston, 1960), p. 60.
[21] Campbell, Gurin, and Miller, *op. cit.*, pp. 187-215.

economic status, on the other hand, are much less likely to have come close enough to the seats of the mighty to feel any sense of control or participation. Similarly, women and Negroes are only recently enfranchised groups and in many respects are still second-class citizens.

We must be careful, however, about drawing conclusions from statistical correlations like those above. It is true that education and higher socioeconomic status tend to promote a sense of involvement and obligations of civic participation, and that lack of education and lower socioeconomic status tend to promote feelings that a vague and powerful "they" are really running things. Partly, at least, this futility is a product of ignorance of the political process and governmental institutions: people tend to fear what they do not understand. But it would be a mistake to assume that education and increased status, for example, are cures for a sense of futility.

The uneducated are more likely to believe that "most major policy decisions are the work of 'wire-pullers' and pressure groups and the product of 'backroom deals.' "[22] But, paradoxically, this is close to one modern sophisticated analysis of the realities of the democratic process. It is, indeed, a reasonably accurate, though somewhat crudely put, restatement of the brokerage model of democratic politics. If the term *wire pullers* is replaced by *lobbyists*, and *committee sessions* and *bargaining situations* are substituted for *backroom deals*, the resulting description is not too wide of the mark.

In addition to this essentially intellectual rejection of the politics of compromise, there is a psychological sense in which increased knowledge of political realities may produce a heightened sense of futility. We have already noted that political interest and motivation may be party-centered, issue-centered, or candidate-centered. And we have noted also that people subjected to cross pressures are less likely to be politically active. Where cross pressures involve conflicts for an individual in these motivational factors (that is, where his party, issue, and candidate preferences cannot be reconciled), the extent of political participation tends to be reduced.[23] The looseness of party lines in a system of broker rule seems likely to increase the incidence of these cross pressures. At the same time, increased education and political knowledge are likely to increase the individual's awareness of these cross pressures where they exist. Here again, education under present conditions may promote, rather than retard, tendencies toward the retreat from politics.

[22] *Ibid.*, p. 188.
[23] *Ibid.*, pp. 157-59.

THE VOTE: REASONED CHOICE OR CONDITIONED RESPONSE?

In the traditional rhetoric of democracy not only was the voter assumed to be interested, he was also described as performing an act of reasoned choice, which was at once informed, principled, and independent. Research has shed light on the extent to which these requirements are typically met by the American electorate. The results reveal a striking contrast between democratic theory and democratic reality. It turns out that a large percentage of voters cast their ballots without much information about the issues, the candidates, and the parties; and they vote on the basis of the influence of family and close associates, economic interests, socioeconomic status, or unconscious, psychological factors. We turn now to a brief review of some of the research findings as they relate to the requirements that the vote be informed, principled, and independent.

The Problem of Information. Everyone is familiar with examples of experiments that show how few voters are able to name or recognize the names of their representatives in Congress, state legislature, or city council. According to the authors of one study of voting behavior, most voters do not consider their vote as carefully or act as knowledgeably as when, for example, they are considering the purchase of a new home or car.[24] Some voters do not see the issues as important or relevant enough to their own immediate concerns to justify the time and effort necessary to inform themselves properly for an intelligent voting decision. Others vote almost habitually out of party commitment and use their allegiance to a party label as a substitute for seeking information and listening to argument.

An informed vote, we may assume, is a vote cast on the issues in a campaign. In order for an issue to affect a voter's decision he must meet three tests:

1. He must be aware of the issue and have some opinion about it.

2. He must feel that the issue is important enough to make a difference; his opinions must be relatively intense.

3. He must see some difference in the way that the political parties will deal with the issue.[25]

---

[24] Berelson, Lazarsfeld, and McPhee, *op. cit.*, p. 310.

[25] Angus Campbell and others, *The American Voter* (New York: Wiley, 1964), Chap. 7.

These are fairly simple and unsophisticated tests, which must be met if a person's vote is to embody any kind of policy choice on the issues in a campaign. Yet, only 25 per cent of the electorate seems to meet even these minimal conditions. The size of this minority that makes rational choices on the issues is reduced even further when we take into account that many of those who perceive differences between the parties do so incorrectly. The general tendency working here seems to be for voters to see the candidates they support as agreeing with *them* on issues and the opposing candidates as disagreeing with them, irrespective of the positions the candidates have publicly taken. For example, 70 per cent of the Republicans who favored price control in 1948 saw the Republican candidate, Thomas E. Dewey, as also favoring price control even though his public speeches and statements clearly indicated his opposition. In 1956, 22 per cent of the voters perceived a difference in the positions of the parties on the issue of whether electric power and housing should be left to private industry. But 25 per cent of these incorrectly saw the Democrats as advocates of *laissez faire*.[26] Voters, in other words, perceive political reality in a highly selective way, so that what Walter Lippmann has called "the pictures inside people's heads" often are falsifications of the political reality outside. The more partisan the voter, the more he is subject to this kind of misperception. The result is that partisanship leads to misperception, which reinforces the original partisanship, which leads to further misperception. These tendencies are aggravated where the actual, objective situation is ambiguous, as it often is in political campaigns.

It is not true, however, that the attitudes of voters toward candidates are stereotypes that cannot be changed by evidence. The more an individual is exposed to the campaign (through newspapers and other mass media and campaign speeches and materials), the more likely he is to perceive the positions of the candidates accurately. Accuracy of perception also increases with education level, interest, and membership in organizations, but exposure to the channels of political communication is the most influential variable. This suggests that much of the misinformation that voters take to the polls is a result of not caring sufficiently to expose themselves to the campaign. We need to recognize, of course, that the fault does not lie entirely with the voters. A failure to see differences in the party positions may be an accurate perception where the parties seek to be all things to all men.

[26] *Ibid.*

Principle or Private Benefits? In the middle of the nineteenth century, John Stuart Mill stated clearly an important premise of traditional democratic thought. The voter, he said, "is bound to give it [his vote] according to his best and most conscientious opinion of the public good."[27] Research suggests that most voters may lack this essentially altruistic motivation, and that most votes are cast for candidates or parties from which the voter expects definite and tangible benefits to accrue to himself. In considerable measure, the arguments of candidates are rationalizations of the interests of the audiences to which they are addressed. Personal advantage, rather than a standard of the public interest, seems to be the major basis of appeal in American politics.

We have noted that the issues in a campaign affect the votes of probably not more than 25 per cent of the electorate. But we cannot conclude from this that one fourth of the ballots are cast on the basis of principle. Many of those who are influenced by issues are motivated by considerations of material self-interest (a low-income voter who votes Democratic to secure benefits from the extension of government welfare services, for example). Only a very small segment of the population is equipped to approach political decisions on the basis of a philosophical commitment or of a general set of norms like those described as ideological *liberalism* and *conservatism* in an earlier chapter. The proportion of the electorate whose vote reflects this kind of principled evaluation of the issues and an accurate perception of the positions of the parties rarely exceeds 10 per cent.[28]

There are two sorts of appeals to private interest that characterize political campaigns. There is first the appeal to the interests of organized groups: promises to farmers to vote for high support prices; promises to labor to vote for increased minimum wage requirements or liberalized industrial accident or unemployment insurance laws; promises to specific industry groups to safeguard local products from foreign competition through tariff; promises to elderly citizens to increase social-security benefits; and so forth.

The second appeal is reflected in the situation in which candidates

---

[27] Quoted in Henry B. Mayo, *An Introduction to Democratic Theory* (New York: Oxford, 1960), p. 75.

[28] Campbell and others, *The American Voter, op. cit.*, Chap. 9. A recent analysis of voting patterns in local elections on expenditure proposals concludes that "the higher the income of a ward or town, the more taste it has for public expenditures of various kinds," including those that will be paid for by higher-income groups but benefit lower-income groups. See James Q. Wilson and Edward C. Banfield, "Public-Regardingness as a Value Premise in Voting Behavior," *American Political Science Review,* December, 1964, pp. 876–87.

promise to secure differential advantages for all their constituents against others. Examples would be the location of a new state college or university in the district; a new county fair ground supported by state funds; reclamation projects, parks and recreational facilities; and government defense installations. This process is revealed in attitudes of California congressmen in the period since World War II. California has twice as much in defense contracts as the next leading state. This means that the protection of this economic advantage has become a major staple in the campaign of incumbent congressmen who claim to be responsible for this pleasant state of affairs and to stand jealous guard over the efforts of less favored states to reverse the situation.

Whichever of these two forms the appeal to private interest takes, one of its consequences is to minimize the role of a public interest in political debate and electoral contests. If politics is a matter of interests, the incumbent can lay claim to effectively representing all interests in his constituency. His opponent is reduced to the difficult task of seeking to maintain that he can do the same thing better. Thus, the tendency on the part of voters to cast their ballots on the basis of their economic interests is reinforced by campaigns in which private interests are the ground of appeal.

Issues or Visceral Responses?   In addition to those whose vote reflects an informed and principled judgment and those whose vote reflects self-interest, there is another large group of voters whose voting decisions seem to be made on grounds in which information about the issues is simply irrelevant. These are the voters whose behavior is based on visceral responses, to use the refined expression—"gut reactions," in Levin's less elegant but more descriptive phrase. Here are some reasons voters offered for their choices of a candidate in a Boston mayoralty campaign: "Don't like his looks"; "smug—looks crooked"; "something about his eyes"; "looked icky, talked funny—the sound of his voice"; "a good man to his family"; "a real gentleman"; "just the way he spoke, I feel he is honest."[29] Considerations equally remote from the issues operate in presidential campaigns; the hair styles and taste in apparel of the candidates' wives, for example, have been matters of political comment and influence.

THE VOTE: AN INDIVIDUAL OR A SOCIAL ACT?

The requirement that the voter be informed was supplemented by the expectation that in casting his ballot he would behave independently

[29] Levin, *op. cit.*, pp. 44, 63.

as an individual. His decision would then reflect his own thinking about public issues and not his ties to socioeconomic status, the pressures of the members of groups to which he belonged, or other types of social compulsion. The evidence available about how people actually behave conflicts with the requirements of the democratic model. Voting decisions of individuals tend to be group rather than individual acts. Voting behavior turns out to be correlated statistically with a wide range of social characteristics. The most significant correlations tie voting behavior to (1) socioeconomic status, (2) group loyalty and allegiances, and (3) geographical and regional characteristics.

We need, however, to remember that statistical correlations do not tell us anything at all about the reasons for any particular individual's vote. "Still," as Professor Clinton Rossiter has put it,

> . . . if we mind our step and are alert to the pitfalls, we can make excellent use of the broad generalizations that the Democrats are a party of the South, the city, the poor, the unions, the hard-luck farmers, the immigrants and their children, Negroes, white supremacists, the young, the least educated, and the most educated; the Republicans a party of the North, the country, suburbia, the rich, the middle class, the business community, the good-luck farmers, the old stock, the middle-aged, and the college graduates. In making these generalizations, we must note that we are speaking of tendencies more than of imperatives. Both parties can still claim to be all things to all men.
>
> Above all, we must be careful to pay homage to American individualism. As we travel over the political landscape we may come across the perfect demographic Democrat—a poor, young, unionized, Roman Catholic, second-generation, un-skilled laborer named Grabowski with an eighth-grade education and a lumpy bed in Buffalo—and find that he votes the straight Republican ticket, or the perfect demographic Republican—a well-to-do, middle-aged, salaried, Protestant, seventh-generation, top-management executive named Hoover with a college degree and a lovely home in Scarsdale—and find that he votes Democratic and, in addition, throws in $500 a year. The Republicans will be happy to have Grabowski's vote, the Democrats will invite Hoover to sit at the head table at the Jefferson-Jackson day dinner, and political demographers will be reminded once again of the hazards of their trade.[30]

Voting and Socioeconomic Status. The most common and well-documented conclusion of all the studies of the behavior of American voters is that persons in lower-income groups tend to vote Democratic

[30] Clinton Rossiter, *Parties and Politics in America* (Ithaca, N.Y. Cornell University Press, 1960), pp. 105-6.

while those in upper-income groups tend to vote Republican. While socioeconomic status is correlated with party affiliation, it is even more closely associated with attitudes toward issues. This fact seems to be best explained as a manifestation of the tendency of voters, especially low-income voters, to act politically on considerations of narrow, immediate self-interest. Thus, lower-status voters are more *liberal* than higher-status voters, and the more direct and obvious the connection between the issue and self-interest, the more *liberal* the lower-status voter tends to be. For example, lower-status voters are more *liberal* on the question of whether government should guarantee employment and on social-security issues than they are on government regulation of business.[31] Of course these attitudes are not necessarily reflected in party preferences. Voters, as we have noted, often do not know enough about politics to translate their self-interest into electoral choice. Where educational level and especially political involvement are low, there is no significant relation between attitudes on issues and party affiliation. Thus, the attitudes of lower-status Republicans on welfare issues that would serve primitive self-interest do not differ greatly from attitudes of lower-status Democrats.[32] The relatively slight differences that do exist go in the direction we would expect—that is, at the same income level —Democrats tend to be more *liberal* than Republicans.

Income appears to be an independent variable in determining voting behavior. Most other variables associated with socioeconomic status— for example, occupation, education, age—turn out to be dependent variables, which cancel out when differences in income are controlled. Thus, except for the very highly educated, the greater the amount of education a citizen has, the more likely it is that he will vote Republican. This does not mean, as Democrats are quick to point out, that there is any connection between being educated and seeing the Republican light, for the correlation between education and political preference turns out really to be an expression of the basic relation between income and political preference. Higher education is associated with higher income, and where income is controlled, educational differences in voting decisions disappear.[33]

The same thing is true of age differences. Younger persons tend to be more liberal and are more likely to vote Democratic, but again this

[31] McClosky, "Issue Conflict and Consensus Among Party Leaders and Followers," *American Political Science Review*, June, 1960.
[32] Campbell and others, *The American Voter*, *op. cit.*, Chap. 8.
[33] Berelson, Lazarsfeld, and McPhee, *op. cit.*, p. 334.

correlation disappears where socioeconomic status is controlled. Religion, however, probably plays an independent role in some limited ways. Political differences among Protestant denominations (a higher percentage of Episcopalians vote Republican than do Baptists) disappear where income and occupation are controlled. But the same does not seem to be true for Catholics and Jews. Even at the same income and occupational levels, Catholics seem to be more Democratic than Protestants, Jews more Democratic than Catholics.

There is one point that needs clarification. If the vote is so largely correlated with socioeconomic status, how do the Republicans ever manage to win elections in the light of the fact that there are many more members of the lower economic classes than of the upper classes? The first factor is that, as we have seen in the earlier section, there is a higher percentage of voters among high-status persons than among wage earners. For example, one study found that 75 per cent of all executives and 74 per cent of all professional workers voted in 1948 and 1952, as compared with only 47 per cent of wage workers.[34]

The second reason is that the correlation between voting preference and socioeconomic ties is by no means unity; that is, there are persons at all levels of socioeconomic status who vote for the candidates of both parties. At the same time, the vote is more cohesive in the higher socioeconomic range than in the lower. In most surveys, fully 75 per cent of those persons engaged in business, professions, and white-collar employment vote Republican. A considerably smaller majority of wage workers vote Democratic, largely for reasons we have already noted. Lower-income groups are also less educated and less involved in politics. They are consequently less able to perceive differences between the parties, and many a lower-status person with Democratic attitudes votes Republican out of ignorance. If it were not so, the Democrats would be perpetual winners.

Group Influences on Voting. Apart from considerations of socioeconomic status, there is another major category of influences that suggests that most voters do not vote independently. These influences flow from the effect of group membership on the individual and the pressures toward group loyalty and conformity. Included here are the influences of the family and of religious, ethnic, occupational, and other primary or reference groups.

[34] Angus Campbell and R. L. Kahn, *The People Elect a President* (Ann Arbor: University of Michigan, Survey Research Center, 1952), p. 109.

The family appears to be the primary unit in fashioning political preferences. Voting studies disclose that, in fully 90 per cent of all family situations, husband and wife agree in their voting decision. In upwards of 70 per cent of the cases, voters adopt the political preferences of their parents and grandparents. These data are even more impressive when we take into account the testimony of psychiatrists that, in a large although undetermined number of cases where individuals depart from the voting preferences of their parents, the reasons are still to be found in primary group relationships. The deviant voter is often expressing his "resentment against his own group, rebellion against authority figures, or the wish to defend himself against an unbearable amount of submissiveness and to show his independence by his deviant vote.[35] Many psychiatrists have testified to the frequency of situations in which a divergence in political opinion and belief between the individual and his parent appears to reflect an unconscious and infantile need to usurp or overthrow the dominance of a parent figure.

Most people, the evidence demonstrates, acquire their party affiliations very early in life and tend to maintain and strengthen them. This is, of course, the period of life in which knowledge of issues and of party positions is the slightest. We are forced to conclude that party preference is predominantly a matter of social pressures to conform, especially those generated within the family.

Beyond the family, the political experience of most people occurs within the framework of like-minded group association. Most political discussions carried on by citizens occur in homogeneous primary groups, and the exchange consists of mutually reinforcing observations on the campaign, candidates, and issues, rather than debates. In most situations in which voters start out with views different from those that prevail among their primary associates, they modify them in the direction of conformity. People who are subjected to cross pressures and conflict in their primary allegiances tend to vacillate and withdraw, or they reinforce one alternative over the other by looking to "wider associations in the surrounding communities."[36]

The available data lead us to the conclusion that voting is primarily a social rather than an individual act, and that most persons in casting their ballots register the preferences and attitudes dominant in the

---

[35] Franz Alexander, "Emotional Factors in Voting Behavior," in Burdick and Brodbeck (eds.) (New York: Free Press, 1959), p. 302.
[36] Berelson, Lazarsfeld, and McPhee, *op. cit.*, p. 100.

groups to which they belong. The average voter votes the way trusted people around him are doing, even though he may be firmly convinced that his decision is uniquely his own, undetermined or uninfluenced by social pressure.

Sectional Influences on Voting. In addition to group influences on voting, there are broader geographical and regional voting patterns in American political life. The most familiar of these is the sectional Democratic vote of the South. With the exception of 1928, when some of the southern states bolted the Democratic ticket because of the Catholicism of candidate Alfred E. Smith, the deep South was solidly in the Democratic camp until 1952, when Stevenson lost Florida, Texas, and Virginia to Eisenhower. The states that border the solid South exhibit a clear tendency toward the Democratic party, although most of them were carried by Eisenhower in the 1952 and 1956 elections. After the Civil War the deep-South states of Mississippi, Alabama, Georgia, and South Carolina had never gone to Republicans until 1964 when, along with Louisiana, they ended up as the only states in the Republican camp. The reason, of course, was what *Newsweek* called "Goldwater's states' righteous 'southern strategy.' " After the election the future of party fortunes in the South was in doubt. Old loyalties had been broken, whether permanently would depend on such factors as the position of the Republican party on the civil-rights issue, the effects of the civil-rights movement, and the 1965 voting rights legislation on Negro registrations.

Until very recently, New England seemed to constitute a Republican hinterland, matching the solid South in its loyalty to the Republican cause. In recent years, however, Massachusetts, Rhode Island, and Connecticut have turned up on occasion in the Democratic camp; Maine and Vermont have, since 1958, elected Democratic candidates in state-wide contests. The Rocky Mountain states, especially Wyoming and Colorado, have been leaning toward the Republicans. The same is true for Oregon. Most of the states, however, have been genuinely two-party states in which the contest is close.

Farm, City, and Suburbs. Within the states themselves, there are varied patterns of community political preference. The large urban centers have been Democratic bastions, which, in election returns, smother the Republican majorities returned by rural areas. Largely since World War II, the phenomenon of the growth of suburbia promises to introduce a new element into the traditional urban-rural split.

During the first quarter of this century, American politics was revolutionized by the migration from farm to city. In the period since 1940 particularly, the major population movement has been from the central city into the suburban community. The following estimated population figures tell the story: in the suburbs of the large metropolitan areas there were fifteen million people in 1920; by 1940, there were twenty-three million; thirty-five million by 1950; and fifty-three million by 1960. By that date, slightly more than one fourth of all Americans lived in suburban communities. In the decade from 1950 to 1960, while the major cities increased in population by about 10.7 per cent, the suburbs of the largest cities increased by 48.6 per cent.[37] Most analyses of the political behavior of suburbanites suggest that there is a suburban *conservatism*. In the elections from 1952 through 1956, Republican majorities in the suburbs overwhelmed the traditional Democratic majorities in the cities proper. Practical politicians, as well as scholars, have noted this trend. On election night in 1952, Jake Arvey, Democratic potentate in Illinois, is reported to have said, "The suburbs beat us."[38]

As scholars have pointed out, in 1952 the commuter country around such large cities as New York, Chicago, Cleveland, Detroit, and Milwaukee rolled up heavier Republican majorities than these cities proper gave the Democrats.[39] In the 1954 congressional elections, New York City voted 65.9 per cent Democratic, while the suburban areas in Suffolk County gave only 30.9 per cent of their votes to the Democrats. Similar results came in from such areas as Chicago, Philadelphia, and most other large metropolitan sections.

The Republican voting pattern of suburbia has been attributed to the exposure of new residents to a conservative and Republican environment, one in which new friends and neighbors share conservative values and in which the political attitudes acquired in large urban Democratic districts are regarded as lower-class habits. Others argue that socioeconomic status considerations are more important. In this view, the new suburbanite is seen to be a person who is already upwardly mobile

[37] Wilbur C. Hallenbeck, *American Urban Communities* (New York: Harper, 1951), p. 202; *U.S. News and World Report*, November 25, 1955, p. 35; and *Statistical Bulletin*, Metropolitan Life Insurance Co., July, 1961, p. 1.

[38] Louis Harris, *Is There a Republican Majority?* (New York: Harper, 1954), p. 124.

[39] Samuel Lubell, *Revolt of the Moderates* (New York: Harper, 1956), p. 112.

before he joins a suburban community. It is a well-established thesis that the impact of social mobility on groups that are climbing their way up the status ladder is to make them more sensitive to the political norms of the groups into which they are climbing. As one observer has said:

> Anyone who aspires to move upward on the social scale will almost certainly sense the fact that the political coloration of the level toward which he is moving is more Republican than the one which he is leaving. This does not mean of course that he will necessarily change his politics as his social status improves, but he will become increasingly aware that Republican values are the accepted standards of the people whose approval he seeks.[40]

Another possible explanation sees suburbia as the habitat of the "other-directed" man and the center of popular culture. Its style of life is epitomized in the quest for diversion and for "belongingness." If so, it is not correct to characterize the political attitudes appropriate to it as conservative in the traditional, middle-class sense (involving a commitment to *laissez faire* and business interests and opposition to progressive taxation and government programs of economic amelioration). The conservative attitudes reflected, after all, certain ideological commitments. And ideology, this argument runs, is contrary to the political style of the typical suburbanite. The attitudes of suburbia, some observers have held, spell "the end of ideology," conservative or otherwise.[41]

In this view, the political style appropriate to the dominant tendencies of suburban life is characterized by moderation and a commitment to the middle of the road. The suburban Republican majorities in the 1950's reflect the fact that, under Eisenhower's leadership, the Republican party had become the party of moderation. Not conservatism, but "conservative liberalism" and "moderate progressivism" were the slogans of the Eisenhower years. If so, the Republicans cannot take for granted a suburban majority. This was indicated in 1960 when the Democrats picked up substantial strength in the suburbs. In 1964, when the Republican campaign permitted the Democrats to occupy the moderate middle, Johnson won the suburbs by 59 per cent.

In addition to the growth of suburbia there have been other homogenizing forces at work on the American electorate in recent years—for example, the growth of mass media, the spread of industrialization

[40] Angus Campbell, "The Case of the Missing Democrats," *New Republic*, July 2, 1956, p. 13.
[41] Daniel Bell, *The End of Ideology* (New York: Free Press, 1960).

into previously rural areas, the importance of defense industry in the economies of most states, the external and internal threats of communism, the dominance of foreign-policy issues, and (with the exception of the Puerto Rican migration to New York) the end of significant new ethnic immigration. The effect of these developments may well be the progressive elimination of ethnic and regional voting patterns.

A PROFILE OF VOTING PREFERENCES

Some over-all idea of the extent to which the American electorate measures up to the demands of democratic theory is provided by an intensive study of the 1956 election conducted at the University of Michigan Survey Research Center.[42] On the basis of responses to interviews voters were classified into four categories, which reflect the extent to which their votes were a function of ideological principle, information, private interests, habit, group loyalty, and emotion. The results are summarized below:

1. *Ideology and Near-ideology.* A vote cast on the basis of ideology is what we have described as a principled vote. The category includes those who use concepts involved in the ideological *liberal-conservative* distinction described in an earlier chapter and who do so in a fairly coherent manner (example: "The Republican Party is more middle of the road, more conservative," along with reactions to specific issues consistent with the over-all appraisal). Only 2½ per cent of those interviewed qualified for this category. As a consequence of the fact that these people are more likely to vote, they constituted 3½ per cent of the actual voters in 1956.

The category of near-ideology includes those who use generalizing ideological concepts but not in a sophisticated or completely consistent manner (example: The Democrats (or Republicans) stand for individual rights, federal control, middle of the road, monopoly, higher standard of living). Even with the addition of those who met this very loose definition only 12 per cent of the electorate (15 per cent of actual voters) qualified in this first category. No more than 12 per cent, that is to say, showed even a fuzzy understanding of the broad principles that might be applied to political issues.

2. *Group Benefits.* A second category base their evaluations of politics on the response of parties and candidates to the interests of

[42] Campbell and others, *The American Voter, op. cit.* The data in the section that follows are drawn from Chap. 9.

groups. Some of these tended to see politics as an arena in which many groups compete for favor (example: "Farmers have always had good times under Democratic administrations; Republican politicians favor Wall Street"). A second subcategory includes those who evaluate political alternatives on the basis of a single group interest with which the person identifies himself (example: "Well, I just don't believe the Republicans are for the laboring people"). A third subcategory includes those whose preferences rest on group benefits but whose group identifications are relatively shallow or vague (example: "I know nothing about politics, but I like the Democratic party because I know they are more for the poorer people; the Republicans are out to help the rich people").

In none of these group-benefit reactions is there any idea of a public interest, of the solution of social problems, or of social justice. In each case persons react to parties and candidates on the basis of whether they are for or against the groups with which the individual is identified. The striking fact is that 42 per cent of citizens (45 per cent of actual voters) fell in this category. The attitudes of a substantial proportion of voters, it would seem, reflect and approve the model of broker rule.

3. *Self-interest in Good Times*. People in this category make some references to public policy but have no abstract or generalized concepts for judging policy and no perception of the relationship of group interests to policy. Instead the economic condition of the person's immediate family is used as a basis for judging that times are good or bad and for praising or blaming the party in power (example: "When the Republicans are in, my husband's investments in stocks are up"). Or one of the parties may be seen as responsible for a specific personal benefit (example: The elderly person living on social-security payments who links his checks with the Democratic party).

Persons in this category are aware of no other issues that influence their preferences. They tend to resent party controversy and to identify it with mudslinging. This category included 24 per cent of the sample and 22 per cent of the voters.

4. *Absence of Issue Content*. Persons in this category exhibit no perception of issues. They either (a) are loyal to a party without any conception of why ("I'm a Democrat, that's all I know"), or (b) are cynical about both parties and concerned only about the personal characteristics of the candidates (looks, sincerity, religion, family life, etc.), or (c) have no attitudes toward politics at all ("Parties are all about the same to me; I don't know about either one of the men

enough to give an opinion"). Still, one fourth of these persons with no opinion voted in 1956.

Those in this fourth category with no issue consciousness at all represented 22 per cent of the sample, 17 per cent of the voters.

The results are summarized in the following table. In the terms we have been using two thirds of the electorate approached their role as citizens on the basis of self-interest (individual or group); nearly a fourth had an irrational basis for their preferences or no preferences at all. By even the loosest definitions, little more than one tenth of the electorate approached their public roles in an informed and principled manner.

Table 1
Summary of the Bases of the Political Preferences of Citizens and Voters in 1956*

BASIS OF POLITICAL PREFERENCE	PROPORTION OF TOTAL SAMPLE		PROPORTION OF VOTERS	
1. Ideological concepts				
(a) Ideology	2½%		3½%	
(b) Near-ideology	9		12	
Total		11½%		15½%
2. Group benefits				
(a) Group interests in multi-group conflict	14		16	
(b) Single-group interest	17		18	
(c) Shallow and vague concepts of group benefits	11		11	
Total		42		45
3. Self-interest in good times		24		22
4. No issue content				
(a) Party loyalty without policy reasons	4		3½	
(b) Candidate preference on personal grounds	9		7	
(c) No political preferences	5		3	
(d) Unclassified	4½		4	
Total		22½		17½
		100%		100%

* Adapted from Chap. 9, Table 9–1 in Campbell and others, *The American Voter, op. cit.*

This profile lends no support to the hope that there are tendencies operating to reinforce a picture of voters as independent, deliberating members of a public organized to make reasoned selections of public policy. The irresponsible voter—threatened into apathy, incapacitated by ignorance, manipulated by group pressures, and motivated by private interests—emerges clearly enough from the data to pose a dramatic challenge to our traditional ideas of what a citizen as voter ought to be.

The Elite and the Electorate

Recent inquiry into the question of how much disagreement exists in the United States on policy questions has disclosed that it is necessary to distinguish between two groups of citizens on the basis of education, socioeconomic status, and political involvement. As we saw earlier in this chapter, the large majority of voters exhibit no firm belief in the democratic universals; the small minority of those who are politically active and influential serve as the carriers of the creed. The same distinction applies in the same way to the question of issues and public policies. The elite, much more nearly than the electorate, meets the democratic demand for principled, informed disagreement on issues.[43]

In contrast to the general electorate, the active party leaders adopt attitudes on the issues that are quite ideologically sophisticated and coherent. The leaders of the two parties are separated by differences large enough to provide the required disagreement and opportunity for significant choice. Their differences conform generally to the *liberal-conservative* ideological cleavage described earlier. Across the whole range of issues significant disagreement holds: Republican leaders are more likely to regard welfare programs as government handouts; to favor greater regulation of unions; to identify with business, free enterprise, and economic conservatism generally. Democratic leaders, to a significant degree, are more friendly to labor, favor welfare programs and economic liberalism in general. The respective party leaders are widely separated on such issues as federal aid to education, slum clearance and public housing, social security, and minimum wage laws. Democrats favor these programs by majorities of from 50 to 78 per cent, while only a minority of Republican leaders (ranging from 16 to 40 per cent) favor them. Democrats, judged by their leaders, are much more willing to use the power of government to extend benefits to the underprivileged.

---

[43] The discussion that follows draws heavily on McClosky, "Issue Conflict and Consensus Among Party Leaders and Followers," *op. cit.*

Republicans, by contrast, are not so much committed to eliminating existing welfare programs as to keeping them from being expanded.

As we have noticed earlier, the general electorate is not characterized by ideological sophistication. Rank-and-file Republican and Democratic voters do not disagree nearly as sharply as do the party leaders. In fact, "the level of consensus among the electorate (with or without regard to party) is fairly high."[44] There is not enough disagreement among the electorate to furnish significant competition over issues. If any segment of the population meets the democratic test of significant, principled disagreement on issues, we must conclude it is a very small political elite.

The Voter and the Crisis in Democratic Theory

So we have come to an impasse, many believe, in the theory of democracy: we are forced to admit that citizens do not cast their votes in the way that traditional theory required for the system to work. Are we, then, to say that the system has not worked, and should we try changing the behavior of voters to fit the model so that it will work? Or are we to say that it has worked, and, therefore, we need to find out how and why it has worked and to revise our theory of democracy accordingly?

In recent years, a significant school of thought has pursued the second of these alternatives. Many theorists argue that there is nothing wrong with the American voter; the problem lies with the traditional theory, which imposed impossible—and unnecessary—demands on him in his role as citizen. In the following section, we present such a case—not the only one, but a representative and leading one.

THE CASE FOR THE IRRATIONAL VOTER

According to this argument, a major difficulty in traditional democratic theory has been that it took as its point of departure the individual citizen rather than the political system. If we can transcend our inherited tendency to think in individualistic terms and think first about what we want a democratic political *system* to do, we will be able to discover why our own has worked as well as it has and why it has even worked better, perhaps, than it would have if voters had behaved as they

[44] *Ibid.*, p. 419.

should. We will even discover that irrational individuals are necessary in order to make the system behave rationally.

What is it then that a democratic *system* ought to do? Although there are many ways of answering this question, there seem to be at least three qualities that have inhered in our own politics and that help to account for the fact that we live under the oldest existing constitutional republic. These qualities are: (1) the provision of a balance between consensus and cleavage; (2) the ability to reconcile stability with flexibility and change; and (3) the creation of a framework within which the conciliation of the rival claims of conflicting groups in society can be peacefully achieved. We shall consider briefly how the actual characteristics of American voting behavior contribute to the meeting of these three tests.

Consensus and Cleavage.   Democracy, we have argued, requires disagreement and debate of public policies; at the same time, it requires agreement on the underlying procedures and values of its political processes. The typical American voter, as we have seen, provides neither. This, however, need not occasion concern, argue the defenders of mass democracy. For what is necessary is not that people verbally express conscious agreement on the validity of principles, but that the existing rules of the game are preserved in practice. Habitual patterns of behavior are more important in preserving democracy than conscious, verbalized agreement on its principles.[45] What people *do* is more important than what they *say* they believe. Fortunately for the democratic system, those who express the most undemocratic principles are least likely to be active in politics at all. A large portion of the people, for example, may not believe that atheists or Negroes or socialists should be allowed to run for public office, but they are too apathetic and alienated to act on their beliefs in concrete situations.

Moreover, there is a saving remnant, a political elite who do tend to share a consensus on fundamental democratic values and who constitute the politically active and influential segment of society. These are the carriers of the creed, and they are sufficient for the purpose.

This same class of political influentials provides the necessary cleavage on policy issues. Unlike the general electorate, its members are characterized by significant disagreement on issues. They tend, then, to fit the traditional model: in their agreement on the procedural principles

---

[45] See, for example, Carl J. Friedrich, *The New Image of the Common Man* (Boston: Beacon, 1950), and Prothro and Grigg, *op. cit.*

of democracy they provide the system with consensus; in their conscious, articulate disagreement on policy they make it possible for the system to adapt continuously to meet changing social problems. The masses, by their very apathy and political inertness or by their tendency to accept the procedures supported by the influentials, permit the game to go on according to the democratic rules.

Stability and Flexibility. Any workable democratic system must provide for both stability and change. It must be capable of adapting itself to new conditions, but, at the same time, it must avoid the instabilities and fluctuations of power that characterize some of the Latin American "democracies" for example. It may be argued that the American system provides a strikingly successful solution to this problem and that it does so because of, rather than in spite of, the fact that its citizens behave irrationally. If all citizens voted independently, the result would be government by fits and starts without the necessary stability and continuity of policy. In the American system, stability is provided by the role of habit in the voting decisions of a majority of citizens. These ties of habit tend to be self-perpetuating, precisely because they are not rational or reflective or principled. Voters do, to be sure, modify their political preferences, but this is a very gradual and, from the point of view of the individual voter, an almost unconscious process.

On the other hand, the element of flexibility in the system is provided by the independent voter who is likely to change his mind during the course of the campaign. As we have seen, the so-called independent is even further from the ideal of what a citizen ought to be than the biological, "my-party-right-or-wrong," partisan. He is likely to be inconsistent in his beliefs, caught in cross pressures, but, unlike the donkey between two bales of hay, not likely to care very much anyway. Thus, two groups of citizens, neither of whom embodies the traditional virtues of citizenship, may provide the political system with the desirable qualities ideal citizens could not furnish.

If democratic pluralism is to be reflected in politics, there must be some correlation between political party membership and socioeconomic, ethnic, and other affiliations. The correlation, however, must not be too close, else there will be "total political war between segments of the society."[46] If, for example, all labor union members or all Catholics or all lower-income families were Democrats, and all business and professional groups or Protestants or high-income families were Republicans,

---

[46] Berelson, Lazarsfeld, and McPhee, *op. cit.*, p. 320.

a stable political system would be impossible. Under such conditions, the losing side in an election would be unwilling to accept a defeat that seemed to mean oppression by the victorious side.

The Peaceful Conciliation of Group Interests. In the view we are considering, perhaps the major problem of politics is seen as the peaceful and willing conciliation of the rival claims made on public policy by competing individuals and groups. The social, cultural, and political conditions that make possible an environment in which a politics of conciliation and compromise can prevail is a central problem for any democratic system. On this assumption, it can be argued that the highly motivated and interested citizen of the traditional model can only increase the temperature of politics to the point where the climate is too heated for an effective politics of accommodation.

We have noted that only a minority of American voters seem highly motivated and interested, still more are mildly involved, and a large and apparently growing group is apathetic. The large number of Americans who stay home on election day may be regarded as indicative of confidence in the basic governmental process, of a unity reflected in the feeling that, whichever way the election goes, things will not turn out badly. Moreover, under any other conditions we should not be able to expect that an electoral decision would be accepted on all sides or that the wounds of a heated campaign would heal rapidly when the election is over. A society in which the voting turnout approaches 100 per cent, in the absence of compulsory voting, is on the verge of revolution. Highly involved voters who see politics as a crusade for their conceptions of social justice are not the ingredients of a situation in which the compromise necessary to democracy can prevail. Indifferent or very lukewarm involvement on the part of large numbers of citizens reflects a general satisfaction with the *status quo* and provides the foundation for the process of conciliation and compromise of interests on which the success of a democratic system rests.

The arguments on each of these three points all emphasize "the collective properties that reside in the electorate as a whole and in the political and social system in which it functions."[47] Citizens are not required to be members of or to aspire to membership in a homogenous electorate characterized by interest, independence, and rationality. What makes the system work, it is held, is that the citizens are a heterogeneous group with a mixture of different and contradictory properties; in the

[47] *Ibid.*, p. 312.

balance of these properties lies the clue to a successfully operating democratic system.

THE CASE FOR TRADITIONAL DEMOCRATIC THEORY

Basically the argument for the existing system is that it works; who can quarrel with success? One answer is that those who are still committed to the ideals of classical democratic thought can, and do. Their case rests essentially on two arguments: (1) the system does not work in any meaningful democratic sense; and (2) its highly valued stability is precarious and threatens constantly to be upset in orgies of antidemocratic excess. Let us examine these arguments more fully.

1. Traditional democratic theory starts by questioning whether the system works. It insists that the verb *works* must be related to some purpose or goal or ideal. Democracy itself must be a normative, rather than a merely descriptive, theory.

It must be admitted that the traditional requirement of the citizen, "if pushed at all, becomes an impossible demand on the democratic electorate," at least in the sense that under modern conditions we are not likely to find anything like a majority of ideal citizens. But the theory of democracy has never claimed to be a description of actual political societies. Its description of the democratic voter was never offered as a picture of the average voter. It is, rather, an ethical norm of behavior. The democratic political system is, among other things, one in which this norm lives as a criterion against which citizens are continually urged to measure their behavior as citizens. The men who formulated this theory were never under the impression that group loyalties, habit, passion, and self-interest could be eliminated from politics. But they understood that they could be contained and superceded only so long as there were public norms of behavior that made contrary demands on citizens.

It would make as much sense to argue that the religious norm of love as a basis for human relations ought to be abandoned because the empirical evidence on prejudice, war, rivalry, and other forms of aggression proves that most men hate. Judged on this basis, not even the most proximate example of a religious society could be found in the world. But the crucial fact is this: insofar as there are differences in the behavior and relations of men in the world, certainly the ideals that men hold help directly to explain them. Every ideal, if it is to be meaningful, makes impossible demands on people; that is what makes it an ideal.

For consciously formulated goals and ideals the brokerage system substitutes consensus among organized groups. It may be fairly doubted that policy proposals meeting the test of such a consensus can move quickly and forcefully enough to cope with the problems of a society undergoing rapid and far-reaching social and economic change. We need to ask about how the system adapts itself to change; what gives direction to the changes that are effected? There would seem to be two possible answers. First, it might be a political elite skilled in the ability to manipulate the anxieties, the emotions, and the desires of the marginal voters—the cross-pressured, uncertain, mildly concerned independent whom we have examined. The second possibility is that campaigns and elections are a largely meaningless façade behind which the real forces of local and special interests operate freely in their incessant struggle for differential advantage. In this case, political change is simply a response to the constantly shifting and changing balance of economic and social forces in a pluralist society. It is aimless, not consciously determined by anyone.

Both of these alternatives involve the surrender of the liberal faith that man might consciously and purposefully steer his course into the future; they invite him, instead, to enjoy the fruits of tranquillity in the present at the necessary price of surrendering his responsibility for the future. They also encourage men to cease struggling against their own irrationality which turns out to be, happily, the very prerequisite of a rational political system. As was the case with the traditional theory of *laissez faire*, private vices are transmuted into public virtues, as if by an unseen hand.

2. The second point that traditional democratic theory would make is that the system is likely to be an unstable one over the long run. The segment of the population that does not accept or understand basic democratic procedures constitutes a large, latent protest vote, which deters leaders from publicly advocating or acting on their own convictions (as, for example, in the case of the bare handful of Congressmen who dare publicly to criticize the actions of the House Committee on Un-American Activities or to vote against its appropriations). The general result is that political leaders are largely incapacitated from protecting the principles they are committed to and fail almost totally to challenge publicly the undemocratic views of a large segment of the electorate. Thus, even an unorganized public opinion opposed to or confused about democratic procedural values operates as a massive deterrent to the protection of those values by the political influentials.

We should note, parenthetically, that the undemocratic segment of mass opinion seems to operate precisely as what group theorists call a potential group. But, whereas in the broker model potential groups are supposed to endow the system with stability and to preserve the rules of the game, the effect of the potential political organization of the undemocratic voter is precisely the opposite.

No doubt this is a basic and crucial cause of the tendency in recent years for the mantle of "defender of the democratic faith" to fall on the shoulders of the "undemocratic" Supreme Court in all of the significant areas of democratic principle: political equality and civil rights, civil liberties, and due process of law. In a later chapter we shall examine more closely the implications of the historical default of political leaders in these areas and the assumption of responsibility by the "nonpolitical" courts. In the present context the point is simply that even the alienated and politically inactive exert powerful pressures on political leaders that make it difficult or impossible for them effectively to play the role of carriers of the democratic creed.

When those segments of the electorate which do not share the democratic consensus become politically active, their activity tends to become cumulative and to obscure and complicate the effort to debate the meaning of democratic principles and to define their limits. This is true because the danger we are discussing does not result from large numbers of voters embracing some antidemocratic ideology; it results, rather, from their failure to understand at all clearly the essential principles on which democracy is grounded. Recall that, typically, there is a consensus on democratic values when they are stated in their most generalized form, but that this consensus disappears when they are applied to actual, concrete situations. The result is a large number of potential activists who will believe themselves to be defending and safeguarding democratic principles while they are actively engaged in undermining them. This phenomenon has been apparent to close political observers of the American scene and to potential leaders of mass movements for a long time. Huey Long, Louisiana politician of the 1930's and perhaps the most powerful demagogue of recent American history, recognized it in his comment that if a dictator ever came to power in America he would do so in the name of democracy and Americanism. It is supported also by empirical studies of the partisans of undemocratic American political movements. One researcher concludes, for example, that support for McCarthyism "represented less a conscious rejection of American democratic ideals than a misguided effort to defend them. We found few McCarthy supporters who genuinely shared the attitudes and values associated with his name."[48]

Professor Herbert McClosky, the author of the research referred to, goes on to offer additional evidence on the point:

> Lacking the intellectual equipment to assess complex political events accurately, the unsophisticated may give support to causes that are contrary to their own or to the national interest. In the name of freedom, democracy, and the Constitution, they may favor a McCarthy, join the John Birch Society, or agitate for the impeachment of a Supreme Court Justice who has worked unstintingly to uphold their constitutional liberties. . . . Our findings on the attitudes shown by ordinary Americans toward "extreme" political beliefs . . . verify that the possibilities just cited are not merely hypothetical. Those who have the least understanding of American politics subscribe least enthusiastically to its principles, and are most frequently "misled" into attacking constitutional values while acting (as they see it) to defend them.[49]

These considerations raise serious doubts about the sort of optimism contained in the conclusion that the apathy of "those who are most confused about democratic ideals" will save the system because "their role in the nation's decision process is so small that their 'misguided' opinions or non-opinions have little practical consequence for stability."[50]

Finally, we would want to insist that any political system is to be judged primarily on its consequences for individuals, including their capacity to participate as citizens in the conscious, reflective choice of public goals and policies. And we would argue that a theory of democracy is inadequate if it involves no greater demands on its citizens than to be their own sweet, apathetic, uninformed, self-interested and manipulated—but indispensable—selves.

Those who argue for replacing the hopelessly idealistic and optimistic eighteenth-century view of the role of the citizen with a realistic model more in keeping with the actual behavior of voters base their case on the desirability of recognizing man as he is. This position neglects, we believe, the basic truth expressed by Goethe: "When we take man as he is, we make him worse; but when we take man as if he were already what he should be, we promote him to what he can be."[51]

---

[48] McClosky, "Consensus and Ideology in American Politics," *op. cit.*, p. 377.
[49] *Ibid.*, p. 379.
[50] *Ibid.*, p. 376.
[51] Quoted in Viktor E. Frankl, *From Death Camp to Existentialism* (Boston: Beacon, 1959), p. 110.

Chapter Eleven

LEGISLATORS AND
THEIR ENVIRONMENT

. . . which examines some of the forces at work within the legislative branch of government that have an impact on public policy.

The Role of the Legislator is an exacting one: innumerable extralegislative demands upon his time compete with his official duty of enacting laws; the complexity of the legislative task in modern industrial society is overwhelming. Still, in the final analysis,

A democracy is a government of **Men,** not of **Laws** in the sense that laws are always subject to change by legislators. Because legislatures reflect the social forces of the society they represent, in a pluralistic society as heterogeneous as the United States it becomes very difficult to understand and evaluate the processes of **Congress.** Such an evaluation must start by asking the question,

What Is a Legislator? and proceed by examining some of the **Models of the Legislative Role.** Three major conceptions of the role and responsibility of a legislator may be classified as (1) The legislator as errand boy and broker, in which combination role he faithfully mirrors his constituency, negotiating for their interests when they speak with a clear voice, serving as neutral broker when their interests conflict. Lacking ideological commitments of his own, his relationship to the voters will emphasize a personality image. (2) The legislator as political hack, who fronts for a party machine, a powerful local interest group, or a newspaper that dictates his vote. (3) The legislator as idealist, whose behavior is dictated by a personal commitment to an ideology or a cause that makes compromise difficult. Political idealists find the brokerage way of life frustrating; although they may recognize compromise to be sometimes necessary, drawing the line becomes almost impossible.

Which of these roles is likely to be dominant will depend on **The Legislative Environment,** which is shaped by both formal and informal forces. The environment of American legislatures creates a close relationship between **Legislators and Lobbyists.** This relationship is enhanced by the strength

325

of the pressures of local constituency interests; by the influence, financial resources, and effective pressure techniques of lobbyists; and by the weakness of the ties between

Political Parties and the Legislator. Where politicians do not depend mainly on their political parties for election and where the parties are not organized effectively in the legislature to promote party policies and to discipline their members for failing to support party policies, the legislator tends to see his future as tied more closely to pressure group support. He also in this environment finds himself faced with

The Dilemmas of a Legislator. Some of these dilemmas are inherent in the legislative task: he must vote "aye" or "nay" when he would prefer to vote "yes, but . . ." In addition, he faces the problem of the relationship of

The Legislator and His Constituents, which is made difficult by the localistic bias of American politics. His electibility depends on voting his district even though this may violate his conscience. Moreover, to protect his district's interests he must bargain away his vote on other issues. This is a special case of the central dilemma of legislators:

Conscience or Compromise? A principled vote will ordinarily have costly consequences; therefore, the problem becomes one of weighing costs against gains and of seeking to draw a line between necessary and justifiable compromises and a surrender of independence and integrity.

Who Are the Legislators? The differences in personal style and outlook among legislators are wide; yet, they have common characteristics (professional, social, religious, and economic) that are relevant to how they function. Moreover, their activities occur within a

Club atmosphere, which establishes and enforces informal rules. These rules provide members with mutual protection and can be violated only at great risk of political punishment. The informal rules of the club tend further to mute party differences in the Congress.

Leadership in the Congress, as in all political bodies, may be either formally established or informally exercised. In any case it flows into the hands of men, widely different in personal temperament, who can effectively organize their party colleagues for power purposes; the extent to which there is also effective leadership for policy purposes varies with circumstance and personalities.

The subtlety and complexity of this environment make difficult the understanding and evaluation of the legislative process and of legislators. Yet, in a democracy, this is an inherent part of the public role of the citizen.

A letter from PRAY (Paul Revere Association, Yeomen, Inc.) predicts that the nuclear test ban will end up with "the Russians and Zionists ruling the world, all Christianity wiped out, and all wives, mothers, and daughters in the brothels of Asia, China and India." George W. ("Wake up Humanity") Adams demands that I "banish organized religion damned quick lest organized religion banish the world a hell of a lot quicker." A neighbor wants to know, "What are you clowns doing in Washington?" A 13-year-old boy asks me if I have ever taken a bribe. A tired-looking woman timidly seeks help in getting veterans' benefits, since she just learned that her husband, who years ago abandoned her with 10 children, had recently died after living with another woman in Brazil.

REPRESENTATIVE CLARENCE D. LONG

Chapter Eleven

LEGISLATORS AND THEIR ENVIRONMENT

CONGRESS and other legislative bodies are the key institutions of representative democracy. As the public's representatives, legislators are carefully observed and sometimes severely upbraided by both professional and amateur observers of their activities, and a vast literature has resulted from these various observations. In this chapter we discuss the legislative environment and its effects on public policy. The next chapter will focus on the complicated machinery through which legislation is made.

The Role of the Legislator

During the 1959 session of the lower house of the California legislature, the Assembly chaplain offered the following prayer:

> *Ever-present God,* We seek immediate attention to our prayer for we think we can afford only a few moments, and, please, God, answer our prayer instantly. If you have any word of guidance for us, speak promptly, but, please, God, do not expect promptness from us. Carelessly some of us waste the time of others who must wait in committee and on Assembly floor while we get ourselves organized. You know our excuses: the telephone, an office visitor, we just couldn't make it on time. We mean we could have, but did not. Forgive our self-deception and our lack of courtesy to others. Help us, O God, to be present and ready for every duty, and thank you, God, for your prompt attention.—AMEN.[1]

The chaplain's candor was refreshing and his implicit plea that the legislative sessions should have first call on the time of a legislator is understandable. It minimizes, however, the great burden of work facing legislators, particularly United States congressmen who represent large constituencies. Much of the work has to do with matters not directly concerned with enacting laws—errands for constituents, correspondence, political party matters, speeches, and other time-consuming duties. All these things distract the legislator from his primary responsibility of acting upon proposals before his legislative house.

In Congress itself, his responsibility is enormous. The matters he must consider and vote upon are staggering in both variety and quantity. He must pass upon legislation in almost every area of human affairs, including appropriations for innumerable governmental activities both domestic and foreign; taxation measures to raise the money for appropriations; proposals to guarantee civil rights and liberties to minority groups; public housing bills; welfare proposals; demands for policy declarations covering the political activities of civil servants and military personnel; agricultural programs; social-security measures; veterans' benefits; debt ceilings; tax depletion allowances; inquiries into foreign policies; federal-state-local governmental relationships; lobbying activities; aid to education; criminal procedures and penalties; immigration matters; bankruptcy regulations; new federal judicial districts and new courts to handle special kinds of cases; atomic energy; defense weapons; wages and hours legislation; and bills for the regulation of interstate commerce,

[1] *Assembly Daily Journal,* May 6, 1959, p. 3281.

communications, securities, aircraft, and other areas of the national economy.

Some sessions of Congress will be more concerned with some of these areas than others. Some Congresses will be known for their action on particular monumental measures such as social security, foreign aid, or land grants for state institutions of higher learning. Others may become known, perhaps unfairly, for their inactivity. For example, President Truman's 1948 campaign included many attacks upon "that no-good, do-nothing Eightieth Congress."

LAWS AND MEN

A time-honored aphorism of American politics holds that "we have a government of laws, not of men." This implies that law is a moral cut or two above the decisions of mere mortals. Many devotees of the law have carried such assumptions to the point where they look to constitutions, statute books, and judicial decisions for answers to moral questions on the premise that within these legal documents lies the key to moral direction. Yet, in a democracy it is obvious that law is made by men, capricious creatures that they are, and law reflects the characteristics of men, including their greatness and their pettiness.

It is for this reason that legislative bodies are the most distinctive structural characteristic of democratic government. When one speaks of the British Parliament, the Congress of the United States, the North Dakota State Legislature, or the Sacramento County Board of Supervisors, he is referring to that body of persons chosen by constituents in a given area to represent them in enacting measures for the public benefit. Democracy assumes that people will participate in shaping their own destiny and will prescribe the rules by which they will proceed to fulfill it. Legislative bodies are the basic means to this end. Laws and ordinances passed by these bodies determine the rules that executives administer and enforce and that courts will judge. Constitutions, executive vetoes, and judicial review may sometimes thwart the legislative will, but the long-run course of public policy is usually set by legislatures.

THE DIFFICULTY OF EVALUATING LEGISLATURES

Legislatures are the locus of most of the social forces of the society they represent. It is here that these forces become pressures for recognition or demands for solutions to social problems. Politics in its most elaborate forms is involved in a bewilderingly complicated way to reach solutions to these problems. Many standards and measurements of legislative activities are applied to attempt an understanding of the process, but these often leave even the most sophisticated observer doubtful of the accuracy of his appraisal. Even at the purely descriptive level it is difficult to discover, for example, how a particular law was passed or why another failed of enactment.

The effort to explain the activities of a legislature involves an assessment of complex pressures, motivations, rules, and procedures not completely intelligible to the participants themselves and likely to leave the citizen who has not been behind the scenes of the legislative pageant hopelessly lost. Did the Civil Rights Bill pass because of any real congressional attitude that such a bill was good, or did it get through Congress because one political party knew it could roast the opposition by presenting it an issue that would tear it to shreds? Or did it pass because politicians of both parties in the North and West were seeking to cultivate significant organized groups of voters? Do we have a tax depletion allowance for the oil industry because it is in the public interest or because it was horse-traded by congressmen partial to the oil lobby for a favorable vote on another issue, such as civil rights?

The answers to these questions are not simple and are sometimes impossible. No one person, even a congressman himself, can have available all the cloakroom conversations, cocktail party chatter, and luncheon talk around the capitol. The personal motivations, ambitions, or fears of a legislator all have an effect on what he does. So does the influence of important bureaucrats, lobbyists, constituents, wives, secretaries, and his political party. The best that can be hoped for is a plausible explanation not too far removed from what happened in particular cases and a broad view of the general characteristics of the decision-making process.

We do know, however, a good deal about some of the methods of persuasion and influence as well as legislative convictions that lead to laws. We also know a good deal about certain congressmen. Senator Doe always votes for the public utilities, and Representative Roe is the man who always supports and often sponsors antitrust legislation. Such information is useful in predicting the outcome of certain bills. It is particularly useful to the lobbyist who accumulates such information so that, for example, labor can predict how many solid votes it has on particular issues or the oil lobby can judge its chances for desired legislation. For the lobbyist, this is important information since he must avoid writing checks on his accumulated good-will account with legislators for what are likely to be lost causes. It also permits him to concentrate his attention on fence sitters. These legislators are given even more thorough attention because it is the fence sitters who often decide important issues and who are most subject to persuasion. Moving a legislator off the fence on an issue to which he is indifferent is one of the greatest tasks and tests of skill of the lobbyist.

Briefly, we can gather a good deal of empirical evidence about legislators and the means they use to achieve their ends. We also can draw some general conclusions about the most significant characteristics of the process through which public policies are adopted. But our picture will surely remain incomplete.

WHAT IS A LEGISLATOR?

After the votes are cast, the political posters swept up, and the autumn air cleansed of the political smog of the preceding months, the victors in the contests for legislative seats emerge triumphant and anxiously await the day they will begin or continue to make laws for the rest of us to obey. But who is this victorious peer and what will he do when he makes our laws? Legislators are representative of the society that chooses them.[2] The appeals and promises of the campaign were many and varied. Yet, in one way or another, each managed to appeal to a majority of the voters in his constituency.

There are sharp differences, though, in the way that a legislator may perceive his role, that is, in the self-image from which he defines his relationship to constituents, interest groups, party, and his own conscience. We can identify three broad models that may define the politician's role, generally, and his conception of the public interest, in particular.

Models of the Legislator's Role. 1. A legislator may conceive himself as a political errand boy or cash register, whose obligation it is to mirror faithfully his constituency and skillfully to negotiate in the legislature for their attitudes or interests, whatever they may be. Such a legislator is inclined to keep his "ear to the ground and his nose to the wind," seeking to gauge shifting public sentiment and attitudes as these are reflected in public-opinion polls, letters from home, and the importunities of delegations of citizens. He is likely to regard what he

[2] Interesting appraisals of what legislators are and do may be found in Richard L. Neuberger's "I Go to the Legislature," *Survey Graphic*, July, 1941, pp. 373-76; Jerry Voorhis' *Confessions of a Congressman* (Garden City, N.Y.: Doubleday, 1947); and Clem Miller's *Member of the House* (New York: Scribners, 1962).

learns as a mandate that deprives him of the right of independent judgment. When his constituents do not speak with a clear, near-unanimous voice—either in their attitudes on such a question as capital punishment or in their interests in such a question as taxation or minimum wage legislation—the appropriate posture for the political errand boy is the role of broker. In this circumstance, he may seek that solution which is tolerable, if not desirable, from the points of view of persons and groups with conflicting attitudes or interests. If this is impossible he can, in the last resort, avoid a position and find occasion to be in a conflicting committee meeting or the men's room when a vote is taken.

Lacking a political philosophy of his own, or at least unwilling to allow it to interfere with his political career, the broker politician who is a political mirror must rely in his campaigns upon organizational support and his personality. Ideally, a 100 per cent American with an attractive wife, war record, broad grin, glad hand extended, three lovely children; of the middle class but from humbler origins; who is hardworking, honest, able, and sincere—such a man offers himself as a charming personality who will do well because he is so typical of what all of us see ourselves to be. He must be able to play the role of egghead before audiences of intellectuals, and to shift to a wholesome folksiness before other groups. He must have a facility at role playing to fit the flexible public image created by professional public relations advisers.

2. Another general type of legislator is the hack, who usually sets the low horizon of remaining in office as the highest virtue. The hack spends his time toiling the vineyards of his party, the political machine, the dominant interest group, or the press that operates in his constituency with enough strength to determine elections. He is often content to front for the political boss, party wheelhorse, or newspaper editor who flashes him signals and pulls his strings on issues of importance. Sometimes the bosses will permit their hacks to join a harmless and popular movement. Thus, a tool of a boss may become known for his righteous stand against narcotic peddlers, or famous as a crusader against pornographic comic books. Still, he knows that his political office and his political future depend upon other backstage forces that can make him or break him at will, and would not hesitate to do so on appropriate occasions.

Hacks are seldom bothered by any great pangs of doubt about the public interest or the rationality of constituent demands. As a result, they are very often noted for their personal services to their supporting constituents. This can take such forms as arranging appointments with bureaucrats for someone seeking a government contract, unsnarling a serviceman's war bride from the Bureau of Immigration's red tape, or getting a job for the boss's nephew just out of college. The hack gladly performs these services so long as they do not arouse the forces for which he fronts.

3. The third general type of legislator is the idealist. Idealists rarely exist in pure form, since the rigors of politics are often fatal to this delicate species unless they make some adaptation to their environment. Idealists are of two general types: the generalist and the specialist.

The generalist refers all political issues to his own conception of the public interest. Sometimes, the idealist is prone to see all issues as black-or-white moral matters and to deliver pious lectures to his colleagues on almost any subject, reminding them that the public interest will be thwarted if his moral guidance is not followed.

The specialist generally embraces a single cause and becomes famous for his dedication to it. He may be dedicated to the repeal of the income tax, the public ownership of basic industries, vegetarianism, prohibition, or other causes. This type is fading in importance in current politics. Champions of single causes usually possess immoderate, if not eccentric, qualities not conducive to winning elections in the political climate of moderation.

Idealists usually try to campaign on issues, but their efforts often fail disastrously if their opponents are distracting the electorate with circus tactics. Many idealists suffer greatly because they know they must often play the advertising game to get elected and the brokerage game to get bills passed in the legislatures. To an idealist, these compromises of conscience do not come easily. He often finds the brokerage way of legislation to be a cynical, if not appalling, threat to his conception of democracy.

The above types of legislators are by no means definitive descriptions of actual individuals. There is a reciprocal relationship between every legislator and his constituency, and the realities and requirements of political life create dilemmas for every legislator. No matter what his self-image, a legislator whose constituency is made up predominantly of labor votes would hesitate to introduce legislation designed to thwart labor unions. Similarly, any legislator is likely to do whatever is necessary to retain a large government installation in his district or to secure an important public-works project for his constituents. Still, the way in which a legislator meets these problems and makes his decisions will tend to hinge on his ideal image of his relationship to the electorate.

The old distinctions between liberal and conservative are on the wane in legislative bodies. Brokerage politics renders both the *noblesse oblige* of the conservative and the majoritarian views of the liberal equally quaint. As we noted in an earlier chapter, the current use of the terms *liberal* and *conservative* tends to denote a stand on particular issues such as the extent of the welfare state, the burden of taxation, and the amount of foreign aid. It is hard to find a liberal or conservative in modern legislatures whose acts display a commitment to a consistent set of principles. The operation of brokerage politics is such that an economic *liberal* might be *conservative* on civil rights without appearing inconsistent. The dominant type of legislator who must survive in the environment discussed throughout this chapter tends to adapt himself to the system. It is a "world they never made;" yet most legislators regard it as real and adjust themselves to it.[3]

The Legislative Environment

The business of a legislature is conducted in an environment that shapes the pressures and sets limits of action in legislative conduct. Part of this environment is formal, derived from structural and constitutional factors and formalized rules of procedure. This formal background is considered in the next chapter. Now we are concerned with those informal arrangements that involve the role of lobbyists and political parties in the legislature and define the relationships of legislators to one another.

LEGISLATORS AND LOBBYISTS

The lobbyist, as well as the journalist and the academician, is interested in the characteristics and the motivations of legislators. Clues to their power drives, vanity, integrity, and other factors may be significant for the lobbyists' tactics. Legislators' constituencies are carefully studied and analyzed by lobbyists to discover the composition of forces they contain. The lobbyist then plans his strategy on the assumption

---

[3] Not surprisingly, however, legislators do not tend to identify themselves with the broker's role. See the findings of John C. Wahlke and others, *The Legislative System* (New York: Wiley, 1962), p. 259.

that the legislator will be influenced by the relative strength in his district of labor, real estate interests, newspaper editors, educational interests, Catholics, professional men, Protestants, small-business interests, Jews, civil servants, ethnic groups, motel operators, liquor interests, the oil industry, manufacturers of various commodities, corn growers, dairy farmers, or local governmental units. Some lobbyists gather and catalogue information about the personal habits of lawmakers. Representative Doe likes two martinis before a roast beef dinner; one of his colleagues does not drink; another likes night clubs with lots of brass in the band and girls in the line; another likes a quiet dinner with good conversation; another, the theatre. Some legislators can be flattered; others like to argue; a racy joke goes over well with some, but angers others; some want information in turgid reports full of facts and figures; others think statistics are lies. Overt requests to some legislators by a lobbyist mean a "no" vote, whereas other legislators seek out the stand of all affected interest groups on an issue.

How is this information used by those attempting to influence legislation? It depends on the legislator; the approach will be tailored to his individual characteristics. Assume a lobbyist is retained by the teachers' organizations in his political jurisdiction to work for higher salaries for the profession. He may drop off a mimeographed report with the secretaries of several legislators, knowing that the legislators are favorably interested and will read the report in order to shore up their arguments. He may arrange a luncheon with a few legislators to talk over the proposal and to point out why he thinks they should vote for it. He may take a few more out on the town that evening and do nothing more than let his guests know whom he represents. For others, he may be able to arrange a block of seats for a good play in town, or he might dig up some information desired by a legislator on a problem totally unrelated to his interest. His task is complicated by the necessity of tailoring his approach to the individual characteristics of legislators. The application of pressure is always delicate: too little may cost him his bill; too much may cost him his job. If he builds up widespread resentment, he becomes ineffectual, and no organization can afford lobbyists who are not well considered by the people they are attempting to influence.

The stereotype of the lobbyist has generally been a portly character dressed in cigar butt and elk tooth, his pockets stuffed with cash for the ready purchase of favor, and followed by a brace of shapely ladies of easy virtue who are readily available to those in influence. There have been such characters and may be a few left, but they have rapidly given way to the new type of lobbyist. He is usually a sincere, professionally trained man, skilled in human relations and the manipulative arts, who really likes people and enjoys the good life. If he is also intellectually committed to the goals of the organization he represents and if, figuratively, his eyes grow moist when his organization's name is mentioned, he is even more effective. A true believer who is competent and intelligent makes the most effective lobbyist. He puts the legislator in a very difficult position. When the legislator dealt with the stereotype lobbyist, he knew he was being used if he gave him aid. When he deals with the new model, he has difficulty sorting out truth from fancy, no doubt because the lobbyist himself is often confused on this point. In a society that increasingly submits to the engineering of desires by public-relations experts, it is difficult for the citizen, the legislator, or even the lobbyist to extricate himself from the quagmire of contrived stratagems.

The influence of the modern lobbyist is increased by the complexity of the legislative task. The legislator is confronted with a range of activity that is virtually impossible for a human mind to comprehend. Generally, he cannot and admits it. He may base many decisions upon party platform, advice from a highly respected colleague, information from public officials, or articulated demands from constituents. But many things remain in doubt, and it is here that the lobbyist can often be of help as well as influence. In many instances, lobbyists will supply information, often of a high quality, on matters in which they have no interest. This serves to help the legislator as well as to ingratiate the lobbyist. It can also muddy the waters of influence to the point where it is increasingly difficult to sort out biased from unbiased information.

In some situations, effective lobbying requires no great skill. There are many constituencies in which a single interest wields, or is thought to wield, a determinate amount of political influence. In these cases, the representative himself may be counted on by the lobbyist to "work the floor"—that is, to line up support from his colleagues. All that is needed to activate him is a word from the lobbyist indicating what his organization seriously wants. The legislator himself then becomes lobbyist, armed with the potent weapon regular lobbyists do not have—his vote on other issues. In every state legislature, for example, the representatives from the districts where the large state offices are located are likely to regard the support of the large number of state government employees in their districts as absolutely essential to their political careers. No matter what their own political philosophies, they are likely to lobby for the legislative program of the state employee's association and against legislation that might reduce the number of state employees or adversely affect their salaries, rights, or privileges. Yet again, the dominant interest might be an economic organization or a newspaper. If a single interest is politically powerful enough, the initiative may even come from the representative himself, as in the case of the state legislator who told one of the authors: "I finally got a good editorial in my home town newspaper, but it took me six bad votes to do it."

The techniques of influence, it would seem, have been polished, refined, and made more subtle in recent years. At the same time, the effort to raise the question of the morality of manipulative techniques or the question of the relation between group pressures and the search for the public interest seems to be generally regarded as old-fashioned, quaintly moralistic fault-finding. These questions, however, are made more rather than less significant and pressing by a recognition of the pervasive influence of lobbies.

POLITICAL PARTIES AND THE LEGISLATOR

Political parties are basic instruments of responsible government. If they are to play this role, however, more is necessary than that they provide voters with significantly different alternatives. They must also be strong enough to organize the debate and the vote in the legislature.

Every legislature must provide organized means for formulating the proposals on which the legislators will finally be called on to say "aye" or "nay." If the parties are not the instruments through which proposals are formulated and alternatives drawn, that function will be performed by other groups. In a pluralist society, it seems that the alternative to party government is pressure-group government.

In the period after 1913, California provided a dramatic and instructive example. During the "progressive" era of Hiram Johnson, Californians were disillusioned with the corruption of political parties and the control exercised over them by dominant interest groups. In revolt, they passed a series of reform measures, including crossfiling, a system that permits candidates in primary elections to run on the opposing party's ballot. These measures were passed with the objective of minimizing the power of the parties. The reforms succeeded—in virtually eliminating effective political parties. But they succeeded also in *increasing* corruption and the power of dominant interest groups. They failed to accomplish their underlying purpose because they rested on a typically American fallacy we have often alluded to—the myth that the problem of controlling political power can be solved by eliminating it. Over a period of time, the reforms created a vacuum in the legislature, which was filled by the pressure groups. Where formerly the legislature was organized by the dominant party it came to be organized on the basis of deals worked out by the lobbyists for the powerful interests. Lobbyists actually negotiated among themselves the appointment of speaker and committee chairmen. Instead of pressure groups seeking a party, candidates sought pressure groups. Within the framework of the pressure system itself, a structure of power developed. A master lobbyist, in the employ of several of the major interests, emerged as the invisible king of the legislature. Holding court in the Senator Hotel, across the street from the Capitol, Artie Samish summoned his minions in the legislature to appear and receive orders.[4] At one point, Earl Warren, then the Governor, pleaded that Artie had more power in the legislature than the Governor (which was very likely the case), and Samish himself on one occasion proclaimed, "The hell with the Governor; I run this state."

The lesson, which it took Californians until 1959 to learn, is that nonpartisan politics means an almost complete surrender of political power to the most powerful interests. Effective power is shifted out of the legislature and into the lobby. Eventually Samish was convicted of income tax evasion and thus removed as an effective influence on legislation. In 1959 California abolished cross filing, which tended to strengthen its political parties and diminish the influence of lobbyists like Samish.

When lobbies dominate legislative bodies the legislator is left with little effective partisan organizational protection and no support. No longer able to look to his party for campaign funds or campaign workers, he looks elsewhere and takes help where he can find it. At the same time, the lack of effective party organization in the legislature means that proposals are usually formulated by pressure groups themselves and the legislator receives neither party pressure on his vote nor party protection. This is not likely to mean that he becomes independent or rises above politics. It only means he is forced to rely heavily on pressure groups for political support.

[4] Lester Velie, "The Secret Boss of California," *Colliers*, August 13 (pp. 12-13; 71-73) and August 20 (pp. 12-13; 60-64), 1949.

The principle seems clear: parties and pressure groups are *alternative* devices for organizing the legislative process; the strength and influence of the one is at the expense of the other. The party with its program based upon its platform and principles is the only instrument yet devised for exerting any responsible control over the power aspirations of groups. It is not, however, a mere matter of the *strength* of party organization. Parties must be able to exert influence over their members in the legislature, but their power must be exerted in the service of party principle and not the mere balancing of interests.

In Congress, the power and effectiveness of party organization is something of an open question. There is agreement on the effectiveness of party discipline in organizing Congress (that is, on such matters as party control over the election of the presiding officers and committee chairmen). There is disagreement, however, on the effectiveness of the parties in formulating a legislative program that reflects party principles and in inducing party members to vote the party position.

One authority has concluded that the pressure of the party is the most important influence on a majority of congressmen. He claims, too, that legislators who are independent of their parties are not treated kindly by the electorate.[5] In the view of others, the party system breaks down in Congress, party lines being crossed so often in the vote that party responsibility becomes impossible. The endemic rash of what one critic has called "coalition fever" means, in this interpretation, that interest coalitions largely displace party policies in congressional voting.[6]

Coalitions can form around a variety of issues or interests. For example, a group of congressmen from gas-producing areas may get together on legislation affecting the gas industry, although their views on other matters might be diametrically opposed. The most enduring and widespread coalition in Congress has been that of southern Democrats with northern Republicans, who, as Senator Dirksen put it, "see through the same spectacles."[7] This coalition was based upon agreements between these two groups on civil rights and economic issues. Southern Democrats would support Republican economic policies, while Republicans would vote to retain the southern Democrats' racially segregated way of life. There are signs, however, that the spectacles minority

---

[5] Julius Turner, *Party and Constituency* (Baltimore: Johns Hopkins Press, 1951), pp. 70-71 and 174-79.

[6] James Burns, *Congress on Trial* (New York: Harper, 1949), p. 43.

[7] Daniel E. Berman, *In Congress Assembled* (New York: Macmillan, 1964), p. 246.

leader Dirksen and his southern friends have been using are badly out of focus. It is also questionable whether a new prescription would fit both of them—particularly since Senator Dirksen has emerged as the Republican leader for strong civil-rights legislation. Many other Republicans have refused to negotiate on civil rights with the result that Southerners have become alarmed that the old basis of their bargaining power has been seriously weakened. The portent of this shift by the Republicans was stated by the Republican Committee on Program and Progress in 1960, when it declared:

> The Republican Party will be false to its historic tradition unless it continues to work for equality of opportunity for every person, regardless of race, creed or ethnic group. Raising the ceiling of opportunity means raising it for all our people and raising it in all fields of human endeavor.[8]

The hopes of the southerners in 1964 for an abandonment of this position by the Republicans were dashed by the election results. In the Congress, southerners had already witnessed the awesome possibilities of losing power when the Civil Rights Bill of 1960 was passed over their objections. Clem Miller described their frustration with both Democrats and Republicans this way:

> Southern Congressmen were urged to refuse to join northerners (Democrats) in organizing the House in 1961. Since they had been trampled on they would retaliate wherever it would be effective. For the first time, they felt the chilling breeze of a hostile coalition, and it was not to their liking. It remains to be seen whether the alliance between southerners and Republicans can be re-formed . . . we could see that the reluctance to cast their lot formally with the Republicans runs very deep.[9]

The passage of the 1965 voting-rights measure by a new coalition of northern Republicans and Democrats has undermined the southern bastion of power in the Congress. When Negroes are able to vote in large numbers, it is very possible that the whole character of southern politics will change and that northern Republicans may find themselves an isolated minority with regard to their positions on economic issues. Republicans have managed to enact many *conservative* economic policies into law with southern help. Breaking this old and tested coalition

[8] *Decision for a Better America* (Garden City, N.Y.: Doubleday, 1960), pp. 37-38.
[9] Miller, *op. cit.*, p. 130.

could strengthen party discipline, but there are many other factors working against strong parties and new coalitions could readily form around other issues.

The weakness of party control in the Congress can be gauged by several other measures. One clue is simply the number of bills introduced during a session. In Congress, the figure is never less than several thousand. By contrast, in the British Parliament, where there is strict party control and discipline, there are likely to be perhaps ninety bills (comprising the majority party's legislative program) considered.

The lack of party discipline in Congress is largely a result of the looseness of the party organization described earlier. The legislator does not owe his election as much to party affiliation, organization, and finances as he does to his own resourcefulness in securing local support. He is likely, therefore, to be much more sensitive and responsive to local interests and needs than to the party's position on national issues. He "tends to vote in the legislature as the local pressures upon him seem likely to influence his fate at the next election."[10] If his party had a greater influence on that fate, he would be more inclined to reflect that influence in his votes.

These pressures acquire special urgency in the House, where the two-year term never permits the legislator to stop running for office. He is made especially anxious to cater to the interests of his constituency and the wishes of the dominant interests in it and is less likely to see issues in terms of his party's conception of a national interest.

The Dilemmas of a Legislator

No matter by what model a legislator defines his role he confronts inevitable dilemmas. Conflicting pressures on him create problems for which there is no simple solution—perhaps no solution at all. Is he entitled completely to neglect his constituents' interests in pursuit of his view of the national interest? To what extent should he serve the powerful interests in his constituency (on which his chances of re-election will largely depend) at the expense of the interests of the unorganized? What compromises of his principles are justifiable in order to secure a part of a political loaf? When does compromise become surrender or give way to expediency?

[10] Henry B. Mayo, *An Introduction to Democratic Theory* (New York: Oxford, 1960), p. 90.

THE LEGISLATOR AND HIS CONSTITUENTS

Because American politics, as we have often noted, is strongly oriented toward local and private interests the problem of constituents for the individual legislator is complicated and difficult. This is true whether he comes from a constituency dominated by a single interest or from one in which there is a variety of sometimes conflicting interests. In the former case—if, for example, he represents a working-class district in Detroit or an important natural-gas-producing state—he is likely to feel that on crucial issues he has no alternative but to vote against a labor reform bill the Auto Workers dislike, or for a bill to exempt natural-gas wells from price regulation. (In 1956, all fifty-eight of the representatives in Congress from the leading gas-producing states of Arkansas, Kansas, Louisiana, Oklahoma, and Texas—liberals and conservatives alike—voted for removing controls on the price of natural gas at the well!) On issues that affect the dominant interest, he is likely to lose his freedom of action and even the opportunity to consider the question of the public interest. On issues unrelated to the dominant constituency interest, however, he may play his hand more freely.

His situation may be more confining if he represents a constituency with a diversity of economic interests. For in this case, it is likely that the lobbyists themselves will not be so prone to identify their interests with the American Way; they are more likely to take a "reasonable" position, which expresses a willingness to compromise with other interests in order to produce a "fair" solution to conflicts. The legislator in these circumstances may play a freer hand, but he is under considerable pressure to perform the neutral function of mediator between conflicting interests. He will often tend to seek solutions that will find a balance agreeable to the several interests. The point is that no matter what the interest group composition of his constituency, the role of interest groups makes it difficult for a legislator to approach his task as the application of a philosophical position to public issues.

The legislator can serve his constituents' interests, as a close observer of and participant in the Washington scene has put it, "only by frequent and perhaps distasteful compromises, and the line between compromise and corruption is often shadowy."[11] The price the legislator pays for being able to serve his constituents' interests successfully may be the

[11] Telford Taylor, "The Ethics of Public Office," *Saturday Evening Post*, April 16, 1960, p. 94.

ability effectively to promote his principles. His constituents' interests may directly conflict with his view of the public interest (as, for example, when he is committed to a low-tariff policy but seeks protection for dominant local industries). More broadly, if he works hard and actively to promote his principles, he is likely to violate the unwritten rules that make it easier for other legislators to satisfy their constituents' interests. If he insists on doing so, he will forfeit his own effectiveness.

This situation was dramatically illustrated during a session of the California State Senate. A freshman senator sought, on the floor, to remove committee amendments emasculating a bill that would have required the marking of gasoline octane ratings on pumps. By long-standing Senate tradition, committee action is seldom challenged on the floor and never by freshman senators. Vigorous pressure for the amendments had come from the powerful oil lobby; no discernible organized pressures sought to protect the bill. The senator had lined up enough votes to remove the amendments on the floor, but just before the vote was taken several of his colleagues asked to be excused from their vote pledge. The senator found the powerful lobby opposing him and the traditions of the Senate itself too formidable a combination. His explanation to the press was frank:

> Some of the men said the heat they were getting from their home districts was too much [the heat, of course, was applied by the petroleum industry, not consumers]. A couple of them won recent elections by close margins and indicated that if they voted with me they would not be returning to the senate.
>
> There's no sense in making an issue of it. Somewhere along the line there would be a rollcall and I'd just be putting people on the spot for a losing cause. Maybe in a couple of years things will be different and we can try again.[12]

It is hard to see what might happen so that "things will be different" —in 1965 octane ratings are still not on the pumps—except a strengthening of political party organization and principles so that legislators are less susceptible to the power of the oil lobby. In the absence of that, it seems more likely that freshman senators will learn to behave according to the rules of a game that gives constituent and private interests priority over the legislator's conception of the pubic interest. It does not follow that all or even most legislators want it this way.

No democratic legislature could ever be a utopia, and complete

---

[12] *The Sacramento Bee,* May 5, 1959.

consistency and unblemished conscience cannot be expected of democratic legislators. The idea that they can be is a dangerous illusion in a democracy for it leads to those efforts to "rise above politics" and those demands for perfection in which "the good becomes the enemy of the better." We may demand more principle in politics, but we need to remember that the demand for uncompromised principle and purity of motive would make the good an impossible goal and the better an unworthy one.

THE LEGISLATOR: CONSCIENCE OR COMPROMISE?

Under what conditions is the legislator justified in sacrificing his own principles to the prevailing sentiment in his constituency or to the compromises worked out in the legislative arena? These are not easy questions. William Benton, former United States Senator from Connecticut, put them to his one-time colleagues in the Senate with interesting results. Ralph Flanders, Republican of Vermont who retired after a long and distinguished career in the Senate, replied:

> There is a saying to the effect that "a Senator's first duty is to get re-elected." This sounds a bit cynical, but there is a real vein of truth in it.
> If I were a Southern Senator and were facing the Little Rock situation, I would be strongly moved to avoid the extreme segregationist position, but would also avoid crusading for anti-segregation. I would join the moderates so far as seemed safe and hope for re-election, knowing that if I were defeated in the primaries my place would be taken by a rabid segregationist.[13]

Another distinguished Republican, Representative John Vorys of Ohio, took an opposite view:

> I am extremely cautious about calling political decisions moral issues. On the other hand, I think that Congressmen and Senators are expendable rather than indispensable, and no Congressman or Senator should cast a vote he knows is wrong in order to be re-elected. It makes no difference whether the wrongness is on a moral, legal, economic or other issue. . . . Taking the example you mention, I think that if a Southern Senator is opposed morally to segregation he should vote his convictions and take his medicine. For one thing, he might be surprised to find how many people admire that kind of courage.

[13] William Benton, "The Big Dilemma: Conscience or Votes," *New York Times Magazine*, April 26, 1959, p. 12. Copyright by The New York Times. Reprinted by permission.

The same position was upheld vigorously by Democratic Senator Wayne Morse of Oregon who replied:

> Too often and too readily politicians—when they vote against something they know is in the public interest—fall back upon the excuse that "I know it is right but people don't understand it."
>
> What these politicians don't understand themselves is that it is part of their function in representative government to get the facts across to the people so they *will* understand. Instead, they become panhandlers for votes. We have many in public life who are afraid or unwilling to be defeated. Winning is their only goal, not true public service.[14]

The question at issue is whether the legislator is justified in doing what is necessary to win elections. If he does so, he may justify his actions with the argument that he is giving the voters what they want. This argument must be rejected on grounds that voters cannot know what they want, in a democratic sense, unless politicians formulate alternatives. Yet, the problem is not so simple. The legislator knows, for example, that his vote on many important issues is overlooked or even unknown to his constituents. He also knows his vote on a single issue, dramatized in his constituency, may cost him an election. He has not one, but many, principles. Should he take defeat for voting to repeal a loyalty oath when he might be re-elected on his votes on other issues if only he could make the voters aware of them? There are no simple answers here.

Another major problem of conscience for the legislator arises from the nature of democratic processes. The issues with which a legislature deals are complex, and there are many approaches to their solution. Yet, when a bill finally reaches the floor, the legislature must vote on a single measure that reflects both the complexity of the problem and compromises among rival viewpoints. The individual can vote aye or nay; there is no opportunity to follow up with qualifying conditions. Unable to vote his convictions in the record, the legislator faces the tremendously difficult problem, as the late President Kennedy put it when he was a Senator, of "wondering when a compromise is one of accommodation or one of principle," and he must do it in "a glare of publicity," in "an irretrievable manner, on a permanent record, and with only the answer of an 'aye' or 'nay' to choose between."[15]

Legislators draw a line at different places. Senator Morse, for example,

---

[14] *Ibid.*, pp. 12 and 83.
[15] *Ibid.*, p. 84.

always has been a stalwart champion of civil rights. In 1957 he was the only senator outside the South who voted against the Civil Rights Bill, because he regarded it as an inadmissable series of compromises with "the civil rights guarantee of the Fourteenth Amendment. I do not accept the view that such a compromise is ever justified."[16] Others, like President (then Senator) Johnson incline to the position that politics requires the acceptance of considerably less than a whole loaf. "It is essential," he commented, for a political leader to yield or withdraw on some issues so that he will be "able to pick the terrain upon which he will give battle."[17] Still others are so concerned with accommodation that their principles are difficult to discern.

"Politics," an old saying goes, "is the art of the possible." This will always express an important truth about democratic politics. But it is not necessarily the whole truth. It may be that what makes what is possible also a movement in the direction of what is desirable is the presence of those politicians in the system who stand firm for the presently impossible. It is a presumptuous and misguided citizen, however, who will judge too quickly, too harshly, or too certainly every vote that appears to be a sacrifice of principle by a legislator.

Who Are the Legislators?

In addition to the general question of the relationship of politician to constituents and to his conscience, every legislator confronts other problems that involve his relationship to his party, to the executive branch, to other legislators, and to particular issues with which he is especially concerned. He also has the problem of adapting his own strengths and weaknesses in interpersonal relations, and the devising of strategy for the legislative situation in order to maximize his effectiveness. As a result, it is possible to categorize legislators into a wide variety of types depending on how they react to this variety of demands. Legislators often get themselves typed during their careers to the point where their political futures may even be determined by their deserved or undeserved reputations. And, like actors, the type may not be deserved or indicate the real or potential qualities of the individual legislator. A

[16] *Ibid.*, p. 83.
[17] *Ibid.*, p. 84. Vice-President Humphrey commented that President Johnson taught him that "half a loaf is better than none if you know where the other half is and can come back and get it later." Editorial, *Saturday Evening Post*, April 10, 1965, p. 18.

legislator, either by his conception of his role or by the evaluations of others, may find himself known to the public as:[18]

1. An agent for the executive branch of government. He may represent the whole program of the administration or a segment of it, such as defense, agriculture, housing, or some other phase of the administration's legislative desires. This role often falls to the leadership of the executive's party in the legislature.

2. An agent for the program of an administrative agency, even though it is in opposition to the executive's desires for the program. A congressman may be known as a spokesman for the program of the Air Force or the Corps of Engineers, for example.

3. A spokesman and champion of a pressure group. Many congressmen have had a difficult time explaining their close associations with the power lobby, the natural-gas lobby, or labor unions. Too close an identity with pressure-group interests often has detrimental effects on aspirations for national office.

4. A champion of a cause, such as civil liberties, antitrust legislation, or lower taxes. Wyoming's Senator O'Mahoney was noted for his championing of antitrust legislation, and Senator Eastland of Mississippi is identified with his desire to preserve the southern way of life in the face of legislation and judicial opinion extending civil rights to minority groups.

5. A strategist and champion of the political position of a party; for example, the late Senator Taft's efforts in behalf of the Republican party, which earned him the title "Mr. Republican."

6. A self-styled statesman in the grand design who rises above the petty aims of party and pressure groups and sees himself as the personification of the Truth. These people often have difficulty finding a haven for their ideas, if not their egos, within any political organization.

7. A "bad boy" (the late Senators Bilbo and McCarthy are examples) whose career is built upon roughshod treatment of the ethical rules of society. Such a role is risky, since one may ride high on an emotional binge, but when sanity returns the comedown is usually abrupt and often complete.

8. A political maverick. Examples are the late Senator Langer of North Dakota and Senator Lausche of Ohio, who tended to run astray of party discipline and have been quite unpredictable.

[18] Journalistic and academic observers of American politics very often discuss politicians as types. Our list is a general assessment of some of these observations, as well as some of our own and is not intended to be definitive.

9. An elder statesman. Senator Hayden of Arizona, for example, does not seek the limelight but is consulted and admired by his colleagues for his wise counsel and great knowledge of legislative affairs.

10. A parliamentarian and strategist able to operate the creaking machinery of the legislative mill and get things done without breaking the machine down. Senator Russell of Georgia is known for his abilities in this direction.

11. A messenger for constituents. He will guide them through the bureaucratic labyrinth, see that appointments are granted to people from home, and arrange for tours of visitors.

12. A "hatchet man" for the party, a role that often falls to a personality type who delights in bursting the pompous poses of the opposition, and whose attack flirts with charges that the opposition is dishonest, subversive, or a dupe of sinister forces. This can also be a risky business relative to one's political future. Such tactics can have a serious boomerang effect.

13. A bright young man with intellectual aspirations. He writes books and articles, sometimes very able ones, about his conception of the theoretical and practical aspects of his job.

14. A compromiser who is famous for his ability to get people together and get bills through Congress, even if it requires virtually emasculating the bill to do it. Several senators are noted for their abilities to reconcile the many opposing forces in Congress.

15. A flowery orator whose purple and bulbous rhetoric appeals to the sentimental and the pious in man. There are still many political figures noted for their uses of embellished oratorical utterances, which cause embarrassment, rapture, or amusement, depending upon their listeners' orientation. Sadly, however, this type seems to be on the wane.

16. A political extremist, either to the right or left of the existing middle, who speaks seriously of a political philosophy of the distant past or dim future. Extremists also find difficulty retaining their positions, particularly when moderation is popular. Congress for a time contained two California members of the John Birch Society, both of whom were defeated in 1962.

17. A nonentity who is colorless, votes right to satisfy enough constituents, and laboriously tends his political fences to prevent a breakthrough of any sort. Legislative bodies, particularly at the state and local levels, ordinarily contain a good number of nonentities, but their chances of reaching the United States Senate are very limited.

A list like this could be extended at some length, but it should illustrate the great variety of personality traits found in every legislative body. None of the above illustrative types is intended as an inclusive description of individual legislators. Most legislators are a combination of types who display these varied characteristics on various occasions. Such variety is both frustrating and fascinating to those politicians, lobbyists, academicians, and others who are constantly attempting to analyze and predict political behavior.

THE CLUB

Most students of organization realize that the power used to make institutional policies often lies somewhere in the organization other than in the top boxes on the organizational chart. A secretary to an executive may have a good deal of influence on corporate policy; an assistant professor may force issues upon equivocating administrators of his college; or a low-ranking budget analyst may throw a large and cumbersome bureaucracy into all sorts of agonizing justifications of its activities. So it is with legislatures. If one posed the question of the locus of power in the United States Congress, he would get a plethora of answers from a host of "informed" sources. Republicans would have one answer, Democrats another; labor leaders would offer their views, manufacturers theirs; leaders of minority groups theirs; and Capitol newspaper correspondents would have still others. But all would probably agree upon several key figures in both houses who had a great deal of influence upon congressional decisions.

The shifting sands of political fortune can change the power structure in Congress quite drastically. This is most noticeable when the political climate changes or the hue and cry goes up, and is successful, to "throw the rascals out." Generally, however, the shift in power alignments is more gradual and has an almost infinite number of factors working continuously to change it. To describe the power structure adequately in any particular Congress is difficult, especially for outsiders, and even the memoirs of insiders are not always completely reliable. Power in legislative bodies rests on such factors as personal charm, seniority, voting strength in the constituency, the ability to compromise and get people together, social prestige, favor with the President, erudition, honesty, cunning, bluntness, dependability, wit, humor, eloquence, or even, as Senator Joseph McCarthy proved, the ability to cow one's colleagues into submission.

Legislatures, however, are more than a haphazard collection of elected representatives who are thrown together to make laws. They are exclusive clubs to which admission is open only to those who have survived the rigorous test of campaigning successfully for office. This is a hard test. Those who survive it soon develop a strong sense of *esprit de corps,* which transcends the verbal discord and power struggles that take place in legislative chambers. The United States Senate is often referred to as the most exclusive club in the United States, open only to one hundred of more than 175 million people. Although there are all kinds of members with a variety of professional backgrounds, upon election to the Senate all of them share an important common attribute —membership in the club.

The late Congressman Clem Miller stated in one of his letters to his constituents that:

> One's overwhelming first impression as a member of Congress is the aura of friendliness that surrounds the life of a Congressman. No wonder that "few die and none resign." Almost everyone is unfailingly polite and courteous. Window washers, clerks, senators—it cuts all ways.
>
> We live in a cocoon of good feeling—no doubt the compensation for the cruel buffeting that is received in the world outside. And we can immediately appreciate how Congress or the Congressmen can shield it or himself from reality, losing touch with the facts of life if not watchful.[19]

While the club protects its members against outsiders, it also has its own internal rules and etiquette. New members are to be seen and not heard. Before they are admitted to high councils of the club, they must serve their apprenticeship and prove their worthiness. The new member must be a workhorse, not a showhorse, tilling the vineyard and leaving the headlines and the glamour to the older hands. The new member gets what office space is left over after his colleagues with previous service have made their choices. He sits at the foot of the table at official dinners. He does not speak on the floor often, for this is a breach of tradition; in fact, he is not even supposed to deliver eulogies and flattery, a practice common among legislators, unless he has been around long enough to have earned the right to praise his colleagues. A veteran senator has illustrated the tradition in this story of a freshman who did not know his place:

[19] Miller, *op. cit.,* p. 93.

When I came to the Senate, I sat next to Senator Borah. A few months later, he had a birthday. A number of the older men got up and made brief, laudatory speeches about it. Borah was pleased. Then a freshman Senator—one who had only been in the Chamber three or four months—got to his feet and started on a similar eulogy. He was an excellent speaker, but between each of his laudatory references to Borah, Borah loudly whispered "That son-of-a-bitch, that son-of-a-bitch." He didn't dislike the speaker personally. He just didn't feel that he should speak so soon.[20]

The Senate folkways are elaborate, and admission to the inner circles of command depends upon one's observance of them before he can expect his elders to bestow on him the longed-for nod of acceptance.

The club not only has serious effects upon behavior but tends to encourage brokerage politics on the part of its members. Whereas integrity is recognized as desirable, brashness and flaunting of erudition is not. One accommodates his fellow club members and is expected to do some careful horse trading, often at a disadvantage since the inner circle has most of the best horses, to get his bills passed. Some members have gained admission to the club eventually by flouting the rules and "kicking the door down," but this takes a rare and dramatic personality as well as the ability, over a period of time, to gain personal respect. If the member attempting this tactic does not kick hard enough, he is in trouble when his bills begin their way through the legislative labyrinth. If a member has served well on unimportant committees, and acted properly in other ways, his bills will meet with some success. If he has flouted or defied the rules, his legislative objectives are likely to suffer and his constituents may be put on a slim diet of "pork." The same is true of committee assignments. The good spots go to the most acceptable applicants if seniority does not dictate otherwise. Pressure groups are aware of the advantages the club provides them, and they carefully cultivate the friendship of its informal directors.

Lower houses of legislative bodies have some of the club atmosphere, but their larger size and frequent elections with consequently higher turnover of members make them less charmed circles than are upper houses. What is true of the United States Senate is also true of the upper houses in most states. State senates are quite exclusive, as many an eager freshman has discovered. In fact, members of most upper houses hardly

[20] From Donald R. Matthews, "The Folkways of the United States Senate: Conformity to Group Norms and Legislative Effectiveness," *American Political Science Review*, December, 1959, p. 1066.

acknowledge the existence of the lower house; when they do, they often refer to it as "that group across the Capitol," "those other fellows," or, as one state senator put it, "that mob over there."

LEGISLATIVE LEADERSHIP

Some legislative leadership is formally established. By definition of their offices and the manner of selection, the speaker of the House, majority leader in the Senate, minority leaders in both houses, and party whips will have a good deal of power. Their partisan colleagues usually have selected them because of some characteristics of leadership. There are, however, some members of Congress who avoid assuming formal positions of leadership, since they feel more effective operating from the sidelines. Many legislators, for example, are very adept at calming troubled waters or at in-fighting in the privacy of offices but are very poor at publicly leading their colleagues.

Positions of prominence, such as majority or minority leader in the Senate, generally go to Senators whose abilities are recognized by both the public and their colleagues. The personal characteristics of the legislative leaders may differ greatly, but they almost without exception have considerable ability in organizing their party colleagues for legislative battle.

Prevailing political attitudes also have an effect on the selection of legislative leadership. If the nation is sharply divided on issues, such as the economic crises of the 1930's, forceful leaders able clearly and emphatically to state their party's views are more in favor. But if the mood is one of harmony and if political success is gained from being moderate, as in the late 1950's, leadership tends to adopt this role. Senator Lyndon Johnson's selection as Democratic majority leader of the Senate in 1954, reflected the desire of his party to be "less controversial" than it would be under a more doctrinaire leader.[21] President Johnson's greatest praise as a senator stemmed from his ability to compromise factions and to get along reasonably well with a President of the opposite political faith. Many members of Senator Johnson's own party grumbled about his propensity to compromise, but for those Democrats who were anxious to avoid the charge of being extremists in a time of moderation he did his job effectively. Without strong party identity on public issues,

[21] See William S. White, "Who Is Lyndon Johnson?" *Harper's*, March, 1958, for an interesting appraisal of then Senator, now President Johnson by a well-respected reporter on national politics.

an increasing number of moderates will probably find a position of leadership. But a revolt of the moderates does not imply a breakdown in party organization and discipline for power purposes. Moderates need power to be moderate just as extremists need power to be extreme. Legislative leaders are likely to continue to be men who can organize their party's quest for power.

Internal fights occasionally develop that reflect the parties' dissatisfaction with the organizational effectiveness of its leadership. An example was the struggle for the House minority leader position between Republican representatives Joseph W. Martin and Charles A. Halleck in the Eighty-Sixth Congress. Martin had been minority floor leader since 1939, with the exception of the Eightieth and Eighty-Third Republican Congresses, in which he was speaker. Halleck was majority leader when Martin was speaker, and Martin's unofficial assistant in the Eighty-Fourth and Eighty-Fifth Congresses. Halleck was a more vigorous fifty-eight years of age, while Martin was seventy-four and not in the most robust health. Each had support from both the liberal and conservative segments of the party, but Martin intimated that Vice-President Nixon had intervened on his opponent's behalf. As he put it, "All I know is that all his [Nixon's] people were against me—actively against me." After it was decided to use a secret ballot, which permitted some reluctant members to vote against Martin without having to do so openly, Halleck emerged triumphant. Martin, after twenty years of leadership, was turned out to pasture.

Cruel treatment, one might say, and reasons for it ranged from Martin's age to the failure of Republicans to win enough congressional seats in the preceding three elections. As Martin said, election reverses "had the boys confused. They wanted a fall guy." As politicians are prone to do, they tried to soften the blow for Martin by offering him a variety of honorary offices, but these were rejected with Martin's succinct statement, "After twenty years as leader, what the hell do I want those for?" Honorary office could not remove the sting of defeat.[22] In 1964 the drama, with new characters, was given its second production. This time Halleck, now the old man, was replaced by Gerald R. Ford, of Michigan.

The game goes on and on. Reporters report, professors analyze, lobbyists manipulate, editors editorialize, and novelists fictionalize while the legislator swims in his goldfish bowl under the bright light of

[22] *Congressional Quarterly*, January 9, 1959, pp. 43-44.

scrutiny, neither completely understood nor misunderstood. Yet citizens must judge legislators, and, if their judgments are to be meaningful, they must be undertaken in the light of what one considers to be the legislator's proper function. Errand boy, broker, or principled party politician? Or a combination in what proportions? The decision is a difficult but vitally important one. And after the citizen has defined the role of the ideal legislator, he must face the difficult task of applying it to men with human motivations operating in the almost bewildering complexity of pressures and forces that an open and pluralistic society produces. This is the public role of the citizen. Dictators have lost their heads for failure to solve simpler problems! The costs of indifference or failure in a democracy are more widely shared but, in the long run, no less severe.

LEGISLATIVE ORGANIZATION AND PROCEDURE

... which is concerned with the elaborate and complicated structure and processes that condition the manner in which the legislative business is conducted.

The **Bicameral** (two-house) character of American legislatures provides the advantage of dual consideration of important policy; at the same time, especially in the absence of effective party liaison between the houses, effective control and accountability are made difficult. Direct responsibility of the legislature to the electorate is diminished by the election of the two houses on different bases and by the ways in which

Legislative District lines are drawn. The gerrymander and the silent gerrymander have historically been used to distort the population basis of legislative districts for partisan purposes. Recent Supreme Court decisions have resulted in

   Reapportionment by Judicial Command. The Court has ordered the House of Representatives and both houses of state legislatures to be reapportioned to conform to the liberal principle of "one man, one vote." The Court's decisions have precipitated political conflict, which raises fundamental questions about the nature of representation and the role of the Court. Both of these questions turn on the role of majorities in the democratic model to which one is committed. The same questions are raised in an examination of the

Legislative Organization and Procedure made necessary by the size of legislative bodies and the complexity of the legislative task. Legislative structure and rules may be judged by their

   Efficiency in enabling Congress to act swiftly and expeditiously on its huge agenda. But in a democracy the responsibility of decision-making processes is at least as important. The conflict between these two goals is apparent in the problem of

   Debate and Its Limitations. Full and free debate is desirable for the public airing of controversy; yet, it may be used, as in the filibuster, in ways that subvert its purpose. The control of debate in the two houses of Congress takes different forms, partly because of the relative size of the bodies, but in neither has an ideal solution to the problem been found.

The problem of legislative responsibility is most clearly apparent in the question of *Party Control of the Legislature*, because political parties are the major vehicles through which legislatures may be organized to permit citizens to hold them accountable. In the Congress parties play a less decisive role than in most other democratic nations. Party control and discipline are nearly complete in the business of selecting
Legislative Leadership and organizing the body and its committees. But party control tends not to extend beyond organizational questions to policy matters. The decentralized, nonprogrammatic character of American parties contributes to the selection of congressional leadership by
The Seniority System, which almost automatically promotes senior members to important posts irrespective of their loyalty to party principles. These characteristics contribute to the brokerage character of congressional processes. So, also, does

The Committee System through which the flow of legislation is controlled. The power of the committees and especially of committee chairmen, the control over the business of the House exercised by its Rules Committee, the power of committees to conduct investigations, and the nature of committee hearings on bills—all of these phenomena contribute to the role played by the committee structure in promoting

Brokerage Politics in Congress. In the absence of effective party government the committee system furnishes an ideal milieu for the dominant influence of organized groups on the legislative process.

The crucial role of committees in congressional organization conditions the processes of *Floor Action and Debate.* There is, however, considerable use of
Floor Amendments and Riders to bills, which are sometimes used as techniques in the brokerage process, and of *Test Votes* designed to avoid a direct confrontation that would put members on the public record.

The central question that emerges from all of these considerations is how *The Legislative Process* can be made to serve the purposes of *Responsible Government.* As prestige, influence, and the capacity for independent initiative have shifted to the President and the Court, the role of Congress becomes a crucial matter for evaluation in the light of our conceptions of what responsibility requires.

We would amend the Holy Bible if it were before us for consideration.

SPEAKER SAM RAYBURN

Chapter Twelve

LEGISLATIVE ORGANIZATION AND PROCEDURE

As WE HAVE SEEN, *complexity* is perhaps the best descriptive term that can be applied to the legislative process—in fact, human beings seldom have devised a more elaborate contrivance of rule, ceremony, regulation, and detail than is found in democratic legislative bodies. Some of the ceremonies seem bizarre to the casual observer from a gallery. The peculiar spectacle of an extended debate and speechmaking while members read newspapers, gossip, and caucus; the general confusion of members coming and going while business is conducted;

358

THE CONSENT OF THE GOVERNED

the steady droning of the voices of clerks reading bills to an inattentive audience; the shuttling of pieces of legislation around to various committees; the befuddling method of taking test votes; and the ceremonial forms of address are a few of the more obvious and superficial spectacles that may seem to the uninitiated to be useless, time-consuming, or silly.

Many visitors to legislative halls are annoyed when they see their representative reading his local newspaper while earnest speeches are being made or hear him refer to a political enemy as his distinguished colleague. Such observations lead to many cynical statements about congressmen, state legislators, and local politicians. The Senator Snort of the cartoons, the Claghorn of the radio, and Senator Phogbound of the comics all attest to this derision. Good humored it may be, but it is a stereotype that contains very little truth and is generally unfair.

In every case, there are good, if not always sufficient, reasons for practices that seem quaint or ridiculous to the uninitiated. Ceremonial forms of address illustrate this. Senator Stephen M. Young of Ohio, attributing the quotation to the late Senator and Vice-President Barkley of Kentucky, described the practice in this way:

> If some colleague refers to you as the "distinguished senator from Ohio" consider yourself lucky. If this same colleague refers to you as "the able and distinguished senator from Ohio" be on your guard, for the knife is getting sharper. If, however, your colleague refers to you as "the able and distinguished senator from Ohio and my friend" then duck fast for he is trying to see if the jugular vein is exposed. And in case your colleague refers to you as "my very good friend, the able, distinguished and outstanding senator from Ohio" then run for your life.[1]

When a congressman uses the elaborately formal modes of address customary in the Congress, there are good and sufficient reasons. Personal animosities must be muted and restrained in a group of men working so closely together and trying to achieve conflicting goals. Formal modes of address—"the honorable gentleman from . . ."—help to concentrate the debate on issues and to avoid personalities. The senator who, more than anyone in recent years, violated the dignity of the Senate and disrupted its orderly procedures, the late Senator Joseph McCarthy, was also most prone to putting his colleagues on a first-name basis. In democratic legislatures, formality and titles of address may be desirable to facilitate the processes of orderly debate of issues.

[1] *Sacramento Bee*, February 10, 1960.

Similarly, if a legislator reads a newspaper while a colleague is speaking, it is probably because this is the only time he has to read it. If he makes ambiguous statements on current issues, it may be that he has been so bombarded by shrill demands for a position that he wants to investigate the matter more deeply before making a declaration of his views. Legislators are often attacked because they do not take a consistent stand on every issue. By necessity, some of them may go along with something they do not like in order to conserve their strength for issues they consider vital.

Some legislative practices are understandable but more difficult to justify. For example, some of the rules of legislative bodies seem designed to provide mutual protection against the pressures and demands of outside forces. Where political parties are too weak to protect an individual against pressure groups or his constituency for an unpopular vote, the organization and procedural methods of the legislature may provide some shelter. This helps explain some procedures and rules, such as voice votes, committee control of bills, closed committee hearings,[2] control of its membership by each house of the legislature, and methods of censuring colleagues who bring disgrace to the legislative institution. In addition to such formal rules and procedures, the informal ethics of the club, as we have seen, also often operate to protect legislators against outside pressures.

Bicameralism

In the United States, the federal government and all the states except Nebraska have bicameral, or two-house legislatures. Nebraska's experiment with a unicameral, or single-house, legislature has not led other jurisdictions to follow in this direction.

It is often argued that two-house legislatures are inefficient. By management analysis standards they are. There is duplication of function, a pet peeve of efficiency experts. Everything is done twice. Hearings on bills are generally held separately. Votes are taken separately in each

[2] About one third of congressional hearings are closed—that is, the public is excluded from attendance while testimony is being taken and decisions are made. Many closed hearings are held on matters where government security is involved and classified information is discussed. Other closed hearings may not involve security but are held because the committee members feel it would be better to conduct them privately. There is considerable unrest over the extensive use of closed hearings. Criticism usually centers around the question of whether the public is entitled to observe committee action unless there are vital reasons why it should be excluded. *Congressional Quarterly*, April 21, 1961, p. 669.

THE CONSENT OF THE GOVERNED

house. Rules apply only to the house that makes them. Each house has its own committees to deal with the same subject matter, and each has its own officers and attaches.

Bicameralism has virtues, however. It gives two full-dress considerations to all important, and even unimportant, measures. Longer terms in upper or smaller houses, such as the United States Senate, may prevent rash or hasty action on emotionally charged bills. Two houses, in short, give a greater range of attention to public policy. In Congress, each of the houses occasionally prevents the passage of a bill rushed through the other on a surge of expediency or emotion.

Bicameralism also presents problems. It leads to delays and bickering. Over forty years ago, one authority described the Senate and House of Representatives as being "strangers to each other." His comments are still appropriate.

> Save for conference committees, they might as well sit at opposite extremes of the continent or at different times of the year. The leaders confer once in a while, no doubt, but for the rank and file there is neither acquaintance nor interest. Rarely does a Senator deign to enter the House. Rarely does a Representative go to the other end of the Capitol from motives other than those of curiosity, unless he has occasion to consult a Senator from his own State in some personal or political matter.[3]

This estrangement partly reflects the weakness of national political parties, and it makes it difficult to fix political responsibility for ignoring or overriding a majority opinion. It also tends to facilitate the occasional irresponsible passage of a bill by one house, in the confidence that the other will let it die in committee.

The absence of effective coordination between the two houses is particularly evident when they pass widely different versions of the same bill. In this circumstance, conference committees are used to resolve differences between the two houses. Very often this results in bargains at halfway points between the bills of each house. If one house knows the other will force a bill to conference by amendments, it very often loads the bill with excessive demands to ensure itself a good bargaining position. When both houses do this, a bill gets so far out of shape when it goes to a conference committee that the eventual resolution of differences may not reflect the intentions of either house.

The idea that popularly representative lower houses are the best

---

[3] Robert Luce, *Legislative Procedure* (Boston: Houghton Mifflin, 1922), p. 141.

vehicles for the expression of a public interest or of majority opinion is questionable. One often finds that civil rights and liberties, for example, receive treatment more in keeping with the basic ideals of democracy in upper than in lower houses of legislatures. It is even difficult to support the position that a more numerous lower house, based on population rather than area, is ordinarily more responsible to majority opinion. In Congress, for example, the Senate in recent years has been more responsive to the problems of urban majorities than has the House. Partly, this is because House members tend more to represent local interests than positions on national or even statewide issues and because even the smallest states have been urbanized in recent years. Partly, it is due to distortions in representation caused by methods of legislative districting discussed in the following section.

Legislative Districts

In 1928, H. L. Mencken, the brilliant and vitriolic social and political commentator of the Jazz Age, took a prophetic look at America's legislatures and sourly commented:

> The yokels hang on because old apportionments give them unfair advantages. The vote of a malarious peasant on the lower Eastern Shore counts as much as the votes of twelve Baltimoreans [where Mencken lived]. But that can't last. It is not only unjust and undemocratic; it is absurd.[4]

Absurd though it may have been to Mr. Mencken, designers of legislative districts continued to ignore population in favor of other more politically attractive criteria. It was the Supreme Court that finally forced the states into the agonizing difficulty of redistricting their legislatures on a population basis. The Court used the Fourteenth Amendment's "equal protection of the laws" and "due process" clauses to insist that states set about the business of assuring their citizens the equality of representation summed up in the phrase "one person, one vote."[5] Until the Supreme Court's edicts, legislative districting always

---

[4] Quoted in J. Anthony Lewis, "Legislative Apportionment and the Federal Courts," *Harvard Law Review*, LXXI, April, 1958. Reprinted in the excellent work on reapportionment by Glendon Schubert, *Reapportionment* (New York: Scribner's Research Anthologies, 1965), p. 83. Another good book on this subject is Howard D. Hamilton, ed., *Legislative Apportionment* (New York: Harper and Row, 1964).

[5] This phrase was used in *Gray v. Sanders*, 372 U.S. 368 (1963), when the Court held that Georgia's "county unit system" of counting votes, which diluted the weight of votes in heavily populated counties, was unconstitutional. The Court said:

had been a matter for the states. Indeed, the Court had been reluctant to intrude into this jealously guarded sanctum, populated in most states by skilled political cartographers and professional distributors of political rewards who seemed partial to Mencken's "yokels."

In 1946 some exasperated citizens of Illinois started through the federal judicial system arguing that they were being denied fair representation in Congress because they lived in a bloated congressional district. The case went to the United States Supreme Court, where Justice Frankfurter wrote the opinion denying their claim on the grounds that the Court should not get involved in political questions. Refusing to do any "verbal fencing about 'jurisdiction'," Frankfurter said:

> To sustain this action would cut very deep into the very being of Congress. Courts ought not to enter this political thicket. The remedy for unfairness in districting is to secure State Legislatures that will apportion properly, or to invoke the ample powers of Congress.[6]

Frankfurter's desire to stay out of "this political thicket" was understandable even though one might detect an element of buck passing. His argument that the remedy lies in state legislatures, themselves oblivious to doctrines of equality of representation, or in Congress, many of whose members were also the beneficiaries of overrepresented districts drawn by state legislatures, was unrealistic. In neither arena is equal representation regarded as a first principle of democracy. Frankfurter's opinion gave the go-ahead, for a while, to the traditionally inequitable practices of state legislatures in districting their own seats and those of the House of Representatives in Congress.

One of the most common devices for legislative districting goes back to 1811, when Elbridge Gerry, governor of Massachusetts, carved out a peculiar-looking congressional district designed to keep his Federalist opponents out of power. Because the boundary lines resembled a salamander, a victimized Federalist said it should be called a "gerrymander" in honor of its creator. Cartoonists put claws, wings, and a face on Gerry's creature, and the term has become part of our political vocabulary as descriptive of partisan geography.

A variation on the gerrymander is the silent gerrymander, a device

---

"The conception of political equality from the Declaration of Independence, to Lincoln's Gettysburg Address, to the Fifteenth, Seventeenth, and Nineteenth Amendments can mean only one thing—one person, one vote."

[6] *Colegrove* v. *Green*, 328 U.S. 549 (1946).

that has been responsible for much of the current controversy. The silent gerrymander is simply a refusal to redraw districts after a shift in population. By silently allowing districts to remain as they always have while the people move from farm to city, many states have become grossly unbalanced in popular representation. The variation in size of constituencies of members of the House of Representatives revealed by the 1960 census is an indication of the silent response to the urban revolution. The census indicated that the average Representative served 410,481 persons. In 1961, the largest number of constituents was served by Representative James B. Utt (R) in California's Twenty-Eighth district. It contained 1,014,460 persons. The smallest district, the Sixth Kansas, represented by Robert Dole (R), had 244,706 constituents. The 1960 election returns showed that the average number of voters for the 262 seats held by Democrats was 359,459, whereas the 174 Republican seats averaged 430,380 voters.[7] The difference in size between Republican and Democratic districts indicates that there are more state legislatures controlled by Democrats. It also indicates another popular ploy in legislative districting, which is to crowd as much of the opposition into as few districts as possible. After doing this, the party in power then deploys its own troops to gain the maximum number of seats possible. For example, when the Republicans redistricted California in 1950, the Twenty-Sixth Congressional District in Los Angeles County was drawn to contain nearly a 90 per cent Democratic majority. In 1960, the Democrats had their turn, and some Republican districts were nearly as lopsided. In both cases, the party in control of the state legislature ensured itself more of the congressional seats than the size of its majority would have justified.

The result of all of these cartographical skills had increasingly tended to disfranchise the urban voter. City dwellers became increasingly restive, but had nowhere to turn for redress. State legislatures were unresponsive —particularly so since they had put the urban voter in his place and intended to keep him there. Congress was in the same situation and declined to respond to the urbanite's demand for first-class citizenship. In *Colegrove* v. *Green*, cited above, the judiciary's answer to the city dweller, when he came for redress, was to go back to the legislature. The Court had not been unanimous, however, and the minority became the city dweller's brightest hope in his circular search for equal representation.

[7] *Congressional Quarterly*, February 17, 1961, p. 275 ff.

In 1962 some city people came back to the Court. They were from Tennessee, and they had been to a federal district court with a claim that Tennessee denied them "equal protection of the laws accorded them by the Fourteenth Amendment to the Constitution of the United States by virtue of the debasement of their votes." The district court based its decision on *Colegrove* v. *Green* and dismissed the case on the grounds that it lacked jurisdiction. The decision was appealed to the Supreme Court.[8]

The Tennessee appellants won their appeal in the Supreme Court in the first of a series of cases that were to shake legislative bodies to their foundations. The Court, in an opinion written by Justice Brennan, used the "equal protection of the laws" and "due process" clauses of the Fourteenth Amendment to order reapportionment of the Tennessee legislature. In a concurring opinion, Justice Clark cited evidence and statistics in support of the view that equal protection had clearly been denied urban voters. Moore County, for example, had a total population of 2,340, whereas Rutherford County had 25,316, but both had the same representation in a Tennessee legislature that had not been redistricted since 1901.

Justice Frankfurter would have stayed with his opinion in *Colegrove* v. *Green.* He dissented in a lengthy opinion, which Justice Clark referred to as "bursting with words that go through so much and conclude with so little." The majority's decision, Frankfurther argued, would "charge courts with the task of accommodating the incommensurable factors of policy which underlie those mathematical puzzles." In Frankfurter's view, the courts were being plunged into a "quagmire" of political considerations to which judicial processes are inadequate and inappropriate.

REAPPORTIONMENT BY JUDICIAL COMMAND

Baker v. *Carr* was only the beginning. Decisions began to flow from the Court that required the districts in both houses of state legislatures and in the House of Representatives to be apportioned on the basis of population.[9]

[8] *Baker* v. *Carr,* 369 U.S. 186 (1962).

[9] To illustrate the extent of judicial involvement in state reapportionment, some of the cases follow: *Reynolds* v. *Sims, Vann* v. *Baggett,* and *McConnell* v. *Baggett* were decided together, 377 U.S. 533 (1964). Other cases are *W.M.C.A. Inc.* v. *Lomenzo,* 337 U.S. 633 (1964), *Maryland Committee for Fair Representation* v. *Tawes,* 377 U.S. 656 (1964), and *Lucas* v. *Forty-Fourth General Assembly of Colorado,* 377 U.S. 713 (1964).

The House of Representatives reapportionment decision, in an opinion written by Justice Black, concluded that congressional districting in Georgia had flagrantly violated equal representation of its citizens.[10] Black pointed out that Georgia's largest district, as of 1960, contained 823,680 people, while the average of the ten districts was 394,312, and the smallest was 272,154, or less than one third of the largest. Black concluded his opinion with the observation that:

> While it may not be possible to draw Congressional districts with mathematical precision, that is no excuse for ignoring our Constitution's plain objective making equal representation for equal numbers of people the fundamental goal for the House of Representatives. That is the high standard of justice and common sense which the founders set for us.

Reactions to the Court's reapportionment orders have varied from passive resistance in some states to serious efforts to redistrict in others. Congress has shown interest in amending the federal Constitution to permit area representation and to negate the Supreme Court's order. Whether the move will prove either popular or successful remains to be seen.

Hanging over the head of states that balk at redistricting is a threat of "at-large" elections, where all voters vote for all members of a legislative body. Courts can order at-large elections and have done so in a few instances. Illinois had an at-large election for its General Assembly in 1963, and presented a ballot providing for the election of its 177 members to the befuddled voter. It took weeks to count the ballots, and the results were so chaotic that other states are not anxious to have a similar experience.

Congressional redistricting occurred in several states following the 1960 census when population shifts resulted in a gain or loss of seats in the House of Representatives. In such instances population was a strong factor in redistricting and congressmen themselves actively took part in realigning their districts.[11]

Reapportionment, especially the Court's orders to reapportion the upper houses of state legislatures, raises interesting theoretical questions. It is often argued that the apportionment of a second house on the basis of geography rather than population is justifiable as an application of the federal principle embodied in Congress. The analogy, however,

[10] *Wesberry* v. *Sanders*, 376 U.S. 1 (1964).
[11] Malcom E. Jewell, "Political Patterns of Reapportionment," reprinted in Schubert, *op. cit.*, p. 34.

simply will not sustain the argument. None of the state constitutions contains the equivalent of federalism or state's rights for local jurisdictions. States are not federal unions and no such provision is a condition of their political existence.

The argument against "one man, one vote" is basically the argument for broker rule. The objective would appear to be the representation of interests rather than individuals and the arrangement of the legislature so that compromise rather than majority rule is likely to be the governing process. Liberals will support the Court's position and it is not clear why conservatives, in the philosophical sense, should support the over-representation of rural districts. Most self-professed *conservatives* have opposed the decision, however. But in a recent "Memorandum to Republican Leaders,"[12] William B. Pendergast argued oversized districts hurt the Republican party and his arguments caused some conservatives to reappraise their position toward the Court's insistence on equal representation.

For the judiciary to order states to be egalitarian and give equal voice to all citizens, urban or rural, is an ironic development in the Court's role in a democracy. The controversy growing out of its decision indicates that some people feel the Court has abandoned its role of preserving traditions.[13] The greatest irony, however, is that legislatures, in liberal theory the repository for the voice of the majority, are being told by the judiciary to be majoritarian. For legislatures to argue against the Court's order is a strange twist, indeed, on the functions of these two branches of government.

The Necessity for Legislative Organization and Procedure

Any deliberative body that makes policy requires some procedural framework, be it *Roberts' Rules of Order* in a student council or the elaborate rules of each house of the United States Congress. Size alone necessitates this, and as size increases, rules and procedures often increasingly limit the freedom of the individual member. For example, the 435-member House of Representatives is over four times as large as the Senate, and the entire membership must face election every two years. To organize such a large institution, which has as its purpose the deliberation and

---

[12] Reprinted in Schubert, *op. cit.*, p. 201.
[13] "Toward the Total State," editorial in *National Review*, April 10, 1962, reprinted in Schubert, *op. cit.*

creation of public policy, requires some necessary restrictions on the activities of its members. Debate must be limited, and a tight control over the measures coming before the House must be exercised. Committees, in such a large body, become important and powerful since they control the flow of legislation.

In the Senate, only one third of the Senators face election every two years so there is a greater guaranteed continuity of membership. This, along with its smaller size, ensures organization and procedures different from those of the House. Its rules and procedures give the individual senator more opportunity to make his views known.

There are many other factors that make organization and procedure essential. The variety of areas and interests represented in a legislature requires some procedural mechanism that guarantees them a fair hearing. The competition of rival political parties must be regulated. Methods must be found to prevent obstructionists from thwarting the flow of legislation; minorities must have protection from tyranny of the majority; members must be protected from legal action for their statements in the legislature; and many other safeguards are necessary.

Rules and regulations are means devised by a legislature to achieve its objectives rather than ends in themselves. The objectives of individual legislators may be diametrically opposed—that is, one legislator may look to procedure as a means of getting a law enacted while one of his colleagues may look to the same procedure as a device to prevent such enactment. Rules and procedure attempt to provide the battlefield and code of conduct on which legislative jousting takes place.

Some legislators are masters of the intricacies of the procedural labyrinth. They can find their way in its endless passageways until their desired goals are obtained. Others flout procedural formalities as much as possible. They emphasize the virtue of their goals and often point out that they are being frustrated by antagonists with procedural roadblocks.

EFFICIENCY OF LEGISLATIVE ORGANIZATION AND PROCEDURE

The economic growth of the United States and the complexity of the problems created by rapid social change have led to dramatic changes in the structure and organization of the executive branch of government. Congress, on the other hand, in spite of these changes, goes along in just about the same way it has for generations. One author summed up the situation, in 1953, as follows:

Congress meanwhile had changed little in the intervening decades. For the most part it was still operating with the same machinery and methods, the same facilities and services, that it had inherited from the era of Thomas Bracket Reed [1800's]. Overworked and underpaid, often lampooned by the press and unfairly criticized by the thoughtless, our national legislature had fallen from its once high estate. Few any longer regarded it as the keystone of the federal arch. With Congress overwhelmed by its great responsibilities, operating under its ancient ritual, the streamlined age of the Giant Clipper, radar, and the atomic bomb seem to have passed it by.[14]

Granted the truth of this statement, the question of how one would gear Congress to the twentieth century remains difficult. To make it bigger would only aggravate the problems. To streamline its procedures might result in more laws being made, but it might also be less democratic in making them.

Making laws does not lend itself to the generally accepted standards of efficiency. For example, a law that had been filibustered, amended countless times, heard by many committees, and sent to several conference committees before it at long last was passed might still be a very efficient action of Congress in that the public interest is well served. It may well be that efficiency is the advantage of tyranny; the strength of democracy lies in the very "inefficiency" of its methods for determining the goals and purposes of political society.

This is not to say that the structure and procedures of Congress now serve this democratic process well. The question we must ask of congressional organization is whether it facilitates the process of democratic decision-making. And, of course, our conclusions will depend on which model of the democratic process we apply. With this in mind we turn to the organization of Congress.

DEBATE AND ITS LIMITATIONS

The responsibility for enacting laws makes legislative bodies a forum for the debate of public issues. Few, if any, of the nation's important laws have been unanimously agreed upon by all members of Congress. Debate reflects the range of political perspectives held or articulated by congressmen. Debate, however, cannot go on forever; pressing issues will not wait.

[14] George G. Galloway, *The Legislative Process in Congress* (New York: Crowell, 1953), p. 8. Even the academic study of government has largely ignored legislative activities. Most government curricula in most colleges deal heavily with the executive and courts but have few courses on legislation.

In Congress, the size of the House of Representatives works against the free debate still used in the Senate. The House Rules Committee is charged with allotting time to debate bills. It does this by a special rule specifying the time for debate allotted to the most important bills (except appropriations). The time is then divided equally between the parties. The chairman of the committee in charge of the bill rations out the time to majority members wishing to speak, while the ranking minority member does the same for the opposition. Sometimes, many members who would like to discuss the bill are eliminated by the time factor, and often those who do enter the debate have only a few minutes to make their views known. Also, debate can be closed by a motion for the previous question, and a majority vote on this motion stops debate (technically called cloture) to bring the issue up for final vote. If the previous question passes before any debate on the measure has been held, a brief time, usually forty minutes equally divided between the parties, is allowed. Floor leaders of the political parties are influential in the managing of debate and in calling for cloture.

In the Senate debate is not easily limited. There is a strong tradition of free discussion that occasionally blossoms into a filibuster—an extended marathon of words and procedural delays that can frustrate the business of the Senate almost indefinitely. From 1949 to 1959, cloture could not be obtained without a two-thirds vote of the entire Senate membership. In 1959, a struggle over this issue ended with the adoption of Rule 22, which made cloture somewhat easier by only requiring a two-thirds vote of members present and voting, rather than of the whole body. But extended debate and delay can still occur, and it is difficult to muster enough votes to stop a real or threatened filibuster.

The history of the filibuster is a colorful story. Filibusters may be extended talks on any subject, since the discussion does not have to be germane to the issue. The individual record was made by Senator Strom Thurmond, who talked for twenty-four hours and eighteen minutes against the Civil Rights Act of 1957. Other individual endurance performances were Senator Morse's twenty-two-hour-and-twenty-six-minute talk against the Tidelands Oil Bill and Huey Long's fifteen-hour-and-thirty-minute talk on an amendment to the National Recovery Act in 1935. Subjects range from Long's elaborate recipes for homemade liquor, turnip greens, and corn pone to the best technique of swinging a golf club, the evils of Wall Street, motherhood, and raising children.

Extended speeches are only one way to conduct filibusters. Other techniques include delaying parliamentary tactics; quorum calls, roll call votes, points of order and appeals from them, and extended questions and answers. Difficult as it is, cloture is usually the only effective weapon against a filibuster, but a strict enforcement of Senate rules can help. Senators have to stand and cannot walk around when speaking, they cannot use nonparliamentary language and can be taken "off their feet" if they do, and they cannot have clerks read their material. A less effective but more sensational technique to combat the filibuster is to keep the Senate in long sessions so that the talkers will become too tired to continue. This tactic has limitations, however, since physical fitness is a prime requisite for verbal endurance tests.

Legislation filibustered to death is often needed or desirable but is killed because it is unpopular with powerful private or sectional interests. Southern Senators, for example, have used the filibuster many times to kill civil-rights legislation. Between 1865 and 1946, thirty-seven measures exclusive of appropriations were killed by filibustering. It is estimated that about four times this many appropriation bills have met their deaths by this same device. On a heated issue it may take a long time to talk a bill to death. In 1890, the southern filibuster against a bill calling for federal supervision of elections lasted twenty-nine days.[15] Filibusters are particularly effective toward the end of a congressional session, since the pressure of time works in favor of dropping the bill being talked to death.

Free debate is susceptible to such obstructionist abuse that there have been repeated attempts to change the rules to make cloture easier. Its chief advantage, however, is that it can assure a full-scale debate as well as a depth of criticism and analysis of measures before the Senate. Even a filibuster can be used to awaken the public to an important issue. These broad considerations have done as much to retain free and full debate in the Senate as have the powerful minority blocs who see it as a device to gain their ends. The abuse of free debate is more possible when political parties lack the strength to discipline members who wish to use their right to unlimited discussion as a power device to enhance a narrow interest. Stronger parties with stronger platforms might do much to make free debate more responsible.

[15] Bertram M. Gross, *The Legislative Struggle* (New York: McGraw-Hill, 1953), pp. 374-75.

Party Control of the Legislature

The political setting of legislative bodies finds two parties, one a majority and the other a minority, contesting for power. This political contest sets the tone of much procedure. Both major political parties fight earnestly, sometimes even viciously, for political control of Congress and other legislative bodies. The power conflicts between the two parties come to focus in their efforts to control the organization of legislatures. Organizational control means the power to designate the presiding officers and committee chairmen, to hold a majority of seats on the committees, and to control the order of business. On these questions, party discipline and cohesion are rigid, and deviation rarely occurs although it is sometimes threatened.

This unity on organizational issues is in sharp contrast to the divisions in Congress on legislative issues, which rarely follow strict party lines. The alignment of southern Democrats with northern Republicans on many issues is a case in point. On organizational questions, the southern Democrats stay with their party; but on other legislative issues, they are inclined to vote with the Republicans.

At the national level, neither party has any wild dreams of ever completely driving out the opposition. Procedure is devised to give the majority party strength but also to assure the voice of the minority party will be heard. Both parties are aware that democratic government demands opposition. They are also conscious that they will themselves almost certainly be a minority at some future time and are therefore sensitive to the rights of the minority party. Moreover, whereas each party unites itself to control the legislature, they do not want such overwhelming control as one might imagine.

Having too large a majority, as President Franklin Roosevelt discovered, aggravates the already serious problem of party discipline and cohesiveness on legislation. If one party has an overwhelming majority, its individual members may feel less personal obligation to support the party's position, and the party tends to break up into internal factions, which quarrel with one another rather than with the opposition. The minority party gains considerable strength, if it is united, from such an occurrence. What most party leaders seek is a comfortable majority that is not so big it becomes indifferent to the opposition but big enough to ensure the passage of the party's legislative program. It is convenient for a party to have a comfortable enough majority so that party members who have some political reason related to their constituency, a major interest group, or their consciences may be allowed to vote against the party on particular issues. But the party's position may be weakened if its majority is so big that the party members ride off in all directions at once.

Briefly, when a political party captures Congress it sets out to organize the institution so that it will be able to get its program under way. If it is fortunate enough to be of the same party as the chief executive, it has both an opportunity and a responsibility to see that it is set up so the executive program will have a good chance of success. If the chief executive is from the other party, it may organize itself so it can saddle the executive and his party with blame for failures and unpopular policies and secure for itself the credit for the successes.

The combination of partisan cohesion on organizational issues, and the abandonment of partisan loyalties on others, causes an endless shifting of alliances among the membership. A majority and minority leader may engage in a bitter parliamentary battle on an organizational question but find themselves close allies on a bill dealing with civil rights. They may break apart again on a tax measure. Constituents, personal convictions, or sympathy toward articulate interest groups is likely to contribute to this.

LEGISLATIVE LEADERSHIP AND ORGANIZATION

The leadership of a legislative body is ordinarily selected from the membership of its majority party. The official presiding officer in the United States Senate, however, is the Vice-President who may not be from the majority party. He is unable to vote except in case of a tie, but his ability to use his position to party advantage has many possibilities. Vice-President Nixon, for example, was a Republican presiding over a Senate controlled by the Democrats for six of the eight years (1954–1960) he held the office. On a few important issues, his vote to break a tie was a distinct advantage to his party. He also used his position as presiding officer to assist his party in many ways, particularly in bringing public attention to political maneuvers by Democratic Senators.

An important official in upper houses is the President *pro tempore*, who presides in the absence of the official leader. In the United States Senate, he assumes the presiding office in the event of the Vice-President's death, resignation, or succession to the Presidency. The majority party's nominee for the office is virtually assured election, although the minority party puts up a candidate as a gesture.

The House of Representatives selects its own presiding officer, who is called the speaker. Each party places a candidate for speaker before the House, but party discipline is such that the majority party is victorious.

The real struggle for leadership occurs in the party caucus or conference. Each house of Congress has its party conferences to select its leaders. In addition to securing agreement on nominees for president *pro tempore* and speaker, as well as secretary to the senate, clerk of the house, and other administrative aides, party conferences are used in both houses to select the majority and minority floor leaders, assistant floor leaders, often referred to as whips, and the membership of each party's committee on committees.

The internal struggles in party conferences sometimes involve a challenge to the existing leadership of the party. Sometimes the challenge is serious but unless it reflects deep-seated grievances, as it did in the case of Minority Leader Martin's difficulty discussed previously, the threat to party unity ordinarily keeps it in bounds and renders it ineffectual.[16]

The selection of committee membership by the committee on committees of each party is a crucial step in the organization of party power. Until 1910, when the House of Representatives rebelled against the iron-fisted rule of Speaker Joseph G. Cannon, the Speaker virtually handpicked members of committees. Since Cannon's dethroning, the House has adopted a method of selecting committees which involves a much broader participation by party members. The party leaderships informally agree upon the total membership and party ratios of each House committee. The Democratic caucus elects their members of the Ways and Means Committee who also serve as the party's committee on committees. This committee then draws up the committee assignments and submits them to a party caucus for approval. When the caucus agrees upon the list, a resolution containing it is submitted to the House.

The Republican committee on committees in the House is made up

[16] In 1959, there developed some rumblings of dissatisfaction within the Democratic party in both the House and the Senate. The "two Texans," the late Speaker Rayburn of the House and then Senate Majority Leader Lyndon Johnson, were criticized by their own party for being both too authoritarian with party members and too much committed to compromise with the opposition.

of one member from each state having at least one Republican in its delegation. It prepares a list which is submitted for approval to the party's policy committee, which in turn reviews the list and incorporates it in a House resolution. The Democrats have developed a list of committee priorities based upon considerations other than strict seniority, but the Republicans follow no firm rule but seniority.[17]

In the Senate, the Democratic Steering Committee and the Republican Committee on Committees each works up a list of committee members. In the case of the Democrats the list must be submitted to the party caucus for approval. The Republicans do not require submission to a caucus. The lists then go to the Senate in the form of resolutions for acceptance. Senate tradition and knowledge of the rituals of seniority make approval almost automatic so that rarely does any adjustment occur on the floor.

THE SENIORITY SYSTEM

Both houses of Congress select committee members on the basis of the personal preferences of the congressmen if the rule of seniority does not interfere. If the number of Senators or Representatives requesting membership on the same committee is so large that all of them will not be able to be placed on it, seniority then applies and those with the longest tenure get the seats. Seniority also applies to the committee itself. That is, the members with the longest service on the committee get the positions of leadership. Thus, a relatively new member of Congress may have committee seniority over one of his elders who joined the committee at a later time. The member of the majority party with the greatest committee seniority becomes chairman; his counterpart in the opposition party will probably be chairman in the future if the political climate changes.

Probably no aspect of congressional procedure has been subjected to such prolonged and fundamental attack as the seniority rule. Its tenacity is partly explained by the two main advantages it provides the legislators. One is that it provides an objective and impartial alternative to the bitter feuding within the party over committee posts that might otherwise occur. No doubt it is largely for this reason that most congressmen find that the longer they are in Congress the better the seniority rule looks and the easier it is to accept. The second advantage

[17] *Congressional Quarterly: 1961–62 Guide to Current American Government,* p. 18.

is that seniority provides a buffer against pressure groups and the executive branch turning on the heat for the location of particular legislators on committees they are anxious to stack.

The chief disadvantage of seniority is that it tends to favor one-party regions, such as the South, which return the same congressmen year after year and thus gain a disproportionate control over Congress. Elections in these one-party areas generally turn on local interests and issues. As a consequence their representatives are likely to be freer to act as political brokers on issues of national or international scope. Seniority also protects mediocrities who continue to be elected. It gives them a means to float to the top positions of power and prestige. Sometimes seniority produces chairman of key committees who are out of sympathy with the objectives of their party and its presidential leadership. Thus, a President devoted to foreign aid might find an old-style isolationist as chairman of the Senate Foreign Relations Committee. Seniority, in short, makes party responsibility and discipline difficult.

THE STRUGGLE FOR COMMITTEE ASSIGNMENT

Aspirations of individuals in Congress to be placed on certain committees run the gamut of human motivations and drives. Some want to be on a committee in order to promote their own views by furthering or frustrating specific legislation; some want an assignment that can be dramatized to their constituents; some want to be on pork-barrel committees that deal with projects of importance to their districts; others feel they can serve various interest groups important to them by being placed on appropriate committees. Still others, particularly aspirants for a national reputation, may feel they can get a lot of publicity and political mileage out of certain strategic committee assignments. Television and the other mass media can put a congressman in the national limelight if he serves on a committee investigating sensational matters and well enough financed to hold public hearings. World-wide travel can also be a lure for membership on some congressional committees. The motivations are almost without limit and in the case of individual legislators are no doubt mixed.

The formal procedures of committee selection are of concern to groups other than Congress itself. Political parties, private-interest groups, the President, government agencies, and geographical areas are all anxious to place elected representatives partial to their interests on appropriate committees. Within the limitations of seniority and other procedural formalities, they often work to influence the choice of members for particular committees.

Political parties work over membership lists with the most extreme care. Key committees must be stocked with enough talent so that if seniority dictates a mediocrity or a maverick as chairman, the party can still have a committee member who is an articulate spokesman for the official party position. There are always some "duty" committees concerned with mundane matters. These committees usually have a membership composed of a large number of freshmen with an occasional oldster or two. Such pork-barrel committees as post offices, civil service, public works, and veterans affairs are carefully staffed and controlled by the majority party to handle available spoils within the limits of civil service. "Pork" committees are also used to get politically advantageous distribution of government construction and other spending projects located in strategic spots throughout the country. Decisions on the location of defense plants and military installations, and the efforts of congressmen and governors to get their fair share of such installations, have become a serious political concern. The composition of the armed services committees, for example, is likely to be reflected in the distribution of military payrolls among the states.

Special-interest groups are ever on the alert when committee members are being selected. They apply pressure on political parties or wherever else it might be effective to see that committees are staffed so that their particular interests will be given a favorable and sympathetic audience. Agricultural groups have been quite effective in loading agriculture committees of both houses of Congress (and most state legislatures) with sympathetic members. Other interest groups, such as business, labor, medicine, law, education, and oil, exert pressure to get members on or keep members off committees in which they are interested.

The Committee System and Legislation

Committees are the basic units of legislative organization. They serve as subgroups of the legislature, permitting work to be divided and the multitude of legislative proposals to be given more attention, albeit by a smaller group, than if the whole house had to deal with them. Committees also control the flow of legislation. Manning the toll gates of the legislative process, committees control the fate of political party programs. While the party that controls a legislature usually controls its committees, this control extends only to party affiliation, and if a member of the majority party not in tune with the official position of his party becomes chairman of a key committee, he can cause his party a good deal of difficulty.

Committee chairmen, by virtue of the power of the chair and by tradition, generally have a great deal of control over their committees. If they are unable to control their committees, on key issues at least, they usually try to rearrange the membership so that they can. Even the threat by a committee chairman to resign if his committee does not support his position may be effective, since such resignations would undermine, in effect, the seniority system.

An illustration of the power of a key committee and its chairman, whose individual views on legislation transcend party discipline, is Howard W. Smith's subjective reign over the House Rules Committee. Judge Smith, a courtly Virginia Democrat, generally looks at legislation from an economically conservative and segregationist viewpoint. The Rules Committee controls the agenda of the House by issuing "rules" which schedule bills for debate on the floor. Chairman Smith's power, therefore, extends to the entire range of legislation as hearings are held before his committee on whether rules should be granted. Civil-rights legislation and spending bills get long and careful scrutiny at hearings, while bills Chairman Smith looks upon favorably have sailed through his committee with alacrity. The Rules Committee's power is essentially negative. While it can delay or withhold legislation altogether, all it can do to help passage of a bill is to give it a rule so it can be debated and voted upon.[18] On numerous occasions the committee, under the paternalistic guidance of its chairman, has bottled up legislation not to its liking by the use of delaying tactics such as dilatory hearings or by refusal to conduct hearings at all. The chairman and his committee may also use their power by having bills amended to conform to their particular viewpoints before issuing a rule. As one congressman put it, the Rules Committee has a "psychological effect. Every committee chairman knows whether the Rules Committee will approve a bill or not. And the chairman will move in the direction of the Rules Committee in trying to get a rule."[19] The Committee can even issue a "special" or "gag" rule, which forbids further amendments to a bill at the time of floor action.

[18] See James A. Robinson, *The House Rules Committee* (New York: Bobbs-Merrill, 1963), pp. 18-19.
[19] *Ibid.*, p. 15.

Judge Smith once described himself as "a horse-trader and son of a horse trader," qualities his colleagues have learned to understand.[20] Some of his trades have included amendments to bills in return for a rule, moving or holding other bills in other committees for a rule, and modifications of a colleague's position for or against other bills or particular features thereof in return for a rule. When all else fails, Chairman Smith occasionally leaves town. On one such occasion, when a barn had burned on Smith's farm, Speaker Rayburn expressed surprise that Judge Smith would resort to arson to deny a hearing to important bills. Judge Smith, in short, is a skilled trader and strategist. He has acquired a lot of good horses well below the market value.

The Rules Committee and its powerful chairman have been the subject of lively controversy in recent years. There is little question that this Committee has blocked, delayed, or forced modification of much popular and necessary legislation. Yet, for a body as large as the House of Representatives, it is necessary to organize and cull out the mass of insignificant legislation introduced in every Congress. The problem is how to make this function responsible not only to the majority party but to the entire Congress and, even more important, to the public interest. Ironically, the power of the Rules Committee originated as an attempt to curtail the power of the speaker to schedule debate. This reform was successful but it resulted in the chairman of the Rules Committee being almost as powerful as the speaker had been.

In 1965 the House revised its rules to restore the "twenty-one-day rule," which had been used in the Eighty-First Congress of 1949–1950. By this device the speaker is granted the discretion, on specific days, to recognize the chairman of a committee who has a bill he wishes debated and that has been before the Rules Committee for twenty-one days. In other words, the Rules Committee's delaying power is limited to twenty-one days if the speaker chooses to recognize a committee chairman for the purpose of bringing a bill before the House.[21] The Speaker is also authorized to entertain motions, which can be passed by a simple majority, to send bills already passed by the House to conference committees. This, too, used to require a special rule from the Rules Committee. Before these changes the Committee could delay debate and conferences indefinitely. This is an important reform and substantially curtails the Committee's power. The chairman's power

20 *Ibid.*, p. 14.
21 *New York Times*, January 10, 1965, p. E1.

also was modified in 1961 by expanding the committee membership so that the majority of the members would be more responsible to party leadership. This was not as significant, however, as the twenty-one-day reform, which gave the speaker power to overrule the Rules Committee on the scheduling of debate.

The power of the Rules Committee has been significantly diminished, but the problem remains. In any legislative body there must be some means of performing the necessary function of sorting out significant legislation from the mountain of inconsequential proposals before it. The problem is to devise ways of doing this that permit the Congress to exert responsible legislative initiative. Ultimately, the only way of accomplishing this seems to lie in the direction of legislative leadership that more closely reflects party policies and is more directly responsible to the views of the members of the majority party in the legislature.

STAFF ASSISTANCE TO COMMITTEES

The staff assistance available to committees depends upon the amount of funds allotted them, the importance of the issues under consideration, and the desire of the legislature to have information. Many legislative committees are able to employ their own staff or consultants, as they are often called. Others must rely upon what help they can get from the executive departments. Since committee chairmen have discretion over whom the committee will employ, there is always a problem of appointing staff members as a repayment for a political debt. Some staff members are zealous partisans of a political cause, others show a particular fondness for certain pressure groups, and others may be embarrassments to the whole legislature, because of either their ineptitude or their independence.[22] On the other hand, many legislative committees avail themselves of the best talent they can find. Some committee staffs have done a monumental job of gathering and analyzing information vital to efficient legislation.

There are, however, problems contingent upon the staffing of committees in relation to minority membership. For example, in the Eighty-Seventh Congress there was complaint from the Republican party, a minority in both houses, that they did not have proper staff assistance

---

[22] The House Special Committee on Legislative Oversight in 1958, which looked into the activities of regulatory commissions, employed a staff member so zealous in his duties that he caused a great deal of discomfort to his committee. He was fired, but out of his zeal several regulatory agencies had trouble. See William S. Fairfield, "Dr. Schwartz Goes to Washington," *Reporter*, March 20, 1958, pp. 24-28.

to do the spadework for positions contrary to those of the majority party. Contributing to this discontent was the fact that the Democrats not only controlled the staff of congressional committees, but had access to information from the executive branch, which their party also controlled.

The problem raised by the Republicans is a serious one that many states have confronted. Some states—Wisconsin is a good example— have helped solve it by establishing a centralized research agency that gathers information requested by legislators from either party. The quality of this research is often excellent and provides, if not a partisan argument, a body of data from which a political position can be derived. Congress has not yet developed such an agency, but with the growing complexity of issues it must resolve, it is quite possible it may do so in the future.

THE INVESTIGATING POWER

In addition to the problem of securing adequate information on the measures before them, the legislature confronts the task of exploring new areas to determine whether laws are necessary or desirable. This investigative function opens the way to potential abuses that have aroused a good deal of political and legal controversy.

Legislative investigations in the past have led to some of our more fundamental laws. In the past several decades, congressional committees have investigated such important and pressing national problems as organized crime, business monopolies, fraudulent stock and bond sales, farm problems, atomic energy, space exploration, education, un-American activities, and political corruption. Laws regulating business and labor relationships, antitrust acts, farm legislation, and the Securities and Exchange Act have resulted from such investigations.

Investigations are sometimes conducted by full committees (standing, special, or joint), but generally they are undertaken by subcommittees. The Eighty-Sixth Congress, for example, had a total in both houses of forty-one investigating committees, most of them subcommittees, which were authorized to spend $15,565,695 for investigations.[23]

The control of the legislative power to investigate is basically a problem for the legislature itself. The informal rules of the club and the ethical purview of legislative bodies have an effect on those who tend to

[23] *Congressional Quarterly*, April 22, 1960, p. 673. This is in addition to the other committee expenditures not connected with investigations. All this money may not be used; the Eighty-Fifth Congress authorized $12,118,280 but spent only $9,717,796.

abuse the power. Senator Joseph McCarthy was halted in his free-swinging investigations because he violated the dignity of the Senate. Others have also been limited by Congress and state legislatures when they have gone too far. Sometimes, however, they have not been halted before extensive and serious damage has been done to the lives and reputations of individuals often innocent of any crime and guilty only of thinking or acting in a way not approved by the investigators.

Proposals to curtail investigating power must be carefully and cautiously considered. The power to legislate requires the power to investigate. Formalized restraints to prevent abuses may seriously curtail access to important information. A decent respect for private rights by the legislature and a public opinion alert to their invasion must be the ultimate safeguards.

INTRODUCTION OF BILLS AND COMMITTEE HEARINGS

Every measure introduced into a legislature is called a bill. It may be a potential statute or one of various types of resolutions.[24] The sponsor of a bill may state a preference for referral to a particular committee and struggle to achieve his preference. In the Senate, bills are assigned to committee by the president *pro tempore* and in the House by the parliamentarian on order of the speaker. Sometimes, however, the decision on referral is vital to the bill's chances, and the real struggle may be to decide whether a favorably or unfavorably disposed committee shall have jurisdiction.

Rarely is a piece of legislation the sole creation of the individual legislator who introduces it; usually, even the idea is not originated by him. A bill may have been drafted by some governmental agency as part of the executive's legislative program; it may be introduced at the request of, perhaps even be written by, a particular interest group; a group of legislators may draw up a bill in which they have a common interest; the legislator may introduce private bills[25] for constituents in

[24] Regular bills introduced into the house of Representatives are entitled "H.R. 500" or whatever the number happens to be, and in the Senate, "S. 500." Joint resolutions, which can become law also, are entitled "H.J. Res. 500" in the House and "S.J. Res. 500" in the Senate. Concurrent resolutions, which do not become law but declare a sentiment or desire of Congress, are entitled "H. Con. Res. 500" in the House and "S. Con. Res. 500" in the Senate. Single-house resolutions, which do not become law but declare an attitude of one house (sometimes aimed at the other), are entitled "H. Res. 500" or "S. Res. 500" in the respective houses. All these bills go to committees.

[25] Private bills are for the benefit of a particular individual. They are used, for example, to appropriate money for the relief of an individual who is unable to sue the government because of its sovereign immunity.

need of special relief; or he may introduce bills at the suggestion of constituents.

Several legislative bodies adopt the practice of allowing the author of a bill to have the words *by request* placed under its title. This is a note either to the speaker to send the bill to the graveyard or to the first committee chairman to administer the *coup de grace* to the bill. This courtesy between legislators allows them to introduce the whims and fantasies of their constituents and then dispose of them for one another by killing them when the phrase *by request* appears. Cynical perhaps, but effective. In Congress *by request* on bills generally means that the author's responsibility has ended with the bill's introduction, and he is not interested in pushing the bill actively through committee. Committee action, it scarcely needs adding, is often negative.

After a bill is referred to a congressional committee, it is placed on the committee calendar. Most proposed legislation dies on the calendar. If the committee fails to hear the bill and report it out, it can be rescued only by a petition of 218 members of the House or a resolution of discharge in the Senate. In both cases, a majority of the total membership is required to remove a bill from the committee's jurisdiction and return it to the floor. Successful withdrawal action is seldom achieved in either the Senate or House of Representatives. The strong tradition of the sanctity of committees is partly responsible for this. So is the possibility of reprisal against the bills of members attempting to call bills back from committees. If the committee does schedule a bill for a hearing, it may assign it to a subcommittee or decide to give it a full committee hearing. Such a decision often depends on the size of the committee and the range of substance in its jurisdiction.

Hearings on bills in committee ordinarily provide pressure groups a favorable climate. Since the purpose of the committee hearing is to take testimony on the bills before it, interested groups appear to present their cases, often in the form of formal reports. Such groups endorse, support, or attempt to amend or kill bills to suit the interests they represent. Although committee members are ordinarily interested in deciding on the merits of a bill, in the setting of a hearing the emphasis is on who is pushing it, trying to kill it, or proposing to amend it. In fact, the question of who favors or supports a bill may often become as important to its fate as its substance. Some legislators are especially sensitive to the position of a particular highly organized lobby; others seek to satisfy the claims and objections of all of the major interested groups. Often the activity of a committee clearly focuses on the effort to amend a bill to make it satisfactory to the contending interests. In many cases, a bill dies because a satisfactory bargain cannot be negotiated among the contending parties. On the other hand, if such powerful interests as labor, manufacturers, and real estate all support a bill, its path through committee is likely to be smooth.

Testimony before committees is an important function of lobbyists, and it is here they apply some of their best techniques of persuasion. The most able of the lobbyists work carefully to appear objective in their testimony. This often involves a dignified and quasi-intellectual approach to the issue, which many times serves to disguise the desires of the interests represented. A favorite device is to equate their interests with the public interest, in order to avoid the charge of being self-seekers.

Most of this approach is for public consumption, however, since legislators are not naïve and know very well what is going on. Very often there have been more intimate conversations on interest group desires. Legislators tend to discount righteous claims to the public interest by lobbyists as "window dressing" or "violin music." Whether committee members or their staff scratch the surface to reveal the true nature of the testimony depends, as much as anything else, on their desire to probe deeply. If a legislator is sympathetic to the lobbyist, he will probably let the testimony stand. In fact, he may bulwark the testimony and make it more plausible by asking leading questions to draw out the lobbyist. On the other hand, an unsympathetic legislator often asks probing and, for the lobbyist, embarrassing questions. He may, if he feels strongly about the measure, expose the testimony as being misleading and publicly censure the lobbyist.

The testimony of lobbyists often appeals to such symbols as the American way of life, creeping socialism, selfish exploitation, and other clichés full of emotion and empty of precision. But in spite of the perfection of the science of persuasion, many arguments by interest groups are paradoxical and almost humorously inconsistent. For example, the steel industry has historically dressed up its case with the slogans of *laissez faire* competition, yet devoted all its energies to legislation legalizing basing-point marketing systems that artificially raise and protect the price of steel. In the same way, labor unions support featherbedding in the form of full-crew laws while at the same time paying deference, when it suits their convenience, to the notions of pride in workmanship.

Appearances before committees by persons other than those employed to do so is uncommon. The testimony of Mr. Harry Golden before a Senate Committee in 1945 put it this way: "Anytime a bill is presented to the Congress, I can close my eyes and visualize who will appear. They will be about the same people who usually testify for or against a bill. You never have any new blood."[26]

The late Congressman Clem Miller colorfully described these central characteristics of committee hearings:

> Many times, the hearings seem to be *pro forma*, just going through the motions, with key decisions already made. They resemble a large verbal orchestration, as a "record" is carefully shaped under the vigilant gavel of the chairman. A standard parade of witnesses files by from the national organizations—A.F. of L., U. S. Chamber of Commerce, National Association of Manufacturers—then a seasoning of University Professors, and so on. The witnesses are carved up or blown up, or tailored to the need. Some are dismissed peremptorily, others are drawn out solicitously.[27]

Ostensibly, the function of committees in hearing bills is to acquire information about the bill, as well as to cull out from the plethora of measures introduced into legislatures those they think are deserving of consideration. This function is often used for other than its original purposes. Many times important bills favored by a majority of the legislature will never reach the floor because they have been bottled up in a powerful committee. On the other hand, committees sometimes duck their responsibilities and report out bills that are not deserving of passage but are so highly pressured the committee passes the buck to the total legislature.

When a bill survives committee hearings, the committee has several possible courses of action in reporting it back to the whole house. It can recommend that the bill be passed as introduced, that it be passed with amendments made by the committee, or that it be defeated. This last alternative of reporting a bill unfavorably is very infrequently used because committees themselves have a most effective means of killing bills, either by not considering them or by tabling them. Few bills dealing with important matters survive committee deliberations without amendment. If, as speaker Rayburn stated, the Bible were before Congress for action, the variety of interest group pressures for amendments would doubtless make the original intent hard to discover.

[26] Quoted in Gross, *op. cit.*, p. 290.
[27] Clem Miller, *Member of the House* (New York: Scribner's, 1962), p. 8.

When there are a large number of amendments suggested by a committee, very often they are put into a clean bill, which is assigned a new number and reported to the floor for action. On the floor, all committee amendments must be acted upon (approved, altered, or rejected) before a vote is taken on the measure itself. Committees do not always make unanimous reports to the whole house. Minority or dissenting opinions by a member or members of the committee are often submitted to the house along with the majority opinion. Dissenting opinions can recommend completely different action or modified action in the form of additional amendments. A bill generally has a better chance for favorable action if the committee is unanimous in its recommendations.

Brokerage Politics and Committees

The process of creating and staffing committees reflects the complex interplay of political forces. To recount accurately or definitively all the factors entering into the final accommodation would be impossible. The result, however, is an intricate balance of prestige, power, ambition, statesmanship, self-interest, and political stratagems of all kinds. Indeed, the test of political leadership in a legislature is often largely measured by how well the committees were put together. If it is a good job, political programs will move. If it is a poor job, programs bog down. If it is a very bad job, there will probably be some changes made in the leadership.

Committee hearings and deliberations are suited perfectly to the free play of pressure groups and the compromise of their differences. Except for executive sessions, committee meetings are open to the public; yet, they are for the most part private and unpublicized. The spotlight of publicity that attends floor debate serves to encourage legislators to frame their arguments in a broad public context. Floor debate and its publicity can also shine the light of public attention on the private interests and their stakes in the outcome. Neither of these conditions ordinarily obtains in the committee room. It is thus especially significant that the role of floor debate in legislative bodies has continuously declined while the power of committees has increased. Even in the Senate, traditionally the central forum of American public life, the role of floor debate has been progressively usurped by committees. The sheer weight of legislative business exerts pressures in this direction.

The process is complicated by the power of committee chairmen. Committees can bottle up a bill the majority wants by simply refusing to take it up or report it out, by referring it to a subcommittee, or by reporting it out too late in the session for action. In most legislative bodies, including Congress, committee chairmen are often powerful enough to frustrate the wishes of a majority of the committee members. A chairman through his control of the agenda and of subcommittees, and with a swift and strong hand on the gavel, can often have his own way. In many committees, there are traditions, part of the rules of the club, that dictate against a frustrated majority demanding a roll call vote of the committee or appealing from a ruling of the chair.

Committee control over the fate of legislation may increase with the growing complexity of the issues themselves. As this happens, group pressures are more intensely applied, bargains are more easily made, and the legislative process more nearly approximates the brokerage model.

Floor Action and Debate

Bills are scheduled for debate by being placed upon the appropriate calendar.[28] In the House, appropriation and other important bills are debated before the Committee of the Whole House. This is a procedure by which the House converts itself into a committee and thus

[28] The House of Representatives has several different calendars, which are used for various types of bills. These are the *Union Calendar*, which contains all appropriation and revenue bills; the *House Calendar*, which lists public bills other than those dealing with financial matters; the *Private Calendar*, which contains all private bills; the *Consent Calendar*, to which noncontroversial bills from the *Union* and *House Calendars* can be removed and considered in order of their listing on the first and third Mondays of each month and passed only if they receive unanimous approval; and the *Discharge Calendar*, where bills with a favorable petition to discharge them from a committee (the petition requires 218 signatures) are placed and considered on the second and fourth Mondays. A sixth calendar contains bills the President has vetoed.

The Senate uses only one legislative calendar but has an *Executive Calendar* reserved for the confirmation of treaties and presidential nominations of officials.

Placing bills on various calendars is virtually automatic, but occasionally some deft maneuvering goes on in efforts to secure unanimous consent through the Consent Calendar. If any objections are raised to a member's bill on the Consent Calendar, it goes back to either the House or Private Calendar from which it came and cannot be put on the Consent Calendar again during the session. Many bills are noncontroversial, and the Consent Calendar speeds up action on these bills, but members at times attempt to move something to the Consent Calendar, often after a good deal of cloakroom conversation, even at the risk of losing it. Timing is important for such moves, since there is a twilight zone between the controversial and noncontroversial.

avoids having to follow the intricate formal procedure with which it has encumbered itself for regular business. The Senate does not use the Committee of the Whole except for treaties.

Debate on legislation displays wide ranges of ability, wit, erudition, and style. There are congressmen who speak with calm and reasoned dispatch and those whose rhetoric virtually lifts the dome off the Capitol in a mist of homilies, biblical references, and sentimental maxims. Great spellbinders seem to be diminishing in the ranks of congressmen, and their loss takes something of the drama out of political debate. Much of the debate, in any event, is for public consumption since committee action and informal commitments give a degree of predictability to the outcome of most legislation.

FLOOR AMENDMENTS AND RIDERS

Congress, unlike many state legislatures, makes extensive use of floor amendments to bills. When an amendment is intended to cut the very heart out of the bill or alter its basic intent it is referred to as a *rider*. Riders are designed to achieve a purpose not originally intended by the bill. On the 1918 agriculture appropriations bill, for example, the "dries" attached a rider calling for the wartime prohibition of intoxicating liquor. Riders can embrace subject matter totally unrelated to the provisions of a bill. Senator Morse, for example, attempted to attach an anti-poll-tax rider onto the Tidelands Oil Bill before the Senate in 1946. Fortunately for the tidelands interests, the rider was killed along the way, although it was not ruled out of order. A threatened filibuster by southern Senators against the anti-poll-tax rider was thus avoided. Riders seem to attach themselves like barnacles to legislation that seems likely to pass without difficulty. Such a situation provides an opportunity for many congressmen to get a free ride for some favorite cause, if they can hook it onto something going by with a lot of momentum.

Often legislative horse trading comes into play at this point, and the sponsor must agree to riders as the price of enough votes to get his bill passed. The effectiveness of the use of the rider also reflects the separation of powers and the fact that the President does not have an item veto power. The item veto, which many states provide their governors, allows the executive to veto, and often to reduce, specific items in appropriation bills. The President's lack of this power precludes him from vetoing riders out of a bill. In short, he must either approve or veto the whole bill. Congress very often attaches riders the President wants to a bill that is otherwise distasteful to him. A reverse situation also applies—that is, an obnoxious rider can be attached to a highly desired piece of administrative legislation.[29]

If the amending process from the floor of a legislative chamber gets too far out of hand, it can result in a practice, occurring in some state legislatures, known as bill hijacking. This is a device by which one legislator takes little more than the number and title of a bill and rewrites it completely by amendment. For example, a bill increasing welfare benefits to the aged by ten dollars a month may be amended to reduce the benefits ten dollars a month and to place restrictions on the receipt of such benefits. The bill has then been hijacked so that its effect is the opposite of what was intended. In many legislatures, including Congress, hijacking is discouraged by informal tradition. Even where it is permissible, it is discouraged by fear of reprisal. Carried very far, it introduces a degree of viciousness and irresponsibility into the legislative process which thwarts the whole system.

Amendments and riders are effective techniques in the brokerage process of politics. Many amendments are designed to satisfy special-interest groups or to make bills politically palatable to constituents. The result of much of the maneuvering that flowers into amendments is legislation that often misses the point it originally tried to make. The strong and straightforward principles of the Truman administration in its original request to Congress for the Full Employment Act (1946) were reduced to legislation qualified to meet the demands of the major industrial, labor, and agricultural interests. Such legislation might be hailed as a victory by those who acclaim the validity of "hammering out laws on the anvil of compromise," but to those who believe the principle of full employment to be vital, the thunderous declaration of an aggressive governmental responsibility for the economic security of its citizens emerged as a mild squeak.

Test Votes. During the course of consideration of bills, a vote on an amendment may be a test vote designed to permit the leadership to discover the prospects for favorable final action without risking the bill itself. Which amendments will be used as tests of the final vote depends upon the stratagems employed by the floor managers. When an amendment, for example, would tend to destroy a bill, the vote is

[29] In 1961, President Kennedy was presented with a bill revising the immigration laws in several respects desirable to him. It also contained a provision changing the appellate jurisdiction on rulings by the Immigration Service from federal district courts to circuit courts, which he reportedly did not want. The bill was signed, however.

usually a test. If the amendment passes, the bill will be dead for all practical purposes, and usually those who support a destructive amendment will vote against final passage of the bill. There are both offensive amendments, designed to cripple bills, and defensive amendments, designed to thwart the offense and preserve the original purpose of the bill. The vote on riders is also very often a test of a bill's strength. If the backers can keep the barnacles off their bills, it is an indication of its strength. If they are unable to do this, the bill may become so encumbered that it could never pass or survive a presidential veto.

Other stratagems used to test legislation under debate are votes on procedural questions, such as the validity of a point of order, a motion to table a bill (which in effect kills it), and a vote on a motion to recommit a bill to committee for further study.

These procedures for dealing with bills under debate do not begin to exhaust the intricacies of procedure. Many a new elected representative of the people has discovered the complexity of the process as he has watched his legislation disappear into the mysterious caverns of procedure. It is both a frustrating and fascinating experience, and most freshmen legislators have taken the sage advice of their more battle-scarred elder brethren to sit quietly on the sidelines and keep their mouths shut and their eyes open.

The Vote. After a bill has been fully debated, and if it survives the laborious process from introduction to final vote, the question put to the House of Representatives is "Shall the bill be engrossed and read the third time?" The vote which follows is on final passage of the bill.

In the votes on the floor, congressmen may pair votes, which means they enter into an agreement with a colleague on the opposite side of an issue to withhold their votes if one or both of them are absent when the vote is taken. In such cases, one is paired for and the other paired against an issue. Pairs are recorded in the *Congressional Record* but are not counted in vote totals.

If members do not want to vote they do not have to, even though they are present; both precedent and procedure guarantee the right to abstain. Voting may be by voice vote, with the speaker deciding which side has it. If the vote is close or a member demands it, the vote may be by division, which requires members to stand and be counted. Or, the vote may be by roll call when a member demands it.

Article I, section 5, of the Constitution provides for the recording in the *Journal* of "yeas and nays of the members of either House on any question . . . at the desire of one-fifth of the members." Any member may arise and ask for the yeas and nays. This request forces his often reluctant colleagues to declare themselves. Because of the necessary declaration of a stand on the bill before the house, the roll call is seldom used. If a roll call is obtained, it is still difficult to get one fifth of the members to demand a recording of the vote in the *Journal*. An alert observer, however, can get the vote on a roll call, and some of the more adept are able to get it on a division by remembering which members stood on each side of the vote.

If the vote on final passage is affirmative, the bill is engrossed; that is, it is reprinted with all of its amendments put in their appropriate places and sent on to the Senate. Senate procedure is similar although simpler than that in the House. If the bill passes the second house without amendment, it goes on to the President for his action. If the two versions are not the same, the bill will go to a conference committee, the members of which are appointed by the presiding officers of the two houses. They usually consist of the interested senior members of the committees that were in charge of the bill in the respective houses. Conference committees report back to their respective chambers on the compromise or agreement reached in conference. Sessions are secret and unrecorded, and the report must be signed by a majority of the conferees from each house. Conference committees theoretically decide only those issues disagreed upon by the two houses—that is, they are not free to change the features of a bill on which both houses were in accord. If the conference report is accepted by both houses, the bill, with modifications contained in the conference report, is passed. If either house votes down the report, a new conference committee may be appointed or the bill may be allowed to die.

The President may approve the bill or veto it and return it to Congress with a message stating his reasons. Or if Congress has adjourned and he cannot send it back, he can effect a pocket veto by not acting upon the bill. If Congress is in session and the President does not either approve or veto the bill, it automatically becomes law ten days after he has received it.

The Legislative Process and Responsible Government

How well does the legislative process work? Our discussion in the last two chapters has shown that a combination of environmental, procedural, political, and legal circumstances makes the legislative process a most complex phenomenon. Perhaps it is this very complexity that has resulted in the rise of executive and judicial power in the United States while Congress suffers comparatively low prestige. A United States senator has argued that legislatures have become the weakest link in the constitutional chain, and that the brokerage character of these bodies, among other things, has turned the public away from legislatures as an effective champion of the public interest. After pointing out that the executive and judicial branches of government operate reasonably well, he says:

> It is the third branch of government, the legislative, where things have gone awry. Whether we look at city councils, the state legislatures, or the Congress of the United States, we react to what we see with scarcely concealed contempt. This is the area where democratic government tends to break down. This is where the vested interest lobbies run riot, where conflict of interest rides unchecked, where demagoguery knows few bounds, where political lag keeps needed action a generation behind the times, where the nineteenth century still reigns supreme in committees, where ignorance is often at a premium and wisdom at a discount, where the evil influence of arrogant and corrupt political machines ignores most successfully the public interest, where the lust for patronage and favors for the faithful do the greatest damage to the public interest.
>
> As a former chief executive of a large American city, as a member of the United States Senate, as a public servant who, in both capacities, has been obliged to know a good deal about the workings of state government, I have no hesitation in stating my deep conviction that the legislatures of America, local, state, and national, are presently the greatest menace to the successful operation of the democratic process.[30]

Senator Clark's indictment is harsh, yet it cannot be casually dismissed. Congress and state legislatures have tended to become brokerage houses for special-interest groups out to gain special favor. What was once conceived to be the branch of government belonging to the people has moved away from a pursuit of a public interest to the point where many citizens look to the executive as their champion. Minorities find redress for their grievances in court, as do the lonely and unattached individuals who do not even have minority-group status. Legislators themselves feel this deterioration of their role, and many of them share Senator Clark's frustration at the blurring of issues by the pressure of constituency interests and by organized power groups seeking bargains.

[30] Joseph S. Clark, "The Increasing Role of Government," in *The Elite and the Electorate* (Santa Barbara, Calif.: Fund for the Republic, 1963), p. 14.

As prestige, influence, and the capacity for independent initiative have shifted to the Presidency and the Court, the discontent with Congress has often taken the form of efforts to make it respond more readily and completely to presidential leadership. It is not clear, however, that we would be better off with a Congress that bends readily to every wind from the White House. It is true that Congress, as it is now organized, is distinguished by its power and inclination to obstruct and to obfuscate a President's program. But perhaps the remedy lies in developing its capacity for independent, responsible initiative rather than making it a rubber stamp.

Chapter Thirteen

THE PRESIDENCY:
THE OFFICE AND THE MAN

. . . Wherein we examine the nature of the office occupied by "the most powerful democratic chief executive in the world," how it got that way, and some of the problems involved in its exercise.

The modern Presidency differs radically from the nonpolitical office occupied by a gentleman-aristocrat envisioned at the Constitutional Convention. *The Emergence of Presidential Power* involved the process by which the office, carefully removed in the Constitution from direct popular control, came to be the major instrument of popular government; and the process by which the sparse and vaguely defined constitutional powers of the office were used as a platform for the expansion of personalized powers of influence and persuasion.

Because the actual powers of the office are not clearly defined by Constitution or custom, the incumbents have operated on *Conflicting Concepts of the Presidency*. These concepts have come to be identified with their chief exemplars, so that it is possible to distinguish "Buchanan Presidents," "Lincoln Presidents," and "Eisenhower Presidents," depending upon how dynamic and extensive, and how deeply involved in politics, the powers of the presidency are seen to be.

The combination of circumstances that surround the office today, however, virtually require Presidents to be strong: "Everybody expects the man inside the White House to do something about everything." The reasons for this are to be found in

The President's Roles. These require him to be, at the same time:

    Chief of State, who serves as symbol and ceremonial spokesman of the nation;

    Chief Legislator, who must provide legislative initiative and leadership if the system of separation of powers is not to bog down at dead center, but who, lacking formal powers or a party mechanism adequate to the task, must devise informal and personal means of influencing an often hostile Congress;

Party Leader, who must seek to build a presidential party out of the decentralized national party machinery and must often struggle for influence with the congressional party;

Chief Executive, who is responsible for the performance of the huge federal bureaucracy (a role examined more closely in the next chapter);

Chief Foreign Policy-Maker, who is in charge of the nation's diplomacy and who, as commander-in-chief, can deploy the nation's armed forces in ways that give him power to conduct undeclared wars;

Chief Politician who, as the only politician whose constituency is the nation, is in a unique position to influence the national electorate. This influence may be directed to developing a charismatic appeal, to organizing a consensus among the major organized groups, or to providing political and moral leadership. To be effective, however, his popular support must be translated into bargaining advantages in his relationship with party, Congress, and the bureaucracy. In short,

Effective Presidential Power has become *Personalized:* A President's real power is measured, not by his formal authority, but by his ability to influence, persuade, cajole, threaten, intimidate, and negotiate with others whose interests and goals are different from his.

This central proposition about presidential power is illustrated by a comparison of the approaches of Presidents Truman and Kennedy to crises in the steel industry: one relied on his formal powers, and lost; the other used his informal influence, and won.

It is also illustrated by the wide variations in *Presidential Styles of Leadership,* which reflect the personalities as well as the conceptions of the presidential role of different Presidents.

The personalization of presidential power raises questions about the role of *Presidential Leadership* in democratic politics, which turn out to be deeply rooted in the system of checks and balances and in the tendencies of mass society.

To make the most of power for himself a President must know what it is made of.

RICHARD E. NEUSTADT

Chapter Thirteen

THE PRESIDENCY:
THE OFFICE AND THE MAN

*I*N THE DEBATE in the Pennsylvania ratifying convention James Wilson informed the delegates that he and his colleagues in the convention of 1787 had been "perplexed with no part of this plan of a Constitution so much as the mode of choosing the President of the United States." The bitterly fought issue was whether the President should be chosen by the national legislature or by state legislatures or executives. There was general agreement that he should be chosen indirectly. Wilson himself had been almost alone in arguing for direct popular election. Yet, notwithstanding the continued formal existence of the Electoral College, the President far more than any other political figure has emerged as the symbol of popular, majoritarian government.

Similarly, the authors of the Constitution did not have in mind a dominant *political* role for the President. The Presidency fitted into the conservative scheme of checks and balances as an office that would provide a symbol of national unity and continuity, provide an objective and dispassionate arbiter of legislative conflict, and "take care that the laws be faithfully executed." They expected the office to be filled, through the process of indirect election, by a gentleman-aristocrat—wise, far-seeing, motivated by the aristocratic creed of *noblesse oblige*. The Presidency was in this sense to be a nonpolitical office, above the strife of rival factions and the strategies of party politics. They did not expect the power of the President to rest on popular or party support for his political program. Indeed, they did not expect him to have a political program and, perhaps above all, they did not contemplate that he would campaign for the office.

Even the Jeffersonians did not see the Presidency as an important instrument of liberal democracy. During the Revolutionary War the forces of liberal democracy in the states had created governments with legislative supremacy. The governors in most of them were elected annually by the legislature. In only one case did a governor have a conditional veto power, and even there it was removed after a brief trial. In most states governors had no power to summon or dismiss the legislature. The Articles of Confederation had not even provided for a head of state or a chief executive. These conditions were due partly to a liberal predilection in favor of legislative supremacy to facilitate popular rule, partly to a distrust and fear of executive power rooted in colonial experiences with royal governors.

Perhaps the definition of executive power in the Constitution was left purposefully vague because a Presidency with broad powers would not have been palatable to the Jeffersonians and to those jealous of the rights of the states. Even as it stood, Hamilton felt it necessary to spend an entire issue of the *Federalist Papers* (No. 69) arguing that the presidential powers were moderate and not to be confused with the powers of the English king.

The Emergence of Presidential Power

In some ways these early views still cast their shadow over American attitudes toward the Presidency. Candidates like to pretend that they are above politics and that the office is seeking them. But this is a thin and transparent facade. The framers designed a system that as nearly as possible would keep all Presidents out of the heat of the political kitchen and seat them in the dignified aloofness of the parlor. But President Truman's advice to those aspiring to high political office was much more descriptive of the modern Presidency: "If you can't stand the heat, get out of the kitchen."

The transformation of the Presidency into a political office and the aggrandizement of presidential power were not long in expressing themselves. The constitutional provisions respecting the powers of the office, as we have indicated, were magnificently ambiguous. "The executive power," Article II declared, "shall be vested in a President of the United States of America." But what are the executive powers? The Constitution enumerates only the following:

To serve as commander-in-chief of the armed forces.

To grant reprieves and pardons for offenses against the United States.

To make treaties with the "advice and consent" of the Senate.

To appoint, with the advice and consent of the Senate, Supreme Court justices, ambassadors, and other public officials.

To call special sessions of Congress.

To address the Congress on the state of the Union and to recommend measures to the Congress.

To receive ambassadors.

To "take care that the laws be faithfully executed."

To approve or to exercise a qualified veto over legislative bills.

On this slender constitutional grant of power the American President has become what one expert has termed "the most powerful democratic chief executive in the world." The process through which this was accomplished had early beginnings. The nation's first President, George Washington, established the principle, left vague in the Constitution, that the President is not an agent of Congress but has independent power when he issued the neutrality proclamation in 1793. And in his forceful action in dispatching federal troops to suppress the Whisky Rebellion he established the precedent that the Presidency has residual power, not spelled out in the Constitution but amounting to virtual dictatorship in situations of national crisis or when widespread disorder is imminent.

It remained to Jefferson, somewhat paradoxically, to establish the ground of the modern power of the Presidency. Jefferson's strict construction of the Constitution meant controls on the powers of the national government and of the Presidency. Yet, as President he accepted the opportunity to effect the purchase of France's Louisiana territory, an exercise of power clearly beyond those expressly delegated in the Constitution. The manner in which he acted, however, is more instructive than the fact that he acted. Having negotiated and ratified the purchase agreement, he belatedly sought and received the approval of Congress. Where Washington had sought legitimacy for his power in the claim to formal constitutional prerogative, Jefferson sought and got the stamp of political consent on his action. The Congress, to be sure, justified its approval on the constitutional ground that the transaction had been an exercise of power implied in the constitutional power of the President to make treaties. But, in fact, Jefferson had got the support of Congress not because he had the constitutional power to act but because he had the political *influence* to make his action stick. This influence was based on his partisan popularity in the nation and on the effectiveness of his political control over his party lieutenants in the Congress. Jefferson's exercise of the power of the Presidency, in short, was the first demonstration of the potential informal power of the office in the hands of a man who had mastered the arts of political organization and influence.

Already, by the end of Jefferson's administration the process was under way that was to lead one of the foremost students of the Presidency to say: "Taken by and large, the history of the presidency has been a history of aggrandizement."[1] The process through which this has occurred confronts us with two related constitutional anomalies: The Presidency, carefully removed in the Constitution from direct popular control, has come to play the role of the major instrument of popular government; and the sparse and ambiguous delegation of constitutional power to the President has been a springboard from which the men who have occupied the office have been elevated to the center of the political stage. The first of these developments seriously weakened the barriers constructed by the Founders against majority rule. The second has undermined the principles of separation of powers and checks and

---

[1] Edward S. Corwin, *The President: Office and Powers, 1787-1957*, 4th rev. ed. (New York: New York University Press, 1957), p. 307.

balances; indeed, in the view of Professor Corwin and others, it has destroyed these principles.

Conflicting Concepts of the Presidency

Because the constitutional definition of the office is ambiguous and because the growth of presidential power over the years has proceeded by fits and starts, there is no clearly agreed upon concept of what the President should be and do. President Theodore Roosevelt clearly sensed the range of possibilities in the office. He divided the Presidents into two groups, "Buchanan Presidents" and "Lincoln Presidents," depending upon their view of the office. His distinction merits further scrutiny.

1. *"Buchanan Presidents."* President Grant expressed this view of the office in his conception of himself as "a purely administrative officer."[2] Other Presidents have shared this view, with Buchanan being perhaps its chief exemplar. In this century it is represented by Presidents Taft, Harding, Coolidge, and Hoover. It rejects the idea that the Presidency is a political office and sees it instead as the administrative arm of the Congress. The President should not seek to lead public opinion or to control Congress in behalf of presidential policy. His constitutional obligation is dignified aloofness from politics and the honest and efficient administration of the public business.

In the Buchanan concept the President has no undefined or residual powers of protecting the public welfare or dealing with national emergencies; he is limited to the powers expressly given him in the Constitution. President Taft, in his argument with Roosevelt over the nature of the office, clearly expressed this strict interpretation of presidential power:

> My judgment is that the view . . . ascribing an undefined residuum of power to the President is an unsafe doctrine and that it might lead under emergencies to results of an arbitrary character, doing irremediable injustice to private right. The mainspring of such a view is that the Executive is charged with responsibility for the welfare of all the people in a general way, that he is to play the part of a Universal Providence and set all things right, and that anything that in his judgment will help the people he ought to do, unless he is expressly forbidden not to do it. The wide field of action that this would give to the Executive one can hardly limit.[3]

[2] Quoted in Sidney Hyman, "What Is the President's True Role?" *The New York Times Magazine*, September 7, 1958.

[3] Quoted in Donald Bruce Johnson and Jack L. Walker, eds., *The Dynamics of the American Presidency* (New York: Wiley, 1964), p. 138.

President Buchanan provided the classic example of the custodial view when he denied that he had legal power to use force against the southern secession in 1860. The reaction of those who saw the matter differently was expressed in the retort of John Sherman of Ohio: "The Constitution provides for every accidental contingency in the executive except a vacancy in the mind of a President."[4]

2. *"Lincoln Presidents."* In this view the Presidency is an intensely political office. The President becomes the nation's first party politician, chief legislator, major source of political goals, leader of public opinion. Presidents before Lincoln had acted on this concept—Jefferson and Jackson are examples—and in this century they have been followed by Wilson, the two Roosevelts, Truman, and Kennedy. The "Lincoln President" takes up political methods where his formal constitutional powers stop. When Theodore Roosevelt encountered difficulty with Congress, he later related, his recourse was an appeal over their heads "to the people, who are the masters of both the Congress and the President."[5]

The powers of the Presidency become as extensive as the political talents of its incumbent allow. The only constitutional limits are those explicitly provided. Theodore Roosevelt effectively summarized the concept:

> The most important factor in getting the right spirit in my Administration, next to insistence upon courage, honesty, and a genuine democracy of desire to serve the plain people, was my insistence upon the theory that the executive power was limited only by specific restrictions and prohibitions appearing in the Constitution or imposed by Congress under its constitutional powers. . . . I declined to adopt this view that what was imperatively necessary for the Nation could not be done by the President, unless he could find some specific authorization to do it. My belief was that it was not only his right but his duty to do anything that the needs of the Nation demanded unless such action was forbidden by the Constitution or by the laws. Under this interpretation of executive power I did and caused to be done many things not previously done by the President and the heads of the departments. I did not usurp power but I did greatly broaden the use of executive power. In other words, I acted for the common well being of all our people whenever and in whatever measure was necessary, unless prevented by direct constitutional or legislative prohibition.[6]

[4] Quoted in Sidney Hyman, "What IS the President?" *San Francisco Chronicle,* September 27, 1964.
[5] Quoted in Johnson and Walker, *op. cit.,* pp. 134-35.
[6] Quoted in *ibid.,* p. 136.

3. *"Eisenhower Presidents."* To the two concepts of the Presidency delineated by Roosevelt we may usefully add a third, the contours of which were marked out by President Eisenhower. The Eisenhower concept of the Presidency borrows something from the other two. Like the Buchanan concept, it eschews any dynamic role of political leadership for the President and involves disengagement from partisan politics and party battles. But the President does not become mere chief administrator. He intervenes to veto or negate ill-advised partisan plans. By rising above politics and political divisions he becomes "the father of all the people." One observer summed up President Eisenhower's approach after six years in office in the following way:

All men are by nature good. Government alone corrupts them. Therefore, to the extent that government can be reduced in importance, the natural goodness of men will assert itself in social cooperation, voluntarily given. However irreconcilable rival interests may seem to be, once their representative men sit down and talk things over without the intervention of government, natural goodness will resolve all difficulties.

His own Presidential function, then, was to be "the President of all the people." He should be a compassionate shaft of light within whose arc all men would want to live up to the better angels of their nature.[7]

As this interpretation suggests, there is something of the idea of the President as chief broker in this approach. The President emerges as spokesman for and symbol of a national consensus when partisan conflicts are transcended and men are encouraged to sit down and talk things over in an atmosphere of good will.

In a speech in the Senate early in 1960, John F. Kennedy implicitly attacked the "Eisenhower Presidency" and argued that "the times" required a "Lincoln President":

They demand a vigorous proponent of the national interest—not a passive broker for conflicting private interests. They demand a man capable of acting as the commander in chief of the Grand Alliance, not merely a bookkeeper who feels that his work is done when the numbers on the balance sheet come out even. They demand that he be the head of a responsible party, not rise so far above politics as to be invisible —a man who will formulate and fight for legislative policies, not be a casual bystander to the legislative process.[8]

[7] Hyman, "What Is the President's True Role?" *op. cit.*
[8] *The Congressional Record*, January 18, 1960, pp. A353-54. Reprinted in Johnson and Walker, *op. cit.*, p. 139.

After two years in office President Kennedy was embroiled in a struggle with "conflicting private interests" and inclined to be more philosophical about the extent to which these interests force the President into the role of "passive broker." When the President's program "is significant and affects important interests and is controversial," he observed, "then there is a fight, and the President is never wholly successful."[9] This recognition of the dominance of organized interests in American politics, and especially in the Congress, probably forced Kennedy into a role he did not want to play and tempered his view of what the Presidency could be.

When President Johnson assumed office after the tragic assassination of Kennedy, he came to it equipped with the taste and talent for exercising presidential power within a brokerage context. A leading student of the Presidency has said of him: "Perhaps it's not entirely fanciful to combine two other men and say that Mr. Johnson is trying to be a 'Rooseveltian Eisenhower'—trying to establish a rather Eisenhower-like stance in the interest of Rooseveltian results."[10] Johnson approached the Presidency with the proclaimed aim of making "the government work within the framework of a preexisting harmony, or consensus." As a close Washington observer has put it:

> He is concerned less with defining goals than arranging means, less with changing aggregates than allocations. His method is the method of the legislative leader, the method of suspending his own commitments, until the commitments of other men are in line—until, that is, the majority is built. "The President," one man who has worked closely with him says, "really doesn't know what he is going to do, until he knows how he is going to do it."[11]

This approach requires direct and continuing contact with "the power centers in government, business, labor, the press, and the local communities that make up the elements of the consensus."[12] Unlike Eisenhower, Johnson seeks to mold and guide the consensus, to move group interests in his direction, to put the impress of his strategy on the grand coalition.

THE NEED FOR PRESIDENTIAL LEADERSHIP

It is difficult even to imagine the possibility of another "Buchanan President" in the middle of the twentieth century. Over a hundred

[9] Televised interview of December 16, 1962. Transcript reprinted in *ibid.*, p. 144.
[10] "How LBJ Is Doing His Job," an interview with Richard E. Neustadt, *U. S. News and World Report*, August 3, 1964, p. 34.
[11] Joseph Kraft, "West Wing Story," *Harper's Magazine*, April, 1965, p. 106.
[12] *Ibid.*

years ago, de Tocqueville said of the American President that "the laws allow him to be strong but circumstances make him weak."[13] Today we must say that circumstances require him to be strong. We have already examined these circumstances in other contexts: the ending of American isolationism and the emergence of the nation as a world leader inevitably broadened the scope of presidential power. Domestically, the decline of *laissez faire* and the rise of the concept of government as an active, controlling force in the economy led in the same direction. Meanwhile the franchise had been extended, the ideal of majority rule had come to dominate men's minds, and informal changes had made the Presidency in effect a popularly elected office. The President, along with the Vice-President, emerged as the only popularly elected official with a national constituency. This combination of circumstances explains why the powers of the national government have grown and why the President has shared in this increase, but they do not explain why "everybody now expects the man inside the White House to do something about everything."[14] The President, after all, occupies only one of three "equal and coordinate" branches established by the Constitution. Why has it become possible to describe him as "the most powerful democratic chief executive in the world"? The answer to this question must be found largely not in aggrandizing Presidents but in the nature of the roles the American political system requires its President to play.

The President's Roles

The President is often said to wear different hats in playing his several roles. He is the ceremonial head of state, serving as symbol of the nation at home and abroad, greeting distinguished visitors, and adding his presence to national ceremonies, which range from throwing out the first baseball of each new season to buying the first box of Girl Scouts cookies and talking by telephone to every returned astronaut. He is the chief legislator to whom the country looks for a legislative program, which he pushes by methods ranging from persuasion to heavy lashes from the political bullwhip. He is the leader of his political party, the chief Republican or Democrat, in charge of party strategy, the distribution of political rewards, and the furthering of party goals. He is chief executive, responsible for the huge bureaucracy that administers the public business. He is chief foreign policy-maker, spokesman for and

[13] Alexis de Tocqueville, *Democracy in America*, Phillips Bradley, ed. (New York: Knopf, 1948), Vol. I, p. 126.
[14] Richard E. Neustadt, *Presidential Power* (New York: Wiley, 1962), p. 6.

leader of the nation in foreign affairs. And, finally, he is chief politician whose constituency is the nation and to whom citizens look for a definition and promotion of the public interest. We may see more clearly the character of his power by examining the demands and opportunities in these roles.

THE PRESIDENT AS CHIEF OF STATE

The American political system does not provide for a royal family. Some of the functions of such an institution have accordingly fallen to the Presidency. He is not only the head of the government but the symbolic and ceremonial head of the nation as well. In ritual and ceremonial functions both at home and abroad he represents the nation as a unified and continuing entity. Many of the duties he performs in this capacity seem trivial—dedicating a new dam, receiving a foreign dignitary, or bestowing a medal—but ritual and ceremony are never trivial. They symbolize the common life and common aspirations of a people.

The President's role as ceremonial chief of state does not endow him with the mystery and awe that sometimes surround a king, but it does provide the office with a certain majesty. Even those who have known him best, who have perhaps been accustomed to calling him Ike or Jack or Lyndon, address the incumbent as Mr. President. Ironically perhaps, it is the public at large who, seeing him as their President, now "know" him familiarly. The President reaps a double advantage in his political role of leadership. The status he acquires as chief of state becomes a powerful vantage point for influencing those with whom he works most closely. A congressman, for example, or the spokesman for a private interest group, will find it difficult to resist a presidential entreaty when he is seated in Mr. President's White House office with its symbolic evidence linking the President with the nation. At the same time the public familiarity and personal sense of possession of the Presidency are a base for the development of charismatic support.

For this symbolic link with the people the President and his family pay an exacting price in almost constant surveillance and publicity. Herbert Hoover is reported to have once remarked: "There are only two occasions when Americans respect privacy, especially in Presidents. Those are prayer and fishing. So that some have taken to fishing."[15]

A President's use of his ceremonial role may also help set the tone

[15] Quoted in Clifton Fadiman, "Please Tap My Wire, I Like It!" *Holiday*, July, 1964, p. 16.

of society and mark his administration with a particular quality. President Kennedy's cultivation of the arts and of artists at White House functions was a case in point. It contrasts sharply with the tone and style of President Johnson's picnic for correspondents and their families on the White House lawn. Here again, ceremonial behavior provides an avenue for developing sources of political support. Intellectuals identified with Kennedy; perhaps picnickers, a much larger group, do the same with Johnson.

The difficulty in separating ceremonial from political roles often handicaps the President's opposition. In a period of crisis, for example, it is not always clear whether a President is speaking as the head of state or as a political leader. For example, a demand by the opposition party for equal time on television to answer a political speech will boomerang if the speech is publicly interpreted to have been above politics.

THE PRESIDENT AS CHIEF LEGISLATOR

The Presidency has become the dominant instrument of national power and sometimes of majoritarian democracy largely because of the default of Congress. Many factors have contributed to congressional incapacity for leadership: the absence of effective political parties, the feudal suzerainty wielded by congressional committees, the seniority system, the power of the Rules Committee in the House, and the filibuster in the Senate. The most significant effect of these structural characteristics, as earlier chapters have indicated, is the dominance in Congress of group and constituency interests. Even Calvin Coolidge, who can hardly be called one of the nation's more aggressive Presidents, was prompted to say: "It is because in their hours of timidity the congress becomes subservient to the importunities of organized minorities that the President comes more and more to stand as the champion of the rights of the whole country."

As Congress became, in Edmund Burke's phrase, "a confused and scuffling bustle of local agency," the pressures mounted on any President to transcend the strife and compromise of rival interests in order to propose solutions to nationwide issues and to speak for a public interest. Particularly in periods of crisis or in the presence of grave national problems (conditions that seem in the mid-twentieth century to have become normal), the American system of checks and balances tends to bog down at dead center without the exercise of presidential initiative and leadership.

In the American constitutional system the problem of effective and responsible policy leadership is posed directly by the separation of powers. In parliamentary systems, like that of Great Britain, where the executive and his cabinet are chosen from the majority party in the legislature, they have almost automatic legislative support for their programs. If they do not, the executive and his cabinet can be removed. This is not the case where the executive is a separate branch of government elected for a fixed term. He may or may not have political support, and his ability to provide legislative leadership and to organize an effective and dynamic administration can suffer severely if he does not. President Hoover in his last two years in office, President Truman during the Eightieth Congress, and, to a lesser extent, President Eisenhower in his second term were all handicapped administratively as well as politically by Congresses dominated by the opposite party.

Even where the Presidency and Congress are controlled by the same party, the weakness of American parties and the concomitant influence of interest groups in Congress force the policy leadership role on the President. At the same time, they put formidable barriers in the way of his ability to generate the necessary congressional support. Presidential-congressional hostility is virtually built into the system. In domestic affairs completely, and in foreign affairs to a limited extent, the President can act only with and through a jealous Congress, suspicious of incursions on its prerogatives and dominated by sectional, local, and economic interests. It is a Congress powerfully equipped to distort and water down the presidential program or to frustrate the President completely by causing his proposals to disappear in the committee structure. President Kennedy, for example, saw some twenty of his legislative proposals strangled in the House Rules Committee from 1961 to 1963.

Congress and the President share in the constitutional power to legislate. What the Constitution separated, American political parties have not been strong enough to bring back together. Party loyalty in the Congress is not an insignificant source of presidential influence. A congressman's political future is tied sufficiently to party fortunes that a President may expect some measure of partisan support for some of his program. But it is almost never enough to ensure success.

The President, therefore, must sharpen other weapons. His only significant formal source of power is the veto. It is not, however, to be underestimated. In practice, since it takes a two-thirds vote of both houses to override it, it is a vote equivalent to the votes of two thirds of the senators and members of the House. Nor is it simply a negative weapon. The threat of a veto may be used effectively to bargain for changes in a bill. Franklin Roosevelt is reported to have asked his aides for "something I can veto" as a reminder to Congress of his power. The reminder was usually addressed to a specific congressman and involved a bill important to his constituents. A President's ability to threaten a public project in a legislator's constituency, for example, is a potent weapon.

In the main, however, legislative leadership rests on a President's use of informal influence. He must seek to persuade, threaten, intimidate, cajole, or pressure congressmen into cooperating with him. His control over the administrative bureaucracy, which may grant or deny a congressman's request on behalf of an influential constituent, may be invoked. More important, perhaps, is the question whether he has solid support in his own national constituency. Promises or threats are more likely to be effective if congressmen are convinced that the political winds from home are blowing in the President's direction. President Franklin D. Roosevelt pressured the Congress into adopting price controls during World War II by threatening to institute the program under his war powers if they refused. His threat was effective because public opinion was on his side.

Congress has powerful weapons to obstruct the President, but it is virtually incapacitated from assuming leadership in response to national issues. This is the crucial task of the President. Without presidential initiative and leadership the Congress is rarely capable of rising much above the level of that annual monument to brokerage politics, the Rivers and Harbors Bill.

Ironically, Congress, while resisting increases in Presidential power, has nonetheless contributed significantly to the process by delegating some of its legislative power to him. Typically, the laws enacted by Congress are, of necessity, formulated in broad terms. The President is often the recipient of delegated legislative power to fill out the details of these broad policies through executive orders.

At the same time, this very expansion in the powers of the executive branch has intensified constitutional conflicts among the three branches of the federal government, conflicts that have existed in varying degrees since the Constitution was adopted. When Theodore Roosevelt had trouble getting appropriations from Congress, he sent the Navy halfway around the world, exhausting his available funds, and then announced it was up to Congress to bring it back. Woodrow Wilson lost his health and his dream of United States leadership in a strong League of Nations when the United States Senate, led in this fight by Senator Henry Cabot Lodge, refused to approve American participation. Both Franklin Roosevelt and Harry Truman came into conflict with the courts and with Congress over the extent of executive power. President Kennedy ran into difficulty in asking Congress for grants of executive power to regulate tariffs and to control recessions. In early 1962, when his bill to create a new cabinet post on urban affairs was bottled up in committee, he forced the House to a roll call vote, which he lost, by exercising his power to reorganize the administrative branch. (Under the existing Reorganization Act, presidential reorganization proposals become effective in the absence of a veto by either house within sixty days.)

As these examples suggest, presidential power, however much it has increased, is still limited by the system of separation of powers and environment of pluralism in which it operates. Our situation is almost the reverse of that described by de Tocqueville: circumstances require the President to provide strong leadership, but constitutional relationships preclude any guarantee that the required leadership will be forthcoming. This is so because, in the absence of effective constitutional, legal, or partisan sources of power, the President must depend largely upon his own personal resources of leadership.

THE PRESIDENT AS PARTY LEADER

In the relations between President and Congress, party ties are not a negligible factor. No President, however, owes his nomination to Congress nor, though he has some influence, does he control the election of congressmen. The congressional party and the presidential party, as we have seen, draw their strength from different sources and are often rivals for power and influence.

Nor can a President rest his national leadership on party loyalties. In the country generally the confederational character of the national political parties and their nonideological character make them a tenuous basis of presidential strength. In the national nominating conventions even a successful presidential nominee does not always have his own way. His choice of a running mate, for example, is often dictated by considerations of strengthening his position among various factions in the party. Even when Roosevelt secured an unprecedented nomination for a third term in 1944, Truman was apparently not his first choice for Vice-President.

The President's influence as party leader is supported by his control over patronage in offices and favors. But it rests fundamentally on his ability to use these and other advantages in order to secure the support of other men whose interests and ambitions may differ sharply from his own and who have independent sources of political support.

THE PRESIDENT AS CHIEF EXECUTIVE

The President is nominally in almost complete charge of the huge federal bureaucracy. The performance of this administrative role is examined in some detail in the next chapter. Here our concern is with the fact that this control is nominal. Even in the President's relations with the officials in the executive branch it is by no means true that he can assume their loyalty and support. Members of the bureaucracy are likely to keep their own ideas and careers in clear focus and they may have independent relationships in Congress or support from pressure groups that enable them to resist presidential directives or to pursue an independent course. The armed forces, for example, with sources of power in the congressional committees and the reserve associations have sometimes been able to get larger appropriations from Congress than the President's budget called for. President Truman, confronted with this situation in 1949, countered by declining to spend some of the appropriated Air Force funds.

The same sorts of informal pressures are operative with respect to the President's power to appoint and remove his administrative subordinates. His formal power to appoint and remove is limited, of course, to those employees (about 10 per cent of the total of approximately 2½ million) not recruited through Civil Service. His appointment of several thousand more must be with "the advice and consent of the Senate." But even in the cases where his formal power is adequate, he is often limited in practice. Many of the departments of government (commerce, labor, and agriculture, for example) have a special clientele. In these and in other agencies officials are likely to be appointed because of their following among the agencies' clientele, which, in turn, strengthens the President's influence among organized groups. But once in office it is quite possible for these officials to increase their independence from the President by strengthening their ties with the groups involved and by developing close and friendly contacts with congressional committees. Should a powerful official fail to support, or even actively oppose, a President's policies, he can be removed by an exercise of the formal power of dismissal. But the exercise of that power by a President may have repercussions that involve political costs for him. The costs may be higher than he is willing to bear. Thus, in his own administrative backyard the role of the President is not the simple role of command. Even here the presidential power to command is far less than adequate to enable him to perform the role with which he is charged.

THE PRESIDENT AS CHIEF FOREIGN POLICY-MAKER

Of all the roles played by the most powerful elective official in the world, none matches in its importance and in the power that attends it the President's position as chief formulator and executor of the nation's foreign policy. The force of circumstance has seen to its importance, while the ineffectiveness of checks and balances in this area has increased the power of the Presidency almost by default.

We have considered elsewhere the character of the revolution in international politics and in the role of the United States that underlies the enormous growth in the power of the executive establishment over foreign policy. Here we need only note that the effect of all these changes was to make the Cold War, as well as preparations for a hot one, a matter of total competition. Every facet of society has a relationship to the struggle. Older distinctions between foreign and domestic policies seem misleading in this new context. An effective foreign policy for carrying on the struggle must be almost a complete and integrated social policy. At the domestic level, it clearly involves the health and the growth rate of the economy, the effectiveness of the educational system, the vitality of the political system, and the elimination of the racial discrimination and segregation that handicap us so seriously in our approach to the underdeveloped areas. At the level of the explicit formulation of foreign policies, total competition requires that these domestic concerns be related to the sources of international tension and conflict described above. Ideally at least, the resulting policies should reflect a clear and realizable national purpose.

In the application of foreign policy, the problem of coordination and control is staggering. Intelligence information on the capabilities and intentions of other countries, strategic military planning, programs of ideological warfare, the conduct of diplomatic relations and of our role in international organizations, the development of economic aid programs—these are but a few of the many considerations that must be meshed into policies applicable to a constantly shifting set of circumstances and opportunities. This is the tremendous burden that, in the main, comes to rest on the President.

The national government, under the Constitution, has exclusive power to make treaties and to carry on relations with other governments. The power to engage in international relations, the Supreme Court has held, is inherent in a nation-state and was acquired by the United States in 1776 when sovereignty was wrested from the British Crown.[16] This power, moreover, has been used as the basis for federal action in areas that would otherwise be beyond the constitutional competence of the national government.

In 1914, for example, Congress passed a law regulating the hunting and killing of birds that migrate between Canada and the United States. The federal district courts ruled that the law was an unconstitutional assertion of congressional power in an area reserved to the states under the Tenth Amendment. Subsequently, the United States entered into a treaty with Canada on this subject and, after the treaty was duly ratified by a two-thirds vote of the Senate, Congress enacted a law providing for even more rigorous protection of the migratory birds. This time, the Supreme Court upheld the power of Congress to act in this area as necessary to comply with a treaty.[17] The Court ruled that, whereas ordinary acts of Congress became "the supreme law of the land" only when made "in pursuance of the Constitution," treaties become "supreme law" when "made under the authority of the United States" in the exercise of a power that must "somewhere reside in every civilized government." The Court added that the treaty-making power is subject to constitutional limitations, but implied that states' rights are not among these. More recent decisions have reinforced this view.

The power acquired by the national government in foreign policy has largely been inherited by the President. This was not always the case. The Monroe Doctrine, for example, was for much of American history a legislative restriction on presidential power in foreign affairs, limiting presidential initiative to the Western hemisphere. When the nation became a world power after World War II, its Latin American

---

[16] *United States v. Curtiss-Wright Export Corporation*, 299 U.S. 304 (1936).
[17] *Missouri v. Holland*, 252 U.S. 416 (1920).

policy became a key instrument of presidential maneuver in the global conflict. The invasion of Cuba in 1961 and the sending of troops to the Dominican Republic in 1965 were completely unilateral decisions by Presidents Kennedy and Johnson. They reflected the almost total power of the modern President to commit the nation anywhere in the world.

The President's power under the Constitution is limited and shared with the Senate. The power to enter into a treaty with a foreign nation, for example, must be exercised "by and with the advice and consent" of two thirds of the senators present. The power that has enabled the President to circumvent this requirement is his ability to make *executive agreements*, which have the force of treaties but do not require Senate ratification. The Presidential power to commit the nation through executive agreements without the consent of Congress is a formidable one, and it has been used to consummate most of the international agreements to which the United States has been a party. Such important commitments as the Atlantic Charter, the Yalta agreements, and Roosevelt's trade of American destroyers for British bases on the eve of World War II were all consummated by the President as executive agreements. They make it easy to understand why the Congress would resent them as evasions of the constitutional role of the Senate in treaty-making.

But, even without the executive agreement, there are factors operating to make the President the chief foreign policy-maker. Partly, his power stems directly from the Constitution. With the consent of the Senate, he appoints ambassadors and all other official representatives in foreign countries, and he has the exclusive power to "receive ambassadors and other public ministers." From this power, the President directly derives the exclusive authority to recognize or refuse to recognize other governments since recognition is formalized by an exchange of ambassadors. The importance of recognition as an instrument of foreign policy was illustrated by Theodore Roosevelt's recognition of Panama within a few hours of an American-backed "revolt," Franklin Roosevelt's recognition of the Soviet Union in 1933, and the controversy over the refusal of American Presidents to recognize Communist China in recent years.

The Constitution also makes the President "Commander-in-Chief of the Army and Navy." Although the power to raise armies and to declare war are expressly delegated to Congress by the Constitution, in practice the President's power as commander in chief permits him to create a state of war that Congress may well find impossible to reverse.

Presidential power has often been used in this way, recent examples being President Truman's commitment of troops to resist North Korean aggression in 1950 and President Johnson's escalation of American involvement in South Vietnam in 1965. In 1958 President Eisenhower sent American forces into Lebanon, though armed conflict was averted. Eisenhower went to Congress for a resolution supporting the move after it was made, not because it is constitutionally necessary, but in order to impress the outside world with the firmness and solidity of American purpose.

The Cuban invasion of 1961 involved the use of American military forces, but more importantly the Central Intelligence Agency (in the Executive Office), which apparently planned, coordinated, and supervised the operation.[18] When the landings at the Bay of Pigs faltered, the President alone decided not to commit American air power to ensure their success. There were two striking characteristics of the ill-starred Cuban invasion attempt. The first is that the plans that had been in preparation for months by the Eisenhower administration were applied by the Kennedy administration, without Congress even being informed of what was going on. And in the second place, the venture was not intended as a prelude to war, but rather as a paramilitary operation disguised as a revolution.

In this new area of undeclared, guerrilla-type conflict, the President's power is virtually unrestrained since he not only can commit American personnel and material, he can do so under the cloak of secrecy. Congress is thereby barred from expressing its disapproval through its power over appointments and appropriations, and, at the same time, presidential decisions in this area are removed from public scrutiny and criticism.

Apart from the specific powers of the President in the field of foreign relations, his position as chief of state makes him the only authoritative representative of, and spokesman for, the nation. No other figure in the country could conceivably represent us at a summit meeting with other heads of state. The Supreme Court recognized this fact in the Curtiss-Wright case when it referred to the President as "the sole organ of the Federal Government in the field of international relations."

The President's real power, however, probably stems as much from the complexity of formulating a foreign policy in an age of ideological

[18] For an account of this bizarre event, see Haynes Johnson, *The Bay of Pigs* (New York: Dell, 1964).

conflict and total war as it does from his constitutional position. The basic fact is simple, and perhaps also disturbing: if the President did not make foreign policy, no one else could. No other individual or agency is in a position to weigh the bewildering variety of relevant considerations and to integrate them into coherent and purposeful policy. The President's access to information as well as to expert advice is not available to Congress, which finds itself at a serious disadvantage in not having the background information that would make possible intelligent appraisal of presidential foreign policy. The system of checks and balances was not designed to ensure responsibility in such circumstances; the effort to apply it would make any coherent foreign policy impossible.

Although the President alone has potential access to the resources and the information necessary for decision, Congress has the power to grant or withhold appropriations for foreign-policy programs. And Congress is often inclined to look at the President's requests with a suspicious eye. In addition to its constant desire to protect congressional prerogative against executive encroachment, the concern of congressmen to protect and advance their constituents' interests and the influence of pressure groups in Congress are likely to lead to congressional-presidential conflict.

When a conflict occurs, the President is at the same disadvantage on foreign-policy issues as he is on other matters. On the whole, the President cannot rely on interest-group support for his policies. Even where executive agencies have the built-in support of private groups—the armed services can count on their own private associations and on the major veterans' groups, for example—it is likely to be exerted against the President through congressional committees.

Nor can the President count on active and knowledgeable public support. All the polls show that not more than one out of four voters has even a basic knowledge or understanding of foreign affairs. Many of those who know something about it show a tendency to oversimplify, to see issues in black and white, and to demand an inflexibility of policy positions incompatible with rapidly changing events.

General public indifference combines with the weakness of pressure-group support for broad national policies to increase the influence of pressure groups who oppose specific aspects of policy. As a result, the alternative to congressional rubber-stamping usually takes the form of nit picking and tampering rather than of sustained review, criticism, and debate of broad policies. Congressional frustration of the President's policies may take other forms. At the behest of national-origin pressure groups, for example, Congress during the 1950's passed several resolutions calling for the liberation of the satellite nations of eastern Europe and even of nationality groups within the Soviet Union that had never been independent nations—"Cossackia," for example. The resolutions had no legal force but they did appear to the Soviet Union as provocative threats in situations in which presidential policies might have dictated an opposite approach. Neither a meaningful consensus nor responsible criticism and debate are possible in this environment.

In the absence of effective political parties, the machinery of checks and balances creaks cumbersomely along where domestic policies are concerned; in the area of foreign policy, it has broken down almost completely. Presidential power over foreign policy is awesome. We have yet to develop the means to make it responsible.

THE PRESIDENT AS CHIEF POLITICIAN

In his relations with Congress, party, and bureaucracy the President tends to be involved in an arena of political conflict in which his power is largely a matter of the techniques of negotiation. In these relations, "power is persuasion and persuasion becomes bargaining."[19] The President, however, is the only party to this bargaining whose constituency is the nation. The President may turn this fact to his bargaining advantage if he can marshal public opinion behind his program, if he exerts a personal charismatic influence on the electorate, or if he can put together a consensus of the major organized groups in society. All three of these sources of popular power are personal in the sense they depend largely on the personal qualities of the man in the White House. And his ability to turn them to account will depend on his talent for using his popular support as a lever in his relations with others in the policy-making process.

At the same time the President's access to the national electorate provides him with a unique opportunity for political and moral leadership. The Presidency, as Theodore Roosevelt put it, can be a "bully pulpit" from which to mobilize a national sense of justice or to promote a conception of the public interest. The difficulty is that when a President's power rests so largely on his ability to negotiate effectively with other power centers, he is likely to see greater political advantage in a

[19] Neustadt, *op. cit.*, p. 38.

charismatic public image or in good relations with the important groups in society than in the exercise of moral and ideological leadership.

The Personalization of Presidential Power

To say that effective presidential power is the power to influence other men rather than the power to command them is to say that it rests to a significant degree on the personal qualities of the incumbent. A President's influence is the measure of his leadership.

The personalized quality of presidential power is inherent in the constitutional scheme. The separation of powers means that the President *shares* powers with others who are involved in making and administering public policy.[20] The others involved draw their political power from other sources and other constituencies than the President; their own interests and power stakes differ from his. His task, then, is to persuade them that it is in their interest to follow his lead.

To be sure, the status as well as the constitutional and legal powers of the office are a powerful vantage point from which to exercise influence. But the effective wielding of power requires that this awesome status and the power to command be used as vantage points for exerting influence. The point was dramatized by President Truman when, nearing the end of his tenure in 1952, he anticipated the problems that General Eisenhower would encounter in the effort to apply his military experience to the office. "He'll sit here, and he'll say, 'Do this! Do that!' *And nothing will happen.* Poor Ike—it won't be a bit like the Army. He'll find it very frustrating."[21] Throughout most of President Eisenhower's eight years in office he was handicapped, as Truman had predicted, by the difficulty of understanding the nature of presidential power. As one authority has put it: "Apparently he could not quite absorb the notion that effective power had to be extracted out of other men's self-interest; neither did he quite absorb the notion that nobody else's interest could be wholly like his own."[22]

The contrast with President Truman himself is instructive. When he was elevated to the Presidency by Roosevelt's death, there was little in his career to suggest that he would be a strong President. Indeed, one journalist characterized the new President as "a sedative in a double-

---

[20] For a classic statement of this view of the Presidency, see Neustadt, *op. cit., passim.*

[21] Quoted in *ibid.,* p. 9.

[22] *Ibid.,* pp. 163-64.

breasted suit."[23] But Truman turned out to have a sure instinct for the uses of presidential power. He was, in short, a skillful politician who made effective use of the status and the formal power of the office. He understood that these are mere vantage points from which an American President builds his influence by playing on the needs and fears of others. He also understood that even those whom he has the legal power to command can resist through the courts, with public opinion, in the Congress, or informally by threatening to frustrate what the President wants. Power, Truman knew, must be used in combination with a keen political sensitivity to the consequences of its use.

The President, in short, is often forced to play the role of negotiator in a power context. The absence of effective national political parties and the nonideological character of American politics deprive him of any regular opportunity to base his leadership on the common ground of party allegiance or a common commitment to principles or programs. On this account the occupant of the White House has sometimes been described as the "loneliest man in the world."

FORMAL AND INFORMAL PRESIDENTIAL POWER: THE CASE OF STEEL

The contrast between the formal power and the informal influence of the Presidency is put into sharp focus by the contrast between the efforts of two Presidents to deal with a crisis in the steel industry. In both cases the issue arose because of the President's effort to forestall wage and price increases in this basic industry that were seen as major threats to economic stability. In each case the resulting clash between President and a powerful private group left a clear mark on American political history.

President Truman had difficulty with the steel industry in 1952. Ten years later, in 1962, President Kennedy collided with the same industry. The circumstances, actions, and results in the two cases were different; taken together they illustrate the range of methods available to a President in exploiting the full power and influence of the office.

Steel represents a large industrial establishment which enters into contractual agreements with its well-organized employees. Labor-management negotiations take the form of industry-wide bargaining and revolve basically around wages and fringe benefits. The historical pattern

[23] Quoted in Sidney Warren, "How to Pick a President," *Saturday Review*, July 4, 1964, p. 11.

is for wage increases to be followed immediately by industry-wide price increases. Steel has been referred to often as the barometer of the economy—that is, when steel goes up in price everything else tends to do so also. Thus, the wage-price spiral in steel exerts inflationary pressure throughout the economy.

For a long time, the price of steel was considered a matter for the industry to determine, but recently there has been a growing body of opinion that holds that steel pricing policies should be consistent with the public interest in economic growth and monetary stability. In 1952, during the Korean War, union and management officials deadlocked in negotiations. Part of the machinery of wartime emergency wage and price controls empowered the Wage Stabilization Board to make findings in labor disputes. In this case, the WSB proposed a package of hourly and fringe benefit increases totaling $.225 as a basis for settlement. Charles E. Wilson, Director of the Office of Defense Mobilization (parent organization of the Wage Stabilization Board), considered the package a "serious threat in our effort to stabilize the economy."[24] President Truman disagreed, and Mr. Wilson resigned. The recommended package was accepted by the union but vigorously opposed by management. If it were enforced, industry officials argued, a twelve-dollar-per-ton price increase would be necessary (although they may have taken less); President Truman responded with the promise that if a price rise is necessary "in the interest of national defense, it will be granted," but he refused to commit himself to any specific amount. Later, steel management presented the union an offer less than the package, and Philip Murray of the union turned it down and served notice of a strike. Industry began banking its furnaces.

President Truman's problem was to avert a strike. He could invoke the politically distasteful cooling-off provisions of the Taft-Hartley Law; he could grant the industry's price request; or, although legal opinion was divided as to his power to do so, he could seize the mills and put them under government operation. He chose to seize the mills.

President Truman's action precipitated a national debate. He defended his position as being in the public interest and within the emergency powers implied in his constitutional position as chief executive and commander in chief of the armed forces. He told his fellow Americans, on April 8, 1952:

[24] Alan F. Westin, *The Anatomy of a Constitutional Law Case* (New York: Macmillan, 1958), p. 4.

You may think this steel dispute doesn't affect you—you may think it's just a matter between the Government and a few greedy companies. But it isn't. If we granted the outrageous prices the steel industry wants, we would scuttle our whole price control program. And that comes pretty close to home to everybody. . . .[25]

On April 9, Clarence Randall, President of Inland Steel, responded for the entire steel industry (he was angry, as his remarks reveal):

I am here to make answer on behalf of the steel industry to charges flung over these microphones last night by the man who stood where I stand now. I am a plain citizen. He was President of the United States . . . but actually it is not the President of the United States to whom I make answer. It is Harry S. Truman, the man, who last night so transgressed his oath of office, so far abused the power which is temporarily his, that he must now stand and take it.[26]

Mr. Randall emphasized the rights of private property and its ownership by "one million .people" and asked parents whether their boys were "making $1.70 an hour in Korea." His response was bitter, stimulated no doubt by the bitterness in the President's attack.

The press took up the battle, but it was not decided there. The steel industry entered suit and, after hasty processing through the lower courts, the Supreme Court upheld its claim.[27] The decision stated that there is no implied grant of emergency power to the President in the Constitution sufficient to justify his abrogation of the separation of powers in this case. The power claimed by the President, the Court ruled, constitutionally resides in the Congress, and the Congress had not expressly delegated it to the President. Truman had lost his battle in the courts.

Ten years later the President and the steel industry faced each other again.[28] This time it was President Kennedy who invoked the public interest against a steel price increase. The then Secretary of Labor, Arthur Goldberg, had persuaded labor to make moderate demands; the matter had been discussed with steel executives, and the President was under the impression that no price increase would be made. But shortly after the contract was signed, on April 10, 1962, United States Steel announced a six-dollar-per-ton increase in price, an action followed

---

[25] *Ibid.,* p. 16.

[26] *Ibid.,* p. 18.

[27] *Youngstown Sheet and Tube Company* v. *Sawyer,* 343 U.S. 579 (1952).

[28] During the Eisenhower administration, in 1960, Vice-President Nixon had persuaded the steel industry not to raise prices immediately after a wage increase.

quickly by the Republic, Bethlehem, Jones and Laughlin, Pittsburgh, National, and Youngstown companies. On April 11, President Kennedy scheduled a nationally televised press conference and icily levelled charges that the decision to raise steel prices was a threat to the public interest:

> Simultaneous and identical actions of United States Steel and other leading steel corporations increasing steel prices by some $6 a ton constitute a wholly unjustifiable and irresponsible defiance of the public interest.
>
> In this serious hour in our Nation's history, when we are confronted with grave crises in Berlin and Southeast Asia, when we are devoting our energies to economic recovery and stability, when we are asking reservists to leave their home and families for months on end and servicemen to risk their lives—and four were killed in the last two days in Vietnam—and asking union members to hold down their wage increases, at a time when restraint and sacrifice are being asked of every citizen, the American people will find it hard, as I do, to accept a situation in which a tiny handful of steel executives whose pursuit of private power and profit exceeds their sense of public responsibility can show such utter contempt for the interests of 185 million Americans.
>
> If this rise in the cost of steel is imitated by the rest of the industry, instead of rescinded, it would increase the cost of homes, autos, appliances, and most other items for every American family. It would increase the cost of machinery and tools to every American businessman and farmer. It would seriously handicap our efforts to prevent an inflationary spiral from eating up the pensions of our older citizens, and our new gains in purchasing power.

The President then pointed to the favorable earnings position of the companies and added some clear threats of executive retribution:

> The facts of the matter are that there is no justification for an increase in the steel prices. The recent settlement between the industry and the union, which does not even take place until July 1st, was widely acknowledged to be non-inflationary, and the whole purpose and effect of the Administration's role, which both parties understood, was to achieve an agreement which would make unnecessary any increase in prices. Steel output per man is rising so fast that labor costs per ton of steel can actually be expected to decline in the next 12 months. And in fact, the Acting Commissioner of the Bureau of Labor Statistics informed me this morning that, and I quote: "Employment costs per unit of steel output in 1961 were essentially the same as they were in 1958."
>
> The cost of the major raw materials, steel scrap and coal, has also

been declining, and for an industry which has been generally operating at less than two-thirds of capacity, its profit rate has been normal and can be expected to rise sharply this year in view of the reduction in idle capacity.

Their lot has been easier than that of 100,000 steel workers thrown out of work in the last three years. The industry's cash dividends have exceeded $600 million in each of the last five years, and earnings in the first quarter of this year were estimated in the February 28th Wall Street Journal to be among the highest in history.

In short, at a time when they could be exploring how more efficient and better prices could be obtained, reducing prices in this industry in recognition of lower costs, their unusually good labor contract, their foreign competition and their increase in production and profits which are coming this year, a few gigantic corporations have decided to increase prices in ruthless disregard of their public responsibilities.

The Steel Workers Union can be proud that it abided by its responsibilities in this agreement. And this government also has responsibilities which we intend to meet. The Department of Justice and the Federal Trade Commission are examining the significance of this action in a free, competitive economy. The Department of Defense and other agencies are reviewing its impact on their policies of procurement and I am informed that steps are underway by those members of the Congress who plan appropriate inquiries into how these price decisions are so quickly made and reached, and what legislative safeguards may be needed to protect the public interest.

His concluding statement raised the whole issue of the public responsibility of powerful private groups:

Price and wage decisions in this country, except for very limited restrictions in the case of monopolies and national emergency strikes, are and ought to be freely and privately made, but the American people have a right to expect in return for that freedom, a higher sense of business responsibility for the welfare of their country than has been shown in the last two days.

Some time ago I asked each American to consider what he would do for his country. And I asked the steel companies. In the last 24 hours we had their answer.[29]

Mr. Roger Blough, board chairman of United States Steel, responded for a part of the steel industry. In contrast to the historical pattern, the industry had not solidly followed United States Steel's price leadership; Inland and Kaiser steel companies announced they would not raise prices. Other steel companies followed suit, particularly when they found the Attorney General and Congress acting to explore violations

29 *Sacramento Bee*, April 12, 1962.

of antitrust statutes and to investigate price collusions. Also, government contracts were awarded to companies not raising their prices. In the face of all these pressures, the industry reconsidered and rescinded the increase. President Kennedy won his battle and graciously stated in his press conference that his administration "harbors no ill will against any individual, any industry, corporation, or any segment of the American economy."

There are many reasons why President Truman lost his case while President Kennedy won his. Both Presidents stood on the public interest as justification for their actions. Both took their cases to the people. But, whereas President Kennedy chose to make this informal arena the decisive battleground, President Truman chose to risk his formal constitutional powers in the courts. But where formal powers had failed, President Kennedy made informal power succeed. It is true that the informal pressures of public opinion that Kennedy exploited were backed by the use of, and by threats to use, such formal executive power as control over the allocation of defense contracts and antitrust prosecutions. His formal power to recommend to Congress and his informal power as party leader were also available to threaten, for example, changes in the tax laws unfavorable to the steel industry.

These case studies illuminate the limits of presidential power. The President is never a completely free agent. If he has enormous potential for influencing the behavior of others, he is also influenced by them. Truman's decision to invoke legal power by seizing the mills, which made him vulnerable to the Court's decision, was influenced by the informal power of others, especially the power of the workers. Truman might have avoided this eventuality by invoking his clear legal power to impose a cooling off period under the Taft-Hartley Act. He was deterred, in part, by the likelihood of wildcat protest strikes, which the leaders of the United Steelworkers could not avert and which would have resulted in loss of production.

These case studies further reveal how closely the President's formal legal and constitutional authority is connected with the informal prestige and influence he commands. Kennedy's formal powers stood behind his informal pressures. In Truman's case, while he lost the formal battle in the Court, he lost it there partly because he had not been able to make his case informally with Congress and the public. One reason why he had not lay in the weakening of his personal influence that followed his decision a year earlier to relieve the very popular General MacArthur of his command in the Korean War.

Moreover, Truman's seizure of the mills could not by itself accomplish his central purpose. At best it gave him time and a vantage point for informally forcing a wage and price agreement that would be compatible with his objectives. He might have been able to accomplish this in the time between seizure and the Court decision if it had not been for the fact that his tactic for forcing a settlement was opposed by his own secretary of commerce, Charles S. Sawyer, who had been directed by executive order to serve as administrator of the mills. The Secretary, directed to follow Truman's tactics, did not refuse but he did drag his feet. By the time the President was able to implement his plan, it was too late; the Court had intervened. The Secretary was the President's subordinate, subject to his command. Why had the President not been able to use his power to command effectively? The answer reveals the limitations in the formal powers of the Presidency. Truman could have pressured Sawyer's compliance by publicly announcing the planned wage and price adjustments he had privately ordered Sawyer to implement. But Sawyer had his own interests to protect and his own potential weapons for protecting them. Presidential publicity might have pressured Sawyer into compliance with the President's directives; it might have led, however, to public defiance. Having just lost his director of defense mobilization in similar circumstances, still suffering from his dismissal of MacArthur, having just fired his attorney general (though for reasons not connected with the steel crisis), Truman could not afford the latter alternative. The President, then, was pressured into tolerating his Secretary's delaying tactics.[30]

Finally, President Kennedy's apparent success is also revealing with respect to the real power of the Presidency. First, his triumph rested in part on a stroke of good fortune when some of the steel companies broke ranks and declined to follow the price leadership of United States Steel. This departure from long-established conditions of administered pricing in the industry was due to the development of new competitive conditions in steel and steel-substitute products. If traditional patterns had prevailed, the President's tactics might well have failed.[31]

In the second place, Kennedy paid a political price for his victory. He acquired the reputation of being anti-big-business in many quarters and incurred sharp opposition from significant groups in the business

[30] See Neustadt, *op. cit.*, p. 22 ff.
[31] See Grant McConnell, *Steel and the Presidency—1962* (New York: Norton, 1963).

community. The exercise of presidential power, we conclude, is always an intensely political affair. It is never simply a case of the legal or constitutional power to command. Its essence is influence—the wielding of the informal capacity to persuade, coerce, intimidate, threaten, or cajole others to do what a President wants done.

PRESIDENTIAL STYLES OF LEADERSHIP

Every occupant of the White House puts the stamp of his personality on the office. It is reflected in his way of handling press conferences, in the character of his close advisers, in his choice of guests at White House functions, and perhaps above all in his speech.

Historian Eric F. Goldman has pointed out that the public statements of Presidents, albeit largely ghost-written, are directly related to the quality of their Presidencies. As he puts it, "what Presidents have done with words has expressed a lot about them, bad and good." He continues with an illustration:

> Go in any place on the long roll of American Chief Executives and the White House words call up the memory of the administrations. Take George Washington, an aging general playing father to a squalling infant nation, and the words are firm, paternal, magisterial. Or Thomas Jefferson, a remarkable combination of the gentleman scholar and the hardheaded politician, using a prose that is a striking amalgam of the elegant and the wily. Or piddling, indecisive James Buchanan, mincing along from flaccidity to inanity. Or Abraham Lincoln, that great President and great human being, incapable of writing even a hasty letter that is not touched with wisdom and compassion. Or the nothing Rutherford B. Hayes, talking and writing a nothing prose. Or the rambunctious Teddy Roosevelt, lecturing the corporations or any other deviator from The Good and The True in sentences that shrill like a runaway calliope.[32]

Goldman observes that Woodrow Wilson, in his prose,

> drove ahead in his God-lashed way, rarely failing to intimate that his program had a decided connection with divine revelation. (The cynical old French Prime Minister Georges Clemenceau put it: "God gave us only Ten Commandments. Wilson brings us Fourteen Points.") The Wilson prose, most of which he hammered out himself on a battered typewriter brought from his Princeton days, had a constant summons to redemption. On the occasion of his famous first inaugural in 1913 the crowd hushed, as if in church, when the new President reached his climax, speaking of lifting "our life as a Nation

[32] Eric F. Goldman, "Presidential Prose," *Holiday*, April, 1962, p. 11.

to the light that shines from the hearthfire of every man's conscience.
. . . The feelings with which we face this new age of right and opportunity sweep across our heartstrings like some air out of God's own
presence, where justice and mercy are reconciled and the judge and the
brother are one."[33]

By contrast, according to Goldman, Truman used a "shoot from-the-
hip decisiveness, a brash confidence in the face of anything"; Coolidge's
prose was "as crabbed as the Coolidge policies"; Eisenhower was adept
at "expressing in a friendly muddle of words his faith in a sunny
muddling through"; and Kennedy's prose was "carefully burnished,
tautly disciplined, astute and hard-driving, humorous in its wary way,
and cool, so very cool."[34]

There is much more to a President than his public speeches, but
since the President is the focal point of the political attention of the
whole nation, his prose will be listened to very carefully. From his words
the people derive hope, despair, frustration, anger, and, above all, a
sense of national purpose.

The importance of a President's speeches is magnified by the absence
of regular, institutionalized sources of leadership such as might be
provided by strong, ideologically oriented national political parties.
At the same time the speeches of Presidents in recent years, while they
reveal something of the style of the man, seem also to be conscious
efforts of professional phrase-makers to create a favorable image. As a
former State Department official has put it:

> Because they have preferred action to words, and because the de-
> mands of action have pressed so hard upon them in any case, our
> Presidents since the Second World War have made the mistake of
> neglecting what is the prime obligation of leadership. They have
> thought that they could leave it to Madison Avenue to supply them
> with words when occasion required. They have thought that they could
> devote their own time to operational decisions and negotiations while
> hired writers, trained in public relations, wrote their public statements
> for them.[35]

Mr. Halle goes on to argue that the "cleverness" reflected in recent
presidential prose "may be all right for selling dishwashers, but it is
fatal to the sense of truth and conviction that goes with genuine vision."

[33] *Ibid.*, pp. 11 and 14.
[34] *Ibid.*, pp. 14, 16, 18, and 19.
[35] Louis J. Halle, "Appraisal of Kennedy as World Leader," *New York Times
Magazine*, June 16, 1963, pp. 40, 42.

Its effect is to substitute the appeal of a charismatic image for policy leadership. It may thus be said to personalize even more the leadership on which the nation depends.

Presidential Leadership and Democratic Theory

Democracy in the modern world requires leadership no less than other governmental forms. The President, by default of other institutions if nothing else, is the nation's political leader. (There is another possibility to be examined in the ensuing chapters: The Court may in some circumstances take up the political initiative.) This growth in the power of the Presidency reveals a paradox in the system of separation of powers and checks and balances: The system devised by the Founders to establish a government of laws in order to minimize *personal* power was fated to maximize it. When leadership was required, only the President could lead and the President tended to have only the tools of personal power and influence.

The dangers to democracy in the personalization of presidential influence are magnified by the growth of mass society. In a mass democracy political leadership tends to elicit the consent of a mass electorate in two ways. The first possibility is that consent will rest on a charismatic relationship with leaders. Unlike the original Greek meaning, in which charisma was associated with magical and superhuman powers, the appeal of a charismatic leader in a mass democracy is to a personal magnetism and charm, sincerity, and good will, which will make things come out right. But like the appeal to magic, the authority of the democratic charismatic leader is personal; it has no basis in the conservative appeal of tradition and *noblesse oblige* or in the liberal ideal of rationally defended goals and principles.

The second way in which consent tends to be generated in a mass democracy is through a passive, responsive style of leadership. Leaders will not lead, predicted de Tocqueville, but will instead seek to "curry favor with the masses" by addressing themselves to the lowest common denominator of their wants.

Both of these possibilities assume that the "mindless masses" are incapable of independent moral decision and political choice. They are at radical odds with any concept of democracy that counts on political leadership to define issues and to formulate broad programs for dealing with them. Perhaps the crucial question to be asked is: Does the leader's performance provide the possibility of meaningful electoral choice? Does it permit criticism and debate? Does it invite a loyal opposition? We must, it appears, look to the White House for leadership. But because presidential power is so largely a matter of personal influence and bargaining, a President's strength is more likely to be promoted by leadership that is charismatic and responsive. It is not clear how such leadership can be made, in any democratic sense, responsible to the freely formed consent of free men.

Chapter Fourteen

THE PRESIDENT
AND THE BUREAUCRACY

. . . which considers the ways in which the vast responsibilities of the modern Presidency are fulfilled and explores the problems of the political responsibility of and executive control over the federal bureaucracy.

The enormity of his task and the personal character of his responsibility make the President peculiarly dependent on a staff of loyal and able assistants. The number and complexity of the decisions for which he is personally responsible require that he be furnished with **Good Advice** by a staff of able advisers.

The problem of establishing **Executive Control** of the huge bureaucracies composing the executive branch requires every incumbent of the Presidency to rely upon the competence and loyalty of
> **The President's Administrative Staff.** The ways in which Presidents have used the staff available to them for assistance in policy-making and in controlling administrative agencies have varied widely, permitting us to speak of

Presidential Styles in Administration. Comparison of the administrations of such Presidents as Roosevelt and Eisenhower offer a striking illustration of the ways in which the personality of the President, his view of the office, and the circumstances of his times affect the way in which he organizes and uses his available staff.

The Problem of Executive Control of the administrative apparatus has been complicated by the growth of federal functions and of federal bureaucracies that are resistant to change and that often develop independent sources of political strength. The President, as a result, must struggle with other centers of power for effective control of the agencies that are formally responsible to him. In this struggle he must rely chiefly on his
> **Administrative Staff.** Those closest to him, and especially selected for their

personal loyalty, are the members of his White House office staff. These close assistants are part of *The Executive Office of the President,* which also includes the Bureau of the Budget, the National Security Council, the Council of Economic Advisers, and other executive aides.

Because of the personalization of and increase in the powers of the Presidency, recent Presidents have come to rely more heavily upon the members of the *Executive Office* whose loyalty is easier to ensure than upon the Secretaries who make up the *Cabinet.* For the same reasons, the *Vice-President* has not become an assistant President, although he does play a more important role than formerly.

The difficulties of securing adequate sources of advice for Presidential decisions and adequate instruments of control and coordination are especially reflected in *The Machinery of Foreign Policy,* the growth of which has matched the increasing complexity of foreign relations. The gravity of the President's problem is revealed when we leave the immediate circle of staff agencies closely connected to the President, to enter

The Bureaucratic Wilderness of administrative agencies that carry out the business of modern government. In addition to the regular government departments, bureaus, and agencies over which the President has formal power to exercise direct control, there are other agencies with substantial autonomy and independence. The leading types are

Government Corporations, established by Congress to provide flexibility and efficiency in certain operations; and *Independent Commissions,* designed to remove regulatory activities from political control. Autonomy from the political process, however, raises *The Problem of Political Responsibility.* Here, as elsewhere, political agencies that are not made effectively accountable to responsible political officials will be shaped by other political forces. Thus, independent commissions take on the character of *Brokerage Politics* as they are subjected to intense pressure to negotiate bargains between the government and the economic interests they are charged with regulating. In a larger sense, this is

The Problem of Bureaucracy: How is the huge and complex administrative establishment, with its necessary procedural rigidity (red tape), to be made responsible to democratically determined public policy? The problem is complicated by:

The necessary *Role of the Expert,* who must be kept on tap but prevented from getting on top; and by the increasing use of *Public Relations* as an administration tool that puts government agencies in the position of selling their programs to the public, rather than implementing programs initiated by free processes of consent.

At the heart of the problem of *Bureaucracy* is the question of how a *Public Interest,* responsive to public opinion, may be made the basis for effective control and coordination of the administrative leviathan of the modern state.

429

To change anything in the Na-a-vy is like punching a feather bed. You punch it with your right and you punch it with your left until you are finally exhausted, and then you find the damn bed just as it was before you started punching.

FRANKLIN D. ROOSEVELT

Chapter Fourteen

THE PRESIDENT
AND THE BUREAUCRACY

*T*HE RESPONSIBILITIES and duties of the President are immense. No man could hope to carry them out without a wide variety of dedicated, loyal, high-quality assistants. He must have personal aides who keep him informed and advised of the conditions in which he must perform the roles described in the preceding chapter. These include political assistants who keep their finger on the pulse of the nation, offer advice on patronage, tend the constant repair of political fences throughout the country, and advise the President on the current status of his image. International specialists must be prepared to offer almost instant analysis of the development of events in every other nation of the world—allies, neutrals, and antagonists alike. Military advisers are always on tap to inform the President on the condition and requirements of the nation's military capability and to offer advice on strategy for employing it in the numerous military commitments in foreign countries.

Technicians of an almost infinite variety are available to the President. He can find out everything from the best seed corn to use in Iowa to the quality of crude oil imported from Saudi Arabia. He is informed of the activities of the Ku Klux Klan and kept abreast of the current rate of the dollar on the international money market or the predicted effect on the domestic economy of a 2 per cent reduction in the excise tax. His congressional advisers, both political and technical, will tell him what to expect when he launches a new piece of legislation, advise him on the best way to draft the bill, and suggest what amendments to his proposal might be necessary in order to get it enacted.

Governmental housekeeping functions are also a presidential responsibility, and there is a vast army of federal employees continuously seeking better and more efficient methods of conducting, controlling, and coordinating the public business, creating and organizing a bewildering array of statistics, researching innumerable problems, purchasing mountains of supplies, auditing a multitude of transactions, and, when night falls, sweeping out Washington's marble temples and less imposing edifices throughout the nation and the world where these hordes of civil servants labor by day. This whole effort employs some two and one-half million people exclusive of the armed forces. The President, in short, is in charge of a very large undertaking.

The Problem of Good Advice

How does the President best tap this massive bureaucracy for appropriate information upon which to act? How does he know he has the right answer when there are often conflicts among the experts? Which decisions should he make and which ones can he delegate to others? What about the opinions of those outside officialdom such as the business, labor, or university communities? One writer put it well when he said that the President "bobs on a vast sea of information and his problem is to avoid being swamped by it":

Theoretically at least, the President has the entire apparatus of Government to keep him informed—the resources of the National Security Council, the Cabinet, 10 executive departments, more than 50 independent Federal agencies and the White House staff.

He also can look to the press, private organizations, political polls, books, magazines, White House mail, elder statesmen and personal friends for a cross-check on Government sources and for the assurance that he is not the captive of a single group of advisers.[1]

Most modern Presidents have come to rely especially upon one or a few very close and completely loyal and dedicated individuals. Woodrow Wilson's Colonel House and Eisenhower's Sherman Adams were almost assistant Presidents; Roosevelt's Harry Hopkins and Kennedy's Theodore Sorenson were more like alter-egos to their chiefs; and President Johnson looks to his private entourage as a loyal band of bright people whom he uses as sounding boards. As one associate put it, "The President bounces ideas off everybody."[2]

There are also numerous people outside of government whom the President looks to for ideas and information—businessmen, labor leaders, entertainers, intellectuals, physicians, novelists, poets, sportsmen, editors, and reporters, for example. How much information a President can absorb depends upon his capacity, curiosity, and desire. President Kennedy used to amaze his inquisitors at press conferences when he could reel off facts and figures about innumerable matters. This was in marked contrast to President Eisenhower, whose press conferences often displayed a series of rehearsed answers to screened questions or desultory reactions to other questions. President Johnson, not enamored of press conferences, is well informed but skillfully evasive of questions framed to drill deeply into matters he does not wish to discuss.

Presidential Styles in Administration

The advice a President seeks and uses gives his administration a definite tone. It also reveals his own qualities and personal characteristics, which are themselves important to the administration. A contrast between the administrations of Franklin Roosevelt and Eisenhower illustrates this point. Roosevelt ran a loose-jointed administration, which was the bane of the efficiency expert who looked to organization charts, clear

[1] Hedrick Smith, "How the President Keeps Informed," *New York Times Magazine*, August 30, 1964, p. 15.
[2] Quoted in *ibid*.

lines of communications, and standard operating procedures as the right and proper way to do things. Roosevelt's cabinet was a quarrelsome collection of able individualists—some of them have been called prima donnas—who went directly to "the boss" with complaints and sought the favor of their chief.[3]

Roosevelt's cabinet leaked like a sieve to the press, although some of the leaks were opened by the President. At times Roosevelt dealt directly with subordinates to the cabinet members in the various departments and, it is alleged, sometimes bypassed his cabinet members by taking charge of things personally. The administrative pattern was also complicated by advisers like Harry Hopkins,[4] who had a great deal of power but no definite place in any structural apparatus. Hopkins served as sort of a personal "trouble shooter" for the President. Roosevelt also piled organization upon organization and had fantastic overlaps of jurisdiction of various governmental agencies. He got things done in spite of this organizational inefficiency, and his administration was creative even though, or perhaps because, it was structurally disorganized.[5]

President Eisenhower operated on a different concept of administration. His military background, and the fact that he was not as intrigued with the political aspects of his job as was Roosevelt, no doubt contributed much to the difference. Where Roosevelt seldom, if ever, avoided the politics of administrative situations, Eisenhower attempted, at least early in his administration, to divorce politics as much as possible from administering the government. Instead of the free-wheeling informality of Roosevelt's cabinet meetings, Eisenhower's cabinet always had a carefully planned agenda, distributed in advance. Discussion was not allowed to roam hither and yon but focused on the issues at hand. Eisenhower also introduced the military staff concept to his cabinet and, in his own words, he gave "way on a number of personal opinions to this gang [the cabinet]."[6] He regarded his cabinet as advisers who were to be respected and whose collective judgment should be a guide to

---

[3] For an interesting account of some of the doings of the cabinet, see Harold Ickes, *The Secret Diary of Harold Ickes: The First Thousand Days* (New York: Simon and Schuster, 1954).

[4] See Robert E. Sherwood, *Roosevelt and Hopkins*, 2 Vols. (New York: Bantam, 1950).

[5] For an account of Roosevelt's organizational creations and his built-in "espionage" system of acquiring information, see Arthur M. Schlesinger, Jr., *The Coming of the New Deal: The Age of Roosevelt* (Boston: Houghton Mifflin, 1959), Vol. 2.

[6] Robert J. Donovan, *Eisenhower: The Inside Story* (New York: Harper, 1956), p. 64.

action, rather than a collection of people with interesting ideas that he might or might not follow. Eisenhower also delegated a great deal of authority to his cabinet officers and other administrators. His knowledge of what was going on in the inner workings of bureaucracy was often severely limited—so much so, that many members of the press accused his administration of drift and lack of direction. He relied mainly upon the techniques of persuasion rather than orders to his subordinates and, unlike Roosevelt, would not circumvent his administrators or short-circuit the lines of authority to get his wishes into action.

Briefly, Roosevelt dominated his administration and got his way, whereas Eisenhower was influenced by his cabinet and often followed its lead. The contrast in power between Roosevelt's various secretaries of state and Eisenhower's Mr. Dulles is a case in point. Roosevelt was, in effect, his own secretary of state, but Eisenhower relied heavily upon Mr. Dulles for foreign-policy decisions. In short, the chief executive's role as chief administrator depends upon his conception of the office and the importance he attaches to administrative matters in comparison with his other duties.

Since the tragic death of President Kennedy and the somber events surrounding President Johnson's ascendancy to the office, there have been numerous comparisons of the two men and their presidential styles. Like Roosevelt and Eisenhower, these men brought different personalities and perspectives to the White House. While it is premature to render any definitive appraisals of Kennedy and Johnson, some tentative analyses have been offered. Professor John P. Roche has stated that

> Kennedy's triumphs were in the sector of politics where administration is decisive. Never had the top levels of the Federal bureaucracy been so effectively managed and coordinated; the creation of a meaningful Defense Department ranks as a spectacular achievement. Foreign relations were handled with a perceptiveness and unified command that dazzled many observers. . . . In domestic affairs, however, where "politics" in its broad sense dominates the field, Kennedy often seemed baffled and overwhelmed. It is clear that even as a member first of the House and then of the Senate he had little affection or respect for Congress as an institution. . . . True, Kennedy always treated Congress with elaborate solicitude, but it was that of a kindergarten teacher who suspects that one of the children has secreted a hand grenade on the premises.[7]

[7] John P. Roche, "How a President Should Use the Intellectuals," *New York Times Magazine*, July 26, 1964, p. 10.

President Johnson has a different relationship with Congress. As Roche points out:

> As Lyndon Johnson's stunning performance indicates . . . Senators and Representatives will accept some pretty rough handling from a President who takes their function (if not their performance) seriously. Like other men, they too want to be loved—but love was not in the Kennedy political lexicon. It is almost incomprehensible, for example, to an apostle of his brand of modern politics that a long-time Senatorial opponent of closure could promise his *friend* the President a vote for closure if it were needed.[8]

President Kennedy's personal strengths, Professor Roche suggests, made him a master executive; Johnson's make domestic politics the scene of his most dramatic accomplishments. But no matter what his personal qualities or preferences, every President must deal with the nation's far-flung and often inflexible bureaucracy and make it respond as he wishes. This is not a simple task, but there are many agencies closely available to the President to assist him in stimulating the often ponderous bureaucratic establishment that lies beyond the White House.

The Problem of Executive Control

The growth of government, over which Americans have been so deeply concerned, occurs primarily in the agencies composing the executive branch of government—by both the creation of new ones and the expansion of old ones. The almost explosive expansion of the executive branch has created intricately complicated problems of over-all coordination, control, and responsibility. In the American constitutional system, the final authority and responsibility for administration remains with the President. As a sign on President Truman's desk put it, "the buck stops here."

President Franklin D. Roosevelt expressed some of the frustrations of final authority when he reportedly made the following comment to one of his aides:

> The Treasury . . . is so large and far-flung and ingrained in its practices that I find it is almost impossible to get the action and results I want—even with Henry [Morgenthau] there. But the Treasury is not to be compared with the State Department. You should go through the experience of trying to get any changes in the thinking,

[8] *Ibid.*, pp. 32-33.

policy, and action of the career diplomats and then you'd know what a real problem was. But the Treasury and the State Department put together are nothing as compared with the Na-a-vy.[9]

Every President has been plagued by the difficulties Roosevelt described. The established bureaucracies are resistant to change and they are adept at resisting and delaying efforts to initiate changes from above. In addition to this organizational inertia, agencies often develop an outlook and policy commitment of their own. When they do, they are usually in a position to become lobbies for their own point of view in the Congress. Peter Woll describes the inherent advantages enjoyed by bureaucratic agencies before Congress:

> Many private groups maintain substantial lobbies in Washington, but they do not have quite the same access and privileges as administrative agencies. They cannot conduct Congressmen on expense-free trips to Europe, provide free medical care, make the life of a Congressman more enjoyable in a number of other respects. Administrative agencies do this and for the most part questions are not raised. When private groups attempt similar activity, charges of "bribery" or worse are likely to be leveled.[10]

In addition to organizational inertia and agency pressure on Congress, the President must struggle for control with other enemies as well. Highly placed bureaucrats, congressmen, and pressure groups all occasionally compete with him for control of administrative agencies.

Probably the classic example of a zealous subordinate pulling the rug out from under a President was General Douglas MacArthur's challenge to President Truman. MacArthur, the popular hero of Corregidor and commander of American forces in the Pacific in World War II, parted company with the President on the conduct of the Korean War. The General, from his Korean headquarters, openly challenged the President's policies in his press communiqués and through his messages to veterans' organizations and other groups. Truman tried desperately to avoid a showdown but finally relieved MacArthur of his command. The challenge to Truman and to the office and power of the Presidency was a serious one: the dismissed General was given a hero's welcome in a gigantic ticker-tape parade down Broadway. President Truman paid a price in popularity, but he had reaffirmed presidential supremacy over military subordinates.

---

[9] Marriner S. Eccles, quoted in Peter Woll, *American Bureaucracy* (New York: Norton, 1963), p. 143.
[10] Woll, *op. cit.*, p. 135.

The separation of powers also tends to weaken Presidential control. It permits Congress to tunnel into the heart of bureaucracy without, at times, the President's knowledge. Occasionally a congressman may plant an explosive within one of these organizational giants and start some interesting political reverberations when he lights the fuse. Senator Joseph McCarthy was adroit at this sort of thing. He had a talent for cultivating subordinates within large agencies who would leak information to him. McCarthy's tactics annoyed more than one President, and when he burrowed deeply into such agencies as the Defense Department, the havoc he created had widespread political repercussions.[11]

Finally, pressure groups also operate on and in administrative agencies. Their networks of informants and supporters within agencies often cause a President serious difficulties. Nearly all recent Presidents have had to force the resignations of officials who became too friendly with organized pressure groups.

THE PRESIDENT'S ADMINISTRATIVE STAFF

The complexities of the federal service and the problems of control and coordination are such that many students of administration feel something must be done to relieve the chief executive of his burdens.[12] Suggestions include giving the Vice-President some administrative duties and creating various assistant President offices, which would be more than advisory in nature. Presidents themselves have chafed at the numerous demands upon their time and have sought out trusted help, yet few have suggested sharing their ultimate responsibility for decisions. Presidents have delegated authority to cabinet members, to administrative assistants, or to other members of their personal staffs, but the President has to take the brunt of criticism if they fail him—often a more unpleasant burden than making the mistake himself. As Woodrow Wilson once said: "Men of ordinary physique and discretion cannot be Presidents and live. If the strain be not somehow relieved, we shall be obliged to be picking our chief magistrates from among wise and prudent athletes—a small class."[13]

[11] See Emile de Antonio and Daniel Talbot, *Point of Order! A Documentary of the Army-McCarthy Hearings* (New York: Norton, 1964); also Richard Rovere, *Senator Joe McCarthy* (New York: Meridian, 1963).

[12] The Hoover Commission of 1949, which recommended many changes in the structure of the federal executive agencies, led to several little Hoover Commissions in the states.

[13] Quoted in F. M. Carney and H. F. Way, *Politics 1960* (San Francisco: Wadsworth, 1960), p. 65.

Even though the White House office staff numbers about four hundred people, many of whom work to organize and funnel information for the President, no one man could possibly expect to acquire or be adequately briefed on all of the information these people collect. When he is not briefed, the press has a field day at the President's expense. A free society is often cruel to its chief executive for he must constantly expose himself to criticism. Unlike a dictator, a President cannot order his critics to be silent, although no doubt he is often tempted.

The Executive Office of the President. Since we have yet to develop a group of supermen from which we could select our Presidents, it has been necessary to equip our chief executive with subordinates who can aid in carrying out the administrative burdens of the office. The most important staff aid is the Executive Office of the President. It took a long time to get the President more than two or three secretaries for help, but in 1937 the President's Committee on Administrative Management, a group of academically and practically trained experts in administration, decided that the President needed more than clerical help and recommended he be given six administrative aides who should have, in the now legendary words, a "passion for anonymity." Two years later, as part of the Reorganization Act, Congress authorized these positions but not without some spirited and eloquent debate regarding the sacred principle of separation of power. Congress also viewed with alarm the growing power of the President. Some of the fears expressed misgivings about the fact that Congress has through the years given the executive branch more and more personnel and more and more power. At the same time, Congress has denied itself much of the same kind of assistance and has delegated away much of its authority to administrative agencies.

The Executive Office of the President now consists of over 2,500 people including the approximately four hundred members of the White House staff mentioned earlier. It also employs a variety of special consultants and temporary help.

In addition to the White House staff, the following are the chief agencies of the Executive Office of the President:

The Bureau of the Budget. This office is composed of economists and administrative analysts who study the national economy and federal governmental agencies and put the executive budget together for presentation to Congress. The staff of the bureau attempts to make use of the best techniques of administrative and budget analysis in preparing the budget. The net result of such efforts is a mass of complex data to support appropriation requests.

Under President Johnson, the Bureau of the Budget has become even more important than it had been in the past. A distinguished reporter recently entitled an article about this agency and its director "The Remarkable Mr. Gorden and His Quiet Power Center."[14] The Bureau of the Budget is now making use of the latest and most sophisticated techniques of economic analysis, not only in preparing the budget but in helping the President manage the government. Kraft quotes one White House aide as saying, "The Bureau has never been stronger than it is now. Other administrations used it. This administration relies on it."

The National Security Council. The National Security Council was made part of the Executive Office of the President by Congress in 1947. It is designed to provide top-level advice on how the nation's foreign, domestic, and military policies can be integrated to protect the national security. The law provides that the membership shall include the President, the Vice-President, the secretaries of state and defense, and the director of the Office of Emergency Planning. The President may also invite others to attend including the chairman of the Joint Chiefs of Staff, the director of the Central Intelligence Agency, the director of the Bureau of the Budget, the ambassador to the United Nations, and various other officials. The President may use this agency to develop long-range policies or to meet crises as they arise. Under Truman, the council wielded an influence that led John Fischer to describe it as "Mr. Truman's Politburo." Mr. Eisenhower also relied on this agency a great deal; President Kennedy paid little attention to it until after the first Cuban crisis in 1961, when he augmented it with personally selected advisers. The National Security Council's role can change dramatically with events; like other agencies in the Executive Office, its role depends largely on the uses a President wishes to make of it.

The Council of Economic Advisers. The Council of Economic Advisers, created by the Employment Act of 1946, consists of three members appointed by the President with Senate confirmation. It has a small but highly professionalized staff. The chief duties of the Council are to make general analyses of the national economy and inform the

---

[14] Joseph Kraft, "The Remarkable Mr. Gorden and His Quiet Power Center," *Harper's Magazine*, May, 1965, p. 40.

President on these matters. The President uses the Council's reports as a basis for his recommendations to Congress in his required annual economic report to that body. The Council has been subject to criticism for being soft-headed as well as eggheaded in its recommendations, particularly when it suggests that increased welfare and public works programs might be desirable. The business community and labor have both chafed under its recommendations upon occasion. Nevertheless, Presidents since 1946 have relied heavily on the Council's advice in formulating programs for avoiding the boom-bust cycles of the past.

Other Executive Aides. There are other agencies within the Executive Office of the President designed to help with specialized functions. The President's scientific adviser keeps him abreast of what is going on in this rapidly expanding area, and his national security adviser consults with him about foreign affairs and military crises. President Kennedy developed the Office of Congressional Relations to a new importance; further President Johnson strengthened it under Kennedy holdover, Lawrence O'Brien. This office, along with Johnson's frequent telephone calls to congressional leaders, not only keeps the President informed of what is going on in Congress, but keeps Congress aware that the President is keeping a close watch on its activities.

Executive Office and Cabinet. There has been a marked tendency in recent years for Presidents to rely more heavily on the members of the Executive Office than on the heads of the regular government departments. There are many reasons for this. Partly it is a matter of the increasing complexity of the presidential task and his increased responsibility for over-all policy leadership and coordination. Particularly in the area of foreign policy in an age in which almost all aspects of society are involved, it is obvious why the President would come to rely on those agencies of coordination and policy planning whose responsibility and vision are not limited to traditional departmental boundaries. The same considerations apply to domestic policy. The Council of Economic Advisers, for example, is in a position to make recommendations on problems of economic stability and growth that cut across the jurisdictions, and the limited perspectives, of the Departments of State, Defense, Labor, Attorney General, Post Office, Commerce, Agriculture, Interior, Treasury, Health, Education and Welfare, and Urban Affairs (which comprise the cabinet), as well as of independent agencies like the Securities and Exchange Commission, the Federal Trade Commission, and the Federal Reserve Board.

Partly, also, the President's reliance on the men in the Executive Office is due to the fact that they are, in a unique sense, "his men." With few exceptions, his hand is free in making appointments, since the requirement of Senate confirmation applicable to the heads of regular departments does not apply. Without the requirement of Senate confirmation, the President need not worry about senatorial courtesy, and he need not consider the damage that might be done his position by the harassment of a single senator on even those nominations that eventually will be confirmed. The appointees to positions in the Executive Office are not likely, therefore, to have their allegiance to the President fragmented by conflicting loyalties.

The Vice-Presidency. These same considerations help to explain why the Vice-President has not emerged as an assistant President. Although the traditions of the presidential nominating conventions of both parties virtually assure the presidential nominee of the power to name his running mate, his actual choice is likely to be circumscribed. The nomination of the party's standard-bearer will most often have involved conflicts among the interest group and ideological factions of the party. The imperative necessity in filling the second place on the slate has been traditionally to heal wounds.

Recently, however, the Vice-Presidency has become a much more important office. The assassination of President Kennedy dramatized to the nation the fact that the Vice-President is never more than a heart beat away from the highest office in the land. This does not mean that the Vice-Presidency itself has become an important office in its own right. Senator Dirksen, for example, scorned rumors of his possible selection in 1964 with the comment that he had little taste for "sharing a jug of goat's milk on some Arabian desert."[15] But the constant possibility of accession to the Presidency dictates that the Vice-President be closely informed. Johnson, like Nixon before him, had been kept abreast of all the important events of the nation, and when the time came he was prepared to take over the office. This does not mean that the Vice-President's relationship with the President will be close and confident. There was an aloofness between Eisenhower and Nixon; Kennedy was by no means close to Johnson; and Vice-President Humphrey, although of much service and highly respected, is not in the innermost circle of presidential confidants.

[15] *Newsweek,* July 20, 1964, p. 27.

THE MACHINERY OF FOREIGN POLICY

The problem of providing the President with adequate sources of advice and adequate instruments of control and coordination is probably most pressing and difficult in the area of foreign policy.

The institutional machinery available to the President in the making and conduct of foreign policy is impressive and, unavoidably, impressively complicated. The Secretary of State is ordinarily the most important cabinet member. The department over which he presides is a prolific source for the gathering and analysis of information on all of the countries of the world; it has responsibility for the conduct of our diplomatic relations and negotiations; it carries on intelligence and research programs; and it has responsibility for the execution of technical and economic assistance programs. It is charged with coordinating the activities of all its own and other governmental agencies engaged in planning and executing foreign policy. And it has a responsibility to advise the President on over-all policy and on specific policy problems.

There are many other agencies outside the State Department involved in foreign-policy activities. In addition to the National Security Council, described above, they include the following:

The Defense Department develops military policy, administers the programs of military aid to other governments, and collects and evaluates intelligence information.

The Department of the Treasury recommends policy on and administers financial and monetary relations with other governments and with international agencies.

The Departments of Commerce, Labor, and Agriculture all contain branches that help formulate and administer phases of our economic relations with other countries.

The United States Tariff Commission's role has been accentuated in recent efforts to work out new relationships with the European Common Market countries.

The Central Intelligence Agency collects and analyzes intelligence data, which, in the modern world, means much more than espionage. The great bulk of the information collected is from open sources and includes data on geography, cultural customs, public opinion, industrial development, political conditions, and transportation systems, as well as on military forces and plans. In an age of total conflict, intelligence also becomes total, and the agency that collects and evaluates it is cast in a more important policy role. The actual power of the CIA and the range of its activities, however, cannot be described because no outsiders, including the Congress, know them. Its operations are highly secret, and its budget is concealed from Congress by distributing it in smaller amounts throughout the budgets for other agencies.

The United States Information Agency carries on propaganda programs through the Voice of America, maintains field offices and libraries in foreign countries, and encourages and helps foreign students to come to the United States for study.

All this elaborate machinery operates to provide the President with advice; the basic policy decisions are his alone. The coordinating mechanisms assist him in the integrated application of policies; the responsibility, however, remains his.

The Bureaucratic Wilderness

Beyond the White House and the comparatively close relationship of the President to his Executive Office lies a vast complex of organizations designed to conduct the nation's business. To wander through the labyrinth of bureaucracy and explain all of the agencies and their activities would require a work of bewildering detail. Both the 1949 and 1955 Hoover Commissions inquiring into government organization found that the federal government was a fantastic collection of all sorts of agencies that had mushroomed and solidified into permanent concerns. "Great confusion," said the 1949 Hoover Commission,[16] as it surveyed this vast mechanism. In addition to the Executive Office of the President and the eleven departments of cabinet rank (State, Treasury, Defense, Justice, Post Office, Interior, Agriculture, Commerce, Labor, Health, Education and Welfare, and Urban Affairs) there are numerous other agencies with various purposes and structural designs. Some of these are directly controlled by the President and some are not.

In addition to program agencies, there are housekeeping agencies, which do not deal directly with the public. These agencies service the bureaucracy with people (the United States Civil Service Commission, headed by three commissioners) or supply it with the bureaucratic fuel of paper, mimeograph ink, desks, charts, pencils, and other supplies and services (the General Services Administration, headed by an administrator).

[16] *Report on the General Management of the Executive Branch* (Washington, D.C.: Government Printing Office, 1949), pp. 3-4.

GOVERNMENT CORPORATIONS

Government corporations are multiheaded, semiautonomous agencies. The Tennessee Valley Authority is without question the most celebrated and controversial example. Corporations are not a new phenomenon in government. The first corporation in which the government took part was the Bank of North America, chartered by the Continental Congress in 1781. In 1791, Congress chartered the First United States Bank. Since that time, the government has been in and out of several governmental corporate activities. Such organizations are very effective in times of emergencies, and during wars and depressions they tend to proliferate. For example, the economic depression of the 1930's created several new agenices, beginning with the Reconstruction Finance Corporation in 1932 and mushrooming into the Roosevelt administration's numerous agencies designed to stimulate the economy. During World War II, over twenty new corporations were created to produce needed commodities in certain areas, such as rubber and metal.

Government corporations are organized something like a private business and are thus freed from many traditional controls by the executive and the legislature. Their budgets are generally brief, and the Bureau of the Budget does not go into details as it does on other agency budgets. The boards of directors or commissioners often are able to make a good deal of policy without specific legislative or executive authorization or direction, even to the extent that profits realized from such activities as the sale of electrical power may be reinvested for the production of other commodities. The Tennessee Valley Authority, for example, has invested in a variety of projects designed to improve the region in which it operates but not specifically authorized by Congress. Government corporations, since they are akin to private business, do not enjoy sovereign immunity and, unlike most government agencies, can be sued, as well as sue. Some of them are permitted to develop their own personnel systems independent of the Civil Service Commission. In recent years, there has been a tendency to restrict the autonomy of government corporations in order to bring them under more direct control by the President and Congress.

A second, and perhaps more important, factor working against government corporations is the hostility aimed at them from defenders of private enterprise. No government agency has aroused the opposition of the power lobby and other economic interests more than the Tennessee

Valley Authority whose activities have often been called creeping social-ism by those who identify democracy with capitalist economic institu-tions.

State and local governments also make use of the corporate device. The compact between New York and New Jersey creating the Port of New York Authority is a good example. This is an administratively efficient operation, but there are protests from several sources that it is not adequately responsive to public demands. As in the federal system, the corporate device makes for more flexible administration, but it raises serious questions about public control. Its flexibility actually results from a lack of accountability to elected representatives and frees the administrator from having to answer for his actions.

INDEPENDENT REGULATORY COMMISSIONS

In the administrative structure of American government, there is a unique type of administrative agency known as the independent regulatory commission. These organizations, sometimes called the headless fourth branch of government, are figuratively adrift from the traditional administrative structure of government. Created by Congress, they are not clearly tied down to either the executive, legislative, or judicial branches of government, although they exercise all three types of power. Commissions serve as their policy-making bodies. The size of the commissions varies—the Interstate Commerce Commission has eleven members and the Federal Power Commission has five—but all commissions are engaged in regulating specific activities of the economy within very broad policy lines established by Congress. They act in a legislative capacity by making rules that have the force of law, in an executive capacity by administering and enforcing the law, and in a judicial capacity by conducting hearings and issuing orders. Commis-sioners are appointed for overlapping terms by the President, who can remove them only for specific reasons.

The leading or big six regulatory commissions are:

1. *The Interstate Commerce Commission.* This Commission was originally created in 1887 to regulate railroads, and its powers have been expanded to include the regulation of routes, rates, and safety of, and conflicts between, all means of interstate transportation except air.

2. *The Federal Trade Commission.* Created in 1914 to regulate eco-nomic competition so it will be "free and fair," it has two basic func-tions: to issue cease-and-desist orders when it finds unfair trade practices

existing; to study and investigate questionable business practices and make reports of its findings.

3. *The Securities and Exchange Commission.* Founded in 1934 after the stock market collapse, it supervises the entire securities market and administers statutes providing for securities regulation.

4. *The Civil Aeronautics Board.* Established in 1938, it makes civil airline rules and regulations (enforced by the Civil Aeronautics Administration), determines rates, allocates routes, adjusts disputes over routes, investigates accidents, and conducts other functions related to air transportation.

5. *The Federal Communications Commission.* This Commission was created in 1934 to regulate radio and telephone, telegraph, and submarine cable communications in interstate and foreign commerce, and its functions have been expanded to include television. It has general supervision over these activities, and it can require the extension of service, award franchises, regulate rates, and conduct investigations.

6. *The Federal Power Commission.* Established in 1920, this commission had as its original responsibility the licensing of hydroelectric projects on navigable waters of the United States. Since then, its functions have been continuously expanded by the Natural Gas Act (1938), which gave it authority over the transportation and sale of natural gas in interstate commerce; the Flood Control Acts of 1938 and 1944, which authorized the Commission to recommend hydroelectric projects at dams held by the Department of the Army and to regulate the price of power so produced; and Executive Order 10485 (1953), which authorized it to issue permits for power projects on the borders of the United States.

The Problem of Political Responsibility. When this type of independent organization drifts too far away from the regular branches of government, the question of who will pull it back into proper constitutional orbit causes much confusion. Franklin Roosevelt found that Presidents cannot remove commissioners on these bodies at will without trouble from the courts and objection from Congress, which provides the conditions for which the President may remove commissioners.[17] Such conditions do not include a political or economic philosophy contrary to that of the President. Congress may, of course, redefine the functions of the commissions, change the size or conditions of their governing bodies, or eliminate them altogether. And the courts may

---

[17] *Humphrey's Executor* v. *United States*, 295 U.S. 602 (1935).

declare that a commission has no statutory authority to perform certain functions, or is required by its organic statute to perform others.

But why are such circuitous measures necessary to change a governmental agency's policy? Part of the answer lies in the structure of the commissions. The structural difficulties stem from the facts that these agencies are governed by commissioners who generally serve longer terms than the President; that commissioners cannot be replaced by the President except for generally few and specific causes set out by Congress; that effective political control is difficult, particularly if there are holdovers from a previous administration or if the law demands bipartisan membership as it nearly always does; and that there is no congressional or executive veto of commission actions. These structural characteristics tend to remove the commissions from responsibility to the elected branches of government. This very independence from political controls operates to make the commissions more susceptible to other, and often less desirable, influences.

Independent Commissions and Brokerage Politics. During the Eisenhower administration, the Special Subcommittee on Legislative Oversight of the House Committee on Interstate and Foreign Commerce conducted a broad investigation of regulatory agencies. The purpose was to deal with an underlying problem that had been evident to close observers for a long time. The commissions, largely freed from responsibility to the regular branches of government and subjected to the pressures of the interests they were designed to regulate, often were improperly influenced or controlled by those interests.[18]

The whole concept of public regulation is based on the assumption that private economic groups are not always governed by a self-discipline that subordinates their interests to broader interests. Business and other private-interest groups, the regulatory concept assumes, will tend to regard whatever they can legally get as legitimate. The purpose of regulation is to subordinate these interests to the public interest. When the agency regulating them is independent of other controls, however, the techniques of lobbying can be sharply focused on a small group of men. The pressure can become most intense, particularly if the general

[18] The Committee had conducted over three years of investigation. The result was legislation aimed at more stringent regulation of improper or corrupt influence on the commissions (H.R. 4800 and H.R. 6774, Eighty-Sixth Congress). These measures, however, failed of passage. At present the issue is relatively dormant but the very nature of regulatory commissions will no doubt cause the problem to flare up from time to time, particularly when incidents of favored treatment or corruption are evident.

attitude of politicians is that the claims of all groups must be, by good brokerage practice, treated "fairly." In the power vacuum created by nonpartisan commissions, the public interest is undefined, and effective power passes into the hands of the well-organized and powerful private interests. Political columnist Doris Fleeson, analyzing the testimony before the Subcommittee, described the regulatory process as one in which "the consumer plays no discernible role . . . beyond that of final bill payer."[19] Lawyer-lobbyists and their utility company clients bring pressure on the commissions in "a kind of gray area between what is allowed by law and what is encouraged by present custom." The result, as the Counsel for the Subcommittee described it, is negotiation, not regulation. The government often makes no serious effort to regulate; instead, treaties are negotiated between commissioners who serve as the government's ambassadors and the lawyer-lobbyists who act as ambassadors for the interests.

Regulation by brokerage is sometimes even more starkly apparent in the structure of regulatory agencies in the states. A classic example is the seven-man California State Board of Forestry. The law reads in part:

> There shall be a State Board of Forestry of seven members appointed by the Governor with advice and consent of the Senate. . . .
> One member shall represent the pine producing industry.
> One member shall represent the redwood producing industry.
> One member shall represent forest land ownership.
> One member shall represent the range livestock industry.
> One member shall represent agriculture.
> One member shall represent the beneficial use of water.
> The aforementioned six members shall be persons of practical knowledge and experience in the field they are to represent. One member shall be appointed from the general public at large.[20]

Brokerage politics could not be more clearly expressed in the law. The public interest has one seventh of the total voice; it would appear that it would have to be loud and clear to be heard above the din of the special interests given a legal voice. It seems much more likely that the lone and lonely public member will be forced to define his role as broker to the other six. And it is highly probable that the protection of the best interests of the people of the state will be identified with the settlements reached by the ambassadors from the affected private interests.

[19] *Sacramento Bee*, May 23, 1960.
[20] *California Public Resources Code*, sec. 505.

The problem of regulating industries so that the public is properly represented continues to be an important one in American government. In one of its aspects, the problem depends on the extent such activities need to be and ought to be regulated. The argument rages between classic concepts of *laissez faire* and increased public control of the economy. But when public regulatory agencies become pressure groups or brokers for the interests they regulate, the public stands little chance to benefit. If the public's interests are to prevail, they must be politically organized. Responsible and competitive political parties, experience teaches us, are the only effective democratic device for accomplishing this purpose. The efforts to accomplish regulation through independent, nonpartisan agencies makes impossible the organization, definition, and protection of a public interest. The resulting vacuum will be filled, as it has been, by those private groups whose organization is strong and whose interests are clearly defined.

The Problem of Bureaucracy

Among the more fashionable parlor games of a large number of Americans is that of damning the governmental bureaucrats. Vice-President Alben Barkley facetiously explained the derisive nature of the word *bureaucrat* when he asked the rhetorical question, "What is a bureaucrat?" He supplied the answer by saying "a bureaucrat is a Democrat who has a job some Republican would like to have." In the public mind, however, all employees of governmental bureaucracies are bureaucrats; whereas those who staff corporate and other private bureaucracies, for some reason, are not. The corporate executive's briefcase is full of know-how; the bureau chief's contains only a rulebook. Status goes to the hard-headed businessman who has met a payroll, whereas the public employee, be he federal, state, or local, must often accept the stigma of being stereotyped as a bumbling plodder with two left hands who enjoys nothing more than packaging the most simple problem in bales of mimeographed minutiae bound with endless yards of red tape. As one participant in and observer of bureaucracy put it:

> To most of us, "bureaucracy" is an I-don't-like-it word. It conjures up crowds of drones at rows of desks, laboring listlessly at dull and repetitive tasks. It reminds one of that gag which originated in the Quartermaster Corps: "Government property is issued in order that a proper record may be kept thereof." The word "bureaucracy," says the

Columbia Encyclopedia, "usually carries a suggestion of reprobation and implies incompetency and parasitism among the functionaries." Now *there's* a bureaucratic sentence for you![21]

In spite of our propensity to stereotype the bureaucrat, public employees are of about the same quality as their business counterparts. Bureaucracy, public or private, leaves much the same marks on those who are the cogs in its wheels. It is often true that there is a high degree of idealism and dedication on the part of the public employee, which focuses upon service to people rather than personal gain. This is an important factor and one that should give many of our public servants a more deserving reputation than they now enjoy. Elevating the bureaucrat to first-class status with his private-enterprise counterpart, however, does not mean that bureaucracy does not present some real problems related to the conduct of public business.

Perhaps it is more realistic to conceive of bureaucracy and the bureaucratic way of life as a phenomenon of size rather than of the public or private nature of the organization. Governments are big—the federal government is huge—but so are the private corporate organizations in which the vast majority of Americans make their livings, the unions by which they are represented, the educational systems in which they get their schooling, and the churches in which they worship. Bureaucratic procedure is usually the result of the necessity of large organizations to prescribe rules, regulations, and formal procedures for carrying out the organization's activities. Paul Appleby has related the bizzare problems he encountered in trying to order an ironing board from a large department store chain with a mail-order service.[22]

Some veterans, on the other hand, have been driven almost to distraction trying to figure out how the forms supplied them by the Veterans Administration should be filled out, and they stand in awe of the elaborate machinery necessary to secure veterans' benefits. Appleby's ironing-board incident indicates what happens occasionally when necessarily formalized procedures are mechanically applied to individual cases. The veteran painfully answering what he considers a host of irrelevant questions does not often consider that such questions may be important factors for deciding cases other than his own. When

---

[21] Harlan Cleveland, "The Case for Bureaucracy," *New York Times Magazine,* October 27, 1963.

[22] Paul H. Appleby, *Big Democracy* (New York: Knopf, 1949), p. 59 ff.

masses of people must be dealt with by large organizations, settled rules and procedures are necessary, and they inevitably will be arbitrary or redundant in individual cases.

Even the strange cant of the bureaucrat—as someone once said, "I love you" becomes "complete assurance of maximum affection is hereby implied"—has a purpose. It is an attempt to get the most widespread understanding possible by deadening prose until it loses any emotional impact. "I love you" causes emotional reactions in the reader of the phrase. "Assurance of maximum affection" transmits the idea without unnecessarily stirring feelings of romance. An absurd basis for a marriage or a friendship, and perhaps a dehumanizing basis for any social relationships, nevertheless it is a necessary price of large-scale, formal organization.

Bertrand Russell, in his Nobel Prize acceptance speech, stated that most officials prefer to say No rather than Yes, since they derive greater feelings of satisfaction and power from turning someone down than by giving him what he wants. Perhaps Lord Russell is correct, but it should be pointed out that bureaucratic procedure is at the heart of the problem. If each public official could arbitrarily decide how persons coming before him should be treated, the basic democratic doctrine of equality before the law would be destroyed. Many individuals feel that their situation is unique and therefore should be treated differently from John Doe's. When the public official applies the rules and decides accordingly, a person who is disappointed often grumbles that the bureaucrat is intellectually and morally bankrupt since he cannot recognize the uniqueness of the case and use his discretion. But discretion is just what rules, regulations, and procedures are designed to prevent. While the denial of discretion prevents the official from considering unusual circumstances, it also stops him from capriciously turning away deserving people. We are all, in short, treated with maddening uniformity, a situation quite difficult for people tending toward individualism to understand. It has been argued that the development of mass society and mass man has led to a greater toleration if not acceptance of bureaucratic treatment. It can also be argued that large bureaucracies acting impartially toward the society they serve may have contributed to the creation of the mass man, since individualism becomes buried under the increasing and necessarily impersonal treatment by big government, big business, big labor, and big education.

BUREAUCRACY AND THE ROLE OF THE EXPERT

Public service on most any level contains almost all the professions and skills society develops. Government agencies employ engineers, physicists, educators of all sorts, doctors, lawyers, professional administrators, typists, clerks, accountants, sanitation experts, social workers, efficiency experts, biologists, chemists, librarians, cooks, loggers, bulldozer operators, carpenters, painters, plumbers, steam fitters, public-relations men, mechanics, policemen, mailmen, key-punch operators, janitors, surveyors, and gardeners. As government assumes new functions such as control of atomic energy or space exploration the diversity of its employees increases. Also, as government grows in both size and complexity, the role of the expert in government becomes increasingly important and problematical. One observer has described American bureaucracy this way:

> Unlike the civil service in almost all other countries, the American bureaucracy is a collection of specialized offices set up to do specific tasks and manned by experts in the field. Each bureaucratic office, accordingly, has a direction and momentum of its own: for example, the Reclamation Bureau of Interior always wants to bring more land into cultivation. Each also, tends to come into conflict with other agencies: the Reclamation Bureau is consistently at odds with those parts of the Agriculture Department trying to cut down on food surpluses. Because they have their own purposes and battles, these offices tend to establish independent lines of alliance with Committees, or at least members of the Congress: there is, for instance, a romance of long standing between the Reclamation Bureau and Carl Hayden of Arizona, the dean of the Senate and Chairman of its Appropriations Committee. Finally, because of its expertise, each bureaucratic office tends to throw up a complex of regulations, traditions, and personnel patterns as protection against interference from outside.[23]

The chief problem connected with experts practicing their *expertise* (bureaucratic jargon for *expertness*) is to keep them in tune with the public interest. To do this, many schemes have been proposed to keep the expert "on tap, not on top." Some of the proposals include continuous surveillance by legislative committees to see that the legislative intent establishing the agency and setting out its powers and duties is carried out. Another is to see that political appointees always dominate the administrative structure so that the chief executive can insist that

[23] Joseph Kraft, "Johnson's Talent Hunt," *Harper's Magazine*, March, 1965, p. 42.

his political desires be reflected in the organization. Thus, the President's cabinet is composed of politically appointed heads of the major agencies of government.

Political control of a bureaucracy composed of experts is rendered difficult, however, because of bureaucratic responsibility to a variety of masters. As one authority on the executive branch of government has put it:

> Like our governmental structure as a whole, the executive establishment consists of separated institutions sharing powers. The President heads one of these; Cabinet officers, agency administrators, and military commanders head others. Below the departmental level, virtually independent bureau chiefs head many more. Under mid-century conditions, Federal operations spill across dividing lines on organization charts; almost every policy entangles many agencies; almost every program calls for interagency collaboration. Everything somehow involves the President. But operating agencies owe their existence least of all to one another—and only in some part to him. Each has a separate statutory base; each has its statutes to administer; each deals with a different set of subcommittees at the Capitol. Each has its own peculiar set of clients, friends, and enemies outside the formal government. Each has a different set of specialized careerists inside its own bailiwick. Our Constitution gives the President the "take-care" clause and the appointive power. Our statutes give him central budgeting and a degree of personnel control. All agency administrators are responsible to him. But they *also* are responsible to Congress, to their clients, to their staffs, and to themselves. In short, they have five masters. Only after all of those do they owe any loyalty to each other.[24]

Even if there were effective political controls, however, the problem of a responsible bureaucracy composed of experts remains. Many writers in the field of public administration concern themselves with this problem, and a quite common theme is that the generalist should dominate the specialist.[25]

What is a generalist? It is often suggested that he is a specialist in generalization trained to have a broad view of things. Unfortunately, however, as an examination of college catalogues in public administration reveals, the specialist in generalization usually comes out of college

---

[24] Richard E. Neustadt, *Presidential Power* (New York: Wiley, 1962), p. 39.

[25] In his address before the American Sociological Society as long ago as December 28, 1936, Arthur E. Morgan succinctly stated the issue: "One plausible explanation for the breakdown of great climaxes of human culture is that there came to be so many specialists and so few generalists that the coordinating and integrating forces of society became too weak to make effective synthesis of the riot of specialization." From J. M. Pfiffner, *Public Administration* (New York: Ronald, 1946), p. 21.

a specialist in public administration just as the engineer, physicist, business administration major, or statistician is a specialist in his field. As in most academic areas, there has been a tendency, with some present signs of reversal, continuously to narrow the base of the discipline of public administration by adding more courses in that area at the expense of electives in other fields. Instead of the student learning to make a decision on the basis of a broad knowledge of the culture, literature, and philosophy of his civilization, he is taught how to do this in a course in decision-making. So even the training of generalists, if such is the goal, tends to become a specialty replete with its own jargon and esoteric literature.

Perhaps the desired generalist should be defined not by formal training but by a state of mind. Thinking big or broadly is not easy in an era of specialization necessitated by complexity. The lure to know more and more about less and less is a built-in temptation of modern life. A political scientist becomes a specialist in public law but further specializes in administrative law and then may narrow this to state administrative law, perhaps the administrative law of Michigan, or maybe even administrative law in Michigan's workman's compensation cases. And so it goes. The amount of data is so great in so many narrow areas that one may be drawn into it so completely that after a while he loses touch with the broader areas of a field.

To maintain a generalist position is most difficult, particularly for the public official whose daily tasks tend to focus on special areas. He has to know his business, but he also has to equate this with the elusive public interest. How he does this depends upon his state of mind and the kind of person he is. This may or may not be a result of his education. People who think small may think just as small had they pursued liberal arts rather than cost accounting.

Experts, however, are necessary. People broadly familiar with literature and the arts could not build atomic submarines without an additional knowledge of physics and engineering, just as the atomic physicist would be unable to prosecute an antitrust suit through the courts without legal training. Government needs experts who know what they are doing. Without expert advice on the consequences of policies, government programs may be doomed in advance to failure (the ill-fated Cuban "invasion" of 1961 was a dramatic example). Similarly, even the best grounded intentions of the public, Congress, or the President will be frustrated where the expertness necessary for implementation is lacking. Such circumstances produce that heightened sense of frustration and futility that undermines popular government.

When the often necessary tent of secrecy has been dropped over the bureaucrat's operation, the frustration becomes even greater. "We must trust our sincere public officials" is often the medicinal dose offered an excited public when secrecy surrounds important policies. In a democratic society, such a dosage goes down hard, even if it is necessary. This is especially true if the questioning of policy is treated as disloyalty. To equate disloyalty with incisive probing into political and administrative blunders or questionable policies is a device used with disappointing frequency and equally disappointing results. The problem of political control of experts is insoluble wherever secrecy is deemed necessary and criticism is stilled by charges of disloyalty. We may have to accept secrecy in some areas; we ought not, however, fool ourselves that it is compatible with democracy.

Generally, perhaps the key to the solution is that the expert must retain a humility and acceptance of the fact that he is a public servant who must submit to the public's orders as expressed by their representatives. This may be a lot to ask of generals, physicists, accountants, and others who are appalled at public and even legislative misinformation about their fields of specialization. But purpose must dominate technique if a democratic public is to be adequately served.

BUREAUCRACY AND PUBLIC RELATIONS

Earlier, we discussed the use of public relations and advertising techniques in electing candidates, influencing them after they are elected, and manipulating public attitudes on specific issues. These same techniques are used increasingly in public administration to sell the public on a governmental or departmental program. The techniques can focus around top political personalities, such as the President or a governor of a state. But they can be directly focused on an agency program, such as the Veterans Administration, a great user of spot announcements on radio and television designed to inform the agency's clientele of what the agency can do for it.

Information officers, as they are called in most jurisdictions, are used to inform the public of agency programs. For example, fish and game departments in many states have made use of information officers to print bulletins and issue press releases on such matters as bag limits for fish, the merits of shooting limited numbers of doe during deer season,

456

the problem of producing adequate pheasants for hunters, and the virtues of fish and game conservation. A real question arises as to whether this type of activity is informing or propagandizing the public.

Federal agencies also use direct promotional devices to win support for their programs. The radio commercials of the Veterans Administration are paralleled by activities of the Department of Agriculture, the Treasury Department, all branches of the Department of Defense, and the Department of Labor; in fact, all government agencies, including independent regulatory commissions, engage in this activity in varying degree.

The basic questions involve the purpose and content of public relations. Is it a matter of informing the public or is it an effort to promote public acceptance of a program? Can this distinction be made? One of the country's leading authorities defines public relations as ". . . the attempt, by information, by persuasion, and adjustment, to engineer public support for an activity, cause, movement, or institution."[26]

Such words as "information, . . . persuasion, and adjustment" are vague enough to cover the whole catalogue of political sins and virtues but it is the engineering of public support that is bothersome. The Civil Service Assembly, an organization devoted to understanding and improving the public service, has recognized the delicacy of governmental use of public-relations techniques and insists that publicly employed public-relations men must use "legitimate" means to "educate" and to "inform" the public. They also add: "Public relations have to do with the development and maintenance by any legitimate means of *favorable* attitudes on the part of the people with whom the agency comes in contact."[27]

It is a peculiar comment on democracy, if we accept Mr. Bernays' definition of public relations, to find the public employing people to persuade them that the public's agencies are doing well by them. It is no answer to say that the agencies are acting on the orders and in behalf of the policies of elected officials. Even where this is true, it means that one of the parties is using the machinery and finances of government not to *administer* its programs but to manipulate public opinion in its favor. Presidents as politicians, and their parties, have a right and an obligation to carry their views to the public. But as chief administrator

[26] Edward L. Bernays, *The Engineering of Consent* (Norman: University of Oklahoma Press, 1955), pp. 3-4.
[27] *Public Relations of Public Personnel Agencies* (Chicago: Civil Service Assembly, 1941), pp. 5-7. Italics added.

of the governmental apparatus the President can have no such democratic right nor can any of his subordinates. The basic principle involved
is simple but important: If the opinions of the public are to control the
government, these opinions must not be controlled by the government.

The problem is aggravated in those situations in which an administrative agency's program is closely linked with the interest of a private
group. In these cases, government machinery and personnel of persuasion may be directly used for the betterment of a private interest. One
observer has provided a striking example in the development of security
programs for defense contractors:

> In the case of the industrial security program, which is in opera-
> tion for classified defense contract work, we find a leading organiza-
> tion of industrialists calling attention to the sweet, nonsecurity uses
> of security. Says the foreword of the National Industrial Conference
> Board Study on Industrial Security (published in 1952): "Even if
> you don't have a trained saboteur in hire, industrial security can pay
> off in peacetime. It can help you rid your plant of agitators who
> create labor unrest, who promote excessive grievances, slowdowns and
> strikes, and encourage worker antipathy toward management. These
> actions cost your company money."
> Believe it or not, this advice to businessmen on the anti-labor
> applications of security was reprinted in 1955 in a pamphlet, "Disaster
> Planning for the Oil and Gas Industries,"* published by the National
> Petroleum Council, an organization which also functions as the
> Petroleum Advisory Council to the Department of Interior of the U.S.
> Government.
> * This pamphlet . . . bears the notation that it is "published in
> response to request of Office of Oil and Gas, Department of
> Interior."[28]

The same techniques may, of course, be employed *against* an administration. According to one report, a public-relations firm persuaded
a governor to veto a bill without ever contacting the governor. It merely
arranged to have objective-sounding propaganda opposing the bill cross
the governor's desk in such a barrage that he changed his mind.[29]

Persuasive techniques employed by private interests on administrative agencies may often strain at ethical limitations. Ordinarily, however, conflicting interests will operate partly to cancel out one another's

[28] Benjamin Ginsburg, *Rededication to Freedom* (New York: Simon and Schuster,
1959), p. 33.
[29] R. L. Heilbroner, "Public Relations: The Invisible Sell," *Harper's Magazine*,
June, 1957, pp. 28-29.

extravagances. In any event, it is difficult in a free society to regulate the private use of manipulative techniques. But this is not a justification for allowing public, administrative agencies to become the province of the professional experts in attitude engineering.

Public information services can be a very useful activity of governmental agencies. If an agency confines itself only to dispensing information requested—favorable and unfavorable from the agency's point of view—it can contribute to public enlightenment. But with agencies whose continuity and growth depend upon public support of their programs, and with personnel generally committed to the programs as well as to keeping their jobs, it is difficult to insist that they forego those efforts to create good public relations that have become so basic to the conduct of all nongovernmental organizations. This, however, is a legitimate demand of democratic citizens. Few people would argue that a "ministry of propaganda" in a government is consistent with the consent of the governed. For the same reason, neither can there be a whole series of smaller propaganda offices and officers attached to specific governmental agencies. The public-relations approach *to* government by private groups poses a constant and unavoidable threat to responsible administration and popular consent; when it is used *by* government to engineer the attitudes of the electorate, the stream of popular, responsible consent is polluted at its source.

BUREAUCRACY AND THE PUBLIC INTEREST

The central problem of bureaucracy is responsibility. How may the vast network of governmental functions and functionaries be made responsible to political processes of democratic policy-making? The first requirement, of course, is executive control since the President is the politically responsible chief of the administrative agencies. When we go beyond that we come back to the political parties, which, alone, can provide the framework of organized competition for office in which the relationship of government and the public interest can be placed before the electorate. Where parties do not play this role, the public employee as well as the politician elected to office is without guidance and support. Individually isolated, he has the same difficulty in pursuing such an abstract concept as does the legislator, judge, or citizen. As a result, bureaucracies very often rely upon brokerage processes to solve problems facing them. The Defense Department is inclined to see that all the services get their share of things; small and large farmers are each given their due by the Department of Agriculture (large farmers are more politically potent; thus, they have more due); the Post Office sees that its clientele (mailers are organized and potent; householders are not) is treated fairly; and the Justice Department spreads itself among the many demands put upon it. Sometimes such brokerage is dictated by the chief executive through his politically controlled cabinet members, but many delegated areas of decision deep down in the organization charts also tend to operate on the brokerage model.

Administrative agencies vie with one another for appropriations from legislatures. In the making of a budget the brokerage process also operates. At both the national and state levels, the method of arriving at a budget is predicated on taking the departmental requests, carving them to the bone through analysis, and coming up with a final figure somewhere between the agency's request and the budget analyst's recommendation. The figure is usually agreed upon at a hearing before the head of the budgeting agency. The claims of the agencies and of the budget analysts are both considered equally legitimate. As a result, budgeting tends to become a game in which the agencies often pump their budgets full of air while the budget analysts try to puncture them, with both sides hoping for a result somewhere near what each really felt was correct.

If one side is able to generate more influence than the other, the agency may end up with a bloated budget or an inadequate one, depending on which side is victorious in the struggle. At times, these differences are taken to the legislature, but this is risky for both sides since the compromises of the legislature are often made on politically different criteria than those of administrative agencies under the executive. Also, since both the budgeting agency and the program agency are ordinarily controlled by the executive, it looks bad to see them quarrel before the legislature, which might very well say, "A plague on both your houses."

The solution of the basic problem of a responsible bureaucracy will largely depend upon whether party organization can overcome the discontinuities and rivalries between Congress and President that are inherent in the separation of powers. Legislative bodies must themselves be organized to make responsible party government possible and to exercise enough control and ask enough questions so that the public will know what goes on. But it is difficult to hope for much more than brokerage if legislatures create a host of agencies dedicated to special interests. This seems to be a trend in many governmental jurisdictions, particularly in the creation of federal regulatory commissions and, on the state and local level, licensing boards, which all too often become tax-supported lobbies for pressure groups.

The President, on his part, can exercise responsible control over the bureaucracy only if, as party and legislative leader, he can protect the principles and programs of his administration from the pressures of private groups operating directly on and through Congress. In the abscence of sustained and strong presidential leadership, the major restraint on the brokerage process in the parties and in the Congress is removed. If parties and Congress are dominated by private interests, it is unrealistic to expect a President to be able to harness the bureaucracy in the service of the national principles and policies on which he was elected. He will be able to do so only insofar as he can apply effective strategies of personal persuasion, influence, and pressure on Congress and on powerful private groups. He is not without weapons in this struggle, but the odds against him are high. And he must constantly bear the burden of knowing that whenever he is outmaneuvered, and segments of the bureaucracy succumb to pressures from outside, the public will not blame the constitutional principle of separation of powers, the weakness and the brokerage character of the political parties, or the dominance of interests in the Congress. The President alone will be held responsible. It is an unfair game, and the President deserves better of enlightened public criticism.

Chapter Fifteen

COURTS AND
THE RULE OF LAW

. . . wherein the relation of law to society and to freedom, the character of the judicial process, and the role of the courts in American politics are considered.

In modern societies *Law* replaces but continues to perform the functions of custom: it ensures predictability in social relations by enforcing commands and prohibitions that are backed by the moral norms and physical force of the community. The existence of a legal order provides the citizen with a legal personality, which defines his rights and obligations; thus,

> *Law* is a necessary condition of *Freedom* since the alternative to a legal order is complete arbitrariness. *Law in Democracy* rests on a distinction between legality and morality: democratic laws only tell citizens "what they must not do; never what they ought to do." Since morality is left to the individual conscience, democratic legal systems face the problem of *Civil Disobedience to Democratic Laws*. The conflict between society's demand that the law be obeyed and democracy's recognition of the primacy of individual conscience poses a paradox. The resulting dilemma is complicated in the American constitutional system, which gives the individual the implicit *Right to Violate Laws* to test their constitutionality. The courts, in effect, vindicate the individual's illegal act if they declare the violated statute unconstitutional.

The *Judicial Process* never operates in a vacuum: "a judicial decision is a social event," which reflects, in addition to law and precedent, "an interaction of social forces." Since judges are human beings,

> *The Nature of Judicial Decisions* cannot be reduced to a mechanical process. The discretionary element is never lacking 'though it may be concealed when judges, like Tom Sawyer, call a *Pickax* a *Case Knife* in order to cloak new situations in established precedent. Underlying every legal system are assumptions about the nature of man that are reflected in its judicial decisions. The conflict between the assumption of rational, moral man, inherent in the Anglo-Saxon legal tradition,

461

and the deterministic assumptions of modern social science pose an important problem for American courts.

American Legal Principles have their primary ***Sources*** in the English ***Common Law and Equity,*** the historical development of which illustrates the way in which judicial decisions may resolve the dilemma of every legal system: the reconciliation of justice and predictability. Predictability requires rules of law hardened into precedent; justice requires that the law reflect changes in circumstance and moral standards. In modern democratic societies this dilemma is solved mainly by the fact that most law is

> ***Statutory Law,*** enacted and amended by legislatures, which limits but does not eliminate judicial discretion. Statutes define, and establish penalties for violations of, both ***Criminal Law*** (offenses against the public) and ***Civil Law*** (offenses committed by one person against another).

The Role of the Courts in American Government is more important than in other democratic nations because they have not only the power of

> ***Statutory Interpretation,*** which is inherent in the judicial process, but also the power of ***Constitutional Interpretation*** in which their decisions are final and binding on the other agencies of government. This power makes the
>
> ***American Courts*** into ***Political Institutions*** since it authorizes them to make political decisions. Because the courts are the final judges (constitutional amendment aside) of their own powers, they must decide whether to adopt a posture of
>
> ***Judicial Activism or Judicial Self-restraint*** in entering the thicket of political decisions. Although judicial activism has been dominant in recent Courts, the issue remains a central one.

The Court Structure in the United States consists generally of a dual system of federal and state courts, each of which is organized into trial courts (courts of original jurisdiction) and appellate courts (which review decisions on appeal). Since the quality of a judicial system depends largely upon the quality of its judges, the best method for

> ***The Selection of Judges*** becomes an important problem to which no ideal solution has been found.
>
> ***The Jurisdiction of the Courts*** in the United States is complicated by the dual system of federal and state courts to which all citizens are subject by definition of their dual federal and state citizenship. In unusual cases jurisdictional questions may be very difficult to decide.

462

A country where judges are faithful to the popular will rather than
to the rule of law, will not be a democratic country worthy of the
name.

ARTHUR J. GOLDBERG

Chapter Fifteen

COURTS AND
THE RULE OF LAW

HAT IS THE LAW?" Socrates used to ask his fellow Athenians. The question is a simple one only at first glance, as many an Athenian discovered. Over the centuries, it has been approached from a variety of vantage points and remains worth asking. We might begin with the proposition that law is the power of a government to control the behavior of its subjects by commanding or forbidding certain actions and by attaching a penalty to a violation of these commands. The content of the law is derived from that body of precepts by which a society lives.

The source of these precepts may be an absolute ruler of some sort; an aristocracy selected on the basis of heredity, wealth, or learning; the people of the society themselves either through representatives or on their own initiative; judges selected either by appointment or election; or a society's traditions with their sources shrouded in the mist of antiquity.

Law and Society

Social control can be exercised by means other than law. Custom, habit, folkways, and mores all influence people to act in certain ways. Law is more formalized, and its command to action is backed with the power of the state. Law continues to perform, however, the major social function performed by tradition in earlier societies. Social life requires some range of predictability; individuals and groups must be able to anticipate the consequences of their actions in the reactions of others. Where the "cake of custom" has been crumbled, law as the command of the state steps in to ensure predictability in social relations. Law is like custom in another respect: its commands and proscriptions have behind them a moral force. Custom may be obeyed in a traditional society because the individual is really unaware of the possibility of alternative actions. The "good" and the customary are interwoven in the fabric of social life and inculcated in the processes by which children are socialized. Law most often develops in society as a codification of group values. Indeed, law is often formalized custom. The effectiveness of law, like the effectiveness of custom, continues to depend upon the acceptance of its moral content by those over whom it would be effective. A legal system is a substitute for physical might. It may be that in matters of the law, as Thomas Hobbes long ago said, "When nothing else is turned up clubs are trumps." But the vitality of a legal system will depend on its ability to make this situation the exception.

The existence of law presupposes a community—that is, a set of values by which a society resolves the issues on which its existence depends. At some stage of its development, the community establishes a basic legal order that determines the methods of creating laws. It also decides how laws are to be interpreted and enforced. Since specific laws always eventuate from conflicts and controversies, the machinery for making and interpreting laws tends to be used by the most powerful and influential segments of society in order to implement their interests or values. Law, then, is never a system of abstract, perfect justice. It must, however, rest on a claim to widely applicable and valid principles of justice from which a moral obligation to obey may be derived.

Freedom and the Law

The role of law, its meaning, and the method by which it is enacted and interpreted are basic expressions of the political philosophy of every society. The distinction between a free and a totalitarian society is directly related to both the sources and the meaning of the law. When we talk of majority rule, we mean the right of the majority to declare the legal rules for society. We are accustomed to thinking of dictatorship as including a system of unjust laws enacted and enforced without the consent of those subject to them. In modern totalitarian regimes, the development and refinement of the techniques of random terror exemplify the importance of even unjust laws. The random use of these techniques—the punishment of people for no apparent reason or without legal justification—means the elimination of law and predictability. The individual is deprived of any legal personality. In this respect, Hannah Arendt argues, the modern totalitarian regime not only destroys the old legal order but also deliberately prevents the creation of a new one. Arbitrary decrees to carry out the demands of a movement and the use of the techniques of random terror deprive the citizen of any legal status.[1]

The citizen of the fully developed totalitarian state is in the same position as those unfortunates in the period following World War I who found themselves stateless, unwanted,. and unaccepted in the legal system of any nation state. Wandering from state to state in Europe without legal personality in any nation, they were dealt with at the whim or caprice of police agencies. They dramatically illustrated the final plight of men who do not live under a law: the only way they could improve their condition was to come under the law by breaking it. For only then did they become legal persons and acquire such minimum legal rights as the right to be saved from starvation in prison. The fullest achievement of human rights requires a particular kind of legal order. The one condition in which there are no human rights whatever is the absence of a legal order altogether.

The necessity for a legal order, maintained by a responsible judiciary, is the essence of the quotation from former Justice Goldberg heading

[1] Hannah Arendt, *Origins of Totalitarianism* (New York: Harcourt, Brace, 1960).

this chapter. It may at first glance appear to be a paradox, but what Goldberg is saying is that the judiciary in a democratic society must be completely independent of the capriciousness of popular whim. Judicial responsiveness to undemocratic public demands could be as ruinous to a free society as a responsiveness to the bigoted prejudices of a dictator. Goldberg's words do not necessarily deny the validity of majority rule, but he does insist that the courts in their decisions must seek to maintain the rule of law and to resist arbitrariness. In this view, then, an independent judiciary is the tribunal that must seek to guarantee the legal personality of citizens.

This is a large responsibility, to be sure. Americans are accustomed to an elaborate and responsible judicial system with a demanding appellate structure designed to assure a high standard of justice. But even Americans must be alert to perversions of the judicial system. In our dual court structure of federal and state courts, which we will examine more thoroughly below, there have been instances when state courts have capitulated to popular prejudice and have failed to guarantee the legal rights of all citizens. Such a perversion of the judicial function unravels the moral fabric of society to the point where disobedience and even violence become commonplace. When the courts themselves accede to unequal treatment before the law, the very foundations of the legal order are undermined.

LAW AND DEMOCRACY

In a free society and a democratic political system the legal personality of citizens is guaranteed by all those requirements of due process described earlier. Due process refers to those procedures designed to guarantee rights to the citizen as a subject of the law. The democratic citizen is creator of the law as well as its subject; thus law and morality bear a distinctive relationship to each other in democratic societies.

In closed societies and authoritarian political systems, law is regarded as the authoritative expression of the values of society. The moral personality of the citizen is identified with his legal personality: not only obedience to the law, but also allegiance to the values it expresses, is the obligation of citizenship.

In a democratic society, legality and morality are never identical. In Arendt's words, "The genius of law in a free society is that it only tells citizens what they must not do; never what they ought to do." This characteristic of democratic laws derives from the fact that they are instruments that express the values of a majority in a climate in which minorities retain the basic right to continue to criticize, oppose, and seek to amend or repeal majority decisions. The empirical question of "what is legal?" is relevant only to the citizen's role as subject of the laws; as maker of the law, it is the value question of "what is right?" that is relevant.

A law-abiding citizenry is necessary to any organized society, but obedience to existing laws in democratic societies cannot require a commitment to the worth of the law in question. Indeed, earlier generations of democratic thinkers went further. In the Revolutionary period, M. R. Cohen says, "Not only Democrats like Jefferson but Federalists like James Wilson, living at a time when the Revolutionary tradition was vivid, found it easy to think that the people had a right to disregard the law when it seemed to them unjust or contrary to conscience."[2]

Civil Disobedience and Democratic Laws. In the development of the American legal tradition, there has been some confusion on the question of disobedience of the law as a matter of conscience. It is not uncommon for a citizen to substitute his private judgment about easing his car through stop signs or playing poker with his friends even though he knows there are laws prohibiting such actions. These are comparatively trivial illustrations but they are, nonetheless, examples of lawbreaking that fit in the same category as such crimes as robbery, embezzlement, and the use of narcotics. They are, that is to say, instances of the violation of a law for the individual's own advantage, and they are committed with the expectation that the act will go undetected and unpunished.

Acts of civil disobedience have a different character and a different purpose. They stem from a conscientious decision that the law must be defied because it is immoral. These acts are aimed at changing the law rather than evading it, and the individual fully intends that his illegal act will be detected and punished.

The question of civil disobedience is a complex and difficult one in any democratic society. In our own it has taken on new urgency in recent years as increasing numbers of people have resorted to deliberate violation of law as a means of protesting what they regard as immoral laws and policies, especially in the areas of foreign policy and civil rights. The basic issue raised for democratic societies can perhaps never be finally resolved. No government, not even the most democratic, can openly grant the right of individuals to substitute their consciences for obedience to the law. But, on the other hand, democracies are unique in

[2] Morris R. Cohen, *American Thought, A Critical Sketch* (New York: Free Press, 1954), p. 143.

their insistence that citizens do have the right to put the *morality* of existing laws to the test of their individual consciences. Democracy is thus the only form of government that raises the question of the moral limits of the demands its legal system is entitled to make on the individual. Ultimately, it encourages the individual to make his own conscience the seat of even this judgment. It is not likely, therefore, that the question of civil disobedience can ever be finally resolved in a free society.

The Right to Violate Unconstitutional Laws. In the American political system the problem is further complicated by the role played by the courts as final, authoritative interpreters of the Constitution. The courts, in the exercise of judicial supremacy, cast laws up against the guarantees of individual liberties and rights embodied in the Constitution. An individual may, as an act of conscience, violate a law in the belief that the court's interpretation of the Constitution will vindicate his conscience and nullify the law. Thus, for example, conscientious objectors to war or to a pledge of secular loyalty have had laws that they violated nullified under the religious clauses of the First Amendment.

Further confusion results from the federal system of government, which often leaves one's legal obligations in doubt. State and local ordinances often conflict with federal laws or constitutional interpretations on the same or related subjects. In such instances, often the only way a federal test of a state or local law or ordinance can be achieved is for a citizen to have himself arrested so a test case will be available for federal interpretation. Since the federal judiciary does not render state and local laws invalid without a specific case before it, martyrdom to test the law is an implicit right in a system of judicial supremacy. Thus, in the sixties the wave of protests, demonstrations, and outright violation of state and local laws and ordinances provides the vehicle for getting a case before the federal courts. To win is to be vindicated—to lose is to suffer but not always without ultimate vindication.[3]

---

[3] Homer Plessy, a one-eighth Negro, had himself arrested and thrown off a train because he refused to ride in the "separate but equal" Jim Crow car. His ultimate conviction was upheld by the United States Supreme Court in 1896 in *Plessy* v. *Ferguson,* 163 U.S. 537, a landmark decision that gave Supreme Court approval to the doctrine of "separate but equal" facilities and therefore racial segregation. Justice Harlan was the lone supporter of Plessy's cause, and the position he took in his eloquent dissenting opinion finally became law in 1954, when the court outlawed segregation in *Brown* v. *The Board of Education,* 347 U.S. 483. Mr. Plessy suffered for his "crime" but he was posthumously rewarded for his martyrdom.

Not all citizens are likely to be candidates for martyrdom. Most men, no doubt, accept in principle an unqualified obligation to obey the law. Yet a democratic citizen cannot take the further step of putting his duties as subject to the law and his obligation to obey it above his obligation to exercise his conscientious judgment of the morality of the law.

The Nature of the Judicial Process

"A judicial decision is a social event," wrote Felix S. Cohen. "Like the enactment of a federal statute or the equipping of police cars with radios, a judicial decision is an interaction of social forces."[4] Such social events do not occur arbitrarily, however, for the legal process is an elaborate and rigorous one, which has developed intricate procedures designed specifically to rule out arbitrary action whenever possible. Most Americans are familiar, perhaps superficially, with the elaborate ceremonials connected with the operation of the legal process. The strange cant of the lawyers liberally sprinkled with Latin phrases; the awesome atmosphere of many courtrooms, which exude dignity and justice; the robed judge sitting remotely upon his raised bench while lawyers, clerks, and other court attachés speak to him in required subservience; the oath taken on the Bible; and the jury box with stern-faced peers attentively listening to the proceedings—all bring to the courtroom a dramatic tenseness. The social events and their drama have not escaped the attention of writers, and the American novel, theatre, movie house, radio, and television have fed us almost as much courtroom drama as they have "horse opera."

The judge is a public servant charged with judging controversies and dispensing justice. As a public servant, his area of operation is disciplined, steeped in tradition, and circumscribed by highly formalized precedents, rules, and procedures. The precedents, rules, and procedures have not been established or developed merely to make the judge's task difficult. They attempt to reduce any tendencies toward arbitrary or capricious action by human beings wearing the judicial ermine. Even the judicial apparatus of a hierarchy of courts with an increasing number of judges is designed to ensure an adequate review of judicial action by the collective review of others skilled in the same discipline. The entire

[4] F. S. Cohen, "Transcendental Nonsense and the Functional Approach," in F. S. Cohen and M. R. Cohen, *Readings in Jurisprudence and Legal Philosophy* (Englewood Cliffs, N.J.: Prentice-Hall, 1951), p. 479.

judicial structure, in fact, is based upon the assumption that human beings, even judges, can err. There are procedures, to ensure against judges' mistakes, by means of which a litigant may challenge in a higher court the validity of the proceedings in a lower one.

THE NATURE OF JUDICIAL DECISIONS

Legal rules and ritual and the structure of the court system are important factors in determining the quality of justice, but equally important are the human beings who wear the judicial robes. How does the judge operate? Do his decisions reflect his own values and philosophy? Or does he deduce them mechanically from precedent? Or does he follow the procedure of Rabelais' irreverent Judge Bridlegoose:

> . . . having well and exactly seen, surveyed, overlooked, reviewed, recognized, read, and read over again, turned and tossed over, seriously perused and examined the bills of complaint, accusations, impeachments, indictments, warnings, citations, summaries . . . I posit on the end of a table in my closet all pokes and bags of the defendant and then allow unto him the first hazard of the dice according to the usual manner of your other worships. . . . That being done, I thereafter lay down upon the other end of the same table in my closet the bags and satchels of the plaintiff . . . and forthwith [give] him his chance. . . .[5]

Most judges would, of course, reject Bridlegoose's theory that judicial decisions have no more foundation than a hazard of the dice, but the theory of the hunch or intuitive process has been well defended by members of the judiciary. Federal Judge Joseph Hutcheson, playing on Rabelais' description of Bridlegoose, once said:

> I, after canvassing all the available material at my command, and duly cogitating upon it, give my imagination play, and brooding over the cause, wait for the feeling, the hunch—that intuitive flash of understanding which makes the jump-spark connection between question and decision, and at the point where the path is darkest for the judicial feet, sheds its light along the way.[6]

This description at least has the merit of emphasizing the inadequacy of the theory that the making of judicial decisions is an essentially mechanical process of applying the law to particular cases. In this me-

---

[5] *Gargantua*, Book III, in Cohen and Cohen, *op. cit.*, p. 441.
[6] Joseph C. Hutcheson, "The Judgment Intuitive: The Function of the 'Hunch' in Judicial Decision," 14 *Cornell Law Review* 277-278 (1929).

chanical view, judges are seen as simply matching the proper tint card of law and precedent to the color of the case, thus producing an automatic decision. In some aspects of judicial decision, however, it is immediately clear that discretion is involved. Thus decisions rendered by different judges for violations of the same law show a wide variation in penalties. For example, the statistician of the City Magistrates' Court of New York reported in 1916 that 17,075 persons were charged before the magistrates with intoxication. Of these cases, 92 per cent were convicted, but the record indicated that one judge dismissed 79 per cent of this class of cases. The same agency also reported that in cases of disorderly conduct one judge heard 566 cases and discharged one person, whereas another judge discharged 18 per cent, and another 54 per cent of the cases.[7] Such unscientific and inconsistent application of the law has led Felix S. Cohen to observe:

> Concretely and specifically we know that Judge So-and-So, a former attorney for a non-union shop, has very definite ideas about labor injunctions, that another judge, who has an unfortunate sex life, is parsimonious in the fixing of alimony; that another judge can be "fixed" by a certain political "boss"; that a series of notorious kidnapings will bring about a wave of maximum sentences in kidnaping cases.[8]

The tendency in this age of objectivity and science is to recoil from such subjectivity, particularly in the administration of justice. It is impossible, however, to avoid the conclusion that judges *interpret* the law and, in the process, apply their own values and are influenced by the political, economic, and social environment in which they act.

Judicial Decisions: Pickax or Case Knife? The discretionary element in judicial decisions and the influence of social and economic forces are often concealed by the ritual and tradition of the judicial process. Confronted with a need to change the law or precedent in response to changed conditions or social forces, courts sometimes resort to legal fictions, which make it possible to pretend that fundamentally nothing has been changed.

This process has been likened to the approach of Tom Sawyer and

[7] Charles G. Haines, "General Observations on the Effects of Personal, Political and Economic Influences in the Decisions of Judges," 17 *Illinois Law Review* 96 (1922).

[8] F. S. Cohen, "Transcendental Nonsense and the Functional Approach," in Cohen and Cohen, *op. cit.*, p. 481.

Huck Finn to digging Jim out of jail.[9] Tom, who was an authority on all matters of the right and proper and traditional ways for prisoners to dig themselves out, explained to Huck that "case knives" (table knives) were the only appropriate tool: ". . . it's the *right* way—and it's the regular way. And there ain't no *other* way, that ever *I* heard of, and I've read all the books that gives any information about these things. They always dig out with a case knife. . . ." Huck, not knowing any better and not caring "shucks for the morality of it, nohow," was all for getting on with the job with picks, but Tom would not "stand by and see the rules broke —because right is right, and wrong is wrong, and a body ain't got no business doing wrong when he ain't ignorant and knows better." After digging until midnight with case knives but with little visible result except blisters, even Tom began to see the advantages of getting on, and said to Huck, "Gimme a case knife." Huck tells the rest of the story:

> He had his own by him, but I handed him mine. He flung it down, and says, "Gimme a *case knife*."
> I didn't know just what to do—but then I thought. I scratched around amongst the old tools, and got a pickax and give it to him, and he took it and went to work, and never said a word.
> He was always just that particular. Full of principle.

And so they dug Jim out with case knives that were really pickaxes, but form, precedent, and rules were followed, as in many judicial decisions where it is necessary to relabel the pickax a case knife.[10]

Legal fictions conceal the subjective elements involved in decisions that modify the law or apply it to new conditions. They also serve to dramatize the broader truth that judicial discretion is not only unavoidable but necessary to the flexibility of the legal system and to the search for justice. Like the concept of the public interest in a democracy, justice is never perfectly or finally achieved but remains an abstraction pursued by men of good intentions within an ordered framework of procedure and precedent.

[9] Roscoe Pound, "Law in Books and Law in Action," in Cohen and Cohen, *op. cit.*, p. 419.

[10] A good example of the case knife–pickax routine would be the situation in California (similar to that in other states), which restricts the legislature from enacting certain statutes relating to a specific county. The courts have allowed the legislature to classify counties, however, and enact legislation for particular classes of counties. California has fifty-eight counties and oddly enough, there are fifty-eight classifications of counties. When the California legislature enacts a law applicable to "all counties of the fourteenth class," it is, of course, enacting a law for only one county. But since the pickax is a case knife, all is well with proper precedent.

Judicial Decisions: Moral Man or Determined Behavior? At the heart of the Anglo-American legal system are certain assumptions about the nature of man. These assumptions hold that man is a rational creature, capable of making rational choices between right and wrong, and that when wrong choices are made he can expect to pay penalties, which he deserves. The view of legal punishment as retribution and atonement for bad or wrong actions follows from these assumptions. Justice Holmes declared bluntly that "the various forms of liability known to modern law spring from the common ground of revenge. . . . In the criminal law and the law of torts it is of the first importance."[11]

The assumptions about human nature and behavior, from which the legal principles of personal responsibility, punishment, and atonement were derived, came to be part of our legal system before the development of modern, scientific analysis of human behavior. The knowledge and the theories of modern sociology and psychology are, on some fundamental points, at odds with the traditional assumptions of the law. Much modern behavioral science selects as its operational assumption a theory of determinism, which holds that the behavior of men, like that of other animals, is to be explained entirely as conditioned responses to stimuli. A person's response to a given situation at a given time is entirely the result of his earlier conditioning. Thus, if enough knowledge of the antecedents were obtainable, it would be possible to predict his actions. In this view free will is meaningless. Responsible choices between the alternatives of right and wrong are never the real basis of behavior. If the wrong choice (from society's point of view) is made, the man making it cannot legitimately be punished by society or held responsible for wrong behavior when he could not in any relevant sense have behaved differently.

The logical end of social determinism would hold that society rather than the criminal must assume responsibility for criminal acts, for it was environmental conditions that caused the criminal to act as he did. The slum theory of juvenile delinquency, the emotional stress theory of alcoholism, and the disturbed mother-father relationship theory of homosexuality are all indications of the effort to find causal factors or determinants of certain types of crimes and misbehaviors.

The search for causal factors is important to justice in its broad sense, and has long been a factor in criminal law. To the common law standards

[11] Oliver Wendell Holmes, *The Common Law* (Boston: Little, Brown, 1881), p. 37.

of defining a crime—that is, both an act and an intent—it adds a reason for committing the act or having the intent. This has sometimes resulted in acquittals in cases in which the accused had committed an illegal act with premeditated intent. A good and not uncommon example of this type of case would be the irate husband who, upon discovering that he is the cuckold in a love triangle, seeks out either his wife or her paramour and kills one or both in a fit of emotional frenzy. If the drama occurs in suburbia rather than the slums, the husband's chances of acquittal are fairly good because, whereas the intent was there as well as the act, his reason for doing his intended act may be considered adequate explanation by many of his peers occupying the jury box.

The courts of most states have relied increasingly upon psychiatric and other expert help in searching out the reasons for many acts. Very often, the question revolves about the issue of the sanity of the individual. The classic standard of legal insanity throughout the English-speaking world is the McNaughten Rule. This rule holds that in a plea of insanity it must be proved that the person making the plea was laboring under such a defect of reason that he was unable to know the nature or quality of his act or was unable to know that his act was wrong.

The McNaughten Rule, however, has been challenged as inconsistent with modern scientific evidence. A recent decision,[12] partly recognizing these objections, caused a stir in both the professions of law and psychiatry. The Durham Rule, resulting from the decision, holds that an accused is not criminally responsible if his unlawful act was the *product* of mental disease or mental defect. The implications of this rule would change the test of legal responsibility in a significant way. The product of a mental illness is a different test from whether, at the time the act was committed, the accused was able to determine right from wrong. It would make a wide range of psychological reasons for an act relevant and admissible.

The current controversy over punishment of criminals calls into question the foundations of Anglo-American law. A report of the committee on psychiatry and law of the Group for the Advancement of Psychiatry, entitled "Criminal Responsibility and Psychiatric Expert Testimony"[13] points up the issue quite clearly:

> Attacks upon the law by psychiatrists and the defense of the legal position by lawyers have engaged a disproportionate share of our attention and exertions at the expense of significant psychological

[12] *Durham* v. *The United States*, 214 F2d 862 (1954).
[13] Report No. 26, 1954.

insights which can no longer be ignored. A re-examination of not only the basic premises of the criminal law but also of its actual operations is needed if lawyers and psychiatrists are to attain a better inter-communication and understanding.

As expressed in contemporary law, responsibility is regarded as a function of the intellect, of conscious volition with definite boundaries and degree. Modern psychiatry recognizes the role of the intellect, but would give to the emotions and unconscious a greater weight in the balance of forces in mental life, and would assert that their boundaries and degree are not readily ascertainable.

The role of punishment by society still has its strong advocates, however. The focus is often put upon organized crime and the necessity of holding out a social whip against those who wish to practice such illegal professions as burglary or embezzlement. Retribution, both severe and certain, is deterrence, and if determinism becomes the basic assumption of criminal acts, say its critics, anyone could do almost anything and explain it by trauma in childhood. "Benevolent social reformers," says M. R. Cohen,

> are apt to ignore the amount of cold calculating business shrewd-ness among criminals. . . . Men will risk their lives if they think that there is some chance of winning something. And while many take long chances, as in lotteries, it is a fact that professional crime, like any other business, ceases to grow in extent where the chances of failure rise. That is why bandits do not try to rob the United States Treasury or the mint.[14]

Both lawyers and behavioral scientists are deeply concerned with the proper treatment of criminals. The scientific approach to human be-havior has not demonstrated the desirability of abandoning the assump-tion of personal responsibility for one's acts. Much carefully tested behavioral evidence shows very clearly, however, that retribution and atonement for a social act are not usually the most effective solution for either society or the individual. On the other hand, lawyers are not anxi-ous to give up traditional approaches to punishment and chart new courses until these new methods of treatment and rehabilitation can be proved a better solution. The dilemma centers around establishing the most meaningful appraisal and understanding of man. This is a problem as old as human history and it is far from resolved.

The burden of dealing with it falls inescapably on the courts. What, no doubt, they will continue to search for will be solutions that reconcile responsibility with justice. Sometimes this may be based upon scientific

---

[14] "Moral Aspects of the Criminal Law," 49 *Yale Law Journal* 987 (1940).

evidence offered by an expert, but at other times it will probably be a subjective selection of the right treatment made by the judge. The basic assumption of individual responsibility over which the courts stand guard is also a basic premise of political democracy. The courts in a democratic system cannot avoid seeking solutions to the dilemmas that this assumption occasions.

Sources of American Legal Principles

If the essence of legal order is summed up in the attributes of justice and predictability, this is also the source of the major problem of law. Particular standards of justice tend to develop into rules or principles of law. In Justice Cardozo's definition, a rule of law is "a principle or rule of conduct so established as to justify a prediction with reasonable certainty that it will be enforced by the courts if its authority is challenged. . . ." Thus, law is not simply a series of particular commands. Every legal system is a body of principles, applicable to a range of discrete social situations, and slowly evolved by the decision of concrete cases. Since the variety of specific human acts and human relationships is almost limitless, only a body of legal principles applicable to a wide range of situations can ensure predictability. Yet, in the nature of the case the general principle cannot contain and include all possible specific cases. Particularly, it cannot encompass new acts and relations that develop from changes in one part of society or another. The problem, for every legal system, is how to reconcile the need for stability of legal principles, which predictability requires, with the need for change and flexibility, which the quest for justice requires in a changing society.

In the United States, there are generally four sources of legal principles: constitutional law, statutory law, common law, and equity. The first two stem from deliberative bodies, which announce new legal principles; the latter two represent judge-made law. Of course, both constitutional principles and legislative enactments have to be interpreted when they are applied to particular cases. Thus, the development of legal principles derived from the Constitution or statutes still allows considerable leeway for the making of law by the courts, particularly if judicial supremacy gives them final authority.

Moreover, even in the areas of common law and equity, where principles of law are developed by judges rather than by legislatures, the principles themselves are hardened into precedent, which limits not only the discretion of judges but also the flexibility of the legal system itself. Thus, judges make law in any legal system, but in none do they make it out of whole cloth. For this reason, every legal system, by virtue of its commitment to predictability, has built-in tendencies to *rigor mortis* that the urge to justice must find ways of overcoming. This problem is illustrated in the common law itself.

COMMON LAW AND EQUITY

The common law developed in England after the Norman Conquest. A system of royal commissioners, empowered by the king to decide cases throughout the realm, was under the obligation to develop rules of law. Originally, all regular matters were handled in the traditional system of local courts that predated the Norman Conquest. Where the local courts proved inadequate—for example, when a controversy arose between litigants from different areas—a petition could be made to the king for intervention. In such extraordinary matters the king might, in the exercise of royal prerogative, hear the case personally or through a Royal Deputy. The decisions of the royal commissioners evolved into the common law. This was a reaction to the necessity of providing relief against the rigors of an established legal system under changed circumstances. In societies where the art of legislation had not matured, this became the function of the ultimate interpreter of law—the king—in the exercise of his "prerogative of grace." The king's grace was gradually evolved into a body of law presided over by judges. Common law, because of its ability to accommodate to social changes, moved far beyond the adjustment of legal relations in feudal society and became the basis of modern Anglo-American law.

By the fourteenth century, the common law had begun to be crystallized into fairly settled rules and principles. It had grown to satisfy the requirement of predictability, but its very development made it a cumbersome way of satisfying the demands of justice in new conditions. The response to the rigors of common law precedent paralleled the development of common law itself. The solution was revived appeals to the king's grace. The king began to formalize the new procedures by referring the numerous petitions addressed to him to his chancellor. From this developed the High Court of Chancery, whose decisions came to be known as equity.

Cases in equity were not subject to ordinary common law or statutory provisions. In its broadest sense, equity implies a natural form of justice based upon right reason. It developed out of appeals to the king's own person to do justice in cases where neither common law nor statutory remedies were available. The type of concern to which equity extended is illustrated by the injunction. The injunction is the strong arm of equity. It is a court order that generally prohibits a person or persons from doing something the court deems unjust or inequitable to some other person or party. Injunctions can be temporary, permanent, or for a specified period of time. They can prevent things from happening that are planned for the future. Cases at law, on the other hand, must wait until the event has occurred before there is a case.[15]

But again, the quest for new principles of justice hardened into precedents that provided predictability. By the latter half of the sixteenth century, the principles upon which cases were decided in the Chancery had tended to become settled and, hence, precedents for the guidance of subsequent chancellors. Equity, however, continued to be characterized by greater opportunity for judicial experimentation and innovation than common law. But with the development of democracy legislation became the major source and method in the quest for principles of justice.

With the development of statutory law, the courts necessarily became involved in the interpretation of statutes. But in his approach to this problem, the judge who operates in the common law tradition will bring to his task the judicial freedom and flexibility of that tradition. Thus we get remarkably different interpretations of laws passed by legislative bodies given by different judges. For example, we find many judges making interpretations of legislative intent that are difficult for other judges, lawyers, and legislators themselves to accept.

STATUTORY LAW

The importance of common law in the United States is increasingly overshadowed by statutory law. Statutory law goes beyond the common law and supersedes it if conflict arises. It takes much of the discretion out of the judges' hands by prescribing definitions of crimes or civil situations and the penalties or rights of contestants under the statutory provisions.

---

[15] Other remedies in equity include nuisance abatement, alimony awards, divorce decrees, mortgage foreclosures, wage garnishment, and bankruptcy receiverships. A few states still have courts of equity, and others provide for equity procedures in their regular courts. In most states, however, the distinction between the common law and equity is disappearing. Also, much of both common law and equity is being put into statutory law.

CRIMINAL AND CIVIL LAW

In all the codified or written law jurisdictions in the United States (federal, state, local), law is divided into the two broad classifications of criminal and civil. Criminal law defines offenses against the public; civil law governs the relations between individuals. Since common law was never taken over by the national government, all federal crimes are statutory crimes, although federal cases involving citizens of different states are tried under the common law of the state wherein the trial is held. Most state crimes have been crimes at common law (for example, assault, battery, kidnaping, rape, homicide, burglary, arson, larceny, forgery), but for the most part they have been embodied in and defined by statute. Except for exclusively federal matters, civil law belongs almost entirely to the states. Although now embodied in statutes for the most part, some of the civil law of the states had common law origins (for example, real property, personal property, contracts, sales, torts, domestic relations, inheritances, wills). Other areas of civil law owe their origins directly to statutes (for example, corporations, bankruptcy, mining, irrigation, taxation, administrative law).

Criminal law is concerned with wrongs against society, and prosecution is by the political jurisdiction against the individual; the United States versus John Doe, California versus Mary Roe, or the City of Syracuse versus John Doe, Jr. Crimes are classified according to their seriousness, the two most common classifications being felonies and misdemeanors. Felonies are major crimes, such as murder, armed robbery, and rape. Felonies are in turn often classified in degrees depending on the intent, premeditation, or other standards prescribed by the legislature. Misdemeanors are minor crimes, which have limited penalties, seldom involving fines above one thousand dollars or more than six months to a year in jail. Traffic tickets, building code violations, petit theft, vagrancy, and other minor infractions of the law are usually misdemeanors. Local government ordinances define misdemeanors only.

The common law holds there is no crime without both an act and an intent to do wrong or to act in a criminal manner. Statutes may make acts crimes without intent, such as statutory rape, which applies to seduction of girls under a certain age although no criminal intent was evident; or they may make intent punishable without an act, such as a conspiracy to advocate the overthrow of the government by force or violence although no act of force or violence occurred.

Criminal trials are exacting in their demands for proof of guilt. The individual on trial must be appropriately brought before the bar. This is done by grand jury indictment in federal cases. A suspect is presumed innocent until proven guilty beyond any reasonable doubt, and if he elects to have a jury, their decision must be unanimous. If convicted, the criminal faces a variety of penalties ranging from death to a lecture by the judge.

One problem with justice in a federal system is that penalties for crimes vary so greatly from state to state. Some states allow the death penalty for the more serious crimes while others do not. At the same time, statutory limits on the penalties for specific crimes vary widely from state to state. In some instances, such as kidnaping and interstate traffic in women for purposes of prostitution, the crime has been made a federal offense in order to ensure adequate punishment and to indicate national disapproval of such crimes.

Civil law governs relations between individuals and between individuals and the public not involving public offenses. Civil law generally revolves around contracts, torts, civil rights, and other such matters. Civil law has been defined as that law which is not criminal and, while this may be similar to saying chemistry is what is not physics, it reflects the difficulty of precise definition.

In civil actions, proof is by a preponderance of evidence rather than beyond any reasonable doubt, as in criminal law. Juries may or may not be used, depending upon the wishes of the contestants and the constitutional provisions of the states. If juries are used, they can often be less than twelve members, and their decision may require only a majority of the jurymen rather than unanimity.

There are instances in which some acts are subject to both civil and criminal action. Many criminal acts are subject to recovery by tort action. For example, under the Sherman Anti-trust Act, a firm may be convicted of the crime of conspiring to "restrain trade"; at the same time, an injured competitor may recover in a civil suit as much as treble the damage it has suffered.

The Role of the Courts in American Government

The separation of powers in the United States gives the judiciary a place of unusual importance and influence. Its unique power stems from its role as final arbiter of the federal and state constitutions. Since

Chief Justice Marshall's opinion established the precedent of judicial review of legislation, American constitutionalism has endowed the courts with the power to serve as guardians of the principles of the Constitution and its amendments.

STATUTORY AND CONSTITUTIONAL INTERPRETATION

The institution of judicial review has been termed *judicial supremacy* since the decisions of the court on constitutional matters are binding on the other branches of government. This doctrine is a unique American contribution to political institutions. To understand its significance, it is necessary to distinguish clearly between statutory interpretation and constitutional interpretation. In a legal system that has an independent judiciary, the courts interpret the statutes they are called upon to apply in the cases that come before them. Did Congress in enacting the Taft-Hartley Act mean to exclude states from legislating in the same area? The courts have said Yes, and have invalidated restrictive state legislation on that ground. But when the court is interpreting a statute, the way is completely open for the legislative body to overrule the court's interpretation through amending the statute to make its intention clear. Thus, in the case of labor legislation, bills were introduced into Congress to amend the Taft-Hartley Act to permit state right-to-work laws to supersede federal law. A partial victory for this point of view was achieved in the Landrum-Griffin labor bill, in the 1959 session, which permitted state labor relations agencies to apply state law to cases that the National Labor Relations Board had declined to hear. But the point is that there is nothing in the court's decision interpreting the statute to prohibit the Congress from going further.

Similarly, a court may decide that a particular law requires a governmental agency to do something that the agency has failed to do. Thus, the Supreme Court held that the Natural Gas Act *requires* the Federal Power Commission to regulate the interstate rates of natural gas. One result of the Court's decision was a political attempt to amend the Act to exempt the rates from federal regulation. In this case, the effort was successful in Congress, although the bill was vetoed by President Eisenhower on grounds that the natural-gas lobby had used undue pressure in its efforts to get the bill passed.

In these cases, the Supreme Court's decision was based on statutory interpretation. The Court had decided only what Congress had intended when it wrote the statute in question. After such cases are decided,

Congress has complete authority to redefine its intent if it disagrees with the Court's interpretation. But when the Court considers the constitutionality of congressional acts its decision is binding on the Congress. The recourse is not amending the law but amending the Constitution or, perhaps, waiting long enough for the judges to change their minds.

THE COURTS AS POLITICAL INSTITUTIONS

There is no question that in the United States the courts, either by interpreting constitutions and statutes or by acting under the common law, have a major influence on our destiny. They may order, in eloquent ambiguity, our reluctant Southland to integrate its schools "with all deliberate speed"; demand that an economic empire break up its holdings because it has competed so well it is becoming a monopoly; tell a religious group its children will have to salute the flag but, upon pondering the matter later, decide they do not have to after all; send people to their deaths; tell children with which parent they must live; keep us from reading books that might corrupt our morals; and tell the President of the United States that he and his cabinet are without power to take over the steel industry.

It is obvious that many of these decisions are *political* in the sense that they lay down or modify the course of public policy and arbitrate between conflicting groups and values in society. The political character of the courts' role is further revealed in the history of judicial review of legislation.

The Constitution (Art. I, sec. 10), for example, is explicit in stating that "no state shall . . . pass any . . . law impairing the obligation of contracts." This is not vague language, and for a long time the Court interpreted it almost literally. In a series of four decisions,[16] Chief Justice Marshall and the Court made the contract clause a powerful instrument for the protection of property rights.

After the Civil War, justices unfavorably disposed to social legislation relied upon the contract clause to protect the right of employers to hire labor as cheaply and for as many hours as possible. At the same time, efforts to organize labor were frustrated by court-supported "yellow-dog" contracts forbidding employees to join unions and by court decisions that unions were monopolies that violated the liberties protected by the

[16] *Fletcher* v. *Peck*, 6 Cranch 87 (1810); *New Jersey* v. *Wilson*, 7 Cranch 164 (1812); *Dartmouth College* v. *Woodward*, 4 Wheaton 518 (1819); and *Sturges* v. *Crowninshield*, 4 Wheaton 122 (1819).

Fifth and Fourteenth Amendments. Such judgments by his colleagues on the Supreme Court led to one of Justice Holmes's sharpest dissents. In *Lochner* v. *New York*, a case invalidating a New York statute limiting to sixty hours the work week of bakers and confectioners, Holmes stated:

> This case is decided upon an economic theory which a large part of the country does not entertain. If it were a question whether I agreed with that theory, I should desire to study it further and long before making up my mind. But I do not conceive that to be my duty, because I strongly believe that my agreement or disagreement has nothing to do with the right of the majority to embody their opinions in law. . . . The Fourteenth Amendment does not enact Mr. Herbert Spencer's Social Statics. . . . Some of these laws [limiting hours of work, etc.] embody convictions or prejudices which judges are likely to share. Some may not. But a constitution is not intended to embody a particular economic theory, whether of paternalism and the organic relation of the citizen to the state or of *laissez-faire*.[17]

As the economy expanded and as efforts to deal with the problems of industrialism began to collide with private property rights, the contract clause lost most of its power. In 1934, the contract clause became almost an historical anachronism when, in *Home Building and Loan Assn.* v. *Blaisdell*,[18] Chief Justice Hughes's opinion in a five-four decision upheld a Minnesota statute preventing foreclosures on property during the Depression. After this decision, the contract clause as a protection of property rights against legislation was seldom used, demonstrating, as Pritchett puts it, "the present-day superfluity of the clause."[19]

The contract clause is still in the Constitution, but circumstances have changed. So have the viewpoints of the justices on the Court, particularly on the relationship of private contracts to the public interest. The Court changes its mind, at times reversing itself, not particularly because the language of the Constitution is vague, but because circumstances and the political demands of society change. Perhaps even more important, justices with different systems of values and perspectives become members of the Court.

Sometimes, the Court's actions have been in accord with popularly held values; at other times its judgments have aroused heated political

---

[17] 198 U.S. 45 (1905).
[18] 290 U.S. 398 (1934).
[19] C. Herman Pritchett. *The American Constitution* (New York: McGraw-Hill, 1959), p. 658.

controversy. When the latter does occur, the Court is catapulted into political conflict over its role in a democratic society. Sometimes, these attacks involve the Court as an institution; at other times, attacks are aimed at particular justices; and sometimes, both the Court and the justices are criticized.

JUDICIAL ACTIVISM OR JUDICIAL SELF-RESTRAINT?

The Court, itself, is not always certain whether it should occupy the center of the stage or retreat toward the wings. There have been some sharp divisions among the justices over the relative merits of an active or restrained use of judicial authority. This is, of course, essentially a political argument involving the whole theory and structure of American government. Activists, such as Justice Black, would use the judicial power to work toward the elimination of social and political inequities and to ensure civil liberties to all citizens of the United States. Such justices would not hesitate to curtail the activities of overly zealous legislative committees when they infringe upon individual rights and liberties, nor would they hesitate to tell a president when he has transcended his constitutional authority.

Those advocating judicial self-restraint, such as former Justice Frankfurter, would argue that the Court has no business imposing its views on the other branches of government or the states unless there is a patent and flagrant violation of the Constitution. The self-restraint philosophy seems, however, to be waning at present. One observer says:

> The Frankfurter influence waned as first Warren, then William Brennan (both Eisenhower appointees) regularly joined those two old New Deal warhorses, Hugo Black and William O. Douglas, in liberal dissent. The occasional addition to this quartet of Potter Stewart (again Eisenhower's choice) now and then turned potential dissent into majority doctrine. Frankfurter could carry only faithful John Harlan with him in his bitter judicial swansong protesting the Court's first entry into the "political thicket" of reapportionment in 1962.[20]

Rodell goes on to say that the activist libertarian view seems well established now even though it is not popular:

> For the first time in the Court's 175-year history, therefore, a consistent—if bare—majority of the justices, scorning self-restraint where individual liberties are at issue, are determined to enforce the

[20] Fred Rodell, "The Warren Court Stands Its Ground," *New York Times Magazine*, September 27, 1964, p. 120.

Bill of Rights (plus the 14th Amendment) against any Government action, state or Federal, that disregards or infringes its guarantees. From the protection of equal voting rights to the protection even of obscene literature from censorship, it is this determination which has brought down on the Court's head the current storm of protest.[21]

Rodell's conclusion that judicial activism is well established was confirmed in striking fashion in a recent decision of the Supreme Court declaring unconstitutional a Connecticut law prohibiting the use of contraceptives by anyone in the state.[22] This law was enacted in 1879, and its enforcement has been both difficult and infrequent. Justice Douglas, for the majority, searched far and wide for a constitutional issue and finally concluded that the Connecticut law violated the "penumbra" of the First Amendment. He also held that the spirit of the Third, Fourth, Fifth, Ninth, and Fourteenth Amendments made the law constitutionally intolerable.

Given the repressive and repugnant character of the Connecticut statute, liberal justices would inevitably be tempted to abolish it. But even for the judicial activists, the Court's right to function as a superlegislature must have constitutional bounds. Justice Douglas and the majority were powerfully aware of this fact, and the opinion distinguished "economic problems, business affairs or social conditions," which legislatures may regulate, from the "intimate relation of husband and wife and their physician's role in one aspect of that relationship."

Evidently the majority of the Court was able to find at least a spiritual civil liberty in the marital relationship, even though it had to be extracted from the spirit of six separate constitutional amendments. The spiritual essence of these amendments will be adequate only for the most thoroughgoing judicial activist.

The split on the Court was in itself remarkable. Justice Harlan, an eloquent advocate of strict constitutionalism, who argued vigorously for self-restraint in the reapportionment cases, voted with the majority. On the other hand, the consistent activist on civil rights and liberties, Justice Black, dissented sharply. He said:

If any broad unlimited power to hold laws unconstitutional because they offend what this court conceives to be "the collective conscience of our people" is vested in this court by the Ninth Amendment, the Fourteenth Amendment, or any other provision of the Constitution,

[21] Ibid.
[22] Griswold v. Connecticut, 381 U.S. 479 (1965).

it was not given by the Framers (of the Constitution) but rather has been bestowed on the Court by the Court.

Justice Stewart, an avowed advocate of planned parenthood, agreed with Black's dissent, and although he felt Connecticut had "an uncommonly silly law," he could not agree to strike it down as unconstitutional on the personal convictions of justices who might "think this law is unwise or even asinine."

The Court divided differently on this case than it had on reapportionment, and a different, and perhaps sharper, focus was put on the issue of judicial activism. Columnist James Reston put it well when he said:

> . . . in deciding that State legislatures had no right to be silly, a rule that would put most of them out of business, the majority inadvertently provided some substance to the main charge that is often leveled against the court: that it occasionally wanders beyond its proper judicial function and acts as a "super-legislature" in striking down laws that violate the sensitivities of the members of the court rather than any specific constitutional provision. . . .
>
> The lawyers will be arguing about this one for a long time. Not since Justice Oliver Wendell Holmes upheld the right of sterilization on the ground that two generations of idiots are enough has there been such a combination of legal controversy and sex.[23]

It is true that since 1937, court decisions have reflected a self-imposed restraint on declaring legislation outside the field of civil liberties and civil rights unconstitutional. Within those areas, however, and in their exercise of the function of statutory interpretation, the courts remain near the center of the political stage. It is always possible, of course, for the Court either to cast off its self-restrain and become even more active or to withdraw itself from political controversy. Whatever it does will depend upon the Justices' conception of the role of the Court in American government.

The Court Structure in the United States

It is through the American judicial system that law gains its meaning and interpretation. The court system is structured to provide for extensive hearings and for appeal and review of legal decisions. Indeed, the very structure of our parallel system of courts in the federal and state

[23] *San Francisco Chronicle*, June 9, 1965, p. 8.

governments is probably one of the most extensive areas for judicial interpretation ever devised.

The structure of courts in the federal judiciary as well as in individual states is a fairly neat hierarchical arrangement. It proceeds from trial courts or courts of original jurisdiction on up to appellate courts and culminates in a Supreme Court that is the capstone of justice. The three-layer system is the most popular, although some more sparsely populated states, such as New Mexico, have only two layers of courts with appeals going from the trial court directly to the supreme court. States also have a variety of minor courts, or courts of limited jurisdiction, such as justices of the peace, juvenile courts, small-claims courts, traffic courts, and family courts.

In the three-level court structure used in the federal system, the trial court or court of original jurisdiction is the federal district court, of which there are over one hundred, some with more than one judge or court, scattered throughout the country and its territories. Above the federal district court are the circuit courts of appeals. There are eleven circuits with the states being grouped into ten of these. The District of Columbia, where federal business is centered, is an eleventh circuit. On top of the pyramid is the United States Supreme Court.

Federal district courts usually operate with only one judge presiding, although some types of cases require three judges. The circuit courts have three judges, and the Supreme Court has nine, so as one proceeds up the ladder of justice he finds that more heads will ponder his fate.

In addition to the three-level hierarchy of courts in the federal system, there are special courts created to hear cases involving military courts-martial, customs, patents, and claims against the United States. All the federal courts, except the Supreme Court, are creatures of Congress, since Article III, section 1, of the Constitution states: "The judicial power of the United States shall be vested in a Supreme Court, and in such inferior courts as Congress shall from time to time ordain and establish."

The authors of the Constitution anticipated such an establishment of courts, and they put in some safeguards on the selection, retention, and compensation of the judges of future inferior courts: "The judges, both of the supreme and inferior courts, shall hold their offices during good behavior and shall, at stated times, receive for their services, a compensation, which shall not be diminished during their continuance in office."

THE SELECTION OF JUDGES

Judges for all federal courts are appointed by the President with the consent of the Senate. Senatorial courtesy[24] is often extended to the senator from the state in which district court appointments are to be made.

The quality of justice in any legal system is very largely dependent upon the quality of appointees to the bench. The appointing power of the President, the tradition of senatorial courtesy, and the selection of judges are all political processes. Judges are appointed basically on the premise that there will be some political mileage gained from their selection. About the best the people can hope for is that their President will be sold on the idea that good justice is good politics. Presidents are usually able to find acceptable appointees from the ranks of their own party, for it would be an indication of political weakness to rely upon the opposite political party for judicial talent.

Like all political appointments, judges must generally satisfy political considerations first and be qualified candidates second. As a result, many eminent jurists have never received the highest reward of their profession, a Supreme Court appointment. If an appointment is made from the ranks of the opposition, it is generally quite evident that this is to take care of some political consideration of pressing importance, or perhaps to reward a good friend from past associations.

Appointments to federal district court judgeships are usually made on the advice of some sort of party organization and after consultation with the senators from the state involved, particularly the ones from the President's own political party if there are such. Over 90 per cent of such vacancies have been filled from the ranks of the President's party during the past seventy years.[25] The Department of Justice, the FBI, and the American Bar Association's Committee on the Federal Judiciary all scrutinize the candidate to see that he is loyal and qualified after the party has determined his political worth. Circuit court appointments follow the same process although political party organizations play a lesser role. Many circuit court appointments are filled by promotion from district courts.

The appointees to the Supreme Court are the most important to the

[24] A practice wherein senators will not vote for nominees who are unacceptable to the senator of a nominee's home state.
[25] Pritchett, op. cit., p. 114.

President and his party. Presidents have all sorts of suggestions offered but generally attempt to place people on the Supreme Court who will bring to the bench a philosophy of government and a value system similar to their own. Very often, Supreme Court justices are selected on the basis of careers outside the judiciary, such as Chief Justice Earl Warren, who distinguished himself as Attorney General and Governor of California. Many former United States Attorneys General—Tom Clark, James C. McReynolds, and Harlan F. Stone are examples—have been elevated to a Supreme Court seat. Several former senators and representatives have found places on the bench; so have cabinet members and others who have brought attention to themselves and their beliefs.

There have been instances when Supreme Court justices have failed to fulfill the expectations of those appointing them. When President Theodore Roosevelt appointed Holmes to the Supreme Court, he expected Holmes to help him "bust" some trusts. There was a good deal of social intercourse and a mutual affection between the two men, based on Roosevelt's fascination with Holmes's erudition and wit and Holmes's admiration of Roosevelt's energy, courage, and candor. But after the Northern Securities case,[26] in which Holmes dissented from the Court's decision upholding the enforcement of the Sherman Anti-trust Act and attacked the whole idea of trust-busting, Roosevelt was furious with his appointee, and the friendship between the two men virtually ended.

A similar instance was the appointment of Justice McReynolds by President Wilson in 1914. McReynolds, as assistant attorney general in charge of antitrust prosecutions under Theodore Roosevelt, and later as Attorney General under Wilson, had shown himself to be an energetic and able lawyer who successfully prosecuted many cases and gained a reputation as a fearless trustbuster. On the Supreme Court, however, he became a cantankerous and ardent champion of *laissez faire* and rugged individualism. He grumbled at his colleagues to the point where Chief Justice Taft described him as "a continual grouch" who "seemed to delight in making others uncomfortable."[27]

In spite of the caution exercised by Presidents in their appointments to the judiciary, candidates may behave differently than expected or hoped for. But the probability that the nominee will act in a predictable fashion sometimes causes the Senate to delay or deny confirmation.

[26] 193 U.S. 197 (1904).
[27] Rocco J. Tresolini, *American Constitutional Law* (New York: Macmillan, 1959), p. 649.

This happened in the case of John J. Parker in 1930, who was held to be antilabor and anti-Negro. The Senate thoroughly aired the political, social, economic, and other views of the candidate before they denied his appointment. Justice Brandeis was only able to gain confirmation by a strict party vote, and Charles E. Hughes was opposed as being overly friendly to the business community when he was nominated and eventually appointed to the Court for the second time in 1931. Earl Warren did not escape some scrutiny before confirmation, and, oddly enough, most of it came from his own party.

Many bar associations are continuously suggesting that prior judicial experience would be advantageous, and bills have been introduced into Congress requiring such experience. This argument, however, rests mainly on a theory of constitutional jurisprudence that gives experience and knowledge of procedure a high value. It loses its force if the judges' role is regarded as more broadly political than narrowly legal and mechanical. Moreover, some of our greatest Supreme Court justices attest to the fact that their backgrounds, which did not include judicial experience, have brought much to American justice. As Herman Pritchett points out,[28] if previous judicial experience had been required in the past, the nation would have been denied Marshall, Storey, Taney, Miller, Bradley, Hughes (first appointment), Brandeis, Stone, Frankfurter, Jackson, and Warren.

Methods of selecting judges for state courts vary widely. Many states retain the electoral process, although some have made judicial elections nonpartisan. Others use appointment by the governor for some or all of the courts. Still others, like California, use a combination of election and appointment for the appellate courts wherein the governor nominates from a screened list, and the people confirm his choice by election. If they do not confirm the governor's appointment, he then appoints some other candidate from the screened list.

The question of how to select a judge is a difficult one. If we rely on appointment, a political hack may get on the bench. But if we rely on election, we may get fooled by eloquent oratorical spellbinders who are incompetent. How does an elector judge a judge? By what standards does he measure the abilities of candidates to weigh precedent against justice? There is no panacea. It is a difficult problem, which many states are considering carefully. Various plans have emerged, and some of them, like California's, are designed to satisfy the demands for the

28 Pritchett, *op. cit.*, p. 115.

popular selection of judges while, at the same time, admitting that a governor may be able to select better candidates than would result from elections.

JURISDICTION OF THE COURTS

In the federal system of government in the United States, there are two court systems to which each citizen is subject. Whether the federal or state courts have jurisdiction depends upon the nature of the case. The federal courts are used for cases arising under the jurisdiction stated in Article III, section 2, of the Constitution as limited by the Eleventh Amendment. This jurisdiction extends to cases arising out of the nature of the controversy and the nature of the parties. Examples of cases arising from the controversy would be those coming under the Constitution, statutes and treaties of the United States, and all cases dealing with admiralty and maritime law. Treason, for example, is a crime defined in the Constitution. The power of setting the penalties is delegated to Congress except that "no attainder of treason shall work corruption of blood, or forfeiture except during the life of the person attainted."

Cases arising out of the nature of the parties include those affecting ambassadors and other diplomats; contests between states, which go directly to the Supreme Court; and controversies to which the United States is a party.

At the trial level state courts are not inferior in any sense to federal courts, but their jurisdiction differs because they have a different legal system to adjudicate. State courts, in short, hear cases arising out of state constitutions and statutes and the common law of their state. (In hearing these cases, of course, state courts apply and interpret the federal Constitution and federal laws.) Federal courts hear cases arising out of the federal Constitution and federal statutes. Courts of unlimited jurisdiction in the states hear cases arising from common law, suits in equity, criminal prosecutions, civil contests, and probate matters. Minor state courts hear only those cases falling within their limited jurisdiction, such as misdemeanors, family matters, traffic violations, and small claims, which usually involve controversies of not more than two or three hundred dollars.

The use of the appellate courts is similar in both federal and state systems. Cases that are appealed to higher courts usually go up on what is called a writ of *certiorari*, which is an order of a higher court to review the decision of a lower court. In such instances, the case is reviewed on matters of law rather than fact, although the question of what is law and what is fact is one that often causes a good deal of legal bickering. The appellate court upon review has a good deal of discretion over the disposition of the case. It can uphold or reverse the lower court's decision, modify the sentence, or order a new trial. Generally, review by a higher court is at the discretion of the higher court, although in several states there is an automatic review by higher courts over some cases. The Supreme Court of California, for example, is required to review all cases where the death penalty has been given. The effect of a refusal by a higher court to grant a review of a lower-court decision is to sustain the judgment below. This is often done, and it serves the purpose of upholding the lower court while avoiding the necessity of saying why.

The hierarchy of courts is a guarantee of thorough review to ensure the criminally accused or contestants in a civil matter not only their "day in court" but their "days in court." They can travel up either the federal or state pyramid, depending on the jurisdiction over their case, and can move from the state supreme court to the federal Supreme Court, if the latter thinks there is a federal issue warranting a grant of *certiorari*. They can appeal the questions whether the procedures in their trials conformed to the requirements of due process and whether the law under which they were convicted is constitutional.

Within this structure and procedure, the courts define and play their political role in society. In this realm, the courts have several options, and, to a considerable extent, they themselves define what their political role will be. In the next chapter, some of these options are described and their political consequences analyzed.

Chapter Sixteen

THE COURTS
IN AMERICAN POLITICS

. . . in which the political roles of the courts in the United States
are subjected to examination in the light of democratic theory.

Armed with the power of judicial review, the Supreme Court in recent
years has played two particular roles, which have raised the fundamental
question of the power of the courts in a democratic society. The Court,
acting as oracle and as guardian of due process, has been put at the center
of political controversy.

The role of **The Supreme Court as Oracle** is rooted in its constitutional
position: its interpretation of the Constitution as higher law will inevitably
define the direction and the limits of public policy.
    The Oracular Role, however, is a flexible one: Sometimes it may be
avoided by judicial self-restraint; when it is exercised it may be, for
example, in ideological defense of *laissez faire* or in philosophical
defense of equality or majority rule. This flexibility is illustrated by the
Court's
    Oracular Judgment that the constitutional guarantee of equal protection
is incompatible with separate facilities for the races. **The Constitutional
and Political Background of Segregation** after Reconstruction reveals
a long struggle in which the courts, the Congress, and the executive
branch failed almost completely to give effect to the Fourteenth
Amendment. Finally, it was the Court that broke dramatically with
precedent to initiate an era of **Judicial Enforcement of Equality,** the
political character of which was clearly revealed in its political repercussions. While the Court was vigorously attacked, its decisions exerted
pressures on Congress and the President, who responded with significant
legislation and executive orders to protect and extend civil rights. The
Court as oracle had initiated a political revolution and forced it on the
political agencies of government, which had been bogged down at dead
center and immobilized by the slow processes of broker rule. The question is posed whether an "undemocratic," oracular Court has become

the only agency of government capable of responding to issues in moral terms.

The *Court* also functions as *Guarantor of Due Process,* a role in which it stands guard over the rights that protect citizens as subjects against arbitrariness in the enforcement of the laws. In the exercise of this role the courts have reviewed both

National and *Local Law Enforcement* practices and have often held that they contravene the provisions of the Bill of Rights and the Fourteenth Amendment. In recent years the Court, under the due-process clause of the Fourteenth Amendment, has restricted the methods and techniques of state and local police agencies by invoking the provisions of the Bill of Rights with respect to *Cruel and Unusual Punishment, Unreasonable Searches and Seizures,* the *Right to Counsel, Freedom from Self-incrimination,* and the *Right to Confront Adverse Witnesses.* In all of these cases the Court generally found itself in the position of defending the rights of low-status or unpopular individuals or of persons implicated in sordid situations. Its decisions made law enforcement more difficult. As a result, the Court was charged with responsibility for increases in crime and violence on the streets; these attacks raise the question whether due process can be reconciled with law and order.

The Court has also applied the test of *Due Process* to *Legislative Investigations.* With respect to congressional and other legislative investigations, the Court has been more restrained in protecting the rights of individuals because of its deference to the principle of separation of powers.

The variety of roles open to the Court permits it to play a large, though not unlimited, part in American politics. When it ventures into the political arena, it raises the question of the relationship between *Judicial Power and Majority Rule.* Whether the Court is the wisest—or the safest—repository of liberty has not been finally settled. But the Court's ultimate role in a democracy will depend on whether citizens respond to its rulings by making the issues they raise part of the public dialogue.

As citizens and realists we may rejoice in "good" Supreme Court decisions and denounce "bad" ones, but at the same time we should in our analytical capacities be aware of the fact that . . . [the Court] is a Platonic graft on the democratic process—a group of wise men insulated from the people . . . acting as institutional chaperones to insure that the sovereign populace and its elected representatives do not act unwisely.

JOHN P. ROCHE

Chapter Sixteen

THE COURTS
IN AMERICAN POLITICS

THE JUDICIARY occupies a special place in the triumvirate of powers in the United States. We have seen in previous chapters that the leaders in the legislative and executive branches of government are plagued with the necessity to yield to the importunities of group pressures and prejudice even though they may be keenly aware of some of the shortcomings of such adjustments. Brokerage has become increasingly the legislative way of life and shows signs of dominating the executive branch.

495

THE CONSENT OF THE GOVERNED

In recent years the judiciary has come to stand virtually alone as the tribunal that unequivocally articulates a democratic philosophy. This is not to say that all judges are philosopher-kings. It is to say, however, that the judicial process, as the last chapter should have made clear, allows judges who are so inclined to state their opinions and judgments in philosophical or ideological terms. It is true that judges can and often do act as brokers among contestants before them, but the point is that judges have enough discretion—ironically, this means enough independence from the political process—to make decisions based on a philosophical or ideological position that clearly transcends the operational model of brokerage politics. They can, in short, defend the proposition that "whatever is, is right," or they can steer the nation in new directions. They can leave the question of the meaning of democracy to the other branches of government, or they can find in the Constitution a model of democracy to be used as a criterion for reviewing the conduct of the other two branches of the federal government or of the states.

The judiciary often outrages many powerful segments of society in rendering its judgments. In deciding legal contests, the courts often disrupt the orderly arrangements of the *status quo* and put philosophical and ideological questions squarely before the public. Judges thus become philosophers, and there is little question that such men as John Marshall, Oliver Wendell Holmes, Benjamin Cardozo, John Marshall Harlan, Charles Evans Hughes, Hugo Black, Felix Frankfurter, and William O. Douglas have not only served their nation well as Supreme Court justices, but have enriched our cultural, philosophical, and ideological heritage as well. The men who occupy the bench are potential sources of ideas and attitudes important to a meaningful democratic dialogue.

The political role of the judiciary lends itself to many interpretations. At any given time it is shaped by the attitudes of judges, by the citizens' expectations of and reactions to judicial decisions, by the effect of judicial pronouncements on other agencies of government, and by the internal conflict within the judiciary regarding its place in the political arena. Activist judges would use the judicial power for all it is worth to resolve political questions; the self-restraint advocated by others would give maximum latitude to the other branches of government and defer to their political decisions. The subjective viewpoint of some judges leads them to bend laws and constitutions to their will; the objective approach to the law would require judges to adhere rigorously to its literal interpretation. When all of these internal and external political forces interact upon and within the judicial system, it becomes a much more controversial and politically involved institution than it does in most other countries.

Historically, the Supreme Court has played many political roles which have given meaning to the legal standards, helped to shape the moral tone, and influenced the basic political philosophy of the country. At one time or another, the judiciary has played the role of umpire between contesting factions locked in economic and social combat. Umpiring is a thankless job, for losers seldom spare the umpire their wrath even though they angrily proceed with the game. At other times, and in the view of other judges, umpiring is not enough. If the game itself is threatened by the intransigence of some of the players, or if harmony is viewed as its object, the courts may decide to act as brokers among the factions and arrange a settlement that will calm the storm but not call anyone out.

We are concerned here, however, with two roles assumed by the Court in recent years which have brought it squarely into the center of political controversy and which raise most directly the question of the role of the courts in a democratic system. In the first of these roles the Court has served the lofty function of oracle, pronouncing basic principles of public policy and proclaiming the meaning and direction of public morality. In the second, the Court has served as guardian of due process of law when other agencies of government fail to live up to appropriate standards or use law-enforcement methods that, as Justice Frankfurter once put it, "shock the conscience" and smack of the "rack and the screw."[1]

These are political roles in which the Court embodies political decisions in its legal judgments. Judicial politics differs from legislative or executive politics, but it has had no less an impact on the American system. Because the courts are not democratically elected, their exercise of political power raises fundamental problems for democratic theory. These problems have been complicated in recent years as the courts, assuming the roles of oracle and guardian of due process, have made political decisions in defense of fundamental democratic values.

[1] *Rochin* v. *California*, 342 U.S. 165 (1952)

The Supreme Court as Oracle

The capstone of justice in the United States is the Supreme Court. Other courts must concern themselves with constitutional issues, but it is the Supreme Court that has the final and authoritative power to interpret and pronounce the meaning of the Constitution. They must declare not only what it legally requires but what it morally implies. This function of extracting moral implications places the justices in the role of the Court is rooted in its constitutional position. The American approached differently by various justices. Some shy away from their oracular function and prefer to concentrate on legalities or, at least, to shroud their moral judgments in legalistic technicalities. Others look to the Constitution as much more than a legal document and emphasize the view that it is a set of basic moral principles by which men conduct their political lives.

Whatever the perspectives of different justices, however, the oracular role of the Court is rooted in its constitutional position. The American judiciary has been charged with the responsibility of saying what the Constitution means in a given set of circumstances. It then becomes the authoritative interpreter of a higher law than legislative statutes or executive orders. The responsibility is unavoidable: when cases come to the Court that involve constitutional questions, they very often pose political and moral as well as legal dilemmas. When this is the case, the Court cannot avoid acting as an oracle, and its decisions will necessarily define the limits and direction of public policy. The Court is thus compelled by our constitutional arrangements to assume an awesome responsibility. Whether it be the Grecian Oracle of Delphi offering ambiguously fateful predictions of things to come or Li'l Abner's cave-dwelling forecaster Ole Man Mose, the proclamations of oracles become highly respected guides to human conduct.

THE FLEXIBILITY OF THE ORACULAR ROLE

We have noted earlier that the Supreme Court has exercised its oracular function differently during various historical periods. During its early period the Court used its power to establish the operating framework of separated power and a federal system of government. During much of the nineteenth and early twentieth centuries, it protected private property from the onslaught of social reform. The New Deal of Franklin Roosevelt saw it briefly hold the line against the bloodless revolution in traditional relationships of the government to private sectors of the society. But even though the Court dramatically changed its position after the 1937 crisis, it did not give up its oracular function.

Since the middle of the twentieth century the Court has given new meaning to the civil rights and liberties of American citizens. It has proclaimed that the Fourteenth Amendment embodies a doctrine of political equality that means "one man, one vote," that liberties of citizens guaranteed by the federal Constitution are not to be abridged by other units of government, and that legal stratification of society on the basis of race contravenes the Constitution. The judicial abolition of racial segregation provides an informative example of how the oracular function of the Supreme Court enables it to proclaim moral postulates that overturn long-established legal and political precedents.

ORACULAR JUDGMENT: SEPARATE OR EQUAL?

The United States has had more than a decade of struggle with the Supreme Court's 1954 announcement that legally sanctioned segregation was incompatible with the Fourteenth Amendment and therefore unconstitutional. Since 1954 the Court has bulwarked this decision with additional proclamations. Each time the Court speaks there are legal, political, and social reactions ranging from scholarly critiques of the Court in law journals to billboards demanding the impeachment of the Chief Justice. The attacks upon the Court come from many quarters and raise many objections, but they tend to divide themselves into two categories. One type of attack holds that in playing oracle the justices usurped a power that properly belongs in the legislature. The other type holds that the justices were bad oracles.

In the following section we review the position of the judiciary in the history of racial segregation as background for analysis of the Court's oracular role.

The Constitutional and Political Background of Segregation. The emancipation of the slaves and the passage of the Thirteenth, Fourteenth, and Fifteenth Amendments, which, respectively, outlawed slavery, extended "equal protection of the laws" to citizens of all states, and guaranteed the right to vote to all citizens of the United States regardless of "race, color or previous condition of servitude," did not liberate the Negro from discrimination. In 1866, Congress passed a civil-rights act shortly before it passed the Fourteenth Amendment. The law was designed to give Negroes equality in the courts and in commercial activities. In part it read:

> Citizens of every race and color [shall have] the same right in every State and Territory . . . to make and enforce contracts, to sue, be parties, and give evidence, to inherit, purchase, lease, sell, hold, and convey real and personal property, and to full and equal benefit of all laws and proceedings for the security of person and property, as is enjoyed by white citizens, and shall be subject to like punishment, pains, and penalties and to none other. . . .

Between 1866 and 1875, a total of five civil-rights and reconstruction acts were passed by the "radical Congress," which were aimed at giving the Negro immediate equality and at thwarting the efforts of state legislatures to curtail the Negroes' rights. The stormy period of reconstruction following the Civil War was one of rising racial tension, particularly in the old Confederacy, and a long contest between Congress and the states developed over the rights of former slaves.

In 1875, Congress passed a civil-rights act designed to prevent any public form of discrimination against Negroes. The law provided that all persons regardless of race or color were entitled to the "full and equal enjoyment of accommodations, advantages, facilities, and privileges of inns, public conveyances on land or water, theatres, and other places of public amusements." This law was based upon the assumption that Congress had the power to enact legislation that would enforce the Fourteenth Amendment, not only by negating state action but also by affirmatively forbidding private individuals from exercising discrimination.

The Supreme Court disagreed, however, and in 1883 it declared the Civil Rights Act of 1875 unconstitutional.[2] Justice Bradley wrote the court's opinion, which held that the Fourteenth Amendment meant that Congress could only enact corrective legislation where states had violated the Amendment's provisions.[3] The opinion held also that Congress had no power to enact "primary and direct" legislation—that is, to pre-empt power to legislate on the subject of equal accommodations. Following

---

[2] *Civil Rights Cases*, 109 U.S. 3 (1883).

[3] One analysis of the Civil Rights Cases states that the opinion "served notice that the federal government could not lawfully protect the Negro against the discrimination which private individuals might choose to exercise against him. This was another way of saying that the system of white supremacy was mainly beyond federal control." Alfred H. Kelly and Winfred A. Harbison, *The American Constitution, Its Origins and Development* (New York: Norton, 1948.), p. 491.

this line of narrow construction, the opinion stated that the Civil Rights Act "superseded and displaced" state legislation rather than just correcting it:

> It [the Civil Rights Act] ignores such legislation, and assumes that the matter is one that belongs to the domain of national regulation. . . . What we have to decide is, whether such plenary power has been conferred upon Congress by the Fourteenth Amendment, and, in our judgment, it has not.

In a lone and lengthy dissent, Justice John M. Harlan stated that the Court's opinion was "too narrow and artificial" and that "the substance and spirit of recent amendments of the Constitution have been sacrificed by a subtle and ingenious verbal criticism." Harlan made a well-documented argument that the Court had inadequately interpreted the intent of the constitutional amendments. His interpretation of the Thirteenth and Fourteenth Amendments included the following:

> If the constitutional amendments be enforced, according to the intent with which, as I conceive, they were adopted, there cannot be, in this republic, any class of human beings in practical subjection to another class, with power in the latter to dole out to the former just such privileges· as they may choose to grant. The supreme law of the land has decreed that no authority shall be exercised in this country upon the basis of discrimination, in respect to civil rights. . . . To that decree—for the due enforcement of which, by appropriate legislation, Congress· has been invested with express power—everyone must bow. . . .[4]

Justice Harlan's views were a long time gaining acceptance. With the blessings of the majority opinion of the Court state restrictions of all sorts in the areas prohibited by the 1875 act befell the Negro. With the resurgence of southern political power in Congress following the Reconstruction Era, civil-rights legislation lapsed. Post-Civil War legislation dealing with civil rights was almost eliminated by 1910, through judicial construction as well as legislative modification.

During the long period of congressional inactivity in the area of civil rights, the status of these provisions depended primarily upon judicial construction. The narrow interpretation of the Civil Rights Cases gave the southern states a basis for enacting a number of laws restricting the freedom of the Negro. Such things as the grandfather clause,[5] poll

---

[4] *Civil Rights Cases*, 109 U.S. 3 (1883).
[5] There were several versions of the grandfather clause, but generally they required descendants of persons who were not qualified to vote before or during the Civil War

taxes, the all-white primary, elaborate tests to qualify for voting, and other laws and ordinances authorizing segregation of the races were passed. Segregation of the races was given judicial sanction in *Plessy* v. *Ferguson*,[6] which upheld a Louisiana statute requiring railroads to provide separate cars for the two races. The Court held that separate but equal facilities were not incompatible with the Fourteenth Amendment. In fact, Justice Brown in the majority opinion held that segregation had nothing to do with superiority or inferiority. The opinion stated:

> We consider the underlying fallacy of the plaintiff's argument to consist in the assumption that enforced separation of the two races stamps the colored race with a badge of inferiority. If this be so, it is not by reason of anything found in the act, but solely because the colored race chooses to put that construction upon it.
> If one race be inferior to another socially the Constitution of the United States cannot put them upon the same plane.

Only Justice Harlan, as in the Civil Rights Cases, dissented. He attacked the reasoning of the Court and argued that segregation recognized classes based upon race, and that "our Constitution is color blind": "The law regards man as man, and takes no account of his surroundings or of his color when his civil rights as guaranteed by the supreme law of the land are involved."

Plessy v. *Ferguson* helped racial segregation become a southern tradition. For a long time, the doctrine of separate but equal lay unmolested although there was growing awareness that while "separate" was well enforced, "equal" was not. Negro facilities were remarkably inferior, and Negroes were often denied an equitable share of tax-supported services and facilities.[7]

By the late 1930's, the court began to take a close look at "equal" facilities. In *Missouri* ex. rel. *Gaines* v. *Canada*,[8] the Court decided that since Missouri had no law school for Negroes it must admit them to its white law school. Like many southern states, Missouri paid the tuition of Negro law students at law schools in other states that accepted them.

---

to pass a maze of literacy and other tests that the rest of the population did not have to take. The court ruled the grandfather clause illegal in both *Guinn* v. *United States,* 238 U.S. 347 (1915), and again in *Lane* v. *Wilson,* 307 U.S. 268 (1939). Both cases applied to Oklahoma's attempts to use this "sophisticated" means of discrimination, as Justice Frankfurter called it.

[6] 163 U.S. 537 (1896).

[7] President's Committee on Civil Rights, *To Secure These Rights* (Washington, D.C.: Government Printing Office, 1947) pp. 81-82.

[8] 305 U.S. 337 (1938).

The court held that this practice did not provide equal treatment to residents of the same state. Equality was denied solely on the basis of color. White students had a law school in Missouri. Negro residents of Missouri were obliged to be educated in the law in another state. Thus there was not equal treatment.

This same doctrine was asserted in *Sipuel* v. *University of Oklahoma*,[9] and in 1950 the Court went a step farther and held that Negroes could not be segregated after being admitted to a graduate school.[10] Separate but equal suffered another blow in *Henderson* v. *United States*,[11] where the court ruled that segregation of Negroes in railroad dining cars under rules of the Interstate Commerce Commission denied equal treatment of the races.

The Plessy doctrine was, in short, increasingly, and steadily being weakened by judicial decisions. In *Sweatt* v. *Painter*,[12] the Court laid the foundation for the final reversal of the separate but equal doctrine. In this case, Sweatt, a Negro, was denied admission to the University of Texas Law School, and when he sued to be admitted he was turned down by the lower court on the grounds that Texas was building a law school for Negroes. The Texas courts all refused to grant Sweatt's request on the grounds that separate but equal facilities would soon be available. When the case reached the United States Supreme Court, Chief Justice Vinson's opinion for the Court carefully compared the facilities of the existing law school with those being prepared for Negroes. He found that the latter would be in no way equal to the established law school and reversed the Texas courts. Vinson, however, carefully avoided a re-examination of the rule of *Plessy* v. *Ferguson*, and the case turned narrowly on the point that the Negro law school would not be equal to the white law school.

Judicial Enforcement of Equality. In 1954, the final reversal of *Plessy* v. *Ferguson* was carried out by the Supreme Court in *Brown et al.* v. *Board of Education*.[13] In effect, the decision foreshadowed an end to the pattern of segregation of the South. Since this decision, the whole structure of racial segregation, which reposed on the separate but equal doctrine, has been weakened. Sit-ins, boycotts, and other protests by the Negro press the issue of equality, and when cases come to the federal

[9] 332 U.S. 631 (1948).
[10] *McLaurin* v. *Oklahoma State Regents,* 339 U.S. 637 (1950).
[11] 339 U.S. 816 (1950).
[12] 339 U.S. 629 (1950).
[13] 347 U.S. 483 (1954).

courts, "separate but equal" no longer provides a convenient way out of the difficulty.

The resulting struggle, aside from its sporadic violence, involves an intense debate over the judicial process. It raises questions, for example, about the role of precedent in the decisions of judges. The pattern of precedent, or *stare decisis*, regarding school facilities for different races had been at one time on the side of separate facilities for the races. "Separate but equal" was the clear precedent for many years, with the courts permitting a strict enforcement of "separate" on a loose interpretation of "equal." In the Brown case, equality of facilities was challenged directly; and the Court, finding some precedent in the law but more justification in psychological and sociological theory, decided that separate but equal was incompatible with the "equal protection of the laws" of the Fourteenth Amendment to the Constitution.

The Political Repercussions. The Court's decision was moral and political as well as constitutional, and it had almost immediate political repercussions. Southern segregationists described the decision itself as "unconstitutional" and charged that it was part of the Communist conspiracy. Bills were introduced in the Congress (and came very close to passage in 1957 and 1958) to exclude school segregation cases from the Court's appellate jurisdiction. Constitutional amendments were initiated to exempt education from any federal intervention and to curb the constitutional power of the Supreme Court. Campaigns were initiated to impeach Chief Justice Warren and some or all of his colleagues.

While the Brown decision elicited attacks on the Court, it also exerted positive political pressures in other areas of American politics. It served to encourage and strengthen the groups involved in the civil-rights movement by putting the Constitution on their side. In striking down laws in southern states, the Court's decisions set off pressures on northern states to protect civil rights in such areas as housing and employment and focused attention on the responsibilities of Congress and the President to implement equal protection through positive legislation. In 1957 a bipartisan coalition in Congress passed the first civil-rights bill since Reconstruction. Its major provisions extended federal authority to sue in the federal district courts for a civil injunction against local authorities who had deprived any person of his right to vote and established the United States Commission on Civil Rights to investigate denials of voting rights and to evaluate federal progress in promoting the equal protection of the laws. In 1960 another Civil Rights Act closed off some of the loopholes for southern evasion of the voting rights provisions of the 1957 Act.

In this same period executive action in the area of civil rights was accelerated by the issuance of executive orders requiring nondiscrimination in the employment practices of the federal government and of government contractors and prohibiting discrimination in federally assisted housing.

The civil-rights movement flourished on its earlier partial successes and in the "long, hot summers" of 1963 and 1964 pushed its demands for equality of voting rights and access to public accommodations in the South and its demands for equality of employment and housing opportunity in the cities of the North. Congress responded with the Civil Rights Act of 1964, the first comprehensive legislation since the 1870's. Its major provisions prohibited discrimination in public accommodations (hotels, restaurants, gas stations, theatres, etc.) that affect interstate commerce or are owned by public agencies; created a federal Fair Employment Practices Commission to enforce its prohibition of discrimination by either an employer or a union in businesses with more than one hundred employees (decreasing by steps to twenty-five in 1968); empowered the President to cut off federal grants to programs in which discrimination is practiced; and created stricter standards to prevent differential treatment in the registration of Negro and white voters.

Meanwhile the Court had followed the Brown decision with similar rulings in a host of other school desegregation suits and had applied its new equal-protection standard in other areas. It had, for example, upheld the voting rights provision of the 1957 Civil Rights Act;[14] it had declared unconstitutional a scheme of legislative districting that minimized the strength of Negro voters;[15] it had outlawed segregation in interstate railroad, bus, and airport facilities.[16] The Court had also reversed the convictions of NAACP officials under punitive state statutes and had nullified the efforts of southern states to harass and eliminate the NAACP.[17]

Outside the South, state and city governments were under pressure

[14] U.S. v. Raines, 362 U.S. 17 (1960).
[15] Gomillion v. Lightfoot, 364 U.S. 339 (1960).
[16] Bailey v. Patterson, 369 U.S. 31 (1962), and Turner v. Memphis, 369 U.S. 350 (1962).
[17] NAACP v. Alabama, 357 U.S. 449 (1958).

to deal with *de facto* school segregation and to legislate in the areas of public accommodations, fair employment, and fair housing. Finally, throughout the nation churches and private business, labor, and civic groups increasingly threw their moral and political weight into the civil-rights struggle on the side of the revolution initiated by the Court.

In the climate generated by the Court's decision, the political system responded in ways that would have been otherwise impossible. President Kennedy had delayed until 1962 the fulfillment of his 1960 campaign pledge to end discrimination in federally assisted housing and had failed to press his civil-rights legislation in Congress for fear of jeopardizing the rest of his legislative program. By 1964 President Johnson, with bipartisan support, had gotten the highly significant Civil Rights Act through the Congress. And in 1965, fired by the brutal suppression of civil-rights demonstrations in parts of the South and by the court-protected march on Montgomery, Johnson pushed through the Congress a voting rights bill that authorizes, under certain conditions, the suspension of discriminatory literacy tests and provides for federal registration of voters.

The "American dilemma" is far from resolved; it has, perhaps, not yet reached the period of crisis through which the nation must go before recovery of its political health is possible. The Court did not create the dilemma, and it was not responsible for the pressures demanding its solution. In any event, the extension of the principles of the American dream to members of minority ethnic groups could not have been postponed much longer. But where the other agencies of American government seemed bogged down close to dead center or doomed to move only through the intolerably slow processes of broker rule, the Court asserted a constitutional and moral principle to which the other formal and informal agencies of politics were forced to respond.

The Supreme Court, in short, has helped make the subject of equal rights in race relations an unavoidable part of political discourse through its decisions on the subject. The exercise of its oracular role has made the Court, in this area, more than the final appellate jurisdiction in the judicial hierarchy. In often eloquent opinions, it declares the moral postulates at issue in the cases that come before it. Sometimes the values expressed reveal sentiments held by individual justices which they try to impose upon the rest of society. Sometimes the moral position asserted by the Court leaves doubt and confusion among many segments of society. The Court can hold back surges of social reform, but it can also force social changes more rapidly than some would prefer. But whether one agrees with Supreme Court interpretations of moral issues, most citizens have a high respect for the Court as an oracular institution. Indeed, when other political agencies default, it often falls to the Court to introduce moral questions into political dialogue. Both majority opinions and sharp dissents are high-quality fuel for the democratic machinery through which public issues are debated.

The Courts as Guarantors of Due Process

The quality of a legal system in any society is largely measured by the character of the agencies through which laws are enforced. Police agencies stand between citizens and the courts, and the conduct of these agencies is often the real measure of a nation's standards of justice. The United States, as we have seen, guarantees the citizen rights *against* the government through the Bill of Rights of the federal Constitution. The restrictions on law enforcement are the procedural guarantees of the Bill of Rights that protect citizens from possible caprice, arbitrariness, overzealousness, or brutality of law enforcement agencies. One observer has commented:

> It is not unjust to suggest that the greatest single area of violation of civil rights is police practices, but because of the character, poverty, and ignorance of the victims, few cases in this sphere are litigated. Until in recent years the spotlight was focused on the problem, standard police procedure in dealing with Negro, Italian, and Puerto Rican "gangs" of juvenile delinquents was to take them to the station house, beat the ears off them, and then send them home to muse on the evils of sin. While the police involved would admit that an innocent lad occasionally got pushed around, they basically endorsed the philosophy of the French *gendarme* that everyone in the world has at least one beating coming to him.[18]

Recently the nation has witnessed some shocking spectacles of police brutality. Civil-rights demonstrations, nationally covered by the press and television, have been broken up by police using clubs, electric cattle prods, and fists. Horse-mounted police have ridden into crowds dispelling demonstrators by whipping them with canes, and demonstrators, some of them children, have been arrested in mass and thrown into totally inadequate jails. Such widely reported events caused

[18] John P. Roche, *Courts and Rights* (New York: Random House, 1961), p. 49.

national public concern about the lack of respect for civil rights and liberties on the part of certain law enforcement officers. Citizen action in these areas, however, is difficult. In the main the task of surveillance of law enforcement methods and the protection of due process of law has fallen to the courts. At both the national and local levels the courts have responded in recent years by insisting on a more rigorous respect for constitutionally guaranteed procedures.

NATIONAL LAW ENFORCEMENT AND DUE PROCESS

In May, 1964, J. Edgar Hoover celebrated his fortieth year as head of the Federal Bureau of Investigation of the Department of Justice. At that time Mr. Hoover was almost a living legend, and President Johnson honored him with these words:

> He is a hero to millions of decent citizens and anathema to evil men. No other American now or in our past has ever served the cause of justice more faithfully or so well. No other American has fought so long or so hard for a safer and better national life.[19]

Shortly after receiving this accolade, Mr. Hoover, in November, 1964, unburdened himself in a rarely held news conference. He talked about "bleeding-heart judges" and referred to Nobel Peace Prize winner, Dr. Martin Luther King, Jr., who had recently criticized the FBI, as "the most notorious liar in the country."[20] Many people were shocked at this indiscretion. King attributed it to fatigue, the troubles the FBI had with law enforcement in Mississippi, and adverse comments in the official report on the assassination of President Kennedy.

Whatever the reason, Hoover's following of idolators and many newspapers were disturbed and his critics were irate. Had a legend ended? Should a bureau chief in a government agency engage in this sort of criticism of the courts and in a public quarrel with the groups who had been victimized by local police brutality? Mr. Hoover's remarks underlined some basic issues of democratic government. His comment about bleeding-heart judges echoed a favorite phrase of the extremist right and raised the question of the appropriate role of law enforcement officials as constitutional experts. His intemperate criticism of Dr. King raised a similar question about his role as social critic.

---

[19] Anthony Lewis, Special Report to the *New York Times*, December 6, 1964, p. 4E. President Johnson also waived the compulsory federal retirement age of seventy for Mr. Hoover in order to permit him to continue in his position indefinitely.
[20] *Ibid.*

The popular respect for and adulation of Mr. Hoover had rested not only on the efficiency of his agency but on a tendency to see him as the nation's foremost authority on the internal Communist threat and arbiter of methods for dealing with it. Perhaps Mr. Hoover's ire was partly attributable to the fact that the Supreme Court had not always shared this adulation and deference. In several cases involving suspected Communist activity the Court had restricted the Bureau's investigative methods to ensure compliance with the Bill of Rights. In *Kremen* v. *United States*,[21] for example, the Court held that the FBI could not search and seize the contents of a cabin without a warrant and use the evidence in court. The use of information supplied by informers to the FBI was seriously curtailed in *Jencks* v. *United States*,[22] when the court held that the source of such information must be disclosed to the defendant. Justice Brennan had this to say:

> We hold that the criminal action must be dismissed when the government, on the ground of privilege, elects not to comply with an order to produce, for the accused's inspection and, for admission in evidence, relevant statements or reports in its possession. . . .
> The burden is the government's . . . to decide whether the public prejudice of allowing the crime to go unpunished is greater than that attendant upon the possible disclosures of state secrets and other confidential information in the government's possession.

These decisions rested on the doctrine that in the American constitutional system the judicially interpreted provisions of the Bill of Rights establish the framework and the limits of the police function. The Court, in effect, told the FBI that it must accept the Court's interpretation of the procedural rights and liberties even though a criminal may occasionally elude a talented agent. The FBI has responded to the Court's purview of individual rights and liberties by improving its methods to conform to judicial limitations on its activities.

LOCAL LAW ENFORCEMENT AND DUE PROCESS

Judicial supervision of state and local law enforcement practices has been more difficult, both because these agencies are usually less professionally staffed and operated and because of the Supreme Court's reluctance, until recently, to incorporate procedural due process into the Fourteenth Amendment and, thus, apply it to state and local law

[21] 353 U.S. 346 (1957).
[22] 353 U.S. 657 (1957).

enforcement activities. In an earlier chapter we have seen how the Court operated for many years under Justice Cardozo's rule for sorting out those principles of the Bill of Rights that are fundamental from those that are not. His test set forth in 1937 in *Palko* v. *Connecticut*,[23] would incorporate into the Fourteenth Amendment only those rights which are essential to "a scheme of ordered liberty."

Unfortunately, the *Palko* doctrine was interpreted in many states as permission to be casual about procedural due process. At the same time the decision was criticized as too lenient by more zealous civil libertarians who would agree with Justice Douglas, concurring in *Joint Antifascist Refugee Committee* v. *McGrath*,[24] that "it is procedure that spells much of the difference between rule by law and rule by whim or caprice."[25]

Applying this principle to the *Palko* rule, the Court in recent years has extended the due process clause of the Fourteenth Amendment to include more of the procedural guarantees in the Bill of Rights. As the Court put it in *Malloy* v. *Hogan*, "This shift reflects recognition that the American system of criminal prosecution is accusatorial, not inquisitorial."[26] Some of the most important of recent decisions are discussed below.

Cruel and Unusual Punishment. The Eighth Amendment to the Constitution prevents "cruel or unusual punishments" from being inflicted. One of the few cases that has come before the Court on cruel and unusual punishment, illustrating the complexity of the Court's task, was *Louisiana* ex. rel. *Francis* v. *Resweber*.[27] Francis, a young Negro sentenced to death for murder, had been placed in the electric chair, but when the switch was thrown some mechanical difficulty prevented his being killed. He tried to prevent a second attempt on the grounds of double jeopardy as well as cruel and unusual punishment, but the Court in a five-four decision turned him down. Justice Reed had this interesting comment for the Court:

> Even the fact that petitioner has already been subjected to a current of electricity does not make his subsequent execution any more cruel in the constitutional sense than any other execution. The cruelty

[23] 302 U.S. 319 (1937).
[24] 341 U.S. 123 (1951).
[25] Justice Frankfurter has said: "The history of American freedom is, in no small measure, the history of procedure," in *Malinski* v. *New York*, 324 U.S. 401 (1945).
[26] 12 L. ed. 2d 653 (1964).
[27] 329 U.S. 459 (1947).

against which the Constitution protects a convicted man is cruelty
inherent in the method of punishment, not the necessary suffering
involved in any method employed to extinguish life humanely. The
fact that an unforeseeable accident prevented the prompt consumma-
tion of the sentence cannot, it seems to us, add an element of cruelty
to a subsequent execution.

After this decision, Francis was again strapped in the electric chair.
This time it worked and he was properly killed. Although the specific
facts in the case are unlikely to be repeated in the future, Justice Reed's
definition of humane execution implies certain limits on state governments in the administration of the death penalty.

In 1962 the Supreme Court applied the cruel-and-unusual-punishment
clause of the Eighth Amendment to the definition of a crime in a state
statute. California, in an attempt to deal with its steadily increasing
narcotics problem, enacted a law making it a crime for a person to be
addicted to narcotics. In a test of the statute, the United States Supreme
Court held that mere addiction to narcotics cannot be construed as
criminal. The statute was found to be "in violation of the Eighth and
Fourteenth Amendments."[28]

Unreasonable Searches and Seizures.   Until recent years the Court
declined to rule that the Fourth Amendment's prohibition against "unreasonable searches and seizures" protected the individual against state
and local police activity. Recent cases, however, have gradually extended the due-process clause of the Fourteenth Amendment to include
the Fourth. The process began with the case of *Elkins* v. *United States*,[29]
which ended the so-called "silver-platter" doctrine, a rule allowing
evidence illegally obtained by *state* officers to be introduced as evidence
in a federal criminal trial, although similar evidence obtained by *federal*
officers was barred by the Fourth Amendment.

Dollree Mapp v. *Ohio*,[30] expanded the Court's application of the
Fourth Amendment to the states. Justice Clark summed up the Court's
position:

Having once recognized that the right to privacy embodied in
the Fourth Amendment is enforceable against the States, and that the
right to be secure against rude invasions by state officers is, therefore,
constitutional in origin, we can no longer permit that right to remain
an empty promise. Because it is enforceable in the same manner and to

[28] *Robinson* v. *California*, 370 U.S. 660 (1962).
[29] 80 S. Ct. 1437 (1960).
[30] 81 S. Ct. 1684 (1961).

like effect as other basic rights secured by the Due Process Clause, we can no longer permit it to be revocable at the whim of any police officer who, in the name of law enforcement itself, chooses to suspend its enjoyment. Our decision, founded on reason and truth, gives to the individual no more than that which the Constitution guarantees him, to the police officer, no less than that to which honest law enforcement is entitled, and, to the courts, that judicial integrity so necessary in the true administration of justice.

The Mapp decision was a blow to law enforcement agencies throughout the country. Charges that their hands had been tied emanated from many police officials throughout the country and many newspapers supported this view. The main theme of the criticism charged the Court with being more concerned with the rights of criminals than with the security of the majority. More responsible police officials, however, stated that they could live with the law and some went further to argue that law enforcement would ultimately benefit from the decision.

Right to Counsel. The dust raised by the Mapp case had hardly settled when the Court moved again. From Florida State Prison, the Supreme Court of the United States received a penciled petition on prison stationery from one Clarence E. Gideon, in-and-out resident of jails for most of his fifty-one years, requesting the Supreme Court grant him a petition of *certiorari*. Gideon stated that he had been convicted of a charge of breaking and entering at a trial in which he was not represented by counsel. The trial court had turned down his request, and the Florida appellate courts let stand the trial court's refusal to appoint counsel. Gideon claimed that the due-process clause of the Fourteenth Amendment required the trial court to appoint a counsel to defend him. He asked the Supreme Court to extend the Sixth Amendment's provision for "the assistance of counsel for his defense" to the states. Gideon also had to be permitted to proceed *in forma pauperis* (in the manner of a pauper) since he was without funds of his own.

The Court ultimately granted his petition and his request to proceed *in forma pauperis* and ensured that he would be ably represented. The Court, recognizing the importance of the issue, appointed one of the country's most prominent lawyers, Mr. Abe Fortas, who is now himself a Supreme Court Justice, as Gideon's attorney. With legal resources at his disposal that few individuals, even if not *pauperis*, could afford, Gideon's case became one of the monumental decisions in constitutional law.

It should be noted that the Supreme Court avoids deciding cases on constitutional grounds if it is possible. It also puts the interest of the individual ahead of other considerations—that is, if a constitutional principle might be raised at the expense of an individual's particular case, which might be won on nonconstitutional grounds, the Court will avoid sacrificing the individual in order to interpret the Constitution.

Mr. Fortas researched his case carefully and concluded that it could only turn on constitutional grounds and would require the Court to reverse its previous judgment in *Betts* v. *Brady*,[31] where the Court held states had to grant counsel to criminals tried in their courts only when "special circumstances" existed. Many Justices, particularly Justice Black, chafed under the elasticity of such a test of the right to counsel and felt it should be rejected in favor of demanding counsel in all criminal cases.

Gideon won his case. Justice Black, who had dissented in the Betts decision, wrote the opinion for a unanimous Court. His opinion attacked the special-circumstances rule of the Betts case and contained this eloquent statement of law in a democratic government:

> . . . Reason and reflection require us to recognize that in our adversary system of criminal justice, any person haled into court, who is too poor to hire a lawyer, cannot be assured a fair trial unless counsel is provided for him. This seems to us to be an obvious truth. Governments, both state and federal, quite properly spend vast sums of money to establish machinery to try defendants accused of crime. Lawyers to prosecute are everywhere deemed essential to protect the public's interest in an orderly society. Similarly, there are few defendants charged with crime, few indeed, who fail to hire the best lawyers they can get to prepare and present their defenses. That government hires lawyers to prosecute defendants and that defendants who have the money hire lawyers to defend them are the strongest indications of the widespread belief that lawyers in criminal courts are necessities, not luxuries. The right of one charged with crime to counsel may not be deemed fundamental and essential to fair trials in some countries, but it is in ours.[32]

The reaction to the Gideon decision by state and local law enforcement officials was swift and bitter. Petitions such as Gideon's flooded into state and federal courts by the tens of thousands, and the Supreme Court was accused of "throwing open the prison doors." Undeterred, the Court refined the Gideon decision, this time five to four, in *Escobedo*

[31] *Betts* v. *Brady*, 316 U.S. 455 (1942).
[32] *Gideon* v. *Wainwright*, 372 U.S. 335 (1963).

v. *Illinois*,[33] where they held that police must honor a criminally accused person's request to consult an attorney during the course of an interrogation.

The Escobedo decision had held that a person suspected of a crime had a right to counsel from the time he was arrested and that he had a right to remain silent during interrogation. Unquestionably this complicated police work as generally practiced. In California, the State Supreme Court extended this doctrine to require that California police officers must advise not only those formally accused but suspects of their right to see an attorney as well as their right to remain silent once an investigation focused upon them.[34] This decision was quickly challenged by many of the state's law enforcement agencies in a petition for rehearing.[35] The petition was filed by the state attorney general with the county district attorneys filing as *amici curiae*, or "friends of the court," in support of the attorney general. Many county sheriffs and city police chiefs supported the petition, which contended that the retroactive application of the decision would free thousands of convicted criminals and that its future application, would make effective police investigation, particularly undercover work, almost impossible. The California Supreme Court conducted a rehearing of the case in which it held its decision not to be retroactive, but reaffirmed its future application.

Freedom from Self-incrimination and the Right to Confront Adverse Witnesses. The trend of Supreme Court decisions bulwarking the rights of accused persons and the presumption that they are innocent until proved guilty has been extended recently into other areas long ignored by many states. The Fifth Amendment contains the provision that no person "shall be compelled in any criminal case to be a witness against himself." While the federal judiciary generally has respected this provision, many state courts have been quite casual about it, and others tended to ignore it when it was not strictly required of them by their state constitution. In 1964 the Supreme Court, again using the Fourteenth Amendment, decided that this basic right of the accused must be standard throughout the nation.[36] Without such a protection many suspected criminals had been convicted in state courts on the

---

[33] 84 S. Ct. 1758 (1964).
[34] *People* v. *Dorado*, Crim. N. 7468, August 31, 1964.
[35] As yet unpublished petition by the Attorney General of California.
[36] *Malloy* v. *Hogan*, 12 L. ed. 653 (1964).

basis of coerced confessions. In this particular case Malloy was arrested during a gambling raid in Hartford, Connecticut, and questioned about his activities. When he refused to answer on the grounds of self-incrimination, a Connecticut court held him in contempt and committed him to prison until he decided to answer the questions. The United States Supreme Court reversed the conviction and held it to be a form of coercion forbidden by the Fifth Amendment's protection against self-incrimination.

Less than a year later the Court further elaborated the rights of accused persons when it decided that states had to guarantee the Sixth Amendment's provision that the accused "be confronted by witnesses against him."[37] No longer can state courts accept testimony of witnesses *in absentia*, no matter how inaccessible they may be at the time of trial.

DUE PROCESS OF LAW IN A DEMOCRATIC SOCIETY

The questions raised by these recent Court decisions became an issue in the 1964 presidential campaign and continue to affect American politics. In defending the rights of criminals has the Court sacrificed the rights of the law-abiding majority to be secure in their persons and effects? Has the Court perilously crippled police agencies in their efforts to enforce the laws? Are the courts responsible for the fact that it is no longer safe to walk the streets of many American cities after dark?

Many who have answered "yes" to these questions have supported their answers with fraudulent phrases and misleading arguments. The Justices do not have bleeding hearts and certainly are not engaged in coddling criminals. The guarantees of due process of law apply not to criminals but to the criminally *accused*; they are the processes that ensure that men are not judged to be criminals lightly or arbitrarily. They ensure that accusations are carefully made, that men are equal before the law, and that guilt must be established beyond any reasonable doubt. They remind us that the presumption of innocence is a great monument to free men.

It is true that many of the cases testing due process involve sordid situations or persons whose race, political or religious beliefs, economic status, or personal habits do not command popular respect or sympathy. A case in point was *United States* v. *Rabinowitz*,[38] which involved a stamp forger (Rabinowitz) who sold his altered and artificial goods to

[37] *Pointer v. Texas*, 32 L. W. 4306 (1965).
[38] 339 U.S. 56 (1950).

collectors. Federal officers acting under a proper warrant arrested him but also ransacked his office for evidence, although they had no warrant to search his premises. The illegal search yielded 573 forged postage stamps, which were later used as evidence to convict him. Rabinowitz appealed, but by a four-three decision the Court upheld the conviction. Commenting in his dissent, Justice Frankfurter entered a plea for the Fourth Amendment as a fundamental liberty and scolded his colleagues for subordinating this Amendment to the unpleasant case before them. He said:

> The old saw that hard cases make bad law has its basis in experience. But petty cases are even more calculated to make bad law. The impact of a sordid little case is apt to obscure the implications of the generalization to which the case gives rise. Only thus can I account for disregard of the history embedded in the Fourth Amendment and the great place which belongs to that Amendment in the body of our liberties as recognized and applied by unanimous decisions over a long stretch of the Court's history.
>
> It is a fair summary of history to say that the safeguards of liberty have frequently been forged in controversies involving not very nice people. And so while we are concerned here with a shabby defrauder, we must deal with his case in the great theme expressed by the Fourth Amendment. A disregard of the historic materials underlying the Amendment does not answer them.

What Justice Frankfurter said of his colleagues is even more true of society generally. It is difficult to arouse the respectable majority over the maltreatment of the "undesirable element" of society, except in a case of extreme cruelty[39] or after it is too late—when an innocent person has been victimized.

The resentment expressed by police agencies against the Court's interference is understandable even when it is unsound and exceeds their legitimate role. Engaged in a difficult and hazardous undertaking, they are likely to feel that the task is thankless as well when the Court reverses the fruits of their labor. Often, however, they are unmindful of the fact that law enforcement is society's first line of defense for the rights of all of its citizens. Occasionally police agencies have even appeared hysterical over attempts to create a body of lay citizens to investigate charges of brutality or corruption. In Los Angeles, the Ameri-

---

[39] A case in which brutality of disgusting proportions was used on a prisoner is *Apodaca* v. *United States,* 188 Fed. 2nd 932 (1951). This type of treatment eventually works to the detriment of good law enforcement, as most leaders of police work will attest.

can Civil Liberties Union and certain civil rights organizations have been charged with misguided efforts if not outright subversion in their attempts to establish a police review board.[40] The same thing has happened in numerous other cities. The big question seems to be whether we wish to allow some criminals to go free rather than compromise the civil liberties all Americans expect to enjoy or whether we are willing to forego some of these liberties in order to give law enforcement officials more efficient means to do their jobs. It is not an easy question, for we demand a peaceful and tranquil society, and law enforcement is difficult in a democracy. We are annoyed when some of our major criminals seem to evade the law or are put behind bars for the evasion of income tax or some other charge because conviction for the real crimes cannot be made—albeit sometimes because of corruption or payoff to appropriate sources of influence. Yet, as Frankfurter so well put it, we cannot allow a "sordid little case" to tear down the structure of American justice.

Justice Frankfurter's words express the principle that the true measure of a democratic civilization is the treatment it accords its minorities, its unfortunates, its "undesirables," its deviants. A legal system that protects only the popular, the affluent, the respectable, and the conformist is not worthy of a Great Society.

LEGISLATIVE INVESTIGATIONS AND DUE PROCESS

The role of the courts as protector of individual rights and guarantor of due process occasionally comes into conflict with its position as one of three presumably equal and independent branches of government. The position of the courts as final arbiters of the Constitution, however, makes them in effect the judges of the constitutional limits of their own power, as well as of the legislative and executive powers. As a result, when the courts' power to accord individuals the guarantees of due process collides with the exercise of legislative and executive powers, it is the courts that decide which must give way. The other agencies may be restrained by the courts; the restraints *on* the courts are largely self-imposed. The constitutional system of separation of powers, however, often operates as a significant source of judicial self-restraint.

[40] See Norman B. Moore (Sergeant, Los Angeles Police Department) "Police Review Boards," *California Peace Officer*, November-December, 1960. The editorial caption reads, "A Page out of the Communist Manual," and a boxed editorial comment opens with the sentence: "No matter what names are used by sponsors of so-called 'Police Review Boards' they exude the obnoxious odor of Communism."

One important arena in which the courts have faced this problem in recent years surrounds actions of Congress and state legislatures in pursuit of their powers of investigation. Legislative bodies have the power to compel witnesses to appear before them and to punish them for contempt if they refuse to cooperate in the inquiries of investigating committees. These inquiries, described in an earlier chapter, often involve a personal examination and cross examination of witnesses in a legislative setting that lacks the procedural rigors of the courtroom. Sometimes the questions asked a witness may be held to infringe upon constitutional rights and rules of due process. If he declines to answer, his recourse is often an appeal to the courts from contempt proceedings of Congress. The courts are then forced to define their role as guarantor of due process in its relation to the legislative power of investigation. The result is that these are hard cases, which often narrowly divide the court.

The rights and powers of congressional investigating committees became a judicial problem after Congress gave itself the power to punish for contempt. In 1789, Congress empowered its committees to administer oaths and take testimony and made false statements by witnesses subject to the "pains, penalties, and liabilities of perjury."[41] The Supreme Court upheld this exercise of congressional authority in *Anderson* v. *Dunn*[42] but held that a person imprisoned under this staute could not be confined beyond the session of Congress in which the contempt occurred. Congress remedied this in 1857 by enacting a law that made contempt a misdemeanor—an indictable offense with appropriate punishment attached.

An early court decision held that Congress is limited in its investigations by the separation of powers. It also held that the subject matter of investigations must be relevant to contemplated legislation, and that the resolution establishing the committee must indicate an interest in legislation on the subject being investigated.[43]

The Court later abandoned the last requirement in a decision that held that it was not necessary for a Senate investigating committee to

---

[41] C. Herman Pritchett, *The American Constitution*, (New York: McGraw-Hill, 1959), p. 192. The chapter on the investigatory power of Congress is an excellent account of its history and use.

[42] 6 Wheaton 204 (1821).

[43] *Kilbourn* v. *Thompson*, 103 U. S. 168 (1881), in which the court held Congress did not have "a general power of making inquiry into the private affairs of a citizen."

declare by resolution what it contemplated doing with the information it gathered—in this case, information on the corruption of senators.[44] In 1927, the Supreme Court received a case arising out of the Teapot Dome scandal. The Senate subpoenaed the brother of Attorney General Harry Daugherty. Lower courts held that the Senate was exceeding its powers in conducting an investigation that seemed to be more in the nature of a trial. The Supreme Court reversed the lower courts and held that it was an appropriate investigation and that the "power of inquiry—with processes to enforce it—is an essential and appropriate auxiliary to the legislative function."[45]

More recent developments have found the court again confronted with the constitutional relationship of individual rights to legislative power. During the span of McCarthy hearings, the Supreme Court had generally exercised self-restraint, refusing to invoke constitutional rights as limits on the investigating activities of the Wisconsin Senator's subcommittee and other investigatory bodies. Later, when the Warren Court adopted a firmly defensive position on civil rights generally, the courts did begin to take cases involving legislative investigations, thus abandoning a strict interpretation of the principle of the separation of powers.

In 1957, the Court, in one day, temporarily placed two explosive charges on the doorsteps of Congress and state legislatures. One of these was the Watkins case,[46] which went to Congress; the other was the Sweezy case,[47] which was delivered to state legislatures.

The Watkins case concerned an official of the Farm Equipment Workers Union who had appeared before a subcommittee of the Committee on un-American Activities in 1954 and had answered all questions about his past activity freely and fully. He denied he had ever been an official member of the Communist party but admitted that he was very cooperative with the Party and its members at certain times in his past. Watkins refused, however, to tell the committee if he knew whether people whose names were read to him had been members of the Communist party. He did not invoke the self-incrimination clause of the Fifth Amendment, which Congress itself had not challenged as a legitimate *constitutional* ground for a refusal to answer (certain

---

[44] *In re Chapman*, 166 U.S. 661 (1897).
[45] *McGrain* v. *Daugherty*, 273 U.S. 135 (1927).
[46] *Watkins* v. *United States*, 354 U.S. 178.
[47] *Sweezy* v. *New Hampshire*, 354 U.S. 234.

congressmen challenged it, however, as a legitimate *moral* ground by helping to popularize the ingenuously vicious phrase, "Fifth Amendment Communist"). Watkins had, instead, based his refusal to answer on his constitutional right to silence where, in his judgment, his answers might lead to unjust harm being visited on others.

The Court's decision, while finding in favor of Watkins, did not turn on the constitutional issue. The case was actually decided on the point that the committee's instructions from Congress did not "spell out that group's jurisdiction and purpose with sufficient particularity." The Court thus left the door open to Congress to remedy the situation. But in spite of the narrowness of the decision, Chief Justice Warren, speaking for the Court, made clear that the investigating power itself was subject to constitutional limitations:

> Clearly, an investigation is subject to the command that the Congress shall make no law abridging freedom of speech or press or assembly. While it is true that there is no statute to be reviewed, and that an investigation is not a law, nevertheless an investigation is part of law-making. It is justified solely as an adjunct to the legislative process. The First Amendment may be invoked against infringement of the protected freedoms by law or by lawmaking.

The Court went even further in taking explicit notice of the fact that infringements on civil liberties and due process by legislative investigators must be judged by the social consequences of the investigative process, as well as on narrowly legal considerations:

> Abuses of the investigative process may imperceptibly lead to an abridgment of protected freedom. The mere summoning of a witness and compelling him to testify, against his will, about his beliefs, expressions or associations is a measure of governmental interference. And when those forced revelations concern matters that are unorthodox, unpopular, or even hateful to the general public, the reaction in the life of the witness may be disastrous.

The Court here expressed concern over the tendencies of legislative committees to act like courts of law without extending to witnesses the customary legal procedural guaranties.

The Sweezy case involved a situation in New Hampshire in which the legislature delegated its investigating power to the state's attorney general, who in turn made sweeping inquiries into un-American activities in New Hampshire. Among those called before the attorney general, acting as a one-man investigating committee, was Professor Sweezy, who lectured at the University of New Hampshire. The attorney general questioned Mr. Sweezy at length on many subjects, including the content of his classroom lectures. Sweezy refused to answer certain questions on the grounds that his constitutional liberties were being invaded. He was convicted for contempt by the New Hampshire courts, and his case went to the United States Supreme Court.

Chief Justice Warren, speaking for the Court, held that the questions asked Sweezy were an invasion of academic freedom. Warren had reservations about the delegation of power to the attorney general because, in his view, it separated the power to investigate from the power to direct its use. Warren also argued that constitutional protection does extend to legislative investigation:

> There is no doubt that legislative investigations whether on a federal or state level, are capable of encroaching upon the constitutional liberties of individuals. It is particularly important that the exercises of the power of compulsory process be carefully circumscribed when the investigative process tends to impinge upon such highly sensitive areas as freedom of speech or press, freedom of political association, and freedom of communication of ideas, particularly in the academic community.

The concurring opinions of Justices Frankfurter and Harlan denied that the internal affairs of New Hampshire were of concern to the Court and joined the majority only on the grounds of an invasion of Sweezy's rights under the First Amendment.

The trend established in the Watkins and Sweezy cases did not continue, however, for in a series of five-four decisions involving legislative investigations the court upheld contempt convictions and would not allow the First Amendment as sufficient grounds for refusing to answer committee questions.

Two years after the Watkins and Sweezy decisions, the Court had a similar pair of cases before them. One of these was *Uphaus* v. *Wyman*,[48] which again involved the one-man legislative investigating committee of New Hampshire—Attorney General Wyman.

Uphaus ran a summer family camp for a group called World Fellowship, which had as one of its purposes the discussion of world peace. Uphaus was a lay clergyman who had been a life-long pacifist. New Hampshire law required the preparation by all public facilities of guest registration lists and required that these lists be available to appropriate

[48] 360 U.S. 72 (1959).

officials. Even though the attorney general had access to them, he demanded a guest list from Uphaus, who refused to give it to him. Uphaus was subsequently convicted of civil contempt. In civil contempt cases, the sentence is indefinite. The convicted person has the key to his release in his pocket, since all he has to do to gain his freedom is comply with the court order: in this case, to deliver the guest list. The appeal from the conviction went to the Supreme Court and was denied. Justice Clark wrote the opinion of the Court upholding the conviction. He put the interests of government, in this case New Hampshire, above the constitutional provisions of the First Amendment. He said: ". . . the governmental interest in self-preservation is sufficiently compelling to subordinate the interest in associational privacy of persons who, at least to the extent of the guest registration statute, made public at the inception the association they now wish to keep private."

The dissenters would have reversed the conviction. Justice Brennan did not feel that New Hampshire had sufficient grounds to invade the privacy of Mr. Uphaus, particularly since the guest list was already available to the attorney general. Brennan also dealt with the social pressures individuals suffer when brought before investigating committees, simply because they hold views contrary to conventional opinions:

> For in an era of mass communication and mass opinion, and of international tensions and domestic anxiety, exposure and group identification by the state of those holding unpopular and dissident views are frought with such serious consequences for the individual as inevitably to inhibit seriously the expression of views the Constitution intended to make free.

In another 1959 decision, which involved a university professor who had been convicted for refusal to answer, the Court upheld the contempt conviction and backed away from its suggestion in the Sweezy case that academic freedom should be accorded special protection.[49]

In a dissenting opinion, Justice Black again dealt with the social consequences of legislative abuse of witness. His views were similar to those expressed by Warren in his opinion for the Court in the Watkins case, and Brennan in his dissent in the Uphaus case. Justice Black said:

> Finally, I think Barenblatt's conviction violates the Constitution because the chief aim and purpose of the House Un-American Activities Committee, as disclosed by its many reports, is to try witnesses and punish them because they are or have been communists or because

[49] *Barenblatt* v. *United States*, 360 U.S. 109.

they refuse to admit or deny communist affiliations. The punishment imposed is generally punishment by humiliation and public shame. There is nothing strange or novel about this kind of punishment. It is in fact one of the oldest forms of governmental punishment known to mankind; branding, the pillory, ostracism, and subjection to public hatred being but a few examples of it.

On the same day in 1961, the court decided two more cases in which they refused to extend the protection of the First Amendment to witnesses appearing before the House un-American Activities Committee.[50] Both cases resulted from a foray of the Committee into Atlanta, Georgia, in search of "un-Americans." Oddly enough, the committee evidently did not consider the perpetrations of violence by white citizen councils and expedient politicians during racial integration struggles as within its purview, and the two cases that finally reached the Supreme Court both involved integrationists and opponents of the committee itself. Wilkinson, a member of an Emergency Committee on Civil Liberties, had a long record of opposition to the committee. He came to Atlanta to speak against and to organize opposition to the committee and was subpoenaed to appear as a witness. The committee put a series of questions to Wilkinson, all of which he refused to answer on the ground of the First Amendent. He was subsequently tried and convicted for contempt.

The Braden case was similar in that Braden, a white integrationist, had sent several letters asking people of both races in the South to write their congressmen protesting the attacks on the Supreme Court that had followed the school desegregation decision and urging that Congress discourage the un-American Activities Committee from harassing integrationists. Braden was called before the committee and refused to answer questions on the grounds of the First Amendment. He, like Wilkinson, was eventually convicted of contempt and his case appealed to the Supreme Court. In both cases, a five-man majority again asserted the Barenblatt decision as ruling and declined to invoke the First Amendment as a defense for refusing to answer the committee's questions. The four dissenters were vigorous in their opposition. Justice Douglas argued that opposition to the committee (quite widespread at the time) was an important factor in the calling up of the witnesses and that such opposition was beyond reach of the committee's legitimate

[50] *Wilkinson* v. *United States*, 81 S. Ct. 567; and *Braden* v. *United States*, 81 S. Ct. 584.

jurisdiction. Justice Black again expressed his fear that the committee's tactics were promoting those conditions in which "government by consent will disappear to be replaced by government by intimidation."

On May 21, 1962, the Supreme Court decided six cases in this area in a single opinion.[51] Four of the cases grew out of investigations of the Internal Security Subcommittee of the Senate Judiciary Committee; the other two involved the House un-American Activities Committee. All the petitioners had been convicted of contempt for refusing to answer questions put by the committees. The Supreme Court held that the indictments were faulty because they did not state the subject under inquiry by the investigating committee. The constitutional issue of the First Amendment was avoided, but in a concurring opinion Justice Douglas stated "no indictment, however drawn, could in my view be sustained under the requirements of the First Amendment." The dissenters, however, regarded the majority opinion as a serious break with the precedent set in the Braden, Wilkinson, and Barenblatt cases. Justice Clark held that the decision "abruptly breaks with the past."

This decision was not happily received by several congressmen. Democratic Senator John B. McClellan, chairman of a Senate subcommittee that has inquired into many things, including the activities of Teamster Union official James Hoffa and the financial affairs of Billie Sol Estes, was particularly unhappy with the majority opinion of the Court. In a statement to the press, he said:

> The action of the Supreme Court . . . seems to make it crystal clear that Congress cannot rely upon the Courts to punish contumacious witnesses who appear before its committees.
>
> Thus, it appears that in these circumstances the only recourse left to Congress, if it is to have any protection at all, is for it to exercise the inherent power of each House to uphold its own prerogatives and to punish directly contempt or contumacy of witnesses appearing before it.[52]

The court's decision and Senator McClellan's reaction to it may presage a new struggle over the separation of powers.

The present position of the Court involves a basic political conflict. A reluctance to restrict the range of inquiry of investigating committees

[51] *Russell* v. *United States; Shelton* v. *United States; Whitman* v. *United States; Liveright* v. *United States; Price* v. *United States;* and *Gojack* v. *United States,* 30 L. W. 4352.

[52] *Los Angeles Times,* May 23, 1962, p. 26.

collides with an obligation to protect individual liberty and due process. The dilemma was well pointed out by Justice Brennan:

> I fully appreciate the delicacy of the judicial task of questioning the workings of a legislative investigation. . . . However, our frame of government also imposes another inescapable duty upon the judiciary, that of protecting the constitutional rights of freedom of speech and assembly from improper invasion, whether by national or state legislatures.[53]

Justice Brennan's statement focuses upon the difficulty of the court's role as the guardian of due process working in a context of separated political power. The Court's inability to translate its concern for due process into rules restraining the investigative power is understandable. Regular standards of law and evidence would provide a straightjacket, seriously crippling the legitimate ends of legislative investigations. Self-restraint by the legislature, in the circumstances, seems the most effective restraint.

It is doubtful whether more vigorous and strict judicial application of the First Amendment and the rules of due process to individual cases would very effectively deal with the problem that has concerned Warren, Black, or Douglas. The most serious invasions of liberty and due process ensuing from investigations involve, in Justice Black's words "disastrous" consequences "in the life of the witness." The courts cannot devise and enforce constitutional rules to protect individuals against a suspicious and intolerant public. In such a political climate, the power to subpoena and compel testimony can result in social punishment even if formal constitutional restraints are enforced. The courts, however, might still play the political role of reminding or persuading legislators and the public of the importance of individual liberties and due process of law in a democratic society.

The Judicial Power and Majority Rule

Chief Justice Hughes once suggested that the "law is what the Court says it is." If so, even a government of laws is rule by men. Within the discipline of the law, it is they who will ultimately decide which balance scales to use. As Justice Frankfurter declared:

> Judges are men, not disembodied spirits. Of course a judge is not free from preferences or, if you will, biases. But he may deprive

[53] *Uphaus* v. *Wyman*, 360 U.S. 72 (1959).

a bias of its meretricious authority by stripping it of the uncritical assumption that it is founded on compelling reason or the conceived power of a syllogism. He will be alert to detect that though a conclusion has a logical form it in fact represents a choice of competing considerations of policy, one of which for the time has won the day.[54]

Choosing among competing considerations of policy involves an assessment by the judge of his place in the structure of American government. To many judges, the right of a majority to enact laws through legislatures must be regarded as a principle to be preserved even though the laws might be foolish. To others, the role of oracle requires the judge to overrule legislative and executive action where it collides with a judicial interpretation of the Constitution.

The judicial process is not a simple one, and the judge often finds he is without the necessary rules and procedures which would make it easier. Former Supreme Court Justice Cardozo summed it up well:

> "They do things better with logarithms." The wail escapes me now and again after putting forth the best that is in me, I look upon the finished product, and cannot say that it is good.
>
> I have given my years to the task, and behind me are untold generations, the judges and lawgivers of old, who strove with a passion as burning. Code and commentary, manor roll and year book, treatise and law-report, reveal the processes of trial and error by which they struggled to attain the truth, enshrine their blunders and their triumphs for warning and example.[55]

Cardozo's sigh for a logarithm is a wistful plea for the certainty of exactness that comes from the iron laws of mathematics applied to problems. It would be much easier and more comfortable to do it this way, but a judge true to his calling, as Cardozo recognized, must be denied such comfort. He has to follow right reason, sometimes to the point of being unreasonable.

The power of the courts and the discretion of judges raise fundamental questions about the relationship of the judiciary to majority rule. The courts can thwart social reform, or they can overturn established customs. They can defy majority demands for changes in the *status quo*, or they can press the sensitive nerve of a national guilt complex

---

[54] Felix Frankfurter, "Some Observations on the Nature of the Judicial Process of Supreme Court Litigation," in Alan F. Westin, ed., *The Supreme Court: Views from the Inside* (New York: Norton, 1961), p. 41.

[55] Benjamin N. Cardozo, *The Paradoxes of Legal Science* (New York: Columbia University Press, 1928), pp. 1-2.

about the second-class treatment of a racial minority. Is such power, exercised by "nine old men" who are removed from public control, compatible with the principles of popular sovereignty and majority rule?

The key to this question, we believe, lies in the realization that the actual political power of the courts will be determined by how citizens, politicians, and political parties view the role of the courts. If the justices are seen as oracles, whose decisions are authoritative pronouncements of the true meaning of the Constitution and of public morality, their decisions will replace public debate and responsible political processes.

On the other hand, if the commitment to democratic processes is deeply rooted and widely shared, the role of the judiciary will be seen as that of clarifying social values and public issues. In these circumstances, judicial decisions may put the focus on an issue that will require the majority not only to think about it but let its views be known. The courts can act as both a brake and accelerator upon popular demands and force a value judgment on issues that otherwise might be expediently avoided. The Supreme Court is an elite, but an elite of oracles can serve a majority, either as a goad to action or as a conscience to stop hysterical overaction. Responsible government may be threatened where the judges' views of public morality are made the law of the land. Responsible government is destroyed where judge-made law becomes an authoritative and closed definition of the public interest no longer subject to public debate and modification by statute or constitutional amendment. The law may be "what the court says it is," but the public must be willing to debate issues raised by judicial decisions.

"We must watch the guardians," we say. "They must answer to us." But who guards the guardians? Somewhere the regress ends and we rest on the unwatched watcher. There, in the end, we must depend on character. Ours?

JOSEPH TUSSMAN

Chapter Seventeen

EPILOGUE . . .
AND PROLOGUE

. . .which is a brief summing up with suggestions for a new agenda of problems to which the politics of mass democracy should be addressed.

W E ARE ENGAGED, all over the world, in a defense of the Western conception of freedom and democracy. Our problem is that we are not at all clear whether in defending democracy we are defending hot dogs, baseball, and Mom's apple pie or the rights of man. And if the latter, what are these rights specifically, and how are they to be realized in a political system?

At the root of our problem is the fact that the actual political system, as we are able to observe it in operation today, is at fundamental odds with the traditional ideas and assumptions on which democratic government was founded. This crisis in the traditional order of democratic politics raises a whole new range of questions.

Unfinished Business of the Old Order

Roughly, from the end of the Civil War to World War II, the political system itself was unquestioned. The problems of politics involved, for the most part, the use of existing political arrangements to extend political and economic opportunities to a wider range of citizens. There remains some unfinished business on the agenda of this traditional order: the extension of full political and civil rights to minority racial groups, particularly the Negro, and the use of governmental power to improve the conditions and opportunities of the unorganized who have not shared in the growing affluence of American society. At the same time, the brokerage character of political processes makes the solution of these problems difficult. Indeed, they remain as problems because, in the nature of the case, they do not respond to brokerage solutions.

The plight of the Negro, for example, can only be intensified, not resolved, by seeing Negroes as an interest group entitled to have their private claims weighed fairly against the claims of other organized groups. The National Association for the Advancement of Colored People was begun not as a Negro organization, but a nonracial organization for the promotion of an ideal held to be valid for all. The principle of equal rights can never be achieved by a Negro lobby, or represented in politics by the response of politicians to the Negro vote in the large industrial areas outside the South. If the problem is approached within the framework of countervailing power and the compromise of group interests, the American dilemma and the international embarrassment that results from it can only be endlessly prolonged.

A similar problem exists with those groups that have not shared very fully in the affluence of the economy. These are the groups of people who are not organized, for whom organization is difficult, and who, even if they were organized, would be dwarfed by the political bargaining power of rival groups. They include migrant farm workers, technologically displaced unskilled workers, and the elderly. They are, in a sense, the left-overs from a system of minorities rule. Such groups are unable to acquire the recognized status of minorities, and even if they were, they would not be dealt fully into the game. Since their present situation is largely the result of the operation of broker rule, it is unlikely to be relieved by continued application of the same rules.

If effective political organization as pressure groups is impossible or unlikely for some, the other side of the coin is the situation in which the power of effectively organized groups is not matched by the counter-vailing power of other groups, and is not likely to be. The farm bloc, for example, is well organized and politically effective. The farm program, on the other hand, is generally admitted to be a colossal and irrational failure. If the interests of farmers are well attended to, the same cannot be said for the public interest in the rational management of farm surpluses and effective land use and conservation. These are public problems that are not susceptible of solution through political processes that respond only to group and constituency interests.

A New Agenda for Politics

It may still be argued that the brokerage process has, on the whole, successfully allocated political power and economic advantage to produce a sharing of the economic pie compatible with a rapid increase in its size. The left-overs aside, American politics has been a successful instrument for the solution of economic problems. But democracy cannot afford to minimize the importance of finding ways of dealing with the remaining pockets of privation and poverty. Solutions will depend on the working of political instruments through which these are seen as public problems rather than simply as private grievances.

THE CHALLENGE OF POVERTY

In the thirties President Roosevelt moved the conscience of the nation with the phrase "one-third of a nation—ill-housed, ill-clad, ill-nourished." But the political climate was different then, and poverty was differently distributed. The important facts about poverty in the sixties are that from one fifth to one fourth of the nation's citizens are still afflicted by it; that their numbers are concentrated among migrants, in rural areas, among the unskilled, among the very young and very old, and especially among the minority groups; and that the rate at which poverty has been decreasing has slowed down alarmingly since the end of World War II. The poor, writes Michael Harrington, are becoming "invisible."[1] Primarily, they are "politically invisible": "without lobbies of their own; they put forward no legislative program. . . . They are atomized . . . no face . . . no voice . . . forty to fifty million people are becoming increasingly invisible."

Politically, the poor are characterized by apathy, cynicism, and aliena-tion. They rarely vote and voting registration drives have not been very successful. When they do vote, they do not lose their cynicism about the political process. Why should they? What they require—the social and economic reforms necessary to deal with their problems—cannot be secured by pressure-group tactics. And in any event, why should those who seek opportunity and some minimum standard of human dignity be satisfied by the concessions ambitious politicians might be pressured into making?

The problem is that the poor are politically invisible because they are *morally* invisible. The human dimensions of their problem have not seeped, through that saving capacity for compassion on which civic decency rests, into the consciences of the affluent. As a result, the egoistic sanction for justice that operates in brokerage politics—"it might happen to me"—does not provide a basis for compassionate concern. Under current conditions only a passion for justice starting with the assumption that "it *has* happened to me" when it has happened to others can make the problem of poverty relevant to the affluent. Poverty, in this respect, is typical of the problems on the new agenda of mass democracies. What they reveal, above all, is the very real poverty of our existing political processes.

THE CHALLENGE OF THE WARFARE STATE

President Eisenhower, in his last major presidential address, issued a solemn warning of the dangers associated with the development of a military-industrial complex that permeates almost every facet of Ameri-can life. The United States, he noted, had been compelled to "create a permanent armaments industry of vast proportions" and to maintain a defense establishment of three and one-half million persons. He con-tinued with a further warning:

[1] Michael Harrington, *The Other America: Poverty in the United States* (New York: Macmillan, 1962).

This conjunction of an immense military establishment and a large arms industry is new in American experience. The total influence—economic, political, even spiritual—is felt in every city, every statehouse, every office of the federal government. We recognize the imperative need for this development. Yet we must not fail to comprehend its grave implications. Our toil, resources, and livelihood are all involved; so is the very structure of our society.

In the councils of government, we must guard against the acquisition of unwarranted influence, whether sought or unsought by the military-industrial complex. The potential for the disastrous use of misplaced power exists and will persist. We must never let the weight of this combination endanger our liberties or democratic processes. We should take nothing for granted. Only an alert and knowledgeable citizenry can compel the proper meshing of the huge industrial and military machinery of defense with our peaceful methods and goals so that security and liberty may prosper together.[2]

Cast in the brokerage system, the military-industrial complex has even wider ramifications. Perhaps it might more adequately be called the military-industrial-labor-state-local complex, since all are involved. Governors descend upon Washington to support their state's congressional representatives' claims for a fair share of defense contracts; local chambers of commerce and other groups vie with one another in making attractive offers to defense plants; economically depressed areas are given defense priorities; and all defense appropriations in the Congress have strong political overtones as bargaining takes place among congressmen eager to better the economic conditions of their constituents.

What the military-industrial complex illustrates is the difficulty of getting a national interest recognized as a basis for judgment in a political setting dominated by organized interest groups and the promotion of constituency interests. National defense requirements, like the other aspects of foreign policy, do not respond to the politics of group accommodation in a climate of countervailing power.

THE CHALLENGE OF FOREIGN POLICY

The problem of devising responsible instruments for the expression and implementation of public goals in the area of foreign policy is further complicated by the absence of organized political debate. In the period since World War II, we have developed a desire for unity of

---

[2] *Congressional Quarterly*, March 24, 1961, p. 464. This issue contains a careful analysis of the impact of the military lobby (pp. 463-78). See also Fred J. Cook, "Juggernaut: The Warfare State," *The Nation*, October 28, 1961.

purpose under the generally agreed-upon assumption that foreign policy should be bipartisan. The late and distinguished Senator Vandenberg, who was one of its major architects, preferred to call it "nonpartisan," thus suggesting that the absence of partisan debate was due to the presence of a clearly discernible national interest about which there was no real room for disagreement. On other occasions, however, he justified the policy as necessary in order that we might "unite our official voice at water's edge so that America speaks with maximum authority."[3] For Senator Vandenberg, as for the rest of us, there has always been some confusion about whether a consensus *exists*, or whether it is necessary that we act *as if* it did.

Whether regarded as bipartisanism or nonpartisanism, what this policy implies is not that politics stops at the water's edge, but rather that it is excluded from the processes of our own political system with respect to policies that involve our relations with the outside world. The difficulty is that the elimination of politics is also the elimination of most of the devices for ensuring political responsibility. So far as the citizen is concerned, his vote, where it involves foreign policy, becomes merely an exercise in patriotism and social solidarity. In the absence of the regular mechanisms of choice and accountability, he endorses a blank check made out to the successful candidates.

The crux of the matter is that our new foreign-policy problems (with all this now implies) cannot even be approached, much less resolved, through the brokerage process, which has come so largely to shape our approach to traditional problems. At the same time, the traditional processes of partisan competition and debate have been ruled out. Where foreign-policy questions have come to be the most important political questions, the problem of devising instruments of responsible government becomes a pressing and fundamental concern.

THE CHALLENGE OF CITIZENSHIP

Even if it were not for the overarching importance of foreign-policy problems, Americans in mid-century still should return to fundamentals and consider again the question of the meaning of democratic government and the institutions and attitudes appropriate to it. As we might expect in a democratic society, the crisis in the political order has its roots in the attitudes of individual citizens toward politics.

[3] Quoted in H. H. Humphrey, "The Senate in Foreign Policy," *Foreign Affairs*, July, 1959, p. 533.

Americans have always prided themselves on their receptivity to change, their flexibility and inventiveness, and their hospitality to new ideas. This quality of openness was transmitted into a sense of the unfinished business of building a democratic society. The pressures of mass society, in the view of one penetrating critic, have not eliminated the average American's eagerness to "try new things and new methods." But they have confined it to those activities that do not "make him look 'different' or 'peculiar.'"[4] Political involvement that reflects one's principles and commitments is one of the earliest casualties of this limitation. Citizens tend to retreat into the private world of consumption where trying the new is the only way to avoid being peculiar. This preoccupation with personal economic affairs, de Tocqueville pointed out, "saps the virtues of public life."

Under these conditions, the consent of the governed ceases to mean that citizens have exercised conscious, reasoned choice. There may still be competitive elections, and the efforts of competing consent engineers may even be said to give the public what it wants. The question, however, is whether consent in a democratiç society is simply a matter of giving people what they want. People are not born with wants; they develop them in a social setting. The character of a society's educational system, its system of mass communications, its group life, and its political system—all contribute to defining the conditions in which human wants are developed. If people are to participate politically in defining the goals of their public life, it is necessary that these institutions be in good democratic repair to open up alternatives, sharpen the skills of critical choice, draw men into a public discourse, and provide information and reasoned argument. Only then can the contest for political power be genuinely competitive. This suggests that education and the mass media should be high on the agenda of a democracy concerned not to give people what they want but what they "think best."[5]

Criticism of the existing order of American politics need not involve either an underestimation of its achievements and virtues or a plea for utopian perfectionism. The politics of group conciliation maintains social peace and order and has resulted in a wider sharing of economic plenty than any other society has every achieved. Moreover, despite its

[4] Gabriel A. Almond, *The American People and Foreign Policy* (New York: Harcourt, Brace, 1956), p. 59.
[5] See Joseph Tussman, *Obligation and the Body Politic* (New York: Oxford, 1960), pp. 110-12.

lack of provision for direct responsibility to majority opinion, the system no doubt responds, cumbersomely but surely, in the direction of widespread and sustained popular desires.

Similarly, if much of the appeal by politicians to citizens is manipulative, there are still advantages in the existence of a plurality of manipulators. Certainly, this condition is preferable to an exclusive monopoly of the instruments of manipulation in the hands of party or state. To borrow a figure from democratic philosopher Boyd Bode, it is much worse to be bawled out by a policeman than by one's wife. But dictatorship and totalitarianism are not the only alternatives to the politics of compromise and manipulation. It is true that they are likely to be the result if, out of frustration and despair and righteous indignation, men seek to elevate politics by transcending it. Perfectionism, as modern conservatives have ably and persistently warned, has a habit of defeating its own purposes. The demand for total victories and total solutions to problems, the cry for leaders who will rise above politics and parties, the tendency to see those who disagree as traitors—these are the characteristics of the modern mass movements that lead to totalitarianism. Democratic alternatives must stay within the bounds of competitive politics, which encompasses pluralism, conflict, disagreement, compromise, and manipulation. The problem is not to *eliminate* self-interest and emotion or the play of pressure groups and public relations. Rather, it is to make the legislative process something more than the result of group pressures, and politicians something more than moral midwives—in short, to make the electoral process something more than a patriotic holiday.

The fundamental problem is to decide what model of democracy is to serve us as a basis for evaluating the existing order. Only then can we make judgments about the adequacy of current organization and function of campaigns and elections, political parties, pressure groups, Congress, the Presidency, and the courts. In any event, there is no simple panacea. The processes of democratic government will reflect the expectations of its citizens and the demands they make on themselves. If citizens generally make the care of their private interests paramount, effective political power will be increasingly transferred to the agents of pressure groups and to those skilled in the uses of the mass media; the effective political process will increasingly reflect the compromise of private claims.

On the other hand, one may find these tendencies to be incompatible with the development of the highest promises of popular government. Insofar as this occurs, the changed demands that citizens will make on themselves and on their politicians and political parties will themselves be the primary instruments of political reform.

APPENDIX

Constitution of the United States

[In Convention, September 17, 1787]

Preamble

We the people of the United States, in order to form a more perfect union, establish justice, insure domestic tranquillity, provide for the common defense, promote the general welfare, and secure the blessings of liberty to ourselves and our posterity, do ordain and establish this Constitution for the United States of America.

Article 1. Legislative Department[1]

Section 1. Congress[1]

Powers Are Vested in Senate and House[1]

1.[1] All legislative powers herein granted shall be vested in a Congress of the United States, which shall consist of a Senate and House of Representatives.

Section 2. House of Representatives

Election of Representatives

1. The House of Representatives shall be composed of members chosen every second year by the people of the several States, and the electors in each State shall have the qualifications requisite for electors of the most numerous branch of the State Legislature.

Qualifications of Representatives

2. No person shall be a Representative who shall not have attained to the age of twenty-five years, and been seven years a citizen of the United States, and who shall not, when elected, be an inhabitant of that State in which he shall be chosen.

Apportionment of Representatives

3. Representatives and direct taxes shall be apportioned among the several States which may be included within this Union, according to their

---

[1] Headings and paragraph numbers have been inserted to assist the reader, and are not part of the Constitution. The original Constitution contains only article and section numbers. These headings and paragraph numbers were prepared under the direction of the chief clerk of the California Assembly.

respective numbers, which shall be determined by adding to the whole number of free persons, including those bound to service for a term of years, and excluding Indians not taxed, three-fifths of all other persons. The actual enumeration shall be made within three years after the first meeting of the Congress of the United States, and within every subsequent term of ten years, in such manner as they shall by law direct. The number of Representatives shall not exceed one for every thirty thousand, but each State shall have at least one Representative; and until such enumeration shall be made, the State of New Hampshire shall be entitled to choose three, Massachusetts eight, Rhode Island and Providence Plantations one, Connecticut five, New York six, New Jersey four, Pennsylvania eight, Delaware one, Maryland six, Virginia ten, North Carolina five, South Carolina five, and Georgia three.

(This clause has been superseded, so far as it relates to representation, by section 2 of the Fourteenth Amendment to the Constitution.)

Vacancies

4. When vacancies happen in the representation from any State, the executive authority thereof shall issue writs of election to fill such vacancies.

Officers of the House—Impeachment

5. The House of Representatives shall choose their Speaker and other officers; and shall have the sole power of impeachment.

Section 3. The Senate

Number of Senators

1. The Senate of the United States shall be composed of two Senators from each State, chosen by the Legislature thereof, for six years; and each Senator shall have one vote.

(Superseded by Amendment XVII.)

Classification of Senators

2. Immediately after they shall be assembled in consequence of the first election, they shall be divided as equally as may be into three classes. The seats of the Senators of the first class shall be vacated at the expiration of the second year, of the second class at the expiration of the fourth year, and of the third class at the expiration of the sixth year, so that one third may be chosen every second year; and if vacancies happen by resignation, or otherwise, during the recess of the Legislature of any State, the executive thereof may make temporary appointments until the next meeting of the Legislature, which shall then fill such vacancies.

(Modified by Amendment XVII.)

Qualifications of Senators

3. No person shall be a Senator who shall not have attained to the age of thirty years, and been nine years a citizen of the United States, and who shall not, when elected, be an inhabitant of that State for which he shall be chosen.

President of Senate

4. The Vice President of the United States shall be President of the Senate, but shall have no vote, unless they be equally divided.

Officers of Senate

5. The Senate shall choose their other officers, and also a President pro Tempore, in the absence of the Vice President, or when he shall exercise the office of President of the United States.

Trial of Impeachment

6. The Senate shall have the sole power to try all impeachments. When sitting for that purpose, they shall be on oath or affirmation. When the President of the United States is tried the Chief Justice shall preside: And no person shall be convicted without the concurrence of two-thirds of the members present.

Judgment on Conviction of Impeachment

7. Judgment in cases of impeachment shall not extend further than to removal from office, and disqualification to hold and enjoy any office of honor, trust or profit under the United States: but the party convicted shall nevertheless be liable and subject to indictment, trial, judgment and punishment, according to law.

Section 4. Election of Senators and Representatives —Meetings of Congress

Election of Members of Congress

1. The times, places and manner of holding elections for Senators and Representatives, shall be prescribed in each State by the Legislature thereof; but the Congress may at any time by law make or alter such regulations, except as to the places of choosing Senators.

(See Amendment XX.)

Congress to Meet Annually

2. The Congress shall assemble at least once in every year, and such meeting shall be on the first Monday in December, unless they shall by law appoint a different day.

(Changed to January 3 by Amendment XX.)

Section 5. Powers and Duties of Each House of Congress

Sole Judge of Qualifications of Members

1. Each House shall be the judge of the elections, returns and qualifications of its own members, and a majority of each shall constitute a quorum to do business; but a smaller number may adjourn from day to day, and may be authorized to compel the attendance of absent members, in such manner, and under such penalties as each House may provide.

Rules of Proceedings—Punishment of Members

2. Each House may determine the rules of its proceedings, punish its

members for disorderly behavior, and, with the concurrence of two-thirds, expel a member.

Journals

3. Each House shall keep a Journal of its proceedings, and from time to time publish the same, excepting such parts as may in their judgment require secrecy; and the yeas and nays of the members of either House on any question shall, at the desire of one-fifth of those present, be entered on the Journal.

Adjournment

4. Neither House, during the session of Congress, shall, without the consent of the other, adjourn for more than three days, nor to any other place than that in which the two Houses shall be sitting.

Section 6. Compensation, Privileges and Disabilities, of Senators and Representatives

Compensation—Privileges

1. The Senators and Representatives shall receive a compensation for their services, to be ascertained by law, and paid out of the Treasury of the United States. They shall in all cases, except treason, felony and breach of the peace, be privileged from arrest during their attendance at the session of their respective Houses, and in going to and returning from the same; and for any speech or debate in either House, they shall not be questioned in any other place.

Disability to Hold Other Offices

2. No Senator or Representative shall, during the time for which he was elected, be appointed to any civil office under the authority of the United States, which shall have been created, or the emoluments whereof shall have been increased during such time; and no person holding any office under the United States, shall be a member of either House during his continuance in office.

(See also section 3 of the Fourteenth Amendment.)

Section 7. Mode of Passing Laws

Special Provision as to Revenue Laws

1. All bills for raising revenue shall originate in the House of Representatives; but the Senate may propose or concur with amendments as on other bills.

Laws, How Enacted

2. Every bill which shall have passed the House of Representatives and the Senate, shall, before it become a law, be presented to the President of the United States; if he approve he shall sign it, but if not he shall return it, with his objections to that House in which it shall have originated who shall enter the objections at large on their Journal, and proceed to

reconsider it. If after such reconsideration two-thirds of that House shall agree to pass the bill, it shall be sent, together with the objections, to the other House, by which it shall likewise be reconsidered, and if approved by two-thirds of that House, it shall become a law. But in all such cases the votes of both Houses shall be determined by yeas and nays, and the names of the persons voting for and against the bill shall be entered on the Journal of each House respectively. If any bill shall not be returned by the President within ten days (Sundays excepted) after it shall have been presented to him, the same shall be a law, in like manner as if he had signed it, unless the Congress by their adjournment prevent its return, in which case it shall not be a law.

Resolutions, Etc.

3. Every order, resolution, or vote to which the concurrence of the Senate and House of Representatives may be necessary (except on a question of adjournment) shall be presented to the President of the United States; and before the same shall take effect, shall be approved by him, or being disapproved by him, shall be repassed by two-thirds of the Senate and House of Representatives, according to the rules and limitations prescribed in the case of a bill.

Section 8. Powers Granted to Congress

Taxation

1. The Congress shall have power to lay and collect taxes, duties, imposts and excises, to pay the debts and provide for the common defense and general welfare of the United States; but all duties, imposts and excises shall be uniform throughout the United States;

Loans

2. To borrow money on the credit of the United States;

Commerce

3. To regulate commerce with foreign nations, and among the several States, and with the Indian tribes;

Naturalization and Bankruptcies

4. To establish an uniform rule of naturalization, and uniform laws on the subject of bankruptcies throughout the United States;

Coin

5. To coin money, regulate the value thereof, and of foreign coin, and fix the standard of weights and measures;

Counterfeiting

6. To provide for the punishment of counterfeiting the securities and current coin of the United States;

Post Office

7. To establish post offices and post roads;

Patents and Copyrights
8. To promote the progress of science and useful arts, by securing for limited times to authors and inventors the exclusive right to their respective writings and discoveries;

Courts
9. To constitute tribunals inferior to the Supreme Court;

Piracies
10. To define and punish piracies and felonies committed on the high seas, and offenses against the law of nations;

War
11. To declare war, grant letters of marque and reprisal, and make rules concerning captures on land and water;

Army
12. To raise and support armies, but no appropriation of money to that use shall be for a longer term than two years;

Navy
13. To provide and maintain a navy;

Military and Naval Rules
14. To make rules for the government and regulation of the land and naval forces;

Militia, Calling Forth
15. To provide for calling forth the militia to execute the laws of the Union, suppress insurrections and repel invasions;

Militia, Organizing and Arming
16. To provide for organizing, arming, and disciplining, the militia, and for governing such part of them as may be employed in the service of the United States, reserving to the States respectively, the appointment of the officers, and the authority of training the militia according to the discipline prescribed by Congress;

Federal District and Other Places
17. To exercise exclusive legislation in all cases whatsoever, over such district (not exceeding ten miles square) as may, by cession of particular States, and the acceptance of Congress, become the seat of the government of the United States, and to exercise like authority over all places purchased by the consent of the Legislature of the State in which the same shall be, for the erection of forts, magazines, arsenals, dockyards, and other needful buildings;—And

Make Laws to Carry out Foregoing Powers
18. To make all laws which shall be necessary and proper for carrying into execution the foregoing powers, and all other powers vested by this

Constitution in the Government of the United States, or in any department or officer thereof.

(For other powers, see Article II, section 1; Article III, sections 2 and 3; Article IV, sections 1-3; Article V; and Amendments XIII-XVI and XIX-XXI.)

Section 9. Limitation on Powers Granted to the United States

Slave Trade

1. The migration or importation of such persons as any of the States now existing shall think proper to admit, shall not be prohibited by the Congress prior to the year one thousand eight hundred and eight, but a tax or duty may be imposed on such importation, not exceeding ten dollars for each person.

Habeas Corpus

2. The privilege of the writ of habeas corpus shall not be suspended, unless when in cases of rebellion or invasion the public safety may require it.

Ex Post Facto Law

3. No bill of attainder or ex post facto law shall be passed.

Direct Taxes

4. No capitation, or other direct, tax shall be laid, unless in proportion to the census or enumeration hereinbefore directed to be taken.

(Modified by Amendment XVI.)

Duties on Exports

5. No tax or duty shall be laid on articles exported from any State.

No Commercial Discrimination to Be Made Between States

6. No preference shall be given by any regulation of commerce or revenue to the ports of one State over those of another; nor shall vessels bound to, or from, one State, be obliged to enter, clear or pay duties in another.

Money, How Drawn from Treasury

7. No money shall be drawn from the Treasury, but in consequence of appropriations made by law; and a regular statement and account of the receipts and expenditures of all public money shall be published from time to time.

Titles of Nobility

8. No title of nobility shall be granted by the United States: And no person holding any office of profit or trust under them, shall, without the consent of the Congress, accept of any present, emolument, office, or title, of any kind whatever, from any King, Prince, or foreign State.

(For other limitations see Amendments I-X.)

Section 10. Powers Prohibited to the States

Powers Prohibited, Absolutely

1. No State shall enter into any treaty, alliance, or confederation; grant letters of marque and reprisal; coin money; emit bills of credit; make

anything but gold and silver coin a tender in payment of debts; pass any bill of attainder, ex post facto law, or law impairing the obligation of contracts, or grant any title of nobility.

Powers Concerning Duties on Imports or Exports

2. No State shall, without the consent of the Congress, lay any imposts or duties on imports or exports, except what may be absolutely necessary for executing its inspection laws: and the net produce of all duties and imposts, laid by any State on imports or exports, shall be for the use of the Treasury of the United States; and all such laws shall be subject to the revision and control of the Congress.

Powers Permitted with Consent of Congress

3. No State shall, without the consent of Congress, lay any duty of tonnage, keep troops, or ships of war in time of peace, enter into any agreement or compact with another State, or with a foreign power, or engage in war, unless actually invaded, or in such imminent danger as will not admit of delay.

ARTICLE II. EXECUTIVE DEPARTMENT

Section 1. The President

Executive Power Vested in President—Term of Office

1. The executive power shall be vested in a President of the United States of America. He shall hold his office during the term of four years, and, together with the Vice President, chosen for the same term, be elected, as follows:

Appointment and Number of Presidential Electors

2. Each State shall appoint, in such manner as the Legislature thereof may direct, a number of electors, equal to the whole number of Senators and Representatives to which the State may be entitled in the Congress: but no Senator or Representative, or person holding an office of trust or profit under the United States, shall be appointed an elector.

Mode of Electing President and Vice President

3. The electors shall meet in their respective States, and vote by ballot for two persons, of whom one at least shall not be an inhabitant of the same State with themselves. And they shall make a list of all the persons voted for, and of the number of votes for each; which list they shall sign and certify, and transmit sealed to the seat of the Government of the United States, directed to the President of the Senate. The President of the Senate shall, in the presence of the Senate and House of Representatives, open all the certificates, and the votes shall then be counted. The person having the greatest number of votes shall be the President, if such number be a majority of the whole number of electors appointed; and if there be more than one who have such majority, and have an equal number of votes, then the House of Representatives shall immediately choose by a ballot one of them

for President; and if no person have a majority, then from the five highest on the list the said House shall in like manner choose the President. But in choosing the President, the votes shall be taken by States, the representation from each State having one vote; a quorum for this purpose shall consist of a member or members from two-thirds of the States, and a majority of all the States shall be necessary to a choice. In every case, after the choice of the President, the person having the greatest number of votes of the electors shall be the Vice President. But if there should remain two or more who have equal votes, the Senate shall choose from them by ballot the Vice President.

(This paragraph has been superseded by the Twelfth Amendment to the Constitution. See Amendment XX.)

Time of Choosing Electors and Casting Electoral Vote

4. The Congress may determine the time of choosing the electors, and the day on which they shall give their votes; which day shall be the same throughout the United States.

Qualifications of President

5. No person except a natural-born citizen, or a citizen of the United States, at the time of the adoption of this Constitution, shall be eligible to the office of President; neither shall any person be eligible to that office who shall not have attained to the age of thirty-five years, and been fourteen years a resident within the United States.

(See also Article II, section 1, and Fourteenth Amendment.)

Presidential Succession

6. In case of the removal of the President from office, or of his death, resignation, or inability to discharge the powers and duties of the said office, the same shall devolve on the Vice President, and the Congress may by law provide for the case of removal, death, resignation or inability, both of the President and Vice President declaring what officer shall then act as President, and such officer shall act accordingly, until the disability be removed, or a President shall be elected.

Salary of President

7. The President shall, at stated times, receive for his services, a compensation, which shall neither be increased nor diminished during the period for which he shall have been elected, and he shall not receive within that period any other emolument from the United States, or any of them.

Oath of Office of President

8. Before he enter on the execution of his office, he shall take the following oath or affirmation:—"I do solemnly swear (or affirm) that I will faithfully execute the office of President of the United States, and will to the best of my ability, preserve, protect and defend the Constitution of the United States."

Section 2. Powers of the President

Commander in Chief

1. The President shall be Commander in Chief of the Army and Navy of the United States, and of the militia of the several States, when called into the actual service of the United States; he may require the opinion, in writing, of the principal officer in each of the executive departments, upon any subject relating to the duties of their respective offices, and he shall have power to grant reprieves and pardons for offenses against the United States, except in cases of impeachment.

Treaties and Appointments

2. He shall have power, by and with the advice and consent of the Senate, to make treaties, provided two-thirds of the Senators present concur; and he shall nominate, and by and with the advice and consent of the Senate, shall appoint ambassadors, other public ministers and consuls, Judges of the Supreme Court, and all other officers of the United States, whose appointments are not herein otherwise provided for, and which shall be established by law: but the Congress may by law vest the appointment of such inferior officers, as they think proper, in the President alone, in the courts of law, or in the heads of departments.

Filling Vacancies

3. The President shall have power to fill up all vacancies that may happen during the recess of the Senate, by granting commissions which shall expire at the end of their next session.

Section 3. Duties of the President

Message to Congress—Adjourn and Call Special Session

He shall from time to time give to the Congress information of the state of the Union, and recommend to their consideration such measures as he shall judge necessary and expedient; he may, on extraordinary occasions, convene both Houses, or either of them, and in case of disagreement between them, with respect to the time of adjournment, he may adjourn them to such time as he shall think proper; he shall receive ambassadors and other public ministers; he shall take care that the laws be faithfully executed, and shall commission all the officers of the United States.

(See also Article I, section 5.)

Section 4. Removal of Executive and Civil Officers

Impeachment of President and Other Officers

The President, Vice President and all civil officers of the United States, shall be removed from office on impeachment for, and conviction of, treason, bribery, or other high crimes and misdemeanors.

(See also Article I, sections 2 and 3.)

ARTICLE III. JUDICIAL DEPARTMENT
Section 1. Judicial Powers Vested in Federal Courts

Courts—Terms of Office and Salary of Judges

The judicial power of the United States, shall be vested in one Supreme Court, and in such inferior courts as the Congress may from time to time ordain and establish. The judges, both of the Supreme and inferior courts, shall hold their offices during good behavior, and shall, at stated times, receive for their services, a compensation, which shall not be diminished during their continuance in office.

Section 2. Jurisdiction of United States Courts

Cases That May Come Before United States Courts

1. The judicial power shall extend to all cases, in law and equity, arising under this Constitution, the laws of the United States, and treaties made, or which shall be made, under their authority;—to all cases affecting ambassadors, other public ministers and consuls;—to all cases of admiralty and maritime jurisdiction;—to controversies to which the United States shall be a party;—to controversies between two or more States;—between a State and citizens of another State;—between citizens of different States; —between citizens of the same State claiming lands under grants of different States, and between a State, or the citizens thereof, and foreign States, citizens or subjects.

(See also Eleventh Amendment.)

Jurisdiction of Supreme and Appellate Courts

2. In all cases affecting ambassadors, other public ministers and consuls, and those in which a State shall be party, the Supreme Court shall have original jurisdiction. In all the other cases before mentioned, the Supreme Court shall have appellate jurisdiction, both as to law and fact, with such exceptions, and under such regulations as the Congress shall make.

Trial of Crimes

3. The trial of all crimes, except in cases of impeachment, shall be by jury; and such trial shall be held in the State where the said crimes shall have been committed; but when not committed within any State, the trial shall be at such place or places as the Congress may by law have directed.

(See also Fifth. Sixth, Seventh, and Eighth Amendments.)

Section 3. Treason

Treason Defined

1. Treason against the United States, shall consist only in levying war against them, or in adhering to their enemies, giving them aid and comfort.

Conviction

2. No person shall be convicted of treason unless on the testimony of two witnesses to the same overt act, or on confession in open court.

Punishment

3. The Congress shall have power to declare the punishment of treason, but no attainder of treason shall work corruption of blood, or forfeiture except during the life of the person attainted.

ARTICLE IV. THE STATES AND THE FEDERAL GOVERNMENT

Section 1. Offical Acts of the States

Full Faith and Credit

Full faith and credit shall be given in each State to the public acts, records, and judicial proceedings of every other State. And the Congress may by general laws prescribe the manner in which such acts, records and proceedings shall be proved, and the effect thereof.

(See also Fourteenth Amendment.)

Section 2. Citizens of the States

Interstate Privileges of Citizens

1. The citizens of each State shall be entitled to all privileges and immunities of citizens in the several States.

Fugitives from Justice

2. A person charged in any State with treason, felony, or other crime, who shall flee from justice, and be found in another State, shall on demand of the executive authority of the State from which he fled, be delivered up, to be removed to the State having jurisdiction of the crime.

Fugitives from Service

3. No person held to service or labor in one State, under the laws thereof, escaping into another, shall, in consequence of any law or regulation therein, be discharged from such service or labor, but shall be delivered up on claim of the party to whom such service or labor may be due.

(*Person* here includes slave. This was the basis of the Fugitive Slave Laws of 1793 and 1850. It is now superseded by the Thirteenth Amendment, by which slavery is prohibited.)

Section 3. New States

Admission or Division of States

1. New States may be admitted by the Congress into this Union; but no new State shall be formed or erected within the jurisdiction of any other State; nor any State be formed by the junction of two or more States, or parts of States, without the consent of the Legislatures of the States concerned as well as of the Congress.

Control of the Property and Territory of the Union

2. The Congress shall have power to dispose of and make all needful rules and regulations respecting the territory or other property belonging

to the United States; and nothing in this Constitution shall be so construed as to prejudice any claims of the United States, or of any particular State.

Section 4. Protection of States Guaranteed

Republican Form of Government

The United States shall guarantee to every State in this Union a republican form of government, and shall protect each of them against invasion; and on application of the Legislature, or of the executive (when the Legislature cannot be convened) against domestic violence.

ARTICLE V. AMENDMENTS

Amendments, How Proposed and Adopted

The Congress, whenever two-thirds of both Houses shall deem it necessary, shall propose amendments to this Constitution, or, on the application of the Legislatures of two-thirds of the several States, shall call a convention for proposing amendments, which, in either case, shall be valid to all intents and purposes, as part of this Constitution, when ratified by the Legislatures of three-fourths of the several States, or by conventions in three-fourths thereof, as the one or the other mode of ratification may be proposed by the Congress; provided that no amendment which may be made prior to the year one thousand eight hundred and eight shall in any manner affect the first and fourth clauses in the ninth section of the first article; and that no State, without its consent, shall be deprived of its equal suffrage in the Senate.

ARTICLE VI. GENERAL PROVISIONS

The Public Debt

1. All debts contracted and engagements entered into, before the adoption of this Constitution, shall be as valid against the United States under this Constitution, as under the Confederation.

(See also Fourteenth Amendment, section 4.)

Supreme Law of the Land

2. This Constitution, and the laws of the United States which shall be made in pursuance thereof; and all treaties made, or which shall be made, under the authority of the United States, shall be the supreme law of the land; and the judges in every State shall be bound thereby, anything in the Constitution or laws of any State to the contrary notwithstanding.

Oath of Office—No Religious Test Required

3. The Senators and Representatives before mentioned, and the members of the several State Legislatures, and all executive and judicial officers, both of the United States and of the several States, shall be bound by oath or affirmation, to support this Constitution; but no religious test shall ever be required as a qualification to any office or public trust under the United States.

ARTICLE VII. RATIFICATION OF THE CONSTITUTION[2]

Ratification of Nine States Required

The ratification of the conventions of nine States, shall be sufficient for the establishment of this Constitution between the States so ratifying the same.

DONE in convention by the unanimous consent of the States present the seventeenth day of September in the year of our Lord one thousand seven hundred and eighty-seven and of the Independence of the United States of America the twelfth. In witness whereof we have hereunto subscribed our names,[3]

G° WASHINGTON—Presid[t] and deputy from Virginia

New Hampshire {JOHN LANGDON
NICHOLAS GILMAN

Massachusetts {NATHANIEL GORHAM
RUFUS KING

Connecticut {W[M] SAM[L] JOHNSON
ROGER SHERMAN

New York   ALEXANDER HAMILTON

New Jersey {WIL: LIVINGSTON
DAVID BREARLEY.
W[M] PATERSON.
JONA: DAYTON

[2] The Constitution was ratified by the States in the following order:
1. Delaware—December 7, 1787.
2. Pennsylvania—December 12, 1787.
3. New Jersey—December 19, 1787.
4. Georgia—January 2, 1788.
5. Connecticut—January 9, 1788.
6. Massachusetts—February 6, 1788.
7. Maryland—April 28, 1788.
8. South Carolina—May 23, 1788.
9. New Hampshire—June 21, 1788.
10. Virginia—June 25, 1788.
11. New York—July 26, 1788.
12. North Carolina—November 21, 1789.
13. Rhode Island—May 29, 1790.

[3] There were sixty-five delegates chosen to the convention; ten did not attend; sixteen declined or failed to sign; thirty-nine signed. Rhode Island sent no delegates.

Pennsylvania
- B Franklin
- Thomas Mifflin
- Rob$^{T.}$ Morris
- Geo. Clymer
- Thos FitzSimons
- Jared Ingersoll
- James Wilson
- Gouv Morris

Delaware
- Geo: Read
- Gunning Bedford jun
- John Dickinson
- Richard Bassett
- Jaco: Broom

Maryland
- James McHenry
- Dan of S^T Thos Jenifer
- Dan^L Carroll

Virginia
- John Blair—
- James Madison Jr.

North Carolina
- W^M Blount
- Rich^D Dobbs Spaight.
- Hu Williamson

South Carolina
- J. Rutledge
- Charles Cotesworth Pinckney
- Charles Pinckney
- Pierce Butler

Georgia
- William Few
- Abr Baldwin

Amendments

AMENDMENT I

Restrictions on Powers of Congress

(SECTION 1.) Congress shall make no law respecting an establishment of religion, or prohibiting the free exercise thereof; or abridging the freedom of speech, or of the press; or the right of the people peaceably to assemble, and to petition the Government for a redress of grievances.

(Proposed September 25, 1789; ratified December 15, 1791.)

AMENDMENT II

Right to Bear Arms

(SECTION 1.) A well-regulated militia, being necessary to the security of a free State, the right of the people to keep and bear arms, shall not be infringed.

(Proposed September 25, 1789; ratified December 15, 1791.)

AMENDMENT III

Billeting of Soldiers

(SECTION 1.) No soldier shall, in time of peace be quartered in any house, without the consent of the owner, nor in time of war, but in a manner to be prescribed by law.

(Proposed September 25, 1789; ratified December 15, 1791.)

AMENDMENT IV

Seizures, Searches and Warrants

(SECTION 1.) The right of the people to be secure in their persons, houses, papers, and effects, against unreasonable searches and seizures, shall not be violated, and no warrants shall issue, but upon probable cause, supported by oath or affirmation, and particularly describing the place to be searched, and the persons or things to be seized.

(Proposed September 25, 1789; ratified December 15, 1791.)

AMENDMENT V

Criminal Proceedings and Condemnation of Property

(SECTION 1). No person shall be held to answer for a capital, or otherwise infamous crime, unless on a presentment or indictment of a grand jury, except in cases arising in the land or naval forces, or in the militia, when in actual service in time of war or public danger; nor shall any person be subject for the same offense to be twice put in jeopardy of life or limb; nor shall be compelled in any criminal case to be a witness against himself, nor be deprived of life, liberty, or property, without due process of law; nor shall private property be taken for public use, without just compensation.

(Proposed September 25, 1789; ratified December 15, 1791.)

AMENDMENT VI

Mode of Trial in Criminal Proceedings

(SECTION 1.) In all criminal prosecutions, the accused shall enjoy the right to a speedy and public trial, by an impartial jury of the State and district wherein the crime shall have been committed, which district shall have been previously ascertained by law, and to be informed of the nature and cause of the accusation; to be confronted with the witnesses against him; to have compulsory process for obtaining witnesses in his favor, and to have the assistance of counsel for his defense.

(Proposed September 25, 1789; ratified December 15, 1791.)

AMENDMENT VII

Trial by Jury

(SECTION 1.) In suits at common law, where the value in controversy shall exceed twenty dollars, the right of trial by jury shall be preserved, and no fact tried by a jury, shall be otherwise re-examined in any court of the United States, than according to the rules of the common law.

(Proposed September 25, 1789; ratified December 15, 1791.)

AMENDMENT VIII

Bails—Fines—Punishments

(SECTION 1.) Excessive bail shall not be required, nor excessive fines imposed, nor cruel and unusual punishments inflicted.

(Proposed September 25, 1789; ratified December 15, 1791.)

AMENDMENT IX

Certain Rights Not Denied to the People

(SECTION 1.) The enumeration in the Constitution, of certain rights, shall not be construed to deny or disparage others retained by the people.

(Proposed September 25, 1789; ratified December 15, 1791.)

AMENDMENT X

State Rights

(SECTION 1.) The powers not delegated to the United States by the Constitution, nor prohibited by it to the States, are reserved to the States respectively, or to the people.

(Proposed September 25, 1789; ratified December 15, 1791.)

AMENDMENT XI

Judicial Powers

(SECTION 1.) The judicial power of the United States shall not be construed to extend to any suit in law or equity, commenced or prosecuted against one of the United States by citizens of another State, or by citizens or subjects of any foreign State.

(Proposed March 4, 1794; ratified February 7, 1795; declared ratified January 8, 1798.)

AMENDMENT XII

Election of President and Vice President

(SECTION 1.) The electors shall meet in their respective States and vote by ballot for President and Vice President, one of whom, at least, shall not be an inhabitant of the same State with themselves; they shall name in their ballots the person voted for as President, and in distinct ballots the person voted for as Vice President, and they shall make distinct lists of all persons voted for as President, and of all persons voted for as Vice President, and of the number of votes for each, which lists they shall sign and certify, and transmit sealed to the seat of the government of the United States, directed to the President of the Senate;—The President of the Senate shall, in the presence of the Senate and House of Representatives, open all the certificates and the votes shall then be counted;—the person having the greatest number of votes for President, shall be the President, if such number be a majority of the whole number of electors appointed; and if no person have such majority, then from the persons having the highest numbers not exceeding three on the list of those voted for as President, the House of Representatives shall choose immediately, by ballot, the President. But in choosing the President, the votes shall be taken by States, the representation from each State having one vote; a quorum for this purpose shall consist of a member or members from two-thirds of the States, and a majority of all the States shall be necessary to a choice. And if the House of Representatives shall not choose a President whenever the right of choice shall devolve upon them, before the fourth day of March next following, then the Vice President shall act as President, as in the case of the death or other constitutional disability of the President—The person having the greatest number of votes, as Vice President, shall be the Vice President, if such a number be a majority of the whole number of electors appointed, and if no person have a majority, then from the two highest numbers on the list, the Senate shall choose the Vice President; a quorum for the purpose shall consist of two-thirds of the whole number of Senators, and a majority of the whole number shall be necessary to a choice. But no person constitutionally ineligible to the office of President shall be eligible to that of Vice President of the United States.

(Proposed December 12, 1803; declared ratified September 25, 1804.)

AMENDMENT XIII

Slavery

(SECTION 1.) Neither slavery nor involuntary servitude, except as a punishment for crime whereof the party shall have been duly convicted, shall exist within the United States, or any place subject to their jurisdiction.

(SECTION 2.) Congress shall have power to enforce this article by appropriate legislation.

(Proposed January 31, 1865; ratified December 6, 1865; certified December 18, 1865.)

AMENDMENT XIV

Citizenship, Representation and Payment of Public Debt

Citizenship

(SECTION 1.) All persons born or naturalized in the United States and subject to the jurisdiction thereof, are citizens of the United States and of the State wherein they reside. No State shall make or enforce any law which shall abridge the privileges or immunities of citizens of the United States; nor shall any State deprive any person of life, liberty, or property, without due process of law; nor deny to any person within its jurisdiction the equal protection of the laws.

Apportionment of Representatives

(SECTION 2.) Representatives shall be apportioned among the several States according to their respective numbers, counting the whole number of persons in each State, excluding Indians not taxed. But when the right to vote at any election for the choice of electors for President and Vice President of the United States, Representatives in Congress, the executive and judicial officers of a State, or the members of the Legislature thereof, is denied to any of the male inhabitants of such State, being twenty-one years of age, and citizens of the United States, or in any way abridged, except for participation in rebellion, or other crime, the basis of representation therein shall be reduced in the proportion which the number of such male citizens shall bear to the whole number of male citizens twenty-one years of age in such State.

Disqualification for Public Office

(SECTION 3.) No person shall be a Senator or Representative in Congress, or elector of President and Vice President, or hold any office, civil or military, under the United States, or under any State, who, having previously taken an oath, as a member of Congress, or as an officer of the United States, or as a member of any State Legislature, or as an executive or judicial officer of any State, to support the Constitution of the United States, shall have engaged in insurrection or rebellion against the same, or given aid or comfort to the enemies thereof. But Congress may by a vote of two-thirds of each House, remove such disability.

Public Debt, Guarantee of

(SECTION 4.) The validity of the public debt of the United States, authorized by law, including debts incurred for payment of pensions and bounties for services in suppressing insurrection or rebellion, shall not be questioned. But neither the United States nor any State shall assume or pay any debt or obligation incurred in aid of insurrection or rebellion against the United States, or any claim for the loss or emancipation of any slave; but all such debts, obligations and claims shall be held illegal and void.

Power of Congress

(SECTION 5.) The Congress shall have power to enforce, by appropriate legislation, the provisions of this article.
(Proposed June 13, 1866; ratified July 9, 1868; certified July 28, 1868.)

AMENDMENT XV

Elective Franchise

Right of Citizens to Vote

(SECTION 1.) The right of citizens of the United States to vote shall not be denied or abridged by the United States or by any State on account of race, color, or previous condition of servitude.

Power of Congress

(SECTION 2.) The Congress shall have power to enforce this article by appropriate legislation.

(Proposed February 26, 1869; ratified February 3, 1870; certified March 30, 1870.)

AMENDMENT XVI

Income Tax—Congress Given Power to Lay and Collect

(SECTION 1.) The Congress shall have power to lay and collect taxes on incomes, from whatever source derived, without apportionment among the several States, and without regard to any census or enumeration.

(Proposed July 12, 1909; ratified February 3, 1913; certified February 25, 1913.)

AMENDMENT XVII

Popular Election of Senators

(SECTION 1.) The Senate of the United States shall be composed of two Senators from each State, elected by the people thereof, for six years; and each Senator shall have one vote. The electors in each State shall have the qualifications requisite for electors of the most numerous branch of the State Legislatures.

(SECTION 2.) When vacancies happen in the representation of any State in the Senate, the executive authority of such State shall issue writs of election to fill such vacancies: *Provided,* That the Legislature of any State may empower the executive thereof to make temporary appointments until the people fill the vacancies by election as the Legislature may direct.

(SECTION 3.) This amendment shall not be so construed as to affect the election or term of any Senator chosen before it becomes valid as part of the Constitution.

(Proposed May 13, 1912; ratified April 8, 1913; certified May 31, 1913.)

NOTE—The Seventeenth Amendment was proposed as a direct amendment of Article I, section 3, of the Constitution.

AMENDMENT XVIII

Prohibition—States Given Concurrent Power to Enforce

(SECTION 1.) After one year from the ratification of this article the manufacture, sale, or transportation of intoxicating liquors within, the importation thereof into, or the exportation thereof from the United States and all territory subject to the jurisdiction thereof for beverage purposes is hereby prohibited.

(SECTION 2.) The Congress and the several States shall have concurrent power to enforce this article by appropriate legislation.

(SECTION 3.) This article shall be inoperative unless it shall have been ratified as an amendment to the Constitution by the Legislatures of the several States, as provided in the Constitution, within seven years from the date of the submission hereof to the States by the Congress.

(Proposed December 18, 1917; ratified January 16, 1919; certified January 29, 1919; effective January 29, 1920. For repeal see Amendment XXI.)

AMENDMENT XIX

Equal Suffrage

(SECTION 1.) The right of citizens of the United States to vote shall not be denied or abridged by the United States or by any State on account of sex.

(SECTION 2.) Congress shall have power to enforce this article by appropriate legislation.

(Proposed June 4, 1919; ratified August 18, 1920; certified August 26, 1920.)

AMENDMENT XX

Commencement of Congressional and Presidential Terms

End of Terms

(SECTION 1.) The terms of the President and Vice President shall end at noon on the 20th day of January, and the terms of Senators and Representatives at noon on the 3d day of January, of the years in which such terms would have ended if this article had not been ratified; and the terms of their successors shall then begin.

Assembling of Congress

(SECTION 2.) The Congress shall assemble at least once in every year, and such meeting shall begin at noon on the 3d day of January, unless they shall by law appoint a different day.

Congress Provides for Acting President

(SECTION 3.) If, at the time fixed for the beginning of the term of the President, the President-elect shall have died, the Vice-President-elect shall become President. If a President shall not have been chosen before the time fixed for the beginning of his term, or if the President-elect shall have failed to qualify, then the Vice-President-elect shall act as President until a President shall have qualified; and the Congress may by law provide for the case wherein neither a President-elect nor a Vice-President-elect shall have qualified, declaring who shall then act as President, or the manner in which one who is to act shall be selected, and such person shall act accordingly until a President or Vice President shall have qualified.

Congress Has Power over Unusual Elections

(SECTION 4.) The Congress may by law provide for the case of the death of any of the persons from whom the House of Representatives may choose a President whenever the right of choice shall have devolved upon them, and for the case of the death of any of the persons from whom the Senate may choose a Vice President whenever the right of choice shall have devolved upon them.

Date in Effect

(SECTION 5.) Sections 1 and 2 shall take effect on the 15th day of October following the ratification of this article.

Conditions of Ratification

(SECTION 6.) This article shall be inoperative unless it shall have been ratified as an amendment to the Constitution by the Legislatures of three-fourths of the several States within seven years from the date of its submission.

(Proposed March 2, 1932; ratified January 23, 1933; certified February 6, 1933.)

AMENDMENT XXI

Repeal of Prohibition

Repeal of 18th Amendment

(SECTION 1.) The eighteenth article of amendment to the Constitution of the United States is hereby repealed.

Control of Interstate Liquor Transportation

(SECTION 2.) The transportation or importation into any State, Territory, or possession of the United States for delivery or use therein of intoxicating liquors, in violation of the laws thereof, is hereby prohibited.

Condition of Ratification

(SECTION 3.) This article shall be inoperative unless it shall have been ratified as an amendment to the Constitution by conventions in the several States, as provided in the Constitution, within seven years from the date of the submission hereof to the States by the Congress.

(Proposed February 20, 1933; ratified December 5, 1933; certified December 5, 1933.)

AMENDMENT XXII

Terms of Office of the President

Limitation on Number of Terms

(SECTION 1.) No person shall be elected to the office of the President more than twice, and no person who has held the office of President, or acted as President, for more than two years of a term to which some other person was elected President shall be elected to the office of the President more than once. But this article shall not apply to any person holding the office of President when this article was proposed by the Congress, and shall not prevent any person who may be holding the office of President, or acting as President, during the term within which this article becomes operative from holding the office of President or acting as President during the remainder of such term.

Condition of Ratification

(SECTION 2.) This article shall be inoperative unless it shall have been ratified as an amendment to the Constitution by the Legislatures of three-fourths of the several States within seven years from the date of its submission to the States by the Congress.

(Proposed March 24, 1947; ratified February 27, 1951; certified March 1, 1951.)

AMENDMENT XXIII

Voting Rights in the District of Columbia

(SECTION 1.) The district constituting the seat of government of the United States shall appoint in such manner as the Congress may direct:

A number of electors of President and Vice President equal to the whole number of Senators and Representatives in Congress to which the District would be entitled if it were a State, but in no event more than the least populous state; they shall be in addition to those appointed by the states, but they shall be considered, for the purposes of the election of President and Vice President, to be electors appointed by a State; and they shall meet in the District and perform such duties as provided by the twelfth article of amendment.

(Certified March 29, 1961.)

AMENDMENT XXIV

Prohibition of Poll Tax

(SECTION 1.) The right of citizens of the United States to vote in any primary or other election for President or Vice President, for electors for President or Vice President, or for Senator or Representative in Congress, shall not be denied or abridged by the United States or any State by reason of failure to pay any poll tax or other tax.

(SECTION 2.) The Congress shall have power to enforce this article by appropriate legislation. (Certified January 23, 1964.)

BIBLIOGRAPHY

*T*HE BOOKS listed below have been selected for their usefulness in providing further information about, insight into, and analysis of the topics and problems covered in the text. This is a highly selective rather than an exhaustive list; many of the books listed contain excellent bibliographies of their own. We have added brief annotations, which indicate the general way in which the various authors treat their subjects.

In addition to the books listed, the footnotes throughout the text refer to many other important publications—books, professional journals, newspapers, magazines, and judicial opinions. An adequate understanding and a sense of the excitement of American politics require regular reading of newspapers and magazines. The ability to reach one's own considered opinions on policy issues requires, especially, regular reading in the opinion periodicals, examples of which are *Commentary, Harper's, Nation, The National Review, The New Republic, New York Times Magazine, The Atlantic Monthly*, and *The Progressive*.

As the text should make clear, we regard the opinions of Supreme Court justices as valuable sources for both understanding and evaluation of American politics. Especially in recent years, Court opinions contain some of the most searching and incisive analyses available of the fundamental problems of the political system. They deserve to be more widely read. A brief description of how easy they are to find may therefore be in order: When, for example, a case is cited as *Debs v. United States*, 249 U.S. 211 (1919), it is to be found at page 211 in Volume 249 of the United States Reports, available in any college library. Court decisions are also contained in other compilations. A reference to *L. ed.* means *Lawyers Edition; L. W.* means *Law Week*, a weekly publication containing the latest decisions. Books marked with an asterisk(*) have paperback editions.

DEMOCRATIC POLITICS AND MASS SOCIETY— CRITIQUES AND ANALYSES (CHAPS. 1, 2, AND 3)

ADORNO, T. W., *et al. The Authoritarian Personality*. New York: Harper, 1950. An effort to define the syndrome of psychological characteristics that

561

are found together in the personality structures of those whose behavior is incompatible with democratic ideals.

* ARENDT, HANNAH. *The Human Condition*. New York: Doubleday, 1958. A provocative existentialist critique of modern industrial mass societies, which argues that the man who is being technologically liberated from labor is incapable of using or deserving the freedom he will gain.

* CARR, E. H. *The New Society*. Boston: Beacon, 1957. A British political scientist surveys the economic, social, and cultural changes that produce mass democracies and develops a proposed way out.

* FEIN, LEONARD J. (ed.). *American Democracy: Essays on Image and Realities*. New York: Holt, Rinehart and Winston, 1964. Interesting and provocative essays on the gulfs between democratic ideals and political realities.

FROMM, ERICH. *Escape from Freedom*. New York: Holt, Rinehart and Winston, 1941. An analysis, from a psychological perspective, of the sources of conformity and of tendencies to escape from the responsibilities of freedom in modern mass societies.

* HOFFER, ERIC. *The True Believer*. New York: New American Library, 1958. Analysis of the social conditions and the psychological characteristics in a democratic society that produce extremists and followers of mass movements.

* LERNER, MAX. *America as a Civilization*. New York: Simon and Schuster, 1957. A critical study of American culture in the 1950's, including many aspects of mass society and popular culture.

* ORTEGA Y GASSET, JOSÉ. *The Revolt of the Masses*. New York: Norton, 1960. A landmark analysis, first published in 1932, of the growth of mass society and the challenges it poses to the traditional order and to democratic values. Written from a conservative perspective by the late, distinguished Spanish philosopher.

* POTTER, DAVID M. *People of Plenty*. Chicago: University of Chicago Press, 1954. An interpretation of American character as related to economic abundance, with challenging and important chapters on status mobility and the rise of the institution of advertising.

* RIESMAN, DAVID. *The Lonely Crowd*. New Haven, Conn.: Yale, 1950. A popular and profound look at the effects of mass society on the American citizen.

* SCHATTSCHNEIDER, E. E. *The Semisovereign People*. New York: Holt, Rinehart, and Winston, 1960. A critical analysis of the condition of modern American democracy and the consequences of lack of participation in government by large numbers of citizens.

STEIN, MAURICE, *et al.* (eds.). *Identity and Anxiety*. New York: Free Press, 1960. Provocative and suggestive essays on the meaning of anxiety. its causes and consequences.

* TOCQUEVILLE, ALEXIS DE. *Democracy in America*. New York: Washington

Square Press, 1964. The classic and prophetic analysis of American democracy during the early nineteenth century by an aristocratic and brilliant Frenchman.

* WHYTE, WILLIAM H., JR. *The Organization Man.* New York: Doubleday, 1957. Much discussed treatment of the impact of modern, large-scale organizations on the values of American culture and the personalities of those who work in them.

THEORIES OF DEMOCRATIC GOVERNMENT
(CHAP. 4)

BENTLEY, ARTHUR F. *The Process of Government.* Bloomington, Ind.: Principia Press, 1949. Landmark analysis of brokerage politics and the role of organized groups in the political process. First published in 1908.

* DAHL, ROBERT A. *A Preface to Democratic Theory.* Chicago: University of Chicago Press, 1956. A criticism of liberal and conservative models and a defense of polyarchy (pluralism and brokerage politics).

* GIRVETZ, HARRY K. *The Evolution of Liberalism.* New York: Collier, 1963. A well-written account of the historical development of modern liberalism from its nineteenth-century origins.

* FRANKEL, CHARLES. *The Case for Modern Man.* New York: Harper, 1955. Criticism of the arguments of some leading conservative theorists and forthright defense of liberal democracy.

HALLOWELL, JOHN H. *The Moral Foundation of Democracy.* Chicago: University of Chicago Press, 1954. A criticism of the secularized politics of compromise and defense of the idea that democracy requires a consensus on the values of the Western religious tradition.

* HARTZ, LOUIS. *The Liberal Tradition in America.* New York: Harcourt, Brace and World, 1955. An influential argument that liberalism as it developed in the United States has dominated American society and politics.

* KIRK, RUSSELL. *Prospect for Conservatives.* New York: Regnery, 1956. A polemical and lively defense of a conservative theory of democracy.

* LIPPMANN, WALTER. *The Public Philosophy.* New York: New American Library, 1956. Exposition and defense of a conservative, antimajoritarian theory of democracy.

MERRIAM, CHARLES E. *American Political Ideas.* New York: Macmillan, 1920. An old but still important work on American political thought.

MYERS, FRANCIS M. *The Warfare of Democratic Ideals.* Yellow Springs, Ohio: Antioch Press, 1956. First-rate critique of philosophical premises of leading conservative and brokerage theorists and defense of a liberal theory of democracy in the tradition of John Dewey.

NEIBUHR, REINHOLD. *The Children of Light and the Children of Darkness.* New York: Scribners, 1944. An exposition of the requirements of democracy from the perspective of a Christian view of the paradoxical nature of human conduct.

* ROSSITER, CLINTON. *Conservatism in America.* New York: Vintage, 1962. A lively account of the ingredients of both theoretical and ideological conservatism in the United States.

SMITH, T. V. *The Legislative Way of Life.* Chicago: University of Chicago Press, 1940. A classic defense of compromise as the method of democratic policy-making.

* TUSSMAN, JOSEPH. *Obligation and the Body Politic.* New York: Oxford, 1960. A sharp analysis of some of the theoretical problems of modern democratic politics and a well-argued defense of a theory of the obligations of democratic citizenship.

CONSTITUTIONAL PRINCIPLES AND THEIR HISTORICAL DEVELOPMENT (CHAPS. 5, 6, AND 7)

* BEARD, CHARLES A. *An Economic Interpretation of the Constitution.* New York: Macmillan, 1939. A controversial analysis, first published in 1913, of the economic motivations of the founders of the American Constitution. See Forrest McDonald's book listed below.

* BELOFF, MAX. *The American Federal Government.* New York: Oxford, 1959. An insightful and critical look at American government by a British professor.

BOWERS, CLAUDE G. *Jefferson and Hamilton.* Boston: Houghton Mifflin, 1925. Comparison and contrasts of the effects these two men have had on American politics, with a discernible pro-Jefferson bias.

* BRYCE, JAMES. *The American Commonwealth.* New York: Macmillan, 1888. A classic look at nineteenth-century America by an astute and scholarly British aristocrat.

FRIEDRICH, CARL J. *Constitutional Government and Democracy.* Boston: Ginn, 1946. A comparative study of constitutional governments.

* HAMILTON, ALEXANDER, JAMES MADISON, and JOHN JAY. *The Federalist Papers.* New York: Liberal Arts Press, 1954. The classic documents about the meaning of and necessity for the Constitution written in 1787–1788. Probably the most important work ever written on political science in the United States.

HOLCOMBE, ARTHUR N. *Our More Perfect Union.* Cambridge, Mass.: Harvard University Press, 1950. An exposition and defense of the Madisonian interpretation of constitutional principles.

* JAMESON, J. F. *The American Revolution Considered as a Social Movement.* Princeton, N.J.: Princeton University Press, 1926. A classic argument for the view that the revolution implied liberal and radical social and political reform.

MACMAHAN, ARTHUR W. (ed.). *Federalism: Mature and Emergent.* New

York: Doubleday, 1955. A collection of essays on political, administrative, and legal problems of federalism.

McDONALD, FORREST. *We the People: The Economic Origins of the Constitution.* Chicago: University of Chicago Press, 1958. A rebuttal to Charles Beard's conclusions on the economic interests of the founders of the American Constitution.

RIKER, WILLIAM H. *Federalism: Origin, Operation, Significance.* Boston: Little, Brown, 1964. A thorough and penetrating analysis of the history and current status of federalism and its relation to democratic theory.

* ROSSITER, CLINTON. *The Political Thought of the American Revolution.* New York: Harcourt, Brace and World, 1963. A highly readable account of the ideas that were reflected in the Constitution.

WRIGHT, BENJAMIN F. *Consensus and Continuity.* Boston: Boston University Press, 1958. Criticism of Beard's economic interpretation and argument that the framers shared a philosophical consensus.

IDEOLOGIES AND ISSUES (CHAP. 8)

* BELL, DANIEL. *The End of Ideology.* New York: Free Press, 1960. A series of essays exploring (and applauding) the sources and consequences of the lack of systematic ideas in contemporary politics.

* BELL, DANIEL, (ed.). *The Radical Right.* Garden City, N.Y.: Doubleday, 1964. A provocative collection of essays emphasizing the social and psychological roots of recent right-wing extremist movements.

* BROGAN, D. W., and DOUGLAS V. VERNEY. *Political Patterns in Today's World.* New York: Harcourt, Brace and World, 1963. A pair of non-Americans look at four liberal democracies with keen and probing insights.

FINER, HERMAN. *Road to Reaction.* Boston: Little Brown, 1945. A vigorous rejoinder to Hayek (see below) and defense of government planning and the welfare state.

GALBRAITH, KENNETH. *The Affluent Society.* Boston: Houghton Mifflin, 1958. An argument that affluence breeds social and political attitudes that complicate the democratic process of serving the public interest.

* GOLDMAN, ERIC F. *Rendezvous with Destiny.* New York: Random House, Vintage, 1961. An interpretive analysis of the rise of the social-service state.

* GOLDWATER, BARRY. *The Conscience of a Conservative.* Shepardsville, Ky.: Victor, 1960. The staunch conservative ideology of the 1964 Republican presidential candidate.

* HARRINGTON, MICHAEL. *The Other America: Poverty in the United States.* Baltimore: Penguin, 1963. A searching look by an American liberal at a nagging American problem that has yet to find solution in our political system.

* HAYEK, F. A. *The Road to Serfdom.* Chicago: University of Chicago

Press, 1944. Thoroughgoing attack on governmental planning and economic intervention from the perspective of economic individualism and *laissez faire.*

LANE, ROBERT E. *Political Ideology.* New York: Free Press, 1962. An exciting analysis in depth of the political attitudes of a group of voters from a psychological and sociological perspective.

LIPSET, SEYMOUR MARTIN. *Political Man.* Garden City, N.Y.: Doubleday, 1960. An analysis by a leading sociologist of the effects of social structure on politics, with emphasis on American political behavior; embodies a brokerage bias.

* McCARTHY, EUGENE J. *The Challenge of Freedom.* New York: Avon, 1960. The Democratic senator from Minnesota describes and defends the credo of a *liberal.*

MADISON, CHARLES A. *Critics and Crusaders.* New York: Ungar, 1961. A history of the Populist and Progressive attacks on the ideology and practices of industrial capitalism.

MILLS, C. WRIGHT. *The Power Elite.* New York: Oxford, 1956. A sociologist looks at the power structure in America and concludes that an elite controls the political system.

OVERSTREET, HARRY, and BONARO OVERSTREET. *The Strange Tactics of Extremism.* New York: Norton, 1964. Highly readable account of extremism of left and right, emphasizing the conflict between extremist tactics and democratic values.

* TOWER, JOHN G. *A Program for Conservatives.* New York: Macfadden, 1962. A superconservative senator offers his views on the direction American government should take.

POLITICAL PARTIES, PRESSURE GROUPS, AND PUBLIC RELATIONS — DESCRIPTIONS, CRITIQUES, AND ANALYSES (CHAP. 9)

AGAR, HERBERT. *The Price of Union.* New York: Houghton Mifflin, 1950. Historical analysis developing and defending the argument that decentralized and loosely disciplined parties are necessary to facilitate the politics of moderation and compromise.

* BAILEY, STEPHEN K. *The Condition of Our National Political Parties.* Santa Barbara, Calif.: The Fund for the Republic, 1959. A critical look at our political parties and a strong plea for their reform.

BERNAYS, EDWARD L. *The Engineering of Consent.* Norman: University of Oklahoma Press, 1955. A study of manipulative techniques used in modern American life by an authority on and defender of public relations.

BINKLEY, WILFRED E. *American Political Parties: Their Natural History,* 4th ed. New York: Knopf, 1964. A well-established text on the historical development of political parties.

BURNS, JAMES MCGREGOR. *The Deadlock of Democracy*. Englewood Cliffs, N.J.: Prentice-Hall, 1963. An analysis of the difficulty of placing political responsibility in view of the conflicts of the presidential and congressional wings of the parties.

KELLY, STANLEY, JR. *Professional Public Relations and Political Power*. Baltimore: Johns Hopkins Press, 1956. A critical look at the hucksters and manipulators working in various political vineyards.

KEY, V. O., JR. *Politics, Parties and Pressure Groups*, 4th ed. New York: Crowell, 1958. A standard text on the subject.

MERRIAM, CHARLES E., and WILLIAM F. GOSNELL. *The American Party System*, 4th ed. New York: Macmillan, 1950. Still a solid and useful work on political parties.

* OWENS, JOHN R., and P. J. STAUDENRAUS (eds.). *The American Party System*. New York: Macmillan, 1965. A collection of readings on political parties.

* POLSBY, NELSON W., and AARON B. WILDAVSKY. *Presidential Elections: Strategies of American Electoral Politics*. New York: Scribners, 1964. An analysis of nominating and campaign politics and strategies, which argues against any fundamental proposals for party reform.

* ROCHE, JOHN P., and LEONARD W. LEVY. *Parties and Pressure Groups*. New York: Harcourt, Brace and World, 1964. A good collection of documents on political parties and pressure groups. Part of a larger series including several topics by the same authors.

ROSSITER, CLINTON. *Parties and Politics in America*. Ithaca, N.Y.: Cornell University Press, 1960. A study of parties in the political process.

SCHATTSCHNEIDER, E. E. *Party Government*. New York: Farrar and Rinehart, 1942. A leader in this school of thought argues the need, from a liberal perspective, for more disciplined and centralized political parties.

* SORAUF, FRANK J. *Political Parties in the American System*. Boston: Little Brown, 1964. An analysis and interpretation of the role of political parties in American politics.

TURNER, JULIUS. *Party and Constituency*. Baltimore: Johns Hopkins Press, 1951. A study of the relationship of parties to the legislative process which holds parties to be the most important influence on a majority of Congressmen.

CITIZENS AND VOTERS: THEORY AND BEHAVIOR (CHAP. 10)

ALMOND, GABRIEL A. *The American People and Foreign Policy*. New York: Harcourt Brace and World, 1950. A critical, thorough, and fascinating analysis of the process through which public opinion on foreign policy is shaped.

BURDICK, EUGENE. *The 480*. New York: McGraw-Hill, 1964. A political scientist-novelist satirizes the uses of public-opinion polling and computer programming in political campaigns.

* CAMPBELL, ANGUS, et al. The American Voter. New York: Wiley, 1964. A paperback abridgment of a longer work, summarizing the research on the American electorate carried on by the Survey Research Center since 1948 and measuring the results against the demands of democratic theory.

KEY, V. O., JR. Southern Politics in State and Nation. New York: Knopf, 1949. Analysis of the impact of race relations on southern politics and the role of southern politicians in national politics.

LANE, ROBERT E. Political Life. New York: Free Press, 1959. An analysis of the motivations and conditions under which Americans become involved in politics.

* LEVIN, MURRAY B. The Alienated Voter. New York: Holt, Rinehart and Winston, 1960. An analysis of political alienation, based on a study of voters in a Boston election.

LOWELL, A. LAWRENCE. Public Opinion and Popular Government. New York: Longmans, Green, 1913. An early analysis of the problems of citizenship and the conditions of freedom in a democracy; still relevant and important.

POLSBY, NELSON W., et al. (eds.). Politics and Social Life. Boston: Houghton Mifflin, 1963. An excellent collection of readings on research in political behavior, including its methods, the psychological and sociological bases of politics, and the relations between political leaders and followers.

STOUFFER, SAMUEL A. Communism, Conformity and Civil Liberties. Garden City, N.Y.: Doubleday, 1955. A study of political attitudes of Americans in the McCarthy period.

LEGISLATURES, LEGISLATORS, AND LEGISLATION (CHAPS. 11 AND 12)

BAILEY, STEPHEN K. Congress Makes a Law. New York: Columbia University Press, 1950. An incisive description and analysis of the legislative history of the Employment Act of 1946, focusing on interest-group pressures in the legislative process. Bailey's critical evaluation of the process should be compared with Latham's appraisal in The Group Basis of Politics listed below.

BERMAN, DAVID M. In Congress Assembled. New York: Macmillan, 1964. A sound text containing some good insights into congressional activity.

BERMAN, DAVID M. A Bill Becomes a Law. New York: Macmillan, 1962. A fine description of how the Civil Rights Act of 1960 became law.

* CLARK, JOSEPH S. Congressional Reform. New York: Crowell, 1965. United States Senator Clark, who thinks Congress could be improved, has assembled a fine collection of readings on the need to get about reform.

* FROMAN, LEWIS A., JR. *Congressman and Their Constituencies.* Chicago: Rand McNally, 1963. Lots of facts, figures, and analysis of the relationship of the congressman to the folks back home.

GALLOWAY, GEORGE B. *The Legislative Process in Congress.* New York: Crowell, 1953. A somewhat dated but thorough textbook. Long a standard.

* HAMILTON, HOWARD D. (ed.). *Legislative Apportionment: Key to Power.* New York: Harper and Row, 1964. A collection of readings on the subject. Some provocative arguments and perspectives are contained in this collection.

KEEFE, WILLIAM J., and MORRIS S. OGUL. *The American Legislative Process: Congress and the States.* Englewood Cliffs, N.J.: Prentice Hall, 1964. A recent and thorough textbook. Contains lots of facts and figures and footnotes to many sources of information.

LATHAM, EARL. *The Group Basis of Politics.* Ithaca, N.Y.: Cornell University Press, 1952. An able study of the history of basing-point legislation in which Latham develops and justifies the brokerage model. Compare his theoretical assumptions with Bailey's in *Congress Makes a Law.*

* MILLER, CLEM. *Member of the House.* New York: Scribner, 1962. Great insight into Congress as seen through his correspondence. Only someone who was a congressman could give us this perspective.

* ROBINSON, JAMES A. *The House Rules Committee.* New York: Bobbs Merrill, 1963. An interesting study of this powerful committee, its members, and its methods.

* ROCHE, JOHN P., and LEONARD W. LEVY. *The Congress: Documents in American Government.* New York: Harcourt, Brace and World, 1964. An interesting collection of documents produced by and about Congress.

* SCHUBERT, GLENDON. *Reapportionment.* New York: Scribners Research Anthologies, 1965. A first-rate study and compilation of documents on the whole problem of reapportionment. Contains much judicial material.

* TAYLOR, TELFORD. *Grand Inquest.* New York: Simon and Schuster, 1955. A critical study of congressional investigations, written from a civil libertarian perspective.

THOMAS, NORMAN C., and KARL A. LAMB. *Congress: Politics and Practice.* New York: Random House, 1964. A brief treatment of politics and procedures in Congress.

WAHLKE, JOHN C., HEINZ EULAU, WILLIAM BUCHANAN, and LEROY G. FERGUSON. *The Legislative System.* New York. Wiley, 1962. A thorough behavioral study of legislators.

* WILSON, WOODROW. *Congressional Government.* New York: Meridian Books, 1956. First published in 1885. A venerable and still-to-be-equaled treatment of congressional power, with particular emphasis on committees.

THE PRESIDENCY, THE PRESIDENT, AND BUREAUCRACY (CHAPS. 13 AND 14)

APPLEBY, PAUL. *Big Democracy*. New York: Knopf, 1945. An ex-public official's comments on large bureaucratic organizations and their relationship to democracy.

BERNSTEIN, MARVER. *Regulating Business by Independent Commission*. Princeton, N.J.: Princeton University Press, 1955. A sharply critical analysis of independent regulatory commissions, explaining how and why they often become creatures of the industries they were designed to regulate.

CHILDS, MARQUIS W. *Eisenhower—Captive Hero: A Critical Study of the General and the President*. New York: Harcourt, Brace and World, 1958. A highly readable account of President Eisenhower's administration by an able, liberal journalist.

CORWIN, EDWARD S. *The President: Office and Powers*, rev. ed. New York: New York University Press, 1957. Thorough and comprehensive treatment of the historical and constitutional development of the office, by a scholar who is concerned about the personalization of its powers.

EGGER, ROWLAND, and JOSEPH P. HARRIS. *The President and Congress*. New York: McGraw-Hill, 1963. A brief account of the interrelationship and struggle for agreement between two of the three branches of American government.

FINER, HERMAN. *The Presidency: Crisis and Regeneration*. Chicago: The University of Chicago Press, 1960. A critical analysis of the burden of presidential responsibility and an argument that the powers of the office need to be shared and institutionalized through a cabinet responsible to the House of Representatives.

* HILL, NORMAN L. *Mr. Secretary of State*. New York: Random House, 1963. An account of the emergence of the Secretary of State as a crucial figure in national policy-making.

ICKES, HAROLD. *The Secret Diary of Harold Ickes: The First Thousand Days*. New York: Simon and Schuster, 1954. A colorful self-styled curmudgeon reveals his activities and complaints as a member of Franklin Roosevelt's cabinet.

JOHNSON, DONALD BRUCE, and JACK L. WALKER (eds.). *The Dynamics of the American Presidency*. New York: Wiley, 1964. A first-rate collection of essays covering all aspects of the modern presidency.

* McCONNELL, GRANT. *Steel and the Presidency—1962*. New York: Norton, 1963. A case study of the power clash between President Kennedy and the steel industry.

* MARTIN, RALPH G. *Ballots and Bandwagons*. New York: Signet, 1964. A lively account of the Republican national convention of 1912 and the Democratic conventions of 1932 and 1956.

* NEUSTADT, RICHARD E. *Presidential Power.* New York: Wiley, 1962. A profound analysis of the modern Presidency, emphasizing its personalized character and describing it as a platform for the exercise of persuasion and influence rather than command.

* ROSSITER, CLINTON. *The American Presidency.* New York: Harcourt, Brace and World, 1960. Well-written introduction to the growth in the power of the Presidency and the roles of its incumbents.

* ROURKE, FRANCIS E. (ed). *Bureaucratic Power in National Politics.* Boston: Little Brown, 1965. An interesting collection of readings on how bureaucracy asserts itself in the political process.

* WHITE, THEODORE H. *The Making of a President, 1960.* New York: Pocket Books, 1961; and *The Making of a President, 1964.* New York: Harper, 1965. Fascinating accounts and interpretations of nominating and campaign politics.

* WILDAVSKY, AARON. *The Politics of the Budgetary Process.* Boston: Little Brown, 1964. A first-rate look at the political pulling and hauling over the federal budget, which clearly illustrates that a budget is political policy with a dollar sign attached.

* WOLL, PETER. *American Bureaucracy.* New York: Norton, 1963. An examination of bureaucratic influence on government policy-making and the problems that result from this phenomenon.

LAW, THE COURTS, AND THE JUDICIAL PROCESS (CHAPS. 15 AND 16)

* CARDOZO, BENJAMIN N. *The Nature of the Judicial Process.* New Haven, Conn.: Yale University Press, 1921. A celebrated justice's insight into the processes judges use in rendering their judgments.

COHEN, FELIX S., and MORRIS R. COHEN. *Readings in Jurisprudence and Legal Philosophy.* Englewood Cliffs, N.J.: Prentice Hall, 1951. A broad-ranging and excellent selection of readings in jurisprudence by two outstanding legal scholars.

* CUSHMAN, ROBERT E. *Leading Constitutional Decisions,* 12th ed. New York: Appleton-Century-Crofts, 1963. A worthy collection of important judicial decisions interpreting the Constitution. Periodically revised and brought up to date.

* DANELSKI, DAVID J. *A Supreme Court Justice Is Appointed.* New York: Random House, 1964. An account of the stormy political events surrounding the appointment of Pierce Butler to the Supreme Court.

FREUND, PAUL A. *On Understanding the Supreme Court.* Boston: Little Brown, 1959. A fine work on the way the Supreme Court approaches constitutional questions.

HAINES, CHARLES G. *The American Doctrine of Judicial Supremacy,* 2nd ed. Berkeley: University of California Press, 1959. A critical analysis and explanation of the final power of the courts to interpret the Constitution.

* HOLMES, OLIVER WENDELL, JR. *The Common Law*. Boston: Little Brown, 1881. A classic statement of the history and meaning of the common law and its adaptability to a changing society.

LEWIS, ANTHONY. *Gideon's Trumpet*. New York: Random House, 1964. An engrossing account of a leading constitutional case and the methods and procedures of the United States Supreme Court.

* ROCHE, JOHN P. *Courts and Rights*. New York: Random House, 1961. A critical analysis of the role of the courts in American politics, written from a liberal, majoritarian perspective.

* ROSENBLUM, VICTOR G. *Law as a Political Instrument*. New York: Doubleday, 1955. An analysis of the role of law and the courts in the political process.

* TRESOLINI, ROCCO J. *American Constitutional Law*, 2nd ed. New York: Macmillan, 1965. A fine textbook on constitutional law, written especially for nonspecialist undergraduate students, yet thorough and comprehensive.

* TRESOLINI, ROCCO J. *Justice and the Supreme Court*. New York: Lippincott, 1963. An interesting account of the trials and tribulations confronting several Supreme Court justices when they made some hard decisions.

* TUSSMAN, JOSEPH, (ed.). *The Supreme Court on Racial Discrimination*. New York: Oxford, 1963. A collection of Court decisions on this important issue.

* WESTIN, ALLEN F. *The Anatomy of a Constitutional Law Case*. New York: Macmillan, 1958. An account of a highly political Supreme Court decision affecting the president's power to control the steel industry.

INDEX OF CASES

INDEX